LAW AND INFLATION

LAW AND INFLATION

KEITH S. ROSENN

UNIVERSITY OF PENNSYLVANIA PRESS
Philadelphia
1982

Library of Congress Cataloging in Publication Data

Rosenn, Keith S.
Law and inflation

Bibliography: p.
Includes index.
1. Money—Law and legislation. 2. Inflation (Finance)
I. Title.
K4431.R67 343'03 81-51139
ISBN 0–8122–7807–0 342.33 AACR2

To My Mother and Father

CONTENTS

Acknowledgments

Many people helped in the preparation of this book, and I am deeply grateful for their assistance. Three of my former colleagues at Ohio State University, Professors Douglas Graham, Earl Finbar Murphy, and Claude Sowle, offered numerous helpful suggestions on early chapters. Professor Leo Raskind, professor of Law at the University of Minnesota, graciously critiqued chapter 9. My colleagues at the University of Miami's Law and Economics Center, Louis De Alessi and Kenneth W. Clarkson, have given me many helpful hints. I owe a special debt of thanks to Arnold Wald, professor of Civil Law at the Law School of the University of the State of Rio de Janeiro, for the many stimulating discussions about monetary correction.

Parts of chapter 5 appeared in *The Business Lawyer,* volume 33, no. 2 (January 1978), 729–47. Parts of chapter 9 appeared in the *Texas International Law Journal,* volume 13, no. 2 (Spring 1978), 165–97. I am grateful to the publishers of both journals for permission to use the material that appeared in these articles.

I am deeply indebted to two of my former students at the Ohio State University College of Law, Jeffry Goldsmith of the Class of 1979 and Adrienne Cantor Lalak of the Class of 1978, for their invaluable editorial and research assistance. Norman Nadorff of OSU's Class of 1980 performed yeoman service in checking my citations. I am also deeply indebted to Matt Dee, Nancy Miller, Ruth Kessler, and Gay Crumpler of the OSU Law Library for their help in obtaining the necessary research materials.

I am most grateful to the secretarial pool at OSU College of Law, where the initial drafts of the manuscript were typed, and to my secretaries at the Law and Economics Center, Evelyn Bavonese, Joanne Davis, and Melanie Vidales, who did the numerous revisions.

I would like to acknowledge a special debt to the University of Miami's Law and Economics Center for financial support to enable me to complete the revision and updating of the manuscript.

My largest debt is to my wife, Silvia, for displaying that notably common Brazilian quality *paciência* in an uncommonly large quantity while I worked on this book.

TABLES AND FIGURES

TABLE OF CASES

Cases discussed in the text are italicized. Cases discussed in the notes or simply cited are in roman type. In some of the civil law countries, case names are infrequently used or are unavailable. Cases cited only by court and date have been omitted from this table.

ARGENTINA

AUSTRALIA

BELGIUM

BRAZIL

CANADA

CHILE

FRANCE

GERMANY

GREAT BRITAIN

ISRAEL

NETHERLANDS

SWEDEN

SWITZERLAND

UNITED STATES

URUGUAY

TABLE OF STATUTES AND DECREES

CANADA

CHILE

GREAT BRITAIN

GREECE

ISRAEL

ITALY

LIBERIA

MEXICO

NETHERLANDS

PERU

POLAND

PORTUGAL

PRUSSIA

SPAIN

SWEDEN

SWITZERLAND

UNITED STATES

Federal

State

ABBREVIATIONS OF NON-ENGLISH PERIODICALS AND REPORTERS

ARGENTINA

J.A.	Jurisprudencia Argentina
La Ley	Revista Juridica Argentina La Ley

BELGIUM

Pas.	Pasichrisie Belge
Rev. Crit. Juris. Belge (R.C.J.B.)	Revue Critique de Jurisprudence Belge
Rev. Gen. Ass. et Resp.	Revue Générale des Assurances et des Responsabilités

BRAZIL

Arch. Jud.	Archivo Judicíaro
Conj. Econ.	Conjuntura Econômica
D. Just.	Diário de Justiça
Rev. Bras. Econ.	Revista Brasileira de Economia
Rev. Dir.	Revista Direito
Rev. Dir. Admin.	Revista de Direito Administrativo
Rev. Dir. Pro. Ger.	Revista do Direito do Procurador Geral
Rev. For.	Revista Forense
Rev. Juris. Guan.	Revista de Jurisprudência do Tribunal de Justiça do Estado da Guanabara
Rev. Trib.	Revista dos Tribunais
R.T.J.	Revista Trimestral de Jurisprudência

CHILE

Rev. Der. Econ.	Revista de Derecho Económico
R.D.J.	Revista de Derecho y Jurisprudencia
Rev. de Der.	Revista de Derecho y Ciencias Sociales
Rev. de Der. Púb.	Revista de Derecho Público

FRANCE

Bull. Civ. I	Bulletin des Arrêts de la Cour de Cassation, Chambres Civiles, 1792-date. Première Section Civile.
Clunet	Journal du Droit International
Crit. Droit Int'l Privé	Critique de Droit International Privé
D.	Recueil Dalloz
D.Jur.	Dalloz, *Jurisprudence,* 1945–55, 1956–64
D.Chron.	Dalloz, Chronique
D.P. I.	Dalloz, *Periodique et Critique,* 1825–1940, Cour de Cassation
D.P. III	Dalloz, *Periodique et Critique,* 1825–1940, Conseil d'État
D.S. Jur. (Chron.)	Dalloz-Sirey, *Jurisprudence,* 1955–56, 1965-date, Chronique
Gaz. Pal.	Gazette du Palais
Gaz. Trib.	Gazette des Tribunaux
J.C.P.	Juris-Classeur Periodique, La Semaine Juridique, 1941–
Rev. Économique	Revue Économique
Rev. Trim. Droit Civ.	Revue Trimestrielle de Droit Civil
Rev. Trim. Droit Comm.	Revue Trimestrielle de Droit Commercial
S.Jur. I	Sirey, *Jurisprudence,* 1791–1955, Cour de Cassation
S.Jur. III	Sirey, *Jurisprudence,* 1791–1955, Jurisprudence Administratif
Travaux Sem. Int'l Droit	Travaux de la Semaine Internationale de Droit

GERMANY

N.J.W.	Neve Juristische Wochenschrift
R.G.Z.	Reichsgericht in Zivilsachen

GREECE

Rev. Hellenique Droit Int'l	Revue Hellenique de Droit International

ITALY

Enci. del Diritto	Enciclopedia del Diritto
Foro Amm.	

Foro Ital. I	Foro Italiano 1876-Corte Cassazione, Corte Coste
Giur. Compl.	Giurisprudenza Italiana
Giur. Ital.	
Rep. Gen. Giur. Ital.	Repertorio Generale della Giurisprudenza Italiana
Rev. Dir. Comm.	Rivista di Diritto Commerciale
SPAIN	
Rev. Admin. Pub.	Revista de Administración Pública
SWITZERLAND	
B.G.E.	Bundesgericht: Entscheidungen des Schweizeriches Bundesgerichts, Amtliche Sammlung, Civil
S.J.Z.	Schweizerische Juristenzeitung
URUGUAY	
Just. Urug.	Revista Juridica La Justicia Uruguaya
Rev. D.J.A.	La Revista de Derecho Jurisprudencia y Administración

PREFACE

> Lenin is said to have declared that the best way to destroy the Capitalist System was to debauch the currency. By a continuing process of inflation, governments can confiscate, secretly and unobserved, an important part of the wealth of their citizens. By this method they not only confiscate, but they confiscate arbitrarily; and, while the process impoverishes many, it actually enriches some. The sight of this arbitrary rearrangement of riches strikes not only at security, but at confidence in the existing distribution of wealth. . . . As the inflation proceeds and the real value of the currency fluctuates wildly from month to month, all permanent relations between debtors and creditors, which form the utimate foundations of capitalism, become so utterly disordered as to be almost meaningless. . . .
>
> Lenin was certainly right. There is no subtler, no surer means of overturning the existing basis of society than to debauch the currency. The process engages all the hidden forces of economic law on the side of destruction, and does it in a manner which not one man in a million is able to diagnose.[1]
>
> John Maynard Keynes

Inflation is currently one of the world's more pressing economic, political, and social problems. We are living in an era in which most countries have experienced double digit inflation, an economic phenomenon that has profound implications for lawyers and jurists. The bulk of our laws and legal doctrines have been formulated upon the assumption that the value of money remains reasonably stable. Unfortunately, this assumption is no longer tenable in much of the world.

Modern legal systems rely heavily on monetary valuations for a wide variety of purposes. Property and income must be assessed for tax purposes. Businesses must record the results of their operations in financial statements. Values have to be placed upon the investment of public utilities for rate-making. Determination of damages in contract, tort, or condemnation suits requires pecuniary valuations. Even the criminal law relies on monetary valuations for determination of the seriousness of certain offenses and the imposition of certain sanctions.

Modern legal systems generally adhere to the nominalist principle: the law presumes that for the purpose of discharging legal obligations the value of money remains constant. In an inflationary milieu, this presumption seriously distorts many legal institutions. For example, despite constitutional guarantees of due process and the protection of private property from confiscation, inflation transfers billions of dollars each year from some socio-economic groups to others. In the United States alone it has been estimated that each one percent of unanticipated inflation in 1971 transferred more than $30 billion from creditors to debtors.[2]

Nominalism is a highly useful fiction, and legislators and courts are understandably reluctant to abandon it. This reluctance stems not only from concerns about national prestige and the desire to avoid upsetting the security of legal transactions, but also from the difficulty of agreeing upon an alternative, for measuring changes in the value of money over time is no simple task. But the failure to discard the nominalist principle during severe inflation subjects many legal institutions to great stress. If severe inflation persists, failure to employ some kind of valoristic adaptation such as indexation will result in the malfunctioning or complete breakdown of certain legal structures.

Inflation affects many legal institutions, and many legal institutions affect inflation. There are a myriad of interrelationships between law and inflation; were one to attempt to deal with all of them, this book would resemble the map of Jorge Luis Borges' mythical kingdom where the science of cartography was so developed that the map of the kingdom was the size of the kingdom. Instead, this book focuses upon three major areas of the law most seriously affected by inflation: contracts, damages, and taxation. A number of important aspects of law and inflation, such as wage and price controls, trusts and estates, and public utility rate regulation, have been omitted entirely.

The first three chapters are introductory. The first explores the meaning and causes of inflation. The second explains the devices by which inflation is measured. The third is designed to provide historical perspective about the value given to money by the law. The next three chapters are devoted to contracts, broadly defined to include various forms of credit transactions, insurance, and annuities. Chapter 4 first depicts the historical experience with legislative and judicial revalorization of contracts whose underlying assumptions have been badly distorted by inflation and then analyzes the difficulties with the various techniques for affording relief. Chapter 5 analyzes the diverse methods for protecting contracts in general from inflationary distortion. Chapter 6 focuses on three types of contractual arrangements particularly susceptible to inflationary distortion: credit transactions, insurance, and pensions and annuities. Chapter 7 examines the diverse ways in which a number of countries have sought to prevent inflation from distorting the compensation awarded in suits for breach of contract, torts, and condemnation. Chapter 8 returns to the problems of inflationary distortions of contracts and damage awards, but with the added layer of complexity of international transactions. Chapter 9 explores the ways in which inflation distorts business and personal income taxation and the techniques for eliminating such distortions. The book concludes with an examination of the implications of instituting widespread indexation and urges the desirability of the adoption of a proposal for partial indexation in countries like the United States.

All translations are by the author unless otherwise noted.

NOTES

1. The Economic Consequences of Peace 235–36 (1920).
2. G. Bach, The New Inflation 24 (1973).

LAW AND INFLATION

1

INFLATION'S CAUSES AND CURES

The term "inflation" is often used loosely in English to mean anything from pomposity to increases in money, income, and profits.[1] For the purposes of this book, inflation is used to refer either to a sustained rise in an economy's general level of prices or to a corresponding fall in the domestic purchasing power of an economy's currency. This working definition implies that inflation is a dynamic process in which the aggregate level of prices is moving upward over time while the purchasing power of money is in corresponding decline. It does not mean that all prices are moving upward uniformly, nor even that all prices are moving upward. It does mean that an economy is undergoing inflation when it presently costs more to purchase a representative sample of goods than it cost in the past.

Inflation and its opposite, deflation, describe changes in a nation's internal price levels or its currency's domestic purchasing power. Changes in a currency's external purchasing power occur through adjustments in the foreign exchange rate. When the value of country A's currency declines relative to the currency of country B, there has been a devaluation of country A's currency. Correspondingly, there has been an upward revaluation in country B's currency relative to country A. In common parlance references to changes in internal and external purchasing power of a currency are frequently commingled; it is not uncommon to find courts confusingly referring to devaluation when they really mean depreciation in domestic purchasing power.[2] In the long run, countries experiencing inflation rates higher than those of customary trading partners will be forced to devalue; however, in the short run, it is frequently possible for countries to maintain the same exchange rate despite substantial domestic inflation, or to devalue by less than the inflation rate differential.[3] Countries also occasionally devalue more rapidly than their domestic inflation rates, such as Germany and France during the 1920s and Brazil in 1979.

Economists customarily categorize inflations by reference to the curious combination of three equine and one infantile gaits: creeping, trotting, galloping, or runaway (sometimes called hyperinflation). There are, however, no clearly defined lines of demarcation. Many economists consider any inflation in which prices are rising less than 4 percent annually as "creeping," and any inflation in which prices are rising at more than 50 percent per month as "runaway."[4] But there seems to be little consensus as to when a trotting inflation breaks into a gallop. Most economists begin to refer to an inflation as "galloping" whenever the general price level increases about 30 to 50 percent per year.

A BRIEF HISTORICAL PERSPECTIVE

Inflation is hardly a recent or rare phenomenon. The ancient Greeks, Romans, and Egyptians all had inflationary experiences.[5] China had severe inflations during the eleventh through fourteenth centuries.[6] The huge influx of gold and silver from the New World generated substantial inflation in Europe during the sixteenth and seventeenth centuries.[7]

There was, however, a significant difference between the early inflations in the Western world and in China. In the Western world money was essentially units of precious metals; consequently early inflations in the West were relatively mild, at least until the end of the seventeenth century. Production costs served as a natural limit on governments' ability to increase the money supply. Discovery of new sources of supply or more efficient extraction techniques occasionally caused an increase in the money supply. If the supply of goods and services remained constant, the purchasing power of each monetary unit declined. Eventually, the decline in the purchasing power of money raised production costs to the point where the marginal mines closed down and less precious metal was produced. There were numerous instances of sovereigns debasing the value of metallic currency either by reducing the gold or silver content of coins or by simply decreeing increases in the nominal value of existing coins. Nonetheless, there were natural limits in the amount of inflation that could be produced by these measures. China, on the other hand, began to use paper money nearly seven centuries before the West. As a result, its early inflations were far more severe than those experienced in the West. Once governments began to make unbacked paper money legal tender, the stage was set for unprecedented galloping and runaway inflation.

The first actors on that stage were the Chinese. Paper money began early in the eleventh century in Szechwan in the form of deposit receipts for iron coins, which people found too bulky to carry. Initially, the government conceded a monopoly upon the issuance of such receipts to sixteen private merchants. In 1016 this was replaced by a government monopoly. In theory these receipts, which came in various denominations and were called promissory notes, were supposed to be redeemed or exchanged for new notes every three years, but the rules about replacing notes and maintaining a fixed quota were quickly broken. The practice of printing notes as a currency gradually spread throughout China, and the number of notes in circulation steadily increased under the two Sung dynasties as the government realized that printing paper money was a convenient way to meet military expenditures. When the notes steadily depreciated, the government issued new notes along with decrees prohibiting further depreciation of the notes. Because the notes were nonredeemable for hard currency, such decrees were ineffective, and inflation continued. In 1260 a new kind of note was issued called a "primary treasure exchange note." These notes were intended to be convertible into silver or copper and were backed by reserves of gold and silver. In addition, gold, silver, and copper were demonetized. For two decades these notes enjoyed the confidence of the people, largely because they were fully backed and tight control was maintained over the issuance of new notes. During the 1270s, however, huge issues of unbacked new notes to finance military expeditions and religious ceremonies once again produced substantial inflation. Even though the notes could be used to pay the tax collector, their value shrank drastically. After 1356 so many unbacked notes had been issued that paper currency became practically worthless, and people were forced to resort to barter and copper coins.[8]

The distinction of having been the first government to issue paper money in Western civilization is usually attributed to the colony of Massachusetts, which issued "bills of credit" in 1690 to finance war against Canada. The value of these bills was originally declared to be equal to money, and like Chinese paper money, they were acceptable for payment in taxes. Two years later Massachusetts declared these bills to be legal tender. From Massachusetts the issuance of paper money soon spread throughout the American colonies. Though there was some depreciation in the value of this early paper money, particularly in Rhode Island, inflation did not really start to gallop until the time of the American Revolution.[9]

The American Revolution of 1776 was financed with massive issues of unbacked paper money called "continentals." Prices rose an average of 8.5 percent per month, and the continental depreciated so quickly in relation to gold that within a few years "Not worth a continental!" had become a colonial colloquialism for expressing valuelessness. In 1790 continentals were redeemed for one cent on a dollar.[10]

The French Revolution of 1789 was largely financed by similar use of the printing press, producing an average price increase of 10 percent per month. The French assignat quickly became about as worthless as the American continental and was similarly withdrawn from circulation.[11] Between 1861 and 1865 the process was repeated in the United States, where the Civil War was financed in the North largely by the issuance of unbacked notes known as "greenbacks" and in the South by the issuance of unbacked Confederate currency. Confederate currency's purchasing power depreciated rapidly during the course of the war, becoming entirely worthless after the military collapse of the South. The greenback, on the other hand, lost only slightly more than half of its nominal value in relation to gold, eventually recuperating to the point that the premium at which the gold dollar had traded disappeared completely.[12]

By far the most spectacular inflations have occurred during the twentieth century, and two factors combined to produce them: One was the enormity of the economic destruction and dislocation resulting from the two world wars. The other was the growth of central banks and bank credit, which greatly amplified the possibilities for monetary expansion through the familiar multiplier effect.[13] The so-called ultimate inflation took place in Germany following its defeat in World War I. After reparations payments were finally set in 1921 at the staggering sum of 132 billion gold or prewar marks (about U.S. $33 billion), both the bottom (and the sides) fell out of the mark market. In the middle of 1921, German prices were about fourteen times higher than in 1913. By the end of 1922, they were 1,475 times higher. By November 1923, the general level of prices had soared to 1,422,900,000,000 times its 1913 level.[14] Although less well known, Hungary's post-World War II inflation actually surpassed the rate of Germany's currency depreciation. Between August 1945 and July 1946, the average monthly inflation rate in Hungary was 19,800 percent. The highest monthly inflation rate was 4.2×10^{16} percent, by far the highest rate ever recorded. In just a little more than twelve months, the general price level in Hungary rose by a factor of 1,366,521,739,130,000.[15]

Austria, Hungary, Poland, and Russia had somewhat less spectacular runaway inflations after World War I, and France narrowly escaped a similar fate. Similar hyperinflations also beset China, Greece, and Rumania in the wake of World War II.[16]

The 1970s introduced a new kind of runaway inflation. Prior to 1970, hyperinflations had always stemmed from economic dislocations caused by war, revolution, or foreign occupation. During the 1970s, Chile and Argentina, two countries in which severe inflation has been chronic, managed to produce annual inflation rates of more than 500 percent through colossal economic mismanagement alone.[17]

The post-World War II era has been characterized by an unparalleled sustained rise in prices in almost all countries of the world. As Table 1 demonstrates, during the 1950s world consumer prices increased by an annual average of 3.2 percent. This figure rose slightly to 4.1 percent in the next decade, and then tripled during the 1970s. Between 1970 and 1979 none of the industrial countries (as classified by the International Monetary Fund) reported a decline or zero increase in consumer prices.

TABLE 1 ANNUAL PERCENTAGE CHANGES IN WORLD CONSUMER PRICES, 1950–80

Year	*Percentage Increase*	*Year*	*Percentage Increase*	*Year*	*Percentage Increase*
1950	.3	1960	2.8	1970	6.0
1951	9.6	1961	2.6	1971	5.9
1952	3.9	1962	3.6	1972	5.8
1953	1.3	1963	4.0	1973	9.6
1954	1.1	1964	4.6	1974	15.3
1955	1.0	1965	5.0	1975	13.4
1956	3.5	1966	5.1	1976	11.1
1957	3.9	1967	4.2	1977	11.4
1958	4.2	1968	4.4	1978	9.8
1959	3.2	1969	5.1	1979	12.2
				1980	15.5

1950–59 Average = 3.2; 1960–69 Average = 4.1; 1970–80 Average = 10.5

SOURCE: IMF, INT'L FINANCIAL STATISTICS YEARBOOK 59 (1980) and 34 INT'L FIN. STAT. 45 (Je. 1981).

CAUSES OF INFLATION

Economists disagree about the causes of inflation in free world economies.[18] They have divided roughly into four camps on this question, with a number pitching their theoretical tents across camp lines.

The Quantity Theory of Money

The oldest theory of inflation, and the dominant theory prior to 1929, is that the quantity of money in circulation determines the level of prices. In its simplest version, which can be traced at least as far back as David Hume in the eighteenth century, the quantity theory postulates that the general level of prices varies directly, though not necessarily in exact proportion, with the quantity of money in circulation and inversely with the total volume of goods sold. It is usually expressed in the form of an equation of exchange:

$$MV = PT$$

where M represents the quantity of money, including bank deposits (and sometimes time deposits as well); V represents the velocity of circulation (the number of times a unit of money changes hands during a given period); P represents the general level of prices; and T represents the total cost of output traded. The theory assumes that the velocity of circulation is relatively constant because of the structure of the economy, savings and shopping habits, and wage payment patterns. It further assumes that the economy is operating at or near full employment.

Three basic criticisms are commonly leveled at the quantity theory. First, the velocity of circulation does not remain constant. Money turns over more rapidly during a period of inflation, as consumers rush to purchase goods before the purchasing power of their currency depreciates further, and turns over less rapidly during a period of deflation, when consumers are reluctant to spend money. Second, economies do have idle capacity and unemployment, a criticism that caused the quantity theory to fall into disfavor during the depression of the 1930s. Third, some economists deny the causality implicit in the quantity theory. Dissenters assert that increases in the money supply do not, as the quantity school claims, cause increases in prices. Instead, they argue increases in prices cause the money supply to increase.

The quantity theory was resuscitated and refurbished by Milton Friedman and his colleagues at the University of Chicago during the 1950s and 1960s. By explicitly cranking in other variables, such as wealth and interest rates, expanding the definition of money, and allowing for lags between changes in money supply and the time in which such changes are reflected in prices, Chicago school economists have been able to use changes in the quantity of money in circulation to explain price level changes fairly accurately.[19]

The "Demand-Pull" Theory

Keynesian economists have tended to view the cause of inflation as the result of attempts by consumers (including government) to buy more goods and services than can be physically produced. Thus, when consumption and investment spending at full employment is greater than gross national product (as occurs when government expenditure is higher than the difference between production and consumption), an "inflationary gap" results. The market process tends to close this gap or eliminate this excess demand, first by bidding up prices and later wages. In turn, the higher prices and wages result in increased income to workers or businessmen, stimulating further increases in demand and further price increases. Prices continue to rise until taxes absorb the excess spending or until the money supply effectively limits demand.[20]

This theory has not been particularly helpful in explaining the sustained inflation since World War II. Much of this inflation has taken place without inflationary gaps.

The "Cost-Push" Theory

Advocates of this theory argue that inflation is caused by the operation of a wage-price spiral. Certain societal groups seek to expand their share of national income at the expense of other groups. Some blame organized pressure groups, especially labor unions, for starting the spiral by pushing for wage increases in excess of productivity, particularly when there is full employment. In order to retain profit margins, businessmen respond by increasing prices. Seeing their wage gains evaporate with increased prices, unions push for further wage increases. Others blame management in monopolistic or oligopolistic industries either for starting the spiral by increasing prices to reap monopoly profits or for responding to increased wage demands with price increases much larger than necessary to cover the increased wage costs.[21]

There has been little empirical evidence to support the cost-push theory, particularly during the post-World War II period in the United States. There is some empirical support for "wage-push" inflation in recent years in parts of Europe, principally Great Britain and Italy, but the evidence is controversial. There is, however, empirical evidence to support the existence of a special type of cost-push inflation stemming from crop failures or the formation of cartels controlling basic commodities. The formation of the Organization of Petroleum Exporting Countries (OPEC) and its cartel on oil exports plus worldwide food shortages during the mid-1970s have produced sharp price increases in basic commodities.[22]

The Structural Theory

A variety of structuralist explanations of inflation have been espoused, particularly in Latin America, where structuralism has attracted a large number of adherents. The basic structuralist approach was developed in the 1950s by a group of economists working for the Economic Commission for Latin America (ECLA) in Santiago, Chile. While admitting that monetary expansion is a crucial factor in propogating inflation, ECLA economists theorized that more fundamental structural maladjustments within a country's economy are the real root of inflation. To these structuralists the basic cause of inflation lay in the pressure of economic growth on underdeveloped social and economic structures.[23]

One maladjustment frequently pointed to in Latin America is the inelasticity of agricultural supply for domestic consumption. Latin American agriculture is dominated by large plantations producing crops for export, large nonmarket-responsive haciendas, and tiny *minifundios* where farmers barely eke out a living. With rapid urbanization and industrialization, the demand for food in urban centers has risen dramatically. With agriculture unable to increase the supply of foodstuffs in response to increased demand, the price of food rises. This stimulates a rise in urban wages, which increases the cost of manufactured goods, which in turn is passed on to the consumers. Thus, a wage-price spiral results from the inelasticity of agricultural supply.

A variant on this theme blames inflation on import inelasticity. Many Latin American countries suffer balance-of-payments problems because of the slow growth of demand for their traditional exports, often accompanied by a decline in the terms of trade. Because Latin American countries are trying to industrialize rapidly, their steadily increasing need to import soon exhausts foreign currency reserves. To remedy their balance-of-payments deficit, Latin American countries are forced to impose import controls and to devalue their currency. These measures produce inflation by boosting the price of imported goods, as well as domestically produced goods with imported components.

Another structuralist variation is that rapid industrialization and urbanization require vast increases in governmental expenditures for services and the creation of a suitable infrastructure for an urban-industrial society. Given the political and administrative inability of many Latin American governments to expand the tax base rapidly and to collect existing tax obligations effectively, the most feasible way for governments to finance development projects is to create money and credit.[24]

Empirical evidence to confirm the structuralist hypothesis about the inelasticity of food supplies does not exist for much of Latin America. There is, however, some empirical confirmation for a reformulated version of structuralist theory with respect to Brazil, Chile, and Mexico.[25]

Still another structuralist variation has emerged recently in the United States under the tutelage of a small group of economists called "supply siders." Supply siders claim that a substantial part of the U.S. inflation is attributable to structural factors in the economy leading to a decline in productivity such as high taxes, inadequate depreciation reserves, and insufficient incentives for savings and investment. Supply siders argue that if these structural deficiencies are corrected, the U.S. economy will reduce its inflation rate sharply and painlessly by producing more goods at lower prices.[26]

The claim that increases in productivity will sharply diminish the inflation rate is dubious. One would have to produce truly phenomenal rates of productivity increase to make much of a dent in a 13 percent annual inflation rate. Even if the rate of productivity growth were doubled from its current 1.5 percent annual rate to its pre-1970 annual rate of 3 percent, by no means an easy task, the economy would still be left with a 10 percent annual inflation rate.[27]

REMEDIES FOR INFLATION

To a large extent the cures an economist prescribes for inflation depend upon what he views as causal factors. Monetarists (those who subscribe to the quantity theory) emphasize restricting the money supply. Keynesians emphasize the use of fiscal policy to absorb excess demand. The cost-push camp urges wage and price controls and vigorous enforcement of the antitrust laws. Latin American structuralists call for the breaking up of existing economic malformations through land reform, agricultural diversification, and increased industrialization. Supply siders call for tax cuts, faster depreciation write offs, and tax incentives for savers and investors.

There has never been a lengthy, severe inflation without large increases in the money supply. Typically, these large increases in the money supply result from financing huge governmental budgetary deficits by creating money, though occasionally, as in Brazil and Uruguay, they result from central bank expansion of credit to the private sector. Inflation can be curtailed by eliminating the inflationary financing of budgetary deficits and tightening private sector credit, thereby sharply constricting the money supply. But that is easier said than done. The kind of austerity program necessary to do so is likely to produce a severe recession or depression, which, in most countries, is not a politically viable alternative. For most economic planners the real choice involves the selection of which mix of policy measures will reduce inflation to acceptable levels without throwing the economy into a tailspin, and a decision as to which societal groups should bear the burden of the decline in real income from austerity measures.

Recently, there has been increasing interest in eclectic solutions called economic incomes policies, particularly one called the tax-based income policy (TIP). The TIP proposal currently receiving greatest attention in the United States was designed by Henry Wallich and Sidney Weintraub in 1971.[28] Operating on the premise that the effective control of inflation requires business firms to refrain from granting wage increases in excess of the average rate of productivity growth, Wallich and Weintraub proposed that large firms which grant wage increases in excess of a governmentally determined standard be subjected to an income tax surcharge, while firms which hold their wage increases below that standard be accorded income tax reductions. Their TIP proposal also contemplated a reduction in the normal corporate income tax rate to offset the average surtax; hence, a firm setting its average wage increase at precisely the TIP guideline would continue to be taxed at the present rate. Another TIP proposal attracting considerable comment was made in 1978 by Arthur Okun, who advocated giving employees of firms that limited average wage increases to a certain percentage a tax credit which would slightly more than offset the average wage reduction.[29] Two TIP schemes were actually implemented in Brazil in 1965–1968, but they had little success in containing Brazil's galloping inflation rate.[30]

THE LIKELIHOOD OF CHRONIC INFLATION

Economists used to believe that there was an analogue to the law of gravity for consumer prices—what went up must come down. But prices throughout the world have been rising steadily since 1939, even during periods of recession. We are now living in an age of inflation, and we are likely to continue living in an age of inflation for many years to come.

There are a variety of reasons for the continuance during the reasonably foreseeable future of substantial inflationary pressures in most nations. These reasons can be summarized under the following six headings.

The Oil Cartel and Imitation Effect

The single most important factor that accounts for the sharp boost in global inflation rates during 1973–74 was the energy crisis provoked by the OPEC cartel formed by the oil producing nations. In one fell swoop, OPEC quadrupled the price of oil. Despite international dissension and price-shaving by a few countries, OPEC has managed to hold together as a cartel. The message has not been lost upon other primary product producing countries, which have attempted to form cartels to boost the prices of commodities such as bananas, copper, and coffee. The developing trend toward cartelization may augur sharply increasing prices for much of the world.[31]

If these were one-time price increases, they could be absorbed into the price structure and cease to be a source of future inflationary pressures.[32] But OPEC nations have been continually increasing oil prices, in part to compensate for the loss in purchasing power in the currencies with which they are paid for their oil exports. OPEC, by successfully pressing its demands for continual price increases, has precipitated a spiral similar to the wage-price spiral and has become a source of continuous worldwide inflationary pressures.

The Sanctity of Nearly Full Employment and the Fall from Grace of the Balanced Budget

The lesson taught by the Great Depression, World War II, and Lord Keynes—that massive governmental deficit spending can put the unemployed back to work—has become an accepted part of the conventional wisdom. Although the once popular notion that balanced budgets prevent inflation is nothing but a myth,[33] it was a useful myth in controlling monetary expansion. The debunking of the myth of the balanced budget makes it harder for political leaders to resist demands for increased governmental spending when the jobless rate rises much beyond a level that has historically been deemed critical. Most people would prefer to trade off moderate inflation for low unemployment. Whether there is such a trade-off is not nearly as important as the fact that most people believe such a trade-off exists.[34]

Increase in Administered Prices and Wages

The strength of labor unions has increased substantially in most countries since the depression of the 1930s. Union organization has spread far beyond the blue collar ranks to include groups like teachers, public employees, and health care workers. Unionization has generated a strong upward pressure on wages, which are a major cost component in modern economies. Consequently, wages have become increasingly ratcheted; they go up, but in most industries they do not go down, despite recession and weak demand. Moreover, some industries have become dominated by a few large corporations with sufficient market power to raise prices without fear of losing customers to competition. Rather than risk interruption of production with a strike, it is easier for such corporations to accede to union demands for substantial wage increases.[35] These increases, as well as something extra, are then passed on to the public.

Concomitantly, organized economic groups have discovered that what the market will not deliver may sometimes be delivered by the legislature. Receipt by industries or other pressure groups of subsidies in the form of price supports, credit, or tariff protection is widespread. Legislatures everywhere have been increasingly willing to intervene in the marketplace to help out groups which used to regard themselves at the mercy of inexorable market forces.[36] To the extent these subsidies are financed through creation of money and credit, they become a source of inflationary pressure.

Increase in Governmental Assumption of Social Welfare Costs and Regulation

Since the Great Depression, governments of most countries have undertaken vast social welfare programs. There have been huge increases in governmental spending directed at those members of the population who are poor, handicapped, or infirm. Not only have the classes of persons entitled to governmental benefits expanded, but the benefit levels have also increased markedly. Welfare and social security beneficiaries have organized to lobby for greater increases in benefits. There is every reason to believe that in most nations social welfare costs will continue to increase substantially. To the extent these benefits are financed by creation of credit rather than taxes, they become a source of inflationary pressure.

Governments have also enacted a steadily increasing amount of legislation regulating economic activity. Industries burning coal are required to install expensive air pollution controls. Transporters are required to maintain uneconomic routes and unnecessary personnel. Automobile manufacturers are required to comply with a series of safety, emission, and fuel economy measures. The burgeoning cost of these regulatory measures is passed on to consumers in the form of higher prices.

Abandonment of the Gold Standard

With all of its defects, and there were many, the gold standard had a decided tendency to check deficit spending and monetary expansion. The limited amount of gold available to back domestic currency or to cover balance of payments deficits served as a natural brake on inflationary spending programs. With the demise of the gold standard in the 1930s and the gradual demonetization of gold, this constraint has disappeared. Although international transactions were linked to gold under the Bretton Woods Agreement of 1944, which set up the International Monetary Fund (IMF), the U.S. dollar was made a "reserve currency." In practice, the dollar became the usual means of payment for international transfers. During the post-World War II era, the U.S. economy was extremely strong, especially in comparison with the war-battered economies of Europe, Japan, and the Soviet Union. There was enormous confidence in the dollar, almost everywhere regarded as good as gold. But the situation gradually changed, as the vast balance-of-payments surplus of the United States dwindled. Between 1949 and 1967 the gold reserves of the United States fell by 50 percent, from $24 billion to $12 billion, some $5.4 billion less than the amount of Eurodollars (U.S. dollars on deposit abroad, principally, but not exclusively, in Europe). Had most of these Eurodollars been redeemed through central banks, the U.S. gold reserves would have been quickly exhausted. Although the United States took a number of measures during the mid-1960s to improve its balance of payments, pressures on the dollar continued to mount. By 1971 they were so great that the United States was forced to torpedo the Bretton Woods Agreement by refusing to redeem dollars for gold held abroad. Gold has now been demonetized, and exchange rates are more or less free to float.

In March of 1980 there were an estimated U.S. $1,200 trillion in the Eurocurrency market.[37] It is widely believed that the vast increase in Eurodollars (852 percent between 1971 and 1980) has in itself been an important source of international inflationary pressure because it has increased the world's money supply. The development of the Eurocurrency market is regarded as an increase in the total supply of money rather than simply a shift in where it is held. Because the Eurodollar banking system is virtually unregulated, banks accepting Eurocurrency deposits can maintain lower reserve requirements with respect to these deposits than the U.S. banks from which the dollars are transferred. This makes the multiplier higher, permitting the Eurocurrency system to create more money with Eurodollars than could regulated U.S. banks.[38]

The Creation of Inflationary Expectations

Once inflation has become chronic, people develop an inflationary psychology. Economic decisions come to include calculations for anticipated inflation. Wage demands are higher than they would otherwise be because workers expect prices to go up during the term of the contract. Rents are set at higher levels than they would be during economic stability to try to ensure an adequate real return on investment. Budgetary calculations factor in the anticipated inflation rate. People reduce their holdings of cash and other unprotected financial assets to a minimum and bid up the price of assets which are commonly regarded as inflation-proof, such as real estate, gold, or precious gems. Interest rates rise, and the terms of long-term credit become shorter and shorter. The velocity with which money circulates increases as people rush to spend or invest cash, while firms shorten payment terms and exact harsher penalties for late payments. This inflationary psychology soon becomes an autonomous cause of inflation. If all other sources of inflationary pressures were suddenly eliminated, prices would continue to rise, at least for some time, simply because people would expect prices to rise. More than thirty-five years of virtually continuous inflation has created inflationary expectations in all but the most unsophisticated individuals.

CONCLUSIONS

These six reasons for the existence of chronic inflationary pressures in most free world economies do not mean that galloping or runaway inflation is likely to beset many countries. As Professor Bach has pointed out,[39] there are countervailing pressures. Competition, where it exists, makes most businessmen hesitate to raise prices. Citizens do resist steadily increasing tax rates and demand constraints on governmental spending. For example, in the United States a recent movement to enact a constitutional amendment requiring balancing of the federal budget has been gathering considerable political support. Most people regard inflation as an evil, even though they may be profiting from it in certain ways, and will oppose political groups that advocate blatantly inflationary policies. Failure to contain inflation has brought down governments in a number of countries. Despite the development of an inflationary psychology, the nominalist illusion still persists. People still tend to regard a dollar as a dollar or a pound as a pound, regardless of when earned or spent.

In short, most countries are likely to undergo chronic creeping or trotting inflation for the reasonably foreseeable future. Complete elimination of inflation is unlikely to be a politically viable strategy for many nations. On the other hand, persistent disregard of inflationary pressures is equally unlikely to be politically viable. The most likely scenario for many countries is the striking of a balance between the policies of restraints on governmental spending and deficit spending that will hold the inflation rate somewhere between 5 and 20 percent per annum.

NOTES

1. The use of the expression "inflation" to describe changes in the value of money or an upward movement of the general price level apparently originated in the United States during the middle of the nineteenth century. Its origins as well as some of the multifarious meanings ascribed to it are explored in Nussbaum, *The Meaning of Inflation,* 58 Pol. Sci. Q. 86 (1943).

2. Examples of judicial confusion about the relationship between domestic inflation rates and exchange rates can be found in Liberty Nat. Bank of N.Y. v. Burr, 270 F. 251, 255 (E.D. Pa. 1921); Kantor v. Aristo Hosiery Co., 222 App. Div. 502, 504, 226 N.Y. Supp. 582, 584 (1st Dept. 1928), *aff'd,* 248 N.Y. 630, 162 N.E. 553 (1928).

3. If there were freely floating exchange rates, no trade barriers, and no shipping costs, exchange rates and relative inflation rates should operate in tandem. Considerable slippage in such linkage occurs, however, from governmental interference in foreign exchange markets to support its currency, tariffs, shipping costs, tourist expenditures, and international capital movements. *See* G. Halm, Monetary Theory 221–28 (2d ed. 1946).

4. Bronfenbrenner, *Inflation and Deflation,* in 7 Int'l Ency. Soc. Sci. 289 (1968).

5. P. Ferreira, A Inflação 36–37 (2d ed. 1967); Schwartz, *Secular Price Change in Historical Perspective,* 5 J. Money, Credit, & Banking 243, 244–46 (1973).

6. L. Yang, Money and Credit in China 51–67 (1952).

7. J. Galbraith, Money: Whence It Came, Where It Went 11–12 (1975). During the sixteenth century prices in Spain rose by a factor of five; in England the rate of increase was roughly half that of Spain. *Id. See also* Schwartz, *supra* note 5, at 250–53.

8. L. Yang, *supra* note 6, at 51–67.

9. A. Nussbaum, Money In The Law: National and International 558–60 (rev. ed. 1950).

10. By the time continentals had been in circulation for six years, their exchange rate varied between $400 and $1,000 for one dollar in specie. A. Hepburn, A History of the Currency of the United States 13–19 (1924); G. Warren & F. Pearson, Prices 328 (rev. ed. 1933); Schwartz, *supra* note 5, at 256.

11. J. Galbraith, *supra* note 7, at 64–66; Schwartz, *supra* note 5, at 256.

12. By January 1865, Confederate currency, which was first issued in May 1861, had fallen to less than one-fiftieth of its nominal value with respect to gold. Four months later Confederate dollars were wholly worthless. Dawson & Cooper, *The Effect of Inflation on Private Contracts: United States, 1861–1879,* 33 Mich. L. Rev. 706, 747 (1935). By January 1865, Northern greenbacks, which were first authorized in February of 1862, fell to 44 percent of their nominal value with respect to gold. The differential between the gold dollar and the greenback gradually diminished and by the end of 1878 disappeared entirely. *Id.* at 854–55.

13. With a 20 percent legal reserve requirement, each dollar deposited in a bank can create five or six dollars through the operation of the multiplier. *See* P. SAMUELSON, ECONOMICS 300–306 (9th ed. 1973).

14. J. GALBRAITH, *supra* note 7, at 154–55.

15. P. FERREIRA, *supra* note 5, at 46. Bomberger & Makinen, *Indexation, Inflationary Finance, and Hyperinflation: The 1945–1946 Hungarian Experience,* 88 J. POL. ECON. 550, 552 (1980). Hungary succeeded in stabilizing its new monetary unit, the *forint,* at a rate of 4×10^{29} *pengo,* its old monetary unit, approximately 400 times 1 billion cubed. Maier, *The Politics of Inflation in the Twentieth Century,* in THE POLITICAL ECONOMY OF INFLATION 37, 47 (F. Hirsch & J. Goldthorpe, eds. 1978).

16. Prewar price levels multiplied roughly 14,000 times in Austria, 23,000 times in Hungary, 2.5 million times in Poland, and 4 billion in Russia. L. YEAGER, INTERNATIONAL MONETARY RELATIONS: THEORY, HISTORY, AND POLICY 312 (2d ed. 1976).

17. The Argentine and Chilean inflation rates would have risen much higher had the Allende and Perón regimes not been ousted by military *coups* and austere stabilization measures instituted. Despite austerity measures Chile's official consumer price index rose by 711 percent from September of 1973 (the date of Allende's demise) to September of 1974, in part because of the military government's dismantling of the widespread subsidies and price controls. 3 Latin America Economic Report 94 (1975). According to the present Argentine government, which came to power in March of 1976, the rate of price increase during the first quarter of 1976 extrapolated to an annual inflation rate of more than 3,000 percent; the increase for the month of March 1976 reportedly extrapolated to an annual rate of more than 17,000 percent. GOBIERNO DE LA REPÚBLICA ARGENTINA, MINISTRY OF ECONOMY, ARGENTINE ECONOMIC DEVELOPMENT 7 (Apr.–Feb. 1976–78). IMF figures place the annual inflation rate for 1976 in Argentina at 599 percent. IMF, 31 INT'L FINANCIAL STATISTICS 42 (No. 4, Apr. 1978).

18. In the centrally planned economies of the Communist countries markets do exist and so does inflation. Inflationary pressures are often attributed to a generalized excess of demand created by the planners. Portes, *Inflation under Central Planning,* in THE POLITICAL ECONOMY OF INFLATION 73, 74 (F. Hirsch & J. Goldthorpe eds. 1978). But inflation in planned economies tends to be repressed. Prices remain stable because the government, which sets prices, refuses to allow them to rise. As a result of suppressed inflationary pressures, shortages develop, and goods are allocated by rationing or the black market. *See* B. GRIFFITHS, INFLATION: THE PRICE OF PROSPERITY 261–66 (1976). Cf. Allen, *The Structure and Reform of the Exchange and Payments Systems of Some East European Countries,* 23 IMF STAFF PAPERS 718 (1976). The discussion in the text is directed only to free market economies.

19. M. FRIEDMAN, *The Supply of Money and Changes in Prices and Output,* in U.S. CONG., JT. ECON. COMM., THE RELATIONSHIP OF PRICES TO ECONOMIC STABILITY AND GROWTH 241 (85th Cong., 2d Sess. 1958); Harberger, *The Dynamics of Inflation in Chile,* in MEASUREMENT IN ECONOMICS: STUDIES IN MATHEMATICAL ECONOMICS IN MEMORY OF YEHUDA GRUNFELD 219 (C. Christ, ed. 1963); Meiselman, *World-wide Inflation: a Monetarist View,* in THE PHENOMENON OF WORLDWIDE INFLATION 69 (D. Meiselman & A. Laffer, eds. 1975).

20. P. SAMUELSON, *supra* note 13, at 242.

21. The wide variety of cost-push explanations of inflation are reviewed in Bronfenbrenner and Holzman, *Survey of Inflation Theory,* 53 AM. ECON. REV. 593 (1963).

22. Gordon, *The Demand for and Supply of Inflation,* 18 J. L. & ECON. 807, 819–23 (1975).

23. S. WACHTER, LATIN AMERICAN INFLATION: THE STRUCTURALIST-MONETARIST DEBATE 4 (1976).

24. This account of Latin America structuralism is largely drawn from Baer, *The Inflation Controversy in Latin America: A Survey,* 2 LATIN AM. RESEARCH REV. 3, 4–19 (1967).

25. M. EDEL, FOOD SUPPLY AND INFLATION IN LATIN AMERICA (1969); S. WACHTER, *supra* note 23.

26. The argument may be spelled out more fully. Tax cuts will increase investment, which will in turn increase labor productivity and total output. Assuming that the productivity increase does not result in an increase in the rate of wage increases, the rate of increase in unit labor costs should fall. Competition should then force prices downward. Supposedly, there should be a corresponding change in monetary conditions with the amount of money needed to finance transactions automatically rising with the increase in total output. Assuming the rate of monetary expansion remains constant, the increase in demand for money would decrease the inflationary gap between monetary supply and demand. The reduction in the excess supply of money and the downward pressure on prices from lowered unit labor costs should reduce inflation without an increase in unemployment. Feldstein, "Inflation and Supply Side Economics," Wall St. J., May 20, 1980.

27. *Id.*; Stein, "Some 'Supply-Side' Propositions," Wall St. J. Mar. 19, 1980.

28. Wallich and Weintraub, *A Tax-Based Incomes Policy,* J. ECON. ISSUES 5 (Je. 1971).

29. Okun, "A Reward TIP," Statement before U.S. Senate Comm. on Banking, Housing, and Urban Affairs, May 22, 1978, reproduced in SOLUTIONS TO INFLATION 176 (D. Colander, ed. 1979).

30. Brazilian TIP legislation granted a variety of tax concessions to firms voluntarily agreeing to hold price increases within certain limits and imposed tax penalties upon those which increased prices by more than certain percentages. This legislation is more fully described in Rosenn, *Adaptations of the Brazilian Income Tax to Inflation,* 21 STAN. L. REV. 58, 85–89 (1968).

31. *See* Bergsten, *Resource Scarcity: Cartelization and Contrived Scarcity,* 24 AM. U. L. REV. 1128 (1975). *See also* Weintraub, *The Example of OPEC and the Possibility of Other Producer Cartels,* 24 AM. U. L. REV. 1097 (1975).

32. Prices would not return to prior levels, but the oil increases would cease to be a source of further price increases. There is, however, a danger that workers who find their real incomes decreased by the inflation during the previous year will press to recoup income previously lost plus anticipated inflation, setting off a wage-price spiral effect.

33. The crucial point is how budgetary deficits are financed. As Arthur Schlesinger has recently reminded those who simple-mindedly seek to solve the inflation problem by balancing the budget, the United States experienced inflation in 1920, despite a budgetary surplus, and had severe deflation in 1930–33, despite unprece-

dented peacetime budgetary deficits. "Inflation: Symbolism vs. Reality," Wall St. J., Apr. 9, 1980, p. 18, cols. 4–6.

34. Until recently, it was fashionable in many economic circles to refer to this trade-off in terms of a downward sloping curve named after Professor A. W. Phillips, who was the first to attempt to quantify the trade-off. The stagflation experienced by many countries during the 1970s, with its combination of high unemployment and high inflation, has cast considerable doubt about the utility of the Phillips curve analysis.

35. This point is more fully developed in J. GALBRAITH, ECONOMICS AND THE PUBLIC PURPOSE 186–94 (1973).

36. *See* G. BACH, THE NEW INFLATION 40–45 (1973).

37. Morgan Guaranty Trust Co. of N.Y., World Financial Markets, Aug. 1980, p. 9. This is a gross figure and includes liabilities to other banks. The net figure is $635 billion. About 74 percent of the Eurocurrency consists of Eurodollars.

38. Salant, *International Transmission of Inflation,* in WORLDWIDE INFLATION 167, 224 (L. Krause & W. Salant, eds. 1977). In addition, the practice of some of the central banks of depositing reserves in the Eurocurrency market also resulted in multiple deposit creation. In the spring of 1971, the Group of Ten Central Banks agreed to stop this practice because of its inflationary effect. *Id.*

39. G. BACH, *supra* note 36.

2

THE MEASUREMENT OF INFLATION

If a legal system is to take inflation into account, the law has to rely on some device to measure inflation. Most legal systems presently assign monetary values to rights and responsibilities. If one is to disregard the fiction that a currency unit is always equal to itself, the law has to find some way of quantifying the adjustments it will have to make to its normal measuring stick, the currency unit. The point is not that the law cannot take account of concepts which cannot be easily measured. Lawyers deal daily with concepts like negligence, pain and suffering, and intent, none of which is easily measurable.

THE PRICE INDEXES

There is no way to know precisely how much inflation any economy is undergoing. There are billions of prices in modern economies, and there is no feasible method to monitor their constant movements. The best approximations are price indexes. The three most commonly used of these yardsticks are (1) the consumer price index (sometimes referred to as the cost-of-living index or the retail price index); (2) the wholesale price index; and (3) the implicit GNP deflator. What are these indexes? How are they constructed? How accurate are they? What universe do they measure? Without a basic understanding of these indexes' derivation, lawyers cannot assess the degree to which their clients are protected from economic loss due to inflation, nor can judges or legislators intelligently appraise the costs and benefits of any inflation adjustment schemes. The next three sections provide a thumbnail sketch of what the three most common inflation indexes actually measure, a brief evaluation of their strengths and weaknesses, and a guide to construction of a price index.

The Consumer Price Index

Consumer price indexes attempt to measure changes over time in the prices of equivalent goods and services that are consumed during the normal course of living. In most countries the consumer price index is the most widely used estimation of the inflation rate. The index numbers typically reflect average annual price changes, from which are calculated the figure usually bandied about, the average annual percentage rate of change. Perhaps more relevant, however, is the year-end rate of change, the percentage change from December to December of each year, or the percentage change in the index over the most recent twelve-month period. If the inflation rate is rising, the year-end and most recent twelve-month percentages will be higher than the average annual rate. On the other hand, if the inflation rate is declining, the average annual rate will be higher.

What does it mean to say that the consumer price index for 1975 rose 11 percent in the United States, 15.9 percent in Great Britain, or 585.9 percent in Chile? What lies behind these figures? How are index numbers derived, and what do they purport to measure?

Constructing a Consumer Price Index

A consumer price index is designed to measure the rate of change in prices paid by the consumer for certain goods and services. But constructing even a simple price index is no easy task. Consider the case of a primitive economy with only five commodities—bananas, coconuts, fish, grass skirts, and rum. Assume that in December of 1979 and 1980 the following price observations were recorded:

Item	*1979 Price*	*1980 Price*
bananas	2	4
coconuts	1	1
fish	3	5
grass skirts	8	15
rum	5	12
Totals	19	37

With this price data, one can construct a crude price index for this economy. If we take 1979 as our base year and set it at 100, we would show that our simple index increased by 94.7 percent in the following year in this fashion:

1979	100
1980	194.7

But do we really know that the cost of living for this hypothetical economy increased by 94.7 percent between 1979 and 1980? By giving the same weight to each commodity, our simple index implicitly gave the greatest weight to those items which had the greatest price increases, specifically bananas and rum. But these items may constitute a relatively small part of the expenditure patterns of the typical inhabitant of this primitive economy. If people in this primitive economy bought more coconuts and fish than bananas and rum, then the cost of living rose by less than 94.7 percent. If they bought more rum and bananas than other commodities, the cost of living rose by more than 94.7 percent. To refine this crude price index, we need to know the quantities of each commodity purchased. This information is generally obtained by a market basket survey in which a representative group is queried about its expenditure patterns. The results of this survey are used to weight each component of the price index.

Suppose a market basket survey revealed that members of this primitive economy in 1979 purchased on the average 30 bananas, 50 coconuts, 50 fish, 1 grass skirt, and 30 bowls of rum. Purchase of this market basket in 1979 cost 418; in 1980 the same market basket cost 795. If one assumes the equivalent quantities of each commodity were purchased in 1980, an assumption whose validity is examined *infra,* [1] our weighted simple price index would look like this:

1979	100
1980	190.2

We would then conclude that the cost of living in this primitive economy increased by 90.2 percent during 1980 rather than 94.7 percent.

The Laspeyres Formula

The formula used for constructing a weighted aggregative price index is largely a function of the question to be answered. A price index is commonly expected to show how much it would cost in the current period to purchase the same market basket purchased in the base period. The formula most widely used to construct an index that answers that question is one devised by Etienne Laspeyres in 1864.

$$I_2 = \frac{\Sigma p_2 q_1}{\Sigma p_1 q_1} \times 100$$

where I_2 is the value of the index number in the second year added to the value in the base year; q_1 represents the quantities purchased in the base year; p_1 represents prices of individual items in the base year; p_2 represents the prices of individual items in the second year; and Σ is the standard symbol for summation. This index is the weighted ratio of two expenditures: the hypothetical current expenditure divided by the actual base period expenditure. The weights and the base are fixed. Plugging the data from our hypothetical primitive economy into this formula, $I_2 = \frac{795}{418} \times 100$

= 190.2. If we set our base year of 1979 at 100, our index would look like this:

1979	100
1980	190.2

This index would tell us that the cost of living rose by 90.2 percent in our economy during 1980, the same result reached more directly above.

The Paasche Formula

Price indexes are also commonly designed to demonstrate how much it would have cost during the base period to purchase the consumer's current market basket of goods. The formula most widely used to construct an index that answers that question was devised by Hermann Paasche in 1874.

$$I_2 = \frac{\Sigma p_2 q_2}{\Sigma p_1 q_2} = 100$$

where I_2 is the value of the index number in the second year added to the value of the base year; p_2 represents the prices of individual items in the second year; p_1 represents prices in the base year; and q_2 represents the quantity purchased in the second year. This formula differs from that of Laspeyres in that it shows the ratio of actual current expenditures to a hypothetical base period expenditure. An annual increase of 8.4 percent on a Paasche index means that the consumer's current market basket costs 8.4 percent more than it would have cost during the base period. Since the Paasche index always compares current expenditures with the base period, year-to-year comparisons are misleading. For example, if our primitive economy's Laspeyres index number for 1980 were to double for 1981, it would be appropriate to interpret the index as showing that the cost of island living during that year rose by 100 percent.

1979	100
1980	190.2
1981	380.4

But such an interpretation of a Paasche-type index would be incorrect. A Paasche-type index with the above values would tell us that 1981's market basket cost 3.804 times as much as it would have cost in 1979. But it does not tell us that the cost of living doubled from 1980 to 1981. The particular selection of commodities being priced changes from 1979 to 1980, distorting direct comparison of current prices with any year but the base year.

Although most countries use some form of Laspeyres formula in constructing their consumer price index, there is considerable variation with respect to which economic groups' spending patterns serve as the basis for the market basket survey and how many items are included in the market basket. West Germany and Italy use sampling techniques designed to reflect a cross section of the entire population. Canada's cost-of-living index reflects the spending patterns of a sample of families earning $2,500 to $7,000 a year and living in cities of more than 30,000 inhabitants. The United States now has two official consumer price indexes. One is based upon a sample of the expenditure patterns of urban wage-earners and clerical workers and their families, who comprise about 45 percent of the entire population. The other, instituted in 1978, is based upon the expenditure patterns of all urban consumers, approximately 80 percent of the population. The number of items represented in consumer price indexes varies considerably—147 items in Belgium, 258 in Canada, 400 in the United States, and 900 in West Germany. The United Kingdom and France revise index weights annually, but most countries allow the weights to remain unchanged for ten to fifteen years.[2]

Consumer price indexes are normally based upon retail prices in particular cities. In some countries, such as the United States, these municipal indexes are aggregated in accordance with weights derived from population data to produce a national consumer price index. In other countries, such as Argentina, the price index for a key city like Buenos Aires is often used as a proxy for the entire country.

In most countries consumer price indexes are compiled on a monthly basis. There are exceptions, however, such as Australia, where the consumer price index appears on a quarterly basis. Great efforts are made to insure that the prices actually paid by the consumer are reflected in the data collected. The items in the market basket are usually described with detailed specifications to try to insure that the same quality and quantity is being priced over time.

The Wholesale Price Index

Wholesale price indexes attempt to measure changes over time in the wholesale prices paid for a selected list of products. They are usually designed to measure changes in prices at the level of their first important commercial transaction. Unlike consumer price indexes, which measure prices in particular localities, wholesale price indexes measure prices in the entire country. Prices collected are f.o.b. production or central marketing point, and any applicable discount is netted out. In the United States some prices are taken from reports by trade associations or from trade publications, while others are obtained by mailing the questionnaires to representative manufacturers. The Bureau of Labor Statistics attempts to obtain transactions prices, but it not infrequently winds up with list or spot prices.

The typical wholesale price index uses the Laspeyres formula, or a variant thereof, and is weighted in accordance with the relative importance of each product to national output. These weights are usually revised every few years in accordance with industrial census data. In the United States about 2,800 items are reflected in the wholesale price index,[3] renamed the "Producer Product Index" in 1978. In some of the less developed countries the number of items priced is often fewer than 100.

The Implicit GNP Deflator

The most comprehensive price indexes available are the Gross National Product (GNP) Implicit Price Deflators. They are the only indexes which cut across all sectors of the economy to include all transactions that affect the general level of prices. They are indexes of the prices of final products, consumer purchases, and business investment.

The GNP deflator is implicit in the relationship between current and constant value estimates of the GNP. Its construction is a rather complicated process. Unlike the wholesale and consumer price indexes, which are usually published on a monthly basis, GNP deflators are usually published quarterly (and in some places only annually). The first step in the production of the GNP deflator is the estimation of GNP in current monetary units. Next, each component of GNP is deflated by subindexes of other price indexes deemed most appropriate. Thus, the gross domestic investment component of GNP would be deflated by various subindexes of the wholesale price index. To the extent that investment represented construction, a cost of construction index would be used. Consumer spending components of GNP would be deflated by the consumer price index. Once the component parts of GNP have been deflated, GNP is then reaggregated to obtain a constant value GNP. Finally, the implicit GNP is determined by dividing the current value GNP by the constant value GNP.

The GNP deflator is a Paasche-type index. Its weights are derived from the composition of GNP during any given period. To the extent that the composition of GNP changes (i.e., change in the relative values of government, consumer, and business spending), the weighting of the implicit GNP deflator changes. The accuracy of the GNP deflator depends upon the accuracy of the GNP estimates and the subindexes being used to deflate the various components of GNP.

Miscellaneous Price Indexes

Most countries compile a variety of price indexes in addition to the consumer and wholesale price index and the GNP deflator. Typically, there are separate indexes for construction costs, prices paid to farmers, prices paid by farmers, import goods, export goods, and a host of other subindexes of the wholesale and consumer price indexes. Some countries also maintain a general price index; for example, in Brazil this index is derived from a weighted average of the wholesale price index, the consumer price index, and the index of construction costs.

LIMITATIONS OF EXISTING PRICE INDEXES

There is a deceptive aura of certainty and simplicity surrounding price indexes. Although technical accuracy has improved enormously in most countries during the past few decades, the little understood art of index-making conceals a number of essentially arbitrary judgments and technical inaccuracies that any policymaker should be aware of before adopting measures in which a substantial amount of money will change hands in accordance with slight movements in index numbers.

Market Basket Changes

Consumers typically change the mix of their market basket in response to changes in relative prices in an attempt to maintain the same living standards. If the price of fish remains the same while the price of meat rises, consumers tend to purchase more fish and less meat. A true cost-of-living index ought to measure the increase in minimum expenditures necessary to maintain a constant level of utility to the consumer. Instead, the Laspeyres price index measures the increase in minimum expenditures necessary to purchase a constant market basket of goods and services. A market basket survey requires continual updating if it is to reflect current expenditure patterns, particularly in a society undergoing rapid inflation.[4] Such surveys, however, are expensive to conduct in complex societies. The U.S. Bureau of Labor Statistics reportedly spent approximately $42 million to complete its most recent market basket survey.[5] This new survey was completed in 1971–72 but was not incorporated into the consumer price index until 1978. Until then, the U.S. calculated its consumer price index on the basis of a 1960–61 market basket survey. This lag is not atypical. Most countries operate with out-of-date market basket surveys; lags of ten to fifteen years are quite common.[6] If one wants to know how much the cost of living has risen from 1962 to 1978, an index that indicates that it cost 90 percent more in 1978 to purchase the collection of goods bought by a representative family in 1962 is of dubious utility. The greater the change in consumption patterns since the market basket survey, the more misleading the index.

The failure to survey consumer spending patterns on a continuing basis causes the consumer price index to exaggerate the real rise in the cost of living. The index assumes that the only way in which a consumer can maintain the same standard of living when certain prices rise is by spending more money. But a consumer may have virtually the same level of satisfaction by spending the same amount of money to purchase a different mix of goods. Yet the magnitude of this substitution bias is not as great as one would expect. A recent fifteen-year empirical study of the U.S. consumer price index places the amount of substitution bias from the use of fixed weights in the Laspeyres formula at 0.1 index points per year.[7]

One technique for mitigating this bias is to chain-link a Laspeyres index. This is accomplished by updating the base each year by using the quantities purchased each year to reweight the index for the following year. The chief difficulty in chain-linking an index lies in securing reliable information about the quantities purchased each year. Estimates are sometimes made from national accounts data; other times an annual family expenditure survey is made. While chain-linking does allow for substitutions in response to price changes more readily than a fixed-weight Laspeyres index, the chain-linked index has a tendency to magnify a succession of sharp price increases. Moreover, it is difficult to interpret. Hence, chain-linking alone is generally not regarded as an adequate solution for eliminating the bias resulting from shifts in consumption patterns.[8]

Another technique for mitigating this bias, proposed many years ago by Irving Fisher, is to construct a comparable consumer price with current year weights and average it with the fixed-weight consumer price index. Because estimates of current year weights have already been developed for calculation of the personal consumption expenditures deflator,[9] and since the Bureau of Labor Statistics recently began a quarterly survey of consumer expenditures, adoption of Fisher's averaging proposal may soon prove practicable.[10]

A related problem is the weighting of certain consumer durables, particularly housing costs. A number of economists argue that the present treatment of housing costs gives the consumer price index an upward bias because the price measured is based solely upon new home sales and current mortgage interest rates; the interest rates on existing mortgages and the prices paid for the existing housing stock does not enter into the calculation. Approximately 6 percent of homeowners bought new houses in the 1972–73 base period; therefore, the weights applied to house prices are based upon the prices paid by the 6 percent who bought new houses, just as automobile prices are based upon the prices paid by those purchasing cars. Many economists believe that purchases of durable goods, such as homes and automobiles, should be treated differently from other goods and services in the consumer price index, because these products are not consumed within a brief period. They argue that only the cost of what is currently consumed should be included in the price index; the remainder should be regarded as investment rather than consumption. If this argument were accepted, the upward pressure resulting from housing costs would be significantly reduced because house prices and home mortgage costs would be an average of the monthly expenditures by all homeowners for amortization and interest payments.[11]

Quality Changes

A perennial problem of price indexes is how to net out changes in the quality of goods being priced. If a 1981 car costs $400 more than a similar 1980 model, how much of that $400 should be allocated to improvements in design, safety features, and gas mileage, and how much should be allocated to inflation?[12] Complex engineering and road tests are necessary to permit the development of quality adjustment factors. Economists have traditionally maintained that an annual inflation rate of 1 to 2 percent is attributable solely to quality improvements in the goods being priced. Richard Ruggles concluded: "If we took quality change into account, there was no secular price rise in the period 1960 to 1965, and in the period 1966 through 1973 prices have risen about half as fast as the indicators show."[13] Other economists argue that these quality changes are much exaggerated and have been substantially offset by declines in quality in other areas, notably services.

A related problem is deciding when to introduce a new product into the index and when to drop a product presently being priced. Entirely new products, such as radios and televisions, are usually reflected in a price index only after a major revision, which is likely to occur long after they have become important consumer items. Although pantyhose may have largely replaced nylon stockings in the marketplace, the price index is likely to ignore such substitution for a good many years. The dilemma faced by the index-maker is determining whether a new product has become firmly entrenched in the buying patterns of the population or is just a passing fad like hula hoops. If one determines that the new product is here to stay, the problem becomes what weight to assign to it. In the absence of a new market basket survey, such weighting is extremely difficult and arbitrary.

Transaction Prices v. List Prices

A price index is supposed to reflect prices actually being paid for goods and services. The wholesale price index frequently uses list or quoted prices rather than actual transaction prices, which may be lower because of discounts or special offers, or higher because of shortages. Consequently, the wholesale price index has a tendency to overstate the inflation rate during normal economic periods, when discounts or rebates are readily available, and to understate the inflation rate when goods become difficult to obtain. In addition, good data are often difficult to obtain, because businessmen tend to be secretive about actual wholesale prices.

Coverage Limitations

A serious limitation upon the adequacy of price indexes is the universe measured by the index. Both the wholesale and consumer price indexes fail to cover important areas of economic activity. For example, the cost of living might increase or decrease substantially because of changes in income or social security taxes or land prices, but such an increase or decrease will not show up directly in the consumer price index.[14] Income taxes and the prices of land or securities are beyond the parameters of the consumer price index as currently constituted. The universe of the consumer price index is usually based upon the expenditure patterns and prices paid by urban dwellers (generally with working-class incomes, married, with two to four children). Prices and expenditure patterns might be quite different for upper-class families, middle class couples, single people, or farm dwellers.

The wholesale price index tells us only what price changes have taken place in certain commodities. It tells us nothing about changes in other costs of doing business, such as wages, advertising, or business services. Also excluded from the universe of the wholesale price index are construction costs, real estate, sales or purchases by the government, military production, securities, and goods produced and consumed within the same plant.

The wholesale price index also has a decided tendency to count certain products several times, for it mixes raw materials and finished products. Thus, if iron ore prices rise, that price increase will show up at least three times in the wholesale price index: first, directly in the price of iron ore; second, in the price of steel; and third, in the price of automobiles. All three of these prices are individual items in the index.[15]

Sampling Errors

All indexes require some kind of sampling. There are billions of prices being set in any modern economy, and it is utterly unrealistic to expect to be able to measure all of them. Sampling techniques are employed at many stages of the construction of price indexes. The choice of items to price, the number of price measurements taken, the frequency of price measurement, the number of firms supplying price data, and the number and characteristics of persons whose expenditure patterns will be surveyed, all afford substantial opportunity for sampling errors. The extent of sampling error is unknown, but it seems probable that for most countries the errors are quite inconsequential for the comprehensive "all items" indexes, but much more significant at the group or subgroup levels.[16]

Seasonal Adjustments

Certain products, particularly foodstuffs, normally display significant seasonal variations. Unless adjusted for these seasonal variations, a price index (especially a subindex) can produce misleading impressions of short-term price behavior. Since 1966 the U.S. Bureau of Labor Statistics has published seasonally adjusted subindexes for the components of the consumer price index most affected by seasonal variations, that is food, apparel, and private transportation. The all-items consumer price index, however, appears to be little affected by such seasonal variations.

Governmental Manipulation

In many countries the inflation rate is a highly charged political issue. Governments frequently predict what the inflation rate will be, and are politically embarrassed if the reported rate is higher than the officially anticipated rate. In some countries governments have perceived that it is easier to control the price indexes than it is to control the inflation rate. The charge that the government has manipulated the price indexes to report a lower rate of inflation is ofttimes voiced in countries undergoing severe inflation, occasionally for good reasons.[17]

Many governments that disdain tampering with the price indexes achieve much the same result indirectly by manipulating prices. Price controls and subsidized prices are common nostrums during inflation. Such measures may succeed in suppressing inflationary pressures for a time; however, shortages and black markets generally follow in their wake. The existence of controls and subsidies poses a severe dilemma for the index-maker. Should he report an item at its official price, even if none or few are to be found at the official price? Should he report the black market price, if such a market exists? Should he average the prices, or perhaps attempt to weight them for quantities? Because most index-makers decide it is more politic to record the official price, price controls and subsidies cause the price indexes to understate the actual rate of inflation.[18]

CONCLUSIONS

Inflation can be viewed either as a sustained rise in the general price level or as a decline in the purchasing power of a country's currency. Whether an economy is undergoing inflation does not depend upon whether the prices of particular goods or services are going up or down or remaining stable. The answer to that question depends upon what is happening to the general or aggregate level of prices over time.

There is no way to know precisely how much inflation any economy is experiencing. There is no feasible way to monitor the constant movements of the myriad prices in modern economies. The best approximations available are price indexes, particularly the consumer price index, the wholesale price index, and the implicit GNP deflator. Only the implicit GNP deflator provides a measure of price level change that reflects the entire economy, but its Paasche formula basis and the three- to twelve-month lag in its publication limit its use as a measure of inflation. Thus, despite their more limited universes, the consumer and wholesale price indexes are more useful proxies for the inflation rate.

All three indexes have serious limitations for making adjustments to inflation. Despite such limitations, the price indexes offer the most promising techniques for adapting legal institutions to inflation.

NOTES

1. *See* pp. 27–28 *infra*.

2. Organization for Economic Co-operation and Development, Consumer Price Indices 10–12 (Nov. 1971).

3. In 1978 the U.S. Bureau of Labor Statistics began the first comprehensive revision of the wholesale price index. The entire revision is not scheduled for completion until 1984, but revised sections are being published as they become available. Thus far, the chief change has been in the index's name; it is now being referred to as the Producer Price Index. The revision will attempt to eliminate multiple counting of price changes by adopting fixed input and output price modes derived from the theory of the firm. In addition, coverage will be expanded significantly. *See* Early, *Improving the Measurement of Producer Price Change,* 101 MONTHLY LABOR REV. 7 (1978).

4. Alsop, "Most Families Become Resourceful and Beat Rise in Consumer Price Index," Wall St. J., Nov. 21, 1980, p. 1, col. 1.

5. Rosenblatt, "CPI: It Changes People's Lives," Los Angeles Times, May 23, 1976, Part VIII, p. 1, 3, col. 2. The new U.S. market basket survey is based upon interviews conducted in 1972–73 of a sample of 20,000 families, selected as representative of the entire urban population from 1970 census data. *Id.*

6. The United Kingdom and France are exceptional in this regard, revising index weights on an annual basis. In the United Kingdom weights are derived from the expenditure patterns of a changing representative sample of households in a continuous Family Expenditure Survey. A moving average of three years of expenditures is used to calculate the weights for each year. R. FOWLER, SOME PROBLEMS OF INDEX NUMBER CONSTRUCTION 10 (1970). In France weights are derived from a combination of consumer surveys and national accounts. Occasionally, countries change index weights for political purposes without bothering to take a new market basket survey. For example, after enacting a statute liberating most housing units from rent control, the Brazilians slashed the weight accorded to rent in the cost-of-living index for Rio de Janeiro from 20 percent to 10.57 percent. See Rosenn, *Controlled Rents and Uncontrolled Inflation: the Brazilian Dilemma,* 17 AM. J. COMP. L. 239, 255, fn. 66 (1969).

7. Braithwait, *The Substitution Bias of the Laspeyres Price Index,* 70 AM. ECON. REV. 64 (1980).

8. W. WALLACE & W. CULLISON, MEASURING PRICE CHANGES: A STUDY OF THE PRICE INDEXES 30–31 (4th ed. 1979).

9. The personal consumer expenditures deflator is implicitly derived in the process of estimating gross national product in constant dollar terms. It represents the value of consumption expenditures by the entire population (including rural areas and private nonprofit institutions) divided by their value in constant (1972) dollars. This deflator is derived by using a constantly changing market basket determined by what items consumers are currently buying.

10. Moore, *Inflation and Statistics,* in CONTEMPORARY ECONOMIC PROBLEMS 1980, 167, 174 (W. Fellner, ed. 1980).

11. *Id.* at 175–76.

12. The U.S. Department of Labor estimated that $59.15, or approximately 16 percent of the average $382.30 price increase in 1977 automobiles, represented quality improvements. Slightly more than one-third of this quality increase represented changes necessary to meet federal safety and pollution control requirements. Wall St. Journal, Nov. 5, 1976, p. 2, Col. 3.

13. Quoted in "Serious Flaws in the Popular Price Indexes," Bus. Week, Apr. 6, 1974, pp. 86, 87.

14. This limitation led to the creation of a new index in Great Britain in 1979 called the Tax and Price Index. The Tories had increased the sales tax in 1979 and had reduced income taxes by an offsetting amount in an effort to persuade people to earn more and spend less. The sales tax hike produced a rise of four percentage points in the consumer price index; the tax cuts did not show up in the index. Revzin, "The Tories Invent New Price Index, But It's Ignored," Wall St. J., Mar. 14, 1980, p. 22, col. 3.

15. Statement of Joel Popkin, former assistant commissioner of the Bureau of Labor Statistics, prepared for U.S. Congress Joint Economic Committee, quoted in Samuelson, "What 8 economic indicators say (or don't say)," 13 COLUM. JOURNALISM REV. 44, 46 (Mar./Apr. 1975).

16. McCarthy, *Index Numbers,* INT'L ENCY. SOC. SCI. 154, 163 (1968).

17. Brazilian manipulation of the price indexes is notorious. In the first quarter of 1966 the weight accorded to rent in Rio's cost-of-living index was virtually halved without conducting any new market basket survey. This reweighting coincided with a period of rapidly rising rents resulting from the relaxation of rent control laws. *See* note 6 *supra.* In October of 1969, when a frost destroyed part of the coffee crop, changes in export prices were eliminated from the wholesale price index used for readjustment of government bonds. J. CHACEL, M. SIMONSEN, & A. WALD, CORREÇÃO MONETÁRIA 310 (1970). In December 1972, when the inflation rate appeared to be declining, the government's estimate of future inflation was given equal weight with the past inflation recorded by the wholesale price index in order to reduce the amount of readjustment in government bonds. "Correção Monetária e Realimentação Inflacionária," Conj. Econ. 88, 92 (June 1976). This estimate of future inflation was eliminated from the index in March of 1974, when it became apparent that the inflation rate was increasing. In 1975, "inflationary accidents," such as acts of God and the Arabs, were eliminated from the index, sharply lowering the reported rate of inflation. 9 Latin Am. 296 (1975). Although the official reported increase in the cost of living was set at 13.7 percent in 1973, a World Bank study and a recently revealed classified governmental study put the 1973 figure at 26.6 percent. *See* chap. 10, *infra,* at note 17.

During the post-World War II period in Finland, when a great many prices were indexed, the government adopted the policy of "buying points" on the cost-of-living index. Large-scale government subsidies were used to hold down the prices of items which most noticeably affected the cost-of-living index. Suviranta, *Wage Inflation in Post War Finland,* in INFLATION 248, 260 (D. C. Hague, ed. 1962). The Israelis have done much the same thing. A special department within the

Ministry of Finance proposed subsidies to keep the cost-of-living index down on the principle "that any disbursement, which is smaller than the anticipated increase in the government budget as the result of the avoided rise in the COL index, is commendable." Rubner, *The Abdication of the Israeli Pound as a Standard of Measurement for Medium and Long-Term Contracts,* 28 REV. ECON. STUDIES 69, 74 (Oct. 1960).

18. For example, for many years the Getúlio Vargas Foundation's cost-of-living index for Rio de Janeiro, generally considered to be the best indicator of the Brazilian inflation rate, adjusted the rental component of its index solely on the basis of official modifications in the rent control statutes. From 1958 to 1966 the rental component of the cost-of-living index rose only 56.7 percent as fast as the rest of the index. From 1954 to 1956, when São Paulo's index indicated rents had risen 44 percent, the Rio index reflected a zero rate of increase. Rosenn, *supra* note 6, at 251.

In 1947 Finnish unions succeeded in replacing the official cost-of-living index with a specially constructed wage regulation index for the purpose of wage adjustments. The wage regulation index emphasized food prices, and included some black market prices. But the wage regulation index was introduced at the same time the government began to dismantle the system of price controls on food. This produced sharp declines in black market prices. Consequently, between 1947 and 1949 the wage regulation index increased by only 13 percent, while the official cost-of-living index increased by 31 percent. Organized labor was only too happy to abandon the concept of a special wage regulation index; instead it pressed hard for price controls and subsidization of crucial products and services. E. HANNI, INFLATION IN POSTWAR FINLAND 156 (1972).

During the Allende period, the official Chilean price indexes were widely believed to have understated the actual inflation rate by a considerable amount because they did not take into account the shortages and widespread black markets spawned by the extensive system of price controls. G. JUD, INFLATION AND THE USE OF INDEXING IN DEVELOPING COUNTRIES 81 (1978). Although the official consumer price index registered a 508 percent rise in 1973, academic studies placed the real rate of increase at close to 1,000 percent. Sergio de Castro Spikula, *Inflation and Financial Discipline in Chile,* in CHILEAN ECONOMIC POLICY 275, 276 (J.C. Méndez ed. 1979).

3

THE VALUE OF MONEY FOR LEGAL PURPOSES

Money and "hard-core" pornography pose similar problems for the juridical mind. Mr. Justice Stewart's classic nondefinition of hard-core pornography—I cannot say what it is, but I know it when I see it[1]—might also be said about money. Common definitions of money, such as "the means established by law . . . for the payment of debts," "the general medium of payment," "a representative of goods and services," "a measure of value," or "a medium of exchange for goods and services," are essentially circular.[2] Indeed, a good case can be made for the proposition that money cannot be defined *a priori.* According to Milton Friedman and Anna Schwartz, "The definition of money is to be sought for not on grounds of principle but on grounds of usefulness in organizing our knowledge of economic relationships. 'Money' is that to which we choose to assign a number of specified operations; . . . it is a tentative scientific construct to be invested, like 'length' or 'temperature' or 'force' in physics."[3]

Legal systems depend upon money to perform three essential functions: money serves as (1) *a means of payment,* facilitating the exchange of goods and services; (2) *a measure of value,* permitting a common method of determining the value of goods and services; and (3) *a store of value,* facilitating savings and the deferred payment of obligations.[4] Hence, one can define money as all assets which perform these three functions. It is readily apparent, however, that no single asset uniquely performs these three functions; in modern economies, a variety of assets perform some or all of these functions in varying degrees. Checks or credit cards may or may not be accepted as means of payment. Even cash may not serve as a means of payment, such as when one tries to pay for gasoline at a late hour with a fifty dollar bill. Depending on the inflation rate, cash may or may not be a store of value or a measure of value. Depending on one's purpose, travelers checks, money market fund deposits with check-writing privileges, NOW accounts, or automatic transfer savings accounts may or may not be considered as money. For the purpose of monitoring monetary policy, countries define the aggregates of their money stock in myriad ways.[5]

This chapter focuses on the value ascribed by law to money and begins with a brief historical introduction to two of the most important doctrines for determining the legal value of money: metallism and nominalism. It then traces the evolution of monetary systems from coins to convertible paper currency to inconvertible paper currency, pausing along the way to show the development of the notion of legal tender and to recount the early American and French experiences with paper money inflations. The next topic examined is the problem of valuing money for international purposes, beginning with the gold standard and ending with the recent reforms of the International Monetary Fund. The chapter concludes with the development of the modern doctrine of valorism and the spread of indexation as a response to sustained inflation.

THE DEVELOPMENT OF COINAGE

Although numerous commodities, such as tobacco, shells, and cattle, have been used as money, "for all practical purposes, for most of the time, money has been a more or less precious metal."[6] Three metals have been perennial monetary favorites: gold, silver, and copper. So long as people exchanged chunks or powders of metal, money was essentially another commodity. The value of money was determined by the economic laws of supply and demand, but the use of metal in the raw as money was enormously inconvenient. Commercial transactions required weighing the quantity tendered and assaying its fineness. At least as early as the seventh or eighth century B.C., merchants began to turn precious metals into coins of predetermined weight and fineness, and to use these coins as means of payment and measures of value.[7]

Soon after the development of coinage, sovereigns fought to make control of the mint part of the royal prerogative.[8] The minting of coins not only offered the opportunity to advance the sovereign's prestige by having his likeness embossed on them, but also presented a chance to improve the sovereign's net worth through "seigniorage" (collection of a duty exceeding coinage expenses) and debasement. As long as coins actually contained their originally determined weight and fineness, there was no difference between their intrinsic (purchasing power) and extrinsic (nominal) value. But few sovereigns could resist the temptation to reduce the precious metal content of coins by slipping in increasing amounts of cheaper metals as alloys or simply reducing the weight of the coins. The Roman emperors were among the worst offenders; by the time of Aurelian (270–275 A.D.) the basic Roman silver coin was about 95 percent copper. Private parties also did their share to reduce the precious metal content of coins by clipping, shaving, or sweating small quantities of metal before passing coins on. Debasement was relatively common and resulted in enormous depreciation in the intrinsic or purchasing power of many early European coins.

Abraham Lincoln's adage about the impossibility of fooling all of the people all of the time might well have been coined to describe what occurred with respect to ancient monetary practices. Sovereigns might get away with debasement of the coinage for a brief period, but merchants quickly detected alterations and either refused to accept debased coins or accepted them at only a fraction of their nominal value. This was particularly true in international transactions where obligations could be discharged only by use of coins whose intrinsic value had not been adulterated.[9]

THE DOCTRINE OF METALLISM

During most of recorded history, legal perception of the value of money has been dominated by metallist theory. Under metallism the value of money is identical with the value of a determined weight and quality of precious metal. Metallism presented few problems so long as money consisted of unaltered coins minted from precious metals. But once debasement became widespread, legal theory had to confront the problem of repayment of a monetary obligation in debased coin. For example, suppose that a debtor agreed to repay ten gold ducats (whose gold content was unspecified in the loan agreement), and that prior to the time for repayment, the sovereign reduced the gold content of the ducat by 20 percent. Was the debtor obligated to repay ten or twelve ducats?

During the Middle Ages it was fairly generally agreed that the debtor was required to repay the quantity of gold rather than the number of monetary units he had borrowed. This conclusion derived partly from Roman law, which, as interpreted by the Glossators and the Post-Glossators, regarded the metallic value of money as the substance of monetary obligations.[10] It also derived from a sense of natural justice. Because canon law deprived the creditor of interest on the loan, it was considered just to protect him against monetary depreciation.[11]

THE ASCENDANCY OF NOMINALISM

This view was seriously challenged in 1546 with the publication of a highly influential treatise, TRACTATUS CONTRACTUUM ET USURARUM, by the French jurist, Charles Dumoulin (Molinaeus). Molinaeus was one of a group of French jurists who sought to consolidate the power of the French monarchy at the expense of feudal princes and the church. In his treatment of usury, Molinaeus discredited the canonists' metallistic interpretation of Roman law and vigorously criticized the view that money is a commodity whose value is determined by its precious metal content. Laying the doctrinal support for nominalism, Molinaeus cogently argued that the value of money is the value imposed by the sovereign.[12] The path from Molinaeus's pen to the French monarch's eye was relatively rapid. Five years after the appearance of Molinaeus' treatise, a French decree was issued requiring all contracts to specify monetary amounts by the nominal value of coins rather than by metallic weights.[13]

The sixteenth and seventeenth centuries were marked by bitter doctrinal disputes between adherents of nominalism and metallism. The former urged that for the purpose of discharging legal obligations, the value of money should be its face or nominal value, which should be presumed constant; the latter urged that legal obligations should be discharged only upon payment of a sum that corresponds to the intrinsic metallic value of the sum at the time the obligation was incurred.[14] Nominal value is attributed to money by the state in terms of multiples of an ideal unit, and this value is presumed to be permanently equal to itself. Nominalism is far more convenient than metallism, for it avoids the difficult task of inquiring into the relative metallic value of goods and services over time. This advantage made nominalism more useful to the development of modern capitalism. This greater utility, coupled with sponsorship by monarchs seeking to augment and centralize powers of the state, ultimately led to widespread acceptance of nominalism during the seventeenth and eighteenth centuries.[15]

One of the world's most influential legal documents, the Napoleonic Code, is decidedly nominalist. The most explicit nominalist statement lies in Article 1895, which provides: "The obligation which results from a loan of money is always only the numerical sum stated in the contract. If the value of money has increased or decreased before the time of payment, the debtor must repay only the numerical sum lent in the lawful currency at the time of payment." Similar provisions can be found in the civil codes of many countries.[16] Although stated only in terms of loans, the nominalist principle is commonly applied to all obligations to pay sums of money.[17]

The nominalist principle has been part of the common law since at least 1604, when the leading case of *Gilbert v. Brett* (also known as the *Case de Mixt Moneys*),[18] was decided. Gilbert had sold goods for "£ 100 sterling current and lawful money of England" to be paid in Dublin. Before payment was due, Queen Elizabeth replaced all Irish currency with an issue of debased coins with the same nominal denominations. A royal proclamation declared these debased coins, popularly known as mixed money, to be the loyal and current money of the realm of Ireland and stated that anyone who refused to accept them at face value should be punished for contempt of the royal prerogative. Gilbert rejected the tender of £ 100 in the debased coins. Relying on the principles of common law, as well as continental authorities such as Molinaeus, the Chief Judges of England held that an obligation to pay £ 100 sterling could be discharged by payment of whatever sum the law recognizes as £ 100 sterling at the date of payment.

THE DEVELOPMENT OF PAPER MONEY

The ascendancy of nominalism coincided with the growth of commercial banking and creation of money via the printing press and the expansion of bank credit. As indicated earlier in Chapter 1, paper money first appeared in China early in the eleventh century in the form of deposit receipts for bulky iron coins. Paper money did not appear in the West until four centuries later. With the development of commercial banks in England and Flanders during the fifteenth century, people began to use bank notes and checks as money.[19] Initially, these took the form of warehouse receipts for deposits of gold or coins. Eventually the words "or bearer" were added after the depositor's name. Since people had confidence that these receipts could be redeemed for gold or specie, the receipts were passed from hand to hand in lieu of money. As bankers recognized the unlikelihood that all depositors would try to redeem these notes simultaneously, banks began to loan out some of their deposits. Because it was more convenient to carry around notes rather than bullion or coins, borrowers also preferred to receive notes. In this fashion the money supply began to expand considerably. So long as banks retained adequate reserves of precious metals or coins with which to redeem the notes, the system operated smoothly. But once the general public suspected that a bank's reserves were inadequate, the inevitable panic to redeem notes and withdraw deposits resulted in the bank's collapse. The dubious distinction of being the first to prove this proposition to the world was a Scottish financial wizard and promotor named John Law.

In 1705 Law had published an essay on money and commerce in which he advocated the issuance of paper money backed by the security of real estate instead of gold or silver.[20] When the Scotch and English rejected his plans for a land bank, Law tried, with a similar lack of success, to interest other European countries in such a venture. In 1716 a nearly bankrupt French government, under the regency of Philippe d'Orleans, finally gave Law the opportunity to put his ideas into practice. Beginning with a private bank, Law soon founded the Mississippi Company *(Compagnie d'Occident)* to exploit the riches of France's Louisiana territory and convinced the French government to grant the company monopolies over immense territory.

Law next transformed his private bank into a state bank, the Banque Royale, through an edict in which the government reimbursed the original stockholders and became the owner of 6 million *livres* of capital. This sum was converted into shares of the Mississippi Company, which served as security for the bank's notes.

In this roundabout fashion Law succeeded in implementing his original idea of a state bank issuing paper money backed by the security of land. Because the first issue of notes had been well received, Law's bank produced two more issues totaling thirty million *livres.* His next step was to acquire three other colonial companies and merge them into a single conglomerate called the Company of the Indies. The third step was to sell stock in this conglomerate to an eager public, which paid for the stock with notes of the Banque Royale.

Until 1720 Law enjoyed phenomenal success. The grateful regent bestowed upon Law the title of the duke of Arkansas and made him comptroller general of France. Had Law actually used the money received from stock sales to mine gold in Louisiana, public confidence in the notes of the Banque Royale might have been sustained for a long period of time. But Law loaned the proceeds of the stock sales to the French government and kept expanding the bank's loans to the private sector. The amount of notes in circulation grew quickly from 100 million *livres* in the spring of 1719 to 1,100 million *livres* at the end of 1719. People who were receiving the notes were using them to buy more and more stock in the Company of the Indies, and the proceeds of the stock sales were being recycled as government loans. Each cycle was larger than its predecessor.

Eventually some of the French public realized that the huge volume of notes and stock which they were holding was backed only by illusory promises of gold and income from Louisiana real estate and loans from an insolvent government. They reacted by selling their stock and redeeming their notes. As the air began to leak from his brilliant bubble, Law sought to patch it with desperate measures. The company began to buy back its own shares, the redeemability of notes into specie was suspended, possession of gold and silver was declared illegal, and bank notes were made legal tender. But all the kings' horses and all the kings' men could not put Law's Humpty-Dumpty together again. Mobs gathered at the offices of the Banque Royale demanding hard money and Law's head. Neither were to be found. Law was smuggled out of the country to die in respectable poverty in Italy. His legacy to the French was huge quantities of worthless bank notes and stock, economic ruin, and a long-lasting suspicion of banks and paper money.[21]

Law's banking scheme, despite its tragic ending, revealed the possibility of indefinite expansion of the money supply by simply printing bank notes if the general public could be convinced both to accept such notes as money and to refrain from redeeming these notes for "hard money."

FROM LEGAL TENDER TO INCONVERTIBLE PAPER CURRENCY

The spread of paper currency was frequently aided by legislatures that designated such currency legal tender. Money designated by the legal system as legal tender is that which will be sufficient at law to discharge a pecuniary debt if properly tendered to the creditor. Though its origins go back to Roman law,[22] the law of tender developed differently at common law from Roman law, and it is from Anglo-American experience that the modern concept of legal tender is derived. At common law if a creditor refused to accept a tender of payment to discharge a debt, the debtor had to "keep tender good." This meant the debtor at all times had to keep the sum whose tender had been refused ready for payment to the creditor if the debtor wished to be able to take advantage of the defense of tender.[23] Several old English cases considered the question of whether a debtor's tender of coins whose intrinsic metallic value was inferior to that of the coins lent or a tender of foreign coins would serve to discharge the debt. The courts consistently held that a tender of whatever money had been made lawful and current in England by royal proclamation would discharge the debt, and that the tendered coins were to be accepted at face value.[24] Although these cases did not specifically use the term "legal tender," the terms "lawful money" or "current money" served as functional equivalents of the modern concept of legal tender.[25]

Paper money was first made legal tender in the Western world in the American colonies,[26] which suffered from a chronic shortage of specie.[27] The first issue was launched in 1690 by Massachusetts, which printed £ 7,000 in bills of credit. The value of these bills, which were akin to negotiable government bonds, depreciated rapidly in relation to specie. In 1692 the Massachusetts legislature tried to bolster their declining value by declaring the bills legal tender. Not only were the bills of credit declared to "pass current within this province equivalent to money," but they were to pass at a premium of 5 percent in all payments made to the colonial treasury.[28] The practice of printing money quickly spread to other colonies, some of which issued bills in huge quantities. Most of these bills depreciated quickly, despite legislative bestowal of full legal tender status. In 1751, alarmed at the flood of paper money and the complaints by English merchants who were being obliged to accept depreciated paper currency to satisfy debts owed by colonists, England enacted a statute requiring the New England colonies to recall all outstanding bills, to emit no more except as emergency measures, and to deny any future emissions the status of legal tender. This statute, which was extended to all of the American colonies in 1764,[29] curtailed paper money issues until the colonies were faced with the problem of financing the American Revolution.

Revolutionary Finance

In 1775 the Continental Congress began to issue bills of credit redeemable in Spanish milled dollars, gold, or silver. These bills were backed only by the faith and credit of the colonies. Instead of laying taxes to redeem these notes, as the members of the Continental Congress had hoped, the thirteen colonies merely provided that the continental notes were legal tender and that anyone who refused to accept them at par should be deemed an enemy of the country.[30] The individual colonies then proceeded to issue large amounts of their own paper money. The result was runaway inflation and the coining of the familiar pejorative: "Not worth a continental!" The continental notes became almost worthless; after 1781 they were bought and sold as a speculative commodity for .05 percent to .001 percent of their face value. They were ultimately redeemed in 1790 for one cent on the dollar.[31]

The French Revolution was financed in a similar fashion. Even though there was a great shortage of coins on the eve of the revolution, vivid memories of the Law fiasco made the French extremely reluctant to accept the reintroduction of paper money. A royal proclamation creating interest-bearing paper money in August 1788 had to be withdrawn the following month because of the storm of public protest.[32] But the revolution demanded large amounts of money, and no viable alternative to the printing press was presented. "The Revolution was accompanied by a reaction against the old obnoxious and oppressive taxes, and by a demoralization of the economic and political organization that made the collection of taxes impossible. Loans were not forthcoming, perhaps because of a dearth of savings, or the uncertainty of the future, or mere administrative weakness."[33] The original financing scheme developed by the French Revolutionists was an innovative measure which would have made John Law proud, though they devoted considerable effort to educating the public to differentiate the revolution's paper issue from that of John Law's Banque Royale.

In 1789 the National Assembly issued 400 million *livres* worth of interest-bearing government bonds secured by lands confiscated from the church and the crown. These bonds, called *assignats,* were to be redeemed within five years by auctioning off these lands. Holders of *assignats* were given special privileges in the purchase of these lands; *assignats* were not, however, made legal tender.[34]

Had the revolutionary government stopped with this initial issue, or even the second or third, the fate of the *assignat* may not have so closely paralleled that of the American continental and Law's notes. But the demands of the revolution for more and more funds were incessant. In April 1790 there was a second issue of *assignats,* followed by a third issue in

October 1790. These notes bore no interest and resembled forced currency more than bonds. Two more issues of *assignats* in smaller denominations were authorized in 1791.

When the *assignats* began to depreciate rapidly with respect to specie,[35] the French government took drastic action. In 1793 the purchase and sale of coins was prohibited, as were contracts requiring the debtor to repay in specie. Punishment for refusal to accept *assignats* was declared to be twenty years in chains, and, in some cases, death.[36] Such Draconian measures proved useless in the face of a limited supply of land and an apparently unlimited supply of *assignats.* In 1795 freedom to deal in gold and silver was restored. By 1796 there were 45.5 billion *livres* in *assignats* in circulation, and their value with respect to specie had fallen to about one-third of 1 percent of their nominal value. In February 1797 France formally abandoned the now worthless *assignats* and returned to gold and silver.

Thus, these early experiences with unbacked or inadequately backed paper money turned out similarly. The notes depreciated rapidly, despite efforts to stem the decline with legal tender legislation backed up by severe economic and penal sanctions. The notes of John Law's Banque Royale, continentals, and *assignats* all became essentially worthless.[37] On the other hand, given the serious constraints on financing the American and French Revolutions by more conventional measures, such as taxation or borrowing, and the severe shortage of available metallic money, paper money served its principal purpose quite well.[38] Quite naturally, there was distinct unhappiness with suffering the side effects of runaway inflation and economic disorder. After the *anciens régimes* had been overthrown and the revolutions secured, both the Americans and the French jettisoned their worthless paper currency and set up monetary systems based upon bimetallic standards.[39]

Nonlegal Tender Paper Money

English experience with paper money during the eighteenth and nineteenth centuries contrasted sharply with the American and French experiences. The Bank of England, founded in 1694, began issuing notes that had no legal tender quality. By the middle of the eighteenth century, these notes had become the dominant form of paper money in England. The Bank of England's notes were readily redeemable in gold or silver coin, but because of the bank's sound financial policies, its notes, unlike those of its smaller rivals, were seldom presented for redemption.[40]

Free convertibility was not suspended until 1797, when the appearance of a French warship off the English coast panicked large numbers of people into redeeming the Bank of England's notes for specie. Fearing a run on the bank, the British parliament ordered suspension of the privilege of redemption. Although not made legal tender,[41] Bank of England notes continued to circulate freely. What disappeared from circulation was gold and silver coin. For many years England operated without any money that was legal tender. Finally, in 1811 and 1812 England enacted curious legislation establishing a purely defensive concept of legal tender. Creditors who sued to collect debts were required to accept bank notes, but these same notes were incapable of discharging debts against creditors' wishes if voluntarily tendered by debtors.[42] Prices rose during this period, but admirable restraint in printing new notes kept inflation from galloping.[43] When the privilege of redemption into specie was restored in 1821, it was possible to reinstitute the same rate of exchange between the notes and gold that had been in effect in 1797. From 1833 through World War I, the notes of the Bank of England were made legal tender only so long as they remained freely convertible into specie.[44]

The lessons of these early experiences with paper money appeared fairly obvious to most nineteenth century money managers. Paper currency was enormously convenient, provided its purchasing power could be kept reasonably stable. This could not be accomplished by legal tender legislation, and the power to make paper legal tender was to be used with great caution.[45] On the other hand, if the supply of paper money were carefully regulated and people were allowed to convert it freely into specie, the value of paper currency could be expected to remain equal to the value of the gold or silver that it represented. Although the nominalist principle might have prevailed in legal theory, during the latter part of the eighteenth century and throughout the nineteenth century, legislators generally opted for metallism by defining the value of the unit of account of national currency in terms of gold or silver or both.

THE RISE OF THE GOLD STANDARD

The modern concept of the gold standard began in England during the seventeenth and eighteenth centuries as a result of a curious historical accident—the undervaluing of gold in relation to silver. The guinea, a gold coin issued in 1663, was officially valued at one pound. At that time England was operating with a loose bimetallic standard. This valuation of the guinea produced a ratio between standard gold and silver of only 1 to 14.485, a ratio considerably lower than that prevailing in the rest of Europe.[46] The operation of Gresham's Law[47] resulted in the virtual disappearance of silver coin from English coffers. An attempt to remedy this situation by statutorily pegging the guinea at 21 shillings, thereby increasing the value of gold with respect to silver by 5 percent, still left gold undervalued with respect to silver. The little silver that remained in circulation consisted primarily of coins so worn down that it was unprofitable either to export or melt them down. As a consequence, the English grew accustomed to conducting monetary transactions with gold rather than silver and eventually confirmed that practice in legislation. In 1774 importation of light silver coinage was prohibited, and tender of more than £ 25 in silver coins ceased to be legal tender. In 1798 the coinage of silver was statutorily suspended to insure that the country would not return to a silver standard.[48] When the guinea was replaced by the sovereign in 1816, the Coinage Act fixed the price of gold at the same rate established in 1717, £ 3, 17 s. 10 1/2d. for a standard ounce of gold, eleven-twelfths fine.[49] The 1816 statute legalized the hitherto *de facto* gold standard by providing "that gold coin made according to the indentures of the Mint should henceforth be the sole standard measure of value and legal tender for payment, without any limitation of amount, and that the silver coin should be a legal tender to a limited amount only, for the facility of exchange and commerce."[50]

After the disastrous experience with the hyperinflation caused by the *assignats,* France returned to bimetallism. Legislation adopted in 1803 defined the franc as a coin containing five grains of silver nine-tenths fine. The French reestablished a bimetallic monetary system in which only gold or silver coins were legal tender. France again adopted the 1 to 15.5 ratio between gold and silver, previously established in 1785.[51] Because the relative prices of gold and silver change with the supply and demand for each metal, countries trying to operate with bimetallic standards have historically had difficulty preventing the operation of Gresham's Law from causing either gold or silver coins to disappear from circulation. Unless all countries maintain the same ratio, each metal tends to move to the country where it is most valued. During the first half of the nineteenth century, silver nearly drove gold coins out of circulation in France. When the world's supply of gold increased dramatically after 1850 because of discoveries in the United States and Australia, France was forced to absorb large influxes of gold. Silver began to trade at a premium over gold and rapidly disappeared from circulation.[52]

During the latter half of the nineteenth century, the gold standard spread throughout the world. This was in good part attributable to England's preeminent position in international trade and finance. London was the headquarters for the world's major banking establishments and the site of the major gold market. The British pound sterling was not only used as a domestic currency in the extensive British colonial empire, but also in financing international trade operations between non-Empire countries.[53] The ascendency of gold was also in part attributable to its being more scarce and hence more valuable than silver. It was less bulky and cumbersome to transport a given value in gold than in silver. Moreover, the cost of coinage of a given value in silver was three or four times that of the same value in gold. Because international wealth transfers involved shipping coins that would be melted down and recoined as a different currency, the higher cost of coinage acted as a tax on international transfers of silver.[54]

In 1871, a major impetus to the expansion of the gold standard resulted from Germany's decision to convert the basis of its monetary system from the silver thaler to the gold mark. As part of this currency reform, Germany suspended free coinage of silver and began dumping large quantities of silver on the world market in exchange for gold.[55] Adding to the glut of silver on the world market were the discovery of new silver deposits in Nevada and elsewhere and the discontinuance of the free coinage of silver in the United States and elsewhere. The result was a sharp increase in the price of gold in relation to silver. Bimetallism, which had always functioned precariously,[56] could not cope with such a sudden change in relative supply and demand for gold and silver. Nation after nation with bimetallic standards elected to demonetize silver and hop on the gold bandwagon. As each new country came aboard, the demand for gold intensified, so that by 1903 the value of gold in relation to silver had increased nearly threefold.[57]

The United States, which had adopted bimetallism in the Coinage Act of 1792,[58] was in effect on a gold standard after 1834, when legislation was enacted pegging the ratio of silver to gold at 15.988 to 1.[59] This ratio was so far above the prevailing market rate, governed by the French ratio of 15.5 to 1, that silver ceased to circulate. The United States demonetized silver (except for coins whose legal tender value was restricted to five dollars) in 1873 and formally adopted the gold standard. Shortly thereafter, however, silver mining interests, buoyed by new Nevada discoveries, flexed their political muscles and forced through a compromise return to bimetallism. In 1879, when the United States abandoned the "greenbacks" first issued during the Civil War era and returned to specie payments, a law was passed authorizing coinage of a minimum of $2 million and a maximum of $4 million silver per month at the previous legal ratio of 15.988 to 1. The law also restored legal tender status to the silver dollar.[60] By 1893 the amount of silver dollars coined became a serious embarrassment and threatened the gold parity of the dollar. In 1893, India and Russia closed their mints to the free coinage of silver, leaving the United States practically alone in the world to defend silver.[61] Finally, in November 1893, the United States abandoned the fight by repealing the legislation requiring the minting of silver dollars.[62] The silver interests were decisively beaten in the election of 1896, and the Gold Standard Act of 1900 formally restored the gold standard.[63]

Countries on the gold standard permitted free import and export of gold, as well as free coinage of gold. Gold coin was legal tender, and paper money was either freely redeemable for gold, or else was not legal tender. Consequently, adoption of the gold standard by most of the world produced a system of fixed exchange rates and a fairly uniform world gold price.[64] Adoption of the gold standard, however, did not insulate a country's economy from inflation or deflation. While on the gold standard, England experienced several lengthy periods during which the general price level rose or fell.[65] Although the periods of rising prices corresponded to substantial increases in world gold production, this correspondence is alone insufficient to explain certain periods of falling prices.[66]

THE DEMISE OF THE GOLD STANDARD

The gold standard gradually disappeared in the wake of the monetary crises flowing from World War I. When the war first broke out, no one expected the enormous costs associated with the hostilities. For the most part, the extraordinary war expenditures were financed by short-term borrowing and the creation of money and credit rather than by taxation.[67] So long as the money supply remained tied to the gold supply, there was a natural limit to the ability of governments to capture resources from the private sector by inflation.[68] War, like revolution, provided governments with sufficient reason for breaking the tie between precious metals and money. In order to finance the war by increasing the means of payment, the belligerents suspended free convertibility of paper money and embargoed the exportation of gold.

Price controls and rationing suppressed the rate of inflation during much of the war, but the postwar relaxation of controls was followed by inflation on an unprecedented scale. The United States escaped with one of the milder inflationary experiences; the consumer price index only doubled between 1914 and 1920. During this same period consumer prices increased by factors of 2.8 in Great Britain, 2.7 in Sweden, 2.4 in Switzerland, and 3.4 in Norway. Inflation was more severe in Italy and France, with consumer prices rising 4.6 and 4.2 times their respective prewar levels by 1920.[69]

Inflation raged totally out of control in five countries: Germany, Austria, Hungary, Poland, and Russia. All except Germany had suffered a breakdown in internal administration. By the end of their post-World War I inflationary experiences, prewar price levels had multiplied by roughly 14,000 times in Austria, 23,000 times in Hungary, 2.5 million times in

Poland, 4 billion times in Russia, and 1.5 trillion times in Germany.[70] In all these countries, the prewar monetary system was totally destroyed by inflation.

The Gold Exchange Standard

Gold flowed into the United States during World War I at a dizzying pace. Some was sent for safekeeping or investment, but the great bulk was used to finance purchase of American goods. Between 1914 and 1917 the gold supply of the United States practically doubled, increasing from $1.5 billion to $2.9 billion.[71] This was more gold than any other country had previously accumulated. Concentration of such a large share of the world's gold supply in one country fundamentally altered the economic and psychological assumptions upon which the gold standard had been constructed.

An unsuccessful effort was made to revive the gold standard after the war, but the gold reserves of most of the former participants were insufficient to make it work. Free convertibility and free export of gold were luxuries that could no longer be permitted. During the war years too much paper currency had been issued and too much gold had been exported. But maldistribution of gold was not the only problem. Rising production costs had reduced world production of gold by about one-third between 1915 and 1922.[72]

Pending restoration of the gold standard, an interim international monetary system called the gold exchange standard operated from 1925 to 1931. The gold exchange standard was designed to secure the advantages of the gold standard to countries with inadequate gold reserves by giving them a free ride on the currencies of countries with gold reserves adequate to permit free convertibility. Under the gold exchange standard, most countries held their currency reserves partly in gold and partly in foreign currencies redeemable in gold. Both exchange rates between currencies and between gold and reserve foreign currencies were pegged within the narrow limits of the gold import and export points.[73] The holder of the paper currency of a nation on the gold exchange standard could freely convert that currency into drafts payable in currencies that could be converted into gold, such as the U.S. dollar, the British pound and, after 1928, the French franc.

The dollar started to displace the British pound as the major international currency under the gold exchange standard. By following severely deflationary policies, England was able to reestablish by 1925 its historical gold exchange rate of £ 3, 17 s. 10 1/2 d. English haste in reestablishing its traditional gold rate, however, was imprudent.[74] Instead of reverting directly to the prewar gold standard, England adopted a modification called the gold bullion standard. Paper currency could be converted only into gold bullion rather than gold coin, which ceased to circulate. Convertibility was placed well beyond the reach of the average citizen by setting the minimum quantity of gold that could be purchased at 400 troy ounces ($8,268 at then prevailing exchange rates).

The gold exchange system crumpled during the Great Depression. Some maintain that the depression caused the collapse of the gold exchange system. Others maintain that the gold exchange system caused the depression. Both positions are overstatements, but each contains a kernel of truth.[75] The instability of the gold exchange standard had long been apparent, for it involved the precarious pyramiding of multinational claims on a narrow base of gold. A consequence of holding monetary reserves in bank accounts and liquid securities instead of gold was that large amounts of funds tended to flow erratically from one financial center to another in response to interest rate differentials, opportunities for arbitrage, and doubts about the soundness of particular currencies. Central banks continually changed the mix of their reserves; large amounts of foreign exchange would be dumped on the market while certain central banks scrambled to acquire gold.[76] Any crisis of confidence in the economies of the United States or England could easily, and ultimately did, undermine the entire system.

The immediate cause of the gold exchange standard's demise was a speculative run on the pound sterling. The British economy had never fully recuperated from the deflationary policies necessary to effect a return to the gold exchange rate first established in 1717. The British had loaned large sums to Austria and Germany. When the largest bank in Austria collapsed in 1931, there was heavy speculation against the British pound. This run on the pound forced England to suspend convertibility into gold bullion in 1931 and to let the pound float. The *coup de grâce* to the gold exchange standard was administered by the United States in 1933, when it devalued the dollar by 41 percent in relation to gold and abandoned free convertibility of dollars into gold.[77]

There were a number of important underlying reasons for the abandonment of the gold standard and its modified successor. First, gold standard theory had little empirical basis. Prices did not invariably decline when gold flowed out of the country. Certain prices and wages were ratchet-like, moving only in an upward direction. Nor did exports invariably increase and imports decrease as gold or foreign exchange reserves diminished. Demand for numerous imports appeared to be price inelastic (relatively unresponsive to price changes). Second, even when the system functioned as envisioned in theory, countries with gold deficits found its domestic effects, such as deflation, high unemployment, and recession, politically intolerable. Changing notions of government responsibility to promote economic growth, prosperity, and full employment were essentially incompatible with the automatic stabilizing mechanism of the gold standard. Even countries with gold surpluses preferred to adopt anti-inflationary policies rather than see their price levels rise because of an influx of gold. Third, the world's gold supply had not grown rapidly enough to meet the world's needs, creating a chronic liquidity crisis. An attempt to make existing supplies perform double duty via the gold exchange standard was not a viable alternative.[78]

The international monetary situation during the Great Depression was chaotic. Countries freely manipulated their exchange rates and tariffs to stimulate exports and protect import-competing industries. This "beggar-thy-neighbor" approach was advantageous only if other countries did not retaliate, but retaliatory policies soon became widespread. The 1930s became a time of rampant economic nationalism, as nations sought to become economically self-sufficient by substituting domestically produced goods for imports. International trade declined drastically, falling from $55.9 billion in 1929 to $21.8 billion in 1932.

By the end of the 1930s, it was apparent to almost all countries that international currency reform was desperately needed. In the long run, competitive devaluations and retaliatory tariffs were detrimental to virtually all concerned.

THE CREATION OF THE INTERNATIONAL MONETARY FUND

In 1944 a group of forty-four countries met at Bretton Woods, New Hampshire at the invitation of the United States and drafted the Articles of Agreement of the International Monetary Fund (IMF).[79] This agreement was designed to promote exchange stability and avoid competitive exchange depreciation by developing and enforcing rules governing exchange rates and controls and by making available resources of the IMF to aid member nations in correcting balance-of-payments maladjustments "without resorting to measures destructive of national or international prosperity."[80] The core of the IMF Agreement was a much strengthened modification of the defunct gold exchange standard. It established a system of stable exchange rates by fixing exchange rates in terms of gold or the U.S. dollar, which was pegged to gold at $35 an ounce. Once set by a member nation, the exchange rate between a country's currency and gold or the dollar was known as "the par value." Each member was obligated to maintain its exchange rate within one percent of its prescribed parity on spot transactions.[81] Members could change par values of their currencies only after consultation with the IMF and only for reasons of "fundamental disequilibrium." The agreement did not define fundamental disequilibrium. In practice, however, it came to mean a persistent imbalance in payments correctable only by controls on current exchange transactions or at the cost of serious unemployment or deflation.[82] If a member changed its par value without IMF permission, it lost its privilege of borrowing from the IMF.

The IMF's resources came from quotas subscribed to by member nations at the time of entry into the agreement. These quotas, which were increased by 50 percent in 1958 and 25 percent in 1966, were payable partly in gold and partly in the member's national currency. The portion payable in gold, called the gold tranche, was, as a minimum, 25 percent of the quota, or 10 percent of the member's net official holdings of gold and U.S. dollars, whichever was the lesser.[83] A nation experiencing a temporary balance-of-payments problem could borrow from the IMF, though the loans were couched in the terminology of purchase and sale. The IMF permitted virtually automatic drawing rights against a member's gold tranche. If a member required more resources, it could ask the IMF to purchase at the official rate the amount of dollars or other foreign currencies that it needed. In exchange, it paid an equivalent amount in its own currency. As soon as it could, the borrower repurchased its own currency by repaying the currency that it had borrowed or a similar acceptable currency. These loans generally had to be repaid within five years (seven to eight years under special policies), and until repayment occurred, the borrower had to pay interest and service charges.[84]

The Articles of Agreement became effective on December 27, 1945. By May 1981 the number of nations belonging to the IMF had increased to 141 from the original 44. The quotas of the IMF members had grown from $7.6 billion in 1945 to the equivalent of $73.23 billion by April 1981. For many years the international monetary system established at Bretton Woods worked well, helping to speed economic recovery after World War II and contributing to an enormous expansion of international trade. With the passage of time, however, several critical and interrelated problems began to emerge and to threaten the underlying structure of the IMF. These problems involved the stability of the U.S. dollar and the role of gold.

THE IMF IN TRANSITION

During the early years of the IMF, the U.S. dollar was practically the only currency in demand for IMF transactions. The dollar was considered as good as gold, if not better, for dollars could earn interest. Even though gold was the "ultimate" reserve asset, the world was plainly on a dollar standard.

During the 1950s, the balance of payments of the United States, which had formerly shown strong surpluses, began to run increasingly large deficits. Initially, these deficits were welcomed by the rest of the world, because they reallocated much of the huge hoard of gold that the United States had accumulated and permitted other countries to build up reserves of U.S. dollars. Moreover, the deficits of the United States were thought to be temporary. By 1960, however, after deficits had continued steadily for a decade, foreign attitudes toward the outpouring of dollars from the United States began to change. Many countries began to have qualms about having so much of their currency reserves in an increasingly anemic-looking currency. France led other countries in cashing dollars for gold. By 1965, the gold reserves of the United States had shrunk to $15 billion, while American short-term obligations and dollars held by foreign countries exceeded $23 billion.[85]

On the other hand, the huge influx of American dollars had contributed to the growth of European prosperity. Many Europeans were understandably reluctant to see any diminution in the flow of dollars. Even worse, from the standpoint of European central bankers, was the prospect of a return to substantial U.S. balance-of-payments surpluses. This would signify a return of gold and dollars to the United States. The concomitant shrinkage in European reserves appeared likely to produce a severe liquidity crisis.

There already was a severe gold liquidity problem. The enormous increase in world trade since World War II had greatly increased the need for international liquidity. But maintenance of a fixed price for gold in the face of continuous inflation since 1944 led to a sharp increase in the speculative demand for gold.[86] Consequently, gold production became increasingly diverted from supplying official reserves to satisfying private demands for the yellow metal on the commodities markets. Because of the excess private demand for gold, the central banks of eight countries in 1961 formed an arrangement called the London Gold Pool to maintain the price of gold on private commodities markets within one percent of official parity. This was accomplished by selling gold from official reserves on the commodities markets. When France dropped out in 1967, the United States picked up the French commitment, bringing the U.S. share up to 59 percent. By 1968 the drain on U.S. gold reserves had become so great that President Johnson decided to terminate the Gold Pool.

This decision gave rise to the two-tier gold system. One tier consisted of the free market, where the gold price was set by supply and demand; the other tier was the official price of $35 an ounce, which was maintained by the central banks of the seven nation Gold Pool solely for effectuating transfers among participating governments. Between 1968 and November of 1973, when the two-tier system was officially terminated, the free market price of gold nearly tripled.[87] Because the participating central banks could no longer purchase gold in the free market to finance official monetary transactions, an increase in international reserve assets was widely perceived as an urgent need.

Creation of Special Drawing Rights

In 1969 the liquidity crisis and confidence crisis in the U.S. dollar led to the first major reform of the IMF agreement, the creation of a new reserve asset called the Special Drawing Right (SDR). The SDR was designed to supplement reliance on the dollar as a reserve currency. Its unit of value was conveniently defined as the gold content of the 1944 U.S. dollar. As of April 30, 1981, a cumulative total of 21.43 billion SDR allocations had been made, amounting to 6.4 percent of the world's currency reserves excluding gold. SDRs can be transferred from one participant to another in exchange for the currency needed to discharge the transferor's foreign exchange obligations. Countries holding more SDRs than their allocations earn interest payable in SDRs, while those holding fewer than their allocations pay interest on the differential. Participating countries are required to maintain an average balance of 15 percent of their cumulative allocation over time and to accept SDRs up to a limit of three times their allocation.

The SDR is a curious international monetary invention that defies classification. With the SDR the alchemists of the IMF created gold from paper, but it is a kind of paper gold that can be held only by a limited group of countries, as a reserve asset, and that is utilized solely to change the composition of a country's currency reserves. The SDR cannot be donated, lent, or deposited as a collateral. Receipt of an allocation of SDRs creates no indebtedness by a recipient to the IMF, nor does the transfer of SDRs between participants create indebtedness or an obligation to reverse the transaction.[88] A unique feature of the SDR is that it adds to the world's reserves without increasing the gold supply or requiring another country to incur a substantial deficit in its balance of payments.

A number of decisions were taken by the IMF in 1978–79 to enhance the role of the SDR and to attempt to turn it into the world's principal reserve asset. Allocations of SDRs, which had stopped in 1972, were resumed at the rate of 4 billion SDRs each year for 1979, 1980, and 1981. The interest rate on SDRs was increased on January 1, 1979, from 60 to 80 percent of the composite of short-term money market rates in France, West Germany, Japan, the United Kingdom, and the United States, making its yield more competitive with other international reserve assets. On the same date, the reconstitution requirement, which had been set at 30 percent, was lowered to 15 percent, enabling participating countries to maintain lower levels of SDRs on a day-to-day basis. In addition, the IMF has allowed wider use of SDRs, such as for settling financial obligations or for repaying loans and interest.[89]

The Demonetization of Gold

During the 1960s, many European nations pressured the United States to put its economic house in order. The United States adopted several unsuccessful measures designed to reduce its balance-of-payments deficit.[90] An oft-voiced complaint of the United States was that the use of the dollar as a reserve currency under the IMF arrangement effectively deprived it of the ability to devalue, a measure essential to curing a fundamental disequilibrium. The United States also complained that the currencies of several of her trading partners, particularly West Germany and Japan, were undervalued in relation to the dollar.

On August 15, 1971, the United States torpedoed the IMF agreement by unilaterally suspending conversion of official foreign dollar holdings into gold or other reserve assets and refusing to maintain the dollar within any margins. At this time, U.S. gold-convertible obligations to foreign central banks had reached five times the dwindling gold holdings available to the U.S. Treasury.[91] The immediate effect of the American action was abrogation of the core of the IMF, the par value arrangement. After August 15, 1971, the monetary authorities of all IMF member nations began to allow their currencies to float in the exchange markets or to adjust their exchange rates without IMF consultation or approval.[92]

The Smithsonian Agreement on Central Rates

The IMF has been listing in limbo since the United States scuttled the 1944 agreement. Attempts to salvage the international monetary system have thus far produced only temporary patch-work arrangements. The Smithsonian Agreement of December 18, 1971 resulted in a provisional system authorizing members to declare "central rates" instead of par values for their currencies. The central rate differed from par value in that the former could be fixed in terms of the SDR or another member nation's currency, as well as in gold. Another difference was that central rates could be changed without consultation or permission of the IMF. Under the Smithsonian Agreement, the margins at which exchange rates were to be maintained were expanded from 1 to 2.25 percent on either side of parity or the central rate. A by-product of the Smithsonian Agreement was a change in the par value of the U.S. dollar to $38 an ounce, a measure taken on May 8, 1972.

Floating Rates

The Smithsonian Agreement did not last long. Speculative pressures in 1972 and early 1973 caused many countries to allow their exchange rates to float. On October 18, 1973, the United States further devalued the dollar with respect to gold, establishing a new rate of $42.22 an ounce. The significance of that gold exchange rate remains only symbolic, for no one can convert dollars to gold. With the market price of gold in June 1981 more than ten times that figure, it is unlikely that anyone will be selling gold to the United States at $42.22 an ounce. The ill-fated attempt to reestablish more or less fixed exchange rates without free convertibility to gold or the U.S. dollar proved a failure.

Presently no IMF member is maintaining a par value for its currency. Exchange rates are floating, though some are floating more freely than others. Some countries have pegged their currencies to the U.S. dollar, French franc, or British pound. Others have pegged their currencies to the SDR or to a combination of currencies. Some have allowed their currencies to float freely, while others have adopted a "managed float," in which central banks intervene to support their currencies if the market becomes too disorderly.[93] In April 1972, nine European Economic Community countries adopted a joint float called "the snake," maintaining their exchange rates within 2.25 percent of each other, but allowing their currencies to float vis-à-vis the dollar and other currencies.[94] On March 13, 1979, the snake was replaced by the European Monetary System. The center of the system is the European Currency Unit (ECU), a basket of fixed amounts of the currencies of the nine Common Market countries. The new agreement essentially maintains the joint float of the snake.[95]

The unit of value of the SDR is no longer the gold dollar. Once the U.S. dollar began to float and the official convertibility of gold into dollars ended, the IMF decided to value the SDR by reference to a weighted combination of the currencies of those member nations with the greatest importance to international trade and finance.[96]

The Second Amendment to the IMF Articles

Efforts have been underway since 1971 to work out a new international monetary system. While the form that system will ultimately take is not entirely clear, what has thus far emerged is a much more flexible system in which gold has been demonetized and deemphasized. The Second Amendment to the Articles of Agreement of the IMF, which went into effect on April 1, 1978, has eliminated gold as the common denominator of the new monetary system. Indeed, gold has no official price under the Second Amendment to the Articles of the IMF. In May 1980, the IMF completed its four-year program to dispose of its gold holdings. Part of the IMF's gold holdings has been sold to its members in four annual installments at 35 SDRs an ounce, and part has been sold to the general public at monthly auctions. The difference between 35 SDRs an ounce and the price received is being used for the benefit of members classified as developing countries.[97]

Whether these efforts to ease gold from the preeminent role it has historically played in international monetary matters will be successful is uncertain. If a decision is made to return to the device of par values, the SDR might serve as a common denominator. There is a substantial risk that returning large quantities of gold to member countries will ultimately lead to restoration of gold's traditional role.[98] The attitudes of people toward gold as the optimal money die hard. Many monetary authorities and some politicians remain convinced that gold may yet play an important role as a monetary asset.[99]

The present system of floating exchange rates will continue under the Second Amendment until such time as the IMF determines, "by an eighty-five percent majority of the total voting power, that international economic conditions permit the introduction of a widespread system of exchange arrangements based upon stable but adjustable par values."[100] If par values are reestablished, the common denominator will not be gold or a particular currency; rather, it will be the SDR or some other common denominator established by the IMF.[101] Even if par values are reestablished by an 85 percent vote of the IMF, any member nation may refrain from establishing a par value for its currency.

THE EMERGENCE OF VALORISM

During most inflations money continues to function at least as a means of payment. Barter is so inconvenient and impractical that only in the ultimate stages of hyperinflation do people refuse to accept money. But currencies of countries that have undergone years of severe inflation cease to function in an economic sense either as a measure or store of value. When that happens, there is often a juridical reaction against rigid application of the nominalist principle, for nominalism presupposes a reasonably stable currency.[102]

Until the twentieth century, reactions against nominalism were largely based upon the metallist theory that the proper measure of the value of pecuniary obligations is the intrinsic value of metallic currency. The legislators who drafted and the judges who applied American and French scaling laws strongly reflected this metallist orientation.[103] But during the highly inflationary post–World War I period, a group of jurists and economists reacted against the injustice resulting from rigid application of nominalism and urged that the legal value of money be ascertained in a new way: by reference to its purchasing power.

During the latter part of the nineteenth century and the beginning of the twentieth century, economists made considerable progress in developing reasonably sophisticated price indexes.[104] By the end of World War I, a number of countries had weighted price indexes published on a regular basis by official or quasi-official agencies. It was to these price indexes rather than gold or silver that many who reacted against nominalism turned for their measure of the value of money. These modern heirs of the metallists have been dubbed "valorists."[105] Their basic tenet was that pecuniary obligations should be discharged only upon payment of a sum that corresponds to the real economic value of the sum lent, the service rendered, or the commodity sold. The real economic value of money was perceived as its purchasing power rather than as the number of units of gold or silver for which it can be exchanged. The valorists correctly realized that the best measure of money's purchasing power is a general price index, such as the cost-of-living or wholesale price indexes, or the implicit GNP deflator.

The valorists were particularly influential in the 1920s in Germany, the only country in which the judiciary both initiated and dominated attempts to revise contractual obligations largely along valoristic lines.[106] Nonetheless, the revalorization conducted by the judiciary in Germany during the 1920s differed in two significant respects from valoristic theory. Although German judges relied heavily upon price indexes, they did not do so exclusively. Other factors, such as the gold exchange value and the relative wealth of the parties, were also considered.[107] More importantly, revalorization was conceived of as a temporary solution to the collapse of the German mark. Once the mark had been stabilized, Germany reverted to nominalism.

Today a modified form of valorism can be found in the intricate web of monetary correction legislation and private indexation that permeates the legal systems of Argentina, Brazil, Chile, Israel, and Uruguay, all of which have been afflicted with severe, chronic inflation.[108] In order to live with inflation, policymakers have turned to indexation or monetary correction of many types of obligations. For example, in Brazil, wages, interest payments, condemnation awards, rents, mortgages, bonds, corporate balance sheets, loans, social security payments, and the tax system are all adjusted periodically in accordance with coefficients derived from the price indexes.[109] This does not mean that the entire legal system has jettisoned nominalism and embraced valorism. Technically, nominalism is still the general rule. Indexation or monetary correction generally applies only if the parties to a contract have so stipulated or there is a specific legal norm mandating that result. Yet even though there are important transactions that are not affected by monetary correction, most legal transactions are structured and most legal disputes in these countries are resolved by taking into account changes in the price indexes.

The Southern cone of South America hardly has a monopoly on indexation. As inflation has become a worldwide phenomenon, many countries have begun to index their tax systems, social security payments, and wages. Index clauses are becoming a standard feature in an increasing variety of private contracts in both developed and developing countries. One indication of the extent to which even judges in a country with relatively stable currency are thinking in valoristic terms is the unprecedented lawsuit recently brought by nearly one-fourth of all federal judges against the United States for failure to maintain the real economic value of judicial salaries, which had been severely eroded by inflation since 1969.[110]

CONCLUSIONS

For a great many years, the answer to the question—what is the value of money?—was simple. Money was a quantity of a precious metal, and its value was the same as that of the precious metal. The value of the metal might change with supply and demand, but such variations were generally gradual and scarcely perceived by most of the population. The value of metals such as gold or silver was assumed to be essentially stable. Once sovereigns began to debase the precious metal content of their coinage, disparities between the metallic value of currency and its nominal value became apparent. This divergence has been accentuated by the nearly universal use of paper currency.

The legal doctrine first developed to deal with this divergence was metallism, which postulates that an obligation to pay a sum of money is discharged only by repayment of the same quantity of precious metal contained in the money borrowed. The number of monetary units owed is not controlling, for metallism regards money as a commodity whose value is determined by its precious metal content.

During the late sixteenth and seventeenth centuries, metallist doctrine was challenged by nominalism, which postulates that an obligation to pay a sum of money is discharged upon payment of the nominal value of the money owed. Nominal value is attributed to money by the government in terms of multiples of an ideal unit, and this value is presumed to be permanently equal to itself. The enormous convenience of nominalism for commercial transactions and its sponsorship by monarchs seeking to aggrandize royal powers ultimately led to its triumph over metallism in the seventeenth and eighteenth centuries in both common law and civil law countries.

Although nominalism may have prevailed in the civil codes and in judicial opinions, metallism dominated popular thought until well into the twentieth century. Indeed, for much of the nineteenth century it made little or no practical difference whether a court applied the doctrine of nominalism or metallism. Most governments were obliged to define their currency units with reference to carefully specified quantities of gold or silver, and to permit holders of paper currency to redeem notes for these quantities of precious metal. So long as governments maintained the same conversion rates and permitted free convertibility, nominalism and metallism produced identical results. In international transactions, metallism failed to displace nominalism; the common denominator for valuing a nation's currency remained, until fairly recently, its gold value.

Nominalism is based upon the assumption of reasonably stable price levels. With the outbreak of World War I and the demise of the gold standard, the world witnessed unprecedented levels of hyperinflation. Because of the massive loss of purchasing power that beset many currencies after the war, many jurists and economists cogently advocated the adoption of valorism. The core proposition of valorism is that the value of money should be determined in accordance with its purchasing power, as measured by a general price index. Although no country has fully accepted this valoristic proposition, several have temporarily come close for the purpose of revalorizing debts in collapsed currencies.

Gold coins disappeared during the 1920s, and the privilege of converting paper currency into gold for domestic transactions disappeared during the following decade. From 1945 to 1971 a modified gold exchange standard existed in international transactions through the IMF Agreement. When the United States closed the "gold window" in 1971 by refusing to allow foreign official dollar holdings to be redeemed for gold any longer, the last legal vestige of metallism vanished. Gold has finally been demonetized. For the present, and perhaps well into the future, the value of currencies for international transactions will continue to be determined by the laws of supply and demand.

In most countries, including the United States, nominalism is still the general rule. In the past two decades, however, there has been renewed interest in the valoristic device of indexing monetary obligations in accordance with coefficients derived from price indexes as a technique for living with inflation. Because of persistent inflation, a growing number of countries have begun indexing many legal obligations in order to maintain the real value of sums stated in nominal terms. Similarly, courts in some countries have shown an increasing willingness to deviate from the rigors of the nominalist principle. If substantial inflationary pressures persist, the tendency to define the value of monetary obligations by reference to purchasing power can be expected to increase. Whether valoristic exceptions will eventually swallow the general rule of nominalism remains to be seen.

NOTES

1. In his famous concurrence in Jacobellis v. Ohio, 378 U.S. 184 (1964), Mr. Justice Stewart wrote: "I shall not today attempt further to define the kinds of material I understand to be embraced within that shorthand description ['hard-core' pornography]; and perhaps I never could succeed in intelligibly doing so. But I know it when I see it, and the motion picture involved in this case is not that." *Compare* the reply of the London accountant named Smith, who in testifying before the Committee on the Resumption of Cash Payments in 1819, was asked to define what he meant by the pound. He replied: "I find it difficult to explain it, but, every gentleman in England knows it." When the Committee repeated the question, Smith responded: "It is something that has existed without variation in this country for eight hundred years—three hundred years before the introduction of gold." Quoted in S. Silard, *Money and Foreign Exchange,* 17 INT'L ENCY. COMP. L., chap. 20, p. 1.

2. *See, e.g.,* K. OLIVECRONA, THE PROBLEM OF THE MONETARY UNIT 9–21 (1957); F. MANN, THE LEGAL ASPECT OF MONEY 3–29 (3d ed. 1971).

3. M. FRIEDMAN & A. SCHWARTZ, MONETARY STATISTICS OF THE UNITED STATES 137 (1970).

4. Doucet, *Le Franc du 8 mars 1803 au décembre 1958,* in INFLUENCE DE LA DÉPRÉCIATION MONÉTAIRE SUR LA VIE JURIDIQUE PRIVÉE 1, 2–3 (P. Durand, ed. 1961); Eder, *Legal Theories of Money,* 20 CORN. L. Q. 52, 55 (1934).

5. For comparisons of the definitions of the national money stock in Canada, France, Germany, Japan, Italy, the United Kingdom, and the United States, *see* Tables 3–1 to 3–8 in R. BRYANT, MONEY AND MONETARY POLICY IN INTERDEPENDENT NATIONS 23–37 (1980).

6. J. GALBRAITH, MONEY: WHENCE IT CAME, WHERE IT WENT 7 (1975).

7. Credit for the first coins is frequently given to the ancient Asia Minor kingdom of Lydia, somewhere about the seventh or eighth centuries B.C. *Id.* at 8; A. NUSSBAUM, MONEY IN THE LAW NATIONAL AND INTERNATIONAL 59 (rev. ed. 1950). Nevertheless, it is quite possible that coins were in use in India several centuries earlier. J. GALBRAITH, *supra* note 6, at 8.

8. The Persian king Darius (521–485 B.C.) made coinage a royal monopoly. It was not until the reign of Diocletian (284–305 A.D.) that the emperor established a complete monopoly over coinage in the Holy Roman Empire. A. NUSSBAUM *supra* note 7, at 32–33. Medieval princes frequently ceded the right of coinage in exchange for a tax called *le fouage* or leased their coinage privileges to others. S. BRECKINRIDGE, LEGAL TENDER 9 (1903); A. NUSSBAUM, *supra* note 7, at 33. During the Middle Ages monetary systems were in great disarray; in Germany as many as 600 mints were operating at the same time. 1 K. HELFFERICH, MONEY 37 (L. Infield, tr. 1927).

9. James, *International Cooperation in the Field of Money: A Strand of Economic*

History, in MONEY AND THE LAW: PROCEEDINGS THE INSTITUTE OF MONEY AND LAW 1, 2–3 (N.Y.U. School of Law 1945).

10. F. MANN, *supra* note 2, at 79. The Post-Glossators distinguished between intrinsic value *(bonitas intrinseca)* and extrinsic value *(bonitas extrinseca);* the former was deemed the subject-matter of monetary obligations. *Id.*

11. A. NUSSBAUM, *supra* note 7, at 176. Until the early seventeenth century, Jewish law, on the other hand, adhered to the nominalist principle in enforcing the Biblical injunction against charging interest. At the start of the seventeenth century, Jewish communities began issuing dispensations in the event of monetary depreciation to divide the loss between creditor and debtor. *See* Rosenbaum v. Zeger, C. A. 248/53 (1954), 2 SELECTED JUDGMENTS OF THE SUPREME COURT OF ISRAEL 10, 27–37 (D. Gotein ed. 1963).

12. F. MANN, *supra* note 2, at 79; A. NUSSBAUM, *supra* note 7, at 177; A. WALD, A CLÁUSULA DE ESCALA MÓVEL 47 (2d ed. 1959).

13. F. MANN, *supra* note 2, at 79–80.

14. T. ASCARELLI, PROBLEMAS DAS SOCIEDADES ANÔNIMAS E DIREITO COMPARADO 194 (1945).

15. *Id.* at 181; F. MANN, *supra* note 2, at 80–84.

16. *E.g.,* Argentina (art. 619); Belgium (art. 1895); Chile (art. 2199); Italy (art. 1277); Mexico (art. 2389); Netherlands (art. 1793); Portugal (art. 727); Spain (art. 312); Venezuela (art. 1737).

The codifier's note to Article 619 of the Argentine Civil Code states: "We abstain from drafting laws to settle the much debated question regarding the obligation of the debtor when there has been an alteration in the currency, for such an alteration would have to be ordered by the national legislature, a nearly impossible event. . . . If one had to lay down a rule of law on the supposition of an alteration in currency, we would accept the article of the Austrian Code."

The Austrian Code provision referred to by the draftsman of the Argentine Civil Code is Article 988, which provides: "Legal currency changes, without alteration of the internal value, are at the risk of the creditor. He shall accept payment in the fixed sort of coin given by him, for example, 1000 imperial ducats or 3000 twenty-kreuzer pieces, without regard to whether or not their external value has been increased or diminished in the meantime. However, if the internal value has been altered, the payment is to be effected in proportion to the internal value which the said sort of coin had at the time the loan was contracted." [Translation from P. BAECK, THE GENERAL CIVIL CODE OF AUSTRIA 191–92 (1972)].

Because both the Argentine and Austrian codifiers were plainly thinking of money in terms of coins with a designated gold or silver content, their statements have an obsolete ring in an era of irredeemable paper money.

17. F. MANN, *supra* note 2, at 80–81. Courts, particularly in France, at one time interpreted Article 1895 as a bar to escalator clauses in private contracts. *See* chap. 5, *infra,* at notes 70–79 and the accompanying text. It is now well settled, even in France, that nominalism is *jus dispositivum* rather than *jus cogens.* Consequently, private parties can avoid the operation of the nominalist principle by inserting maintenance-of-value stipulations in their agreements. F. MANN, *supra* note 2, at 146.

18. 2 James I [Davies' Reports] (A.D. 1605); 2 Cobbett's Complete Collection

of State Trials 114 (1809). The case is reported in law French at J. Davis, Les Reports des cases and matters en Ley 18 (1674).

19. James, *supra* note 9, at 3. Nonpaper bank-created money originated much earlier with the establishment of the Bank of Venice about 1171. Depositors received imaginary banco-coins measured by constant silver or gold weight. These imaginary coins were frequently used by merchants during the Middle Ages to settle accounts. I. FISHER, STABLE MONEY: A HISTORY OF THE MOVEMENT 8–9 (1934).

20. 2 R. GONNARD, HISTOIRE DES DOCTRINES MONÉTAIRES 28 (1936). Law believed that paper money was inherently superior to metallic money, the value of which fluctuated with the supply and demand for gold and silver and which was constantly being subjected to debasement. Paper money was said to be easier to transport, store, utilize as a means of payment, and more difficult to counterfeit. Law further argued that paper money's value could be kept stable by maintaining public confidence in it through backing the currency with something that had a surplus of value, such as the nation's supply of land. *Id.* at 31–36.

21. This account of Law's adventure is drawn from J. GALBRAITH, *supra* note 6, at 22–27 and 2 R. GONNARD, *supra* note 20, at 28–53.

22. Roman law made it a criminal offense *(lese majesty)* to refuse to accept coins stamped with the royal effigy. A. WALD, *supra* note 12, at 55–56. It also required that unaltered Roman coins be accepted at their nominal value irrespective of their actual metallic content, 1 K. HELFFERICH, *supra* note 8, at 31; 1 T. MOMMSEN, HISTOIRE DE LA MONNAIE ROMAINE 209–10 (1865).

23. If before suit the debtor tenders the exact amount owed in lawful money and remains ready and willing to pay, and after suit has been brought, pays the debt into court, the debtor is not responsible for further interest and costs. F. MANN, *supra* note 2, at 38–39; A. NUSSBAUM, *supra* note 7, at 51–53. Moreover, parties secondarily liable are discharged and securities in property are lost. Oliphant, *The Theory of Money in the Law of Commercial Instruments,* 29 YALE L. J. 606, 609 (1920); A. NUSSBAUM, *supra* note 7, at 51–53. Roman law originally allowed the debtor whose tender had been refused to throw away the tender. Eventually, Roman law evolved to grant the debtor the right to secure discharge by depositing the object of the debt at the creditor's expense. The civil law did not develop the rather cumbersome common law notion of tender. *Id.* at 52.

24. Pong v. deLindsay et al, 1 Dyer's Reports 82a (1552) (tender of a baser money called Pollards is good tender to discharge a debt denominated in sterling because Pollards had been declared current in England); The Case of the Mixt Money, *supra* note 18; Foxcraft v. Wade, 5 Coke's Reports 114a (1601) (requirement of payment of £ 250 in *legalis monetae Angliae* met by tender of a mixed bag of English pounds, Spanish pistolets, and French crowns, because the Spanish and French coins had been declared current and lawful money of England by royal proclamation).

25. A. KEMP, THE LEGAL QUALITIES OF MONEY 18 (1956). The first English statute using the modern terminology of legal tender was passed in 1751 as an attempt to prevent the American colonies from abusing paper money denominated legal tender. *Id.* at 19. *See* the text to note 29 *infra.*

26. *See* S. BRECKINRIDGE, *supra* note 8, at 56–57. The notes of the Bank of

England, founded in 1694, did not become legal tender until 1833, when the Bank of England Act provided that the bank's notes should be legal tender for all sums above five pounds "so long as the Bank of England shall continue to pay on demand their said notes in legal coin." F. MANN, *supra* note 2, at 39–40. *But see* the curious quasi-legal tender statute in effect from 1812 to 1821, note 42 *infra*. The notes of John Law's bank were not made legal tender until shortly before the bank's collapse in 1720. 2 R. GONNARD, *supra* note 20, at 49, 51.

The Chinese, who began printing paper money more than 400 years before the West, apparently were the first to develop a legal tender concept. Marco Polo reported that during the thirteenth century rejection of imperial paper money was a capital offense. A. NUSSBAUM, *supra* note 7, at 53.

27. Coin was so scarce in the colonies that Indian wampum, corn, bullets, beaver skins, and tobacco were all used as money. The earliest American legal tender legislation was a Massachusetts statute of 1631 providing that corn shall pass in payment of all debts at the usual market rate, unless money or beaver had been expressly named in the contract. S. BRECKINRIDGE, *supra* note 8, at 52–54.

28. *Id.* at 58–60.

29. *Id.* at 61–63.

30. Resolution of July 11, 1776, set out in A. HEPBURN, A HISTORY OF CURRENCY OF THE UNITED STATES 14 (1915). The greater the depreciation, the more drastic the penalties for refusing to accept the bills. In some cases the penalty consisted of discharge of the debt; in other states the offender was subjected to fines, imprisonment, or the cutting off of his ears. A. KEMP, *supra* note 25, at 51.

31. *Id.* at 50–51.

32. S. HARRIS, THE ASSIGNATS 8 (1930).

33. *Id.* at 8–9.

34. *Id.* at 12.

35. From the beginning of 1792 the *assignat* was no longer accepted at face value in private transactions, but its value remained reasonably high until the end of 1794. The *assignat*'s value declined from 30 percent of face value in January 1795 to 20 percent in April 1795, and to 1 percent by November 1795. *Id.* at 206–207.

36. A. NUSSBAUM, *supra* note 7, at 23, 53.

37. Efforts were made in both the United States and France to stabilize the currency by issuing new kinds of money and by scaling debts in continentals and *assignats*. These efforts are discussed in chap. 4, *infra*, at notes 1–18 and the accompanying text.

38. In a letter in 1779 deploring the depreciation in Continental currency, Benjamin Franklin wrote:

> The only consolation under the evil is, that the public debt is proportionately diminished by the depreciation; and this by a kind of imperceptible tax, every one having paid a part of it in the fall of value that took place between the receiving and paying such sums as passed through his hands. . . . [It] is a mystery even to the politicians, how we have been able to continue a war four years without money, and how we could pay with paper, that had no previously fixed fund appropriated specially to redeem it. This currency, as we manage it, is a wonderful machine. It performs its office when we issue it; it pays and clothes troops, and provides victuals and ammunition.

Quoted in the concurring opinion of Mr. Justice Bradley in The Legal Tender Cases, 79 U.S. (12 Wall.) 457, 557–58 (1870).

39. *See* notes 51 and 58 *infra* and the accompanying text.

40. J. GALBRAITH, *supra* note 6, at 34.

41. Grigby v. Oakes et al, 2 Bos. & Pul. 527 (1801), rejected the defense that the notes of the Bank of England were legal tender when the holder of a note of a country bank refused payment in notes of the Bank of England and demanded payment in specie.

42. 51 Geo. III, ch. 127; 52 Geo. III, ch. 50.

43. Prices in banknotes from 1797 to 1821 were never more than 31 percent higher than in 1796. *See* Table 8 in G. WARREN & F. PEARSON, PRICES 75 (rev. 1933).

44. A. NUSSBAUM, *supra* note 7, at 48.

45. This was perhaps most clearly expressed in the 1806 report of the French Tribunal to the Corps Legislatif with regard to the notes of the Banque de France: "These notes will never be legal tender. We shall have as security the sacred word of [Napoleon]. His Majesty has wished it clearly expressed that no alteration in the value of paper money shall take place. The notes of the Bank shall always be, in the eyes of the State, only notes of trust; never, shall they be recognized as obligatory." MATER, TRAITÉ JURIDIQUE DE LA MONNAIE ET DU CHANGE 101 (1925), cited in French in A. NUSSBAUM, *supra* note 7, at 47, fn. 8 [translation by the author].

Concern about avoiding repetition of the disastrous paper money inflations of the colonial and revolutionary periods was frequently voiced during the debates on the adoption of the U.S. Constitution. This concern led the framers to include in the Constitution an explicit denial to the states of the powers to make anything but gold or silver coin legal tender and to emit bills of credit (Art. I, Sect. 10). The evils of issuing paper money were frequently mentioned in the debates on the U.S. Constitution, and many of the framers expressed the view that even the federal government should be denied the power to make paper money legal tender. 2 M. FARRAND, THE RECORDS OF THE FEDERAL CONVENTION 309–10 (1911).

Although the debates on the Constitution clearly restricted the power of the federal government to issue paper money, there was also some support in the text and the legislative history for the proposition that Congress was granted some authority to issue paper money, at least in an emergency. J. W. HURST, A LEGAL HISTORY OF MONEY IN THE UNITED STATES, 1774–1970, 15–16 (1973). The power of Congress to issue paper money with legal tender quality was vigorously debated in 1862 when the financial exigencies of the Civil War moved Congress to issue "greenbacks." The issue was ultimately resolved in the U.S. Supreme Court. In Hepburn v. Griswold, 75 U.S. (8 Wall.) 603 (1869) the Court, by a vote of 5–3, held the statutes making "greenbacks" legal tender unconstitutional. But in 1870 two new members were appointed to the Court. After a "remarkable public altercation," the Court voted to rehear arguments on the legal tender issue. In Knox v. Lee and Parker v. Davis, known as The Legal Tender Cases, 79 U.S. (12 Wall.) 457 (1871), the Court reversed itself by a 5–4 vote and sustained the constitutionality of the "greenbacks." In a series of subsequent cases the constitutionality of the legal tender laws was reaffirmed, "with a constantly dwindling but increasingly voluble minority." Dawson & Cooper, *The Effect of Inflation on Private Contracts: United States, 1861–1879,* 33 MICH. L. REV. 852, 860 fn. 174 (1935).

46. R. HAWTREY, THE GOLD STANDARD IN THEORY AND PRACTICE 66 (5th ed. 1947).

47. The principle that "bad money drives out good" was erroneously attributed to Sir Thomas Gresham by H. D. MACLEOD'S DICTIONARY OF POLITICAL ECONOMY 17, 18 (1863). There is no evidence that Gresham was even aware of "Gresham's Law." F. MANN, *supra* note 2, at 20, fn. 6.

48. W. SHAW, THE HISTORY OF CURRENCY 238–39 (2d ed. 1896).

49. A. FEAVERYEAR, THE POUND STERLING 154 (2d ed. 1963), cited in F. MANN, *supra* note 2, at 32.

50. 56 Geo. III, ch. 68.

51. Doucet, *supra* note 4, at 9–10.

52. R. HAWTREY, *supra* note 46, at 71–72.

53. S. ROLFE, GOLD AND WORLD POWER 59 (1966); M. Heilperin, *Monetary Internationalism and its Crisis,* in ASPECTS OF THE PATHOLOGY OF MONEY 75, 85 (M. Heilperin 1968). The pound and gold were inextricably linked in nineteenth century perception: "Actually, it hardly occurred to people in those days to speak of sterling as convertible: there was nothing better to convert it into. The identity of gold and sterling seemed almost a law of nature. Even more than the link with gold, sterling's general acceptability and unrestricted transferability promoted confidence" L. YEAGER, INTERNATIONAL MONETARY RELATIONS: THEORY, HISTORY, AND POLICY 299 (2d ed. 1976).

54. R. HAWTREY, *supra* note 46, at 79–80.

55. Between 1871 and 1873 Germany acquired and coined $240,000,000 worth of gold, which was more than the world's bullion markets could stand without a sharp increase in the price of gold. *Id.* at 74.

56. The precariousness stems from the strong likelihood that the existing relation between the supply and demand curves for each metal will be altered over time. A country operating with a fixed bimetallic standard becomes a dealer offering to buy and sell unlimited quantities of both metals at fixed prices. If the value of silver begins to decline in relation to gold, a bimetallic country finds itself having to purchase large quantities of silver. If the decline continues, the country finds itself importing silver and exporting gold. If a bimetallic country exhausts its gold supply, the country becomes on a silver standard *de facto.* During the fourteenth and fifteenth centuries, France was forced to change the ratio between gold and silver more than 150 times in 100 years "with a roughness that is quite inconceivable to the modern mind." W. SHAW, *supra* note 48, at 31. During the first half of the nineteenth century, however, France held sufficient quantities of gold and silver to effectively govern the world prices for gold and silver. R. HAWTREY, *supra* note 46, at 70–71.

57. *See id.* at 82.

58. Act of Apr. 2, 1792, ch. 16, sec. 9, 1 U.S. Stat. 246.

59. W. SHAW, *supra* note 48, at 257.

60. *Id.* at 262.

61. Russia and Japan formally adopted the gold standard in 1897. Among the

major nations only China clung to silver until World War I. L. YEAGER, *supra* note 53, at 298.

62. W. SHAW, *supra* note 48, at 264–65.

63. L. YEAGER, *supra* note 53, at 297–98.

64. Because national currencies were defined in terms of a fixed amount of gold and there was free convertibility and exchange of gold, actual exchange rates could fluctuate only within the narrow limits defined by the cost of transporting gold between countries. Under the gold standard, there was an automatic adjustment mechanism to eliminate disequilibriums in balance-of-payments, which were settled by transfer of gold from the deficit to the surplus country. In theory, the transfer was supposed to cause the country running a balance-of-payments surplus to increase its money supply and inflate domestic prices. An opposite contraction was supposed to occur in the country running a deficit. These reciprocal changes in the money supply were believed to cause the appropriate movements in prices, income, and interest rates to eliminate the disequilibrium. In practice, central banks frequently offset the effects of gold movements on domestic currency supplies, and countries running balance-of-payments surpluses generally experienced inflation or deflation at the same time as countries experiencing balance-of-payments deficits. Nevertheless, the gold standard system functioned surprisingly well during the pre-World War I era for a variety of reasons peculiar to that period. *See* S. ROLFE, *supra* note 53, at 60–62; L. YEAGER, *supra* note 53, at 303–8.

65. R. HAWTREY *supra* note 46, at 84.

66. *Id.* at 84–85.

67. Heilperin, *Post-War European Inflations, World War I A Study of Selected Cases,* in ASPECTS OF THE PATHOLOGY OF MONEY 97, 98–99 (M. Heilperin 1968).

68. Currency authorities generally maintained, either as a custom or legal requirement, a certain supply of gold or silver as a reserve against the contingencies of note redemption or adverse balance of payments. The Bank of England usually kept its gold reserve at about 40 percent of its deposit liability. The reserve was usually higher in France. R. HAWTREY, *supra* note 46, at 53–54.

69. L. YEAGER, *supra* note 53, at 312.

70. *Id.;* J. GALBRAITH, *supra* note 6, at 154–55.

71. These dollar values are calculated at the then prevailing exchange rate of $20.67 per ounce. J. GALBRAITH, *supra* note 6, at 137.

72. S. HORIE, THE INTERNATIONAL MONETARY FUND 13 (1964).

73. S. ROLFE, *supra* note 53, at 63.

74. S. HORIE, *supra* note 72, at 17–18.

75. S. ROLFE, *supra* note 53, at 65–66.

76. *See* L. YEAGER, *supra* note 53, at 331; S. HORIE, *supra* note 72, at 19–23.

77. The primary reason for this measure appears to have been the belief that this would raise domestic price levels. Buchanan and Tideman, *Gold, Money and the Law: The Limits of Governmental Monetary Authority,* in GOLD, MONEY AND THE LAW 9, 33, 35 (H. Manne & R. Miller eds. 1975). *See also* Perry v. United States, 294 U.S. 330, 373 (1935) (dissenting opinion of McReynolds, J.).

78. H. STEINER & D. VAGTS, TRANSNATIONAL LEGAL PROBLEMS 1108 (1st ed. 1968).

79. The Articles of Agreement of the International Monetary Fund (July 22,

1944) are reproduced in 3 THE INTERNATIONAL MONETARY FUND 1945–1965, 185–214 (J. Horsefield, ed. 1969).

80. Art. I (v).

81. Art. IV, sec. 3(i). A spot transaction is one that occurs within two banking days. All other foreign exchange transactions are considered forward transactions; parity is not set for forward transactions.

The Articles of the IMF did not spell out how parity was to be maintained. Normal techniques for doing so were (1) requiring all foreign exchange sales to be made through a central agency; or (2) allowing the rate to be set by the free market, but intervening through the central bank or its surrogate when necessary to prevent any substantial deviations from parity.

A third technique, utilized only by the United States, allowed purchase or sale of gold in international transactions.

82. de Vries, *Exchange Rate Adjustment,* in 2 THE INTERNATIONAL MONETARY FUND 1945–1965, 90, 92 (J. Horsefield ed. 1969); Gold, *Law and Reform of the International Monetary System,* 10 J. INT'L L. & ECON. 371, 374–75 (1975).

83. Art. III, sec. 3(b).

84. *See* Gold, *supra* note 82, at 378.

85. *See* S. ROLFE, *supra* note 53, at 6.

86. If gold's price had risen at the same rate as the consumer price index in the United States between 1944 and 1968, its price would have been approximately $70 rather than $35 an ounce.

87. A. LOWENFELD, THE INTERNATIONAL MONETARY SYSTEM 93–98 (1977); Kafka, *The International Monetary System in Transition—Part I,* 13 VA. J. INT'L L. 135, 146–47 (1972); Comment, *Termination of Two-Tier Gold,* 7 L. & POL. INT'L BUS. 273, 274–85 (1975). Prior to 1961 the central banks had agreed to refrain from buying gold on the private market. Kafka, *supra,* 13 VA. J. INT'L L. at 147.

88. Gold, *Law and Change in International Monetary Relations* 31 RECORD ASSOC. BAR OF CITY OF N.Y. 223, 229 (1976).

89. INT'L MONETARY FUND, 1979 ANNUAL REPORT, pp. 65–67.

90. *See* S. ROLFE, *supra* note 53, at 175–87 for a description of these measures.

91. Triffin, *Basic Considerations in International Monetary Reform,* in INFLATION, TRADE, AND TAXES 119, 121 (D. Belsley et al., eds. 1976).

92. Kafka, *supra* note 87, at 135; Gold, *supra* note 82, at 390.

93. As of June 30, 1975 the currencies of fifty-four countries were pegged to the U.S. dollar; thirteen were pegged to the French franc; ten were pegged to the pound sterling; three were pegged to the South African rand; and one was pegged to the Spanish peseta. Five countries pegged their currencies to the SDR, while fourteen countries tied their currencies to miscellaneous composite arrangements. Eleven countries allowed their currencies to float freely or adopted a "managed float." J. GOLD, FLOATING CURRENCIES, GOLD AND SDRS: SOME RECENT LEGAL DEVELOPMENTS 7 (IMF Pamphlet No. 19, 1976).

As of April 30, 1981, the number of countries pegging their currency to the U.S. dollar dropped to forty, the number pegged to the French franc rose to fourteen; the number pegged to the pound sterling fell to one; and the number pegged to the South African rand fell to two. The number of countries pegging their currency to the SDR increased to fifteen, while the number of countries tying their currencies to a different composite arrangement increased to twenty-two. Eight countries were participating in the joint float of the European monetary system, and thirty-seven either allowed their currencies to float freely or used some other form of changing exchange rates. IMF, 34 INT'L FIN. STATISTICS 11 (Je. 1981).

94. The snake began with nine countries in 1972. Great Britain dropped out in 1972, followed by Italy in 1973, France in 1974 and again in 1976, and Sweden in 1977. Day, *A Reform of the European Currency Snake,* 23 IMF STAFF PAPERS 580 (1976); "Joint Currency Float, Although Shadow of Former Self, Is Still Taken Seriously," Wall St. J., Sept. 12, 1977, p. 20, cols. 1–2.

95. Great Britain has not yet agreed to join the intervention arrangement.

96. *See* chap. 8 *infra,* at note 39 and the accompanying text.

97. Wall St. J., May 8, 1980, at p. 10.

98. To try to reduce that risk, the Group of Ten (United States, Great Britain, France, Germany, the Netherlands, Japan, Italy, Canada, Belgium, and Sweden) on August 31, 1975 agreed that they would take no action to peg the price of gold and that they would not seek to acquire more gold. That agreement was not renewed when it expired on January 23, 1978 on the theory that the experience of the past two years had made such an arrangement unnecessary. "Gold Arrangements End Following a Review by Parties to the Accord," IMF Survey, Feb. 6, 1978, at 34.

99. Gold, *supra* note 88, at 236.

100. Art. IV, sec. 4.

101. Schedule C, sec. 1.

102. "Nominalism primarily applies to fluctuations in the value of money, which are slow, gradual, and moderate. There is no certainty how English law would react in the unlikely event of the pound sterling depreciating in so violent, sudden, and extreme a manner as to lead to a collapse of the monetary system. Experience proves that in such a contingency nominalism cannot, in practice, be maintained and that the legislator or, failing him, the judge must afford relief." F. MANN, *supra* note 2, at 92.

103. *See* chap. 4 *infra,* at notes 3–28 and the accompanying text.

104. A. NUSSBAUM, *supra* note 7, at 28–29; G. WARREN & F. PEARSON, *supra* note 43, at 18–23; Walsh, Index Numbers, 7–8 ENCYCLOPEDIA OF THE SOC. SCIENCES 652–54 (rev. ed. 1937).

105. E. HIRSCHBERG, THE NOMINALISTIC PRINCIPLE 74–75 (1971).

106. *See* A. NUSSBAUM, *supra* note 7, at 215.

107. Dawson, *Effects of Inflation on Private Contracts: Germany, 1914–1924,* 33 MICH. L. REV. 171, 222–33 (1934); E. HIRSCHBERG, *supra* note 105, at 70–71.

108. A study of inflation rates in fifty-three countries for which price data were available between 1949 and 1965 placed six countries in a class by themselves, far surpassing all other countries. One of these countries was Korea, which had been a battlefield during part of the period under study. The other five countries—Argentina, Bolivia, Brazil, Chile, and Uruguay—had no wars to blame for their inflations. Bolivia managed to get its inflationary problems under control between 1956 and 1962. *See* G. EDER, INFLATION AND DEVELOPMENT IN LATIN AMERICA: A CASE HISTORY OF INFLATION AND STABILIZATION IN BOLIVIA 587–91 (1968). This was not the case in the other four South American countries. Between 1960 and 1965 the four countries in the study with the highest annual inflation rates were Brazil

with 58 percent, Uruguay with 32 percent, Chile with 25 percent, and Argentina with 24 percent. Adekunle, *Rates of Inflation in Industrial, Other Developed, and Less Developed Countries, 1949–1965,* 15 IMF STAFF PAPERS 531 (1968). During the 1970s, these four countries retained their positions as the most inflationary countries of the world. From 1970 to 1979 Argentina's inflation rate averaged 132.7 percent annually, Brazil's averaged 25.3 percent, Chile's averaged a whopping 174.1, and Uruguay's averaged 59.3 percent. Calculated from IMF, INT'L FIN. STATISTICS YEARBOOK 61 (1980).

109. Kafka, *Indexing for Inflation in Brazil,* in ESSAYS ON INFLATION AND INDEXATION 87–98 (H. Giersch ed. 1974); Simonsen, *Correção Monetária—a Experiência Brasileira,* 29 Conj. Econ. 65 (Jy. 1975).

110. Atkins v. United States, 214 Ct. Cl. 186, 556 F. 2d 1028 (Ct. Cls. 1977), *cert. denied* 434 U.S. 1009 (1978); Rosenn, *The Constitutional Guaranty against Diminution of Judicial Compensation,* 24 U.C.L.A. L. REV. 308 (1976). *See also* United States v. Will, 101 S. Ct. 471 (1980), where the Supreme Court declared unconstitutional certain Congressional statutes nullifying previously authorized judicial salary increases.

4

STATUTORY AND JUDICIAL REVISION OF INFLATION-DISTORTED CONTRACTS

During severe inflation, the nominalist principle generally comes under greatest pressure in the area of contracts. Performance of agreements entered into upon the assumption that the value of money is relatively stable causes severe hardships when inflation vitiates that assumption. This hardship is most apparent in contracts whose performance is deferred over a considerable period of time, such as construction contracts, mortgages, leases, insurance policies, annuities, and installment sales. Banks discover that it costs more to carry mortgage loans on the books than they receive in amortization and interest payments. Beneficiaries find that the proceeds of life insurance policies do not even cover burial expenses. Annuitants and pensioners who once believed they could retire on a comfortable income are forced to seek supplemental means of support just to subsist. Unfinished construction projects dot the landscape, monuments to bankruptcies of contractors unable to perform fixed-price construction contracts.

Insofar as it undermines the presumption of economic equilibrium underlying contract law, inflation presents essentially three kinds of problems for legal systems:

1. In which circumstances should the legislature or courts intervene to relieve parties from contracts that inflation has made more burdensome than the parties anticipated? If the legal system is to intervene, to what extent should it interfere with executed and partly executed contracts in the interest of mitigating injustice caused by inflation?
2. How should parties structure their contracts to protect themselves against inflation?
3. To what extent should existing legal impediments to protecting contracts from inflation be removed?

This chapter primarily emphasizes the first set of problems. It is concerned with how legislatures and courts have sought to mitigate the hardships caused to contracting parties by inflation. Chapter 5 will focus primarily on the second set of problems with more specific attention given to techniques that can be utilized by contracting parties to protect their bargains from inflationary distortions. Chapter 6 treats the second and third sets of problems in more detail in the context of four types of contractual arrangements that are very badly distorted by inflation: credit transactions, insurance, pensions, and annuities. Chapter 7, in its treatment of contract damages, will touch upon all three sets of issues. Chapter 8 will also deal with the second and third sets of issues in the context of international contracts. Finally, the last chapter will return to the second and third sets of issues in the general context of indexation.

This chapter is divided into two parts: legislative relief and judicial relief. The first part will focus on legislative revalorization of contractual obligations in the wake of severe inflation. The second part will examine judicial techniques that relieve parties from contractual obligations made unduly burdensome by inflation.

LEGISLATIVE REVALORIZATION

A sharp surge in the inflation rate produces considerable pressures on legislatures from two distinct economic classes: promisors whose contractual obligations are unduly burdensome because of unanticipated inflation, and creditors whose claims will be practically wiped out if debtors are permitted to discharge them in badly depreciated currency. These pressures produce a serious dilemma for legislatures. Should they permit revaluation of contractual obligations? If so, which categories of obligations should be revalued and on what bases? Should legislatures merely attempt to lay down broad guidelines and authorize the courts to proceed to do justice on a case-by-case basis? Or should they enact laws specifying certain categories of obligations entitled to relief? Should they go even further to define specifically what relief each category should receive?

The economic, social, and legal problems involved in any legislative or judicial attempt at revaluation of obligations are immense. First and foremost is the intractable problem of what standard of value to substitute for money. Prices gyrate wildly during severe inflation. The foreign exchange rate or the exchange value of gold or silver is generally a misleading indicator of value, reflecting speculative pressures and panicky flights into foreign currency or commodities whose values appear comparatively protected from inflation. Even well-constructed price indexes are unlikely to reflect the mercurial swings in the prices of many goods and services. These swings may vary greatly from region to region and from day to day. Price controls and accompanying shortages are usually part of the economic scene when there is severe inflation, exacerbating distortions in the price indexes. Moreover, the particular contracting parties may be affected by inflation much more or less than a general price index would suggest.

Second, it is extremely difficult to reconstruct the intentions of parties who have contracted in depreciating currency without a value maintenance device. One of the parties has assumed the risk of some inflation, but is it reasonable to assume that he assumed the risk of any inflation rate? If not, how can one determine how much risk of inflation has been assumed? Revaluing contractual obligations on the assumption that the parties contemplated a stable currency is likely to be grossly unfair to debtors; revaluing on the assumption that the parties contemplated runaway inflation is likely to be equally unfair to creditors. Reconstruction of the fantastically complex network of shifting economic equilibria is an awesome task.

Third, it is difficult to draw the line between classes of transactions that should be revalued and those which should not. The stickiest question is whether to revise completed transactions. If completed transactions are subject to revaluation, the lid of Pandora's box swings open wide. Hardships result if debtors who incur new obligations in reasonable reliance on the belief that their prior debts had been discharged by repayment are required to make additional payments. Moreover, the limits of retroactivity are exceedingly difficult to define. How far back does one go? But if one revalues only unpaid obligations, the position of the creditor who complied with legal tender laws is much worse than that of the creditor who did not comply or had the good fortune to have his obligation fall due only after the legislature mandated revaluation. Should one revalue all or just part of those debts that have been partly paid? If private contractual debts are to be revalued, should one also revalue government bonds and cash? What should be done about bank deposits, insurance policies, and insurance premiums? If mortgage debts are to be revalued, what should be done about the security of junior lienholders? Should revaluation of the first mortgage take precedence over the nominal liens of the second or third mortgagees? What should be done about debts which have been assigned? If heavily discounted for inflation at the time of assignment, should part of the revaluation be paid over to the assignor? Should revaluation also extend to obligations owed by trustees, executors, collecting agents, and other fiduciaries?

In short, revaluation is an extraordinarily complicated and ambitious undertaking. The earliest large scale efforts were undertaken by American, Austrian, and French legislators, who attempted to work rough justice by enacting scaling laws. These statutes revalued limited categories of obligations expressed in depreciated paper currency in accordance with fairly crude scales of values in specie or another currency. More ambitious and sophisticated scaling laws were enacted by Poland and Germany following World War I.

Early U.S. Scaling Statutes

The pioneers in the field of scaling laws were U.S. and French legislators.[1] During the period immediately after the American and French Revolutions, both groups were faced with the undeniable fact that the unbacked flood of paper money used to finance the revolutions (continentals in the United States and *assignats* in France) had ceased to function as either a store or measure of value.[2] Both improvised a variation on a theme from *The Arabian Nights* as a remedy for the collapse of their currencies: substitution of a new paper currency for the worthless old, and both enacted laws providing for revaluation by scaling of limited categories of obligations expressed in continentals or *assignats.* Neither had any success in stabilizing the currency through the device of new notes for old,[3] but these early scaling statutes achieved a measure of rough justice for certain classes of creditors.

Revaluation scales in the U.S. state statutes were crudely constructed. The percentage by which an obligation was scaled from its nominal value in continentals to its new value in specie or "hard" currency varied in accordance with the silver value of the continental at the date the obligation was incurred. Because there were no sophisticated price indexes, legislators simply operated on the assumption that the value of metallic money remained constant. Although this assumption was economically unsound, specie certainly did have the appearance of stability in comparison with paper money. The monthly variations in the specie conversion rate of the continental served as the sole standard of value in the scaling laws enacted in all but one of the American states. That exception was South Carolina, which derived its scale from the mean of the specie conversion rate and the prices of rice, indigo, and slaves, three items then regarded as important commodities.[4] State scaling statutes did not affect debts denominated in foreign currency or specie, or debts incurred prior to depreciation of the continentals. These were paid in specie or in the new paper issue (called New Tenor notes), unless these notes had also depreciated, in which event the debtor was required to readjust the amount so that he paid the real value of the debt. Nor did the scaling laws apply to debts already paid, even if paid in depreciated currency.[5] But unpaid debts contracted in continental currency were reduced to scale and repaid in specie.[6]

State legislation differed with respect to creditors who had disregarded the legal tender statutes by refusing to accept a tender of repayment in continentals. Some states referred these cases to arbitrators for equitable settlement, while others declared that such creditors should receive only the nominal value of their debts in depreciated continentals.[7]

French Scaling Statutes

France enacted a complex scaling statute to revalue outstanding contracts in April of 1796, soon after the new paper currency, the *mandat,* had been made legal tender. Contracts made prior to *assignat* depreciation and those calling for specie payments were to be paid in full in *mandats.* All other contractual amounts were to be reduced according to an elaborate depreciation scale and paid in *mandats.* All private contracts entered into after January 1, 1792, were divided into sixteen categories, depending on the date of the contract. The more recent the contract, the lower the percentage of its nominal value due in *mandats.*[8] This depreciation scale was based on a combination of the specie exchange rate, the foreign exchange rate, and prices of subsistence commodities.[9]

This depreciation scale was much criticized on technical grounds by representatives of both debtors and creditors. Indeed, the scale had an inherent flaw; it was based upon the assumption that the *mandat*'s value would remain stable, an assumption that quickly became blatantly untenable.

The French government next tried indexing the value of the *mandat* to the price of corn,[10] an arrangement which worked poorly. French policymakers finally decided that the only feasible solution to the standard of value problem was the use of the specie exchange rate. After August of 1796 tax payments could be made only in *mandats au cours* or specie.[11] For this purpose the government published the specie exchange rate every five days until the demonetization of the *mandat* in February of 1797.

In July of 1796 a law was passed abolishing the *mandat*'s legal tender status.[12] This produced a number of proposals for scaling private contracts. But there was much disagreement about what to use for a standard of value and whether a uniform scale should be established for the entire country. Not until the following year was legislation enacted which provided scaling of private debts arising from loans contracted in paper currency.[13] Each *département* (political subdivision) was directed to construct its own scale of depreciation for *assignats* and *mandats,* taking into account the specie exchange rate, and the prices paid for real estate, foodstuffs, and merchandise.[14] There were, as might be expected, considerable variations from *département* to *département* in the construction of the scales. Price data were sparse and difficult to come by, and little was known about the construction of price indexes.

The scaling statutes did not apply to all private contracts. Their application was limited to debts arising from loans in paper money between 1791 and July of 1796.[15] Debts originating prior to 1791 had to be paid in full in specie. Debts contracted after July 17, 1796, which were payable over more than a two year term were subject to reduction only if the debtor offered to pay the principal reduced to scale within a year. No reduction was available for debts that had been assigned to third parties.[16]

A series of statutes were enacted in 1797–98 to deal with the special problems presented by *rentes* (long-term leases or annuities), sales of real property, and rentals. Most private *rentes* were reduced by scaling down either the capital or the interest. The government in effect declared bankruptcy on public *rentes;* public *rentiers* realized only a tiny fraction of the nominal value of their *rentes* from the government.[17] Three alternatives were provided for adjusting values in the sales of real property. First, the property could be appraised by experts to determine its real value in specie at the time of sale. Second, the seller could avoid appraisal by agreeing to reduce the purchase price in accordance with the scale of depreciation adopted within the *département* where the property was located. Third, the buyer, in certain situations, could rescind the contract and recover the value (according to the depreciation scale) of any installments already paid. Rents were fixed according to 1790 levels or by expert valuation.[18]

Austria's Scaling Law of 1811

The American and French experience with scaling laws was soon repeated in Austria, where nonlegal tender notes of the Vienna Bank had been circulating since 1762. After the Vienna Bank became a state institution, the amount of notes in circulation increased steadily to finance chronic governmental budgetary deficits. In 1800, when specie circulated at a premium over bank notes, the government made bank notes legal tender and suspended convertibility.[19] Further financial difficulties, which led to further increases of the amount of notes in circulation, aggravated the depreciation of Austria's paper money.

The Austrians in 1811 were not in the dire financial straits confronting the Americans in 1780 and the French in 1796. The Austrian *florin* had not collapsed, but it had depreciated by about 850 percent in relation to specie. In 1811 Austria enacted a monetary reform that reduced all bank notes to one-fifth their nominal value. Existing bank notes were to be gradually exchanged over the course of a year for new notes known as *Einlosungsscheine* (Redemption Notes) at the rate of 5 to 1. The *Einlosungsscheine* were issued at a par with specie and were to be limited to one-fifth the amount of bank notes in circulation. Contractual debts were revalued according to a scale of depreciation which incorporated this five to one ratio. This ratio was chosen arbitrarily and greatly overvalued the new notes in relation to specie.[20]

U.S. Post–Civil War Scaling Statutes

Scaling statutes were again enacted in the United States following the Civil War to deal with the specific problem of obligations contracted in Confederate currency. After the military defeat of the Confederacy, Confederate currency was not only worthless but illegal. The only legally valid currency was that of the United States. Requiring discharge of obligations contracted in Confederate dollars in U.S. dollars would have been grossly unfair to debtors; requiring acceptance of payment in worthless Confederate currency would have been grossly unfair to creditors. The scaling statutes enacted by state legislatures in the former Confederate states in the 1865–67 period generally directed the courts to revalue unsatisfied contractual obligations payable in Confederate currency.[21] In most Southern states no attempt was made by legislatures to fix a uniform value of Confederate money for all classes of obligations. Instead courts were directed to utilize the value of the consideration given as the revalorization standard. Although this standard was eventually rejected on constitutional grounds by the U.S. Supreme Court,[22] by then the state courts had largely completed the task of revaluing Confederate currency claims.[23]

Polish Scaling Statutes

Far more complex scaling laws were enacted in 1924 in Poland, which had experienced catastrophic inflation after World War I. The Polish mark, created by German occupation troops and taken over by Polish authorities after Germany's defeat, fell from 6.2 to the dollar in December of 1918 to 6,460,000 to the dollar by January of 1924.[24] The *zloty,* a new currency unit equal to one gold franc, was adopted in 1924, and executory obligations payable in Polish marks were revalorized in *zlotys* in accordance with a complicated scale. Polish law also provided for revalorization of contracts in which the unit of account was expressed in German marks, Russian rubles, or Austrian crowns, so long as the unit of payment was the Polish mark.[25] The law converted the values of such contracts into *zlotys* at exchange rates in effect at the time the obligation was formed.

Polish scaling laws accorded creditors a fraction of the gold value of their original obligations. That fraction varied with the type of contract, the region of the country, and the debtor's economic position. For example, holders of government bonds received between 10 and 30 percent of the original value of the bonds.[26] Mortgagees of real estate received from 25 to 15 percent, depending on the region in which the property was located. Holders of chattel mortgages received between 50 and 15 percent.[27] Most creditors received only 10 percent. Special rates were established for most categories of debts. Where the statute was omissive, the courts were directed to take account of the expressed desires of the parties, good faith, and equity.[28]

Post–World War I German Scaling Legislation

The German experience differed from prior legislative revalorization efforts in several significant respects. First, the Germany judiciary, acting in advance of any legislative direction, had already begun the Herculean task of revaluing obligations payable in depreciated currency. This judicial odyssey into revalorization, which was belatedly joined by the legislature, is treated in more detail in the second part of this chapter.[29] Second, German revalorization was far more complex and ambitious than any other previous revalorization schemes, none of which had attempted to revalorize fully executed transactions. But the German courts and later the legislature refused to draw a line between executed and executory obligations for the purpose of revalorization. Third, German revalorization used a multiplicity of more sophisticated standards of value instead of the simplistic percentage scales of the earlier legislation.

The need for some kind of revalorization relief was manifest because of the speed and magnitude of Germany's economic collapse. In June 1918, 5.31 marks were required to purchase a U.S. dollar. By December of 1922 one needed 7,589 marks. One month later, as the French and Belgian troops occupied the Ruhr area to insure payment of vast reparations obligations, the exchange rate more than doubled. By November 1923, the dollar was being quoted at the astronomical exchange rate of 1 trillion marks.[30] Moderate interest rates were running 6 percent a day.[31] It was calculated at this time that the physical quantity of one dollar's worth of one mark notes would fill between 60,000 and 70,000 freight cars.[32]

On November 15, 1923, the German government issued a new currency called the *rentenmark,* whose value was declared to be equal to one gold mark. Following John Law's precedent, the German government issued this currency as notes of the Rentenbank and made them convertible into interest-bearing bonds secured by a mortgage on all of Germany's agricultural land and special taxes levied on German industry and commerce. Ultimately, the German currency was stabilized at the ratio of 4.2 trillion marks to one gold mark; in 1924 the *rentenmark* was replaced with a new currency unit called the *reichsmark,* which also had the value of one gold mark.[33]

Soon after the German courts began revalorizing contracts, the German legislature seriously contemplated prohibiting any revalorization. There were important commercial and industrial interests that were opposed to any revalorization whatsoever.[34] The response of the German judges to legislative consideration of this proposal was a truly extraordinary example of judicial jujitsu. On January 8, 1924, the board of the Association of the Judges of the *Reichsgericht,* Germany's highest court, issued a proclamation advising the legislature that the good faith principle embodied in Article 242 of the Civil Code, which had served as the legal basis for judicial revalorization, was superior to any "individual statutory rule." The German judges warned that any legislative attempt to prohibit judicial revalorization might be considered an unconstitutional taking of property without compensation or a general tax of unequal incidence.[35] This highly unusual piece of anticipatory judicial review did not prevent the German legislature from enacting revalorization legislation, but it did have the intended effect of helping insure that revalorization efforts begun by the judiciary would be allowed to continue. Indeed, the legislature left a large area of contractual obligations entirely within the province of judicial revalorization. As a result, Germany had two distinct types of revalorization proceeding simultaneously: statutory and judicial (sometimes called "free").

Legislative revalorization began with the Third Emergency Tax Ordinance of February 14, 1924. This hastily drafted measure provided for revalorization of certain bonds and mortgages at 15 percent of the original gold-mark value. It also imposed a substantial tax on the inflation gains of debtors who were able to discharge their debts in depreciated currency. The Third Emergency Tax Ordinance generated great controversy and was made provisional by legislation adopted at the end of 1924. It was eventually supplanted by the Revalorization Law *(Aufwertungsgesetz)* of July 16, 1925.[36]

The 1925 Revalorization Law was considerably more complex than its predecessor. It applied principally to three classes of money obligations: (1) mortgages on real property or ships; (2) negotiable bonds; and (3) insurance claims and savings accounts. Mortgages were revalorized at 25 percent of their original gold mark value. There were, however, two exceptions to this general rule. If the mortgagor could show that payment of this revalorized debt would create a serious hardship, the court, upon prompt application, had the power to reduce the revalorization rate to 10 percent.[37] The revalorization rate was also left to the discretion of the courts for purchase money mortgages and mortgages securing participation in a partnership or a support obligation.[38] Although a court might set the revalorization on a mortgage higher than 25 percent, the excess constituted only an unsecured personal debt. If the revalorization rate were set below 25 percent, the *in rem* obligation would be correspondingly reduced. This statutory quirk occasionally produced anomalous results where mortgagors had sold or assigned the mortgaged property.[39]

Negotiable bonds were generally revalorized at 15 percent of their original gold value. This rate could also be reduced by timely application and a showing of hardship by the debtor. Those bondholders who had acquired industrial bonds prior to July 1, 1920, and held them until revalorization were also entitled to *Genussrechte* (special nonvoting shares), which allowed them to share in the firm's net profits and to receive a share of any surplus upon liquidation. The *Genussrechte* was set at 10 percent of the gold-mark value of the obligation at the time of purchase.[40]

The third class of money obligations—claims against insurance companies, savings banks, and mortgage banks—was treated differently. Revalorization of mortgages and negotiable bonds would have resulted in an increase in the assets of banks and insurance companies. Therefore, the Revalorization Law created partial receiverships for these kinds of entities. Their revalorized assets were transferred to trustees for pro rata distribution to creditors.[41]

Unlike prior scaling laws, the German Revalorization Law applied retrospectively to reopen certain completed transactions. In no case, however, did either the 1924 or 1925 laws reopen any obligations that had been discharged prior to January 1, 1918. If the mortgagee or bondholder, in accepting payment, had expressly reserved his "right" to demand greater payment, retroactive revalorization was expressly allowed. This provision had a basis in German practice, for by the spring of 1922 it was common for creditors to accept payment only with such a reservation.[42] Retroactive revalorization was also expressly provided for mortgages satisfied between June 15, 1922 and February 14, 1924, regardless of whether there had been a reservation of the right to demand a greater payment. Unconditional acceptance of payment of a negotiable bond and surrender of the instrument effectively foreclosed revalorization.[43]

Only one important class of obligations, commercial bank deposits, was expressly excepted from revalorization. As might have been expected, efforts to have holders of cash reimbursed for their losses were unsuccessful.[44] Holders of government bonds were treated only slightly better, receiving 2.5 percent of the original gold value of their bonds.[45]

Legislative adoption of a percentage of the gold value of the original obligation by no means solved the difficult problem of the revalorization amount. First, the legislature had to determine when the original obligation arose. The original value of mortgages was measured as of the date of acquisition by the present owner. For negotiable bonds the original value was measured at the date of issuance by the obligor. The German legislature tried to differentiate between original holders and those who had acquired these obligations later for speculative purposes. But the date of acquisition criterion was too simplistic; the legislature was forced to place those who had acquired bonds and mortgages through inheritance, gift, or matrimony in the shoes of their transferors.[46] Second, the legislature had to determine how to translate values stated in rapidly depreciating marks into original gold values. The 1924 Emergency Tax Ordinance had used the current value of the mark's foreign exchange rate. This was rejected in the 1925 Revalorization Law as unfair to debtors because the domestic purchasing power of the mark, at least until the final stages of its collapse, had depreciated less rapidly than its foreign exchange rate.[47] The retail price index was rejected as a standard of value on the curious ground that in the normal case the lender would not have been able to use the loan proceeds to purchase consumer goods.[48] By default the legislature adopted the mean between the domestic wholesale price index and the dollar foreign exchange rate. An elaborate scale appended to the 1925 Revalorization Law set out the conversion rate on a monthly basis for 1918 and 1919, for ten-day periods between 1920 and June 1, 1923, and on a daily basis thereafter.

A six-and-one-half year moratorium was granted to enable debtors to raise the necessary funds to pay off their revalorized obligations. The creditor could not demand payment of a revalorized obligation prior to January 1, 1932. In cases of extreme hardship, the debtor could extend the period for payment by liquidating his debt in installments up to 1938. To protect the creditor from the possibility of inflation during the intervening period, all revalorized debts were declared to be gold-mark debts. Interest on revalorized debts began to run on January 1, 1925. The annual interest rate rose gradually from 1.2 percent to 5 percent on January 1, 1928.[49]

The German Revalorization Law made no effort to restore the real value of obligations contracted in depreciated currency. It represented a political compromise between those who wanted complete revalorization and those who wanted none. Certain classes of creditors were intentionally wiped out, while others were permitted to recover only a small fraction of the real value of their claims. By substantially narrowing the range of litigation and establishing special revalorization tribunals,[50] the Revalorization Law was an enormous aid to the regular courts in trying to cope with the massive amounts of litigation generated by revalorization.

Currency Reform in Post–World War II Germany

Despite the enormous increase of the amount of *reichsmarks* under the Nazis, Germany did not repeat its cataclysmic experience with inflation after its World War II defeat. Prices rose slowly during the first year of the Allied Occupation. Instead, there was massive flight from the use of German currency into barter and money substitutes, such as cigarettes. Distrust of the *reichsmark* was spurred by widely debated proposals for invalidating or scaling down a large part of the currency in circulation.[51] So pervasive and well-founded was this distrust of the currency that the Federal Supreme Court held that while currency reform was pending, promisors could withhold performance, and rights to repurchase could not be exercised.[52] Finally, in June 1948, the Allied military governments promulgated a series of laws that resulted in a 90 percent contraction in the money supply.[53]

The estimated 135 billion *reichsmarks* in circulation were cancelled and replaced with approximately 12.6 billion *deutsche marks,* a newly created currency. Individuals and businesses were allowed to convert 600 *reichsmarks* into *deutsche marks* at a 10 to 1 ratio, with the exception of 60 marks per person or employee, which could be converted at a 1 to 1 ratio. For persons holding more than 600 marks, the conversion ratio jumped to roughly 16 to 1.[54] The currency reform legislation also scaled down all bonds, mortgages, annuities, and other debt obligations to 10 percent of their former value.[55] The Allies required the German authorities to impose a tax on gains realized by debtors from the currency reform.[56]

This currency reform approach effectively wiped out a great deal of pecuniary wealth and reinstituted a money economy. As in the 1920s, the sacrifice of huge amounts of the nation's wealth was to some extent made more palatable by taxation of the gains accruing to debtors as a result of reduction of their debts by 90 percent. Although in 1948 the law scaled debts down rather than up, the practical effect was the same. The currency reform approach lacked much of the complexity and sophistication of the 1925 Revalorization Law. The standard of value problem was finessed by simply substituting new currency for old and valuing all *reichsmark* obligations, regardless of when contracted, at their face amounts. The method was crude and harshly unjust in many instances, but it was extremely effective in helping to restore Germany's battered economy to a sound footing.

SUMMARY

The problems of revalorizing contractual obligations expressed in currency that has become largely worthless because of hyperinflation are extraordinarily difficult. None of the scaling statutes succeeded in finding an alternative standard of value for money. Only occasionally did the specie exchange rate or the foreign exchange rate equal the rate of depreciation of the currency's purchasing power. Even with sophisticated price indexes, any attempt to measure the inflation rate during hyperinflation was a hit or miss proposition. Legislatures were able to achieve rough justice for some creditors by scaling obligations, but in numerous instances the scaling laws merely exacerbated the economic disruption and willy-nilly income redistribution stemming from hyperinflation. It has even been argued that post-World War I German revalorization legislation impeded the reconstruction of the capital market.[57]

Not all countries whose currency collapsed following war or revolution enacted revalorization legislation. Some deemed it politically desirable to allow inflation to wipe out creditors' claims or decided that revalorization was more trouble than it was worth. Thus, despite the collapse of the Austrian crown after World War I, the Austrian legislature and courts resisted efforts to secure revalorization.[58] Russia and Greece also refused to revalorize debts after the collapse of their currencies.[59]

JUDICIAL RELIEF FROM INFLATION-DISTORTED CONTRACTS

When the performance of contracts becomes unduly burdensome because of unanticipated inflation, courts are forced to confront a series of dilemmas. Should they deny all such claims for relief until the legislature directs them to do otherwise? Or should they intervene to try to bail out parties from contracts obviously rendered inequitable because of inflation? If courts decide to intervene, what should be the doctrinal basis for doing so? Should they expand traditional concepts of *force majeure,* frustration, or impossibility? Should they imply a condition relieving obligors of performances that have become unduly onerous? Should they develop a doctrine of commercial impracticability?

If the courts decide to intervene, what kinds of remedies should they employ? Rescission? Revocation? Termination? Should the courts attempt to modify the terms of a contract to make it "fair"? Should they offer the other party the option of accepting such modification or terminating the contract? Or should they simply adjust the damage remedy to cushion the pecuniary effects of nonperformance? To what extent should it matter that the contract is executory, partially executed, or fully performed?

This next part will explore the responses that courts have given to these questions. Particular emphasis will be placed on the development of doctrinal solutions, some of which have been enacted into positive law.

CIVIL LAW FRUSTRATION DOCTRINES

Civil law countries have evolved a variety of frustration doctrines capable of affording relief to hapless promisors whose performance has become unduly onerous due to inflation. Most of these doctrines have their roots in the medieval theory of *rebus sic stantibus.*[60]

Rebus Sic Stantibus

The doctrine of *rebus sic stantibus* posits that every contract contains a tacit clause (or implicit condition subsequent) ending or modifying its obligatory force whenever a substantial change in the state of facts at the time the contract was made would render its performance unjust. This theory was espoused by the canonists of the twelfth and thirteenth centuries and applied by the ecclesiastical courts, who suspected usury whenever one party's bargain seemed too good. It was elaborated by the Post-Glossators under Bartolus, enacted into some of the early eighteenth century codifications,[61] and incorporated into Italian and German doctrine until the eighteenth century. But even as early as the fifteenth century, the popularity of the theory of *rebus sic stantibus* had begun to wane, largely because of protests from burgeoning commercial interests against the climate of transactional insecurity produced by the theory's widespread application. By the end of the eighteenth century, *pacta sunt servanda* reigned supreme, and the theory of *rebus sic stantibus* had been relegated to the doctrinal scrap heap.[62] Contributing to its demise were the rise of scientific positivism, and the increasing emphasis on individual autonomy and liberty of contract.[63]

In the face of the economic disequilibrium resulting from World War I, many European jurists sought theoretical justifications for excusing promisors from contracts whose performance had become exceedingly burdensome. The doctrine of *rebus sic stantibus* was reclaimed and recycled under a variety of names, each with a somewhat different nuance. French, Italian, and Polish law developed the *théorie de l'imprévision;* German and Swiss law developed the doctrines of *Geschäftsgrundlage,* economic ruin, equivalence of performances, and good faith; and the Scandinavian countries expanded the concept of impossibility to include economic impossibility. The contours of these doctrines will now be briefly explored.

The Théorie de l'Imprévision

There is no single definition of the *théorie de l'imprévision,* but its core concept is that a court may annul or revise a contract whenever there has been a substantial and unforeseen change in the economic conditions prevailing at the time the contract was made, rendering performance by the obligor exceedingly onerous, though not objectively impossible. The leading case is the 1916 decision of the *Conseil d'État,* France's highest administrative tribunal, in *Compagnie Générale d'Éclairage de Bordeaux v. Ville de Bordeaux.*[64] This case involved a suit by a gas company for an increase in rates because of a more than 400 percent increase in the price of coal, the material from which the gas was manufactured. This vast increase in coal prices was the result of the German occupation of the coal fields and the economic dislocations of the war. The *Conseil d'État* held that revision was proper because the increase in the cost of performing the contract "certainly exceeds the outer limits of the increases that could have been contemplated by the parties when the contract of concession was concluded; as a result . . . the contractual equilibrium *(l'économie du contrat)* is completely destroyed. . . ."[65] In the interest of maintaining uninterrupted gas service to the public, the court ordered that the rates be revised to reflect present costs, after first deducting the portion of the cost increase that was reasonably foreseeable.

In France the *théorie de l'imprévision* did not develop into anything more than a method for relieving governmental contractors of unforeseeable hardships to insure the uninterrupted functioning of public services. In practice, the theory has been applied only to three types of contracts: (1) public works, (2) governmental supplies, and (3) concessions such as gas and electricity.[66] Attempts to expand the doctrine of *imprévision* to private contracts have been regularly frustrated by the *Cour de Cassation,* France's highest court, which has been inclined to excuse performance of contractual obligations only if such performance is literally impossible.[67] Being aware of this judicial attitude, French lawyers and businessmen are generally careful to insert an arbitration clause, index clause (if lawful), or some similar provision to deal with an unexpected change in conditions.[68] To the extent the French courts have relieved private parties of the hardships caused by supervening economic events, such as inflation or deflation, it has been the work of lower courts in construing contractual terms and manipulating damage remedies, areas generally beyond the control of the *Cour de Cassation.*[69] When defaulting sellers are sued for damages by buyers who have to pay more for goods because of inflation, the lower courts in France have generally refused to believe that the buyers have suffered substantial damage simply because they have to pay greater nominal amounts for goods whose real economic value has remained the same. In addition, the French legislature from time to time has intervened by enacting statutes temporarily permitting the courts to terminate or revise contracts, particularly *rentes* (long-term leases and annuities), because of substantial unforeseen changes in economic conditions.[70]

The doctrine of *imprévision* was implanted in more fertile soil in five other civil law countries. After World War I, the Polish Supreme Court, through a variety of constructions, in effect adopted the doctrine of *imprévision.*[71] This case-law orientation was codified in 1933 as article 269 of the Code of Obligations, which provides:

> When, in consequence of exceptional circumstances, such as war, epidemic, total loss of harvests or other natural cataclysms, performance causes excessive difficulty or threatens one of the parties with an exorbitant loss, which the parties could not have foreseen at the conclusion of the contract, the court may, in its discretion, according to the principles of good faith and taking into consideration the interests of the two parties, determine the mode of execution, the amount of performance, or even pronounce the resolution of the contract.

Italy in 1915 adopted transitional legislation providing that discharge of contractual obligations warranted by the doctrine of *force majeure* should not be restricted to cases of absolute impossibility, but should be extended to include cases in which the war had made performance extremely onerous to one party.[72] For a brief period Italian case law seemed to accept the doctrine of *imprévision,* either by finding that *rebus sic stantibus* constitutes a general principle of law, or by stretching the notion of *force majeure* to include contracts that had become unduly burdensome because of unforeseen events.[73] But the cassation courts *(Cortes di Cassazione)* of Florence, Rome, and Turin firmly rejected *imprévision* soon thereafter. Until World War II, Italian law insisted upon objective impossibility to excuse contractual obligations.[74] However, with the adoption of the Italian Civil Code of 1942, which in general was less enamored of individual autonomy and freedom of contract than its predecessor, *imprévision* was explicitly returned to Italian law in the form of Articles 1467–69.[75]

Despite many attempts by Greek doctrinal writers to convince Greek tribunals to release promisors from obligations rendered excessively burdensome by the enormous monetary depreciation that accompanied both World Wars, the Greek *Areopagus* (Cassation Court), like the French *Cour de Cassation,* steadfastly refused to do so without a showing of fault on the part of the promisee.[76] The framers of the Greek Civil Code of 1946 rejected that position; instead they adopted a blend of the German doctrine of good faith and the French *théorie de l'imprévision* in Article 388:

> In case of subsequent change in the circumstances on which the contracting parties, under consideration of the principles of good faith and fairness in transactions, have mainly founded a reciprocal contract, the change being due to extraordinary and unforeseen events, and where because of such a change the obligation of the promisor—in comparison with the obligation of the promisee—has become excessively onerous to him, the court may, at the request of the promisor, reduce his obligation to the proper extent, or decree the discharge of the contract as a whole or the extent of the non-performed part. In the case in which the discharge of the contract has been decreed, all the obligations arising from it cease to exist, and the parties are mutually obliged to return all they have received according to the provisions relating to unjustifiable enrichment.[77]

Imprévision has also spread to Argentina and Brazil. It began in Argentina as an extraordinary post–World War II measure to permit readjustment of public construction contracts for increased costs.[78] Though early efforts to convince Argentine courts to accept the doctrine of *imprévision* in private contracts were rebuffed, after the inflation rate exceeded 30 percent for three consecutive years, as it did in 1950–1952, Argentine courts began to release promisors from their obligations on the theory of *imprévision.*[79] This case law development of the theory of *imprévision* was enshrined in positive law by a 1968 amendment to the Argentine Civil Code.[80]

Imprévision tentatively crept into Brazilian case law for the first time in the 1930s as a device for permitting escape from contractual obligations that had become more burdensome because of deflation or the economic dislocation accompanying the Great Depression.[81] *Imprévision* has become important in Brazil, however, only in the area of construction contracts. During the 1940s, when construction prices soared because of the war, a number of cases permitted revision or termination of unduly burdensome contracts,[82] despite the explicit language of Article 1246 of the Civil Code prohibiting such readjustment.[83] Since the 1950s, the decided tendency of the case law has been to accept the doctrine of *imprévision* in theory, but to deny its application to the facts of the case before the court.[84] After so many years of continuous inflation, the claim that inflation is unforeseeable in Brazil has come to have a hollow ring. Moreover, since 1965 virtually all private construction contracts have been indexed.[85] With rare exception, the Brazilian courts have continued to apply the theory of *imprévision* only to public construction contracts,[86] returning to the original French administrative law origins of the doctrine. Unlike Argentina, Brazil has never adopted legislation applying *imprévision* to private contracts. It, however, has provided for revision of contracts for the supply of goods and services to the federal and state governments in accordance with a mathematical formula that allocates 90 percent of the inflation cost to the government contracting agency and 10 percent to the contractor.[87]

Like the Brazilian courts, the Argentine and Italian courts initially utilized the doctrine of *imprévision* to relieve promisors of obligations made more onerous by inflation. After years of continuous inflation, however, they have also taken the position that inflation is plainly foreseeable in both countries and is normally an insufficient justification for invoking the doctrine of *imprévision.*[88] Nevertheless, when a sudden surge in the inflation rate makes it much greater than could have reasonably been anticipated, the courts in both countries have once again begun to relieve promisors through application of the theory of *imprévision.*[89]

Economic Ruin

In 1920, as the pace of inflation quickened in Germany, the *Reichsgericht* began to permit rescission of executory contracts for the sale of goods and services where performance would lead to the debtor's ruin.[90] The doctrine of economic ruin was a judicial invention to relieve obligors in cases of extreme hardship, but which avoided having to revise or rescind most commercial contracts because of inflation. Later cases extended the doctrine to permit the obligor to terminate a contract of which performance, by itself, may not have been ruinous, but, when taken together with his other contracts, would have led to the obligor's bankruptcy.[91] For a time it was criticized by some as a serious threat to security of transactions and as too narrow a form of relief by others. Quixotically, it acted as a boon to marginal businesses and penalized the most solvent firms. By 1922 the decline in the mark's purchasing power was so rapid that the *Reichsgericht* abandoned its insistence on economic ruin in favor of the theories of the equivalence of performances or *Geschäftsgrundlage,* which are discussed in the next two sections. The doctrine of financial ruin was also applied for a time by the Swiss courts, often in conjunction with the doctrine of economic impossibility. More recent Swiss decisions, however, have rejected the doctrine of financial ruin.[92]

The Equivalence of Performances

The theory of the equivalence of performances in bilateral contracts was first advanced by the *Reichsgericht* in 1921.[93] The theory postulates that an essential attribute of bilateral contracts is that the performances required on both sides be roughly equivalent or adequate. When this economic equation is skewed because of supervening events, such as inflation, the courts must intervene to restore the balance. Application of this doctrine results in the courts' modifying the contract price in a reasonable manner, affording the party for whom the price had been increased the option of paying the increase or permitting rescission.[94] This theory has also found its way into Swiss law.[95]

Geschäftsgrundlage (Foundation of the Contract)

The theory of the foundation of the contract, developed by a prominent German scholar named Oertmann, postulates that: "[E]very contract is conditioned upon the continued existence of those facts which, in the contemplation of the parties, are necessary for its performance. As soon as the foundation, constituted by such facts, is disturbed, the express provisions of the contract are no longer effective."[96] This theory was accepted by the *Reichsgericht* in 1922 as an alternative to the theory of equivalence of performances and used to afford relief to a party to a buyout agreement for dissolution of a partnership at a price that had become hopelessly inadequate because of severe inflation. The *Reichsgericht* considered monetary depreciation to have undermined the foundation of the contract, thereby justifying judicial revision of the price term to make the contract fair.[97] Today this theory has largely displaced other frustration theories in German and Swiss law, and has also been accepted by the Scandinavian courts.[98]

The doctrine of *Geschäftsgrundlage* strongly resembles *rebus sic stantibus,* and a number of German courts and commentators have equated the two doctrines.[99] It also resembles the theory of *imprévision.*[100] The foundation of the contract is said to be disturbed or ruptured by an unforeseeable change in circumstances that renders continued performance unconscionable or unduly harsh.[101]

The remedy for destruction of the foundation of the contract is judicial adjustment of the terms of the contract. This has taken many forms, such as increasing the price, extending time limits for performance, or decreasing the amount of performance required. If the contract cannot be modified to permit its continuance, rescission or termination becomes the appropriate remedy.[102]

Good Faith (Treu und Glauben)

Good faith in German and Swiss law is something more than the *bona fides* of Roman law, *bonne foi* of French law, or good faith in Anglo-American law. It expresses an ethical notion of mutual confidence and the interdependence of the parties.[103] As one of the celebrated "general provisions" in the German Civil Code, it has served as a positivistic mandate for the courts to do what is ethical under the circumstances. Thus, it should not be surprising that good faith served as the principal legal basis for the German courts' revalorizing contracts during the 1920s. Nor should it be surprising that the Swiss tribunals invoked the good faith provision of the Swiss Code of Obligations to revalorize debts expressed in worthless German marks, even for obligations governed by Swiss substantive law.[104]

JUDICIAL REVALORIZATION OF CONTRACTS IN POST–WORLD WAR I GERMANY

As the pace of German inflation accelerated sharply in 1921 and 1922, a few German doctrinal writers advocated jettisoning nominalism and substituting valorism.[105] Initially, the German courts declined the invitation. They did, however, relieve certain obligors from contractual obligations that inflation had rendered unduly onerous by expanding the Civil Code requirement of "good faith" in the interpretation and performance of contracts to include such doctrinal escape hatches as economic ruin, *Geschäftsgrundlage,* and equivalence of performances.[106] But by 1923, when the mark's purchasing power began to plummet at startling speed, legal commentators increasingly urged German courts to disregard the nominalist principle and to revalue generally all obligations expressed in marks.[107] On November 28, 1923, when the domestic price level had reached 1,422,900,000,000 times its 1913 level, the Fifth Civil Senate of the *Reichsgericht,* Germany's highest court, took the plunge into valorism. In the celebrated case of *ST. v. R.,* the mortgagee of real estate in the former German protectorate in Southwest Africa refused to cancel the mortgage unless repaid a sum equivalent in value to the money loaned in 1913. The court held that legal tender laws to the contrary notwithstanding, the paper mark would no longer be valued legally at par, and that monetary obligations were to be revalued judicially.[108]

Although the result is appealing from a standpoint of equity, the *Reichsgericht's* opinion is unconvincing. The court dismissed legal tender legislation, the foremost obstacle to revalorization, on two dubious grounds: (1) that at the time of enactment of the legal tender statute the legislature had assumed there would be no paper money inflation and that the value of specie and paper money would remain equal; and (2) that recent legislation requiring taxes to be paid on a gold basis, readjusting certain annuities, and indexing fines and court fees to the cost-of-living index constituted an implicit abrogation of the legal tender laws. But there is little point in making paper money legal tender if one assumes that such notes will remain equal to specie in value. Legislatures declare paper money legal tender precisely because they contemplate paper money inflation and expect that the populace will not accept inconvertible paper money at a par with specie. Furthermore, the German legislation dealing with taxes, annuities, and fines in no way constituted a general legislative repudiation of legal tender laws.

The juridical springboard for the court's valoristic somersault was Article 242 of the German Civil Code, which requires that obligations be performed in good faith, taking ordinary commercial practice into consideration.[109] But it was hardly ordinary commercial practice for debtors to revalorize their debts voluntarily, or, for that matter, for creditors to refuse to accept repayment of debts unless the debtor revalorized the loan. The German court made the following equally dubious assumption about the intent of the parties: "In the case of money loans the debtor's duty (and usually also the parties' intentions) is not only to repay the same amount of money, but also to repay in money of the same value. When the parties stipulate that the loan is to be repaid in their national currency, they do so trusting that this currency constitutes, within the limits of certain normal variations, a steady and a permanent measure of value."[110] Given the extraordinarily high interest rates (6 percent a day) prevailing at the time of the decision, the court's valoristic assumption seems highly suspect.

An even greater deficiency of the court's opinion was its vagueness about how revalorization was to be accomplished. The court specifically refused to set out a general formula or guideline for revalorization. Instead, it directed the lower courts to balance an array of equities on a case by case basis.

> Under Article 242 of the Civil Code, the requirements of good faith, taking into account commercial practice, must be considered in the individual case. A fair consideration of the interests of both sides is required. It follows from this that a general principle requiring the revalorization of every mortgage debt cannot be established. Nor will the extent of the revalorization . . . be the same in each case. It will be necessary to take into account, besides the increase in terms of paper marks of the value of the real property, which will have the principal weight, also the other circumstances of the cases: for example, the economic ability of the debtor to perform under the circumstances, whether agricultural, industrial, or city property is involved. There must also be taken into account the public charges that the property must pay. In the case of rental property the reduction of income resulting from the measures taken to protect renters deserves consideration.[111]

Subsequent decisions of the *Reichsgericht* did little to clarify these nebulous guidelines for the lower courts. Instead the *Reichsgericht* candidly admitted that "revaluation is not a legally defined concept" and urged the lower courts to consider all of the interests of the parties, taking into account all of the ascertainable facts.[112]

The *Reichsgericht's* refusal to adopt standards for revalorization of obligations superimposed juridical confusion on economic chaos. Within a few years, the German courts were deluged with more than three million revalorization suits.[113] Not only were major increases in personnel required by the courts, but also three reporter systems had to be established solely for revalorization cases.[114]

The German courts failed to develop a single standard of value for revaluing obligations. The three most commonly used revaluation standards were the foreign exchange rate, the consumer price index, and the wholesale price index.[115] Also used as standards of value were the market prices of specific goods and a special index prepared privately by Zeiler, one of the judges on the *Reichsgericht.*[116] Given the enormity of Germany's economic dislocation, the choice of revaluation standard frequently made a huge difference in the amount of an obligation. During most of the 1914–24 period the foreign exchange rate or gold value of the mark depreciated considerably more rapidly than its domestic purchasing power, so that use of this standard unfairly disadvantaged most debtors.[117] There was also a very wide gap between the rates at which the wholesale and consumer price indexes were increasing. In most inflationary periods, price increases tend to show up in the wholesale price index several months prior to their being reflected in the consumer price index. This customary lag was accentuated in Germany by price controls, which, though ineffective, served to slow retail prices more than wholesale prices.[118] There were also huge differences in the rates at which particular groups of prices rose in both the consumer and wholesale price index. Price controls and an undervalued exchange rate, which disproportionately increased the prices of imported goods, compounded normal differences in price fluctuations.

The German courts have received both high praise and severe criticism for undertaking to revalorize contractual obligations. Professor Dawson has hailed the decision in *ST. v. R.* as "a landmark in German legal history and a fitting climax to the magnificent work of the Reichsgericht in guiding a great nation through its darkest hours."[119] Professor Nussbaum, on the other hand, characterized the experience as "one of thoroughgoing judicial aberration and confusion."[120] There is little doubt that the juridical situation was chaotic during revalorization, but this was inevitable once the decision had been made to intervene in the nation's economic chaos. Given the enormity of the injustice resulting from the collapse of the country's currency, the case for intervention seems well founded. The most difficult question is whether the courts should have intervened without waiting for legislation to resolve some of the myriad difficulties, for the courts, as an institution, were not terribly well equipped to deal with the extremely difficult redistributional issues involved in revalorization. However, the legislature was not much better equipped, and perhaps would not have intervened at all had the courts not forced it to act.

SUMMARY

These are the basic theories by which the courts in civil law countries have relieved obligors of contractual obligations made exceedingly difficult because of inflation. They are not, however, the only theories. For example, the Scandinavian courts have evolved an economic impossibility doctrine from the 1905 Sale of Goods Act and German doctrines such as *Geschäftsgrundlage.*[121] Japanese law has developed the theory of *jijō henkō no gensoku* (change in circumstances), a blend of *imprévision* and good faith.[122] Swiss and German courts have also invoked the doctrines of *rebus sic stantibus, Ausbeutung* (Exploitation), *Lückenausfüllende Auslegung* (the Gap Filling Doctrine), and *Unzumutbarkeit* (Nonimputability).[123] Frequently, assorted combinations of several of these doctrines are employed simultaneously with good faith or *Geschäftsgrundlage.*

Although there are many differences among these frustration doctrines, four common characteristics have been pointed out. First, there must be an unforeseeable change of circumstances. Second, that change must be truly exceptional, exceeding the normal risks assumed by the parties. Third, that change must render performance unduly onerous for one of the parties. Fourth, the change must not occur as the result of the fault of one of the parties.[124]

It is difficult to predict how much more expensive performance has to become to trigger these frustration doctrines, because so much depends on consideration of the facts of each case. Originally, German courts insisted upon an 80 percent decrease in the value of the monetary performance; this was progressively decreased to two-thirds, one-half, and then to one-third.

> The decisions next adopted the principle that the disproportion between claim and performance justifying the increase in value need not be strictly defined nor expressed in monetary terms. [Citations omitted] In subsequent decisions of the Reichsgericht, the thought is expressed that under special conditions an increase in value could appear justified where the decrease in the value of the performance was only moderate. [Citations omitted] The "strict principles of the law" . . . have been more and more replaced by the principles of good faith and a fair weighing of the demands of all parties considering the special circumstances of the particular case. . . . [E]ach decision should seek to find the solution that is the most just and fair under the circumstances.[125]

There is also another civil law doctrine that, on occasion, has been pressed into service to relieve certain parties of contractual obligations which inflation has made unduly onerous. Because this doctrine, *laesio enormis* (gross price inadequacy), is technically a defect of consent rather than a frustration doctrine, it will be taken up separately in the next section.

LAESIO ENORMIS OR *LÉSION*

The source of the doctrine of *laesio enormis* (gross price inadequacy) is a rescript of Diocletian, reproduced by Justinian's compilers. This rescript permitted sellers of land to demand rescission if the price received were less than half the true value of the land. The buyer, however, could avert rescission by providing additional consideration sufficient to equal true value of the land.[126] The doctrine of *laesio enormis* dovetailed neatly with medieval notions about "just price"; consequently, the Glossators and the Post-Glossators soon expanded the Roman law doctrine to include buyers as well as sellers, personalty as well as realty, and its application to a broad variety of contracts beyond sales.[127]

In France *laesio enormis* almost failed to survive the highly inflationary period that followed the Revolution. The rapid depreciation of the *assignats* and *mandats* during the 1790s produced a flood of suits by vendors of land to rescind sales that had become highly unprofitable. The legislature reacted by abolishing *laesio enormis,* or *lésion* as it is called in France, for all future land sales, and rescission actions already filed were indefinitely suspended.[128]

The great emphasis on individualism and freedom of contract led most nineteenth century codifiers to reject the doctrine of *lésion. Lésion* was accepted, however, in the most influential of all civil codes, the French Civil Code. The French codifiers confined *lésion* to its Roman origins, limiting the remedy of rescission to vendors of land who receive less than five-twelfths of the land's true value, as determined by a commission of three experts. The action to rescind has to be brought within two years. The vendee can avoid rescission by increasing the consideration to nine-tenths of the land's true value; one tenth is assumed to be his just profit.[129] Subsequent French statutes have extended the notion of *lésion* by granting parties to certain other contracts the right to termination or revision if the price is excessive.[130]

The doctrine of *lésion* has also become law in several other countries. In some, such as Belgium, Haiti, and the Dominican Republic, acceptance of the doctrine of *lésion* was a by-product of the adoption of the French Civil Code as their own. The Chilean Civil Code of 1885 and the Colombian Civil Code of 1887 accepted an earlier form of *lésion.* In Chile and Colombia, both vendor and vendee have the right to rescind contracts for the sale of land for *lésion enorme,* which is said to exist if the consideration is less than one-half the just price.[131]

The German Civil Code of 1900 (BGB) rejected the narrow, objective concept of *lésion* adopted by the Napoleonic Code and its progeny. Instead, it substituted a broad, subjective concept of usury or economic duress.[132] Article 138(2) of the BGB voids all contracts (not just in sales of real property) where there is a striking disproportion in the economic value of the performances, if this disparity is the result of the exploitation of the necessity, thoughtlessness, or inexperience of the other party. Article 21 of the Swiss Code of Obligations of 1911 embodies the same rule, though it merely makes such contracts voidable.

The Italian Civil Code of 1942 combined aspects of the objective French notion of *lésion* with the broader, subjective German and Swiss concepts of usury. The Italian Civil Code permits rescission in all except aleatory contracts if there is a disproportion in performances resulting from one party taking advantage of the need of the other. The disproportion, however, must exceed one-half of the value of the performance of the exploited party and must continue to exist at the time the complaint is filed. The other party can avoid rescission by offering to modify the contract to make it equitable.[133]

Argentina has recently amended its Civil Code to adopt the more generalized and subjective concept of *lésion* found in Article 138(2) of the BGB.[134] Although rejected by the draftsman of the Brazilian Civil Code, *lésion* has entered Brazilian law through the side door of a statute making it a criminal offense to "obtain or stipulate in any contract, abusing the pressing necessity, inexperience or levity of the other party, a patrimonial profit in excess of one-fifth of the current or just value of the performance rendered or promised."[135]

Lésion becomes a device for relieving contracting parties from the effects of inflation only if the date for determining the adequacy of the price is subsequent to the time the parties agreed on that price. In Germany the expansive concept of usury had no real utility in relieving promisors from obligations that inflation had made exceedingly burdensome because the disproportion was determined as of the date the contract was celebrated. Despite the suggestion by some commentators that the courts afford relief through the concept of usury, the German courts preferred to utilize other doctrines, such as good faith, to relieve the effects of inflation on contracts.[136] Similarly, in Argentina the calculation of disproportion has to be made in accordance with values at the time of the contract, and the disproportion must continue to exist up to the time of the filing of the complaint.

The French and Belgian civil courts have utilized the doctrine of *lésion* to relieve a select group from the effects of inflation. In cases where land was sold by option or purchase agreement, Article 1675 of the Napoleonic Code ambiguously states: "In order to determine whether there has been *lésion* of more than seven-twelfths, one must value the real property . . . as of the moment of the sale." In option sales the date of the sale might refer either to the time of the signing of the option or to the time of its exercise. If one views *lésion* as a defect in consent, as did the medievalists and many modern writers, the relevant date would be the signing of the option, and a few French cases initially so held.[137] Nevertheless, the French and Belgian *Cours de Cassation,* confronted with options granted prior to World War I being exercised during the postwar inflation, decided to protect sellers from the effects of monetary depreciation by construing the term "moment of the sale" to refer to the date of the exercise of the option.[138] Thus, *lésion* was made to serve the functions of the doctrine of *imprévision* for option sales made unduly onerous by unanticipated inflation.

The opposite rule has been applied to land sales by purchase agreement. In such cases, the relevant date for determining the existence of *lésion* is considered to be the signing of the purchase agreement rather than the completion of the sale.[139] For those who purchase land on installments, determination of *lésion* as of the date of the completion of the sale, as was done for a time in Chile,[140] is quite unfair to the buyer. The real value of each successive installment is diminished by ongoing inflation, while the real value of the land is being correspondingly increased.

French courts have also sought to protect sellers of land from inflation by advancing the date at which the property is to be valued if the buyer elects to increase the price to avoid rescission for *lésion.* Until recently it had been assumed that the just price referred to the date of the sale.[141] However, long delays between the institution of actions for rescission and judicial decision, substantial inflation, and inadequate legal interest rates made the use of the just price at the date of the sale unfair to the seller. In two 1966 decisions[142] the *Cour de Cassation* placed its seal of approval on a burgeoning line of cases[143] holding that for the purpose of the buyer's supplementing the purchase price, the just price of the property refers to its present market value. This means there are two just prices: one for calculation of the existence of *lésion,* and the other for calculating how much price supplementation must be made by the buyer to stave off rescission. Fairness to the buyer, however, would seem to require that the price already paid be revalued upward by a coefficient from a general price index so that the just price and the allowance for moneys paid are both in present-day francs.

At best *lésion* is an awkward doctrine for mitigating the effects of inflation on contracts. There is no present justification for affording vendors of land protection against inflation that is denied to other contracting parties. In an inflationary economy, all unindexed option or installment sales contain an implicit allowance for inflation. There is no single "just price" or fair market value for land that is sold over a period of time. Fair market value is a function of the terms of the sale. The longer the seller has to wait to receive payment, the higher the price he must charge in order to be assured the same real economic value as a cash sale. Focusing solely on the nominal amount of money paid over time in an inflationary economy in order to determine the existence of a legally significant disproportion in price makes little sense. From the standpoint of transactional security, *lésion* is a nightmare. Buyers must wait for years to find out what their acquisition costs will ultimately be. Moreover, the peculiar nature of the doctrine of *lésion* makes it rational for the buyer to pay something extra to the seller to minimize the risk that the sales price might fall below 41.7 percent of the fair market value in order to avoid having to pay 90 percent of fair market value at some later date.

RELIEF UNDER ANGLO-AMERICAN LAW

Anglo-American courts have been far more reluctant than the courts of many civil law countries to relieve obligors from the effects of inflation on contracts. Traditionally, Anglo-American courts have been emphatic in denying claims for relief because of inflation. Consider the facts of *Anderson v. Equitable L. Assur. Soc.*,[144] where the equitable claim for relief could not have been clearer. An Englishman residing in Russia in 1887 had purchased a semi-tontine life insurance policy from the German branch of an American insurance company. The death benefit was fixed at 60,000 German marks, payable in London. The policy was fully paid up by 1907, long before the mark began to depreciate. The insured died in 1922, and the insurance company paid his widow what was then the equivalent of 60,000 paper marks, or less than a shilling. Because the policy was governed by English law, the English Courts reluctantly ruled that the widow was legally entitled to nothing more, though some judges expressed the hope that the insurance company would gratuitously pay her an additional sum. American courts have taken similar positions with respect to debts expressed in collapsed currencies.[145] Not even where the lessee is an arm of the federal government, the chief beneficiary of inflation, will American courts mitigate the effects of inflation on long-term leases.[146]

This reluctance to intervene is largely attributable to three factors. First, Anglo-American courts are much more uncomfortable than civil law courts about remaking contracts for the parties.[147] Traditionally, Anglo-American courts operate with the assumption that the only kind of relief that they may grant in cases where inflation has made performance unduly burdensome is rescission, denial of specific performance, or termination. This means that losses generally cannot be apportioned; rather they are borne entirely by one party or the other.

Second, Anglo-American countries have generally been spared the galloping and runaway inflations that have plagued many of the civil law countries during the twentieth century. When faced with runaway inflation shortly after the U.S. Civil War, the courts of some, but by no means all, of the Southern states did revalorize contract claims in worthless Confederate currency. But these cases never served as the basis for the development of a coherent doctrine for American courts to revise contracts due to changes in the value of money.[148]

Third, the common law has been much slower than the civil law in developing a doctrinal basis for granting relief for supervening impossibility.[149] *Rebus sic stantibus* and *laesio enormis* have deep roots in the civil law. With few exceptions, however, the common law originally adhered to the position that when a party agreed to the terms of a contract, he was bound to perform or respond in damages irrespective of any unforeseen circumstances. Not until 1863 did the common law develop a doctrine for relieving a promisor whose performance had become impossible,[150] and not until the beginning of the twentieth century did the common law begin to excuse performance when the basic purpose of the contract was frustrated by some unforeseen event.[151]

Impossibility and Frustration

The common law has developed two somewhat overlapping doctrines, impossibility and frustration, which can be utilized to mitigate the effects of inflation on contracts. Impossibility comes into play when there is an inability to perform because of supervening events, such as a governmental restriction, death, or destruction of the subject matter of the contract, and the contract does not expressly allocate the risk of the event's occurrence to either party. If discharging the party incapable of performing conforms to customary notions about risk allocation, courts are inclined to invoke the doctrine of impossibility to discharge the promisor. The doctrine of frustration, on the other hand, normally comes into play in situations in which performance is possible, but, as a result of unforeseen circumstances, performance by one party would no longer give the other party what induced him to enter the contract. "Discharge under this doctrine has been limited to instances where a virtually cataclysmic, wholly unforeseeable event renders the contract valueless to one party."[152]

Impossibility originally meant absolute physical impossibility or legal impossibility. The more modern doctrinal view is articulated in §454 of the American Law Institute's First Restatement of Contracts: ". . . [I]mpossibility means not only strict impossibility but impracticability because of extreme and unreasonable difficulty, expense, injury or loss involved." Under the First Restatement's view, either existing or supervening impossibility will discharge the promisor if he neither knew nor had reason to know of the facts that made the performance impossible.[153] This section of the Restatement is, however, more a statement of what its authors think the law should be rather than what the law actually is. The notion that a promisor should be excused on the ground of economic impracticability has received a cool reception from the courts.[154]

There are only a handful of American cases which have accepted the excuse of economic impracticability, and three come from one jurisdiction, California. The leading case is *Mineral Park Land Co. v. Howard,*[155] where the defendants, who were constructing a concrete bridge, agreed to remove and purchase all of the gravel and earth necessary for the construction from the plaintiff's land. The parties apparently assumed that there was enough earth and gravel on the plaintiff's land to satisfy construction needs without digging below the waterline. After defendants had hauled away all of the earth and gravel above the waterline, some 50,000 cubic yards worth, they found they needed another 50,000 cubic yards to complete the bridge. Rather than dredge and dry the subaquatic material, the defendants sensibly purchased the necessary gravel and earth from another source. The expense of dredging and drying would have increased the cost of the fill by ten to twelve times the usual cost. The California Supreme Court held that the defendants were discharged from their promise to take all of their fill from plaintiff's land because the huge increase in cost made performance impracticable, which it regarded as legally tantamount to impossibility. "A thing is impossible in legal contemplation when it is not practicable; and a thing is impracticable when it only can be done at an excessive and unreasonable cost."[156]

In *Transbay Construction Co. v. City and County of San Francisco,*[157] the city had estimated the amount of rock that had to be excavated to enlarge a dam at 30,000 cubic yards. The amount actually excavated turned out to be 84,000 cubic yards, 280 percent more than the original estimate. Because this unanticipated event had radically changed the nature of the performance, the court felt it would be unjust to hold the contractor to the contract price. It, therefore, abrogated the contract and permitted the contractor to recover his increased costs in *quantum meruit.*

The third case coming from California is difficult to comprehend and is probably wrong. In *City of Vernon v. City of Los Angeles,*[158] the City of Los Angeles was excused from its contract to dispose of the City of Vernon's sewage because Los Angeles' own rapid growth required it to build a new sewage treatment plant at a cost of $41 million. Vernon had already paid a substantial sum in advance for sewage disposal service, but the majority apparently believed that the parties contracted only with the continued existence of the old sewage treatment plant in mind. The rationale for this conclusion is never made clear in the majority opinion. Nor does it, as the dissent cogently points out, come to grips with the basic economic impracticability question: How much more would it have cost Los Angeles when constructing its new plant to add on capacity to treat Vernon's sewage?

There are also two American cases that can be read as allowing discharge of a promisor on the ground of economic impracticability, though both contain language suggesting physical impossibility as an alternative ground. In both cases performance as originally contemplated proved physically impossible. The courts refused to order more expensive alternative modes of performance.[159]

Most states continue to adhere to the rule that a promisor will be legally excused only if his performance has become absolutely impossible because of an act of God, the law, or some act by the promisee. The general rule, to the extent it makes sense to talk about general rules in an area such as this, still is: "[U]nexpected difficulty, expense, or hardship involved in performance of a contract will not excuse the promisor from rendering due performance of his undertaking and is not a defense to his breach of contract by nonperformance, where the terms of the contract do not provide otherwise, and the difficulty or obstacle does not make performance objectively impossible."[160]

The Anglo-American concept of frustration is still a doctrine in search of a theory. Like the doctrine of *rebus sic stantibus,* the common law doctrine of frustration originated in an implied condition that certain circumstances would continue to exist.[161] Moreover, the notion of the implied condition has generated much the same kind of criticism in the frustration doctrine as it did in the doctrine of *rebus sic stantibus.* It is logically difficult to accept the fiction that the parties actually contemplated the continued existence of a specific state of facts with respect to the occurrence of unforeseen events. A variety of theories have been offered to explain the content of this implied condition. There are both subjective and objective implied term theories, true construction, and gap filling theories, as well as Oertmann's theory of foundation of the contract.[162] One British judge candidly admitted that the frustration doctrine boiled down to the court's doing what appeared just and reasonable under the circumstances.[163] Judicial reaction to such candor was that, like negligence in the air, it would simply not do. In *Davis Contractors Ltd. v. Fareham Urban District Council,*[164] the House of Lords specifically disapproved of the "just and reasonable solution" theory, but failed to agree upon a new doctrinal synthesis. The judges, however, did agree that an increase of approximately 19 percent in the cost of performing a construction contract due to postwar economic dislocation would not be excused on the ground of frustration. Similarly, in the batch of cases arising from the closing of the Suez Canal, the House of Lords agreed that increased cost in performance because of an unforeseen event would not be a sufficient basis for finding frustration.[165]

Although both American and English courts frequently pay lip service to the doctrine of frustration, there has been a tendency in practice to confine relief for frustration very narrowly. It is difficult to find a single Anglo-American case where the courts have actually been willing to excuse nonperformance on a theory of frustration because of increased costs of performance.[166]

Commercial Impracticability

Until recently the doctrines of frustration and impossibility were treated separately. The notion of impracticability was subsumed by the Restatement of Contracts under the generic doctrine of impossibility. The Uniform Commercial Code (UCC) and the drafts of the Second Restatement of Contracts have combined the concepts of impossibility and frustration into a new doctrine called commercial impracticability. The doctrine of commercial impractibility is set out in the UCC in Section 2–615(a), which curiously applies only in the narrow circumstance in which a seller of goods is seeking discharge from his contractual responsibility.

> §2–615. Except so far as a seller may have assumed a greater obligation and subject to the preceding section on substituted performance:
> (a) Delay in delivery or non-delivery in whole or in part by a seller who complies with paragraphs (b) and (c) is not a breach of his duty under a contract of sale if performance as agreed has been made impracticable by the occurrence of a contingency the non-occurrence of which was a basic assumption on which the contract was made.

The tentative draft of the Second Restatement proposes to apply the doctrine of commercial impracticability to contracts generally. Section 281 provides: "Where, after a contract is made, a party's performance is made impracticable without his fault by the occurrence of an event the nonoccurrence of which was a basic assumption on which the contract was made, his duty to render that performance is discharged, unless the language or the circumstances indicate the contrary."[167]

This new doctrine of commercial impracticability is broad enough to permit courts to relieve obligors from contracts made unduly burdensome by inflation, but there are several problems in doing so. One problem is that neither the UCC nor the Restatement is particularly helpful in indicating how sharp a cost increase must be to render performance impracticable. Official Comment 4 to UCC §2–615 enigmatically states:

> Increased cost alone does not excuse performance unless the rise in cost is due to some unforeseen contingency which alters the essential nature of the performance. Neither is a rise or a collapse in the market in itself a justification, for that is exactly the type of business risk which business contracts made at fixed prices are intended to cover. But a severe shortage of raw materials or of supplies due to a contingency such as war, embargo, local crop failure, unforeseen shutdown of major sources of supply or the like, which either causes a marked increase in cost or altogether prevents the seller from securing supplies necessary to his performance, is within the contemplation of this section.

This comment is puzzling because it is internally inconsistent. If X agrees to sell widgets at a price of 10 cents a widget, the essential nature of his performance would seem to be to sell widgets regardless of whether X's cost per widget is 5 cents or 50 dollars. It would appear that the drafters are seeking to differentiate between normal price fluctuations, which are a usual risk assumed and allocated by the parties, and extraordinary price fluctuations, which are beyond the contemplation of the parties. The First

Restatement used the illustration of a contract to mine a minimum of 10,000 tons of ore and to pay a royalty on that tonnage being discharged if the mineral deposit is so exhausted that the cost of mining further ore is ten times the value of the ore.[168]

The Reporter's comments to §281 of the Tentative Draft of the Second Restatement of Contracts regard "an abrupt tenfold increase in cost" as an example of a circumstance that might well be sufficient to excuse performance. Professor James White, on the other hand, has argued that even a tenfold price increase should not be sufficient to excuse performance because "Increase in price, even rather radical increase in price, is a thing contracts are designed to protect against."[169]

A second problem is proving that a large increase in cost was a contingency whose nonoccurrence was a basic assumption upon which the contract was made. Obviously, anyone who enters a contract that turns out to be unprofitable can claim that he would not have entered the deal had he known that future prices were going to change in a particular fashion. If the courts are going to discharge all promisors who failed to foresee disadvantageous price fluctuations, there would be a deluge of cases and a markedly reduced incentive for persons to enter into contracts. On the other hand, broadly speaking, virtually any contingency is foreseeable. Certainly, inflation is foreseeable. If the common law test of foreseeability is read into the doctrine of commercial impracticability, inflation itself will never excuse nonperformance.

Section 2–615 of the UCC does not specifically refer to foreseeability, nor does §281 of the Tentative Draft of the Second Restatement. Official Comments 1 and 4 make it clear that the supervening circumstance must be unforeseen in order to excuse the seller,[170] but there is a significant difference between an unforeseeable contingency and an unforeseen contingency. Whether a contingency has been foreseen depends upon the actual intent of the parties and whether they had contemplated its existence. Whether a contingency is foreseeable depends upon whether a reasonably prudent person could have been expected to have foreseen it. The doctrine of commercial impracticability, as conceived by the framers of the UCC and the Draft of the Second Restatement of Contracts, requires only that a contingency be unforeseen, not that it be unforeseeable.[171] Yet, even if the doctrine of commercial impracticability is interpreted to require only that a contingency have been unforeseen rather than unforeseeable, few obligors are likely to be excused from performing contracts because of inflation. Inflation has become such a conspicuous feature on the economic horizon that very few parties to contracts that are to be performed over time can successfully claim that they did not take inflation into account. Nonetheless, suppose the inflation rate had been consistently running about 5 percent annually at the time a contract was made, and the inflation rate suddenly surges to 20 percent a year. Should a party be able to seek relief upon the ground of commercial impracticability? Is the relevant contingency inflation *per se* or a particular inflation rate? The reason for asking these questions is ultimately to determine whether the parties have allocated or assumed the risk involved. Just because one party agrees to assume the risk of the continuance of a 5 percent inflation does not mean that the party has assumed the risk of a sudden quadrupling of the inflation rate. This point comes out most clearly in the Reporter's comments to §281 of the Second Restatement of Contracts.

> Determining whether the non-occurrence of a particular event was or was not a basic assumption involves a judgment as to which party assumed the risk of its occurrence. In contracting for the manufacture and delivery of goods at a price fixed in the contract, for example, the seller assumes the risk of increased costs within the normal range. If, however, a disaster results in an abrupt tenfold increase in cost to the seller, a court might determine that the seller did not assume this risk by concluding the non-occurrence of the disaster was a "basic assumption on which the contract was made." In making such determinations, a court will look at all circumstances, including the terms of the contract. The fact that the event was unforeseeable is significant as suggesting that its non-occurrence was a basic assumption. However, the fact that it was foreseeable, or even foreseen, does not, of itself, argue for a contrary conclusion, since the parties might not have thought it sufficiently important a risk to have made it a subject of their bargaining. Another significant factor may be the relative bargaining positions of the parties and the relative ease with which either party could have included a clause.[172]

Thus, the relevant inquiry any time there is a sharp surge in the inflation rate ought to be whether such a surge had been within the contemplation of the parties and not whether inflation itself was reasonably foreseeable or foreseen.

Both the UCC and the Restatement commercial impracticability provisions are invitations to the courts to do justice under the peculiar circumstances of the case at hand. Thus far, the courts have been hesitant to find that justice requires much relief from contractual obligations. Only in a few cases has the defense of commercial impracticability been accepted. Generally, the courts have been reluctant to interpret the UCC and Restatement provisions liberally. Rather they have preferred to cling to the narrow interpretations which courts have traditionally placed upon the doctrines of the impossibility and frustration. With one recent exception, none of the cases that have permitted the defense of commercial impracticability squarely hold that substantial price increases will excuse the promisor.

In *Mansfield Propane Gas Co., Inc. v. Folger Gas Co.*[173] the Georgia Supreme Court permitted a gas company to allocate its supplies of gas pursuant to §2–615(b) because the energy crisis had caused a scarcity of supply. There is no discussion in the opinion of how much more burdensome it would have been for the gas company to have performed its requirements contract with its customers. In the recent case of *Eastern Air Lines, Inc. v. McDonnell Douglas Corp.*,[174] the court reversed the district court for refusing to allow an airplane manufacturer to rely on commercial impracticability under §2–615 to excuse its delay in delivery of planes. The impracticability arose from the government's demand for aircraft for the Vietnam War. In *Mishara Construction Co., Inc. v. Transit Mixed Corp.*,[175] the defendant failed to deliver concrete because of a strike at the building project. The court accepted the argument that a strike could amount to commercial impracticability within the meaning of §2–615. In *Gay v. Seafarer Fiberglass Yachts, Inc.*,[176] the defendant refused to perform his contract to build a fiberglass yacht for the plaintiff because of a sharp rise in the price of polyester resin resulting from the energy crisis. The plaintiff's motion for summary judgment seeking specific performance was denied because the claim of impracticability raised a triable issue of fact.

The exception is the recent case of *Aluminum Co. of America v. Essex Group, Inc.*,[177] where a federal district court permitted revision of a long-term toll conversion service contract on the grounds of mutual mistake, frustration and commercial impracticability. In 1967 ALCOA agreed to smelt alumina into molten aluminum for Essex until 1983 at a charge of $ .15 per pound. The contract contained a tripartite indexing provision to protect ALCOA from cost increases. One-third of the initial price was indexed to a construction cost index in the *Engineering News Record;* one-fifth of the initial price was linked to ALCOA's average hourly wage cost at its Warrick, Indiana, plant; and one-fifth of the initial price was linked to the industrial commodities component of the wholesale price index. The adjusted price contained an overall cap of 65 percent of the price of a specified type of aluminum as reported in a trade journal. The contract became unprofitable for ALCOA in 1977 because of huge increases in electricity prices resulting from OPEC's actions and unanticipated pollution control costs. ALCOA introduced evidence showing that continued performance of its contractual obligations would result in a loss of approximately $75,000,000. Astonishingly, Judge Teitelbaum concluded that the contract should be reformed because of mutual mistake of fact. Anticipating possible reversal on this point on appeal, the court also held that ALCOA was entitled to relief on the theories of frustration and commercial impracticability.[178] Previous U.S. cases refusing similar relief were distinguished on the ground that the potential economic loss in this case was much greater and that the circumstances indicated that the parties did not intend to allocate to ALCOA the risk of extraordinary cost increases. Behaving more like a civil law than a common law court, Judge Teitelbaum reformed the contract to set the price at a figure yielding ALCOA a $ .01 profit on each pound of aluminum converted for Essex.

The court's opinion views the problem in the case as defining an appropriate legal response to inflation's skewing the terms of long-term contracts.

> Finally, the Court notes that this case presents a problem of the appropriate legal response to problems of inflation. There are many long term contracts extant where inflation has upset the basic equivalence of the agreement. Courts will increasingly have to attend to problems like the present one. Bearing in mind the hazards of premature generalization, the Court would suggest that four factors considered in this decision will likely prove to be of durable importance in deciding whether to modify contracts: (1) the parties' prevision of the problems which eventually upset the balance of the agreements and their allocation of the associated risks; (2) the parties' attempts at risk limitation; (3) the existence of severe out of pocket losses and (4) the customs and expectations of the particular business community.
>
> The problem of inflation is most frequently encountered as a change in the value of money to purchase things of all sorts. Long term fixed price contracts are most apt to be deranged by the process of inflation and are most apt to require judicial remedies. But inflation is not a coherent phenomenon. Prices of different things change at different rates. The record in this case shows clearly that the price of energy-intensive services has increased since 1973 much more rapidly than has the general Wholesale Price Index. An indexed price term in a contract may prevent or minimize the hardship of inflation, but if it fails to do so, as was true in this case, a court should look beyond the fact of the parties' prevision of the general problem of inflation and should ask if the deviation between the index and the pertinent costs of the parties was adequately foreseen and its risk allocated in the contract. Indexing may speak more forcefully of a general purpose to limit the risks of a long term contract than of the prevision of the specific problem which the parties encounter.
>
> The existence of severe out of pocket losses should be essential to the award of relief. . . . Only a showing of unusual circumstances strongly suggesting the parties intended to allow the seller an excuse for performing in these circumstances should justify relief. . . .
>
> The limitation of judicial relief to cases where the parties evidence a desire to limit their risks, where one party suffers severe out of pocket losses not adequately foreseen and provided for by the parties seems adequate to prevent a general disruption of commercial life by inflation. This limitation also seems generally compatible with the fair needs and understanding of responsible businessmen. Little more can be asked of the courts in the development of the law.[179]

While it is heartening to see evidence that U.S. courts are becoming sensitive to the problems of inflation, the disruption of the financial equation of the contract before the court was not caused by inflation but by a change in relative prices. Moreover, the court's opinion is unconvincing on the central issue of risk allocation. The complex indexation provisions, which were drafted by ALCOA, are strong evidence that the parties had allocated to ALCOA the risk of extraordinary increases in relative prices, while Essex had assumed the risk of increases in the general level of wholesale prices and labor costs.

Most of the American courts confronting a claim of commercial impracticability have denied the defense on the facts. One of the first cases to interpret the meaning of commercial impracticability under UCC §2–615 was *Transatlantic Finance Corp. v. United States,*[180] one of the plethora of cases arising from the closing of the Suez Canal. The plaintiff company's ship was required to sail around the Cape of Good Hope, which increased its costs about 14 percent. In rejecting the claim that the closing of the Canal had made performance commercial impracticable, the court noted that contract law had been gradually shifting away from strict impossibility towards commercial impracticability.

> The doctrine ultimately represents the evershifting line drawn by courts hopefully responsive to commercial practices and mores, at which the community's interest in having contracts enforced according to their terms is outweighed by the commercial senselessness of requiring performance. When the issue is raised, the court is asked to construct a condition of performance based upon the changed circumstances, a process which involves at least three reasonably defined steps. First, a contingency—something unexpected—must have occurred. Second, the risk of the unexpected contingency must not have been allocated either by agreement or by custom. Finally, occurrence of the contingency must have rendered performance commercially impracticable.[181]

The plaintiff passed the first two steps, but came a cropper on commercial impracticability. The additional cost was only $43,972, which, when compared with the contract price of $305,842, was not enough.

> While it may be an overstatement to say that increased cost and difficulty of performance never constitute impracticability, to justify relief there must be more of a variation between expected cost and the cost of performing by an available alternative than is present in this case, where the promisor can legitimately be presumed to have accepted some degree of abnormal risk, and where impracticability is urged on the basis of added expense alone.[182]

In another Suez Canal closing case, *American Trading & Prod. Corp. v. Shell Int'l Marine Ltd.,*[183] the court found that an additional expense of $131,978 over the agreed upon price of $417,327, an increase of less than a third, was insufficient to constitute commercial impracticability.

In *Maple Farms, Inc. v. City School District of the City of Elimira, New York,*[184] the plaintiff requested a declaratory judgment to terminate its contract to supply milk to the schools because the cost of milk had increased by 23 percent between June and December 1973. This price increase was said to arise from unforeseeable events, namely the sale of huge amounts of grain to Russia and unanticipated crop failures. The court declined to let the plaintiff out of the contract on commercial impracticability. After holding that the plaintiff failed to pass all three of the steps set out in *Transatlantic,* the court's opinion concluded with this observation:

> There is no precise point, though such could conceivably be reached, at which an increase in price of raw goods above the norm would be so disproportionate to the risk assumed as to amount to "impracticality" in a commercial sense. However, we cannot say on these facts that the increase here has reached the point of "impracticality" in performance of this contract in light of the risks that we find were assumed by the plaintiff.[185]

Publicker Industries Inc. v. Union Carbide Corp.[186] involved a contract made in 1972 to supply a substance called ethanol for three years. The seller's costs nearly doubled because of the energy crisis. The contract contained an escalator clause, but that clause provided a ceiling. The court denied a claim for relief on the ground of impracticability, stating:

> We are not aware of any cases where something less than a 100% cost increase has been held to make a seller's performance "impracticable." It is clear that in the present case, the contract contemplated that foreseeable cost increases would be passed on to the buyer. However, the existence of a specific provision which put a ceiling on contract price increases resulting from a rise in the cost of Ethylene impels the conclusion that parties intended that the risk of a substantial and unforeseen rise in its cost would be borne by the seller, Union Carbide.[187]

In *Eastern Air Lines, Inc. v. Gulf Oil Corp.*,[188] Gulf attempted to escape from a requirements contract to supply aviation fuel to Eastern by claiming that the contract had been rendered commercially impracticable by a combination of the energy crisis, the actions of OPEC boosting the price of crude oil by 400 percent, and the federal government's two-tier price control system. In rejecting Gulf's claim, in large part because of Gulf's failure to show that it was not earning intracompany profits on the contract, the court went out of its way to interpret Section 2–615 of the UCC to require that the contingency be unforeseeable rather than merely unforeseen.

> [E]ven if Gulf had established great hardship under U.C.C. §2–615, which it has not, Gulf would not prevail because the events associated with the so-called energy crisis were reasonably foreseeable at the time the contract was executed. . . . If a contingency is foreseeable, it and its consequences are taken outside the scope of U.C.C. §2–615, because the party disadvantaged by fruition of the contingency might have protected himself in the contract.[189]

The most celebrated of the commercial impracticability cases has been the recent litigation brought by a group of public utilities against Westinghouse Electric Corporation for cancellation of contracts to supply the utilities with uranium for twenty years at prices averaging $9.50 per pound, plus certain escalation provisions. In 1973 world uranium prices began to rise sharply to approximately $40 per pound, an increase of about 500 percent, and far in excess of the escalation provisions. Westinghouse had an inventory of only 15 million pounds and had promised to supply 80 million tons. Purchase of the difference at market prices was estimated to cost Westinghouse at least $2 billion. In September 1975 Westinghouse sought to escape liability under these contracts by invoking §2–615 of the UCC. Westinghouse alleged that the steep rise in uranium prices was attributable to an international cartel, an allegation presently the subject of other ongoing litigation. In approving a settlement in 1977 of a suit brought by three utilities in the Pennsylvania Court of Common Pleas, the trial judge observed that "Westinghouse introduced extremely persuasive competent evidence that a number of interrelated contingencies . . . not foreseen by the parties . . . rendered the performance of the asserted contracts commercially impracticable."[190] In similar suits brought by thirteen utilities, however, the United States District Court for the Eastern District of Virginia, after a six-month consolidated trial, issued a ruling without opinion that Westinghouse had failed to meet its burden of proof under §2–615 of the UCC and was therefore liable under the contracts.[191]

This review of the cases suggests that despite the enactment of commercial impracticability into positive law, American courts are unwilling to utilize the doctrine liberally to relieve obligors from the effects of unanticipated price increases.

Relief Through Common Law Contractual Interpretation

On occasion common law courts will achieve results quite similar to civil law *imprévision* cases through liberal interpretation of the terms of the contract. There are cases in which English courts have allowed obligors to escape from contracts to furnish goods or services at a fixed price for an indefinite time by implying a right to terminate.[192] The most recent of these cases is *Staffordshire Area Health Authority v. South Staffordshire Waterworks Co.*,[193] where a company sought to escape from a 1929 contract to supply a hospital's water needs at a fixed price "for all times hereafter." In reversing the lower court, which had read the terms of the contract literally, Lord Denning's opinion explicitly stated that inflation had spawned a modern rule of construction for contracts such as these:

> . . .[I]t is possible to detect a new principle emerging as to the effect of inflation and the fall in the value of money. . . . The time has come when we may have to revise our views about the principle of nominalism. Dr. F. A. Mann in his book, The Legal Aspect of Money, said: "If the trend of inflation which has clouded the last few decades continues some relief in the case of long-term obligations will become unavoidable." That was written in 1971. Inflation has been more rampant since that time. Here we have in the present case a striking instance of a long term obligation entered into 50 years ago. . . . In these 50 years, . . . the cost of supplying the water has increased twentyfold. It is likely to increase with every year that passes. . . . It seems to me that we have reached the point which Viscount Simon contemplated in *British Movietonenews Ltd v. London and District Cinemas Ltd.* Speaking apropos of a depreciation of currency, he envisaged a situation where:
>
> > . . . a consideration of the terms of the contract, in the light of the circumstances existing when it was made, shows that they never agreed to be bound in a fundamentally different situation which has now unexpectedly emerged [and he went on to say that when such a situation emerges], the contract ceases to bind at that point—not because the court in its discretion thinks it just and reasonable to qualify the terms of the contract, but because on its true construction it does not apply in that situation.
>
> That is the forerunner of the modern rule of construction.
>
> So here the situation has changed so radically since the contract was made 50 years ago that the terms of the contract "at all times hereafter" ceases to bind: it is open to the court to hold that the contract is terminated by reasonable notice.[194]

The two concurring judges, however, declined to admit the existence of Lord Denning's "modern rule of construction," preferring to rest their inference of a power to terminate upon the totality of the circumstances surrounding formation of the agreement.

CONCLUSIONS

The question of what steps legislatures and courts should take to relieve obligors from undue hardships caused by unanticipated inflation is a difficult one. One of the most frequently asserted reasons for judicial refusal to revise contracts made inequitable because of inflation has been legal tender legislation. The French courts have found the combination of the principles of *cours forcé* and nominalism an insuperable obstacle to explicit judicial revalorization of obligations made inequitable because of inflation. Until the ultimate stages of the German post–World War I inflation, when obligations had been reduced to one billionth or even a trillionth of their original value, the German courts regarded the legal tender statute as a barrier to judicial relief. But this barrier was more apparent than real.

Legal tender statutes are designed to assure that a nation's currency circulates at par. They speak to the discharge of debts by payment of the nominal sum due in the currency declared to be legal tender. Read literally, legal tender statutes would seem to be no barrier to judicial revision of any contracts but money debts. Even as to such debts, there are a variety of doctrinal devices, such as frustration, *imprevision, lésion,* good faith, or commercial impracticability, to which the courts can resort to adjust the sum actually due without literally violating the legal tender laws.

Nevertheless, there are several good reasons that both courts and legislatures should be extremely reluctant to plunge headlong into the thorny thicket of revising contracts for the parties. Changes in the price of commodities and services are typical business risks. A primary purpose of contract law is to permit the parties to fix that type of risk. There is no feasible way for the courts to differentiate between price changes resulting from fluctuations in the value of goods and services and those resulting from changes in the value of money. The value of money depends on the quantities of goods and services which one can purchase with it. Trying to separate one from the other is a hopeless task. Courts would be required to attempt to make such complex economic judgments that the outcomes would be quite unpredictable. But contracting parties could easily predict protracted and expensive litigation, which would give obligors whose performance has become more expensive because of inflation a substantial incentive to breach. Repudiation or threat thereof would become the order of the day. The resulting uncertainty would make economic planning difficult and undermine the public interest in the security of transactions.

The undermining of the security of transactions becomes particularly acute if revision is made retroactive to already executed contracts. Extension of revalorization to already executed contracts resulted in juridical chaos in Germany. Yet it appeared inequitable to accord relief to obligees who disregarded the legal tender statute and refused to accept payment in depreciated currency, and to deny relief to those who complied with the statute. It also appeared inequitable to differentiate between those obligees whose performance came due shortly before the decision to revalorize and those whose performance came due shortly thereafter.

The French experience suggests an additional reason for judicial reluctance to revise contracts in the wake of inflation. The notorious unwillingness of the French courts to intercede has caused parties contracting for future performance to include some sort of protective clause allocating the risk of inflation. It is preferable for the parties themselves specifically to allocate the risk of inflation than for the courts to guess at a later date about how the parties would have allocated the risk had they thought about it. To the extent that the courts are willing to intercede readily, the parties are relieved of the pressure to work through the allocation of the risk of inflation on their own.

Much of the doctrinal basis for judicial revision of contracts which have become unduly onerous revolves around unforeseeability. But in modern economies inflation is hardly unforeseeable. Indeed, inflation has become the norm, and monetary stability the exception. The more realistic inquiry should be whether the rate of inflation actually experienced substantially exceeds the range of inflation which might reasonably have been contemplated by the parties. This kind of inquiry is doubly difficult because "the price reflects the aggregate expectations of market participants, but the litigating parties may have different subjective views as to the expected fluctuation range. This may not be unusual in markets where speculation is frequent, as people apparently speculate because they hold unrepresentative beliefs as to future prices. . . . Thus, a court may sometimes have to find two expected price fluctuations curves, not one."[195]

Nevertheless, at some point the rate of inflation becomes so substantial that the courts and legislatures should intercede to relieve contractual obligors. This point is not simply a function of whether the inflation rate is 40 or 50 percent per annum; it is also a function of how sudden a spurt there has been in the inflation rate. If a society has reached an annual inflation rate of 50 percent by gradual increases over a ten-year period, an increase to 75 or 100 percent in one year is likely to cause undue hardship to fewer contracting parties than a jump to 20 percent in an economy where inflation had been averaging 5 percent per year.

If a determination is made to revalorize contracts, which makes more sense than simply rescinding them and letting the damages fall where they may, courts and legislatures must confront the largely intractable problem of a valuation standard. No country that has attempted to revalorize contractual claims has been able to resolve this problem satisfactorily. The gold exchange value of currency, which has historically been a popular standard, is no longer a viable alternative. The foreign exchange rate has seldom been an adequate reflector of changes in the domestic purchasing power, particularly in the short run. Despite previously discussed technical difficulties, the best revaluation standard is one of the general price indexes.

The most feasible solution would be monetary correction of the price. This means that the stipulated price must be broken down and restated in terms of units of currency with the same purchasing power. The Israeli courts have been toying with this idea in recent cases involving specific performance of contracts where inflation has rendered the purchase price grossly inadequate. Indeed, in one case decided in 1975 the Israeli Supreme Court revalorized a contract with reference to both the changes in the dollar exchange rate and the cost-of-living index,[196] thereby achieving a result similar to the U.S. Supreme Court in the celebrated case of *Willard v. Tayloe.*[197] The Israeli courts, however, have generally shied away from such revalorization because of the complexity of the issues.[198]

The issues are quite complex. Not only should the price be monetarily corrected, but that monetarily corrected price should also be discounted or augmented to reflect the outside risk of inflation reasonably contemplated by the parties at the time of entry into the contract. This implies an objective test of what a reasonably prudent person would have estimated as the inflation rate over the life of the contract. The difference between that price and the price actually paid should be awarded to the aggrieved party.

For example, let us suppose in 1975 S agreed to sell and B agreed to buy Greenacre for $5,000. The price was to be paid $1,000 down, and the balance in four equal installments of $1,000 each. Let us further suppose that the inflation rate had been averaging 5 percent per annum from 1965 to 1975, but increased sharply soon after the contract was signed. This can be seen from the following consumer price index (assumed to be the best proxy for the purchasing power of money in our hypothetical society):

1975 = 100
1976 = 110
1977 = 165
1978 = 330
1979 = 660

After B performs, S refused to convey Greenacre without an upward revision in price. Greenacre's fair market value increased to $40,000 by 1979. S will have received over the five-year period a total consideration of $19,600 in 1979 dollars, or $2,969.69 in 1975 dollars.[199] Though no interest rate is stated, the contract contains an implicit interest component that reflects the time value of money, the expected inflation rate, and the risk of default. Suppose the court determines that the implicit interest factor is 10 percent a year (8 percent as the outside inflation risk, 2 percent as the real rate of interest, and a negligible risk of default). It should then reduce the $4,000 paid in installments to 1975 values by applying a 10 percent discount factor. This would mean that S could reasonably have expected to receive for Greenacre $4,169 in 1975 dollars, or $27,515.40 in 1979 dollars.[200] Therefore, S should receive an increase in the price of $7,915.40 in 1979 dollars ($27,515.40–$19,600).

To be sure, there are numerous problems with this kind of monetarily corrected revalorization. During galloping inflation, and especially during runaway inflation, the price indexes are often seriously distorted. The price fluctuations are moving so rapidly that good price information is hard to come by. Moreover, the indexes themselves are likely to be distorted by price controls. And a fair amount of arbitrariness is bound to be involved in determining what the parties might reasonably have contemplated the range of inflation to be. Nevertheless, this kind of revalorization would seem to be as good as one can expect courts or legislatures to accomplish.

NOTES

1. Scaling laws date back as early as the Middle Ages, but the American and French experiences are the first important experiences. *See* A. NUSSBAUM, MONEY IN THE LAW NATIONAL AND INTERNATIONAL 204–205 (rev. ed. 1950).

2. See chap. 3, *supra,* notes 30–38 and the accompanying text.

3. The U.S. Congress issued a new batch of paper money called New Tenor notes. These were supposed to be accepted at a par with silver, but Congress neglected to provide for their free convertibility into specie. E. HARGREAVES, RESTORING CURRENCY STANDARDS 6 (1926). The French issued a new batch of paper money called *mandats. Assignats* were to be redeemed for *mandats* at the rate of 30 to 1. Like the American New Tenor notes, *mandats* were rated on a par with specie and their acceptance was mandated for all payments.

Neither country generated a genie. Both the New Tenor notes and the *mandats* were a fiasco. Both issues quickly became worthless. What is most striking about the *mandat* experience is that once it had become apparent that the *mandat* was depreciating rapidly and the return to specie was in the offing, the French government surreptitiously hired a private firm to dump government-supplied mandats on the public and thereby erode any remaining purchasing power from the currency. S. HARRIS, THE ASSIGNATS 210 (1930).

4. E. HARGREAVES, *supra* note 3, at 11. Some statutes did, however, authorize courts to resolve cases on an equitable basis whenever application of the scale would be unjust. In Faw v. Marsteller, 6 U.S. (2 Cranch) 10 (1804), the U.S. Supreme Court revalued a ground rent pursuant to a Virginia scaling statute in accordance with the value of the consideration, declaring this to be the most just and equitable test, as well as the only standard the court could perceive for revaluing the debt in question.

5. *Id.* at 11, 18. State law with respect to debts which had been partly paid differed. Some left such cases up to the discretion of the courts, but most states denied creditors any revaluation on installment payments already made. *Id.* at 19.

6. *Id.* at 12.

7. *Id.* at 12–13, 23.

8. S. HARRIS, *supra* note 3, at 214.

9. E. HARGREAVES, *supra* note 3, at 49.

10. A law of June 26, 1796, decreed that for the purposes of payment of land tax, each franc of assessment should be grossed up to the price of ten pounds of corn. *Id.* at 38–39. A law of July 9, 1796, fixed the price of corn at 16 *sous* in *mandats,* which meant that for each franc due in *mandats,* the taxpayer had to pay eight francs (10 × 16 sous). This made the official value of the *mandat* one-eighth its face value; however, it was estimated that at this time the *mandat*'s exchange value in specie had fallen to one fourteenth its nominal value. *Id.* at 39.

11. *Id.* at 40.

12. Law of Jy. 16, 1796, described in E. HARGREAVES, *supra* note 3, at 41.

13. Law of Dec. 1, 1797, described in *id.* at 54–55.

14. The statute ordering preparation of depreciation scales was enacted on June 23, 1797, more than five months prior to the law requiring scaling of private debts. *Id.* at 48–50. *Départments* generally used the unweighted average of the four factors that the statute directed be taken into account, though modifications were often introduced for periods in which the fluctuations were unusually violent. The scales were more sophisticated than those used in the American scaling statutes.

15. Loans between January 1, 1791 and July 17, 1796 were presumed to be in paper currency, unless proven otherwise. *Id.* at 54. Paper money loans repayable in commodities could be reduced to scale if the debtor could prove that the value of the commodities at the time of the making of the loan was worth more than 1.5 times the sum lent. *Id.* at 55.

16. *Id.* at 55, 65.

17. *Id.* at 58–59.

18. Leases with a term greater than nine years could be cancelled by either party if the lessee had not yet taken possession. Cancellation could be avoided, however, if the lessee agreed to pay the rent in full, or if the lessor agreed to accept rent reduced in accordance with the depreciation scale. *Id.* at 58–64.

19. *Id.* at 73.

20. By the time of the reform, the ratio of a florin in specie to one in paper had already fallen as low as 8.5 to 1. *Id.* at 80.

21. Dawson & Cooper, *The Effect of Inflation on Private Contracts: The United States, 1861–1879,* 33 MICH. L. REV. 706, 727 (1935).

22. Wilmington and Weldon R.R. v. King, 91 U.S. 3 (1875); Effinger v. Kenney, 115 U.S. 566 (1885).

23. Dawson & Cooper, *supra* note 21, at 739.

24. Kuratow-Kuratowski, *Les Problèmes de la Baisse du Mark Polonais dans le Domaine du Droit Privé,* 54 BULL. SOC. LEGIS. COMP. 96, 99 (1925). *See also* Picard, *Le Remboursement des Dettes et la Valorisation des Créances dans les Pays à Monnaie Dépréciée,* 51 Clunet 918, 922–28 (1924).

25. Kuratow-Kuratowski, *supra* note 24, at 111.

26. *Id.* at 110.

27. *Id.* at 114.

28. *Id.* at 117.

29. *See infra,* notes 105–20 and the accompanying text.

30. A. NUSSBAUM, *supra* note 1, at 200.

31. *Id.* at 165.

32. JASTROW, PRINCIPIENRAGEN IN DEN AUFWERTUNGSDEBATTEN 61 (1937), cited in A. NUSSBAUM, *supra* note 1, at 201, fn. 33.

33. *Id.* at 201–202.

34. Dawson, *Effects of Inflation On Private Contracts: Germany, 1914–1924,* 33 MICH. L. REV. 171, 211–12 (1934).

35. *Id.* at 212; A. NUSSBAUM, *supra* note 1, at 211–12.

36. A. NUSSBAUM, *supra* note 1, at 212.

37. Dawson, *supra* note 34, at 215, fn. 135. Hardship situations were statutorily defined to include the debtor's poor financial situation, the loss of one's

fortune, sale of the property for a small price, or that the debtor had to sell the property for much less than its true value because of action taken by the creditor. Fischer, *The German Revalorization Act, 1925,* 10 J. COMP. LEGIS. 94, 96 (3d Ser., Part I, 1928).

38. *Id.* at 95.

39. *Ibid.*

40. *Id.* at 98.

41. *Id.* at 98–99; Dawson, *supra* note 34, at 220–21.

42. This reservation served the valuable function of placing the debtor on notice that the creditor might pursue a further claim for the value of the debt. Dawson, *supra* note 34, at 219.

43. *Ibid.*

44. H. SCHACT, THE STABILIZATION OF THE MARK 213–14 (1927).

45. Dawson, *supra* note 34, at 220.

46. *Id.* at 215–16, fn. 136.

47. D. GRAHAM, EXCHANGE, PRICES, AND PRODUCTION IN HYPERINFLATION: GERMANY, 1920–1923, 156–59 (1930). Professor Dawson, *supra* note 34, at 226, suggested that the use of the foreign exchange rate as a standard of value would "reduce very greatly the creditor's recovery." However, this seems an obvious case of stating precisely the opposite of what the author meant, and in no way detracts from this superb piece of scholarly writing.

48. This dubious conclusion rested on three grounds: (1) the creditor could only consume so much himself; (2) hoarding of commodities for speculation or investment would have contravened the criminal law; and (3) if creditors had hoarded on a broad scale, consumer prices would have been pushed up even further. Dawson, *supra* note 34, at 228, fn. 188. The difficulties with both the retail and wholesale price indexes at this time in Germany are discussed in the text to note 118 *infra.*

49. Fischer, *supra* note 37, at 96–97.

50. These special tribunals were empowered to determine the extent of revalorization, but not whether a right to revalorization existed. The latter question had to be decided by the ordinary courts in the event that both parties failed to submit voluntarily to the jurisdiction of a revalorization tribunal. *Id.* at 97.

51. Klopstock, *Monetary Reform in Western Germany,* 57 J. POL. ECON. 277, 278–79 (1949).

52. Judgment of Feb. 28, 1951, 1951 N.J.W. 399, cited in F. MANN, THE LEGAL ASPECT OF MONEY 123, fn. 5 (3d ed. 1971).

53. Heller, *Tax and Monetary Reform in Occupied Germany,* 2 NAT'L TAX J. 215, 216–18 (1949).

54. *Id.* at 216–17.

55. *Ibid.*

56. *Id.* at 218.

57. *See* H. SCHACT, *supra* note 44, at 212.

58. A. NUSSBAUM, *supra* note 1, at 211; Rashba, *Debts in Collapsed Foreign Currencies,* 54 YALE L. J. 1, 13 (1944).

59. After the revolution, Soviet law, in an effort to destroy the economic classes against which the revolt was directed, expressly prohibited the courts from

taking jurisdiction of pre-revolutionary monetary claims. Rashba, *supra* note 58, at 12. Nevertheless, Russian tribunals, on occasion, did award damages for currency depreciation where claims for unpaid wages and intergovernmental agency debts were involved. *Id.* at 12–13; A. NUSSBAUM, *supra* note 1, at 216. After both world wars, despite fantastic currency depreciation (old drachmas were converted into new at the ratio of 50,000,000,000 to 1), Greece refused to revalorize debts contracted in depreciated currency. Massouridis, *Les Prestations Dues en Monnaie Dévaluée,* 3 Rev. Hellenique Droit Int'l 20 (1950).

60. The entire Latin maxim is *Contractus qui habent tractum succesivum et depentiam de future rebus sic stantibus intelliguntur* (Implicit in contracts of periodic performance and which depend on the future is that things remain as they are.)

61. Bavarian *Landrecht,* IV, c. 15 §12; Prussian *Allgemeines Landrecht* I.5, §378.

62. *See* 6 PLANIOL & RIPERT, TRAITÉ PRATIQUE DE DROIT CIVIL FRANÇAIS 526–27 (2d ed. by P. Esmein 1952); A. MEDEIROS DA FONSECA, CASO FORTUITO E TEORIA DA IMPREVISÃO 198–200 (3d ed. 1958).

63. Hay, *Frustration and its Solution in German Law,* 10 AM. J. COMP. L. 345–46 (1961).

64. March 30, 1916, [1916] D.P. III, 25; [1916] S. Jur. III, 17 (1916), translated in A. VON MEHREN, THE CIVIL LAW SYSTEM 709–10 (1st ed. 1957). The *Bordeaux* case has its roots in prior decisions of the *Conseil d'État*'s modifying contracts to meet changed circumstances resulting from governmental acts. The circumstances justifying revision were gradually extended to other political acts and to the presence of unforeseeably great difficulties in performing public construction contracts. *Id.* at 710.

65. *Id.* at 709–10.

66. *Id.* at 712.

67. 6 PLANIOL & RIPERT, *supra* note 62, at 532–33; Noirel, *L'Influence de la Dépréciation Monétaire dans les Contrats de Droit Privé,* in INFLUENCE DE LA DÉPRÉCIATION MONÉTAIRE SUR LA VIE JURIDIQUE PRIVÉE 100–101 (P. Durand, ed. 1961); Cooper, *Effects of Inflation on Private Contracts: France, 1916–1926,* 6 DET. L. REV. 63, 72 (1936).

68. David, *Frustration of Contract in French Law,* 28 J. COMP. LEGIS. 11, 13–14 (pts. 3 & 4, 1946).

69. Rashba, *supra* note 58, at 16; Dawson & Cooper, *supra* note 21, at 890; Comment, *The Energy Crisis and Economic Impossibility in Louisiana Fuel Requirements Contracts: A Gameplan for Reform,* 49 TUL. L. REV. 605, 610, fn. 39 (1975). *See also* Smit, *Frustration of Contract: A Comparative Attempt at Consolidation,* 58 COLUM. L. REV. 287, 303 (1958).

70. The most famous of these statutes is the *Loi Faillot* of January 21, 1918. For the duration of the war and three months after the cessation of hostilities, this statute permitted termination of all commercial contracts concluded prior to August 1, 1914 involving successive or delayed performance "if it is established that, because of the state of war, performance of the obligations of one of the contracting parties would incur costs or prejudice him much more than he could reasonably have contemplated at the date of the conclusion of the contract" (Art. 2). If termination were ordered, the judge had discretion to award damages; if damages were awarded, they were to be reduced by the amount the war caused them to

exceed what the contracting parties could have foreseen. There do not seem to be any reported cases applying the *Loi Faillot.* Cooper, *supra* note 67, at 88. A similar statute was enacted on April 22, 1949 to deal with undue hardship caused by World War II. 6 PLANIOL & RIPERT, *supra* note 62, at 531–32.

Several statutes have been passed to permit revision of *rentes* whose real economic value has become too low because of inflation. Pursuant to these statutes French courts have even revised indexed annuities and long-term leases if the index device has failed to maintain the economic equilibrium of the contract. *See* 2 RIPERT & BOULANGER, TRAITÉ ELEMENTAIRE DE DROIT CIVIL DE PLANIOL 173 (4th ed. 1952); Bergel, *La Révision Judiciaire des Rentes Viagères entre Particuliers,* 71 Rev. Trim. Droit Civ. 45 (1973).

However, neither the *théorie de l'imprévision* nor statutes like the *Loi Faillot* are considered applicable to pecuniary loans whose value is seriously diminished or augmented by inflation or deflation; such application would infringe the nominalist principle of Article 1895 of the French Civil Code. 6 PLANIOL & RIPERT, *supra* note 62, at 538; A. VON MEHREN, *supra* note 64, at 532–33.

71. A. FONSECA, *supra* note 62, at 256; Przybylowski, *Der Einfluss veranderter Umstände auf die Schuldverhaltnisse in der polnischen Rechtsprechung und Literatur,* 3 Zeitschrift fur Ostrecht 169, 170 (1929); Longchamps de Berier, *La Révision des Contrats par le Juge en Droit Civil Polonais,* 2 Travaux Sem. Int'l Droit 105, 111–14 (1937).

72. A. FONSECA, *supra* note 62, at 261.

73. App. Florence, March 3, 1914, Riv. Dir. Comm. II, 148 (1915); App. Parma, August 12, 1915, Riv. Dir. Comm. II, 48 (1916); App. Turin, March 16, 1916, Riv. Dir. Comm. II, 649 (1916); App. Asti, April 6, 1918, Riv. Dir. Comm. II, 92 (1919).

74. Cass. Florence, Nov. 14, 1918, Foro Ital. I, 117 (1919); Cass. Rome, Nov. 25, 1919, Riv. Dir. Comm. II, 1 (1921); Cass. Turin, Jan. 16, 1920, Riv. Dir. Comm. II, 490 (1920).

75. "Art. 1467. Contract for mutual counterperformances. In contracts for continuous or periodic performances or for deferred performance, if extraordinary and unforeseeable events make the performance of one of the parties excessively onerous, the party who owes such performance can demand dissolution of the contract, with the effects set forth in article 1458. [This article provides that dissolution shall have retroactive effects, except for contracts of continuous or periodic performance. As to the latter, dissolution does not extend to performance already rendered.]

"Dissolution cannot be demanded if the supervening onerousness is part of the normal risk of the contract.

"A party against whom dissolution is demanded can avoid it by offering to modify equitably the conditions of the contract.

"Art. 1468. Contracts with obligations of one party only. In the case contemplated in the preceding article, if the contract is one in which only one of the parties has assumed obligations, he can demand a reduction in his performance or a modification of the manner of performance, sufficient to restore it to an equitable basis.

"Art. 1469. Aleatory contracts. The provisions of the preceding articles (1467 f.) do not apply to contracts that are aleatory by their nature or by the intention of the parties." As translated in M. Beltramo et al., The Italian Civil Code 372–73 (1969).

76. Zepos, *Frustration of Contract in Comparative Law and in the New Greek Civil Code of 1946 (Article 388),* 11 Modern L. Rev. 36, 41 (1948).

77. *Id.* at 42.

78. Law No. 12.910 of May 19, 1947, as amended by Law No. 15.285. See generally, Barra, *La Teoría de la Imprévision y el Régimen de los Mayores Costos en la Obra Pública,* 19–20 Rev. Der. Púb. 323 (Chile 1976).

79. Two early Argentine cases rejecting the doctrine of *imprévision* are Ponzano v. Banco El Hogar Argentino, 29 J.A. 576 (App. Rosario 1929) and Pirán de Flores v. Dose y Cía., 9 La Ley 576 (1st Cam. Civ. B.A. 1937). Early cases accepting imprevision are Grau Bassas v. Fernández, 1952–IV J.A. 381 (2d Cam. Civ. y Com. Eva Perón 1952); Cabal v. Madero, 75 La Ley 254 (CNCiv., Sala C 1953). *But see* Staudt y Cía. v. Padua, 1953–IV J.A. 30 (App. Paraná 1953), criticized in a note by Spota, but *aff'd* 75 La Ley 411 (Sup. Ct. 1954).

80. Law 17.711 of April 22, 1968, amending Art. 1198 of the Argentine Civil Code, translated in K. Karst & K. Rosenn, Law and Development in Latin America 470 (1975). This statute is modeled after Article 1467 of the Italian Civil Code.

81. The first Brazilian case to apply the theory of *imprévision* was Carlos Conteville & Cia. v. Maison F. Eloi & Cia., S.A., 100 Rev. Dir. 178 (1930), *aff'd* 77 Rev. For. 79 (Sup. Fed. Trib. 1938). *See generally,* A. Fonseca, *supra* note 62, at 310–20.

82. *E.g.,* Santos Filho & Cia. v. Rodrigues Tavares, 151 Rev. Trib. 712, 68 Arch. Jud. 344 (5th Cam. Civ. of Court of Appeal of Fed. Dis. 1943); Durante v. Teixeira, 166 Rev. Trib. 786, 104 Rev. For. 269 (3rd Cam. Civ. of Court of Appeal Fed. Dis. 1945). *But see* Processo M.T.I.C.N. 231.800–44, 2 Rev. Dir. Admin. 812 (Fasc. II 1945).

83. Art. 1246 provides: "The architect or builder who contracts to build in accordance with plans accepted by the owner, shall not have the right to demand an increment in the price, even if salaries or materials become more expensive, or there has been an alteration or increase in the amount of work specified in the plans, unless such increment or alteration is done in accordance with written instructions from the owner and exhibited by the architect or builder."

84. Constructora Imobiliaria Comercial S.A. v. Orlando France, 36 R.T.J. 104 (3d Term Sup. Fed. Trib. 1965); Beckhauser v. Pascoa Ceccato, 35 R.T.J. 597 (1st Term Sup. Fed. Trib. 1965); ECAL v. Araújo Pereira, 4 Rev. Juris. Guan. 208 (5th Cam. Civ., No. 10, 1964); Banco Americano de Crédito S.A. v. Espólio de Pinto de Macedo, 5 Rev. Juris. Guan. 183 (3d Group of Cam. Civ., No. 13, 1965); Auerback v. Coelho Pinto, 210 Rev. For. 145 (5th Cam. Civ. Guan. 1961); Lustman v. da Costa Barros, 41 R.T.J. 725 (1st Term Sup. Fed. Trib. 1967).

85. Lefcoe, *Monetary Correction and Mortgage Lending in Brazil: Observations for the United States,* 21 Stan. L. Rev. 106, 126 (1968).

86. *E.g.,* Prefeitura Municipal de Santos v. Daniel Domingos & Irmãos, Ltda., 41 R.T.J. 709 (3d Term Sup. Fed. Trib. 1966).

87. Brazilian Decree-Law No. 185 of Feb. 23, 1967, translated in K. Karst & K. Rosenn, *supra* note 80, at 475. Similar legislation has been adopted in the states of Rio de Janeiro and São Paulo. J. Chacel, M. Simonsen, & A. Wald, Correção Monetária 73–80 (1970).

88. The Italian cases and doctrine are collected in 4 C. GIANNATTASIO, RASSEGNA DI GIURISPRUDENZA SUL CODICE CIVILLE 368, 394–95 (1971). Sample Argentine cases are: Dir. Gral. de Fabricaciones Militares v. Scheinin, 3 J.A. 27 (C. Fed. Cap., sala C 1969); Correa v. Lo Valvo, 9 J.A. 376 (C. Civ. Cap., sala B, 1970); Barder de Magni v. Municipalidad de la Capital, 128 La Ley 485 (CNCiv., sala C 1967); Martín de Dursi v. Teitelbaum, 117 La Ley 379 (CNCiv., sala A 1964).

89. The sharp surge in the inflation rate in Argentina, where the average annual increase in the consumer price index jumped from 24.2 percent in 1974 to 182.7 percent in 1975 and 444.3 percent in 1976, led a number of Argentine courts to allow obligors to escape from their contracts on the theory of imprevision. Aycor S.A. v. Parrone, 1977 J.A.–III 618 (C Nac. Civ., Sala C 1977) and cases cited in Bianchi, *Sobre Inflación e Imprevisión,* 1977 J.A.–III 619, 620, fn. 3. *But see* Tomelleri v. Murúa (C Nac. Civ. 11/15/77), J.A., Jy. 5, 1978, p. 22; Erifa, S.C.A. v. Waterling, S.R.L. (Cam. Esp. Civ. y Com., sala 5, 6/30/78), La Ley, Sept. 20, 1978, p. 5. There is also a recent decision of Brazil's highest court upholding revision of a private construction contract entered into in 1962 on the theory that the sudden burst of inflation in 1963–64 was unforeseeable. Companhia Vale do Rio Doce v. Décio Silviano Brandão, Engenharia, R.E. No. 85,714 (STF 1st Term, June 19, 1979).

90. Dawson, *supra* note 34, at 187–88.

91. Cohn, *Frustration of Contract in German Law,* 28 J. COMP. LEGIS. 15, 18 (3d Ser., Parts III–IV, 1946).

92. Smit, *supra* note 69, at 291; Deschenaux, *La Révision des Contrats en Droit Suisse,* 30 J. COMP. LEGIS. 55, 62 (3d Ser., Parts III–IV, 1948).

93. Dawson, *supra* note 34, at 192–93.

94. *Id.* at 194–95.

95. Deschenaux, *supra* note 92, at 60–61.

96. Smit, *supra* note 69, at 289–90.

97. 103 R.G.Z. 328 (Feb. 3, 1922).

98. Rodhe, *Adjustment of Contracts on Account of Changed Conditions,* 3 SCAND. STUD. IN L. 151, 167 (1959).

99. Cohn, *supra* note 91, at 22.

100. Hay, *supra* note 63, at 368, fn. 131.

101. In a recent German case denying rescission to a landlord whose fixed-dollar leasing arrangement had become unprofitable because of domestic inflation and upward revaluation of the mark, the Court of Appeals stated:

> A claim on account of the disappearance of a transaction basis [*Geschäftsgrundlage*] presupposes a subsequently appearing shift in the balance between performance and counter-performance which was unforeseeable at the time of concluding the contract, a shift of such decisiveness that adherence to the original contract cannot be expected of the contract partner thereby prejudiced. . . . At the time of the signing of the contract fluctuations in the U.S. dollar exchange rate were foreseeable by both parties, even if not to the extent which later occurred.

United States of America v. INDUS, G.m.b.H., Court of Appeals, Karlsruhe, Feb. 13, 1976, 1 A.S.I.L.S. INT'L L.J. 145 (1977).

102. Hay, *supra* note 63, at 364.

103. Deschenaux, *supra* note 92, at 59. The following excerpt from the opinion of the Civil Senate of the High Court of the British zone in M. & Co. v. M., July 15, 1948, cited in A. VON MEHREN, *supra* note 64, at 754, reflects the peculiarly broad quality of good faith in German law:

> Under Article 242 of the Civil Code every obligation is subject to the general principle of good faith. Legal doctrine and judicial decision have deduced from this principle, with many minor deviations, that a decisive change in the assumptions upon which, insofar as it appears, a given contractual relationship was, in the thinking of both or at least one party, based, affects the content of the obligation to perform to the extent that good faith requires. . . . For moral and commercial reasons it is important to hold a person to his word so that an intervention in the existing obligation is possible only in the most exceptional cases, but such interventions are permissible where a rigid adherence to the contract would lead to results that cannot be squared with the requirement of good faith.

104. Hinrichsen et Cie v. Brann et Cie, Je. 3, 1925, 53 Clunet 1118 (1926), and cases cited in F. MANN, *supra* note 52, at 278, fn. 2. Courts of a number of countries have required revalorization of obligations expressed in worthless marks where the governing law was German. *Id.* at 277–78. Switzerland is unusual in revalorizing where the law of the obligation is Swiss. *Compare* the decisions of the Anglo-American courts cited in notes 144–45 *infra.* Switzerland has no general revalorization doctrine, and normally the Swiss courts ignore currency depreciation. However, in cases involving currencies that have collapsed, Swiss courts have held that the good faith requirement of Swiss law requires revalorization.

105. Dawson, *supra* note 34, at 191.

106. *Id.* at 192–93. *See also* notes 90–102, *supra,* and the accompanying text.

107. Dawson, *supra* note 34, at 203–204.

108. 107 R.G.Z. 78. Prior to rendering its decision, the Fifth Civil Senate took the extraordinary step of securing the agreement of all the other civil senates of the *Reichsgericht.* The decision is translated into English in A. VON MEHREN, *supra* note 64, at 743.

109. Art. 242 provides: "The debtor is bound to effect the performance according to the requirements of good faith, ordinary usage being taken into consideration."

110. Translation by A. VON MEHREN, *supra* note 64, at 746.

111. *Id.* at 744–45.

112. A. NUSSBAUM, *supra* note 1, at 208.

113. Nussbaum reports that by January 1928, 2,864,217 revalorization cases had been brought before the Prussian courts, and 522,656 revalorization cases had already been decided by the Bavarian courts. *Id.* at 210, fn. 40. A large number of these cases involved application of statutory rather than judicial revalorization standards.

114. *Id.* at 209–10.

115. Dawson, *supra* note 34, at 225.

116. A. NUSSBAUM, *supra* note 1, at 208.

117. *See* note 47 *supra.*

118. Dawson, *supra* note 34, at 225–26.

119. *Id.* at 205.

120. A. NUSSBAUM, *supra* note 1, at 210.

121. Section 24 of the Swedish Sale of Goods Act of 1905, which has also been adopted by Denmark and Norway, permits the seller to escape contractual responsibility where "performance can be considered impossible owing to a circumstance that the seller could not reasonably have foreseen at the formation of the contract, such as the destruction of all goods of the kind in question or of the parcel to which the purchase refers, or war, import prohibition, or similar occurrence." During the First World War era, the Scandinavian countries relied on this statute to permit sellers to escape whenever prices had risen steeply, or there was some other supervening hardship. Rodhe, *supra* note 98, at 159, 165.

122. This theory, as stated by its leading exponent, Professor Katsumoto, is: "When the change in circumstances occurs, without the fault of either party, between the formation of the contract and the time fixed for performance, and when the change in circumstances was so unforeseeable and of such character that the continuation of the obligation to perform is inconsistent with the rule of Good Faith, then the legal obligation should . . . be governed by the principle of Good Faith rather than the stricter law." Katsumoto's theory has been accepted by the Japanese courts in allowing sellers to rescind or modify equitably agreements for the sale of land entered into prior to, but to be performed after, the onset of the great inflation brought on by World War II. J. SAWADA, SUBSEQUENT CONDUCT AND SUPERVENING EVENTS 140–53 (1968); Igarashi and Rieke, *Impossibility and Frustration in Sales Contracts,* 42 WASH. L. REV. 445, 452–54 (1967). However, both the Japanese courts and legislature declined to follow the German example and revalorize long-term debts which had become greatly reduced in real value through inflation. *Id.* at 455.

123. Article 373 of the Swiss Code of Obligations of 1911 enacts what some writers call *rebus sic stantibus* and others *imprévision* for the special case of construction contracts. The first paragraph of Article 373 prohibits the contractor from increasing the price, even if the cost of completion is greater than he had anticipated. The second paragraph states: "But where extraordinary circumstances which could not be foreseen, or which were excluded by the basis upon which both parties entered into the contract, prevent or unduly impede the completion, the court may, at its discretion, increase the price or rescind the contract." After World War I some of the Swiss courts began to extend this rule of *rebus sic stantibus* or *imprévision* to other kinds of contracts. For example, in Rogenmoser v. Tiefengrund A.G., 59 BGE II 372 (1st Civ. Div., Oct. 10, 1933), the Swiss Federal Court stated that in an appropriate case *rebus sic stantibus,* as "limited by the higher principle of good faith," would be a proper basis for rescinding or modifying a long-term lease. In subsequent litigation between the same parties the court terminated the lease, relying on Article 269 of the Code of Obligations, which permits termination on payment of compensation if the lease becomes intolerable for either party. 60 BGE II 205 (May 29, 1934). Ultimately, the court reduced the damages awarded pursuant to Article 269 to slightly less than one-fifth of the damages shown by the landlord. 61 BGE II 259 (Oct. 29, 1935).

Some of the German cases from the early 1920s also invoked *rebus sic stantibus.* A. NUSSBAUM, *supra* note 1, at 202; Dawson, *supra* note 34, 186, 195. But later cases have specifically rejected reliance on *rebus sic stantibus.* A. NUSSBAUM, *supra* note 1, at 202–203.

The doctrine of *Ausbeutung* (Exploitation) is designed to set aside manifestly one-sided contracts resulting from one party exploiting the inexperience or distress of the other. However, the Swiss *Bundesgericht* has occasionally (and generally in conjunction with another theory) invoked the underlying principle of *Ausbeutung* to set aside contracts made manifestly disproportionate because of subsequent events like inflation. Smit, *supra* note 69, at 292.

Lückenausfüllende Auslegung (the Gap Filling Doctrine) is designed to supplement contracts by supplying provisions to which the parties would presumably have agreed had they foreseen the possibility of the occurrence of changed circumstances. This has been a technique adopted by Swiss and German courts for remaking contracts for the parties. *Id.* at 293–95, 297–99.

Unzumutbarkeit (Nonimputability) requires discharge of a contract if a promisee acts unreasonably and in violation of accepted standards of fair dealing. Insistence on performance of a contract which has become excessively onerous because of unanticipated inflation can be considered unreasonable behavior on the part of the promisee. This doctrine has almost invariably been utilized in conjunction with other theories by Swiss and German courts. *Id.* at 292–93, 297.

124. Hay, *supra* note 63, at 355.

125. G. Co. v. J.G.R. & S. Co., 147 R.G.Z. 286 (3d Civ. Sen., Reichsgericht, Apr. 2, 1935), translated in A. VON MEHREN, *supra* note 64, at 751.

126. Dawson, *Economic Duress and the Fair Exchange in French and German Law,* 11 TUL. L. REV. 345, 364 (Part I, 1937). Modern writers have cast serious doubt about the authenticity of the rescript. *Ibid.*

127. *Id.* at 365–66.

128. *Id.* at 370, 6 PLAINOL & RIPERT, *supra* note 62, at 254.

129. Art. 1674–81. *Lésion* also applied to partition agreements, but not to sales of land by the courts. Arts. 887, 1079, and 1684.

130. 6 PLAINOL & RIPERT, *supra* note 62, at 255–56. For example, Law of July 8, 1907, designed to protect cultivators against unscrupulous sellers, gives the buyer of animal feed an action for reduction in price and for interest if the price exceeds the true value by more than one-fourth. Law of March 10, 1937 extended this statute to purchasers of seeds and plants for agricultural use.

131. Civil Code of Chile, arts. 1888–91. Civil Code of Colombia, arts. 1946–54. As in France, rescission can be avoided if the other party consents to make up the difference in the just price, less one tenth. Art. 1890 of the Chilean Civil Code; art. 1948 of the Colombian Civil Code.

132. Dawson, *supra* note 126, 12 TUL. L. REV. 42, 48–50 (Part II, 1937).

133. Arts. 1448–50.

134. Law No. 17.711 of Apr. 22, 1968, amending art. 954 of the Argentine Civil Code, and translated in K. KARST & K. ROSENN, *supra* note 80, at 401.

135. Brazilian Decree-Law No. 869 of Nov. 18, 1938, as amended by art. 4(b) of Law No. 1.521 of Dec. 26, 1951. *Lésion* has also been proposed by articles 62–64 in the Draft of the Code of Obligations. *See generally,* C. SILVA PEREIRA, LESÃO NOS CONTRATOS 151–69 (2d ed. 1959).

136. Dawson, *supra* note 126, at 58.

137. *See* 10 PLAINOL & RIPERT, TRAITÉ PRATIQUE DE DROIT CIVIL FRANÇAIS 297–98 (2d ed. by J. Hamel 1956); Noirel, *supra* note 67, at 98.

138. The French cases are collected in the authorities cited in note 137 *supra;* Belgium: Vaxelaire et Consorts v. Steens, Cass., Jy. 13, 1923, [1923] Pas. I, 441; Veuve D'Hoosche et Consorts v. Wauters et Desmet, Cass. Oct. 7, 1926, [1927] Pas. I, 62. The French courts virtually unanimously adopted the position of the *Cour de Cassation.* Curiously, the French legislature decided to fix that case law position in legislative concrete; Law of Nov. 28, 1949 added to Article 1675 of the French Civil Code this paragraph: "In the case of an option, *lésion* is determined as of the date of the completion of the sale."

139. Boyer, *Promesse de Vente,* in 6 DALLOZ ENCY. JURID. §187 (2d ed. 1975).

140. Gómez T. v. Cantillana V., 57 R.D.J. 30, 33 (Nos. 5 & 6, 2d Part, 2d Sec., C. de Santiago, Aug. 4, 1960); Avendaño Cueto v. Allesandri Altamirano, 46 R.D.J. 780 (Nos. 5 & 6, 1st Part, 2d Sec., Sup. Ct. Aug. 25, 1949). *Cf.* Jungk S. v. Wagner Sch., 58 R.D.J. 47, 2d Part, 1st Sec., Sup. Ct. 1961). In 1968 the Chilean Supreme Court modified this line of cases and held that the relevant time for determining the existence of *lésion* where land is bought on installments pursuant to a purchase agreement is the date of the purchase agreement and not the date of the completion of the sale. Perlwitz v. Zambrano, 65 R.D.J. 210 (2d Part, 1st Sec. 1968).

141. Although Article 1681 of the Civil Code simply provides that "When rescission is allowed, the buyer can . . . retain [the property], paying the just price, after deducting one-tenth of the total value," it had been assumed that the proper date for determining just price was the date of the sale for two reasons. First, Article 1675 stipulates that the determination of the just price for the purpose of ascertaining the existence of *lésion* should be the date of the sale. Second, Article 1682 requires the buyer who wishes to complete the purchase price to pay interest on the supplementary payment from the date the action for rescission was instituted, suggesting that the just price would be determined no later than as of the day the action was instituted.

142. Dame Goffet, veuve Henry v. Dame Desmarais, Cass. 1re Civ., Je. 7, 1966, [1967] J.C.P. II, 15049; Consorts Vidal v. Dame Pradier, Cass. 1re Civ., Je. 7, 1966, [1966] Bull. Civ. I, No. 346, 264.

143. The cases are collected in Griel, *La Jurisprudence Récente Concernant la Lésion dans la Vente Immoblière,* [1967] D.S. Jur. 57 (Chron.).

144. 134 L.T. 557, 42 T.L.R. 302 [1926]. All three judges expressed the hope that the insurance company would voluntarily pay something to the beneficiary out of considerations of justice and equity. The result is criticized as unnecessarily harsh in 6 CORBIN ON CONTRACTS §1360, at 487 (2d ed. 1962). Yet the decision is explicable in terms of conflicts of law considerations and would probably not have been decided differently even if the suit had been filed in a German court. F. MANN, *supra* note 52, at 279–80, 352–53, fn. 7.

145. Tillman v. Russo Asiatic Bank, 51 F.2d 1023 (2d Cir. 1931), *cert. denied,* 285 U.S. 539; Tillman v. National City Bank, 118 F.2d 631 (2d Cir. 1941), *cert. denied,* 314 U.S. 650 (1941); Dougherty v. Equitable Life Assurance Society, 266 N.Y. 71, 193 N.E. 897 (1934).

146. Brubrad Company v. United States Postal Service, 404 F. Supp. 691 (E.D.N.Y. 1975). *See also* Columbus Ry. & Power v. Columbus, 249 U.S. 399 (1919).

147. The rule of Paradine v. Jane, 82 Eng. Rep. 897 [K.B. 1647] came to stand for the proposition that the courts do not make contracts but simply enforce them as made. Walton v. Waterhouse, 85 Eng. Rep. 1233, 1234, fn. 2 [K.B. 1684].

148. The great bulk of this revalorization was accomplished pursuant to the legislative directive of crude scaling statutes rather than by the courts acting on their own. *See* notes 21 to 23 *supra* and the accompanying text. Moreover, the U.S. Supreme Court, after the business of revalorization was largely accomplished, declared the principal revalorization standard employed by the Southern courts—the value of the consideration—invalid and held that no more could be recovered on the contract than the value of the Confederate currency in U.S. currency at the date of the celebration of the contract. Thorington v. Smith, 75 U.S. (8 Wall.) 1 (1868); Stewart v. Salamon, 94 U.S. 434 (1876); Rives v. Duke, 105 U.S. 132 (1881). The Supreme Court went on to declare unconstitutional two of the scaling statutes as impairments of the obligation of contracts. Wilmington and Weldon R.R. v. King, 91 U.S. 3 (1875); Effinger v. Kenney, 115 U.S. 566 (1885). Allowing judges and juries to revise contracts by placing their own notions rather than those of the parties to the contract on the value of the consideration would, in the view of the Supreme Court, "create an insecurity in business transactions which would be intolerable." Wilmington and Weldon R.R. v. King, *supra,* 91 U.S. at 5. There is also language in the Supreme Court opinions strongly suggesting that the Confederate notes, which had never been made legal tender, were commodities rather than money; therefore, the principle by which they might be revised did not apply to money obligations. 91 U.S. at 6; Effinger v. Kenney, *supra,* 115 U.S. at 575–76 (Bradley, J. dissenting).

In the North, where inflation resulting from the Civil War reduced the purchasing power of the dollar by about half, the courts did not rescind or revise contracts because of monetary depreciation. Dawson and Cooper, *supra* note 21, at 878, 893. In the celebrated case of Willard v. Tayloe, 75 U.S. (8 Wall.) 557 (1869), the Supreme Court did condition specific performance of a contract to sell real estate on tendering the purchase price in gold rather than in depreciated paper currency. But with the disappearance of a dual monetary system, this form of relief has been foreclosed. American courts can withhold specific performance if inflation produces extreme hardship. But the obstacles to doing so are formidable. *See* Dawson & Cooper, *supra* note 21, at 869–73.

149. *See* McElroy, *Frustration and Force Majeure: The Common Law and the Common Market,* 1963 N. Z. L. J. 185, 186.

150. Taylor v. Caldwell, 3 B. & S. 826, 122 Eng. Rep. 309 [1863].

151. Krell v. Henry, 2 K.B. 740 [1903] (excusing defendant's failure to pay the rent on a suite of rooms to view the cancelled coronation of King Edward VII).

152. United States v. Gen. Douglas MacArthur Sr. Vil., Inc., 508 F.2d 377, 381 (2d Cir. 1974).

153. Restatement of Contracts §§456 and 457 (1933).

154. The cases are collected in the American Law Review's Annotation, *Modern Status of the Rules Regarding Impossibility of Performance as Defense in Action for Breach of Contract* [hereinafter cited as ALR Annot.], 84 A.L.R. 2d 12 (1962). The author of this annotation concluded:

> . . . [T]he view to the effect that extreme impracticability of performance may be regarded, in law, as amounting to impossibility which excuses the promisor from liability for nonperformance, seems not to have been adopted very extensively, so far as the representative cases covered in this comment note indicate. Its application would seem to require a difficult distinction between mere difficulty, expense or hardship (rather generally regarded as no excuse for nonperformance) . . . and (in the Restatement's words) "impracticability because of extreme and unreasonable difficulty, expense, injury or loss involved." 84 A.L.R.2d at 62.

155. 172 Cal. 289, 156 P. 458 (1916).

156. *Id.* 156 P. at 460, citing 1 BEACH ON CONTRACTS §216.

157. 35 F. Supp. 433 (N.D. Cal. 1940).

158. 45 Cal. 2d 710, 290 P.2d 841 (1956).

159. Northern Corporation v. Chugach Elec. Ass'n, 518 P.2d 76 (Sup. Ct. Alaska 1974); Kansas, Oklahoma & G. Ry. Co. v. Grand Lake Grain Co., 434 P.2d 153 (Sup. Ct. Okla. 1967).

160. ALR Annot., *supra* note 154, at 27. *See also* 17 Am. Jur. 2d, Contracts §402, at 848.

161. *See* Dawson & Cooper, *supra* note 21, at 894, fn. 266.

162. Schlegel, *Of Nuts, and Ships, and Sealing Wax, Suez and Frustrating Things-The Doctrine of Impossibility of Performance,* 23 RUT. L. REV. 419, 425, 442–46 (1969). *See also* A. MCNAIR & A. WATTS, THE LEGAL EFFECTS OF WAR 167 (4th ed. 1966).

163. Lord Wright in Denny, Mott & Dickson, Ltd. v. James B. Fraser & Co., [1944] A.C. 265, 274–76; Joseph Constantine S.S. Line, Ltd. v. Imperial Smelting Corp., [1942] A.C. 154, 182–87.

164. [1956] A.C. 696.

165. Schlegel, *supra* note 162, at 429–38; Birmingham, *A Second Look at the Suez Canal Cases: Excuse for Nonperformance of Contractual Obligations in the Light of Economic Theory,* 20 HASTINGS L. J. 1393, 1400–1406 (1969).

166. Indeed, it is hard to find cases where frustration has been successfully invoked. E. PETERS, COMMERCIAL TRANSACTIONS 218 (1971); McElroy, *supra* note 149, at 209. *See also* Anderson, *Frustration of a Contract-A Rejected Doctrine,* 3 DE PAUL L. REV. 1 (1953).

167. RESTATEMENT (SECOND) OF CONTRACTS §281 (Tent. Draft No. 9, Apr. 1974).

168. Illustration 2 to §460. Illustration 3 refers to a fiftyfold price increase.

169. *Impossibility, Impracticability, and Supervening Illegality,* in PLI, BREACH OF CONTRACT IN A SHORTAGE ECONOMY 9, 19–20 (1974).

170. Official Comment 1 to UCC §2–615 states that a seller is excused "where his performance has become commercially impracticable because of unforeseen supervening circumstances not within the contemplation of the parties at the time of contracting." Official Comment 4 states that increased cost will not excuse a seller unless "due to some unforeseen contingency. . . ."

171. Comment, *Contractual Flexibility in a Volatile Economy: Saving U.C.C. Section 2-615 from the Common Law,* 72 N.W.U.L. REV. 1032, 1037–39 (1978).

172. RESTATEMENT (SECOND) OF CONTRACTS 42–43 (Tent. Draft No. 9, Apr., 1974).

173. 231 Ga. 868, 204 S.E.2d 625 (1974).

174. 532 F.2d 957 (5th Cir. 1976).

175. 310 N.E.2d 363 (Sup. Ct. Mass. 1974).

176. N.Y.L.J., Jy. 22, 1974, p. 13, 14 UCC Rep. Serv. 1335 (N.Y. Sup. Ct. Suffolk Cty.)

177. 499 F.Supp. 53 (W.D. Pa. 1980).

178. Since UCC §2–615 applies only to contracts for the sale of goods and this contract involved a sale of service, the court invoked the doctrine of commercial impracticability embodied in §281 of the Restatement of Contracts 2d (Tent. Draft No. 10).

179. 499 F. Supp. at 92–93.

180. 363 F.2d 312 (D.C. Cir. 1966).

181. *Id.* at 315.

182. *Id.* at 319.

183. 453 F.2d 939 (2d Cir. 1972).

184. 76 Misc.2d 1080, 352 N.Y.S. 2d 784 (N.Y. Sup. Ct. 1974).

185. 352 N.Y.S.2d at 790.

186. 17 UCC Rep. Ser. 989 (E.D. Pa. 1975).

187. 17 UCC Rep. Ser. at 992.

188. 415 F. Supp. 429 (S.D. Fla. 1975).

189. 415 F. Supp. at 441.

190. "Westinghouse Settles Lawsuit by 3 Utilities," Wall St. J., March 31, 1977, at p. 4, cols. 1–3.

191. Ruling of October 27, 1978, discussed in Note, *Commercial Impracticability as a Contractual Defense,* 47 UMKC L. Rev. 650 (1979). A similar result was reached in another uranium suit, Iowa Elec. Light & Power Co. v. Atlas Corp., 23 UCC Rep. Ser. 1171 (N.D. Iowa 1978), where the court held that Atlas, a uranium supplier, had failed to prove that it could not have protected itself contractually from some of the risks of a dramatic increase in uranium prices. For useful economic analyses of the litigation, *see* Joskow, *Commercial Impossibility, the Uranium Market and the Westinghouse Case,* 6 J. Leg. Stud. 119 (1977); Posner & Rosenfield, *Impossibility and Related Doctrines in Contract Law: an Economic Analysis,* 6 J. Leg. Stud. 83, 94–95 (1977). As of March 1981 Westinghouse had settled all but one of the suits brought against it by public utilities for cash and services worth an estimated $927.2 million. N.Y. Times, Mar. 15, 1981, Sect. F, at p. 22, cols. 4–5.

192. Martin-Baker Aircraft Co. Ltd. v. Canadian Flight Craft Equipment Ltd., [1955] All E.R. 722, [1955] 2 QB 556; Winter Garden Theatre (London) Ltd. v. Millennium Productions Ltd., [1947] 2 All E.R. 331, [1948] AC 173; Re Spenborough Urban District Council's Agreement, [1967] 1 All E.R. 959, [1968] Ch. 139; Beverley Corpn. v. Richard Hodgson & Sons Ltd., [1972] 225 Estates Gazette 799.

193. [1978] 3 All E.R. 769.

194. *Id.* at 776–77

195. Schwartz, *Sales Law and Inflations,* 50 S. Calif. L. Rev. 1, 13, fn. 30 (1976).

196. Yekutieli v. Berman, CA. 682174, 29 P.D. (2) 751 (1975).

197. *Supra,* note 148.

198. Yadin, *Problems of Devaluation before Israeli Courts,* in Internationales

RECHT UND WIRTSCHAFTSORDNUNG 846, 848–49 (W. Flume et al, eds. 1977). There have been, however, several recent Israeli supreme court cases, most of which have remained unpublished, in which specific performance has been conditioned upon readjusting the price or interest rate because of inflation. *See* the note on Ritberg v. Nisim, 34 P.D.(3)314(1980), 16 ISRAEL L. REV. 110 (1981).

199.

1975	$\$1,000 \times \frac{660}{100}$	=	$ 6,600
1976	$\$1,000 \times \frac{660}{110}$	=	$ 6,000
1977	$\$1,000 \times \frac{660}{165}$	=	$ 4,000
1978	$\$1,000 \times \frac{660}{330}$	=	$ 2,000
1979	$\$1,000 \times 1$	=	$ 1,000
Total			$19,600 in 1979 dollars.
1975			$1,000.00
1976	$\frac{100}{110} \times 1,000$	=	$ 909.09
1977	$\frac{100}{165} \times 1,000$	=	$ 606.06
1978	$\frac{100}{330} \times 1,000$	=	$ 303.03
1979	$\frac{100}{660} \times 1,000$	=	$ 151.51
Total			$2,969.69 in 1975 dollars.

200. At a 10 percent discount rate, the present value of the future payments in 1975 dollars will be:

1976	$ 909
1977	826
1978	751
1979	683
Subtotal	$3,169
Down Payment	1,000
Total	$4,169

5

PROTECTING CONTRACTS FROM INFLATION

Rather than have judges or legislatures remake contracts for parties, it is preferable for contracting parties to consider the contingency of inflation and make express provision for it. Given legislative and judicial reluctance to permit escape from contractual obligations made burdensome by inflation, except under extreme circumstances, it is not surprising that lawyers have developed a variety of techniques for protecting the economic equilibrium of contracts from inflationary distortions. These techniques range in sophistication from simply avoiding any contracts that call for future performance at fixed prices to sophisticated index adjustments with complex mathematical formulae.

This chapter will examine the kinds of consensual devices that have been developed to prevent inflation from distorting contracts, focusing on four types of stabilization clauses; (1) commodity clauses, (2) gold clauses, (3) foreign currency clauses, and (4) index clauses. Then these protective devices will be analyzed both in terms of the legal problems they pose and their effectiveness in protecting the economic value of contractual arrangements. Finally, a number of practical suggestions about drafting stabilization clauses will be offered.

THE SHUNNING OF FIXED-PRICE CONTRACTS

A common response to a surge in the inflation rate is the avoidance of long-term and fixed-price contracts. Instead of quoting fixed prices for products that will not be delivered immediately, manufacturers and suppliers attempt to take orders on the basis of "price in effect at the time of delivery." Faced with an inability to project their own rapidly rising costs, price-at-date-of-shipment contracts are rational responses for manufacturers and suppliers, but are plainly less than satisfactory from the viewpoint of the buyer. Purchasers generally enter into deferred performance contracts for the sale of goods not only to fix a source of supply, but also to fix the price. Inability to ascertain costs may induce prospective buyers to withhold advance orders, which impedes orderly production planning by the supplier.

Sometimes the bargaining process produces a compromise in which the seller will agree to a fixed price, provided his costs prior to delivery do not rise above a fixed percentage; any cost increase above that percentage will either be absorbed by the buyer or divided. Another common form of compromise is for the buyer to pay for cost increases up to a fixed percentage; any increase in excess of that percentage is either absorbed by the seller or divided. The extent to which sellers can shift all or part of the risk of inflation to purchasers by these kinds of open-ended contractual arrangements depends upon relative bargaining positions. If demand is weak or the buyer possesses great economic leverage, sellers may be forced to absorb much of the risk of increased costs. Traditionally, periods of substantial inflation have been characterized by brisk rather than weak demand, but since the onset of "stagflation" during the past decade, it is not uncommon to encounter the combination of brisk inflation and weak demand.

Landlords may decide to enter only into short-term leases or month-to-month tenancies. They may well prefer to renegotiate the rent every few months rather than lock themselves into a typical long-term rental arrangement. The effect of this kind of response to inflation is to increase transaction costs substantially. If the parties cannot come to a new agreement each time, the landlord has the additional expenses of reletting the premises, and the tenant has the additional expenses of moving and finding another rental. The insecurity of this kind of arrangement may discourage both landlord and tenant from making any but minimal investment in the leasehold.

The existence of price controls or legal constraints on interest rates may cause certain contracts to disappear entirely. Thus, if enforcement of usury laws prevents lenders from receiving a real rate of return, credit will quickly dry up. If rent control statutes prevent landlords from earning a real rate of return on their investment, the rental market will shrivel. New rental property will not be constructed, and existing structures will be converted into condominiums or cooperatives as quickly as possible.

"GUESSTIMATING" THE INFLATION RATE

Another common response to a surge in the inflation rate is for the parties to build into the contract, either explicitly or implicitly, their best guess as to what the inflation rate will be over the life of the contract. For example, if the parties expect that inflation will be 12 percent annually, a three-year apartment lease may contain a clause providing for a 12 percent increase in the rent after the first year, and an additional 12 percent increase after the second year. Alternatively, the initial rental might be fixed 8 percent higher in the expectation that the inflation rate will average out over the life of the lease. (Neither of these common adjustments, however, actually adjusts for a 12 percent annual inflation rate.)[1] If the parties grossly miscalculate, an attempt is generally made to adjust if there is a renewal.

Both guesstimating the rate of inflation and shunning fixed-price contracts have a number of undesirable features. The chances of correctly predicting the inflation rate are not especially good. Even if the inflation rate is correctly predicted by both parties, the adjustment figure tacked onto the price is likely to be erroneous. Moreover, there is a tendency of the party with the greater leverage to tack on something extra, a practice which, taken in the aggregate, is likely to exacerbate existing inflationary pressures. Most people like to know how much something is going to cost before they order. If all future price increases are shifted to the buyer, he is likely to have justifiable concern about the seller's honesty, or at least as to how much effort the seller will make to keep future cost increases to a minimum. Consequently, where not prohibited by law, most parties prefer to maintain the real economic value of their contracts by inserting stabilization clauses.

STABILIZATION CLAUSES

Stabilization clauses, which date back at least to the Middle Ages,[2] are the most sophisticated method of protecting the real value of the parties' bargain from changes in the value of money. All stabilization clauses can be regarded as commodity clauses in the sense that they tie the underlying value of an obligation to the price of a commodity or group of commodities rather than to money. Nevertheless, it is useful for analytical purposes to break these clauses down into four categories: (1) commodity clauses, (2) gold and silver clauses, (3) foreign money clauses, and (4) index clauses.

Commodity Clauses

The simplest technique for insulating an agreement from the operation of the nominalist principle is by using commodities as both a measure of value and a means of payment. Rental of farmland on a sharecropping basis is a common form of such an arrangement. Because the ultimate value of the lease or rental varies with the yield and the market price for the commodities produced, both parties share all risk of a change in the value of money inhering in the transaction.

A second type of commodities clause, the commodity-index clause, utilizes the price of a commodity or group of commodities only as a measure of value. The means of payment is normally currency.[3] Commodities such as wheat, corn, rye, and barley have long been used to stabilize the value of pecuniary obligations. Perhaps the most extensive use of commodity clauses occurred in Germany during the highly inflationary period between 1918 and 1923, when many German corporations issued bonds indexed to the price of rye or coal. Emergency legislation was adopted during this period permitting indexing of the amount of mortgage debts to the price of rye, wheat, potash, or coal. "Rye mortgage bonds," issued by financial institutions to obtain funds to relend on "rye mortgages," became a popular form of financing.[4] Commodity clauses linked only to the economic activity of the debtor have sometimes been utilized in long-term bonds. This practice has become relatively common in Israel and France, and is detailed in chapter 6 *infra.*

The commodity clause is generally only a crude maintenance of value device, for the price of a given commodity is subject to volatile fluctuations which may have nothing to do with the purchasing power of money. No single or small group of commodities is an adequate proxy for a general price index, though wheat has come surprisingly close in a number of years.[5] The German rye bonds proved to be an inadequate device to protect creditors from monetary depreciation. Dates had to be fixed well in advance of maturity in order to collect the data on rye prices necessary to calculate amounts due on the bonds, and the courts held that average prices over a given period should be used rather than the price on a particular day. Given the rapidity of the mark's depreciation, the effect of shifting the date of calculation backwards was to reduce the value of the creditor's claim to a small fraction of the actual gold value of the stipulated quantity of rye on the maturity date. Eventually, rye bonds and mortgages were transformed into gold-mark mortgages.[6]

Contracts that utilize commodities both as the means of payment and the measure of value have been universally upheld in the courts, unless the stipulated commodities happen to be gold, silver, or foreign money. Courts in some countries, however, particularly France, have sometimes invalidated commodity-index clauses in agreements where money was the means of payment on the dubious theories that such clauses violate the nominalist principle, legal tender laws, usury laws, or public policy. Consideration of these cases will be deferred until pp. 142–45, *infra.* Gold and silver clauses, which analytically might well be treated as commodity clauses, present special problems and will be taken up next.

Gold Clauses

As pointed out in chapter 3, people have been accustomed, until recently, to thinking about the value of money in metallic terms. The value of a coin was the quantity and fineness of gold or silver it contained; the value of a bank note was equal to the amount of gold or silver to which it could be converted. Although the value of gold and silver fluctuated with supply and demand, the fluctuations were generally so mild that most people scarcely perceived them. Hence, gold or silver clauses were the most common form of protecting creditors from the risk of monetary depreciation. Such clauses were particularly popular in France and the United States, where memories of depreciated currencies, such as *assignats, mandats,* continentals, greenbacks, and Confederate dollars were deeply etched in national consciousness.[7]

Types of Gold Clauses

At least three types of gold or silver clauses were in vogue prior to the 1930s. The most common was the gold or silver coin clause, which required that the sum owed be paid in specified gold or silver coins. Typically, such a clause would spell out both the type of coin and the quantity of gold or silver it contained, such as "fifteen pounds current money of Maryland, payable in English golden guineas weighing five pennyweights and six grains, at thirty-five shillings each. . . ."[8] A second type of gold or silver clause often used was the gold or silver value clause, which required payment of a sum of money equal to the value of a specified quantity of gold or silver. Seldom were such clauses employed alone; generally they were linked in the alternative to a gold or silver coin clause, such as a promise to pay a given sum in gold or silver coin or its equivalent value.[9] The third type of clause was the gold or silver bullion clause, which called for payment of a determined weight and fineness of gold or silver. Occasionally, lawyers linked all three types of clauses, such as an 1894 lease that stipulated payment of "a quantity of gold which shall be equal in amount to fifteen hundred ($1500) dollars of the gold coin of the United States of the standard of weight and fineness of the year 1894, or the equivalent of this commodity in United States currency."[10]

From time to time courts have been willing to imply a gold or silver clause in the process of construing contracts in accordance with the probable intention of the parties. In one of the early leading American cases on specific performance, *Willard v. Tayloe,*[11] the defendant leased a building in 1854 for ten years with an option to buy at a price of $22,500. At the time of the lease, only gold and silver coin were legal tender. In 1864, when the plaintiff sought to exercise his option, inconvertible paper money ("greenbacks") had been declared legal tender at a par with gold or silver dollars. Despite such legislation, about $1.80 in paper money was required to purchase a gold dollar. Although the lease did not expressly require payment in gold or silver coin, the U.S. Supreme Court found that the parties could only have contemplated payment in gold or silver dollars;

accordingly, it conditioned its decree of specific performance upon tendering of the purchase price in gold or silver coin. But such cases are rare. Most courts have declined to find tacit gold clauses in contracts irrespective of the probable intention of the parties.[12] There are also a number of cases in which courts have refused to find that a gold clause was intended, despite contractual language strongly suggestive of such an intention.[13]

Legal Obstacles to Gold Clauses

With the introduction of paper money as compulsory legal tender, both courts and legislatures displayed considerable hostility towards gold clauses. In some countries, such as the United States and France, courts declared gold clauses invalid because of a conflict with legal tender laws.[14] In the United States this line of cases, decided by state supreme courts, was overturned in 1869 by the U.S. Supreme Court in *Bronson v. Rodes,* [15] which denied any inconsistency between the principle of legal tender and gold clauses. A similar conclusion was reached by the highest courts of of Argentina, Chile, Great Britain, and Switzerland.[16] On the other hand, the French *Cour de Cassation* for more than eighty years adhered to its position that the principle of *cours forcé* (domestically inconvertible legal tender) invalidated all gold clauses except in contracts involving international payments.[17] The reasoning of the French cases was summarized in these terms by a leading French commentator: "[Gold clauses] in effect tend to conflict with the law on *cours forcé,* a law of *ordre public* [an analogue to, though somewhat broader than, the Anglo-American concept of public policy], by virtue of which paper-francs are deemed to have the same value as gold-francs, even though paper-francs are no longer being exchanged for gold-francs."[18] The Belgian courts have followed this doctrine laid down by the French courts with regard to gold coin clauses,[19] though they have declined to follow the French courts' extension of that doctrine to invalidate gold value, index, and foreign money clauses.[20] Not until 1957, in the celebrated case of *Guyot v. Praquin,* [21] did the French *Cour de Cassation* reverse this long line of cases. In the process of upholding a loan of 350,000 francs indexed to the price of wheat, the court categorically rejected the argument that *ordre public* and the laws establishing *cours forcé* required invalidation of stabilization clauses. In 1962 the *Cour de Cassation*, pushing its reasoning in the *Guyot* case to its logical conclusion, sustained, for the first time since the introduction of *cours forcé,* a gold value clause in a purely domestic contract.[22]

So long as countries were on the gold standard, creditors cared little about whether they were paid in gold coins or paper currency freely convertible into gold. But during monetary crises, when gold coin disappeared and free convertibility was suspended, it mattered a great deal to creditors that they were paid either in gold coin or inconvertible paper currency. In several countries, courts nullified gold coin clauses by refusing to construe them as gold value clauses when gold coin became unavailable.[23] Such construction, which was rejected in most countries,[24] made no sense, for a gold coin clause became relevant only when the debtor had a juridical excuse for not paying in gold coin, such as the law's making nonconvertible paper money legal tender.

During the monetary crises stemming from World War I and the Great Depression of the 1930s, a great many countries enacted legislation abrogating or restricting the use of gold clauses.[25] One of the most celebrated of these enactments was the 1933 Joint Resolution of the U.S. Congress:

> That . . . every provision . . . which purports to give the obligee a right to require payment in gold or a particular kind of currency, or in amount in money of the United States measured thereby, is . . . against public policy. . . . Every obligation, heretofore or hereinafter incurred, whether or not any such provision is contained therein or made with respect thereto, shall be discharged upon payment, dollar for dollar, in any coin or currency which at the time of payment is legal tender for public and private debts.[26]

Subsequent legislation provided for melting down all existing gold coin and prohibited private ownership and dealings in gold.[27] The constitutionality of the Joint Resolution was upheld, though barely, in a series of Supreme Court decisions,[28] thereby ending the widespread use of gold coin and gold value clauses in the United States. Gold bullion clauses theoretically remained unaffected by the Joint Resolution,[29] but legislation restricting the ability of Americans to hold gold and the real possibility that such clauses would be construed by the courts as gold value clauses[30] meant their virtual disappearance from use.

The ban on gold ownership and the use of gold clauses in the United States has recently been lifted. On December 31, 1974, Americans regained the right to hold and deal in gold. Although neither the legislation removing the restrictions on private gold ownership nor its legislative history makes direct mention of gold clauses or the Joint Resolution, the statute states: "No provision of any law in effect at the date of enactment of this Act, and no rule, regulation, or order under authority of any such law, may be construed to prohibit any person from purchasing, holding, selling, *or otherwise dealing with gold* in the United States or abroad" [emphasis added]."[31] The argument that Congress impliedly repealed the Joint Resolution's invalidation of gold clauses by the phrase *otherwise dealing in gold* has been rejected in three recent cases involving attempts to enforce gold clauses in pre-1933 bonds or leases.[32] Congress has, however, recently enacted legislation that the Joint Resolution inapplicable to obligations issued on or after October 28, 1977,[33] thereby making it possible for prospective obligations governed by U.S. law to contain enforceable gold clauses.

The use of gold clauses in France has been severely circumscribed by legislation enacted in 1958 and 1959 as part of De Gaulle's program to stabilize the franc. This legislation, which is discussed in more detail in the next section, prohibits all "contractual provisions resulting in indexation based upon . . . the price of goods, products or services not having a direct relation to the object . . . of the contract or with the activity of one of the parties. . . ."[34] Unless one of the parties is a jeweler or dentist, it is difficult to contend that a gold clause is directly related to the object of the contract or the economic activity of one of the parties.[35] One respected French commentator has argued, however, that gold clauses should be valid in contracts to which a banker is a party, for a banker trades in gold.[36] The case law is presently unclear about the present validity of gold clauses in domestic transactions, though they would appear to be valid in international contracts.[37]

Beginning in 1949, West Germany adopted the policy of requiring approval of the Deutsche Bundesbank to validate stabilization clauses for money debts payable in German marks.[38] Agreements will not be approved if the amount owed is tied to the future price of gold.

It presently makes little sense to prohibit gold clauses. Of course, gold clauses have themselves become anachronisms except for dentists, jewelers, or industrial users of gold. Even prior to demonetization, gold had become a highly speculative commodity. Today its price swings widely on commodity markets for reasons that are frequently unrelated to the real purchasing power of national currency units.

Although gold clauses have practically disappeared in most countries,[39] they remain important in international conventions, where they have been a favorite technique for maintaining the real economic value of damage limitation provisions. International aspects of gold clauses are explored in chapter 8, *infra.*

Foreign Currency Clauses

Another stabilization device commonly employed in countries suffering from severe inflation is requiring payment in a "hard" (relatively stable) foreign currency. The foreign currency may serve as the unit of account or the unit of payment. For example, a Chilean landlord might insist on a lease that required the tenant to pay a monthly rental of U.S. $100, in which case the U.S. dollar would be both the unit of account and the unit of payment. Alternatively, the lease might stipulate that the rental will be $100 U.S. per month, payable in Chilean pesos at the official exchange rate in force at the first day of each month, in which case the U.S. dollar would be the unit of account and the Chilean peso the unit of payment. Unless there is a black market for U.S. currency, the economic effect of both versions of the foreign currency clause should be identical.

There are a number of variations of the foreign currency clause. A common one is the multiple currency clause, which gives the creditor the option of demanding repayment in one of several currencies. Another variation is a composite arrangement, such as the European Unit of Account or the European Composite Unit, in which the amount to be repaid varies in accordance with exchange rate fluctuations in a group of linked currencies. Such maintenance-of-value arrangements in international transactions are examined in greater detail in chapter 8, *infra.*

Legal Obstacles to Foreign Currency Clauses

Generally speaking, foreign currency clauses have been upheld in international contracts.[40] Most countries also permit such clauses in purely domestic transactions.[41] Another group of countries, albeit a minority, bars or severely restricts the use of foreign currency clauses in domestic contracts. The latter group includes Brazil, Colombia, Costa Rica, Mexico, West Germany, the Netherlands, Peru, and Poland, all of which have specific legislation regulating the use of foreign currency clauses.[42] For example, Brazilian law declares null and void all obligations to be performed in Brazil that stipulate payment in gold or foreign currency except for: (a) import or export contracts, (b) financing agreements for export of Brazilian goods, (c) contracts for the buying or selling of foreign exchange, and (d) contracts where neither the debtor not the creditor is a Brazilian resident or domiciliary, unless the contract involves a lease of real property situated in Brazil.[43]

The French courts took it upon themselves to invalidate contracts with foreign currency clauses on the dubious theory that such clauses conflicted with the principle of *cours forcé,*[44] but the French courts upheld foreign currency clauses in international payments, a concept that French case law has expanded to include several instances of what most countries would regard as domestic contracts, such as contracts involving the resale of imported goods where both parties are French nationals.[45] Since the *Cour de Cassation's* about-face on index clauses,[46] French courts have been sustaining foreign currency clauses, irrespective of international character, in contracts entered into prior to 1958;[47] however, post-1958 domestic contracts that would appear to be valid only if they have "a direct relation to the object . . . of the contract or with an activity of one of the parties. . . ."[48] Whether international contracts will have to meet this vague direct relation test is not yet clear.[49]

The Deutsche Bundesbank categorically refuses to approve foreign currency clauses in which the mark is the unit of payment in leases with a term of less than ten years and loans or other financial transactions. The only types of contracts in which foreign currency may serve as a unit of account if the unit of payment is the mark are those connected with imports and exports or maritime matters.[50]

Before the recent modification of the U.S. Joint Resolution, multiple currency clauses that included the U.S. dollar as a possible currency of payment were invalid in the United States.[51] On the other hand, multiple currency clauses in which the U.S. dollar was not a currency of payment have been honored by the U.S. courts.[52] Multiple currency clauses contained in obligations issued on or after October 28, 1977 are enforceable in the United States even if the U.S. dollar is one of the currencies of payment.[53]

Usefulness in Protecting against Inflation

Foreign currency clauses are a convenient technique for shifting exchange risks in international transactions, but they are far from ideal devices for protecting domestic contracts against inflation. Although the dollar might appear stable to a landlord in Chile, whose peso declined staggeringly vis-à-vis the dollar between 1971 and 1977,[54] the purchasing power of the dollar declined by approximately 50 percent during that same period. A foreign currency clause offers no protection against inflation in the "hard" currency country. Moreover, as has been previously indicated, in the short run countries can delay devaluation despite substantial inflation or devalue by far less than the differential between their inflation rates and those of their customary trading partners.[55] When this occurs, as it commonly does, a creditor who relies on a foreign currency clause for inflation protection will be sorely disappointed if exchange controls prevent him from converting the soft currency payment into hard currency, or economic commitments require him to expend the soft currency. Irrespective of the creditor's situation, maintenance of an overvalued exchange rate subsidizes a country's borrowers of foreign currency or those whose debts are indexed to foreign currency exchange rates. Conversely, when the foreign exchange rate declines faster than the domestic inflation rate, as happened in Germany during the early 1920s, the creditor with a foreign currency clause reaps a windfall at the debtor's expense.

Index Clauses

The most effective way for most contracting parties to protect themselves against inflation is by linking the value of their bargain to a broadly based price index, such as the consumer or wholesale price index, or the implicit

GNP deflator. Because such indexes vary more or less with the purchasing power of money, such clauses are far better tailored to inflation-proofing contracts than commodity, gold, or foreign money clauses. Since the development of sophisticated price indexes, index clauses (also referred to as escalator, sliding-scale, monetary correction, or cost-of-living clauses) have become enormously popular during periods of monetary instability.

The origins of the index clause can be traced back at least to 1707 when William Fleetwood, a Cambridge don, monetarily corrected the amount of outside income college fellows were allowed to earn by calculating price changes over six hundred years.[56] The colony of Massachusetts, in 1777, paid its soldiers in special notes whose value varied in accordance with crude standards of purchasing power.[57] Shortly after the American and French Revolutions, attempts were made to adjust debt values in accordance with changes in prices of basic commodities,[58] but, as Arnold Wald has observed, "The real and practical importance of [index] clauses dates from the twentieth century and is linked to the monetary depreciation which followed the First World War."[59]

Uses of Index Clauses

The most common contractual use of index clauses is in collective bargaining agreements. Particularly during periods of substantial inflation, collective labor contracts, as well as governmental determinations of wages and pensions, are likely to be indexed. The indexing format, however, varies widely. In Belgium, Canada, Chile, Israel, Luxembourg, New Zealand, Switzerland, Great Britain, and the United States, wage agreements are usually indexed to the consumer price index.[60] In Denmark, a "wage-regularization" index is used; this index differs from the regular consumer price index in weighting, in its inclusion of public subsidies, and its reflection of the average wages of the preceding quarter.[61] In Austria, France, and the Netherlands the average wage is widely used for indexing.[62]

There is enormous variation in the formats used for wage indexation. Some index clauses adjust wages by only a percentage of the increase in the relevant price index; others adjust by the entire percentage increase, and occasionally by more than the entire percentage increase. Some indexation schemes require a minimum rise in the relevant price index to trigger a wage increase. Ceilings or caps limiting the maximum amount of indexation are a common feature in some countries. *Ex ante* indexing is commonly employed in several European countries; after the index rises by a predetermined amount, wages either go up by a predetermined amount, or a new contract must be negotiated.[63]

In the United States, the most common form of escalator clause in collective bargaining agreements calls for a one cent rise in hourly wages for 0.3 point increase in the consumer price index. This formula has the virtue of being easy to apply and understand, but it accords lower paid workers higher percentage cost-of-living adjustments. Moreover, as the consumer price index rises, each 1 percent increase in the inflation rate produces a greater numerical rise in the index. Most U.S. workers are receiving only partial inflation protection from escalator clauses; in 1979 cost-of-living clauses boosted the wages of the average worker covered by such clauses by only 51 percent of the increase in the consumer price index.[64]

Wage indexation in Europe is most widespread in Italy, which has had a somewhat unique system. A portion of an employee's wage, known as the cost-of-living allowance, is adjusted quarterly in accordance with changes in a special index, called "the consumer price index for wage earners' and salaried employees' families." If this index number rises by at least one point during a given quarter (or falls by at least one point in each of two consecutive quarters), the cost-of-living allowance is adjusted by multiplying the numerical change in the index by a lire figure whose amount varies with occupational groups and family status of the employee.

A particular difficulty with this form of indexing was that the value of a one point rise in the index, which was based upon the year 1956, had been steadily diminishing as the index numbers mounted.[65] Moreover, because only a fraction of each worker's total wages was indexed, each wage increase meant that a smaller fraction of total wages was indexed. Consequently, indexing was gradually losing its effectiveness as a device for ensuring that wages were being protected from inflationary erosion.

The Italian system of wage indexation was substantially reformed in January 1975. The index base was changed so that the August-October quarter of 1974 became 100 instead of 252 on the 1956 base. This had the effect of increasing the value of each point by a factor of 2.52. Instead of multiplying the numerical change in the index by an amount that varied with occupational groups, the indexing system shifted in successive stages to multiplication by a single value—the lire amount applied to the top category of employees. This modification has the effect of equalizing wage increases between top and bottom wage earners, but it will also have the decidedly inflationary effect of increasing average wages by more than the increase in the cost of living.[66]

In November 1979 Brazil adopted a similar wage indexation law, designed to use inflation to redistribute income from higher to lower wage earners.[67] Those earning up to three multiples of the minimum wage have their wages automatically readjusted each six months by 110 percent of the increase in the consumer price index. Those earning between 3 and 10 multiples of the minimum wage receive 100 percent of the increase in the index, and those earning more than 10 multiples of the minimum wage receive only 80 percent of the increase. The formula was modified in November 1980 to free employees earning more than twenty multiples of the minimum wage to negotiate increases directly with management, and to reduce the mandatory wage hikes for those earning between fifteen and twenty multiples of the minimum wage from 80 percent of the increase in the consumer price index to 50 percent. The inflation adjustment is determined by a new National Consumer Price Index prepared by weighting preexisting consumer price indexes for Brazil's principal cities. Productivity increases have been left to collective bargaining and the labor courts. This wage policy has been subjected to a great deal of criticism in Brazil. Some is directed to its unfairness to highly skilled workers; some is directed to the inflationary pressure resulting from raising real wages of the great bulk of the labor in excess of productivity growth.

Indexation is commonly used in a variety of other kinds of legal transactions in inflationary economies. It is an integral feature of credit transactions, insurance, pensions, and social security benefits, which are treated in greater detail in chapter 6, *infra.* It is also an important component of income taxation in many countries, a development treated in detail in chapter 9, *infra.* Finally, the overall implications of indexation are explored in chapter 10, *infra.*

Legal Obstacles to Index Clauses

Unless prohibited by specific legislation, index clauses are generally considered valid and enforceable. The High Court of Australia stated in upholding an index clause in a domestic contract: "There is no principle of law preventing parties adopting a fixed figure as the primary monetary expression of a liability and then proceeding to effect a substantive variation of the liability by providing that more or less money must be actually paid according as index numbers evidence a variation of price levels. That is only a method of measuring the actual liability contracted for."[68] Nevertheless, a number of courts and commentators have been hostile towards index clauses. The reasons underlying this hostility would appear to be the fear that index clauses exacerbate inflationary pressures, impose inequitable burdens on certain debtors, and unfairly allow a few societal members to avoid paying the implicit tax levied upon society through the mechanism of inflation.[69]

The Confused French Experience

The invalidity of index clauses because of the nominalist principle, legal tender laws, or public policy was most frequently asserted in France, the country with by far the most confusing (and confused) case law, doctrine, and legislation concerning this subject.[70] Between 1939 and 1957 many French cases struck down both commodity-index and index clauses, particularly those in money loans indexed to the consumer or wholesale price index, or the minimum wage. One theory for doing so was that the principle of nominalism, embodied in Article 1895 of the Civil Code,[71] was *jus cogens* and had a public law character; therefore, it could not be defeated by private contract. The Court of Lyon succinctly articulated this rationale, albeit in conclusory rather than analytical terms: "This provision [Article 1895], which embodies less a rule of private law than a principle of monetary law, shares the latter's character [as a norm] of internal *ordre public.* Inspired by the desire to maintain one of the essential functions of the currency, this *article is imperative.* The terms used in the article clearly convey the will of the legislator in this respect. Any clause which, either directly or indirectly, impairs this article is null. . . ."[72] By this kind of interpretive alchemy, a provision designed to avoid judicial revision of a contract when the parties failed to provide for such revision was converted into a principle of public policy whose invisible radiations mandated judicial invalidation of contracts where the parties had themselves agreed to price revision. It is most unlikely that the drafters of the Civil Code intended Article 1895 to bar index clauses, particularly when one considers Articles 1896 and 1897, which expressly permit gold clauses and commodity clauses.[73]

A more commonly utilized theory for invalidating index clauses has been a perceived conflict with the principle of *cours forcé.* Cases resting on this theory seldom contained an explanation of why such a conflict exists, but the underlying reasoning would appear to be that indexes such as the consumer or wholesale price index actually measure fluctuations in the value of money; therefore, their use in pecuniary obligations prevents the franc from having the value obligatorily attributed to it by the legislature.[74] But not all index clauses were deemed to undermine the franc as inconvertible legal tender. The doctrine and cases differentiated between index clauses with a monetary character and those with an economic character; the former were unlawful, while the latter were valid. The proper characterization of an index clause as monetary or economic was deemed to turn on whether the parties intended to protect themselves against monetary depreciation.[75] Because virtually all index clauses, especially in monetary loans, are designed to protect the creditor against the consequences of monetary depreciation, the French cases in this area read like something out of the theater of the absurd. They turn on such bizarre criteria as whether the court could find some language in the contract indicative of an intent to speculate against the currency, whether the parties were friends, whether the reference index bore a direct relationship to the common economic sphere of either the lender or the borrower, or the use to which the borrowed funds were put.[76]

The French decisions were about evenly divided prior to 1957,[77] when the *Cour de Cassation* untangled this snarl of case law in its celebrated decision in *Guyot v. Praquin.*[78] Ignoring the argument of the procurator general, who contended that commodity-index clauses contravened public policy, the First Civil Chamber of France's highest court sustained a loan of 350,000 francs indexed to the price of wheat. The court's opinion went far beyond merely upholding commodity-index clauses. It included the following forthright rejection of the doctrinal positions that had been used to invalidate all types of index clauses:

> . . . [P]ublic policy does not require, in the lending of money, protection of borrowers from their free acceptance of the risk that the sum to be paid back may increase, in order to ensure that the purchasing power of the sum lent, will be maintained in terms of the cost of a specified commodity. . . . One can no longer pretend to justify the imperative nature of [Art. 1895 of the Civil Code] by principles of monetary policy, which should be imposed because of the danger these clauses pose to monetary stability. The inflationary effect of these clauses appears too uncertain to justify their nullification, which would be a severe threat to the security of savings and credit. Characterizing this article as imperative is inconsistent with the provisions of Article 1897, dealing with loans of goods. If the price of the goods borrowed increases for any reason, Article 1897 places the risk of that increase on the borrower in all cases. Nor does the nullity of the clause being litigated result from monetary legislation now in force, for none of this legislation implies the invariability of the purchasing power of money, which varies in accordance with the price of goods. None of this legislation prohibits lenders of money, any more than it does other types of creditors, from taking into account changes in purchasing power.[79]

Unfortunately, the doctrinal waters that had finally been cleared in the *Guyot* case were quickly muddied by the De Gaulle regime, which regarded index clauses as a threat to the stability of the franc. At the end of 1958, as part of a comprehensive financial and monetary reform program, a decree was enacted that severely restricted the use of index clauses. As amended in February of 1959, the decree provides:

> 1. All general regulations, whether legislative or administrative, providing for the automatic indexation of the price of goods or services, are hereby abrogated. . . .
>
> 2. Nevertheless, Article 31xa of the Labor Code regarding indexation of the minimum guaranteed interoccupational wage (SMIG) shall remain in force.
>
> 3. Hereafter, no contractual or collective bargaining agreement resulting in indexation based upon the . . . [SMIG] or upon the general level of prices or salaries, or upon the price of goods, products or services which bears no direct relation to the object of the collective

> agreement or contract or to the activity of one of the parties, shall be lawful, except for those provisions relating to personal support or maintenance.
>
> With respect to collective or contractual provisions presently in effect, those authorizing the kind of indexation prohibited above shall be ineffective beyond the level reached at the time of the last adjustment prior to December 31, 1958, in all bilateral contracts involving the continuing performance of reciprocal obligations.[80]

This poorly conceived and badly drafted piece of legislation was primarily aimed at the elimination of escalator clauses in wage agreements and agricultural prices, but its language was broad enough to reach virtually all index clauses. It also curtailed a substantial number of prior statutes and decrees explicitly authorizing or mandating indexation of certain kinds of contracts.[81] Solicitude for the debtor whose income may not keep pace with the rate of indexation would explain barring index clauses that bore no direct relationship to the debtor's economic activity, but by also permitting index clauses linked to the creditor's economic activity, the legislature undercut this rationale. The validity of a few types of indexation, such as agricultural rents with commodities as the unit of account and currency as the unit of payment,[82] indexed lifetime annuities settled between individuals,[83] and linking of residential construction costs to the national index of the cost of construction,[84] has been specifically reaffirmed by subsequent statutes.

The legality of other types of indexation depends on whether the indexing device chosen bears a direct relation to the object of the contract or to the activity of one of the parties to the contract. Initially, the French courts were reluctant to sustain an index clause as directly related to the object of the contract.[85] In recent years, however, the French courts have become far more liberal in sustaining index clauses on the theory they are directly related to the contract's object.[86] A similar liberalizing case law evolution has occurred sustaining index clauses on the theory that they are directly related to the economic activity of one of the parties.[87]

Other countries outside the Communist bloc that have legislatively restricted the use of index clauses include Belgium, Brazil, Chile, Finland, Greece, and West Germany. Virtually all index clauses have been banned in Greece and Finland. Germany has restricted index clauses to certain narrowly defined circumstances. Belgium has recently restricted index clauses in commercial and industrial sales contracts to 80 percent of the real increase in the seller's costs. Brazil, where indexation has become a way of life, has required that index clauses be tied to a single official index. Chile, where indexation has also become a way of life, has prohibited indexation of short-term credit transactions.

The Finnish and Greek Bans

Indexation was widespread in Finland until 1968, when the Economic Special Powers Act banned the use of index clauses in loans, savings deposits, rental contracts and leases, wage agreements, and domestic contracts for the sale or delivery of goods. Insurance policies, pensions, and preexisting bonds were excepted from the ban. The ban on index clauses in Finland was motivated by fear that the increase in import prices resulting from a 24 percent exchange rate devaluation would set off an inflationary spiral propagated through the extensive index linkages. Legal restrictions on indexation have been gradually relaxed to permit their use in long-term leases and construction contracts.[88]

Greece, which experienced hyperinflation after World War II, banned all index clauses in 1945. The ban does not, however, extend to commodity clauses.[89]

West Germany's Prior Restraint

The West German Currency Law prohibits all clauses in which the value of a sum stated in German marks is tied to another currency, to the price or quantity of gold, or to the future price of other goods or services, without the authorization of the Bundesbank.[90] The guidelines published by the Bundesbank provide that index clauses will not be approved in any loan transactions; nor will they be approved in lease agreements for a term shorter than ten years or the life of the lessor. Irrespective of the type of contract, index clauses will not be approved if:

(*a*) they do not provide for the possibility of price decreases;
(*b*) they do not clearly set out the index or prices to which the adjustment is tied;
(*c*) the index is the future price of gold;
(*d*) they are tied to the cost-of-living index, except for annuities or recurring payments to be made either until the recipient can become gainfully employed or reaches a specific educational goal, or which exceed a ten-year period;
(*e*) they are tied to individual or average wages or pensions, except for annuities, or recurring payments to be made either until the recipient can become gainfully employed or reaches a specific educational goal, or where the changes in the wages or salaries exercise a material influence on the creditor's costs; or
(*f*) they are linked to a future price or value of other dissimilar goods and services (i.e., a general price index) except when the amount owed is dependent upon the movement of prices of goods or services which are produced, sold or rendered by the debtor, or materially influence the cost incurred by the creditor.[91]

The German courts have provided lawyers with fairly easy techniques for avoiding the requirement of prior approval by the Bundesbank. They have held that Article 3 of the Currency Law does not apply to contracts that require an equitable adjustment of wages or rents in the event of increases in the cost of living, or to loan agreements where the borrower agrees to repay a determined quantity of marks or the price of a quantity of wheat, whichever is higher.[92] The number of permits granted by the Bundesbank has been steadily increasing, rising from 7,122 out of 10,485 applications in 1960 to 24,999 out of 33,796 applications in 1970.[93]

Belgium's 80 Percent Constraint

Concern about potential inflationary feedback from indexation led Belgium in 1976 to enact a statute placing a curious ceiling upon price readjustments from index clauses.[94] As of March 30, 1976, no contract for the sale of an industrial or commercial product or service may be indexed to a general price index. The only price revision clauses valid in Belgium in industrial and commercial contracts are those by which the seller passes on to the buyer actual cost increases. Moreover, the seller cannot use such clauses to pass through more than 80 percent of his actual cost increases.[95] In December 1976, Belgium also passed a statute prohibiting salaries and wages from escalating faster in 1977 than the cost of living index.[96]

Brazil's Effort to Standardize the Index

Brazil, which has become concerned about the inflationary feedback effects of its widespread system of monetary correction, enacted a law in June 1977 restricting the indexation of practically all pecuniary obligations to the changes in the value of Readjustable Treasury Bonds (ORTNs).[97] Although readjustment of ORTNs is supposedly based upon changes in the whole wholesale price index, manipulation of the adjustment mechanism in recent years has kept the rate of increase in the value of these bonds well below that of the wholesale price index.[98]

Between January and November of 1980 Brazil temporarily abandoned the concept of *ex post* monetary correction. ORTNs were readjusted two months in advance in accordance with a presumed rate of inflation, set at 45 percent for the entire year of 1980. This prefixed monetary correction rate was subsequently raised to 50 percent on a June-to-June basis in the wake of an inflation rate that rose by nearly 100 percent between June of 1979 and June of 1980. Because Brazilian law requires virtually all monetary correction in private contracts, with the significant exception of wage agreements, be linked to the rate of adjustment of ORTNs, this meant that Brazil had effectively banned the use of all *ex post* index clauses. In November 1980 the government conceded that this policy had been a failure and had significantly lowered the savings rate; it therefore reverted to complete *ex ante* indexing of the ORTN. One important change in the nature of the indexing is that instead of its former link to the wholesale price index, the ORTN is now linked to the national consumer price index used for wage indexing.

Chile's Ban on Short-Term Loan Indexation

Faced with a soaring inflation rate, the Chilean military government in 1974 enacted legislation which is Janus-faced with respect to nominalism. Decree-Law No. 455 of May 25, 1974 expressly repealed Civil Code Article 2199, a provision explicitly adopting the nominalist principle but permitting the use of index clauses.[99] Instead, on the one hand, Decree-Law No. 455 expressly prohibits the use of index clauses in all credit transactions with a term of less than one year (reduced to three months in 1976) and in all obligations where the unit of account is foreign currency.[100] On the other hand, all medium and long-term credit transactions are to be indexed automatically, in accordance with variations in the consumer price index, unless the parties have explicitly stipulated to the contrary.[101] Because this decree-law also frees interest rates from nominalist usury constraints,[102] short-term lenders are free to build inflationary expectations into interest rates.

Miscellaneous Judicial Decisions

In addition, there have been isolated cases in which misguided courts of other countries have invalidated index clauses because of perceived conflicts with currency statutes. In 1953 the Argentine Supreme Court invalidated a clause in a lease which stipulated that if the value of the peso declined by more than 40 percent during the life of the lease, the lessor was entitled to secure an equivalent readjustment in the rent.[103] The court concluded that the invalidated clause undermined the legal tender statute by interfering with the statute's prefixing of the value of money. The logic of this decision is difficult to grasp, and it has been subjected to severe criticism by commentators.[104] It has not been followed by the Argentine courts,[105] and by 1964 was dismissed by one Argentine jurist as "an isolated and obsolete precedent."[106]

For forty-two years it had simply been assumed that there was no conflict between index clauses and the U. S. Joint Resolution of 1933, the so-called Gold Clause Resolution.[107] But in 1975 in *Aztec Prop. v. Union Planters Nat. Bank,*[108] the Supreme Court of Tennessee achieved the dubious distinction of being the first American court to discover that such a conflict existed. In striking down a clause in a $50,000 bank loan whose principal was indexed to the consumer price index, the court held: "It would be contrary to the national policy, as expressed by the Congress and as interpreted in several cases by the United States Supreme Court, to permit a lender to require of a borrower a different quantity or number of dollars from that loaned, insofar as the principal amount is concerned."[109] In support of this proposition, the Tennessee court cited three U.S. Supreme Court cases, none of which as on point: *Guaranty Trust Co. v. Henwood, Norman v. Baltimore & Ohio Ry. Co.*, and *Holyoke Water Power Co. v. American Writing Paper Co.* The first struck down a multiple currency clause where one of the currencies of payment was the dollar; the other two cases involved gold clauses.[110]

There is nothing in the legislative history or the language of the Joint Resolution to support the conclusion that Congress intended to bar index clauses. Given the 24 percent decline in the consumer price index between 1929 and 1933, debtors with obligations indexed to that index would have been far better off than those debtors whose obligations had no such clause. The latter had to discharge their debts in appreciated dollars, giving their creditors a substantial windfall. But Congress had a very different concern—to prevent creditors fortunate enough to have gold clauses from reaping another substantial windfall from devaluation of the dollar with respect to gold.[111]

The language in the Joint Resolution on which the Tennessee court relied was: "Every obligation . . . shall be discharged upon payment, dollar for dollar, in any coin or currency which at the time of payment is legal tender for public and private debts." The court's construction of this sentence is implausible. An obligation to pay a number of dollars multipled by a coefficient derived from a price index is no less dischargeable dollar for dollar than an obligation to pay for a foreign currency futures contract or the cost of a child's college education. The "dollar for dollar" language was inserted at a time when the United States had a currency system divided between gold and paper dollars. Indeed, as set out in the Preamble, a prime purpose of the Joint Resolution was to unify the currency, a goal long since accomplished.

Congress' tacit acceptance for forty-two years of the conventional wisdom that the Joint Resolution was not designed to affect the validity of index clauses, while hardly conclusive, is fairly convincing evidence that the conventional wisdom is correct. As a matter of economic and social policy, it is indefensible for a state court to expand enormously the sweep of an outmoded federal statute by placing on it a novel construction that, if followed by other courts, would have threatened a large number of credit transactions throughout the nation.

Had the Tennessee court simply interpreted the "dollar for dollar" language to invalidate all index clauses, it would have been wrong, but its decision would at least have had the virtue of internal consistency. Instead the court went on to draw an untenable distinction reminiscent of the pre-1957 French index clause cases:

> It is recognized, of course, that "indexing" is a current and very legitimate concept in modern business transactions. Nothing in this opinion should be taken to suggest that there is an impropriety in measuring future rentals by a consumer price index, or some comparable standard, in leasing agreements. Nor is there anything improper in computing future wages or salaries by such an index in collective bargaining or employment contracts. As long as there is a national currency, however, which by law is legal tender for the payment of public and private debts, we hold that the indexing device cannot properly be applied to the principal of a debt evidenced by a promissory note payable in that currency.[112]

By distinguishing between index clauses in loans and in other types of contracts, the court restricted the mischief of its decision, but committed mayhem on its internal logic. As the French experience shows, attempts to differentiate between monetary and economic index clauses lead to absurd results.[113] Moreover, there is nothing in the language of the Joint Resolution or its legislative history that suggests an intent to differentiate between loans and other forms of obligations. Fortunately, the potential for this kind of decision to wreak havoc with contracts is sharply limited by the recent amendment, which makes the Joint Resolution inapplicable to obligations issued on or after October 28, 1977.[114]

There are also occasional Brazilian decisions invalidating index clauses because of an asserted conflict with Decree No. 23.501 of November 27, 1933, Brazil's analogue to the U. S. Gold Clause Resolution. Unlike the U. S. Resolution, the Brazilian decree goes on to nullify every contract to be performed in Brazil "that stipulates payment in money other than by its current legal value."[115] This ambiguous language has been interpreted by some Brazilian jurists as forbidding index clauses unless specifically authorized by the legislature.[116] Because of lingering doubts about the validity of index clauses, the Brazilian military government, which came to power in 1964, felt it necessary to enact laws specifically authorizing the use of index clauses in certain circumstances and under certain conditions.[117] There has never been an across-the-board legalization of index clauses in Brazil, but the case law has come to recognize their validity unless they conflict with a specific legislative norm.[118]

Drafting Index Clauses

There is no "ideal" index clause. Clauses vary considerably, depending upon the skill of the draftsman, the intention and the sophistication of the parties, the type and quality of price indexes available, and the prevailing legal ambience. Some examples of index clauses are included in the Appendixes. Index clauses are not particularly difficult to draft, provided the draftsman has a rudimentary understanding of how price indexes work and anticipates the kinds of problems indexation is likely to generate. If one decides to include an index clause in a contract, the following nine considerations should be borne in mind:

1. The index clause should be kept as simple as possible, especially if any party is relatively unsophisticated. During the 1960s Brazil produced chaos by enacting a statute requiring that residential rents be monetarily corrected in accordance with a mathematical formula so complicated that landlords and tenants had difficulty calculating the rent without the services of a lawyer and an accountant.[119]

2. The index most appropriate to the needs of the parties should be chosen. Most nations publish a broad range of economic indexes, along with numerous subindexes. Which index is most appropriate depends upon which risks the parties wish to shift or hedge by indexing. A lender primarily interested in protecting his capital against monetary depreciation may deem the implicit GNP deflator the most appropriate index because, despite its defects, the GNP deflator is the best yardstick of the purchasing power of money.[120] But the GNP deflator is available only on a quarterly basis after a substantial lag, which may lead a rational lender to opt for the consumer price index. A borrowing company may deem an index that fluctuates in the same manner as the borrower's revenues to be most appropriate. A number of European companies have pushed this thinking a step further and have issued debentures indexed to the price of their products or their net revenues.[121]

An index clause designed to neutralize inflation, such as one tied to the wholesale or consumer price index, may offer scant protection against changes in relative prices. This point was illustrated vividly in *Aluminum Co. of America v. Essex Group, Inc.*,[122] where an elaborate indexation arrangement designed by an eminent economist failed to protect his client against huge cost increases resulting from the soaring price of energy because he had linked the nonlabor cost component to the wholesale price index. Had the court not taken the extraordinary step of reforming the contract on the ground of mutual mistake, his client stood to lose an estimated $75,000,000 in performing the long-term service contract. The draftsman of a long-term requirement or deferred performance contract should be careful to link the price to a specialized index or a component of a general price index that closely reflects price changes in the subject matter of the contract. For example, construction contracts are commonly tied to an index of construction costs, while contracts to deliver metal products are often tied to a specific metals component of the wholesale price index.[123] The more specific or specialized the index, the closer the contract approaches a commodity clause or a price-at-time-of-delivery contract.

The most appropriate index in some contracts may be a compromise between the conflicting interests of the parties. A landlord may wish to index the rent he is charging to the rental component of the consumer price index or to the costs of services he is required to supply to the building; the tenant may be unwilling to agree to commit himself to any rental increase unless his income also rises. The parties may ultimately compromise on the consumer price index or the minimum wage.[124]

3. Care should be taken to insure that the index provision does not produce excessive cost escalation. If the purpose of including an index clause in a supply contract is to reimburse the supplier for his future cost increases, that portion of the purchase price representing the supplier's fixed costs should not be indexed. Similarly, if installment payments are being made, escalation of the portion of the total price represented by such payments should cease, irrespective of the date of shipment or delivery. Unless a buyer is willing to accept blindly the escalating cost figures of his supplier, care should be taken by the buyer's attorney to specify what kinds of substantiation are required for cost increases and whether an audit is necessary.[125]

4. The index or its component should be described with considerable care and specificity. If a contract is linked to the consumer price index, the clause should specify whether the parties intend to use the national version or the index for a particular city or region; the all-items column or a component column; the seasonally adjusted version or the unadjusted version. Particularly when contracting with the federal government, great pains should be taken to spell out precisely the commodity or group of commodities intended to serve as a reference for indexation.[126] The contract should also specify what happens in the event of a change in the index such as a switch to a new base year, new market basket survey, or a cessation of publication.[127] Prudence suggests providing for these contingencies, by stipulation of a substitute index or conversion formula, by designating an impartial third party to choose a new index, or by renegotiating the contract.

5. The manner in which the adjustment is to occur should be drafted with great care. Is the adjustment to be made annually, quarterly, monthly, or only when the index moves by a specified number of points or by a specified percentage? The higher the index number in relation to the base year, the lower the significance in percentage terms of a one point increase. Is the obligation to increase by the entire change in the index, or only a fraction thereof? Is the obligation to decrease if the index falls? Is there to be both a floor and a ceiling to any escalation? In an indexed loan, is interest as well as principal to be adjusted?

6. In some jurisdictions indexed loans may be held to violate usury laws if the stipulated interest and the adjustment exceed the maximum allowable interest rate.[128] In such jurisdictions, the maximum rate compat-

ible with the usury law should be included as a ceiling for any readjustment.

7. Inclusion of an index clause in a negotiable instrument will almost surely destroy its negotiability.[129] If negotiability is an important feature, indexation should be eschewed.

8. In drafting an indexed security agreement by virtue of which certain creditors will be senior lienholders and others junior lienholders, the draftsman should specify whether any increase in the senior lienholders' claims resulting from indexation takes precedence over the junior lienholders' claims.

9. Regardless of how closely the index chosen reflects changes in the currency's purchasing power, an index clause will not completely neutralize the effects of inflation unless it contains a mechanism to compensate for ongoing inflation between adjustment periods. Price indexes record previously experienced price changes; hence, the corrective effect of indexation lags behind actual changes in the purchasing power of money. This is a particularly difficult problem in wage or pension index clauses, for no sooner are wages or pensions restored to a real income peak than inflationary erosion begins converting that peak into a valley. An attempt to avoid this lag in federal civil service and military pensions in the United States by adding a one percent "kicker" recently generated so much controversy that it had to be aborted.[130] In the mid-1960s the Brazilians came up with an approach to adjusting wages that offered, at least in principle, a way to maintain real income stability. Nominal wages were adjusted to compensate for the actual inflation rate in the previous period plus productivity increases and one-half the anticipated inflation rate during the next year. The theory was that during the first six months of the coming year, workers would enjoy an increase in real income. This would gradually disappear because of inflation, so that by the middle of the wage period, real wages would be approximately equal to the average real wage during the previous period, and gradually decline during the final half of the next year.[131]

CONCLUSIONS

Generally, the best way to protect contracts from inflationary distortions is by indexation. Considerable care must be taken, however, in tailoring an index clause to the needs and purposes of the parties. Regardless of how closely the index chosen reflects changes in the currency's purchasing power or changes in the prices of specific goods or services, an index clause will offer incomplete protection against rapid price level changes unless it contains a mechanism to compensate for ongoing inflation between adjustment periods.

Index clauses do not work well for all types of contractual arrangements. Many parties find it difficult to live with contracts where their nominal costs cannot be determined in advance.[132] Borrowers frequently find themselves unable to meet indexed loan obligations during inflation unless their incomes rise at least as fast as their debts. Many may prefer to fix their costs, even if it ultimately costs them more, rather than live with the uncertainty of indexation. Despite the problems index clauses bring, they offer the best way to allocate the risks created by inflation and to protect the economic integrity of contractual bargains in inflationary economies.

NOTES

1. In nominal terms each method would result in a total increment of 24 percent over the life of the lease. But the year-end adjustment method does not adequately compensate for the decrease in purchasing power in each monthly rental payment during the year; it merely restores the initial peak. After the thirteenth month, the landlord will again be receiving less than the initial rental in real terms. Assuming that inflation is spread evenly over the course of the year, the second method will overcompensate the landlord in the first year by 2 percent, and undercompensate him in the remaining two years of the lease.

2. A. Wald, A Cláusula de Escala Móvel 63 (2d ed. 1959); A. Nussbaum, Money in the Law National and International 223 (rev. ed. 1950).

3. Occasionally, a commodity clause in which the stated means of payment is a commodity is actually paid in money. A one thousand year lease entered into in Boston in 1817 for a yearly rental of ten tons of first quality iron has reportedly been paid in the currency value of the requisite quantity of iron. I. Fisher, The Money Illusion 116 (1928).

4. A. Nussbaum, *supra* note 2, at 301. French farmers leasing lands were required by law in 1796 to pay one-fourth of their rent in kind and three-fourths in paper money indexed to the price of wheat. S. Harris, The Assignats 210 (1930). In debates on the drafting of provisions of the United States Constitution protecting judicial independence, James Madison suggested that the salaries of the federal judges be protected from inflation by indexing in accordance with the price of wheat. 2 M. Farrand, The Records of the Federal Convention of 1787, 45 (1911).

5. In G. Warren & F. Pearson, Prices 28 (rev. ed. 1933), Figure 12 graphically depicts the close congruence between wheat and a general commodity index between 1798 and 1932.

6. A. Nussbaum, *supra* note 2, at 301–302.

7. A. Nussbaum, *supra* note 2, at 227.

8. From a 1791 lease cited in Butler v. Horwitz, 74 U.S. (7 Wall.) 258, 259 (1868).

9. Very common in the United States was a clause requiring that payment of principal and interest "will be made . . . in gold coin of the United States of America of or equal to the standard of weight and fineness existing on February 1, 1930." Cited in Norman v. Baltimore & Ohio R. Co., 294 U.S. 240 (1935).

10. Cited in Holyoke Water Power Co. v. American Writing Paper Co., 300 U.S. 324, 333 (1937). *See also* the 1859 lease calling for a yearly rental of "two hundred and sixty ounces troy weight of silver of the standard value and fineness of the silver coin of the United States coinage of the year one thousand eight hundred and fifty-nine, or its equivalent in gold," quoted in Holyoke Water Power Co. v. American Writing Paper Co., 68 F. 2d 261, 262 (1st Cir. 1933).

11. 75 U.S. (8 Wall.) 557 (1868).

12. A. Nussbaum, *supra* note 2, at 238–42; F. Mann, The Legal Aspect of Money 131 (3d ed. 1971).

13. *See* the cases cited and discussed in A. Nussbaum, *supra* note 2, at 243–47; F. Mann, *supra* note 12, at 126–27.

14. All but a handful of the state courts in the United States considering this question between 1863 and 1868 invalidated the gold clause. The cases are collected in Dawson, *The Gold Clause Decisions,* 33 Mich. L. Rev. 647, 674 fn. 54 (1935). The French *Cour de Cassation* held that the legal tender law of 1870 invalidated gold clauses in the celebrated case of Do-Delattre v. Scouteten, Cass. Civ., Feb. 11, 1873, [1873] S. Jur. I, 97; [1873] D.P.I., 177.

15. 74 U.S. (7 Wall.) 229 (1868).

16. Bentivoglio v. Arana de Jordán, L.I., 129 La Ley 779, 1967–VI J.A. 528 (Sup. Ct. Buenos Aires Prov., Argentina 1967); Mujica v. Vergara, 35 R.D.J. 318 (2d part, 1st sec., Sup. Ct. Chile 1938); Feist v. Societé Intercommunale Belge d'Electricité, [1934] A.C. 161 (Eng. House of Lords); 64 BGE II 88 (Swiss Fed. Trib. 1938).

17. A. Nussbaum, *supra* note 2, at 263–66; F. Mann, *supra* note 12, at 151–53. The French doctrine of international payments is discussed at notes 45–49 *infra,* and the accompanying text, and in chap. 8, *infra,* at note 3 and accompanying text.

18. Noirel, *L'Influence de la Dépréciation Monétaire dans les Contrats de Droit Privé,* in Influence de la Dépréciation Monétaire sur la Vie Juridique Privée 69, 118 (P. Durand, ed. 1961).

19. Cass., Je. 12, 1930, [1930] Pas. I, 245; Cass. Apr. 27, 1933 [1933] Pas. I, 208, 60 Clunet 739 (1933).

20. Cass., May 30, 1929, [1929] Pas. I, 206; Cass., May 12, 1932, [1932] Pas. I, 167; Cass., Dec. 1, 1966, Rev. Crit. Juris. Belge 419 (1968). The French cases on index and foreign currency clauses are discussed *infra,* notes 44 to 49 and the accompanying text.

21. Cass. Civ. lre, Je. 27, 1957, [1957] D.Jur. 649; [1957] J.C.P. II, 10093.

22. Rolland v. Fournet, Cass Civ. lre, Dec. 4, 1962, [1963] J.C.P. II, No. 63, 13033. The French high court took the position that the legal tender laws prohibited only payments in gold, and not payments in francs measured by the value of gold. The court summarily dismissed the argument that the nominalist principle of Article 1895 of the Civil Code prohibited the gold-indexed loan on the ground that provision was not *jus cogens* and could, therefore, be supplanted by express contractual stipulation. Both the French and English translation of the case, along with a note on the case by Berthold Goldman, appear in 90 Clunet 750 (1963).

One consequence of the French *Cour de Cassation's* 1957 reversal of prior case law hostility to index clauses was the enactment of legislation in 1958 and 1959 severely limiting the permissible scope of stabilization clauses. Because Rolland v. Fournet involved a loan made in 1952, the court did not consider the impact of the 1958 and 1959 legislation. This legislation is analyzed at pp. 144–45.

23. *See* F. Mann, *supra* note 12, at 153, fn. 5.

24. *Id.* at 153, fn. 6.

25. Countries that restricted gold clauses during and in the wake of World

War I include: Belgium, Bulgaria, Egypt, Germany, Greece, Italy, Romania, Uruguay, and Yugoslavia. Countries restricting gold clauses since 1930 include: Austria, Brazil, Canada, Chile, Costa Rica, Colombia, Cuba, Denmark, Ecuador, Egypt, El Salvador, Estonia, France, Germany, Guatemala, Hungary, Luxembourg, Netherlands, Poland, Sweden, Turkey, Union of South Africa, and the United States. *See* J. REISS, PORTÉE INTERNATIONALE DES LOIS INTERDISANT LA CLAUSE-OR (1936); A. WALD, *supra* note 2, at 65; Nussbaum, *Comparative and International Aspects of American Gold Clause Abrogation,* 44 YALE L. J. 53, 60–61 (1934). The case law rule of the French courts invalidating gold clauses except for international payments was made statutory for a time by the Stabilization Law of June 25, 1928. *Id.* at 61.

There are some important differences in these statutues. Most invalidate only gold clauses in obligations expressed in domestic currency; however, the Canadian Act of April 10, 1937, 1 Geo. 6, c. 33, invalidates all gold clauses, regardless of the currency of account. Most of the statutes apply both prospectively and retrospectively; however, the Belgian Royal Decree of April 11, 1935 and the Netherlands Act of May 24, 1937 do not bar gold clauses agreed to subsequent to the enactment of these statutes. Van Hecke, *Currency,* in 3 INT'L ENCY. COMP. L. 36–38 (1972). Generally, whether a statute restricting gold clauses applies to a contract depends upon the proper law of the contract. However, the Polish, Austrian, and German statutes are exceptional in this regard. *Id.* at 36–10.

26. 48 Stat. 112; 31 U.S.C. § 463 (1976).

27. *See* Holzer, *How Americans Lost Their Right to Own Gold—and Became Criminals in the Process,* 39 BROOK. L. REV. 517 (1973).

28. Norman v. Baltimore & Ohio R. Co. and United States v. Bankers Trust, 294 U.S. 240 (1935), sustained the abrogation of gold clauses in private contractual obligations as a valid exercise of Congressional power to regulate the value of U.S. currency. Nortz v. United States, 294 U.S. 317 (1935), and Perry v. United States, 294 U.S. 330 (1935), held that the Joint Resolution exceeded Congressional power in seeking to invalidate the gold clauses contained in U.S. government bonds, but that the plaintiffs were unable to show any damages stemming from their receipt of paper money rather than gold.

29. Emery Bird Thayer Dry Goods Co. v. Williams, 98 F.2d 166, 172 (8th Cir. 1938), 107 F.2d 965, 968 (8th Cir. 1939), *cert. denied,* 309 U.S. 655 (1940); Dawson, *supra* note 14, at 669, 677.

30. In Holyoke Water Power Co. v. American Writing Paper Co., 300 U.S. 324 (1937), the Supreme Court construed a clause requiring payment of "a quantity of gold which shall be equal in amount to fifteen hundred ($1,500) dollars of the gold coin of the United States of the standard of weight and fineness of the year 1894 or the equivalent of this commodity in United States currency" as a gold value clause barred by the Joint Resolution. In Emery Bird Thayer Dry Goods Co. v. Williams, 107 F.2d 965 (8th Cir. 1939), *cert. denied* 309 U.S. 655 (1940) the court similarly construed a ninety-nine year lease at a rental of 557,280 grams of pure gold, subject to a provision that the lessor could require payment of $6,000 quarterly in lawful U.S. currency, as an ineffective gold clause.

In both cases whether the Joint Resolution applied ultimately turned on whether the parties' purpose in inserting the gold bullion clause in the lease was to use gold to stabilize the value of the dollar.

31. Pub. L. 93–110, § 3(a), Sept. 21, 1973, 87 Stat. 352; as amended, Pub. L. 93–373, §2, Aug. 14, 1974, 88 Stat. 445.

32. Feldman v. Great Northern Ry. Co., 428 F. Supp. 979 (S.D. N.Y. 1977); Equitable Life Assur. Soc. v. Grosvenor, 426 F. Supp. 67 (W.D. Tenn. 1976); Henderson v. Mann Theatres Corp., 65 Cal. App. 3d 397, 135 Cal. Rptr. 266 (1976).

33. Pub. L. 95–147, §4(c), Oct. 28, 1977, 91 Stat. 1229.

34. Ordinance No. 58–1374 of Dec. 30, 1958, art. 79; as amended by Ordinance No. 59–246 of Feb. 4, 1959, art. 14.

35. Hauser, *Index Clauses in Private Loans since the Advent of the Fifth French Republic in 1958,* 13 AM. J. COMP. L. 606, 610 (1964).

36. Goldman, *Note on Rolland v. Fournet,* 90 Clunet 752, 754 (1963).

37. *See* Malaurie, *Des Clauses Monétaires Stipulées dans un Contrat International. Jurisprudence Matter et Réglementation des Changes,* 93 Clunet 571 (1966); Eck, *Place Actuelle de la Théorie du Paiement International dans le Droit Monétaire Français,* Rev. Crit. Droit Int'l Privé 441 (1964). *But see* Goldman, *Note,* 94 Clunet 91 (1967), suggesting that this question is still clouded with doubts.

38. Deutsche Bundesbank, *Value Guaranty Clauses: Synopsis of the Bundesbank's Policy in Granting Permits* [hereinafter cited as Value Guaranty Clauses], 23 MONTHLY REPORT OF THE DEUTSCHE BUNDESBANK, No. 4, Apr. 1971, at 24 (reprinted in OECD, REPORT BY COMM. ON FINANCIAL MARKETS, INDEXATION OF FIXED-INTEREST SECURITIES 39–48 (1973).

39. *See* G. DELAUME, LEGAL ASPECTS OF INTERNATIONAL LENDING AND ECONOMIC DEVELOPMENT FINANCING 267 (1967); Silard, *Maintenance-of-Value Arrangements in International Transactions,* 5 L. & POL. INT'L BUS. 398, 424 (1973).

40. A. WALD, *supra* note 2, at 67. There are, however, cases, particularly in Germany, holding that foreign currency clauses stipulating a gold standard currency as the unit of account were actually gold clauses and therefore invalid. F. MANN, *supra* note 12, at 195.

41. Nussbaum states that "there is, outside France, hardly an instance of judicial invalidation of foreign currency debts." A. NUSSBAUM, *supra* note 2, at 348. (As the rest of his paragraph makes clear, Nussbaum was referring only to countries where the legislature had not specifically prohibited foreign money clauses.) Nussbaum's statement used to need qualification for Uruguay, where the courts had regularly invalidated foreign currency clauses. The cases are collected and criticized in Capurro Calamet, *Algo Más sobre la Pretendida Vigencia del Curso Forzoso y el Problema de la Eficacia Jurídica de las Obligaciones Internas Pactadas en Moneda Extranjera,* 64 Rev. D.J.A. 1 (1967). Legislation adopted in 1976 has now legalized foreign currency clauses in Uruguay. Law No. 14.500 of Feb. 25, 1976, art. 10.

Many countries permitting foreign currency clauses require that actual payment be made in national currency at the exchange rate in effect at the time the obligation becomes due, thereby converting all foreign money clauses into foreign money-value clauses. *E.g.,* Atlas S.A. v. Valentine, 105 La Ley 691 (CN Com., Sala C, Arg. 1961); Schwarz v. Cortazar, 60 R.D.J. 169 (2d Sec., Ct. of Santiago, Chile 1963). The English House of Lords has recently reversed a long-standing rule that judgments of British courts could be given only in sterling, even on foreign currency claims. In Miliangos v. George Frank (Textiles) Ltd., [1975] 3 All E.R. 801,

[1975] 3 W.L.R. 758, the House of Lords held that judgment could be granted in a foreign currency and the date for conversion into sterling is the day of payment where a foreign currency claim arises from a contract whose proper law is that of a foreign country and the money of account and payment is of that country. *See generally,* chap. 8, *infra,* at notes 84–86 and the accompanying text.

42. *See* A. NUSSBAUM, *supra* note 2, at 348; A. WALD, *supra* note 2, at 67; Van Hecke, *supra* note 25, at 36–12. In 1933 Norway adopted a statute requiring that all claims stipulated in more than one currency be repayable in Norwegian *kroner* so long as the *kroner* is one of the stipulated currencies. Smith, *Legal Principles in Monetary and Credit Policy,* 18 SCAND. STUD. IN L. 179, 213 (1974). Peruvian Decree-Law No. 18.275 of May 15, 1970, art. 2, prohibited foreign currency clauses in all contracts performed in Peru except to pay for the services of nonresidents. This statute was revoked by Decree-Law No. 21.953 of Oct. 7, 1977, but foreign currency clauses are still permitted only under limited circumstances in Peru. Cent. Bank Resol. Cambiaria No. 1–/77-EF–90 of Oct. 8, 1977.

43. Brazilian Decree-Law No. 857 of Sept. 11, 1969. Legislative restriction of foreign currency clauses in Brazil dates back to 1933, when the *de facto* government of Getúlio Vargas issued a decree barring the use of gold clauses and "the stipulation of payment in money which is not the official currency, by its legal value, . . . in contracts executable in Brazil. . . ." Decree No. 23.501 of Nov. 27, 1933. Law No. 28 of Feb. 15, 1935 created an exception for contracts to import merchandise, while Decree-Law No. 6.650 of Je. 29, 1944 created a further exception for "obligations contracted abroad in foreign currency to be executed in Brazil."

44. *E.g.,* Cons. Bernat v. Virneron, Cass. Civ., Mar. 10, 1942, 35 Rev. Crit. Droit Int'l Privé 96 (1946).

45. A. NUSSBAUM, *supra* note 2, at 346–47.

46. *See* notes 78–79, *infra,* and the accompanying text.

47. *E.g.,* Colombo v. Catapodis, Cass. Civ. lre, May 10, 1966, 94 Clunet 90 (1967).

48. Goldman, *Note on Colombo v. Catapodis, id.* at 93.

49. The Cour de Cassation recently had an opportunity to clarify this area in Société E.F.E.C. v. Girbal, Cass. Com.; Feb. 8, 1972, [1973] J.C.P. II, 17386, where the court sustained a foreign currency clause in a post-1958 contract involving the sale of a press by a Swedish firm to a French firm. But as Philippe Kahn observes in his note on the case, clarification of the problem must await future decisions.

50. Value Guaranty Clauses, *supra* note 38, at 28.

51. Guaranty Trust Co. v. Henwood, 307 U.S. 247 (1939); Bethlehem Steel Co. v. Zurich Ins. Co., 307 U.S. 265 (1939).

52. English Transcontinental, Limited et al v. Puebla Tramway, Light and Power Co., 186 Misc. 481, 61 N.Y.S.2d 356 (Sup. Ct., N.Y. Cty, 1946).

53. *See* note 33, *supra,* and the accompanying text.

54. Between 1971 and 1977 the Chilean peso was devalued by 174,650 percent against the U.S. dollar, falling from .016 pesos = U.S. $1 to 27.96 pesos = $1. IMF, INT'L FIN. STAT. YEARBOOK 139(1980). Moreover, Chilean law prohibits indexation of debts contracted in foreign currency. Decree-Law No. 455 of May 25, 1974, art. 24.

55. Chap. 1, *supra,* at note 2, and the accompanying text.

56. Friedman, *Monetary Correction,* in ESSAYS ON INFLATION AND INDEXATION 25, 35 (H. Giersch et al 1974).

57. These special notes carried the following inscription: ". . . Both Principal and Interest to be paid in the then current Money of said State, in a greater or less Sum, according as Five Bushels of Corn, Sixty-eight Pounds and four-seventh Parts of a Pound of Beef, Ten Pounds of Sheeps Wool, and Sixteen Pounds of Sole Leather shall then cost, more or less than One Hundred and Thirty Pounds of Current Money, at the then current Prices of said Articles. . . ." Quoted in I. FISHER, STABLE MONEY 12–13 (1934). In 1780 Massachusetts issued "soldiers depreciation notes," which offered additional compensation to soldiers in the event of a rise in the prices of certain commodities. Fisher, *The Tabular Standard in Massachusetts History,* 27 Q. J. ECON. 417, 536 (1913).

58. *See* chap. 4, *supra,* at notes 1–7 and the accompanying text.

59. A. WALD, *supra* note 2, at 102.

60. Page and Trollope, *An International Survey of Indexing and its Effects,* NAT'L INSTITUTE ECON. REV. 46, 47–48 (No. 70, Nov. 1974); Braun, *Indexation of Wages and Salaries in Developed Economies,* 23 IMF STAFF PAPERS 226, 262–68 (1976); European Economic Community Commission Report, Machinery for Adjusting Wages and Salaries to the Cost of Living (mimeo 1974) [hereafter cited as EEC Report]. Since 1974 Chile has automatically indexed wages, pensions, and the minimum wage for 100 percent of the increase in the consumer price index since the prior adjustment. Decree-Law No. 670 of Oct. 1, 1974, art. 70.

The U.S. automobile industry has escalated wages in accordance with an unusual binational composite index. The formula calls for converting the U.S. and Canadian consumer price indexes to the same base, weighting the U.S. index by a factor of 9 and the Canadian by a factor of 1, and increasing wages by one cent an hour for each 0.3 point rise in the composite index. LeRoy, *Scheduled Wage Increases and Escalator Provisions in 1977,* 100 MONTHLY LAB. REV. 20 (Jan. 1977).

61. EEC Report, *supra* note 60, at 6.

62. Page and Trollope, *supra* note 60, at 47–48.

63. "*Ex-ante* indexing" of wages is widely used in Switzerland, the Netherlands, France, and Great Britain. Giersch, *Index Clauses and the Fight Against Inflation,* in ESSAYS ON INFLATION AND INDEXATION 1, 16–18 (H. Giersch et al 1974). It was also widely used in Norway until 1966. Braun, *supra* note 60, at 255. In Germany, where indexing is generally prohibited, a limited number of collective bargaining agreements provide for renegotiation if the consumer price index rises by a predetermined amount. *Id.* at 264.

64. 103 MONTHLY LAB. REV. 50 (July 1980). In the United States, it has been estimated that one-fourth of all employees with cost-of-living adjustments had caps on these adjustment clauses. Sheifer, *Cost-of-Living Adjustment: Keeping up with Inflation?,* 102 MONTHLY LAB. REV. 14, 16 (June 1979).

65. EEC Report, *supra* note 60, at 8–9.

66. Faustini, *Wage Indexing and Inflation in Italy,* BANCA NAZIONALE DEL LAVORO Q. REV. 364 (Dec. 1976). Between January 1975 and February 1977 the value of a point increased from 1.235 lire per month to 2,389 lire per month. This meant that only half of the average wage was being indexed in January 1975, but that more

than 100 percent of the average wage was being indexed by February 1977. *Id.* at 368, 372–73.

67. Law No. 6.708 of Oct. 30, 1979.

68. Stanwell Park Hotel Co. Ltd. v. Leslie, 85 C.L.R. 189, 201 [1952].

69. *See* Vasseur, *French Monetary Depreciation and Methods Used to Remedy It,* 30 Tul. L. Rev. 73, 78–84 (1955). *See also,* Lévy, *"Sliding Scale" or "Indexation" Clauses in French Law,* 16 Am. U. L. Rev. 35, 38–49 (1966) for a description of the variety of legal arguments and counterarguments articulated in France manifesting this hostility towards index clauses.

70. The literature describing this controversy is immense. *See e.g.,* Noirel, *supra* note 18; Toulemon, *Évolution de la Jurisprudence en Matière de Clauses d'Échelle Mobile et des Clauses de Variation suivant Indices,* 4 Rev. Trim. Droit Comm. 663 (1951); Toulemon, *Les Obligations Indexées et l'Indice-or,* 16 Rev. Trim. Droit Comm. 443 (1963); Hamel, *Clauses d'Échelle Mobile et le Droit Monétaire Français,* Rev. Économique 167 (1955); Hubert, *Observations sur la Nature et la Validité de la Clause d'Échelle Mobile,* 45 Rev. Trim. Droit Civ. 1 (1947); Vasseur, *Le Droit des Clauses Monétaires et les Enseignements de l'Économie Politique,* 50 Rev. Trim. Droit Civ. 431 (1952); Frejaville, *Les Clauses d'Échelle Mobile,* D. Chron. 31 (1952); Esmein, *La Variation du Montant des Dettes de Sommes d'Argent en Fonction d'un Indice Économique,* [1951] Gaz. Pal. II, Doct. 1; [1952] Gaz. Pal. II, Doct. 4. Useful articles in English are Vasseur, *supra* note 69; Lévy, *supra* note 69; Hauser, *The Use of Index Clauses in Private Loans,* 7 Am. J. Comp. L. 350 (1958); Hauser, *Index Clauses in Private Loans since the Advent of the Fifth French Republic,* 13 Am. J. Comp. L. 606 (1964).

71. Article 1895 is set out in chap. 3, *supra,* at p. 39.

72. Decision of Je. 25, 1951, [1951] D., 725.

73. Article 1896 provides: "The rule set out in the previous article does not apply where a loan has been made in bullion." Article 1897 provides: "If bullion or provisions have been lent, the debtor must always pay back the same quantity and quality, regardless of any increase or decrease in their price, and he need not repay anything else."

74. Lévy, *supra* note 69, at 44.

75. Collel v. Wild, Cass. 1re Civ. Nov. 3, 1953, [1954] S. Jur. I, 18; Cass Civ., Nov. 22, 1951, [1951] J.C.P. II 6649; Cass. Civ., July 24, 1939, Gaz. Trib., Feb. 3, 1940. *See also* Hauser, *supra* note 70, 7 Am. J. Comp. L., at 354–56.

76. *See, e.g.,* Compain v. Pavageau, Trib. Civ. Nantes, 2d Cham., Feb. 17, 1953, [1954] S. Jur. II, 149. One thoughtful commentator observed that "The French case law . . . with regard to escalator clauses is characterized by an absence of criteria." A. Wald, *supra* note 2, at 123. *See also* Lévy, *supra* note 69, at 51–52.

77. *See* Lévy, *supra* note 69, at 50, and cases cited in footnotes 28 and 29. *See also* Hauser, *supra* note 70, 7 Am. J. Comp. L. at 354–55 and cases cited in footnote 21.

78. Cass. 1re Civ. (after deliberation in the *chambre du conseil*), Je. 27, 1957, [1957] D. Jur. 649, with note by Ripert; [1957] J.C.P. II, 10093.

79. [1957] D. Jur. at 649.

80. Ordonnance No. 58–1374 of Dec. 30, 1958, art. 79; as amended by Ordonnance No. 59–246 of Feb. 4, 1959, art. 14. The term "collective bargaining" agreement is used to translate the French word *statut* used in the text. Collective

bargaining agreements are frequently promulgated by ministerial decrees called *statuts.*

81. Index clauses in commercial leases were specifically authorized by the Decrees of Jy. 1, 1939 and Sept. 30, 1953, art. 28. Agricultural rentals fixed in produce may be paid in currency according to commodity prices, as provided in the Ordonnance of Oct. 17, 1945. Decree No. 53–700 of Aug. 9, 1953 linked residential rents with the minimum guaranteed interoccupational wage (SMIG), which had previously been linked to the cost-of-living index for Paris by the Law of Jy. 18, 1952. Law of Sept. 2, 1954, art. 10, provided for the indexing of workmen's compensation. Law of Apr. 15, 1953 authorized indexation of mortgages guaranteeing construction loans, and a Decree of Jan. 4, 1955 authorized indexing of mortgages generally. The use of indexed loans and bonds by a number of public corporations and land banks was authorized by legislation in 1953. *See generally* Vasseur, *supra* note 69, at 77–78.

82. Decree of Jan. 7, 1959 sanctioned the prior commodity-indexing system. The substance of this decree has been repromulgated regularly. Lévy, *supra* note 69, at 60.

83. Law of Jy. 13, 1963, art. 4.

84. Law No. 70–600 of Jy. 9, 1970, whose second article explicitly prohibits the use of index clauses tied to the rental component of the general consumer price index.

85. Lévy, *supra* note 69, at 64–67.

86. Époux Faure-Brac v. Société Civile Immobilière, Cass. Civ. 1re, Jan. 9, 1974, [1974] J.C.P. II, 17806, with note by Lévy; Paralitici v. Dame Leroy, Cass. Civ. 1re, Apr. 12, 1972, [1972] J.C.P. II, 17235, with note by Lévy; Époux Maréchal, Cass. Civ. 1re, July 3, 1973 [1973] J.C.P. IV, p. 317; Tendler, *Indexation et Ordre Public,* [1977] D.S. Chron. 245, 246–47; *See also* Marnierre, *Observations sur l'Indexation comme Mesure de Valeur,* 76 Rev. Trim. Droit Civ. 54, 74–81 (1977). *But see* Gabert v. Époux Lovera et Cravero, Cass. Civ. 1re, Feb. 18, 1976, [1976] J.C.P. II, 13465, with note by Lévy.

87. Époux Couasse v. Consorts Lemoux, Cass. Civ. 3d, Feb. 15, 1972, [1973] D.S. Jur. 417, with note by Ghestin; [1972] J.C.P. II, 17094, with note by Lévy; Tendler, *supra* note 86, at 246. The issue is a question of fact whose resolution is up to the lower courts. Gilly v. Sté des Grands Moulins de la Méditerranée, Cass. Civ. 3d, Jy. 11, 1968, [1969] J.C.P. II, 15942; Soc. de Gestion des Magasins du Midi v. Veuve Maynial et Brambilla, Cass. Civ. 3d, Jy. 16, 1974, [1974] D.S. Jur. 681.

88. The Economic Special Powers Act, Law No. 207 of Apr. 9, 1968, is translated in relevant portion in S. Mukherjee & C. Orlans, Indexation in an Inflationary Economy: A Case Study of Finland 106 (1975). In 1969 and 1970 index clauses were permitted upon authorization by the Ministry of Finance in contracts and leases with a minimum term of ten years. In 1972 the minimum term was reduced to five years. In 1974 the ban was further relaxed for construction contracts and business rentals. Builders with a contract to be performed over at least one year can pass on to the buyer two-thirds of the increases in the building cost index. With Ministry of Finance permission indexation is permissible in business rentals with a term as short as two years. *Id.* at 76–77. Nevertheless, as a practical matter, the requirement of Ministry of Finance permission has prevented most

people from utilizing index clauses. In 1975 it was reported that only twenty to thirty permits had been granted. *Id.* at 77.

89. Law No. 263 of Je. 4, 1945, cited in Vasseur, *L'Indexation a l'Étranger,* Rev. Économique 275, 294 (1955).

90. Currency Law of Je. 20, 1949, art. 3, in conjunction with Law on Foreign Trade and Payments, art. 49, par. 2.

91. Value Guaranty Clauses, *supra* note 38, at 28.

92. F. MANN, *supra* note 12, at 158.

93. Value Guaranty Clauses, *supra* note 38, at 26.

94. Law of Mar. 30, 1976, art. 57.

95. The 80 percent limitation is imposed upon component prices of the contract price. Thus, if labor costs rise by 10 percent and material costs rise by 20 percent in a contract in which the labor component represents twice the cost of material, all that can be passed on to the buyer is a 16 percent increase in the labor component of the contract and an 8 percent increase in the materials component. *See* Andersen, *Les Instruments Juridiques de la Politique des Prix,* 37 Annales de Droit 351, 363–68 (1977).

96. Law of Dec. 24, 1976, art. 11.

97. Law No. 6.423 of Je. 17, 1977. The statute excepts only contracts for the future delivery of goods or services whose price may vary with the cost of production and certain contracts already in force.

98. Between 1975 and 1976 the value of ORTNs increased by 30.1 percent, while the wholesale price index increased by 41.3 percent. Between September 1978 and August 1979 ORTNs increased by only 39.3 percent, while the inflation rate registered 51.9 percent. Calculated from data appearing in Conj. Econ. The evolution in the calculation of monetary correction for Readjustable Treasury Bonds is shown in "Correção Monetária e Realimentação Inflacionária," 30 Conj. Econ. 88, 92–94 (Je. 1976). For an in-depth analysis of the government's manipulation of monetary correction, *see* Roe, *Finance, Rules and the Indexation of Brazilian Government Bonds,* 12 VAND. J. TRANSNAT'L L. 1 (1979).

99. Art. 2199 of the Chilean Civil Code provided:

> If one has lent money, one is owed only the numerical sum stated in the contract. One can repay one class of money for another, despite the wishes of the lender, so long as the sums are adjusted for the relationship established by law between the two classes of money; but the lender shall not be obligated to receive small change or copper, except within the limits which special laws have established or shall establish.

100. Decree-Law No. 455 of May 25, 1974, arts. 3, 17, 19, and 24, as modified by Decree-Law No. 1.533 of Jy. 26, 1976, art. 6.

101. Decree-Law No. 455 of May 25, 1974, art. 19.

102. In short-term credit transactions the interest rate can be freely set by the parties, up to a maximum of 50 percent above the going market or bank rate. *Id.* at art. 5. For legal and fiscal purposes interest is defined to exclude monetary correction of the principal lent. *Id.* at art. 4.

103. Bustillo v. Café Paulista, 1953–III J.A. 89, 70 La Ley 399 (1953).

104. A. WALD, *supra* note 2, at 115; López Olaciregui, *Validez de las Cláusulas Convencionales que Prevén la Desvalorización de la Moneda,* 1953–III J.A. 89. In Novem-

ber 1959, the Sixth National Conference of the Argentine Bar approved the resolution affirming the validity of stabilization clauses, and the Third National Congress of Civil Law at Cordoba in October of 1961 and the Sessions of Civil Law at Santa Fe in November of 1963 did likewise. Guastavino, *El Derecho Civil ante la Inflación,* 116 La Ley 1080, 1111–13 (1964).

105. *E.g.,* Bentivoglio v. Arana de Jordán, L.I., 1967–VI J.A. 528, 129 La Ley 779 (Sup. Ct. Buenos Aires 1967) (upholding a gold clause in a lease).

106. Guastavino, *supra* note 104, at 1093–94.

107. There are no cases on point prior to Aztec Prop. v. Union Planters Nat. Bank, discussed *infra,* in the text to notes 108–13 because the assumption of validity was so widespread that no one bothered to litigate the point. But the commentators have been unanimous that the Gold Clause Resolution did not bar index clauses. F. MANN, *supra* note 12, at 157, fn. 2; A. NUSSBAUM, *supra* note 2, at 307; Call, *Money and the Sliding Scale Clause in Contracts,* 24 MO. L. REV. 44 (1959); Dach, *Validity of Price-Index Clauses under the Gold Coin Joint Resolution,* 13 GEO WASH. L. REV. 328 (1945); Dawson, *supra* note 14, at 683; Dawson & Coultrap, *Contracting by Reference to Price Indices,* 33 MICH. L. REV. 685 (1935); McClintock, *The Probable Legal Consequences of Inserting Price-Index Clauses in Long-Term Corporate Obligations,* 18 HASTINGS L. J. 959, 964 (1967).

108. 530 S.W.2d 756 (1975), *cert. denied,* 425 U.S. 975 (1976).

109. 530 S.W.2d at 760. This is an alternative holding. The Court also held that the indexed note violated the Tennessee usury statute, a problem that is dealt with in chap. 6, *infra,* at pp. 202–03.

110. The *Norman* case is discussed in note 28, *supra;* and the *Holyoke Water Power Co.* case is discussed in note 30, *supra.*

111. Buchanan & Tideman, *Gold, Money and the Law: The Limits of Governmental Monetary Authority,* in GOLD, MONEY AND THE LAW 9, 25–26 (H. Manne & R. Miller eds. 1975). *Cf.* Dawson, *supra* note 14, at 675.

112. 530 S.W.2d at 761.

113. *See* the text to notes 75–78 *supra.*

114. *See* note 33, *supra,* and the accompanying text.

115. Art. 2. The decree is translated in K. KARST & K. ROSENN, LAW AND DEVELOPMENT IN LATIN AMERICA 444–45 (1975).

116. Caio Mario da Silva Pereira, *Estabelecimento de Cláusula de Escala Móvel nas Obrigações em Dinheiro,* 234 Rev. Trib. 3; 157 Rev. For. 50 (1955). One of Brazil's most eminent jurists, Santiago Dantas, took the position that an escalator clause was valid so long as it did not use a cost-of-living index. He reasoned that cost-of-living increments are inversely proportioned to the decline in the purchasing power of the nation's currency, and that use of the cost-of-living index would detract from the legal value of the currency, thereby violating Decree No. 23.501. A. WALD, *supra* note 2, at 160–61.

Article 144 of the draft Code of Obligations of 1965 considers index clauses invalid unless specifically authorized by legislation.

117. This legislation is described in J. CHACEL, M. SIMONSEN, & A. WALD, CORREÇÃO MONETÁRIA (1970).

118. *Id.* at 58–59. An example of such a norm is Law No. 5.441 of May 24, 1968, restricting increments in residential rentals resulting from the use of escala-

tor clauses to a maximum of two-thirds of the percentage increase in the minimum wage.

119. Rosenn, *Controlled Rents and Uncontrolled Inflation: the Brazilian Dilemma,* 17 AM. J. COMP. L. 239, 251–54 (1969).

120. *See* the discussion in chap. 2, supra, p. 26.

121. *See* chap. 6, *infra,* at notes 12–17 and the accompanying text.

122. 499 F. Supp. 53 (W.D. Pa. 1980) discussed more fully in chap. 4, *supra,* at notes 177–79 and the accompanying text.

123. *See* Department of W. & P. v. Okonite-Callender C. Co., 181 F.2d 375 (9th Cir. 1950).

124. For a discussion of various techniques for protecting the value of long-term leases from inflation, *see* Denz, *Lease Provisions Designed to Meet Changing Economic Conditions,* 1952 U. ILL. L. FOR. 344; Hecht, *Variable Rental Provisions in Long Term Ground Leases,* 72 COLUM. L. REV. 625 (1972). Courts in the United States have uniformly upheld index clauses in rental agreements and leases. The cases are collected in Annot., *Lease Provisions Providing for Rent Adjustment Based on Event or Formula Outside Control of Parties,* 87 A.L.R.3d 986 (1978). Indeed, the Florida courts have held that a Florida statute prohibiting inclusion or enforcement of escalator clauses in leases for recreational facilities and management services of condominiums is unconstitutional if applied retroactively to existing leases. Fleeman v. Case, 342 So.2d 815 (Fla. 1976); Kaufman v. Shere, 347 So.2d 627 (Fla. App. D3, 1977) *cert. denied,* 355 So.2d 517 (Fla.).

125. *See generally,* Roman, *Controlling Escalation in Long-term Contracts,* PUB. UTIL. FORTNIGHTLY 28 (Jan. 31, 1980).

126. *See* Firestone Tire & Rubber Company v. U.S., 444 F.2d 547 (Ct. Cl. 1971), where the court found that the escalation clause "under reference 1014" of the wholesale price index was ambiguous.

127. In Tanner v. Stocks & Realty (Premises) Pty. Ltd., [1972] 2 N.S.W.L.R. 722, the Supreme Court of New South Wales reversed the lower courts to bail out a party who had failed to provide for the contingency of a shift in the index's base year. On the other hand, when the French government discontinued publication of economic indexes in World War II, some of the French cases voided contracts indexed to these discontinued indexes for lack of price terms. One French court held that the contract should be governed by the last index number, published in 1939, regardless of any subsequent inflation. Although this decision was reversed on appeal, the solution of the appellate court, which called for reinstatement of the originally stipulated contract price, treated the lessor even more harshly. A rent fixed by contract at 16,000 francs in 1935, and which had escalated to 23,375 francs by 1939, was in 1941 reduced to 16,000 francs because of the cessation in publication of the index. Lévy, *supra* note 69, at 52. Eventually, these irrational positions were abandoned by the French courts in favor of substituting new indexes or allowing experts to determine an equitable adjustment. *Ibid.*

128. The issue of usury and indexation is discussed in chap. 6, *infra,* at notes 125–40 and the accompanying text.

129. Section 3–104 of the Uniform Commercial Code conditions negotiability upon the instrument's containing "an unconditional promise or order to pay a sum certain in money. . . ." The Draftsmen's Comment to Section 3–106, which elabo-

rates on the meaning of "sum certain" states: "The computation must be one which can be made from the instrument itself without reference to any outside source. . . ." Because one must refer to an outside source, *i.e.,* the consumer price index, to compute the amount due under an indexed obligation, the instrument would not be negotiable under §3–104. Poser, *Special Report: Can You Use Price Adjustment and Gold Clauses in Loan Agreements,* SEC. REG. & TRANS. REPORT, Feb. 26, 1975, pp. 4–5; Comment, *The Variable Interest Note: An Answer to Uncertainty in a Fluctuating Money Market,* 1971 L. & SOC. ORDER 600, 606–8. *Cf.* McClintock, *supra* note 107, at 967–69 (suggesting that an imaginative court might analogize an index clause to a foreign money clause).

If an adjustable note is a "security" within the meaning of art. 8 of the Uniform Commercial Code (an instrument which "is of a type commonly dealt in upon securities exchanges or markets or commonly recognized in any area in which it is issued or dealt in as a medium for investment . . .") 8–102 (1) (a)ii, then the presence of the index clause should not prevent it from being negotiable. While indexed instruments are not commonly dealt in by securities exchanges in the United States, since 1974 Citicorp and other U.S. corporations have issued floating notes with interest rates adjustable in accordance with the variations in three-month U.S. Treasury bills. Such indexed obligations would appear to meet the requirements of negotiability under Article 8–105 of the Uniform Commercial Code. Poser, *supra. See also* McClintock, *supra* note 107, at 969–71.

130. 5 U.S.C. §8340 was amended in 1969 to provide that any time the consumer price index remains for three consecutive months at least three percent above the index at the last adjustment, retirement benefits shall be increased by one percent plus the percentage rise in the price index. Thus, if the index rose by three percent a year, retirement benefits would rise by four percent; if the index rose by three percent a quarter (12.6 percent for the year), retirement benefits would go up by 17 percent a year. Pub. L. 94–440, §1306(a) (1976) eliminated the extra one percent adjustment.

131. *See* chap. 10, *infra,* at notes 91–93 and the accompanying text.

132. *See* the Brazilian experience with *ex ante* monetary correction in loan transactions, chap. 6, *infra,* at the text to notes 67–74.

6

LONG-TERM CREDIT TRANSACTIONS, INSURANCE, PENSIONS, AND ANNUITIES

The effects of chronic inflation are particularly pernicious with respect to three types of legal arrangements: (1) credit transactions extending over substantial periods of time, (2) insurance, and (3) pensions and annuities. All three might have been covered under the general topic of contracts; instead, each has been treated separately because each presents special problems in inflationary economics. Generally, these three areas have been the object of special legislation designed to counteract the adverse effects of inflation.

The credit market is especially sensitive to an increase in the inflation rate. As soon as inflation exceeds a trot, long- and medium-term loans become practically unobtainable. Interest rates quickly rise beyond the ceilings imposed by usury laws. If these ceilings are not raised and the government attempts to enforce the usury laws, credit either disappears entirely or is camouflaged by elaborate simulations. Mortgage funds dry up as lenders and savers seek higher rates of return. The bond market is also likely to vanish unless potential issuers are willing to insert maintenance-of-value clauses in their debt obligations.

The insurance industry is similarly affected by inflation. Purchasers of life insurance tend to shift from whole life policies to term insurance as they perceive the relative unprofitability of whole life as a savings vehicle. Many forsake life insurance and annuities altogether because of their fear that the purchasing power of the sums eventually realized will be trifling. Inflation also produces a sharp increase in policy loans, for the low interest rates at which such loans are typically made appear increasingly attractive as inflation progresses. This, in turn, produces a drain on companies' reserves. Companies must liquidate long-term investments, often at substantial losses, to maintain sufficient liquidity to extend loans to policyholders. Fire and casualty insurance companies can be catapulted into bankruptcy by severe inflation because premiums are calculated on the basis of the values of prior years, paid in present value currency, and used to pay off claims at future values. The soaring costs of medical expenses, reconstruction and compensation are factored into rate structures only after a lag of several years. Rate hikes must be approved by regulatory agencies, and typically require an empirical demonstration of inadequacy. Moreover, presently established deductible amounts quickly become poor devices for forestalling trivial claims.[1]

As a class, pensioners and annuitants are likely to suffer most from inflation. Members of this class often discover that inflation so reduces the purchasing power of their benefits that supplemental income is needed for survival. Fairness requires that governments with severe inflation adopt measures to readjust pensions and annuities for inflation.

If the credit market, the insurance industry, and social security systems are to function effectively in an inflationary environment, traditional legal structures must be modified. This chapter will describe the distorting effects of inflation on the credit market, the insurance industry, and the social security systems. It will then describe measures for modifying such institutions to permit their effective functioning during inflation. Finally, it will assess the advantages and disadvantages of these adaptive techniques.

INFLATION AND THE CREDIT MARKET

Inflation tends to distort the economic allocation of capital among competing investment opportunities. Investors shy away from sinking their capital into long-term fixed-return securities. Instead they prefer to purchase real property, gold or silver coins, rare paintings, "hard" foreign currency, or even consumer durables, such as automobiles, in an effort to protect their capital from monetary depreciation. Funds that in stable times would have been utilized to finance productive investment or lent to the government are diverted in inflationary times into consumption or into economically nonproductive hedges against inflation. Moreover, the rate of capital formation tends to decline during inflation, an economically pernicious phenomenon which is exacerbated by traditional accounting conventions which generally overstate profits. As a result, business firms often decapitalize themselves unintentionally.[2] Correspondingly, people tend to save less; it makes little economic sense to defer consumption if the real value of one's savings and interest is steadily depreciating.

Three factors significantly impair the credit market's ability to adjust to inflation: (1) the inability of investors to forecast the inflation rate accurately, (2) tax laws that operate with a nominalist conception of income, and (3) governmental restrictions on maximum interest rates that can be paid to savers and charged to borrowers. If potential lenders were able to predict the rate of inflation correctly and there were no governmental constraints on interest rates, the cost of credit would theoretically adjust to retain the real rates of interest that prevail in times of economic stability. For example, investors willing to purchase ten-year government bonds with a 4 percent rate of return during a period of price stability might demand at least a 13 percent rate of return if they estimated the inflation rate at 9 percent per annum over the life of the bonds. But this calculation fails to take into account the effect of income tax laws that fail to differentiate between real and nominal interest. As chapter 9 more fully explains, most tax systems do not differentiate between real and nominal interest income. If a country has a progressive income tax system that taxes nominal and real interest at the same rate, the rate of return necessary to attract investors varies with marginal income tax rates. An investor with a marginal tax rate of 30 percent, who considers the minimum acceptable rate of return on a government bond during stable times to be 4 percent, would require a nominal return of 16.9 percent with a 9 percent annual inflation rate. Similarly, a taxpayer with a marginal rate of 50 percent would require a 22 percent nominal return to assure the same real disposable income as a 4 percent return with no inflation. With an 18 percent annual inflation rate, an investor with a 50 percent marginal rate requires a 44 percent nominal return in order to receive a pretax return of 4 percent in real terms, eleven times the interest rate required in a stable economy.[3]

Investors cannot, however, accurately predict what the inflation rate will be over any appreciable period of time. If the rate of inflation jumps substantially, investors who have underestimated the rate of inflation in the past will not only revise their predictions upward. They will also include a factor for the risk of underestimating inflation, in much the same fashion as they include a factor for risk of nonrepayment. This inflation risk factor will have the effect of increasing the minimum acceptable rate of return for investors or lenders.

The third factor preventing the credit market from adjusting to inflation is legal restrictions on interest rates. Most countries have usury laws, which typically limit the maximum interest that can be charged for the use of money to about 6 to 12 percent per annum. It takes relatively little inflation to turn the typical usury statute into an artificial limitation on a market rate of interest. Many countries also impose legal restrictions upon the amount of interest banks and savings institutions can pay their depositors. Similarly, relatively little inflation is required to turn these interest ceilings into negative rates of interest, causing depositors to reduce their balances and search for higher rates of return.

MAINTENANCE-OF-VALUE PROVISIONS IN LONG-TERM BONDS

One sector of the credit market most directly affected by inflation is the long-term bond market. Without some kind of maintenance-of-value provision, long-term debt obligations cease to be attractive investments during inflationary periods.

Gold Clauses

The most common maintenance-of-value provision in long-term bonds used to be a gold clause. But the Great Depression of the 1930s forced both the wholesale abandonment of the gold exchange standard as well as free convertibility of paper currency into gold. If they had not already barred the use of gold clauses during the monetary chaos that followed World War I, many countries did so during the 1930s.[4] Although special legislation is occasionally enacted from time to time authorizing a governmental issue of a gold-linked bond,[5] as a practical matter, the gold clause has been rendered obsolete. As indicated in chapter 5, *supra,* demonetization has made gold an even more ill-suited maintenance-of-value device.[6]

Foreign Exchange Linked Bonds

Another maintenance-of-value technique is the linking of the value of bonds to the foreign exchange rate. After World War II, a number of countries adopted the practice of making their bonds payable in so-called hard-currency, such as U.S. dollars or British pounds, or linking their value to the foreign exchange rate for these currencies. For example, in 1947 China issued one series of bonds redeemable in U.S. dollars and another linked to the dollar exchange rate.[7] Between 1948 and 1955 the Israeli government linked the value of its bonds to the U.S. dollar, and between 1955 and 1962, offered purchasers the choice between linkage to the exchange rate or the cost-of-living index.[8]

Foreign exchange rate linkage has been a troublesome maintenance-of-value technique. No currency has remained immune to inflation, and devaluations have tended to be substantial and unpredictable. During periods of fixed exchange rates, governments frequently maintained the same exchange rate for long periods of substantial domestic inflation, thereby sharply reducing the effectiveness of foreign exchange linkage as an inflation hedge. On occasion, governments have devalued by far more than was necessary to equalize any inflation rate differential with its trading partners. Despite IMF disapproval, a number of countries from time to time have set multiple exchange rates, a contingency for which exchange rate-linked bonds often make no provision. In 1953 Israeli adoption of multiple exchange rates resulted in litigation about the extent of the government's obligation in redeeming its dollar-linked bonds. The government maintained that it was obligated to pay only at the lowest exchange rate, 1 I£ = U.S. $2.80, while the bondholders insisted on payment at the highest exchange rate, 1 I£ = U.S. $1.00. The Israeli Supreme Court ultimately resolved the issue in favor of the bondholders.[9] Since 1971, when many exchange rates began to float, exchange rate linkage has become a somewhat better inflation hedge, but a renewal of interest in bonds tied to foreign exchange rates seems unlikely.

Of course, a great many bonds denominated in "hard currencies," such as the U.S. dollar and the German mark, continue to be issued by foreign governments or corporations seeking to tap the U.S. or European bond markets. The U.S. dollar, followed by the German mark, has been the most popular currency of denomination for Eurobonds.[10] In recent years a number of companies have successfully marketed bonds payable in dollars but denominated in Special Drawing Rights (SDRs) of the International Monetary Fund. Maintenance-of-value arrangements in international loans are considered in more detail in chapter 8, *infra.*

Floating-Rate Bonds and Notes

In 1970 floating-rate bonds and notes were introduced in the Euromarket and have since become a standard feature. Loans in Eurocurrency, money on deposit outside the county of issuance, are generally made at interest rates which are periodically readjusted in accordance with the interbank offered rate (IBOR), most commonly in the London market (LIBOR). This is the rate at which prime banks receive deposits in Eurocurrencies from other banks. The interest rate in a typical floating-rate loan is redetermined every six months at a spread .75 to 2 percent above the current IBOR. In 1974 Citicorp, a New York bank holding company, inaugurated floating rate notes in the United States with a $650 million offering, due in 1989, with an interest rate pegged at 1 percent above the average three-month rate on U.S. Treasury bills. Other banks and corporations quickly followed Citicorp's lead so that there are now about $3.9 billion worth of corporate floating notes outstanding in the U.S. market.

Some U.S. borrowers have issued floating-rate notes convertible into fixed-rate long-term bonds, with an interest rate usually set at about 8.5

percent. Three companies, General Motors Acceptance, General Felt, and Gulf Oil, have linked floating-rate notes to the yields of ten-, twenty-, and thirty-year Treasury bonds respectively.[11]

Floating-rate loans have worked reasonably well from the standpoint of institutional lenders, who are essentially interested in preserving the spread between their cost of funds and their loan income. Floating-rate loans have been less satisfactory from the standpoint of noninstitutional lenders and borrowers, who find their yields and loan costs soaring or falling because of fluctuations in the Treasury bill rate or liquidity of Eurocurrency markets for reasons often unrelated to inflation or to the businesses of the borrowers. Even though short-term interest rates tend to go up during inflation and to fall during deflation, floating-rate loans leave much to be desired as a maintenance-of-value technique. All too often, institutional constraints and unanticipated inflation produce negative or nearly negative short-term interest rates over substantial periods. Because Treasury bills are generally deemed the safest and most liquid of all investments, yields tend to fall below those of alternative investments. For example, the yield on Citicorp's initial floating note offer dipped below 6 percent a year in 1975–76, well below what could be earned on other debt instruments; consequently, investors redeemed their notes in droves, leaving only about $160 million of the original issue still outstanding. The six month interest adjustment period has also created problems in today's highly volatile short-term credit market; Citicorp attempted to rectify this problem in its 1980 issue by providing for monthly adjustment of the interest rate. In addition, the floating interest rate technique tends to do little to protect the value of the principal from inflationary erosion.

Commodity-Linked Bonds

Linking the value of bonds and similar debt instruments to the price of a commodity or small group of commodities is a maintenance-of-value technique that dates back at least to the special notes issued by Massachusetts in 1742 and 1777. As indicated in chapter 5, during Germany's post–World War I runaway inflation, bonds were frequently and unsatisfactorily linked to the price of rye or coal. Commodity-linked bonds, however, did not become an important economic phenomenon until after World War II.

During the 1950s, "variable return" bonds, linked to a wide variety of commodities, dominated the bond market in Israel and France. As one would expect, these bonds were generally linked to commodities where prices were directly related to the issuer's profits. Thus, the Palestine Development Company issued 5 percent debentures convertible into common stock or plots of the company's urban land at predetermined prices.

The Nesher Palestine Portland Cement Works Ltd. issued a series of debentures with principal and interest linked to the official price of cement, and a second series with coupons entitling the bearer to purchase cement at a fixed price. Israel-Rassco Investment Company, a real estate developer, issued debentures convertible into common stock or redeemable for apartments from the company at predetermined prices.[12] Électricité de France issued bonds with principal and interest linked to the average price of a kilowatt-hour of electricity. Charbonnages de France issued bonds whose principal was linked to the price of coal. The French railroad (S.N.C.F.) issued bonds linked to the price of third-class railway tickets with the option of receiving interest in railway tickets good for two years.[13]

The recent surge in the inflation rate in the United States has revived interest in commodity-linked bonds. In April 1980 Sunshine Mining Co. issued a fifteen-year bond granting the bondholder the option of receiving at maturity either $1,000 or 50 ounces of silver. This bond carried an 8.5 percent interest rate, well below the market rate had the bond not contained the silver linkage. This issue reportedly created problems for the U.S. Securities and Exchange Commission, which was unsure whether to call it a bond or a certificate. The Securities and Exchange Commission also requested assurance from Sunshine Mining that it was not monetizing silver.[14]

One problem with commodity-linked bonds is that the purchaser must bear the risk that the price of the commodity to which the security is linked will lag behind the general price level. This risk is significantly exacerbated if a bond's value is linked to goods or services provided by a public utility, such as electricity or train tickets, commodities subject to direct price controls, or highly speculative commodities. On the other hand, bonds giving the holder the right to acquire land, cement, apartments, or railway tickets at predetermined prices are designed as hedges against the risk that these commodities will appreciate in price faster than the general level of prices. They combine aspects of a loan, an option, and an advance purchase of a commodity. Where the issuing company has linked its bonds to a commodity which it sells or produces, the commodity-linked bond tends to protect the issuer from the risk that its income will not rise enough to cover the increased cost of servicing and amortizing a variable debenture in an inflationary economy.[15]

Many companies have made the tie between their earnings and the rates of return on their bonds even more explicit. Firms in Belgium, Finland, France, the Netherlands, and Switzerland have issued "participating debentures" that link interest payments to the issuer's dividend rate. The bonds offered by Pechiney in 1953 featured an interest rate that varied with the company's earnings and dividends; Sidelor bonds of 1954 had an interest rate that varied with the company's dividends and reserves; debt service on the 1955 issue of Michelin bonds was tied to the price of rubber and the company's sales.[16] The practical effect of such linking devices is to convert bonds into hybrid securities. To the extent that his return rises and falls with the earnings of the company, the bondholder's debt interest takes on characteristics of equity. Such hybrid securities make eminent sense as investment devices, resembling in some respects convertible debentures. Issuing companies have been able to borrow at lower rates because of the opportunity for higher returns; moreover, the nature of the commodity or earnings clause substantially protects companies from becoming saddled with interest expense they cannot shoulder in the event of a downturn in the economy.

Some companies have linked their bonds to several variables. In France, for example, the Monod issue of 1952 was tied to a nonlinear function of wages, and steel and cement prices, and the SOMUA issue of 1953 linked its return to the ratio of the value of total sales to the number of hours of direct labor in the year preceding payment and in the base year of 1952.[17] The larger the group of variables to which the bond is linked, the more it takes on the characteristics of an indexed bond.

Indexed Bonds

Currently, the most important maintenance-of-value device for bonds is index-linking. The first sophisticated index bond that attempted to compensate for changes in the purchasing power of money was issued in the United States in 1925 by the Rand Kardex Company. This was done at the instigation of Irving Fisher, an enormously influential economist, who also happened to be one of the owners of Rand Kardex. These bonds obligated Rand Kardex to pay to the bondholder:

> [S]uch sum of money as shall possess the present purchasing power of one thousand dollars (1,000) with interest thereon at the rate of seven percent per annum, payable quarterly . . . in such sums as shall, at the respective times of payment, equal in purchasing power one and seventy-five one-hundredths percent (1.75%) of said purchasing power of one thousand dollars ($1,000) all to be based upon an index number of the price of commodities [the wholesale price index of the U.S. Bureau of Labor Statistics].

But the bonds attracted little interest, perhaps because the indexing provision did not come into play until the wholesale price index had risen 10 percent. These indexed bonds were replaced with conventional bonds a few years later when Rand Kardex merged with another company.[18]

Not until after World War II was there a surge of interest in index-linked bonds and other credit instruments. Since that time, index-linking of bonds and other credit instruments has been widely used in many countries, particularly Argentina, Brazil, Chile, Colombia, Finland, France, and Israel.[19] A wide variety of formulae has been used in these countries to index debt instruments. In some cases, only principal is indexed; in others, only interest is indexed; still others feature indexation of both principal and interest. Additional sums payable on account of the readjustment of the principal are often tax exempt, particularly in the case of government bonds. Generally, principal and interest are increased by 100 percent of the increase registered by the applicable index, but there are a substantial number of bonds in which the amount of the escalation is limited to a fraction of the percentage increase in the index. Because the great majority of creditors want to be assured that they will receive at least the nominal value of the sum lent, it is unusual to find index clauses that permit repayment of less than the nominal amount borrowed in the event the index declines. Bonds have been linked to such diverse economic indicators as consumer or wholesale price indexes, indexes of stock market values, and industrial production indexes.

Finland

Finland was the trailblazer, launching the first major issue of indexed government bonds in 1945. These were ten-year bonds issued to compensate owners of property ceded to Russia. They were fully indexed to the wholesale price index and bore 4 percent interest on current nominal value; however, a 10 percent increment in the price index was required to trigger the readjustment mechanism. Moreover, the government capped the index clause with a provision suspending indexation if the index number more than doubled. After May 1955, the Finnish government's bonds were adjusted for only one-half the change in the price index. With the sole exception of a 1963 issue linked to the wholesale price index for Finnish goods, all of the indexed government bonds issued between 1955 and 1968 were tied to the cost-of-living index.[20] The indexation provisions in nongovernment bonds after 1955 also guaranteed the purchaser only 50 percent of the index rise. A wide variety of indexes was employed. Some were linked to the cost-of-living index, the wholesale price index (or its domestic subindex), the export price index or the official exchange rate for sterling. Indexation rapidly spread throughout the bond market, so that by the end of 1967, when Finland abandoned indexation, 76 percent of all government bonds, 85 percent of the bonds of all financial institutions, and just over 30 percent of all nonfinancial corporate bonds were indexed.[21]

France

The country with the most unusual array of indexed bonds is France. This is in large part attributable to the bewildering assortment of cases and statutes invalidating certain kinds of index clauses.[22] A national loan issued in 1956 to finance the Algerian conflict was indexed to the average quotations of French stocks on the Paris Exchange. Another 1956 issue by the Équipement Industriel et Agricole tied interest payments to the index of industrial production. In 1957 the French government issued bonds whose value was linked to the stock exchange index of non-fixed-income securities, and in 1973 the French government issued bonds denominated in the European unit of account.[23]

Brazil

The country with the most extensive experience with indexed bonds is Brazil. By 1964, when the military seized power, the bond market had virtually disappeared. With an inflation rate that averaged 37.5 percent per year between 1954 and 1964, the yield on government securities purchased at par was negative by more than 30 percent per annum. Moreover, the risk of nonrepayment was substantial.[24] The market for Brazilian government bonds was so depressed prior to 1964 that the government could market them only by making their purchase compulsory. Because the government did not bother to repay these "compulsory loans," most Brazilians understandably regarded these exactions as taxes.

In an imaginative attempt to recreate a market for government securities at a time when the annual inflation rate was 92 percent, the government authorized the issuance in 1964 of Cr $700 billion (then about U.S. $580 million) worth of Readjustable Treasury Bonds (ORTNs) with maturity occurring anywhere between 3 and 20 years and an annual minimum interest rate of 6 percent,[25] calculated on the readjusted value of the bond's principal. This value was readjusted in accordance with changes in the wholesale price index. The increase in nominal value resulting from monetary correction was specifically exempted from income taxation.

Despite the seemingly high rates of return on the ORTNs, the Brazilian public gave them an initially cool reception. This was partly because Brazilian investors had little faith in their government's trustworthiness as a debtor, and partly because they did not trust Brazilian price indexes.[26] The great bulk (73 percent) of all ORTN placements occurring during 1964 were involuntary in the sense that they were held by government agencies or purchased by taxpayers as a way of reducing their income tax.[27] By 1966 ORTN subscriptions had increased to 1.4 billion cruzeiros (U.S. $ 630,450,000), an increase of 16.5 times in real terms over 1964 sales.

Only 17 percent of the ORTNs placed in 1966 were involuntary, and by 1974 involuntary subscriptions had been reduced to 3 percent.[28]

The ORTN has been a very useful device in the fight against inflation. It has enabled the government to finance its budgetary deficit by borrowing from the public instead of resorting to the printing press or the creation of credit. By reestablishing both the government's credit reputation and a market for government securities, the ORTN paved the way for the institution of open market operations.[29]

In 1965 private corporations were authorized to issue indexed bonds and convertible debentures, provided the maturity date was at least one year in the future and inflation adjustments were made no more often than quarterly. An example of an indexed convertible debenture is the Unipar Debenture, translated in Appendix C. There have been, however, relatively few such issues. As Professor Ness explained, "businessmen appear to have feared manipulation of the monetary correction index by the government or departure of their industry's prices and costs from national patterns."[30]

The suspicion that the monetary correction index might be manipulated proved to be well founded. The inflation readjustment was originally based upon a comparison between the wholesale price index for the prior quarter and the present quarter, with a three month hiatus before the adjustment would take effect.[31] Without the benefit of legislation, the government has from time to time changed the method of calculating the readjustment and computing the index. In recent years, the inflation adjustment for ORTNs has increased significantly less rapidly than has the wholesale price index. Consequently, the theoretically automatic readjustment mechanism has in practice become highly discretionary.[32] Because legislation adopted in June 1977 has mandated that virtually all indexed private obligations be adjusted at the same rate as ORTNs,[33] the government has also been able to manipulate the rate of private sector indexation.

On January 16, 1980 the National Monetary Council suddenly abandoned the concept of *ex post* monetary correction for ORTNs, thereby effectively prohibiting indexation of virtually all transactions. Until November of 1980, when this policy was dramatically reversed, ORTNs were being readjusted every two months in accordance with a presumed rate of inflation, optimistically set by the National Monetary Council at 45 percent for all of 1980 (subsequently reset at 50 percent for the twelve months beginning with June 1980). With the actual inflation rate running at approximately twice the presumed inflation rate, there was a substantial shift from indexed obligations into other forms of investment. Since January 1981, ORTNs have been fully indexed to the national consumer price index.

Israel

In 1955 the Israeli government, which had been issuing small amounts of dollar-linked bonds since 1948, began to offer investors the option of bonds tied to the cost-of-living index or the dollar exchange rate. The latter option was eliminated in 1962. Initially, only 50 to 70 percent of the value of bonds was readjusted, depending on term to maturity. Over the years the percentage of indexation rose to 100. It declined to 90 percent at the end of 1975, and in 1977 was further reduced to 80 percent, producing a sharp decline in government bond sales.

The Israeli indexed bond market, unlike that of most countries, is by no means restricted to governmental issues. A substantial number of issues by private corporations has resulted from linkage insurance, made available by the Israeli government since 1966. For a modest premium, private Israeli corporations can insure themselves against rises in the index. Because the premium does not cover the costs of the program, the government has effectively subsidized indexed borrowers. Indexed bonds have totally dominated the Israeli bond market; however, they have not prevented the development of a viable capital market for equity shares.[34]

Argentina

Argentina began issuing indexed bonds in 1972. These paid 7 percent annual interest plus a readjustment of the face value in accordance with variations in the wholesale price index for nonagricultural products, less 5 percent. The 5 percent reduction in the inflation adjustment was supposed to equal the average inflation rate experienced by the majority of countries with so-called stable currencies, though the relevance of this rate to an internal obligation is not readily apparent. The interest and the inflation adjustment are both tax exempt.

The most popular of these adjustable bonds, National Adjustable Values (VNAs), were freely traded on the stock exchange and became immensely popular as inflation accelerated sharply. By 1975 indexed government bonds totally dominated the stock market, accounting for 96.7 percent of the total value of all securities traded. In 1973 indexed bonds represented only slightly more than 1 percent of the total financial assets held by the Argentine public. By 1975 indexed bonds accounted for approximately one-third of the public's financial assets.[35]

Other Countries

In 1952 the Swedish Cooperative Society floated bonds whose principal was linked to increases in the consumer price index. The index clause was capped; the total increase in the adjusted value of the principal could not exceed 50 percent of the bond's original face value.[36]

In 1955 Iceland began issuing bonds tied to the consumer price index, but in 1964 switched to the building cost index. These bonds have maturities of 10 to 14 years and pay an annual interst of 5 to 7.2 percent. Both principal and interest are readjusted each year. In 1972 Iceland started to issue lottery bonds for road construction. These ten-year bonds are indexed to the cost-of-living index. They carry no interest, but 7 to 9 percent of the nominal principal is distributed each year in an annual lottery. In the same year, the Icelandic government began offering private pension funds fifteen-year indexed bonds. These bonds carry 5 percent annual interest and are linked to the building cost index.[37]

Chile's Land Reform Law of 1967 made compensation for expropriation payable partly in cash and partly in bonds. Seventy percent of the bonds issued to each owner had their principal readjusted annually on the basis of consumer price index. The 3 percent annual interest has been readjusted by half the proportionate adjustment in the principal.[38]

In 1967 the Colombian government began issuing indexed bonds as reserve assets for the Social Security Institute, the only entity authorized to purchase these bonds. The bonds paid 6 percent annual interest plus a readjustment equal to 70 percent of the annual change in the wholesale price index.[39]

Indexed bonds have never caught on in the leading financial centers. Despite the urging of a number of economists, the governments of England and the United States have never issued indexed bonds. Nor have private corporations rushed to do so. Other than the abortive experiment of Rand Kardex in 1925, there have been only a few, small companies that have issued indexed debentures.[40]

LINKAGE OF LOANS AND BANK DEPOSITS

Financial markets are interrelated. If investors are offered index-linked bonds, banks and savings and loan associations come under great pressure to index time deposits to prevent substantial withdrawals. If bank deposits are indexed, loans must also be indexed in order to maintain the normal spread between the cost of money to banks and their loan earnings. Thus, it is not surprising that most countries that have issued indexed bonds have also permitted indexation of commercial loans and bank deposits.

Finland

In 1946, one year after the Finnish government issued its first indexed bond, the Finnish Public Pension Institute began making indexed loans.

Borrowers were obligated to adjust amortization of principal and interest by 50 percent of the variations in the wholesale price index. These loans were atypical in that their principal would have decreased below the amount originally lent had the wholesale price index actually declined. In 1947–48 private insurance companies began offering similarly indexed loans. Large government loans to industry were generally linked to one-half or one-fourth of the movement in the wholesale or consumer price indexes, though in one instance they were tied to one-third of the sterling exchange rate. Loans to individuals from the government were generally not indexed. In 1955 indexation was extended to all commercial and savings bank deposits left for a minimum of one year. In 1957 a separate class of deposits was created to attract the depositor with a high marginal tax rate. This new class of deposits was indexed to reflect only 50 percent of the variations in the cost-of-living index and bore a slightly higher interest rate than fully indexed deposits. Unlike fully indexed deposits, half-indexed deposits were tax-exempt. When the privilege of tax exemption was conferred on fully indexed deposits in 1964, half-indexed deposits disappeared.[41] Commercial bank loans were correspondingly indexed to assure the lending bank an acceptable spread between its lending rate and borrowing costs. The indexation of loans and deposits was prohibited in 1968 by the Economic Special Powers Act.[42]

Communist China

With prices rising more than 7,000 percent in 1949, the Chinese Communists introduced the device of "parity deposits" to permit the continued function of the banking system. Chinese banks linked the value of their deposits to the price of a "parity basket" of four essential commodities: rice, cotton fabric, peanut oil, and coal briquettes. The value of the parity basket was estimated on a daily basis, and deposits were readjusted immediately. Bank loans were placed on a similar basis. When prices began to fall in 1950, this adjustment mechanism was abandoned, for it contained no floor on the downward readjustment of the value of deposits. Instead, banks linked deposits to certain regionally important commodities. The linkage mechanism, however, contained a ratchet; the nominal value of the deposits did not decrease in the event of a decline in commodity prices. These linked deposits were abandoned in 1952.[43]

Israel

In 1955 the Israeli government decided to index most of its medium and long-term loans to the private sector. The terms of these loans mirrored those for indexed government bonds. The borrower was given the option of having his loan linked to either the cost-of-living index or the exchange rate, and the percentage of the loan indexed varied directly with the length of the loan. Great difficulty with loans linked to the foreign exchange rate resulted from the government's policy of postponing devaluation for several years and then making a massive readjustment. Thus, in 1962 a 67 percent devaluation of the Israeli pound created severe hardships for the many borrowers who had opted to have their loans linked to the exchange rate. The government was forced to modify the linkage arrangement, permitting borrowers whose loans were linked to the exchange rate the following options: (1) exchanging their dollar-linked loans for cost-of-living linked loans, retroactive to the date of the loan; (2) prepaying the outstanding balance at the former exchange rate, plus a 3 percent commission; or (3) extending the remaining repayment term by one-third. In addition, mortgagors were granted reductions of 5 to 15 percent on the balance of their loans. Private mortgage banks were compensated for their losses in carrying out these relief provisions.[44]

The Israelis have also had difficulty with loans, particularly mortgages, linked to the cost-of-living index. Many borrowers failed to understand the implications of indexation of future payments. Moreover, many found their incomes rising less rapidly than their loan payments, particularly in the short run. Rising popular discontent and undue optimism about the potentiality for future monetary stability led the Israeli government to stop indexing its loans in 1967 in exchange for an annual inflation premium of 3 or 4 percent of the amount of the loan. Because Israel's annual inflation rate averaged 24.2 percent between 1969 and 1976, this shift in policy resulted in a substantial subsidy to those fortunate enough to be able to borrow from the government. Israeli commercial banks and private lenders are not so generous; they have continued to link virtually all medium- and long-term loans to the cost-of-living index.[45]

Israel has utilized several techniques to protect the value of savings deposits. In 1955 the government inaugurated a "Savings for Housing Plan," which paid savers a tax-exempt nominal interest rate ranging between 4 and 6 percent, depending on the length of time the money had been left on deposit. The value of the deposit was linked to the cost of apartment construction. The savings of depositors who wished to withdraw from the scheme were readjusted in accordance with the cost-of-living index. Home mortgages were also linked to the cost-of-living index under this program. Similar programs were offered by private mortgage banks.

More recent arrangements have offered savers the option of an unlinked relatively high rate of interest (up to a tax-free 9 percent annually), or a much lower rate of interest (up to a tax-free 4 percent annually) linked to the cost-of-living index.[46] In addition, recipients of German restitution payments and nonresidents have been allowed to maintain deposits in foreign currency at annual interest rates up to 7 percent free from tax. The restitution payments may be drawn on in foreign currency only for specified purposes. Otherwise withdrawals must be made in Israeli currency, but depositors are protected against devaluation.[47]

Chile

During the late 1950s, Chile began linking credit transactions to the U.S. dollar. Banking regulations adopted in 1958–59 permitted commercial banks to accept interest-bearing deposits in U.S. dollars and to make loans in dollars. These regulations were designed to encourage Chileans to repatriate their foreign holdings by providing domestic inflation protection and an attractive dollar interest rate.[48] Because devaluation of the Chilean peso has lagged considerably behind the domestic inflation rate, these dollar accounts offered limited protection against the Chilean inflation. Foreign currency deposits as a percentage of time deposits in the Chilean banking system have declined dramatically from 35.3 percent in 1975 to 6.4 percent in 1980.[49]

Legislation adopted in Chile in 1960 authorized the governmental Corporation for Production Development (CORFU) to make peso loans to the agricultural sector with U.S. dollars as the unit of account. The borrower had to repay the loans in Chilean currency reflecting the same number of dollars borrowed at the exchange rate in effect at the date of repayment, plus interest of up to nine percent per annum. CORFU was also authorized to make peso loans indexed to three subindexes of the wholesale price index: agricultural, industrial, or mineral.[50]

In 1959, after chronic inflation sent most traditional suppliers of mortgage credit into bankruptcy, Chile initiated an indexed housing finance system along Israeli lines. Chilean D.F.L. No. 2 of July 31, 1959 authorized the State Bank to accept savings deposit quotas bearing 3 percent annual interest. The principal of these quotas was readjusted annually in accordance with most of the variation in an official wage and salary index.[51] The interest and inflation adjustment were tax-exempt. Savers who had amassed the requisite amount of quotas were assured of mortgage loans, which were supposed to have been readjusted by the same index. D.F.L. No. 205 of April 25, 1960 created the National Saving and Loan System (SINAP), a system of private savings and loan associations along the lines developed in the United States, but maintained the same readjustment system. The system was modified in 1963 by a law that limited the amount of adjustment by the State Bank (subsequently extended to the private savings and loan associations) to the lesser of the increase in the wage and salary index or the cost-of-living index.[52] Because the wage and salary index rose more rapidly than the cost-of-living index until in 1972, this legislation constituted a subsidy to the borrower. The reverse occurred in 1972 and 1973, resulting in Decree-Law 162 of November 26, 1973, which indexed all savings and loan operations to the consumer price index. Because of the high rates of inflation, readjustments have been made quarterly and later monthly.[53]

The Chilean system has been fairly successful in capturing savings, but the system, or perhaps lack thereof, has worked poorly in practice.

> Until recently, the government savings and loan system has been hopelessly confused and economically unsatisfactory. Over twelve different savings plans were available, at least in theory. Terms, interest rates, and down payments varied arbitrarily. Though savings was to be a major condition for obtaining a loan, the granting of loans was not in fact closely related to an aspirant's savings record. Loans did not constitute an effective response to the demand for housing. Finally, loans were not adequately tailored to meet the costs of borrowers.[54]

The Chilean savings and loan system was restructured in 1967 to eliminate some of these difficulties, but problems have remained.

Chile has had a high default rate on its readjustable mortgages. Even though wages were rising more rapidly than the rate of mortgage readjustment, it was estimated that in the late 1960s approximately 80 percent of the 150,000 borrowers were behind on at least one payment, and that the average arrearage was ten payments.[55] Enforcement attempts were lackadaisical, for democratically elected governments in Chile were politically incapable of insisting upon strict collection of readjustable mortgage payments. In addition, during the 1960s the rate of upward readjustment of mortgage payments was held to less than one-half the rate of increase in the consumer price index.[56] With good reason Chileans used to repeat the refrain: "Casa CORVI, casa gratis" (A house from CORVI [the government Housing Corporation] is a house for free).[57]

During the late 1960s and early 1970s, the savings and loan system had a decided advantage in attracting savings because it was able to offer an indexed rate of return, while the commercial banks and finance companies were permitted to pay only a fixed-rate of return. This fixed-rate of return was sharply negative, and became even more so as inflation began to shift into high gear in 1972 and 1973. In 1974 the Pinochet government decided to liberalize interest rates and encourage indexation of most credit transactions. Decree-Law No. 455 of May 25, 1974 mandated that all credit transactions with a maturity of one year (later reduced to three months) or more had to be indexed to the consumer price index unless the parties specially decline to do so. The interest rate ceiling on nonindexed commercial bank operations with a maturity of less than one year was raised to 200 percent a year, and the ceiling for loans by finance companies was set at 250 percent a year. Shortly thereafter, the interest rates that commercial banks could pay on time deposits and earn on their loans were freed entirely. By the end of 1975 approximately 56 percent of all Chilean financial obligations were still indexed. Although interest rates have declined sharply since then, there has still been a sizable flow of funds away from the indexed savings and loan system into fixed-rate, short-term finance company operations, which offer much higher real rates of return to investors.[58]

Brazil

Since the mid-1960s, the great bulk of loans and savings deposits in Brazil have been monetarily corrected. There is, however, considerable variation in the types of monetary correction and the degree to which they correct for inflation. Systems of *ex post* and *ex ante* monetary correction have grown up side by side.

In 1964, in addition to indexing government bonds, Brazil set up a far reaching National Housing Plan based upon the principle of *ex post* monetary correction. The National Housing Bank (BNH) was set up to serve as the conduit for investment and application of funds in residential housing. The BNH's resources are derived from a monetarily corrected national pension fund administered by the bank, and from the sale of monetarily corrected real estate bills to private investors.[59] In addition, savings and loan associations affiliated with the BNH are able to attract mortgage funds by paying similar rates of interest plus monetary correction. Funds invested or deposited in the National Housing System receive a return of 6 (formerly 8) percent annually, plus tax-free monetary correction calculated in the same manner as the ORTNs, the readjustable government bonds. The Brazilian housing finance system has been enormously successful in financing the construction of large numbers of new homes and apartments.[60]

The Brazilians have encountered a problem similar to that of the Israelis and Chileans with respect to indexed mortgages, but have handled it better. Initially, all borrowers from the financial entities comprising the National Housing Program had their loans subjected to the same kind of monetary correction utilized to readjust the ORTNs. Instead of being adjusted quarterly, however, mortgage loans were monetarily corrected only after the government changed the minimum wage (normally about once a year). Before two years had elapsed, the number of borrowers in arrears on their monthly mortgage payments had reached alarming proportions. One reason for the large number of defaults was apparent: the wholesale price index rose 76 percent from February 1964 to February 1965, while the highest minimum wage rose by only 57 percent. Consequently, the BNH adopted a program permitting low-cost housing loans to be readjusted on the basis of the percentage increment in the minimum wage, while retaining the ORTN-wholesale price index as the yardstick for higher cost housing.[61]

To make up the difference between actual payments and what should have been paid if the original plan of monetary correction had been adhered to, BNH readjusted the term of the mortgage. To meet the complaint that payments might go on forever, BNH set a limit of 1.5 times the original mortgage term; to insure against possible losses resulting from this limitation on repayment obligatons, BNH set up a Compensation Fund for Salary Variations. Borrowers paid one monthly installment into the fund in exchange for the fund's guaranty to liquidate any balance remaining at the end of the expanded term of the mortgage.

There was great dissatisfaction with this scheme, but much of the dissatisfaction was psychological in origin. Low-income mortgagors had difficulty understanding the intricacies of constantly shifting mortgage payments and terms, and lacked the economic sophistication to comprehend the concept of monetary correction. In 1969 the bank felt constrained to replace this program with the Plan of Salary Equivalence. Under this new plan, participation in which was optional, the maximum number of mortgage payments was fixed (though the borrower could prepay), and all payments by the borrower to the Compensation Fund were eliminated. The system of monetary correction for low-income borrowers was geared to the minimum wage. If wages rose faster than the ORTN index over the life of the mortgage, the borrower would wind up paying more cruzeiros than he would have under the original program.[62] To the extent the minimum wage lagged behind the wholesale price index, the Compensation Fund subsidized the low-income borrower.

Since 1969 the minimum wage has generally been increasing as fast as or a bit more rapidly than the wholesale price index, which in turn has been increasing considerably more rapidly than the Standard Capital Unit (UPC),[63] the standard for readjustment for high-income borrowers. This is partly the result of an attempt since 1969 to compensate for the squeeze on wages in the preceding years, and partly the result of the government's manipulation of the ORTN index, which in turn readjusts the UPC. This means that the bite of monetary correction has fallen more heavily on low-income borrowers who opted for the Plan of Salary Equivalence than upon nonparticipants and high-income borrowers.[64] It also means that contributors to the FGTS pension system, savings depositors, and purchasers of housing bills have been subsidizing the mortgages of higher-income borrowers. On the other hand, the nominal interest rates paid by low-income borrowers (1 to 6 percent annually) have been considerably below those paid by higher-income borrowers (10 to 12 percent annually). Thus, the higher-income borrowers have been subsidizing the lower-income borrowers. Moreover, the minimum wage has generally been increasing as fast as the monetary correction mechanism. These two factors may explain why Brazil has had a manageable delinquency problem on its housing loans. Though estimates on arrearages vary widely, BNH claims that only 3 percent of its low-income homes have been vacated because of an inability to meet payments.[65]

In 1965 Brazil enacted a comprehensive statute designed to stimulate the development of capital markets.[66] Known as the Capital Markets Law, this statute authorized the issuance of a variety of financial instruments, such as promissory notes, loans, and bills of exchange, with tax-free monetary correction. Banks and finance companies were also authorized to pay monetary correction on deposits. Monetary correction was based upon the same index as the ORTNs. Deposits and debt instruments were required to have a minimum term of one year to be eligible for monetary correction.

The Capital Markets Law has had little success in stimulating long and medium-term monetarily corrected debt instruments. Lenders have preferred to extend credit only for short terms, in part because of the lack of a market for the resale of commercial paper. The government, therefore, had to reduce the minimum term for eligibility for monetary correction from one year to six months. Moreover, Brazilian borrowers have been reluctant to enter into loan transactions whose costs remained uncertain until the date fixed for repayment and ultimately depended upon something as unpredictable as the reported inflation rate.

To facilitate advance determination of the cost of money and to circumvent the 12 percent interest limitation of the usury law, at least at a semantic level, the government authorized the use of "prefixed monetary correction" for loans and bank deposits. In 1967 Brazilian finance companies began issuing bills of exchange with prefixed monetary correction. Banks also began to use prefixed monetary correction on short-term loans, certificates of deposit, and time deposits. The total interest and estimated monetary correction rate were fixed in advance, but no attempt was made to separate interest from monetary correction until the official calculation of the ORTN inflation adjustment became available. At that time any amount paid in excess of the officially permitted level of monetary correction was labelled interest and the balance, if any, was considered tax-exempt monetary correction.[67] At the end of 1968, the government issued a decree-law that attempted to discourage prefixed monetary correction and to encourage longer term credit by imposing withholding tax on prefixed monetary correction for loans and bills of exchange, although not deposits. The withholding tax rate varied inversely with the life of the loan, with a high of 10 percent on loans between 180 and 269 days, and a low of 4 percent on loans of more than 720 days.[68]

In 1978 Brazil modified its taxation of prefixed monetary correction. Starting in fiscal year 1979 all financial instruments and bank deposits with prefixed monetary correction were subject withholding tax of 50 percent on their "real yield," statutorily defined as 20 percent of their total nominal yield. The National Monetary Council, however, is specifically authorized to redefine that percentage from time to time, taking into account the length of term and the inflation rate.[69] That power has been exercised through Central Bank Resolutions 503 of 1978 and 525 of 1979, as well as Circular 491 of 1980, so that the percentage of nominal yield of prefixed monetary correction obligations now subject to the 50 percent withholding tax varies from 20 percent for those with a term shorter than 360 days to 14 percent for those with a term longer than 719 days. Income realized by individuals from prefixed monetary correction is taxed exclusively through withholding and need not be included in individual returns, but legal entities must include prefixed monetary correction in income and take a credit for the withholding tax paid. *Ex post* monetary correction gains on deposits and investments have remained tax-exempt for individuals, provided the monetary correction conforms to readjustments of the ORTN. On the other hand, since 1975, juridical entities have been required to include all monetary correction gains in taxable income.[70] Some, however, eventually exclude these gains in computing a tax-free reserve for working capital.

In 1974 Central Bank Resolution No. 286 attempted to convert prefixed monetary correction on certificates of deposit, bills of exchange, and time deposits of more than two years into *ex post* monetary correction. The monetary authorities were concerned that present expectations of inflation rates, formed in a period when the inflation rate had suddenly increased, would be transmitted into future years if prefixed monetary correction were permitted in obligations with a term of more than two years. This created a difficult problem for various finance companies. Their response was the issuance of bills with an intriguing blend of prefixed and *ex post* monetary correction. The nominal interest rate was fixed, but the term of the loan varied in accordance with the number of payments needed to conform to the inflation rate reported by the ORTN index.[71]

Loans and deposits with prefixed monetary correction have thus far been exempted from the requirement of linkage to the rate of monetary correction of the ORTNs, provided they are made or paid through financial institutions. Instead, the government has directly regulated the interest rates paid and received by financial institutions. In 1980 the regulated rates were held well below the actual inflation rate as part of the government's pursuit of two mutually inconsistent goals: reduction in the amount of credit and reduction in interest rates.

Brazil has never applied the principle of monetary correction to all long-term loans. Loans to agriculture have typically been made by the Brazilian government at sharply negative rates as a deliberate subsidy.[72] Certain governmental financing institutions, such as the National Development Bank (BNDE), make long-term priority loans to private sector Brazilian-owned firms at negative interest rates. In 1980 the percentage of monetary correction imposed on such loans was sharply increased, but the interest rates still remain quite negative. Because most of the loan funds come from pension and trust funds which are supposed to be insulated from inflationary erosion by complete monetary correction, the labor force has been making substantial subsidies to Brazilian industry and agriculture.[73]

In January 1980, Brazil inaugurated a short-lived experiment with compulsory under-indexation. Monetary correction of credit transactions continued to be linked to the ORTN index, but the government began to readjust the ORTNs *ex ante* rather than *ex post.* In other words, virtually all Brazilian monetary correction became prefixed two months in advance in accordance with a presumed rate of inflation. The presumed rate of inflation was set at approximately half the actual rate of inflation for two reasons. One was the government's belief that monetary correction was generating inflationary feedback, which had to be reduced. The other was that people's expectations about the future rate of inflation had to be lowered as part of the government's anti-inflationary economic program. The results of this experiment were a substantial redistribution of income from creditors to debtors, a drying up of credit and investment, a significant decline in the savings rate, and an increase in credit transaction costs as lenders developed a variety of techniques for circumventing governmental constraints on interest rates. In November 1980 the government conceded the failure of this compulsory under-indexation policy. In a significant about face, Brazil returned to the concept of *ex post* monetary correction. Instead of linking monetary correction to the wholesale price index, however, Brazil has decided to use the national consumer price index created in 1979 for wage indexation.[74]

Colombia

Colombia has had a chronic shortage of urban housing. This shortage has in large part been caused by the sharply negative rates of interest paid to savers. Although inflation averaged 11 percent during the 1960s, the highest interest rate payable on passbook savings deposits was 4 percent per annum. In 1971 the interest rate on savings deposits was raised to 8.5 percent per annum, but that measure was ineffective in stimulating the necessary increase in savings. In 1972 Colombia followed the Brazilian and Chilean examples and instituted a monetarily corrected savings and loan system.[75] Savings and loan accounts were stated in terms of constant purchasing power units (UPACs). At first UPACs were linked to a three-month moving average of the cost-of-living index. But as inflation accelerated, the monetary authorities shifted the calculation of the inflation adjustment to a twelve-month and then to a twenty-four-month moving average in order to reduce the size of the adjustment.

Deposits denominated in UPACs enjoyed huge advantages over conventional savings deposits and mortgage bonds. Thus, in 1973, when conventional savings deposits and mortgage bonds were earning annual yields of 7 and 11 percent, respectively, UPACs were yielding 28 to 28.5 percent. Moreover, only the 5 to 5.5 percent portion of the UPAC yield denominated as interest was subject to income taxation. Not surprisingly, UPAC deposits increased by 1800 percent in real terms during 1973, while the amount of conventional savings deposits declined in real terms.[76] Because of a strong surge in the inflation rate and great pressure from the banks to increase the money supply to make up for the loss of deposits being transferred to UPAC accounts, in 1974 the Colombian government issued Decrees Nos. 1728 and 2274 reducing the nominal yield on UPAC accounts, restricting the monetary correction adjustment to 20 percent a year, and subjecting monetary correction in excess of 8 percent *per annum* to capital gains tax. This restriction on monetary correction was further reduced in 1975 and 1976, making the yields negative in real terms. Decree No. 664 of 1979 placed a maximum limit of 19 percent a year on the UPAC, making the return negative by 5 percent that year. Decline in the real rate of return and the promotion of alternative fixed rate of return savings instruments have sharply slowed the rush of funds into UPAC accounts.[77]

Other Countries

A number of other countries have indexed mortgages and/or deposits. In 1957, Denmark instituted a successful indexed savings scheme.[78] Iceland has for many years been indexing mortgage loans to the average blue collar wage rate. In 1971, however, borrower dissatisfaction led the government to place a ceiling of 3.5 percent on the inflation adjustment so that the total cost of interest and indexing could not exceed 7.75 percent per year. This ceiling was modified three years later to permit the State Building Fund to pass on the cost of its own indexed borrowing as a surcharge.[79]

In 1966 Bolivia set up a system of readjustable savings deposits and home mortgages. The law provides for linkage to an average of the change in the cost-of-living index, a wage-salary index, and the foreign exchange rate. Nevertheless, in practice, only the exchange rate has been used.[80] Between 1966 and 1974, when the system was abolished, the Swedish government made parity loans for housing and education. Payment of part of the interest was postponed and added to principal, which was linked to a construction cost index. The system was intended to defer repayment of principal and part of the interest for approximately eight years with eventual amortization after twenty-five to thirty years. But interest rates rose to more than 7 percent a year, while the index of construction costs increased by less than 3 percent a year. In this curious, unanticipated circumstance, many of the government parity loans would never have been repaid in full.[81] In 1969, Uruguay set up a readjustable savings and mortgage system. All loans and savings deposits are linked to a readjustable unit, which is adjusted by the average wage index for workers.[82]

In 1976, Argentina began indexing savings deposits and home mortgages to the wholesale price index for nonagricultural products. In February 1977, the Argentine government unilaterally revoked a huge subsidy by imposing revaluation of all unindexed debts and mortgages contracted with the National Mortgage Bank, whose receipts had become insufficient to pay its operating expenses, let alone maintain its capital. These debts and mortgages had to be monetarily corrected in accordance with coefficients derived from an industrial wage index for Buenos Aires; however, debtors were afforded the option of avoiding monetary correction by paying off these debts in full within ninety days of the statute's effective date.[83]

VARIABLE RATE MORTGAGES

Another technique for coping with the deleterious effect of inflation on mortgage financing is the variable rate mortgage. Variable rate mortgages are widely used in Australia, England, Germany, South Africa, Sweden, Switzerland, and the United States.[84] Only the interest rate, but not the principal, of these mortgages varies generally in accordance with some barometer of the tightness of money. For example, in the United States the interest rate on variable mortgages is usually linked either to the average cost of savings deposits and borrowings to savings and loan associations or to the national average interest rate on new mortgages. In England the Building Societies Association recommends interest rate changes to members on the basis of the savings rate, the cost of bank operations, and the rates on new mortgages.[85]

A variation of the variable rate mortgage, called a renegotiable rate mortgage, has recently appeared in the United States.[86] Renegotiable rate mortgages are a series of short-term loans for periods varying between three and five years, automatically renewable at equal intervals, and secured by a long-term mortgage of up to thirty years. The initial interest rate is set by the lender at whatever the market will bear and local usury laws will permit. The interest rate offered on renewal of each short-term loan is tied to the national average mortgage index, which reflects the national average of mortgage interest rates currently charged by savings and loan associations on the purchase of previously occupied homes. Irrespective of the movement of the index, the maximum increase or decrease permitted under federal regulations is one-half of one percentage point for each year in the loan term of adjustment period, with a maximum total increase or decrease of five percentage points over the life of the mortgage. Downward adjustments in the interest rate are mandatory; upward adjustments are optional with the lender. At the expiration of each short-term loan, the borrower may prepay the remaining principal balance without penalty.

Variable rate and renegotiable mortgages are notably inferior to indexed mortgages as a device for offsetting inflationary distortions. When the applicable rate of interest moves upward, the change in the borrower's payments tends to be quite large and wholly unrelated to either the inflation rate or the presumably concomitant rise in the borrower's income. For example, an increase in the interest rate from 3 to 5 percent on a variable rate mortgage will produce a 24 percent increase in annual payments, whereas an increase in the inflation rate from 3 to 5 percent on an indexed mortgage will produce only a 2 percent increase in annual payments.[87] The variable rate mortgage imposes upon the borrower a substantial, additional real risk, for it effectively produces a higher front-end load. Increases in the nominal interest rates on variable rate mortgages are hardest on new borrowers, whose mortgage payments consist almost entirely of interest.[88] Thus, payments of all mortgage borrowers are significantly affected by slight changes in the nominal rate, and borrowers as a political constituency are likely to exert substantial pressure to retard upward movements of the interest rate to which their payments are linked. The resulting delay may significantly inhibit the process of adopting proper monetary policies to stabilize the economy.

ALTERNATIVE MORTGAGE FINANCING TECHNIQUES

A variety of alternative methods of mortgage financing has been developed in recent years to attempt to offset the effects of inflation. For commercial property, mortgages are being written with clauses entitling the lender to a percentage of the income generated by the property. For example, a mortgage on a hotel might require the borrower to repay a fixed amount plus 2 percent of the gross room rental receipts, or a shopping center mortgage might require a "kicker" of 10 percent of the net income from rentals. Fear of being locked into long-term mortgages at interest rates well below market has led to the development of renegotiable mortgages, where the interest rate is reset every few years in light of then prevailing rates. Many lenders in the United States are currently experimenting with seven-year renegotiable mortgages. A recent development in the United States has been the shared appreciation participation mortgage. In exchange for a below market interest rate, mortgage borrowers agree to assign to the lender part of any capital gain (usually one-third) whenever the mortgaged home is sold.

None of these measures is as precise in offsetting the effects of inflation as indexing, yet they have the distinct advantage of assuring the borrower that his ability to pay will keep pace with any increase in his mortgage obligation. The shared appreciation mortgage, however, seems likely to generate a host of problems and may prove impossible to administer without extensive litigation. Homes may be conveyed to straw parties. Valuation of improvements is virtually certain to create problems, as will long-term leases. Some lenders are considering reappraisal after certain periods regardless of whether the borrower has sold the property, but such measures are likely to create substantial administrative problems.

INFLATION'S EFFECT ON INSURANCE

Another legal and financial institution severely affected by inflation is insurance. In a stable economy, insurance companies play a vital role in the capital and financial markets by investing their policy reserves in long-term obligations such as bonds, mortgages and large development projects. Inflation adversely affects the ability of insurance companies to function as mainstays of these markets in several ways. During extended periods of substantial inflation, fewer people purchase insurance because the value of the protection declines over time. If the face value of the policy is fixed in nominal terms, inflation will render the policy's proceeds inadequate to rebuild the home destroyed by fire or support a deceased's spouse and family. Inflation will also reduce the real income earned by insurance companies from their investment portfolios.

Life insurance companies simultaneously profit and lose from inflation. The terms of most whole life policies obligate the insurance companies to loan a sum equivalent to a policy's cash value at modest rates of interest. The number of policy loans increases rapidly during inflation, for these modest interest rates quickly become effectively negative. To meet the increased demand for policy loans, insurers must liquidate some of their long-term investments. These liquidations are at depressed terms, for the demand for long-term investments dries up during inflation. In addition, yields on the unliquidated portion of insurers' investment portfolios become increasingly negative as inflation progresses. On the other hand, as inflation progresses, liabilities of the insurance companies to policyholders, annuitants, and pensioners become proportionately less expensive to discharge in real terms.

Because policy terms are typically much shorter, fire, casualty, and health insurance companies do not enjoy the same inflation hedge as life insurance companies. The former companies are adversely affected by inflation on account of the calculation of premiums on the basis of nominal outlays from past experience. Because the costs of health care, construction, and repair work increase rapidly with inflation, an increasing percentage of claims approach the policy limits. With severe inflation, virtually every claim exceeds deductible limits. Yields on invested reserves, like those of the life insurance companies, tend to become negative, but unlike life insurance companies, fire and casualty insurers can adjust their rate structures every year to current costs. Moreover, many legal systems permit insured defendants to take limited advantage of inflation's ability to reduce the real value of tort and contract claims by delaying payment or calculating damages as of the date of the injury rather than the date of actual payment.[89] Thus, liability insurers have an inflation hedge, because they can satisfy claims in depreciated currency.

Insurance Claims as Debts of Value

In those countries accepting the doctrine of debts of value,[90] there is considerable disagreement about the proper characterization of insurance indemnities and annuities. Nussbaum denies that insurance contracts give rise to debts of value.[91] Ascarelli, on the other hand, maintains that indemnities arising from the insurance of property are debts of value, but he denies such treatment to life insurance policies.[92] The Austrian Supreme Court in 1926 held that an insurance annuity contract created a debt of value.[93] The issue has been considered in a number of recent Argentine cases, primarily in the context of subrogation suits by insurance companies after damage claims have been paid. The great majority of these cases conclude that insurance policies create pecuniary obligations and not debts of value.[94]

The rate structure of the insurance industry makes the debt of value a poor vehicle to resolve the distortions stemming from inflation. To be sure, there are cases such as *Anderson v. Equitable L. Assurance Society,*[95] where it would have been eminently just to utilize the concept of a debt of value to prevent inflation from completely wiping out the value of a paid-up life insurance policy. But there are many cases in which it would be grossly unfair to calculate in real terms the sums of an insurance company must pay when its rates have been calculated on the assumption of nominalism.

Indexed Insurance Policies

Indexing insurance policies for inflation was tried in Germany after World War I. The experiment, which was limited to liability and property insurance, was soon abandoned, in large part because of the inability of insurance companies to place their reserves in correspondingly indexed investments.[96]

In 1948, Finnish insurance companies began issuing policies with face values and premiums linked to the cost-of-living index. Term policies have been fully indexed; since 1957 whole life policies have been only 50 percent indexed. A 10 percent increase in the cost-of-living index has been required to trigger the index adjustment. Insurance companies also began indexing their loans to the wholesale price index, using the linkage proceeds to raise values on old policies in force. Although indexing was generally abolished in Finland in 1968, it has been retained for the insurance industry. The general ban against indexing, however, has created a serious problem in maintaining indexed policies in force, for the insurance companies have been unable to invest their reserves in similarly indexed obligations.[97]

Insurance policies linked to the cost-of-living index have been used in a number of countries, such as Argentina, Belgium, Spain, and Uruguay, for many years.[98] Until 1959, when index clauses were generally prohibited, French insurance companies commonly indexed their policies and premiums to the cost-of-living index. An exception was fire insurance policies, which were generally indexed to the cost of construction in the Paris region, though the indexation feature could be waived at the option of the insured. Not until 1969 did the French government adopt measures permitting insurance companies even minimally to adapt their policies to inflation by issuance of variable life policies,[99] a form of insurance discussed *infra.*

In Israel, Chile, and Brazil the insurance industry has been resuscitated through indexation. Inflation in all three countries had caused consumer avoidance of fixed-amount policies. Since the mid-1950s Israeli and Chilean insurance companies have indexed their policies and premiums to the cost-of-living index, and have invested their reserves in correspondingly linked bonds and securities.[100] Since 1966 Brazilian insurance companies have been authorized to issue monetarily corrected policies.[101] Premiums and policy values are linked to the same index as Readjustable Treasury Bonds (ORTNs). The insurance companies are required to maintain their reserves in ORTNs or in financing operations, such as loans through the National Economic Development Bank, with similar monetary correction.[102]

A number of Canadian and U.S. companies have recently initiated indexed policies. North American Life Assurance Co. of Toronto, which began issuing term and whole life insurance policies linked to the consumer price index in 1969, has been one of the pioneers.[103] Fire and homeowner policies are now being routinely issued with coverage limits indexed to construction costs, and an increasing number of U.S. and Canadian companies are linking face amounts of life insurance to the consumer price index. Examples of index clauses currently in use by U.S. companies for readjusting life and homeowner's coverage are shown in Appendices D and E.

Variable Life Insurance

Insurance companies in several countries, including Canada, England, France, the Netherlands, and the United States, have been offering variable life insurance policies for a number of years. The face amount of these policies fluctuates in accordance with the investment experience of a separate equity securities account. The value of the policy during any given time period is adjusted by a factor that reflects the relationship between the actual net investment experience of the underlying separate account and the interest rate assumed for calculating net premiums and reserves. To maintain actuarial balance under the Dutch program, the premiums also vary in accordance with the adjustment to the face value. Thus, if the investment experience under this program produces a doubling of the face amount, the premium will also double.[104] Several U.S. insurance companies have developed variable life insurance policies with fixed premiums and minimum fixed benefits.[105] Variable life insurance policies provide inflation protection only if the value of the equity portfolio in which the underlying separate account is invested accompanies the inflation rate, an often dubious proposition.

ADJUSTING PENSIONS AND ANNUITIES TO INFLATION

A third area of legal relationships severely affected by inflation is pensions and annuities. In most countries the chief source of pensions and annuities is a governmental social insurance system. During the late 1950s most of the industrial nations perceived the need to readjust social security pensions and annuities because of the post-World War II inflation. Five different readjustment methods have been utilized. One is to revise the formula for computing benefits to place more or exclusive weight on the earnings level in the period just prior to retirement, when earnings are much higher than in earlier years. A second achieves similar results by revaluing the earnings base to bring the average earnings figure up to current levels. A third has been *ad hoc* adjustment from time to time to bring benefit levels up to currently acceptable standards. A fourth is an automatic review of benefit levels triggered by a percentage rise in a price or wage index, and a fifth approach is the automatic indexing of benefit levels to a price or wage index.[106]

Changing the Benefits Formula

Most countries have abandoned the traditional method of computing benefits on the basis of average lifetime earnings because earnings of early years dragged down the average to an unacceptably low figure. In 1961 only twenty-eight countries calculated social security benefits on the basis of fifteen or fewer years of earnings; by 1975 the number of countries doing so had increased to fifty.[107] Many countries now base their benefit calculations only on the last few years of earnings. For example, Austria uses the last five years of earnings; Panama the highest five of the last fifteen years; Iraq the last three years; and Spain the highest two of the last seven years.[108]

Revaluation of the Earnings Base

In the late 1950s France and Germany began to revalue prior earnings records that inflation had rendered hopelessly obsolete. Both countries now use different updating methods. The revaluation of earnings method has also been used or is still in use in nine other countries—Algeria, Austria, Belgium, Canada, Chile, Portugal, Switzerland, Turkey and Yugoslavia.[109]

Ad Hoc Changes

A steadily decreasing number of countries lack regular review procedures for adjusting pension and annuity benefits. As inflation mounts, pressure from retirees induces legislatures to enact *ad hoc* legislation improving benefits. Sometimes the object of these *ad hoc* changes is simply to restore the real level of benefits; more frequently the aim is to improve preexisting real income levels and give retirees some of the benefit of increases in real wage levels by the active labor force. The frequency of these *ad hoc* adjustments varies considerably. In the Netherlands six adjustments were made in the 1967–69 period alone.[110] In Great Britain adjustments have been made at least once a year since 1960, and since 1967, a "forecast" method has been employed. To avoid lags, the inflation rate between the day of review and the date the readjustment goes into effect is estimated and included in the readjusted figure.[111]

Automatic Review Triggered by an Index Rise

A number of countries have adopted a semiautomatic indexation approach to updating social security benefits. Under this approach each time the appropriate index rises by an indicated amount, benefits are increased. The precise amount of increase, however, is determined by review committees or the legislature. The most frequently used indexes are the consumer price index, a general wage index, or a minimum wage index. For example, since 1977 Switzerland readjusts pension benefits automatically every two years in accordance with the mean of the consumer price index and a wage index. Readjustments are to be made more often if the combined index rises by more than 8 percent in a year and may be postponed if the index rises by less than 5 percent in two years.[112] In Germany, a pension adjustment is automatically calculated each year on the basis of the national average wage index lagged by two to three years. The Social Insurance Council then each year recommends to the legislature its proposal for adjusting benefits, taking into account the percentage increase in the index and national productivity changes.[113]

Automatic Indexation of Social Security Benefits

A few countries have automatically indexed social security benefits to the consumer price index, a general wage index, or the minimum wage. Brazil automatically indexes social security benefits to the minimum wage, which is, in turn, automatically indexed to a national consumer price index.[114] Chile automatically indexes social security benefits to the consumer price index.[115] In theory a decline in these indexes could result in a decline in benefits, but this has apparently never occurred.[116] Generally, a 1 to 5 percent increase in the relevant index is necessary to trigger a rise in benefits. For example, Swedish retirement pensions are automatically adjusted whenever the cost-of-living index rises or falls by 3 (originally 5) percentage points. In the United States a rise of at least 3 percent in the consumer price index is also required to trigger an adjustment of social security benefits. Before the adjustment is actually made, however, the Secretary of Health, Education and Welfare must file a financial impact statement and recommendation with the Senate Finance Committee and the House Ways and Means Committee. Congress can then make an *ad hoc* adjustment or let the automatic indexation provisions take effect.[117]

As can be seen from Table 2, in a number of industrialized countries pensions have more than kept up with inflation since 1960. This is largely the result of policies designed to permit retirees to share in real income gains of the active working force during that period. But these policies have created serious questions about the actuarial soundness of social insurance programs. In many countries benefits have been increasing significantly more rapidly than employee and employer contributions. These shortfalls will have to be made up from general tax revenues and/or increased contributions from employers and employees. The problems associated with financing these shortfalls may eventually lead to a reexamination of the social desirability of present readjustment schemes.

Private Sector Indexed Pensions and Variable Annuities

Very few private companies appear to have adopted pension plans which automatically index benefits, primarily because of fears about funding such open-ended liability. An exception is National Airlines' plan for pilots and communications employees, whose pensions are adjusted every six months after retirement in accordance with changes in the consumer price index.[118] Other exceptions are Bell Canada, which readjusts pensions every five years in accordance with the consumer price index, subject to a 10 percent cap, and Shell Canada, which indexes annually to the con-

TABLE 2 CHANGES IN PENSIONS, AVERAGE WEEKLY WAGES, AND CONSUMER PRICE INDEXES, IN EIGHT INDUSTRIAL COUNTRIES, 1960–74

Country and index	*1960*	*1965*	*1970*	*1971*	*1972*	*1973*	*1974*
Austria:							
Pensions[1]	100	109	111	151	162	178	203
Wages[2]	100	143	213	242	270	304	390
Prices	100	121	142	149	158	170	187
France:							
Pensions[3]	100	173	254	280	310	344	379
Wages	100	113	219	241	268	322	347
Prices	100	120	149	157	166	179	203
Germany, Federal Republic of:							
Pensions[4]	100	143	203	216	237	264	293
Wages	100	153	219	241	260	297	311
Prices	100	115	131	138	145	155	162
Netherlands:							
Pensions[5]	100	232	381	442	473	547	645
Wages	100	118	229	260	287	325	[6]
Prices	100	118	149	160	173	187	204
Sweden:	100						
Pensions[7]	100	154	209	232	245	259	295
Wages[2]	100	148	212	229	249	264	[6]
Prices	100	120	149	160	169	181	198
Switzerland:							
Pensions[8]	100	173	260	285	285	519	649
Wages	100	140	196	221	246	276	310
Prices	100	117	139	148	158	172	189
United Kingdom:							
Pensions[9]	100	160	208	240	270	310	400
Wages	100	127	182	197	228	261	309
Prices	100	119	149	163	174	191	221
United States:							
Pensions[10]	100	107	139	153	184	184	205
Wages	100	120	149	158	172	185	197
Prices	100	107	131	137	141	150	167

NOTE: Italics indicate main index used in specific country. [1]Based on ad hoc increases and, since 1966, wage-related coefficient of indexing. [2]Average monthly wage. [3]Based on wage-related coefficient of indexing since 1965; ad hoc adjustments used previously. [4]General computation base. [5]Increases in flat-rate benefit amount. [6]Data not available. [7]Increases in universal pension only; excludes earning-related pension. [8]Based on increases in the maximum benefit amounts that apply equally to benefits in force; indexing instituted in 1969. [9]Increases in flat-rate benefit amount; based on ad hoc adjustments until 1971. [10]Ad hoc percentage increases in benefit. Benefit changes based on price index, effective beginning 1975.

SOURCE: 39 SOCIAL SECURITY BULLETIN 39, Table 2 (Nov. 1976).

sumer price index, with a ten percent cap.[119] Finland has a system of mandatory private pensions to supplement social security, as well as voluntary private pensions, both of which are administered by insurance companies. Pensions under both plans must be automatically adjusted for a combined consumer price index and wage index.[120]

Countries with substantial groups of private annuitants have found it necessary to revalorize annuities during periods of substantial inflation. The post-World War I German inflation would have wiped out the interests of annuitants entirely if the legislature had not passed special legislation partially revalorizing annuities.[121] France in 1949 and 1953 felt compelled to adopt legislation revalorizing annuities because of inflation. Annuities constituted prior to 1939 were increased by 750 percent; those set up between 1939 and 1946 were increased by 250 percent; and those set up between 1946 and 1949 went up by 100 percent. These increases were financed by a fund sustained by the combination of private insurance companies, the French government, and a surcharge on the premiums of certain annuity contracts.[122]

In countries like Argentina, Brazil, Chile, or Israel, where insurance companies can readily invest reserves in indexed obligations, there is little difficulty in funding indexed annuities, though there is a real risk that the indexation may be less than the actual inflation rate. In countries like the United States, where insurance companies have no such investment opportunity, few companies offer indexed annuities. Those that do place caps of 2 to 3 percent on annual escalations.[123]

Since 1952 variable annuities have been used in the United States to offer the prospective annuitant some kind of inflation protection. Like variable life insurance, the return on variable annuities is linked to the performance of a fund of equity securities, debt obligations, or some combination thereof.[124] In recent years the performance of the mutual funds in which variable annuity policy reserves have been invested has left much to be desired as an inflation hedge.

DIFFICULTIES ASSOCIATED WITH INDEXING CREDIT TRANSACTIONS, INSURANCE, AND PENSIONS

Indexation would appear to be the ideal way to adapt credit instruments, insurance, and pension programs to inflation. Yet indexation entails several serious legal and practical problems that must be resolved. These include conflict with usury statutes, high debtor default rates, potential distortion of financial markets, and the actuarial unsoundness of creating indexed insurance without correspondingly indexed supporting financial instruments. The more general question of whether a society should adopt a broad range indexation program is dealt with in the final chapter.

Indexed Loans and Usury Statutes

A number of countries have statutes that limit the maximum interest rate that can be charged on money loans.[125] These usury laws are relics of medieval times, when people believed that charging interest was sinful. They reflect a curious faith that there is a just price for money, and that legislation can successfully control the price of money despite the dismal failure of legislative attempts to control the price of other commodities. The simplistic mentality underlying usury statutes has been neatly satirized by a distinguished Brazilian economist's proposed statute to reduce high interest rates despite inflation:

> Decree-Law No. 001. Regulates the Law of Supply and Demand and prohibits the scarcity of money or goods.
> *Article 1.* The Law of Supply is maintained.
> *Article 2.* The Law of Demand is repealed.
> *Article 3.* The natural or artificial scarcity of money or any other commodity is permanently prohibited.
> *Article 4.* The just profit shall be equal to 10 percent per annum because we are all born with ten fingers on our hands.[126]

Usury laws would be intolerable in modern economies if they were not largely eviscerated by exceptions and riddled with escape valves. In some jurisdictions courts have sanctioned evasion of usury statutes by upholding the relabeling of excess interest as points, commissions, or fees. In others, courts have insisted on more elaborate simulations, such as prepaid interest, linked bank accounts, artificial sales and leasebacks, special incorporations, discounted bills of exchange, wrap-around mortgages, or disguised partnerships.[127]

Usury statutes present a problem for indexed loans because of the possibility that a court will categorize the inflation adjustment as interest rather than as a recapture or maintenance of capital. If the sum resulting from indexation is added to interest, even a relatively mild inflation rate will often turn a loan with a conventional nominal interest rate into a usurious one.

Where indexed loans have not been specifically authorized by statute, courts have occasionally declared that such loans violate usury laws. Even in countries like Brazil and Chile, where indexation is widespread, courts have occasionally allowed usury statutes to trap the unwary. Despite introduction of monetary correction into Brazilian legislation, the Supreme Federal Tribunal (STF), the nation's highest court, several times declared that reasonable (in the context of prevailing inflation rates) interest charges were usurious because the creditor had failed to label the additional interest as commissions or monetary correction.[128] The STF has, however, established a case law rule creatively interpreting banking legislation to exempt transactions with financial institutions from the usury law.[129] Astonishingly, in 1970 the Chilean Court of Appeals for Santiago upheld the criminal conviction for usury of a moneylender whose loans, which bore a nonusurious nominal interest rate, were readjusted in accordance with variations in the official cost-of-living index.[130] Fortunately, such cases are rare.

In the United States, where diverse state usury laws have given rise to an awesome amount of usury litigation, there have been only two cases holding that indexed loans violate state usury laws. In *Aztec Prop. v. Union Planters Nat. Bank*[131] the Supreme Court of Tennessee recently declared usurious a $50,000 commercial bank loan whose principal was indexed to the consumer price index. The gist of the court's reasoning process is contained in this magnificent *non sequitur:*

> We have found no case holding that an intentional increase in the face value of the principal to account for inflation does not constitute interest. In practice the lender has long borne the risk of inflation in this state. The interest charged by a lender is not profit, strictly speaking, but compensation for the use of money and for bearing the risk that the borrower might not repay or the principal might depreciate in value. We accordingly hold that the "indexed principal" constitutes usurious interest.[132]

In *Olwine v. Torrens,*[133] the other reported U.S. case on the question, the Pennsylvania Superior Court concluded that the state's usury statute was violated by a 6 percent mortgage whose principal was indexed to the variations in the consumer price index. The court also reasoned that the sum resulting from indexing is interest rather than principal, because the creditor bears the risk of inflation.

The traditional wisdom that the creditor always bears the risk of inflation is questionable. Much depends on the interest rate and other conditions of the loan. It would be more accurate to state that the creditor bears the risk of unanticipated inflation, for creditors have almost always managed to shift the risk of anticipated inflation back to the debtor. More importantly, a determination that the creditor normally bears the risk of inflation hardly answers the question whether an indexed loan violates a usury statute. A creditor can shift the risk of nonrepayment by requiring a wealthy guarantor, but the requirement of a guarantor has not been regarded as an increase in the interest rate for the purposes of a usury statute.

Israeli and Canadian courts have reached just the opposite conclusion from the Tennessee and Pennsylvania courts on the question of whether an inflation adjustment constitutes interest for the purposes of a usury statute. In *Rosenbaum v. Zeger,*[134] a scholarly opinion by the Israeli Supreme Court concluded that a purchase-money mortgage indexed to the value of the real property securing the loan did not violate the usury law inherited by Israel from the Ottoman Empire. After a lengthy examination of Anglo-American cases and Talmudic law, the court sustained the maintenance-of-value clause on two theories: (1) it did not reflect the corrupt intent or overreaching by the creditor that the usury law was designed to prevent, and (2) the indexed sum constituted a return of principal rather than interest. This second theory was also adopted by a Canadian appellate court in 1966 to uphold a mortgage indexed to the consumer price index.[135]

It makes no sense to strike down legitimate, nonextortionate transactions by stretching arcane usury statutes to cover indexed loans in an inflationary economy. Indexed loans are a highly useful technique for preserving continuation of credit markets during inflation. Recognition of their validity avoids the undesirable alternatives of a dearth of credit, or the resort to complex and expensive simulations. If possible, courts should construe usury statutes in ways that confine them to extortionate loans and that will not interfere with legitimate commercial credit transactions. At least three techniques for doing so were available to the Tennessee and Pennsylvania courts. The simplest technique was to characterize the extra amount resulting from indexation as a return of principal rather than interest, as did the Israeli and Canadian courts. A second technique was to find that a corrupt, usurious intent is lacking, as did the Israeli Supreme Court, and a third technique was to hold that indexed loans are excepted from the usury laws as contingent obligations within the meaning of Restatement of Contracts § 527.[136] Instead, both U.S. courts substituted conclusions for analysis and simply announced the infelicitous result that indexed loans run afoul of usury laws if the total of the interest and the principal readjustment exceeds the maximum interest rate permitted by statute. Hopefully, other courts will choose not to follow these ill-considered precedents.

In some countries, legislatures have resolved the problem by defining interest to exclude inflation adjustments. Thus, in 1957 Israel adopted a usury law which provided that sums resulting from maintenance-of-value clauses are not to be considered as interest.[137] Chile followed suit in 1974 by defining interest to exclude readjustment of principal in accordance with variations in the consumer price index.[138]

On March 31, 1980, the United States adopted the Depository Institutions Deregulation and Monetary Control Act,[139] which preempts state usury laws on four kinds of transactions: (1) first mortgage residential loans by specified institutional lenders, (2) business and agricultural loans of $25,000 or more, (3) obligations of depository institutions, and (4) obligations of small business investment companies. A growing number of states in the United States have alleviated the problem by wholly or partially indexing their usury statutes.[140] While these innovations do not avoid potential conflicts between usury laws and indexed loans, they do represent a step in the right direction by recognizing the futility of maintaining a fixed usury limit in an inflationary economy.

High Default Rate

A second problem with indexation of credit transactions is that the borrower's income may not keep pace with the index to which his obligation is linked. This has proven to be an exceedingly difficult problem with mortgage loans in Israel, Chile, and Brazil. Governments can increase revenues or borrow more funds to service their indexed bonds during periods of rising inflation. Corporations that have issued indexed bonds have carefully considered where they will find the funds to service these bonds, and have frequently tied their obligations to the price of their products. But individuals who saddle themselves with indexed home mortgages lack the resources of governments and business corporations. Moreover, individual borrowers often fail to comprehend the implications of indexing their obligations.

The Brazilians would appear to have solved this rather intractable problem insofar as is possible. Care is taken to explain indexation to low-income borrowers, and to try to insure that the borrower's income will rise at least the same rate as the mortgage payment. The option of extending the period of time over which mortgage payments must be made has also been accorded. Another option has been the purchase of insurance against the risk that the mortgage will have to be paid indefinitely. Given the relatively low premiums and the actuarial uncertainty, this option smacks of a fair amount of subsidy. Nevertheless, people respond much better to having their debts monetarily-corrected when the inflation rate decreases or remains constant. Popular discontent is bound to rise when the inflation rate rises sharply.

Subsidization and Redistribution of Wealth

A third difficulty with indexation of bonds and other financial instruments is the tendency of governments, with an eye toward wealth redistribution and political advantage, to tamper with the readjustment mechanism. There is nothing novel or immoral about governments redistributing wealth. What is objectionable about manipulation of indexation of credit instruments is that the processes of subsidization and confiscation are obscured from public view. In countries with indexed government bonds, such as Brazil and Israel, governments have been tempted to manipulate the index to subsidize debtors. Because the government is the chief debtor, such policies make it easier for the government to service the national debt. With substantial inflation and indexed government bonds, the cost of servicing that debt can quickly become burdensome. It is also politically advantageous to report a lower rate of inflation. The complexities of constructing price indexes and monetary correction formulae give the government considerable leeway to manipulate indexation to its own advantage. If a government were to attempt to reduce the nominal interest rate on its bonds merely to enhance its ability to pay, the public outcry would probably be deafening. But if a government achieves the same result through index manipulation, the protest level is much lower. Nevertheless, index manipulation lessens governmental accountability and causes a loss of faith in governmental integrity. Once savers and investors perceive that the government has attempted to diminish their wealth by deceptively manipulating the index, they may once again withdraw their wealth from the financial markets.

Skewing the Credit Market

Offering investors only one type of monetarily corrected credit instrument during substantial inflation, while maintaining low, negative yields on alternative forms of investment and savings, is likely to create chaos in the credit market. Colombia discovered this from 1972 to 1974 when it launched its program to stimulate the housing industry through the use of monetarily corrected mortgages and savings deposits.[141] Savings and loan associations quickly attracted an excessively large share of investment to the urban housing market by paying depositors 28 to 28.5 percent annual yields (23 percent partly tax-exempt monetary correction, and 5 to 5.5 percent interest), a net after-tax rate of return 18 percent higher than traditional savings deposits and 12 percent higher than the highest yielding nonindexed securities issued by investment banks. Even after August 1974, when a ceiling of 20 percent was placed on monetary correction and the interest rates were reduced by a point, savings and loan associations continued to attract large numbers of depositors.

The financial markets are interrelated, and money will gravitate to where the returns are highest. If certain financial instruments are indexed, and other forms of financing are not, liquidity crises in one sector or the other appear whenever creditors change preferences *en masse.* The Chilean experience of 1975, when interest rates on nonindexed short-term financial instruments were freed from regulation and caused massive withdrawals from indexed savings and loan deposits, forced the Chilean government to create large amounts of credit to maintain the soundness of the savings and loan system. Similar liquidity crises have occurred in Brazil and Israel, with similar expansions of credit by the government to relieve the sector suffering from withdrawal pangs. It has been cogently argued that so long as nonindexed instruments are allowed to coexist with indexed instruments, this liquidity crisis phenomenon makes indexation a source of inflation.[142]

Interference with Business Planning

Business firms have found business planning difficult with indexation. The costs of credit operations cannot be accurately projected with indexed loans. Lenders and borrowers must wait until an official index number is published at some future date to determine the actual cost of credit. Nor do lenders know how much they should require as collateral. Private pension managers have strenuously resisted indexation because of uncertainty about their liquidity requirements in future years, particularly if they do not have correspondingly indexed investment income to fund these open-ended payouts.

Because they had difficulty living with such uncertainty, Brazilian commercial borrowers and lenders developed the useful fiction of prefixed monetary correction. Prefixed monetary correction has served the important functions of facilitating avoidance of Brazil's usury statute and forcing the parties to state explicitly their assumptions about the presumed rate of inflation, but it is unclear whether courts in other countries will permit their usury statutes to be avoided so easily. If lenders can offer indexed loans without running afoul of usury laws but cannot use the fiction of prefixed monetary correction, all loan funds will ultimately become indexed because the returns are higher. But indexed loans will not meet the needs of a substantial group of borrowers, who will probably be forced into more costly simulations to avoid the usury laws. Realistically speaking, permitting indexed loans implies the relaxation of usury limits.

The Appropriate Index

There are built-in conflicts in the choice of indexes. Individual investors and savers generally prefer to use the consumer price index, because it most closely reflects the value of money to them. Individual borrowers generally prefer a wage index, for it closely reflects their changes in income. Commercial borrowers generally prefer an index component closely related to their firms' profits. Banks and insurance companies tend to be more indifferent on the choice of indexes. Their primary concern is to match their liabilities and assets to similar indexes to avoid being caught in a bind. Although most indexed pension schemes use the consumer price index, there is considerable concern that this index may overstate the cost of living for retirees.

Alan Blinder recently proposed an ingenious idea for a new kind of intermediary to resolve conflicting index preferences on financial transactions. He has recommended creation of a mutual fund that would hold bonds linked to the output prices of a wide variety of firms. Because the total interest received would resemble the return on a bond indexed to a general price index, the mutual fund would then be able to pay its depositors a similar return.[143] Despite its difficulties,[144] this intriguing proposal offers a possible solution to the conflict of index problems.

CONCLUSIONS

Credit and financial markets are seriously distorted by inflation. Their continued functioning requires changes in existing legal institutions. Legal restrictions on interest rates, coupled with a nominalist income tax structure, result in the disappearance of the credit market during severe inflation, or its reincarnation with elaborate simulations. A country can insist on interest restrictions only to a very limited extent during inflation. Lenders and savers will not be content with negative returns indefinitely. Unless it is prepared to forego the benefits of credit and insurance, a country has to decide whether to encourage indexing or to liberate interest rates. There is a more preferable alternative—eliminating inflation—but that is easier said than done.

Indexation is clearly not a panacea for the inflationary distortions of the credit and financial markets. It is difficult for many companies and businessmen to live with credit costs which can be calculated only *ex post facto.* It is also difficult for borrowers to make sure that their incomes will rise at the same rate as their indexed obligations. In some cases the effect of indexation will be to raise the total cost of credit to borrowers, which may have inflationary ramifications. More importantly, to the extent the presence of indexed and unindexed sectors generates liquidity crises financed by credit creation, inflation will be exacerbated.

As long as inflation persists, however, there are decided advantages to indexing credit and financial markets. Indexation at least permits banks, savings and loan associations, insurance companies, and other financial intermediaries to operate in a more or less normal fashion despite inflation. Indexation prevents financial disintermediation, which tends to paralyze the construction industry and dry up mortgage money. It permits long-range planning and investment despite inflation. Pensioners, annuitants, and social security recipients can look forward to maintaining the real value of their benefits with indexation. The existence of indexed securities greatly facilitates estate planning and the management of trusts and estates, which are all too often substantially eroded by inflation. Finally, indexation promotes social justice by offering the saver, particularly the small saver, the opportunity to protect his capital from inflationary erosion and to enjoy a real rate of return. The resulting increase in the savings and investment rate should produce substantial productivity gains.

NOTES

1. The effect of a relatively moderate surge in inflation rates in the United States in 1974 and 1975 was that 900 property and casualty insurers reported some $7 billion in underwriting losses. International Insurance Monitor, Jy.–Aug. 1976, p. 10.

2. See chap. 9, *infra,* at notes 27–30 and accompanying text.

3. Tanzi, *Inflation and the Incidence of Income Taxes on Interest Income: Some Results for the United States, 1972–1974,* 24 IMF STAFF PAPERS 500 (1977). The formula for calculating the required return is $R_i^* = R + \frac{\alpha I}{1-t_i}$
Where R_i^* is the required rate of return at a given marginal tax rate;
R is the acceptable annual interest rate if there is no inflation;
αI is the annual rate of inflation; and
t_i is the marginal tax rate on interest income.
Id. at 502. These required interest rates would decrease in the event the tax brackets were indexed for inflation, or legislation were adopted from time to time to adjust brackets to offset the shifts produced by inflation. Bossons, *Indexing Financial Instruments for Inflation,* 22 CAN. TAX J. 107, 111 (1974).

4. *See* chap. 5, *supra,* at note 25.

5. The so-called Pinay loans, issued by the French government in 1952 and 1958 were tied to the value of the 20 franc gold piece. One of the bond issues of the French government in 1973 was also tied to gold. OECD, REPORT BY COMM. ON FINANCIAL MARKETS, INDEXATION OF FIXED-INTEREST SECURITIES 34 (1973) [hereafter cited as OECD INDEXATION REPORT]; Page and Trollope, *An International Survey of Indexing and its Effects,* NAT'L INSTITUTE ECON. REV. 46, 51 (No. 70, Nov. 1974). In 1962 Argentina issued tax-exempt bonds paying 7 percent annual interest, with both principal and interest readjusted for any decline in the value of the peso with respect to gold. Decree No. 6.590 of 1962.

6. *See* chap. 5, *supra,* at p. 136.

7. C. KIA-NGAU, THE INFLATIONARY SPIRAL: THE EXPERIENCE IN CHINA, 1939–1950, 73 (1958).

8. OECD INDEXATION REPORT, *supra* note 5, at 34. In 1950 the Israeli government required its citizens to exchange foreign securities for "Tave-dollar" bonds, whose principal and interest were linked to the U.S. dollar exchange rate. Rubner, *The Abdication of the Israeli Pound as a Standard of Measurement for Medium and Long-Term Contracts,* 28 REV. ECON. STUDIES 69, 72 (Oct. 1960). Between 1954 and 1962 the purchasers of Israeli bonds were accorded the option of linking the value of the obligation to the official cost-of-living index or the dollar exchange rate. Robinson, *Readjustable Mortgages in an Inflationary Economy—A Study of the Israeli Experience,* 5 J. INT'L L. & ECON. 169, 175 (1971). The percentage of the obligation linked increased from 50 percent for a two to five year bond to 70 percent for a bond with a maturity of more than eight years. *Id.*

The Brazilian government has offered investors a similar option. In 1965 and 1966 purchasers of Readjustable Treasury Bonds (ORTNs), were offered the option of using U.S. $1 = Cr$1.85 as a basis for readjustment at a time when the exchange rate was already U.S. $1 = Cr$2.20, thereby insuring a return of 26 percent per annum in dollars. Devaluation of the cruzeiro to 2.70 to the dollar in February of 1967 actually produced an annual return of 55 percent to those who exercised the exchange rate option. During this same period the inflation rate was less than 40 percent. Simonsen, *Inflation and the Money and Capital Markets of Brazil,* in THE ECONOMY OF BRAZIL 133, 157–58 (H. Ellis ed. 1969). Several subsequent exchange rate stimuli to the purchase of Readjustable Treasury Bonds are described in Sant'ana, *As Obrigações Reajustáveis do Tesouro Nacional e a Técnica Operacional de sua Utilização no Mercado de Capitais,* 4 APEC ESTUDOS ECONÔMICOS BRASILEIROS 148 (1969).

9. Morag, *Value-Linking of Loans in Israel,* in FISCAL AND MONETARY PROBLEMS IN DEVELOPING STATES 148, 151 (D. Krivine, ed. 1967).

10. New issues of Eurobonds in 1979 totalled U.S. $18,726 million. Of this amount, $12,565 million was denominated in U.S. dollars, $3,626 million in German marks, $531 million in Dutch guilders, $425 million in Canadian dollars, $253 million in European units of account, and $1,326 in some other currency. Morgan Guaranty Trust Co., World Financial Markets, p. 11, Aug. 1980.

11. Quint, "Inflation and Floating Rate Notes," N.Y. Times, Mar. 1, 1981.

12. U.N., Fiscal & Fin. Branch, Bur. of Econ. Affairs, *Index Clause in Deferred Payments,* 2 ECON. BULL. LAT. AM. 73, 74–75 (No. 2, Oct. 1957) [hereafter cited as U.N. STUDY].

13. *Id.* at 75; Rozental, *Variable-Return Bonds—The French Experience,* 14 J. FINANCE 520, 521, 523 (1959); Viaux, *L'Indexation des Valeurs Mobilières dans la Pratique,* Rev. Économique 249, 264–72 (No. 2, 1955). A similar principle was followed in Chilean D.F.L. No. 357 of Jy. 25, 1953, which authorized the Banco del Estado de Chile to issue commodity-linked bonds for housing and agricultural purposes. Those issued for agricultural purposes were to be adjusted annually in accordance with agricultural products, while those used for construction purposes were to be readjusted annually in accordance with some measure related to construction prices. With the exception of a fifteen-year bond linked to the price of wheat, issued in 1956 to finance a potable water project, this system of readjustment has had no real practical application. *See* Moreno, *Sistemas Legales de Reajustes en los Valores Monetarios,* 2 Rev. Der. Econ. 57, 64 (No. 6, 1964).

14. Lowenstein, "Drexel Officer Devises Inflation Plan: Investing in Commodity-Backed Bonds," Wall St. J., Je. 17, 1980, at p. 6, cols. 1 and 2.

15. There is always the possibility that some form of "cost-push" inflation will drive up a firm's selling price in a way which will not permit a corresponding increase in profits; for most firms, however, indexing their debt service to the price of their output is a desirable inflation hedge. *See* Blinder, *Indexing the Economy through Financial Intermediation,* in STABILIZATION OF THE DOMESTIC AND INTERNATIONAL ECONOMY 69, 96–101 (K. Brunner & A. Meltzer, eds. 1977).

16. Rozental, *supra* note 13, at 524–26; OECD INDEXATION REPORT, *supra* note 5, at 32, 34.

17. Rozental, *supra* note 13, at 525–26, fn. 17.

18. McClintock, *The Probable Legal Consequences of Inserting Price-Index Clauses in Long-Term Corporate Obligations,* 18 HASTINGS, L. J. 959, 961–62, fn. 18 (1967).

19. Indexed bonds have also been issued in Austria, China, Denmark, Iceland, Japan, Great Britain, Luxembourg, Sweden, Switzerland, and the United States. Hein, *A Note on the Use of Index Clauses Abroad,* 15 J. FINANCE 546, 547 (1960); Robinson, *supra* note 8, at 170.

20. S. MUKHERJEE & C. ORLANS, INDEXATION IN AN INFLATIONARY ECONOMY: A CASE STUDY OF FINLAND 60–61 (1975).

21. OECD INDEXATION REPORT, *supra* note 5, at 31.

22. *See* chap. 5, *supra,* at notes 70–87 and the accompanying text.

23. OECD INDEXATION REPORT, *supra* note 5, at 32–33; Page and Trollope, *supra* note 5, at 51. The origin of the European unit of account is explained in chap. 8, *infra,* at pp. 275–77.

24. The Brazilian government's poor payment record was so notorious that a lower court decision refusing to require a railroad to purchase government bonds to fund a pension for a tort victim was affirmed in these terms by Brazil's highest court: "The self-funded pension is better than a deposit of capital, for the accident victim will be paid at the counters of the railroad more advantageously and punctually than at the counters of the National Treasury. . . ." Rêde Ferroviária Federal S.A. v. Pampillon, R.E. 58.252, 38 R.T.J. 215 (Sup. Fed. Trib. 3d Term 1966) (vote of Gonçalves de Oliveira). The Ten-Year Plan for Economic and Social Development prepared by the Ministry of Planning and Economic Coordination candidly acknowledged the "poor paying habits of the Government, which made it a tradition not to redeem its obligations when due. . . ." Ministério do Planejamento e Coordenação Econômica, 2 POLÍTICA MONETÁRIA E MERCADO DE CAPITAIS 48 (prelim. version Mar. 1967).

25. Law No. 4.357 of Jy. 16, 1964. Starting in 1967, interest rates on ORTNs varied with maturity dates. One-year bonds paid 4 percent per annum, while five-year bonds paid 7 percent.

26. D. SYVRUD, FOUNDATIONS OF BRAZILIAN ECONOMIC GROWTH 134 (1974).

27. Firms could avoid paying a 5 percent tax on revaluation gains by purchasing ORTNs in double the amount of the tax due. Law No. 4.357 of Jy. 16, 1964, art. 3, § 8. And taxpayers were entitled to deduct from gross income 30 percent of the face amount of ORTNs purchased.

28. This dramatic turnaround in investor confidence resulted from a combination of three factors: (1) the public was offered the option of purchasing ORTNs linked to the dollar exchange rate under extremely advantageous terms; (2) commercial banks were permitted to satisfy a portion of their compulsory reserve requirements by holding ORTNs; and (3) the government's credit-worthiness was bolstered by punctual repayment of principal and interest.

29. The ORTN has proven cumbersome, however, for short-term operations because of lags in calculating the inflation adjustment. Hence, its open market role has been taken over by nonindexed, shorter-term treasury bills. The amount of ORTNs and treasury bills in circulation as a percentage of Gross Domestic Product increased from .2 percent in 1964 to 9.9 percent in 1973. "Correção Monetária—Tema de Interêsse Internacional," 28 Conj. Econ. 110, 112, Table 2 (May 1974).

30. Ness, *Financial Markets Innovation as a Development Strategy: Initial Results from the Brazilian Experience,* 22 ECON. DEVELOP. & CULT. CHANGE 453, 458 (1974).

31. "Correção Monetária das O.R.T.N.—Formas de Cálculo," 28 Conj. Econ. 92 (Dec. 1974).

32. W. NESS, A INFLUÊNCIA DA CORREÇÃO MONETÁRIA NO SISTEMA FINANCEIRO 40–44 (1977); Roe, *Finance, Rules and the Indexation of Brazilian Government Bonds,* 12 VAND. J. TRANSNAT'L L. 1 (1979).

33. Law No. 6.423 of June 17, 1977. Only the following types of indexation are exempted from the ORTN linkage requirement: collective bargaining agreements, social security benefits, instruments with prefixed monetary correction issued by financial institutions, and contracts for the future delivery of goods or services where the price is readjusted as a function of costs.

34. 33 THE ISRAEL ECONOMIST 10 (Jan./Feb. 1977); Sarnat, *Monetary Risk, Stagflation, and the Uneasy Case for Indexation,* in INFLATION AND CAPITAL MARKETS 179, 194–201 (M. SARNAT, ed. 1978).

35. G. JUD, INFLATION AND THE USE OF INDEXING IN DEVELOPING COUNTRIES 104–107 (1978). These indexed bonds were authorized first by Law No. 19.978 of Nov. 28, 1972. For more recent versions, *see* Decrees No. 754 of Feb. 24, 1976 and No. 439 of May 14, 1976.

36. OECD INDEXATION REPORT, *supra* note 5, at 33–34.

37. OECD INDEXATION OF FINANCIAL ASSETS 13–15, 41 (1975) [hereafter cited as OECD FIN. ASSETS STUDY].

38. *See* chap. 7, *infra,* at note 110 and accompanying text.

39. Decree-Law No. 687 of Apr. 20, 1967.

40. In 1952 two United States firms, the Christiansen Corporation and the Utility Trailer Company, issued virtually identical debentures in which both principal and interest were indexed to changes in the consumer price index. The Christiansen debenture is set out in Appendix B, and the Utility Trailer debenture is described in Utility Trailer Mfg. Co. v. United States, 212 F. Supp. 773 S.D. Calif. 1962). The only significant difference between the two issues was that the Christiansen Corporation limited the maximum payment on its debenture to 150 percent of the face amount at maturity, while Utility Trailer Company established no such limitation. In 1973 Western Credit, a British company, issued a three-year bond with an interest rate of 9.5 percent, adjustable in accordance with changes in the consumer price index, but not to exceed a maximum interest rate of 15 percent a year.

41. OECD FIN. ASSETS STUDY, *supra* note 37, at 17–20; B. GRIFFITHS, INFLATION: THE PRICE OF PROSPERITY 207 (1976).

42. OECD INDEXATION REPORT, *supra* note 5, at 37.

43. U.N. STUDY, *supra* note 12, at 76; Campbell and Tullock, *Hyperinflation in China, 1937–1949,* 62 J. POL. ECON. 236, 239, 243 (1954).

44. Robinson, *supra* note 8, at 176–177; U.N. STUDY, *supra* note 12, at 75.

45. Kleiman, *Monetary Correction and Indexation: The Brazilian and Israeli Experience,* in INDEXATION, THE BRAZILIAN EXPERIENCE, 4 EXPLORATIONS IN ECONOMIC RESEARCH 141, 147 (M. Nadiri & A. Pastore eds., No. 1, 1977); Robinson, *supra* note 8, at 176–77.

46. M. HETH, BANKING INSTITUTIONS IN ISRAEL 326 (1966).

47. *Id.* at 137–38, 327.

48. Harberger, *Some Notes on Inflation,* in INFLATION AND GROWTH IN LATIN AMERICA 319, 334 (W. Baer & I. Kerstenetzky, eds. 1964).

49. Calculated from IMF, 34 INT'L FIN. STATISTICS 110 (Je. 1981).

50. D.F.L. No. 211 of Apr. 6, 1960, as modified by Law 15.077 of Dec. 17, 1962. The operation of this law is described in Pardo Torres, *La Readjustabilidad de los Créditos Agrícolas de la CORFO,* 2 Rev. Der. Econ. 69 (Jy.-Dec. 1964), and Moreno, *supra* note 13, at 89–92.

51. The wage and salary index excluded agricultural wages, copper and petroleum workers' wages, and the earnings of those employed in the manufacture of paper and cellulose. This represented an attempt to prevent the lowest and highest paid wages from distorting the pattern of wage movements. The annual variation registered in this index was to be reduced by one percentage point and any fraction of a percentage point. Thus, a 15.7 percent increase in the index would be reduced to 14 percent. Moreno, *supra* note 13, at 66–67.

52. Decree-Law 205 of 1960, as modified by Law 15.163 of Feb. 13, 1963. Law 16.391 of 1965 extended this limitation to private savings and loans.

53. J. LOPEZ-SANTA MARIA, LE DROIT DES OBLIGATIONS ET DES CONTRATS ET L'INFLATION MONÉTAIRE 92 (1980).

54. Burke, *Law and Development: The Chilean Housing Program,* 2 LAW. AM. 173, 353 (1970).

55. *Id.* at 360–63.

56. R. Merrill, Toward a Structural Housing Policy: An Analysis of Chile's Low Income Housing Program, Jan. 1971 (Ph.D. thesis, Cornell Univ.), at 94–95.

57. Le Gates, *A Decade of Struggle for Housing in Chile,* 28 INTER-AM. ECON. AFFAIRS 51, 58 (Autumn 1974).

58. Galbis, *Inflation and Interest Rate Policies in Latin America, 1967–76,* 26 IMF STAFF PAPERS 334, 342, 346 (1979). Interest rates have fluctuated wildly in Chile, with finance companies charging borrowers as much as 15.3 percent a month in real terms and paying investors as much as 9.1 percent a month in real terms. Calculated from Cuadro 1 in Jeftanovic, *Política Financiera,* in COMENTARIOS SOBRE LA SITUACION ECONOMICA 71, 74 (Univ. of Chile, Dept. of Econ., Pub. No. 30, 1976).

59. This pension fund, called the Fund for the Guaranty of Length of Service (FGTS) was set up by Law No. 5.107 of September 13, 1966 as an alternative to a troublesome tenure provision in the Labor Code. Each employer is required to deposit 8 percent of every employee's total pay into the FGTS. The deposit is in the name of each employee, bears interest, and is subject to monetary correction.

Real estate bills *(letras imobiliárias)* are letters of credit secured by the mortgage portfolios of real estate credit societies (stock-held savings associations) and guaranteed by a special fund of the BNH. Lefcoe, *Monetary Correction and Mortgage Lending in Brazil: Observations for the United States,* 21 STAN. L. REV. 106, 121–22 (1968). Purchase of these bills has been compulsory for certain landlords, construction operations, and the Social Services of Industry and Commerce. The BNH has authorized two types of real estate bills: (1) three-year income bills with interest and monetary correction paid trimestrally in cash; and (2) one-year savings bills with monetary correction and interest capitalized until maturation. However, the great bulk of the real estate bills marketed have been three-year income bills. The annual interest rate was 8 percent until 1972, when it was reduced to 6 percent. Many of these bills are redeemed prior to three years if the buyer wishes through a rediscount fund maintained by the BNH. *See* J. CHACEL, M. SIMONSEN, & A. WALD, CORREÇÃO MONETÁRIA 129 (1970).

60. Reynolds & Carpenter, *Housing Finance in Brazil: Towards a New Distribution of Wealth,* 5 LATIN AM. URBAN RESEARCH 147 (W. Cornelius & F. Trueblood, eds. 1975).

61. Banco Nacional de Habitações, Resolution No. 5/66.

62. *See* BNH Resolution 36/69, discussed in 24 Conj. Econ. No. 3, p. 65 (Mar. 1970) (Vol. 17, No. 3, p. 37 of the English language version). For a useful overview of monetary correction in Brazilian housing finance, *see* Vianna de Lima, *A Correção Monetária no Sistema Imobiliário,* in O MERCADO DE CAPITAIS 173 (A. Wald., ed. 1970).

63. The UPC is an ideal monetary unit, defined in Law No. 4.380 of Aug. 21, 1964, art. 52 § 1, as corresponding to the purchasing power of Cr$10,000 in February 1964.

64. Law No. 6.205 of Apr. 29, 1975 eliminated prospectively the use of the minimum wage as a monetary correction device and substituted the ORTN index.

65. Reynolds and Carpenter, *supra* note 60, at 169.

66. Brazilian Law No. 4.728 of Jy. 14, 1965. For a useful analysis of this law, *see* D. TRUBEK, LAW, PLANNING, AND THE DEVELOPMENT OF THE BRAZILIAN CAPITAL MARKET: A STUDY OF LAW IN ECONOMIC CHANGE (Yale Law School Stud. in Law & Modernization No. 3, Reprinted from Bull. of N.Y.U. Grad. School of Bus. Admin., Nos. 72 & 73, Apr. 1971).

67. Rosenn, *Adaptations of the Brazilian Income Tax to Inflation,* 21 STAN. L. REV. 58, 96 (1968). Brazilian lenders generally avoided the tax on excess pre-fixed monetary correction by reselling the bill or note to a distributing firm.

68. Brazilian Decree-Law No. 403 of Dec. 30, 1968. Central Bank Resolution No. 294 of 1974 upped the highest withholding tax rate on prefixed monetary correction to 11 percent and reduced the lowest to 2 percent.

69. Decree-Law No. 1.641 of Dec. 7, 1978, art. 7. Between 1976 and the end of 1978 financial instruments and bank deposits with prefixed monetary correction were subjected to a flat 10 percent withholding tax by Decree-Law No. 1.494 of Dec. 7, 1976, art. 1.

70. Some companies eventually exclude these gains in computing a tax-free reserve for working capital. Brazilian Decree-Law No. 1.338 of Jy. 23, 1974. The effect of this statute is discussed in chap. 9, *infra,* p. 325.

71. Lemgruber, *Inflation in Brazil,* in WORLDWIDE INFLATION: THEORY AND RECENT EXPERIENCE 395, 416 (L. Krause & W. Salant, eds. 1977); "Mercado de Capitais," 28 Conj. Econ. 70, 73–74 (Aug. 1974). Resolution No. 286 was repealed in 1976 by Resolution No. 367.

72. Baer, *The Brazilian Growth and Development Experience: 1964–1975,* in BRAZIL IN THE SEVENTIES 41, 60 (R. Roett, ed. 1976).

73. Decree-Law No. 1.452 of Mar. 30, 1976, arts. 2 & 3, provides for some offset of this subsidy by granting income tax credits and ORTNs to lending agencies.

74. Bus. Lat. Am., Nov. 12, 1980, at 361.

75. Decree Nos. 677 and 678 of May 2, 1972.

76. G. JUD, *supra* note 35, at 125–29.

77. *See* Findley, *Presidential Intervention in the Economy and the Rule of Law in Colombia,* 28 AM. J. COMP. L. 423 (1980).

78. B. GRIFFITHS, *supra* note 41, at 208.

79. OECD FIN. ASSETS STUDY, *supra* note 37, at 34.

80. Robinson, *supra* note 8, at 180.

81. Stahl, *The Rise and Fall of Index Loans in Sweden,* SKANDINAVISKA ENSKILDA BANKEN Q. REV. 14, 17 (No. 1, 1975). OECD, COMM. ON FINANCIAL MARKETS, HOUSING FINANCE: PRESENT PROBLEMS 24–25 (1974) [hereafter cited as HOUSING FINANCE].

82. Robinson, *supra* note 8, at 182.

83. Resolution No. 21 of the Argentine Caja Federal de Ahorro y Préstamo para la Vivienda of Dec. 30, 1975. Legislation authorizing readjustable deposits and mortgages was enacted in the mid-1960s, but was virtually unused until recently. *See* Robinson, *supra* note 8, at 180. Revaluation of all debts with the National Mortgage Bank was required by Law No. 21.508 of Feb. 21, 1977.

84. *See* W. CANDILIS, VARIABLE RATE MORTGAGE PLANS 24 (American Bankers Assoc. Research Paper No. 7, 1971); Comment, *Adjustable Interest Rates in Home Mortgages: A Reconsideration,* 1975 WIS. L. REV. 742, 746–47 [hereafter cited as WIS. COMMENT].

85. W. CANDILIS, *supra* note 84, at 24. HOUSING FINANCE, *supra* note 81, at 16–18; WIS. COMMENT, *supra* note 84, at 746, 764. *See also* Comment, *The Variable Interest Rate Clause and its Use in California Real Estate Transactions,* 19 U.C.L.A. L. REV. 468 (1972). At least one large insurance company in the United States has recently linked a $25 million shopping center mortgage to the interest rate on high-grade utility bonds. Carberry, "Long-Term Commercial Mortgages Fade; Innovations in Financing Will Raise Costs," Wall St. J., Apr. 11, 1980, p. 44, cols. 1–3.

86. Renegotiable rate mortgages were authorized on April 3, 1980 by Federal Home Loan Bank Board Resolution, 45 Fed. Reg. 67, 059 (1980), 12 C.F.R. § 545.6–4a. *See generally* Comment, *Renegotiable Rate Mortgages: Keeping Pace with a Fluctuating Economy and Equalizing Competition within the Home Financing Industry,* 10 STETSON L. REV. 293 (1981).

87. F. Modigliani, "Some Economic Implications of the Indexing of Financial Assets with Special Reference to Mortgages," M.I.T. MORTGAGE STUDY REPORTS, No. 1 (Sept. 1974), at pp. 18–19.

88. *See* Whitley, *Mortgages: The Case for Index-Linking,* NAT'L INSTITUTE ECON. REV. 75 (Nov. 1974); Whitley, *Index-linked Mortgages,* in INDEXING FOR INFLATION 77 (T. Liesner & M. King, eds. 1975).

89. *See* chapter 7, *infra,* at pp. 221–22, 234–37.

90. The concept of the debt of value is explored in chapter 7, *infra,* at pp. 222–24.

91. A. NUSSBAUM, MONEY IN THE LAW NATIONAL AND INTERNATIONAL 186, fn. 65 (rev. ed. 1950).

92. T. ASCARELLI, PROBLEMAS DAS SOCIEDADES ANÔNIMAS E DIREITO COMPARADO 207 (1945).

93. Decision of Apr. 20, 1926, DIE RECHTSPRECHUNG 135 (1926), cited in A. NUSSBAUM, *supra* note 91, at 186, fn. 65.

94. The cases are collected in Monaco & Alonso, *Desvalorización de la Moneda,* J.A. RESEÑAS 345, 396–402 (1974). *See also* Chiaromonte, *Depreciación Monetaria: Sus Causas y Efectos frente a las Obligaciones de Dinero y Valor. "El Contrato de Seguro,"* 148 La Ley 296 (1972).

95. 134 L.T. 557, 42 T.L.R. 302, [1926] ALL E. R. 93 (Court of Appeal 1926), discussed in chap. 4, *supra* at note 144, and the accompanying text.

96. A. NUSSBAUM, *supra* note 91, at 304.

97. U.N. STUDY, *supra* note 12, at 74; OECD INDEXATION REPORT, *supra* note 5, at 31–32, 37; Page, *International Experience of Indexing,* in INDEXING FOR INFLATION 97, 98 (T. Liesner & M. King, eds., 1975); S. MUKHERJEE & C. ORLANS, *supra* note 20, at 64–65.

98. Di Veroli, *La Inflación en la Argentina y sus Repercusiones en los Seguros de Ramos Elementales,* 3 REV. DER. COM. Y OBLIG. 53, 56, 68 (Feb. 1970).

99. 11 PLAINOL & RIPERT, TRAITÉ PRATIQUE DE DROIT CIVIL FRANÇAIS 741–42 (2d ed. 1954); J. CHACEL et al., *supra* note 59, at 258–59.

100. M. HETH, THE LEGAL FRAMEWORK OF ECONOMIC ACTIVITY IN ISRAEL 158 (1967); Chilean Decree-Law No. 210 of 1953, art. 18.

101. Decree-Law No. 73 of Nov. 21, 1966, art. 14.; Law No. 5.488 of Aug. 27, 1968.

102. Central Bank Resolution No. 113 of Apr. 28, 1969. For an example of a monetarily corrected policy, *see* J. CHACEL et al., *supra* note 59, at 261, fn. 21.

103. Starting in the third year of North American's indexed policy, the face value increases by the same percentage as the consumer price index. There is a maximum increase of the lesser of 6 percent of the prior year's face value or 10 percent of the original face value. The term insurance premium is not indexed; it varies with the amount of insurance in force and the insured's age. The whole life premium increases with the amount of insurance in force, but not with age of the insured. Paid-up additions are in part used to support the increased costs. If the consumer price index goes down, the face value of both types of policies remains the same. Waylett, *Indexed Life Insurance: Actual Product Answers to Inflation,* 77 BESTS REV. (LIFE) 16 (Apr. 1977).

104. Sternhell, *Variable Life Insurance—The Break Through,* 26 RECORD OF N.Y.C.B.A. 433, 434 (1971).

105. *Id.* at 434–37; Frankel, *Regulation of Variable Life Insurance* 48 NOTRE DAME LAWYER 1017, 1018–19 (1973). *See also Proceedings of Conference on Variable Annuities and Variable Life Insurance,* 32 BUS. LAWYER 675 (Spec. Issue Mar. 1977).

106. Tracy, *Maintaining Value of Social Security Benefits During Inflation: Foreign Experience,* 39 SOCIAL SECURITY BULL. 33 (Nov. 1976).

107. *Id.* at 34.

108. Tracy, *World Developments and Trends in Social Security,* 39 SOCIAL SECURITY BULL. 14, 15–16 (Apr. 1976).

109. Tracy, *supra* note 106, at 34–35.

110. *Id.* at 35.

111. R. MYERS, INDEXATION OF PENSIONS AND OTHER BENEFITS 114–15 (1978).

112. *Id.* at 115.

113. The automatic feature was suspended in 1978 for the 1979–81 period. Instead *ad hoc* increases of 4.5 percent for 1979 and 4 percent for 1980 and 1981 have been mandated. *Id.* at 115.

114. Decree-Law No. 15 of Jy. 29, 1966. Productivity gains, however, have been specifically excluded from the minimum wage in calculating most social security benefits. Law No. 6.205 of Apr. 29, 1975.

115. Decree-Law No. 2.448 of Feb. 1979.

116. Horlick and Tracy, *Adjustment of Old-Age Pensions in Foreign Programs,* 37 Soc. Security Bull. 33 (Jy. 1974). The wording of the U.S. statute increasing social security benefits, however, precludes an automatic decrease in benefits.

117. There was overcompensation for inflation under the U.S. Social Security Act because benefits escalated with respect to both inflation and wage increases. The 1977 Amendments, Pub. L. 95–216, § 201(b) and (g), ensure that benefits will not rise by more than the cost-of-living index. *See* Moffit, "Social Security Will Provide a Smaller Part of Retirement Income Despite Big Tax Bite," Wall St. J., Feb. 6, 1978, at p. 28, cols. 1–3.

118. The pension is increased only for index changes in excess of 5 percent, and the first 5 percent changes is ignored. R. Myers, *supra* note 111, at 118–19.

119. *Id.* at 129. Additional exceptions are described at pp. 120–25.

120. *Id.* at 133.

121. A statute enacted on Aug. 18, 1923 authorized revision of annuities for support of relatives. The General Revalorization Act of 1925 permitted special annuity payments for a narrowly defined class of "necessitous" persons. Other holders of annuities with insurance companies received a proportionate share of revalorized insurance company assets. *See* Dawson, *Effects of Inflation on Private Contracts: Germany, 1914–1924,* 33 Mich. L. Rev. 171, 220–21 (1934).

122. 11 Plainol & Ripert, *supra* note 99, at 580. A different schedule of readjustment was adopted for annuities resulting from alienation of property. *Id.* at 579.

123. Comment, *Damages for Loss of Future Income: Accounting for Inflation,* 6 S. F. L. Rev. 311, 322, fn. 54 (1972).

124. Johnson, *The Variable Annuity—Insurance, Investment, or Both?,* 48 Geo. L. J. 641 (1960); Frankel, *Variable Annuities, Variable Insurance and Separate Accounts,* 51 B.U.L. Rev. 177 (1971).

125. Usury laws, however, are by no means universal. A large group of European countries abrogated their usury laws during the middle of the 19th century. *See* Benfield, *Money, Mortgages, and Migraine—the Usury Headache,* 19 Case W. Res. L. Rev. 819, 821 (1968).

126. Campos, *Os Pseudojuristas,* in R. Campos, Ensaios contra a Maré 47, 50 (1969).

127. *See* M. Simonsen, *Brazilian Inflation: Postwar Experience and Outcome of the 1964 Reforms,* in Economic Development Issues: Latin America 261, 301–305 (Comm. for Econ. Develop. Supp. Paper No. 21, 1967); Benfield, *supra* note 125, at 838–72; Comment, *Wrap-Around Financing: A Technique for Skirting the Usury Laws?,* 1972 Duke L. J. 785.

128. Figueiredo v. Gutierre, R.E. No. 58.414, 36 R.T.J. 46 (STF, 1st Term, 1965); In re Albino de Cruz Ferro, R.E. No. 65.424, 47 R.T.J. 558 (STF, 1st Term,

1968); B. Prates & Cia. Ltda. v. Toyota do Brasil S.A., R.E. No. 64.473, 53 R.T.J. 21 (STF *en banc* 1969). In the *Prates* case, *supra,* the Supreme Federal Tribunal intimated for the first time that usury laws would not invalidate payments specifically labelled as monetary correction in private contracts. *See also* Wald, *Da Correção Monetária dos Débitos Comerciais na Jurisprudência,* RT Informa, Jan. 30, 1971, at 17, 18.

129. Súmula No. 596.

130. Wagemann Ehrenfeld, Julio, 67 R.D.J. 42 (2d Part, 4th Sec. 1970).

131. 530 S.W.2d 756 (1975), *cert. denied,* 425 U.S. 975 (1976). The alternative holding—that the index clause violated the Gold Clause Resolution—is discussed in chapter 5, *supra,* at pp. 148–50.

132. 530 S.W.2d at 759.

133. 236 Pa. Super. Ct. 51, 344 A.2d 665 (1975).

134. C.A. 248/53 (1954), 2 SELECTED JUDGMENTS OF THE SUPREME COURT OF ISRAEL 10 (D. Goitein ed. 1963).

135. Commonwealth Savings Plan Ltd. v. Triangle "C" Cattle Co. Ltd., 56 D.L.R. (2d) 453 (B.C.C.A. 1966).

136. This section provides: "A promise, made as the consideration for a loan . . . to give the creditor a greater profit than the highest permissible rate of interest upon the occurrence of a condition, is not usurious if the repayment promised on failure of the condition to occur is materially less than the amount of the loan or debt with the highest permissible interest unless a transaction is given this form as a colorable device to obtain a greater profit than is permissible. In that case it is usurious."

137. M. HETH, *supra* note 100, at 153.

138. Chilean Decree-Law No. 455 of May 25, 1974, art. 4.

139. Pub. L. No. 96–221, 94 Stat. 132. The states can take themselves out of this statute's reach by affirmatively legislating such withdrawal within three years.

140. For example, on loans contracted in Alaska after June 4, 1976, the usury rate is 5 percent above the annual rate charged member banks for advances by the Twelfth Federal Reserve District in the month prior to the loan. ALASKA STAT., § 45.45.010(b) (1976 Cum. Supp.). In 1979 California amended its constitution to set the usury ceiling on nonpersonal loans at the greater of 10 percent annually or 5 percent per annum more than the discount rate of the Federal Reserve Bank of San Francisco. CALIF. CONST., art. 18, § 4. Ohio's usury rate for residential mortgages is defined as 3 percent above the federal reserve bank's discount rate on ninety-day commercial paper. PAGE'S OHIO REV. CODE § 1343.01(B)(4) (1976 Supp.). Pennsylvania pegs its usury rate for residential mortgages at 2.5 percent above the Monthly Index of Long Term United States Government Bond Yields for the second calendar month preceding the making of the loan. PURDON'S PA. STAT. ANN., tit. 41 § 101–605 (Purdon Supp. 1979). Georgia, Illinois, Iowa, New York, and West Virginia follow the Pennsylvania approach of indexing usury limits to the U.S. government bond yields. Delaware follows the Alaskan approach to indexing to the Federal Reserve discount rate for member banks. Nevada and Puerto Rico to a limited extent index to the prime rate. Minnesota, Montana, and Kentucky follow the Ohio approach with respect to certain loans and index to the ninety-day commercial paper discount

rate. *See* Long, *Trends in Usury Legislation—Current Interest,* 34 U. MIAMI L. REV. 325, 333–37 (1980).

141. Findley, *supra* note 77, at 440.

142. Baer & Beckerman, *The Trouble with Index-Linking: Reflections on the Recent Brazilian Experience,* WORLD DEVELOPMENT (August 1980).

143. Blinder, *supra* note 15.

144. For critical comments on Blinder's proposal, *see* Phelps, *Indexation Issues: A Comment on the Blinder and Fischer Papers,* Parkin, *Indexing the Economy Through Financial Intermediation: A Comment,* and Smith, *On the Indexation of Contracts under Uncertainty: A Comment on the Blinder Paper,* in STABILIZATION OF THE DOMESTIC AND INTERNATIONAL ECONOMY 149, 169, 173 (K. Brunner & A. Meltzer, eds. 1977).

7

MONETARY COMPENSATION AND INFLATION

Chronic inflation can play havoc with monetary compensation awarded by the courts for such common actions as tort, breach of contract, and condemnation. The nominalist principle and a steadily depreciating currency, operating in tandem, effectively thwart the basic purpose of indemnification—restoration of the *status quo ante* to the extent monetarily possible.

Inflation erodes the value of monetary damages in a variety of ways. Where damages are liquidated or are calculated as of the date of the tort, breach of contract, or taking, inflation between that date and the day of judgment will reduce the value of the compensation awarded. If there is a time lapse between the day of judgment and date of payment, inflation will further reduce the value of the award, unless the legal interest rate is higher than the inflation rate. The real value of the plaintiff's recovery is likely to vary inversely with the length of time required to secure judicial relief.

A second source of distortion appears when a plaintiff seeks compensation for future injuries, such as lost earnings or future medical expenses. To the extent the courts fix such sums in terms of present values, inflation will make the award insufficient to secure *restitutio in integrum.*

A third source of distortion can be found in statutory limitations upon the amount of damages that can be recovered in certain types of actions. Statutory ceilings upon damage awards are especially common in wrongful death suits. Unless these limits are periodically raised, inflation can effectively convert these causes of action into rights without remedies.

This chapter will examine the ways in which inflation distorts damage awards, and the techniques that have been evolved to attempt to correct these distortions.

TORT DAMAGE AWARDS

Courts have been asked to consider the effects of inflation on tort damage awards in essentially four different contexts. First, when asked to set aside a verdict upon the ground that it is excessive, courts commonly compare the challenged verdict with prior awards. Second, courts are commonly asked to consider the effect of inflation between the date of the tort and the date of the trial or judgment. Third, appellate courts are sometimes asked to revise an award because of inflation which has occurred between the date of the judgment and the date of the appeal. Lastly, courts are often asked to consider inflation in determining damages for future loss, such as lost earnings or future medical expenses.

Comparison of Verdicts

Common law courts exercise a general supervisory power over tort verdicts to insure that awards do not become excessive. It is common practice to compare current verdicts with those rendered in the past on similar sets of facts. In comparing verdicts, it is well settled that courts will take into account inflation since the time past verdicts were rendered.[1] Indeed, on occasion American courts will even utilize price indexes to compare verdicts.

Inflation between Tort and Trial

In an inflationary economy substantial delay between the date of the trial and the date of the tort may make an important difference in the amount of recoverable damage. Suppose a plaintiff's car is damaged in 1976 in an automobile accident in which the defendant is entirely at fault. Damage to the car is estimated at $1,000 the day after the accident. The case does not come up for trial until 1980, when the cost of repairing the car is $2,000. Is the plaintiff entitled to collect more than $1,000?

Anglo-American courts are still likely to apply a nominalist solution and presume that a dollar or a pound is always equal to itself, regardless of changes in relative purchasing power.[2] Whether the car has been repaired or not, common law courts will generally assess damages to property as of the date of the accident and ignore any subsequent price-level changes. As Denning, L.J. explained, in *Philips v. Ward,* where a British court rejected a claim for damages resulting from an increase in the cost of repairing a house between the date of the damage and the date of the judgment: "A fall thereafter in the value of money does not in law affect the figure, for the simple reason that sterling is taken to be constant in value."[3] Although there are a few American cases suggesting that the proper measure of recovery would be the adjusted value of expenditures for repairs in present-day depreciated dollars,[4] the great majority of United States courts assess damages as of the date of the tort and consider inflation irrelevant. The present state of the law is accurately reflected in the Second Restatement of Torts: "The value of money is assumed to be constant in actions for money tortiously taken or destroyed and in actions to obtain the value of property or services at a particular time. In both of such cases the measure of recovery is unaffected by a subsequent increase or decrease in the purchasing power of money, that is, its value with reference to commodities."[5]

The Anglo-American position has nothing to commend it save simplicity. From a policy standpoint it makes no sense whatsoever to force the innocent tort victim to shoulder the burden of monetary depreciation, and to reward the tortfeasor with the windfall of being able to pay off his obligation in depreciated currency. Through no fault of his own, the tort victim is forced to accept less than a complete indemnity. To a limited extent this inequity may be offset by the allowance of legal interest.[6] In most countries, however, the legal interest rate has been set at a fixed rate ranging between 4 to 8 percent *per annum,* a level that is insufficient to offset even a moderate rate of inflation. Moreover, in some countries, such as the United States, allowance of prejudgment interest is usually up to the discretion of the court and is rarely allowed unless a claim is liquidated or reasonably certain. Many civil law countries have adapted to inflation by shifting the date for valuing damages from the day of the injury to the day of judgment. Some countries, such as France, have made this shift directly.[7] Others have employed the intriguing doctrinal device of the debt of value.

The Debt of Value or Adaptable Debt

An important doctrinal device for shifting the onus of monetary depreciation to the tortfeasor has been the differentiation between debts of value *(Wertschuld, debito di valore, deuda de valor)* and pecuniary debts. A debt of value, sometimes called an adaptable debt,[8] requires the obligor to pay an economic value rather than a fixed pecuniary sum. Child support and alimony are classic examples; if the needs of the child or former spouse change, or the purchasing power of the currency declines, the support obligation may be revalued. In theory one distinguishes between debts of value and pecuniary debts by determining whether the object of the obligation is the payment of an essentially nonpecuniary value or the payment of a sum of money. If the obligation's object is the former, the debt is one of value and by definition, readjustable for inflation. This theory, however, draws a distinction where there is no real difference. Unless one postulates a world peopled by numismatists, the object of all pecuniary obligations is the receipt of value. Therefore, it is not surprising that there is no conceptual conformity. The writers and cases diverge considerably, both as to which kinds of obligations should be characterized as debts of value, and as to whether a debt of value becomes a pecuniary debt as soon as it is liquidated (in the sense of being valued in currency), or remains a debt of value until judgment or actual payment.[9]

The debt of value is essentially a doctrinal device for placing the risk of monetary depreciation on the obligor when it appears just to do so. During times of severe inflation, there is a natural tendency on the part of doctrinal writers and lawyers to attempt to expand the scope of debts of value. There is little dispute among jurists who recognize the concept that tort damages are debts of value, but there is little agreement as to whether such damages become pecuniary debts once liquidated. Thus, the highest courts of Austria and Germany have considered tort damages as debts of value and have placed on the tortfeasor the onus of monetary depreciation by requiring assessment of damages in terms of values in effect at the date of the judgment.[10] Nevertheless, if the tort victim proceeds to have his damaged property repaired at his own expense, French and German cases hold that the obligation is thereby converted from one of repairing an injury into paying a pecuniary obligation. The nominalist principle then comes into play and requires assessment of this injury as of the moment the tort victim has paid for the repair of the damage.[11] The highest courts of Belgium[12] and Italy[13] have also adopted the position that tort damages are debts of value, and that damages must therefore be calculated as of the date of the judgment. The Belgian *Cour de Cassation,* unlike its Italian counterpart, has rejected the French and German position that the tort victim who has repaired his own property prior to judgment is the holder of a pecuniary obligation.[14]

Severe inflation and the influence of European doctrine and case law have recently led the courts of Argentina and Brazil to accept the doctrine of the debt of value and to shift the time for calculating tort damages from the date of the accident to the date of the judgment.[15] The Argentine courts are, however, badly divided on the question of whether the victim's prejudgment expenditures for repairs are debts of value or pecuniary debts.[16] Uruguayan lower courts and doctrinal writers have accepted the concept of the debt of value in tort cases;[17] however, this breach in the dam of nominalism has thus far been sandbagged by the Supreme Court.[18] Chilean doctrine is split on whether to accept the doctrine of the debt of value, but thus far no Chilean courts have invoked the doctrine. Nonetheless, Chilean courts have recently changed their orientation to permit monetary correction of a damage award to compensate for monetary depreciation between the date of the accident and the date of payment of the judgment.[19]

Several years of sustained galloping inflation has recently led the Israeli Supreme Court to replace its traditional Anglo-Saxon damages approach with a "revaluation remedy," which in result, though not in theory, is virtually identical with the debt of value approach. Starting with a basic premise of the Anglo-American approach to damages—that the defendant is responsible for all direct and foreseeable consequences of his tortious conduct—, the Israeli Supreme Court reasoned that because inflation is foreseeable, depreciation in the nominal value of assessed tort damages is a direct consequence of the tort. Therefore, the damage resulting from inflation's erosion of the nominal amount of damages is also compensable.[20] The misnamed "revaluation remedy" ordered by the Israeli Supreme Court is actually the assessment of damages as of, or as close as feasible to, the day of judgment.

In 1978, soon after the Israeli courts began to develop this "revaluation remedy," the legislature enacted a Linkage Law authorizing the courts to link the value of damage awards to the consumer price index.[21] The decision of whether to index an award is up to the discretion of the court. If an award is indexed, however, the court's power to award interest is restricted to an annual rate of 3 percent. Although it is difficult to defend the discretionary aspect of the Linkage Law, indexation of the damage award is conceptually much more likely to approximate the goal of *restitutio in integrum* than the "revaluation remedy" or the debt of value of approach.

Whether or not one subscribes to the doctrinal construct of the debt of value, the end result of revaluing damage awards at the date of judgment is far preferable to that which occurs with the traditional view of assessing damage as of the date of the injury. The traditional view is unworkable in an inflationary economy. Not only does it prevent the plaintiff from being made whole, but it also gives the defendant an enormous economic incentive to delay the litigation as much as possible. Application of the nominalist principle to damages that have become liquidated by virtue of the victim's payment makes no sense whatsoever. In terms of social policy, it is unwise to have a legal rule that discourages persons from repairing damaged property for substantial periods. In terms of legal theory, the tort victim is an involuntary creditor. He never assumed the risk of monetary depreciation and is unprotected against it. The risk appropriately belongs on the shoulders of the tortfeasor, who otherwise profits from being able to pay off his obligation in depreciated currency.

Revision of Unpaid Judgments

If the value of a court judgment depreciates because of inflation while the case is on appeal or the judgment remains otherwise unpaid, plaintiff's sole remedy in most jurisdictions is legal interest. The obligation is deemed pecuniary in nature and governed by the nominalist principle. This solution, conceived under the assumption of a stable currency,[22] creates an obvious injustice in an inflationary economy, where the legal interest rate, typically 4 to 8 percent *per annum,* is likely to be sharply negative. Consequently, the tort victim receives something less than is required to make him whole.

Recognizing the injustice of this nominalist solution, which is particularly egregious in a case that wends its way slowly through the judicial system, courts have reached more equitable solutions in France, Italy, Argentina, Brazil, and Chile. Starting from the proposition that reparation of tort damage must be integral, French doctrine and case law have concluded that damage awards on appeal must be revised to correct for inflation between the date of judgment and payment, unless the defendant deposits the amount of the judgment for the plaintiff's use during the appeal.[23] Starting from the proposition that tort damage awards are debts of value, Italian doctrine and case law have taken the position that a damage award does not lose its character as a debt of value until the moment of payment.[24] Argentine doctrine and case law have reached a similar conclusion.[25] In Brazil and Chile, where the courts have been influenced by legislation mandating monetary correction in tax and other matters, as well as by French and Italian doctrine, tort damage awards are being monetarily corrected in accordance with variations in price indexes between the date of the judgment and the date of actual payment.[26]

In Uruguay the problem has been resolved by a 1976 statute, which provides that monetary depreciation shall be taken into account in liquidating the value of all pecuniary obligations whose performance is the subject of a lawsuit or arbitral proceeding.[27] Monetary depreciation is to be determined by the difference between the consumer price index on the date the obligation arises and on the date it is paid. Interest is calculated on the readjusted value.

Future Earnings and Medical Expenses

There are two widely used methods of compensating the plaintiff in a wrongful death or disablement case: (1) a pension or periodical payments, and (2) a lump sum award. Periodical payments have to be used in most of the Socialist countries and in some of the Latin American countries. The common law countries, civil law jurisdictions that have close common law ties (Quebec, South Africa, Louisiana, and Scotland), Denmark, Norway, and some of the Latin American countries generally use only lump sum settlements. Most of the civil law countries permit either form of payment, though in France and Germany the lump sum arrangement is used in virtually all cases.[28] Both methods are likely to undercompensate the plaintiff in an inflationary economy.

The Pension or Periodical Payments

The distortion that can be caused to a traditional pension award is dramatically illustrated by the facts of the Chilean case of *Guzmán v. Empresa de los Ferrocarriles del Estado.*[29] In 1959 Sra. Guzmán attempted to secure judicial revision of her monthly pension of 500 pesos, awarded in 1942 for life or until remarriage to indemnify her for the wrongful death of her husband, killed in a train accident. Her pension was based upon her deceased husband's earnings at the time of his death in 1934, when 500 pesos was worth about U.S. $21. By 1942, when she finally began receiving her pension, inflation had already reduced its purchasing power by more than half. By 1959 her pension had lost 99.4 percent of its 1934 value. Although he could find no legal basis to revise the widow's pension, the trial judge increased it anyway, citing general considerations of equity. The Court of Appeals, however, reversed on the ground that the judgment violated the principle of *res judicata,* a reversal sustained by the Chilean Supreme Court.[30]

Courts in most countries now assess a claim for lost earnings or future medical expenses in terms of wages or costs in effect at the date of judgment rather than those prevailing at the date of the accident.[31] This solution avoids part of the problem of the *Guzmán* case, but it does nothing to prevent pensions from losing their value because of postjudgment inflation.

A more important adaptation has developed in Brazil, and to a lesser extent in Belgium and France, where courts have been awarding indexed pensions. During the galloping inflation of the late 1950s and early 1960s, Brazilian courts began to index pensions awarded in accident cases to the prevailing minimum wage. The problem was particularly acute in Brazil because procedural law required compensation for lost earning capacity be in the form of a pension. Despite initial hostility to this innovation, after 1963 the Supreme Federal Tribunal, Brazil's highest court, began confirming indexed awards.[32] By 1969 the Supreme Federal Tribunal's decisions had become sufficiently uniform on the subject for the court to promulgate the following *Súmula* or case law rule: "The pension corresponding to compensation for civil responsibility must be calculated on the basis of the minimum wage prevailing at the time of the judgment and shall be adjusted for subsequent variations."[33] In most cases, Brazilian courts require the tortfeasor to purchase and deposit with the court government bonds with a yield sufficient to fund the pension.[34] Since the introduction of indexed government bonds in 1964, Brazilian courts have been funding indexed pensions for accident victims with such bonds.[35]

In 1959 and 1960 Belgian courts began to award pensions tied to wage levels or the cost-of-living index.[36] Since the Belgian *Cour de Cassation* has yet to approve such awards,[37] their validity is still doubtful.[38]

Only recently has the legality of indexed pensions become firmly established in France. In 1952 two decisions of the French *Cour de Cassation* invalidated indexed pensions for reparation of personal injuries on the ground that indexation offended the nominalist principle.[39] Although in 1957 the *Cour de Cassation* rejected the contention that index clauses conflicted with the principle of nominalism in the celebrated case of *Guyot v. Praquin,*[40] the French legislature banned virtually all index clauses the following year.[41] In 1961 the *Cour de Cassation* quashed a decision that awarded an accident victim requiring permanent internment in a psychiatric hospital a lifetime pension indexed to the cost of hospitalization.[42] Nonetheless, subsequent passage of two statutes—one authorizing indexation of annuities "constituted by private parties,"[43] and the other in 1972 authorizing judges to award variable alimentary pensions where permitted by law[44]—has led several doctrinal writers to argue that the legislature has implicitly authorized the award of indexed pensions in tort suits.[45] In 1972 and 1973, a number of the French lower courts, supported by a strong doctrinal current critical of the *Cour de Cassation's* position,[46] began awarding indexed pensions to accident victims. The index utilized varied. Some courts chose the trimestral hourly wage index; others chose the consumer price index, or even the European unit of account.[47] Finally, in 1974 the *chambre mixte* of the *Cour de Cassation,* composed of the presidents of the high court's various senates, affirmed a decision indexing a damage award to the trimestral hourly wage index.[48]

The French legislature promptly reacted by enacting a statute authorizing the indexing of all pensions awarded to victims of automobile accidents involving death or disability of at least 75 percent. The reference index is an annual wage index used to update social security benefits, but the amount of the adjustment cannot exceed an annually adjusted maximum. The statute provides for the updating of all tort pensions, regardless of whether the accident occurred prior to the effective date of the act, or whether the pension resulted from a judgment or a settlement.[49] Pension increases resulting from indexing are funded from a common pool financed by all automobile insurance companies. The statute continues to allow courts discretion to award either lump sums or periodical payments. With respect to awards not covered by the act, French courts retain complete discretion whether to index and in choice of index. They do not have discretion, however, to revise nonindexed awards that are not covered by this statute.

Brazilian, German, Greek, and Portuguese courts, on the other hand, do have the power to revise pension awards because of subsequent inflation. Since the 1960s, Brazilian courts, adhering to the doctrinal position that pensions for lost earnings are debts of value, have been ordering revision of previously fixed pensions in accordance with subsequent increases in the minimum wage.[50] German courts have long permitted pension revision if there is a significant increase in the cost of living or a general wage increase. An increase in the general price level of at least 20 percent is usually required, though some courts have revised pensions for as little as a 10 percent increase.[51] Greek law requires a substantial alteration of circumstances as a condition for pension revision, but explicitly defines a change in the cost of living as a substantial change of circumstances.[52] Portugal's 1966 Civil Code explicitly permits revision of pension awards for momentary depreciation in accordance with price indexes.[53]

In 1967 Sweden enacted a statute revalorizing preexisting pension awards stemming from automobile accidents. Revalorization percentages ranged from 225 percent for pre-1940 pensions, to 5 percent for pensions awarded as recently as 1965. Post-1967 pensions have been indexed to the cost-of-living.[54] In 1973 similar indexation was statutorily extended to periodical payment awards in all tort cases. Concern about adequate funding resulted in imposition of a ceiling of 5 percent *per annum* on readjustments under both statutes. Consequently, Swedish pension awards have failed to keep pace with inflation in recent years.[55]

New Zealand, which in 1974 replaced its lump sum system of tort awards with pensions fixed at 80 percent of pre-injury earnings levels, has had to devise a technique for insuring that pension levels keep up with inflation. The original recommendation was to tie pensions to the consumer price index, a proposal successfully opposed by the treasury as inflationary.[56] Instead, since 1975 New Zealand has linked tort pensions to the Industrial Commission's general wage orders, thereby according tort victims the benefits of any productivity increases.[57]

In the United States a Model Act for the Periodic Payment of Judgments has recently been approved by the National Conference on Commissioners on Uniform State Laws.[58] If eventually enacted, either party in cases involving bodily injuries in excess of $100,000 will be able to elect trial under it, provided the defendant can put up $500,000 in security to ensure payment of the judgment. Although the Model Act forbids consideration of inflation,[59] it includes a provision for adjusting the periodical payments for inflation by indexing them to the interest rate on fifty-two-week U.S. Treasury bills.[60] This admittedly less than optimal indexing device was chosen because no inflation-adjusted annuity is presently marketed. Defendants can fund these adjusted periodical payments by investing in Treasury bills. The Model Act also provides for a 3 percent discount factor to reduce awards of future damages to present value.[61] This Act is highly controversial and is virtually certain to incur the enmity of the personal injury bar. Since the case is never closed during the victim's lifetime, the Act is also likely to incur hostility from insurance companies and defense counsel. Even if enacted, the Model Act might not survive constitutional challenge.[62]

In other countries with substantial inflation one who is compensated for lost earnings or future medical expenses through a fixed pension is likely to be in the unenviable position of the widow in the *Guzmán* case, whose pension is today worthless. This helps explain, at least in part, why in countries that permit or even require periodical payments, the great bulk of claims for lost earnings or future medical expenses are likely to be settled for a lump sum. Where there is provision for periodic updating, however, pension awards would appear to offer plaintiffs better protection against inflationary erosion than lump sum awards. Still, even if periodical awards are automatically updated or the economy is stable, both parties to a tort suit are likely to prefer lump sum awards.[63]

Lump Sum Awards

Use of a lump sum award by no means avoids the problem of inflation, though it is clearly much fairer to the plaintiff than a fixed pension in an inflationary economy. A lump sum award means that all damages, both past and future, must be taken into account at the time of the trial. This necessarily entails considerable speculation about unknown events and quantities. Despite their willingness to speculate about a vast array of contingencies, most courts granting lump sum awards refuse to take future inflation into account in calculating damages for lost earning capacity or future medical expenses.[64] To be sure, there are occasional decisions that have permitted consideration of future inflation.[65] There is also a recent decision of the English House of Lords, *Taylor v. O'Connor,*[66] sustaining an increase in a wrongful death award because of future inflation, that has been variously interpreted as approving or disapproving such an allowance for future inflation.[67] But for the accident victim who requires expensive future medical treatment or compensation for a permanent loss in earning capacity, the majority position, which bases future damages upon a projection of current medical costs or earnings, is likely to be grossly inadequate in an inflationary economy.

Professors Harper and James have provided one of the most insightful explanations for the refusal of courts to consider projections of inflationary trends:

> Future trends in the value of money are necessarily unknown and so always render such damages speculative in a way we cannot escape. If the estimates represent a straight-line projection of present living costs, they will be frustrated by fluctuations either way. If prophecy of

> change is heeded, frustration will follow if no change, or the opposite change, occurs. When courts have consciously grappled with the problem they have either found all prophecy too speculative and so, perforce, have taken the equally speculative course of betting on a continuance of the status quo; or they have made intuitive and not always very wise judgments that present conditions represent a departure from some imaginary norm to which they think we shall rapidly return. It is not at all clear that courts would be willing to hear experts on the matter, or that they would get much real help if they did. For the most part the problem—which is inevitably present in every case of future loss—is not analyzed and the present value of money is assumed to be the proper basis.[68]

Yet after forty years of virtually continuous inflation, which has persisted even during severe recessions, any prophecy of price stability seems highly speculative, and any prophecy of deflation seems lunatical. Courts and juries regularly speculate about contingencies easily as indefinite as future inflation rates in making lump sum awards, such as the extent and value of pain and suffering, loss of companionship, and loss of consortium; life expectancy; merit salary increases; the earning capacity of students and young children; income tax rates; and present value discount rates. Branding economic projections of future inflation rates as "too speculative" for judicial consideration is simply arbitrary.[69]

Another justification which courts sometimes assert for refusing to admit evidence about future inflation in determining lost earning capacity is that offsetting factors are not taken into account, thereby producing on balance a fair result. A commonly claimed offset is failure to deduct income taxes on the foregone earnings. The leading case is Judge Friendly's opinion for the Second Circuit in *McWeeney v. New York, N.H. & H.R.R. Co.,*[70] denying consideration of income taxes on lost earnings on the theory that lack of adjustment for inflation and attorney's fees are offsetting factors. The balance struck in *McWeeney,* however, tilts heavily in the defendant's favor. A typical U.S. attorney's fee in a successful tort suit is one-third of the total recovery. Median family income in the United States in 1975 was $13,500; assuming a family of four with deductions of 16 percent of gross income, the average effective federal income tax rate is approximately 11 percent. Moreover, if the lump sum award is invested, interest and capital gains are taxable.[71] If we make the simplifying assumptions that the effective tax rate on the income earned by the investment of the award is one-half that of the average family (since the capital will be steadily depleted over time) and that there are no capital gains or losses, the *McWeeney* offset can be expressed in this *balancette.*

Attorney's fees (33%)	Income Tax on Earnings (11%)
Income Tax on Interest (5.5%)	
Inflation (?)	

It is probable that juries in many cases attempt to compensate the plaintiff for attorney's fees by increasing the amount awarded for pain and suffering. Nevertheless, if one ignores this probable offset, as Judge Friendly does in *McWeeney*, the above *balancette* is in balance only with an inflation rate of −27.5 percent.

A more sophisticated offset approach is to attempt to factor out inflation from the interest rate used to discount a future damage award to present value. Generally, courts discount sums awarded for future damages to take into account the earning power of the lump sum award during the years between the date of the award and the time the money is actually spent. If a plaintiff suffers an earnings loss of $10,000 annually for the next twenty years because of the defendant's wrongful act, a lump sum award of $200,000 at the start of the twenty-year period will over compensate the plaintiff in a stable economy. To determine how much capital is necessary to provide the plaintiff with $10,000 a year for the next twenty years, the court must determine how much the award should yield if safely invested. If the risk-free rate of return is estimated at 6 percent *per annum,* utilization of a standard annuity table will reduce a $200,000 award to $114,699; with a 4 percent discount rate, the net award falls to $135,903. But interest rates are in large part a function of anticipated inflation rates. The higher the anticipated inflation rate, the higher the interest rate.[72] Because of this functional interrelationship, one can argue that it is unjust first to refuse to increase an award by allowing for inflation in calculating future earnings or medical expenses, and then to turn around and decrease the award by discounting it to present value with an interest rate that reflects inflation. In *Feldman v. Allegheny Airlines, Inc.,*[73] a recent federal case that has attracted widespread attention, Judge Blumenfeld developed a sophisticated method for netting out the inflationary component from the risk-free interest rate. By subtracting the average annual increase in the consumer price index from average annual yields on U.S. government securities between 1940 and 1972, he arrived at the unusually low discount rate of 1.5 percent.[74]

In a quartet of cases decided in 1978,[75] Canada's Supreme Court adopted a similar approach but with strikingly different results. Rejecting the traditional view that future inflation should be ignored, the Canadian Supreme Court decided to discount damage awards for future earnings and medical expenses at a 7 percent rate. This figure was reached by subtracting a 3.5 percent projected long-term inflation rate from the 10.5 percent rate of return then available on long-term safe investments. Upon closer examination, however, it is apparent that the court's projected 3.5 percent annual inflation rate over the next forty years was a wholly illusory figure. It was supposedly based upon a 1973 forecast by Dr. Deutsch, former head of the Economic Council of Canada, but it is doubtful that he ever made such a forecast. Even if such a forecast had been made in 1973, it should have been obvious that economic events of the next five years had rendered such a forecast obsolete.[76] From a methodological standpoint, Judge Blumenfeld's effort to derive a real rate of interest by projecting the actual experience of the past 32 years was far sounder.

Neither the *Feldman* approach nor the Canadian variation resolves the debate about whether future inflation should be taken into account. Adjusting the discount rate for inflation merely locates the conflict in a different phase of the process by which damages are calculated. As a practical matter, subtracting a projected inflation rate from the discount rate produces virtually the same result as allowing for a projected inflation rate in computing the original value of the award, and using a current discount rate. Theoretically, the plaintiff should be able to take advantage of current high interest rates by investing in long-term government and corporate bonds, which should become even more attractive investments once interest rates fall to "normal" levels. But there are two practical problems. First, the plaintiff will have to make steady withdrawals from principal to meet his expenses. The award is not calculated to enable him to live solely off the income. This means that bonds will have to be sold from time to time, or that the award will have to be invested in short-term obligations, such as a money fund or certificates of deposit. If interest rates have risen when the bonds must be sold, the plaintiff will be forced to incur capital losses. If interest rates decline, the plaintiff who has elected to invest his award in short-term obligations will experience a decline in income. A sophisticated investor might well decide to hedge and divide his portfolio between long-term bonds and short-term obligations. It does not seem fair to force the innocent victim, who is unlikely to be a sophisticated investor, to bear the risk of loss from future interest rate fluctuations. Second, the plaintiff has to pay income tax on the interest, dividends, or capital gains earned on investing the award. As is shown in chapter 9, *infra,* much of that so-called "income" will actually be illusory, since it is offset by the real loss stemming from inflationary erosion of capital. Fairness would seem to require that the discount rate be based upon the yields of AAA or AA rated tax-free municipal bonds rather than the higher yields of taxable government or corporate issues, especially in a jurisdiction which requires that the award be reduced because income taxes need not be paid on the foregone earnings. On the other hand, netting inflation from the discount rate does have the distinct advantage of simplifying the task of the court or jury by reducing the number of calculations needed to take inflation into account. Moreover, it may be fairer to the plaintiff because the jury will not be misled by the illusory lavishness of an inflation-adjusted award prior to its being discounted to present value.

A less sophisticated, but even more desirable approach is simply to exclude consideration of future inflation in determining the principal sum, and to refuse to discount that sum to present value. A number of American jurisdictions refuse to discount to present value an award for future medical expenses or future pain and suffering.[77] Such a refusal is usually rationalized in one of two ways. One is concern about the potential for confusing the jury with unnecessary calculations. The other is concern that the plaintiff may need to have money for future medical expenses in a liquid form. Curiously, courts adopting this approach usually evince little concern about the effects of inflation. However, in the often-cited but seldom followed case of *Beaulieu* v. *Elliot,*[78] the Alaskan Supreme Court refused to discount an award for lost earnings to present value primarily because of the likelihood that future inflation would cancel out the earnings on the award.

> Annual inflation at a varying rate is and has been with us for many years. There is no reason to expect that it will not be with us in the future. The rate of depreciation offsets the interest that could be earned on government bonds and many other "safe" investments. As a result the plaintiff, who through no fault of his own is given his future earnings reduced to present value must, in order to realize his full earnings and not be penalized by reduction of future earnings to present value, invest his money in enterprises, other than those which are considered "safe" investments, which promise a return in interest or dividends greater than the offsetting rate of annual inflation . . . [I]nstead of being assured of earnings at rates greater than the annual rate of inflation, the injured plaintiff stands a chance of entirely losing his future earnings by unlucky or unwise investments. Since the plaintiff through the defendant's fault and not his own, has been placed in the position of having no assurance that his award of future earnings, reduced to present value, can be utilized so that he will ultimately realize his full earnings, we believe that justice will be best served by permitting the trier of facts to compute loss of future earnings without reduction to present value. The plaintiff is more likely to be restored to his original condition under the rule we adopt than under the prevailing rule which calls for discounting of the future earnings. . . .
>
> [I]f there is any fear that failure to reduce [to] present value will give the plaintiff more than he is entitled to because of the possibility of his making successful investments of the sum awarded at returns greater than the annual rate of inflation, such fear is obviated by the fact that the award may well be deficient in that it does not take into account probable wage increases the plaintiff would ordinarily be expected to receive in the future.[79]

The approach of the Alaskan court has much to recommend it. A few American courts have reached the same result after consideration of expert testimony to that effect.[80] If one assumes that the plaintiff is likely to be an unsophisticated investor and is going to have to maintain a substantial part of his capital in relatively liquid form so that he can draw on it as needed for expenses, it becomes even more reasonable. Preventing one's capital from being eroded by inflation is difficult in today's world, even for the sophisticated investor.[81] Real interest rates are often negative in inflationary economies.[82] It takes a sophisticated investor or considerable luck, and sometimes both, to earn a positive rate of return in most inflationary economies. The typical tort plaintiff is not a sophisticated investor, and it is unfair to hold him to such a standard. Investment in long-term bonds or in real estate, generally regarded as one of the best hedges against inflation, is usually difficult for someone who needs to use up capital to live or pay medical expenses. Short-term investments entail high transaction costs and require considerable investment expertise. There is empirical evidence to suggest that the recipients of lump sum awards frequently dissipate them in a few years.[83] Few countries offer indexed government bonds or savings accounts; even where available, governmental manipulation of the index may prevent the returns on such investments from being positive in real terms. It seems fairer to build in a margin for error on the side of the innocent tort victim rather than on the side of the tortfeasor. In addition, the approach of the Alaskan Supreme Court has the decided advantages of simplicity, predictability, and economy of effort. It may also eliminate opportunities for confusing the jury and courts that are inherent in speculation about both interest and inflation rates.[84]

Ideally, the lump sum award should provide the plaintiff with funds sufficient to purchase an annuity that will accompany the changes in the cost of living plus a real interest component equivalent to the present value discount rate employed. Unfortunately, such annuities are presently available in few countries. Where there are sizeable future medical expenses, such as a victim who will require permanent institutionalization, periodic payments indexed to the cost of hospital care make eminent sense. A rational alternative, recently rejected in a tort case where the U.S. government was the defendant, was the establishment of a trust fund of $500,000, replenishable if necessary, to provide institutional care for the rest of the victim's life.[85] Where the procedural system is not geared to periodical payments, or where there is difficulty in funding an indexed annuity, the most sensible solution would seem to be to forget about both inflation and discounting an award to present value. This is not a perfect solution, but it achieves a fair and practical result.

CONTRACT DAMAGES

The purpose of damages for breach of contract is to place the nonbreaching party in as good a position as he would have enjoyed had the other party performed the contract.[86] During inflationary periods, however, the interaction of three factors—the nominalist principle, the proper date for assessing damages, and the inadequacy of the legal interest rate—causes contract damage awards to fall considerably short of achieving that purpose.

One kind of contract remedy commonly affected by inflation is the creditor's action for damages arising from the debtor's failure to repay a debt on time. In this situation most countries restrict the creditor's damage remedy to legal interest,[87] which has historically been set at such modest fixed rates that inflation renders it negative in real economic terms. Invocation of the nominalist principle prevents the creditor from recovering for monetary depreciation, because the value of money is presumed to be permanently equal to itself. During the term of the loan, imposition of the risk of monetary depreciation on the creditor makes sense, because it is fair to assume that the creditor has allowed for that risk in determining the interest rate, or could have protected himself against the risk with an index clause. But it makes little sense to assume that the creditor assumed the risk of monetary depreciation beyond the time set for repayment.[88] Most countries fail to differentiate between monetary depreciation during the term of the loan and after default. The nondefaulting creditor is prejudiced by being forced to accept repayment in cheaper currency. The defaulting debtor receives a corresponding windfall.

There are a few countries, however, where a creditor is permitted to recover more than legal interest if a debtor fails to repay his debt during a period of inflation. Uruguay and Brazil have recently adopted statutes specifically providing for monetary correction of pecuniary obligations in accordance with price index variations between the date of maturity and the date of actual payment.[89] Spurred by hyperinflation since 1975 and a strong doctrinal current,[90] the Argentine courts have recently jettisoned the nominalism of the country's French-inspired Civil Code and have permitted recovery for monetary depreciation for delay in repayment of a pecuniary obligation.[91] In reaching this result, Argentine courts and commentators have been aided by the suggestive comment of Vélez Sársfield, the draftsman of the Argentine Civil Code, that had he been contemplating a change in the value of money (which he was not), he would have chosen the solution of the Austrian rather than the French Civil Code.[92] Although the question is not free from doubt, Chile seems to have rejected the nominalist solution of the French Civil Code and now permits recovery for monetary depreciation for delay in payment of pecuniary obligations.[93]

Italy, Israel, Austria, Germany, and Switzerland permit recovery of more than legal interest if a debtor fails to repay a pecuniary obligation on time, but the creditor must prove actual damages above and beyond monetary depreciation. Thus, Article 1224 of the Italian Civil Code expressly permits the creditor of an overdue pecuniary obligation to recover compensation in addition to legal interest. This article has been interpreted, however, to require a showing that the creditor has been damaged by more than monetary depreciation in order to harmonize it with the nominalist principle enshrined in Article 1277 of the Italian Civil Code.[94] Despite this restrictive interpretation, some of the Italian courts have recently decided to revalue unpaid but liquidated wage claims in accordance with price index changes.[95] Under Section 10 and 12 of the Israeli Remedies Law, a plaintiff can recover more than legal interest for the failure to repay a debt on time, provided he can prove special damages in accordance with the use he would have made of the money had it been repaid on time. Merely showing monetary depreciation is insufficient.[96] Austria, Switzerland, and Germany also require the creditor to prove special damages; however, Germany accords a non-German creditor whose domestic currency is stable the benefit of a presumption that he would have converted the repayment of the debt into his domestic currency.[97]

There are also a few countries that have mitigated the creditor's loss to inflation by allowing their legal interest rate to float. Argentina, Germany, and Switzerland have long linked their legal interest rates to bank discount rates.[98] France recently enacted a statute tying the legal interest rate to the discount rate of the Bank of France,[99] and similar legislation has been proposed in several other countries.[100] In a country like Argentina, where severe inflation has been chronic, linkage to the discount rate of the Bank of the Nation has not kept the legal interest rate abreast of the inflation rate. Nonetheless, a floating legal interest rate is a significant improvement on a fixed rate during inflationary periods.

Inflation similarly distorts contractual damages in nonloan transactions where the loss is liquidated. Thus, if a buyer wrongfully breaches a contract for the sale of goods, and the seller resells the goods for less than the contract price, his loss will be judicially regarded as liquidated. In a suit for damages for the breach, recovery in most countries will be limited to the difference between the contract price and the resale price, plus any expenses of the resale and legal interest. Similarly, if the seller defaults and the buyer covers at a higher price, his damages will be limited to the difference between the contract price and the cover purchase, plus any expenses of the cover purchase and legal interest.[101] In both cases the loss is regarded as a pecuniary obligation; hence, as with simple debts, the nominalist principle will prevent recovery of damages for depreciation in the purchasing power of the loss between the date of the breach and the date of judgment.[102]

Indeed, it is quite possible for the nominalist principle to prevent recovery of any damages on a sales contract where breach has caused real prejudice to the buyer. For example, suppose a buyer agrees to buy a horse for $100 and defaults on the agreement. The seller disposes of the horse for $100 two months later, when the currency has depreciated by 10 percent. If the transaction is viewed through the astigmatic lens of nominalism, the seller would have no loss, but if one peers through the spectacles of economic reality, the seller has lost $10 because of the buyer's breach.

Where contract damages remain unascertained or unliquidated prior to judgment, the date for assessing damages becomes critical in an inflationary economy. The rule in Anglo-American countries is that damages should be assessed as of the date of breach.[103] This rule has the unfortunate effect of placing the risk of monetary depreciation on the nonbreaching party, because inflation between the date of the breach and the date of judgment will reduce the real value of the damages awarded. In addition, courts frequently refuse to allow recovery of interest from the date of the breach when the damages are unliquidated.[104]

During inflation, most of the civil law countries treat the plaintiff suing for unliquidated damages more favorably than the common law countries. Contractual damages are treated similarly to tort damages, which means that the relevant time for assessing for their assessment is commonly the date of judgment.[105] This rule places the risk of monetary depreciation on the defaulting party. In some countries, such as Argentina, Belgium, Brazil, and Italy, contractual damages, like tort damages, are considered debts of value.[106] Consequently, if there is monetary depreciation between the date of judgment and the date of eventual payment, such as when an appeal is taken, the amount of the obligation will be revalued to reflect the interim inflation.

In an inflationary economy the Anglo-American rule requiring assessment of damages as of the date of the breach is plainly undesirable. It significantly undercompensates the plaintiff, and gives the defendant a substantial economic incentive to default and to delay judgment as long as possible. The civilian approach of assessing damages as of the day of judgment is therefore fairer to the plaintiff. Nonetheless, the day of judgment rule is also flawed, for it gives the plaintiff a significant speculative advantage. For example, French law does not require the plaintiff to mitigate damages by covering or reselling in the open market. Hence, if the price of the goods rises more rapidly than the general price index, the plaintiff may recover far more than his original loss plus monetary depreciation. Plaintiff has the same free ride under the debt of value theory, and there the speculative advantage may continue even longer. The preferable solution would be to assess damages as of the date of the breach, correct for monetary depreciation between that date and eventual payment, and add a real rate of interest on to that total. This solution encourages mitigation of damages, and fully compensates the plaintiff for his loss from both the breach and from monetary depreciation.

BANKRUPTCY DEBTS

A closely related damage problem arises in the context of bankruptcy. In inflationary periods, securing discharge of one's debts in bankruptcy or through a composition of creditors can be a profitable enterprise for debtors, particularly for those with substantial noncash assets. The greater the delay in paying off creditors, the cheaper one's debts become in real economic terms.

Argentina appears to be the first country to enact legislation to protect creditors by imposing monetary correction on debts liquidated in bankruptcy or composition proceedings. A statute enacted at the end of 1976 provides that all debts discharged under the aegis of the bankruptcy courts shall be updated by coefficients reflecting the change in the wholesale price index for nonagricultural products plus 6 percent interest.[107] For creditors to whom debts were due before the debtor invoked the protection of the bankruptcy court, monetary correction begins with the index number for the month preceding the decree of bankruptcy and continues until discharge. For those to whom debts became due thereafter, monetary correction begins with the index number of the month preceding the date the debts became due. Other systems of indexation, such as those contained in index clauses, do not apply after the date the debtor has been declared a bankrupt.[108] Israel in 1978 instituted a similar, albeit weaker, measure granting bankruptcy courts discretion to permit creditors to index the value of past due debts to the consumer price index.[109] These statutes represent a significant step toward fair treatment of creditors in an inflationary economy. Not only do they avoid the unjust result of treating as equals creditors who have been owed the same nominal sum by a bankrupt debtor for varying lengths of time, but they also prevent debtors with substantial noncash assets from significantly lightening their debts as a result of compositions or arrangements in the bankruptcy courts.

EMINENT DOMAIN AWARDS

In many countries private property can be taken for public use only after payment of just compensation. In theory, just compensation should provide the former owner with sufficient funds to replace his property with another of similar value. Nonetheless, condemnees seldom receive just compensation in inflationary economies. Inflation almost invariably distorts condemnation processes and results in disguised confiscation.

Guises of Confiscation

Inflation produces disguised confiscation in five ways. First, there are invariable delays between the time the property is valued and the date compensation is paid. Inflation itself tends to prolong normal delays in the condemnation process by making appropriations for public works inadequate. Realistic budgeting requires inclusion of a substantial component for future inflation, but inclusion of such sums is tantamount to the government's confessing its inability to control inflation. Hard pressed governmental officials readily perceive that a policy of "Take Now, Pay Later" stretches inadequate project budgets, because condemnation awards can be paid off in depreciated currency.

Second, "quick take" statutes, which permit the condemnor to obtain possession upon deposit of a sum linked to tax appraisal values, are used extensively in many countries. Tax appraisal values seldom correspond to fair market value, and rapid inflation sharply accentuates the disparity. Consequently, a substantial portion of the compensation that should be paid prior to the actual taking is not paid until lengthy court proceedings have been completed.

Third, as with tort and contract damage awards, the only legal remedy for delay in payment of an award has traditionally been legal interest. Because legal interest rates quickly become negative during inflation, the longer the delay until payment, the greater the inflationary erosion of the real value of the compensation.

Fourth, governments occasionally decide to nationalize companies by taking their stock rather than their physical assets. In the process shareholders may be compensated for their shares at book value. If the tax or corporation laws do not require or permit monetary correction of corporate balance sheets, inflation is likely to assure that book value will be below the actual value of corporate stock.

Fifth, governments engaging in a substantial amount of expropriation sometimes compensate former property owners with long-term bonds rather than cash. To the extent that the principal and interest are unprotected against inflation, the result is confiscation. Occasionally, it is obvious that the drafters of expropriation legislation have deliberately built inflationary confiscation into the system, as was done in Chile's 1967 Agrarian Reform Law.[110] Under the regime established by this law, compensation for land expropriated for agrarian reform purposes was to be paid partly in cash and the balance in bonds bearing 3 percent annual interest. The bonds were in three classes with maturity dates varying from 5 to 30 years. Each class was divided into two series. The first series had its principal readjusted annually in accordance with variations in the consumer price index, and the interest received half the inflation adjustment of the principal. The second series bonds had neither principal nor interest readjusted for inflation. Each property owner received 70 percent of the unpaid balance in first series bonds, and 30 percent in second series bonds.

Judicial and Legislative Efforts to Maintain Just Compensation

The U.S. Approach

The reactions of courts to the disguised confiscation resulting from inflation's distortion of the eminent domain process have varied considerably. One reaction, exemplified by the American courts, has been to imitate ostriches. U.S. courts generally value property as of the date of the taking[111] and ignore inflation. Efforts to advance the date of valuation to the day of judgment, or to invite the jury to consider the effects of inflation, have been flatly rejected.[112] Most of the cases blithely proceed on the premise that legal interest, usually fixed at 6 percent *per annum,* is sufficient to compensate the condemnee for any delays in the process.[113]

The British Approach

On the other hand, the English House of Lords recently withdrew its collective head from the sand and scrapped its traditional practice of valuing condemned property as of the filing of a "notice to treat" (a formal notification served on the condemnee advising that the condemnor wishes to acquire the property). In *Birmingham City Corporation v. West Midland Baptist (Trust) Association,* [114] a notice to treat had been served in 1947, when the cost of relocating the condemnee church in a similar chapel would have been £50,025. The property was not actually taken until 1961, when the cost of reinstatement had increased to £89,575. Because adherence to valuation as of the date of the filing of the notice to treat was manifestly unfair to the condemnee in an inflationary economy, the House of Lords held that the appropriate date for determining the amount of compensation due was the date when reinstatement could reasonably begin.[115] Most condemnees electing the reinstatement procedure do so to be able to utilize the compensation award to pay the expenses of their relocation. Therefore, the date when reinstatement can reasonably begin coincides with that of effective payment, but a condemnee can opt for reinstatement only when the property is "devoted to a purpose of such a nature that there is no general demand or market for land for that purpose. . . ." In the more common situation, condemned property is valued by what it would bring in a voluntary sale on the open market. By way of *dictum,* the House of Lords suggested that the relevant date for determining the amount of compensation in the usual condemnation case is when the agreement for compensation is reached, or the date of judicial decision determining compensation. If, however, possession has been taken prior to either of those dates, the House of Lords suggested that the date of possession ought to be the relevant time for valuation. The relevance of the date of possession has been forcefully questioned as inconsistent with the rest of the opinion and potentially unjust for the condemnee.[116]

In addition to shifting forward the time for appraising the value of condemned property, the British have significantly upped the legal interest rate payable under the Land Compensation Act. As of January 4, 1979 the legal interest rate on condemnation awards was set at 14 percent *per annum.*[117]

The Debt of Value Approach

Some courts that have utilized the doctrine of the debt of value to revise tort damage awards for inflation have refused to employ the doctrine to revise condemnation awards. The Belgian courts have insisted on valuing condemned property as of the date of transference of possession despite substantial increases in the value of the property prior to payment.[118] Only when the gold value of the franc had been modified by law between the taking and payment did Belgian courts order an increase in compensation.[119] Although several Italian jurists and courts have taken the position that a condemnation award is a debt of value and should be updated for monetary depreciation until the date of payment,[120] the dominant position of Italian case law regards the obligation of compensation as a debt of value only until the date of valuation, after which it is considered a pecuniary obligation. The somewhat dubious rationale is that at that point condemnation in effect becomes a forced sale.[121]

The inconsistency of interpretation manifested by the courts and doctrinal writers who accept the debt of value indicates that a basic difficulty with the concept is its imprecision. Nevertheless, if one accepts the validity of the doctrine of a debt of value, eminent domain awards should certainly fall within its parameters. Because the debt of value is designed to place the risk of inflation on the debtor when it appears just to do so, there is no good reason for failing to categorize the eminent domain award as a debt of value. Here, as in the tort context, the condemnee is an involuntary creditor who never assumed the risk of monetary depreciation and is unprotected against it. It is particularly appropriate to place the loss resulting from inflation on the condemnor. The condemnor profits from the inflation by being able to discharge its obligation in depreciated currency.

Moreover, the condemnor initiated the eminent domain process and is generally the party responsible for the delay. In fact, certain condemnors may ultimately be responsible for much of the inflation. Even if it may not be fair to charge a particular state agency with being a cause of inflation, through taxation the state can spread the losses from monetary depreciation in the condemnation process over the general public, the ultimate beneficiary of the condemnation. The individual condemnee has no such loss-spreading prerogatives.

During the early 1960s, despite consistent Supreme Court rejection of the argument,[122] a substantial number of Argentine and Brazilian lower courts, faced with condemnation awards which remained unpaid for ten to twenty years of severe inflation, held that condemnation awards were debts of value and revised them to take intervening inflation into account.[123]

Judicial Revaluation: The Approaches of Argentina, Spain, and Uruguay

For a great many years the Argentine Supreme Court maintained that legal interest was the sole remedy for delay in payment of an expropriation award. In 1967, after a military *coup d'état* had produced a complete change in its personnel, the Argentine Supreme Court overruled its prior line of cases and held:

> [I]n order to maintain inviolate the principle of just compensation in the face of continued depreciation of the currency, the value of the condemned property must be fixed on the day of the final decision, assuming that the property is then transferred and that payment follows that decision without delay. If this is not so, it would then be necessary to protect the right of the condemnee to compensation for the harm resulting from the unjustified delay.[124]

Recognizing that this standard, if interpreted literally, might require a new appraisal in every case, the Argentine Supreme Court went on to suggest that lower courts perform the task of revaluation themselves by taking into account monetary depreciation and any other factors that might affect the property's actual value. As a practical matter the Argentine courts have had to utilize the Brazilian system of monetary correction, updating old valuations by coefficients derived from price indexes.[125] German, Austrian, and, for a time, French courts adopted a similar position, valuing property as of the day of judgment during inflationary periods.[126] German courts, nevertheless, will adhere to the original valuation if it appears that the condemnee caused the delay by unjustifiably invoking judicial proceedings.[127]

The Spanish courts have ordered new valuations or revisions of delayed condemnation awards by invoking the medieval doctrine of *rebus sic stantibus.*[128] In a celebrated 1953 decision involving a pre–Civil War expropriation, where the expropriating agency had attempted to compensate the condemnee in 1948 at 1934 prices, the Supreme Court held that *rebus sic stantibus* required revision of the compensation or a new valuation whenever inflation and a long delay have combined to produce a disequilibrium in the economic conditions under which compensation has been awarded.[129] In 1954 Spain revised its condemnation statute to require a new valuation whenever a compensation award remains unpaid for more than two years.[130]

Article 32 of Uruguay's 1967 Constitution specifically protects the condemnee from loss because of monetary depreciation by providing: "Whenever expropriation is ordered because of public necessity or for a public use, property owners shall be indemnified for loss or damages which they may suffer from delay, ... including those incurred because of variations in the value of the currency." Despite doctrinal urging of monetary correction of condemnation awards,[131] the Uruguayan courts have preferred to implement this constitutional guarantee by revaluation in accordance with expert appraisals.[132]

Supplementary Damage Actions

During the 1950s and 1960s, a great many Brazilian courts began to allow supplementary damage actions against condemnors. The theory of the action was that substantial delay in paying the condemnation award constituted fault *(culpa)* which had caused injury to the plaintiffs. These courts either awarded damages, as measured by the difference between the original award and current value of the property, or ordered a new valuation.[133] Until the late 1960s, the Brazilian Supreme Federal Tribunal rejected supplementary damage actions as inconsistent with *res judicata* and Article 1061 of the Civil Code (limiting loss and damages in pecuniary obligations to legal interest of 6 percent *per annum*);[134] however, after 1967 it abandoned its case law rule, *Súmula* 416,[135] and has since been affirming these damage awards.[136] Despite rejection of the debt of value theory, or perhaps because of its rejection, Italian courts have also permitted supplementary damage actions under Article 1224 of the Civil Code for money depreciation if the expropriating party has unjustifiably delayed payment of the compensation award.[137]

Monetary Correction: The Approach of Brazil, Chile, and Israel

In 1965 the Brazilian legislature enacted the following statute: "After the lapse of more than a year from the date of valuation, the judge or court, prior to final decision, shall determine monetary correction of the value set."[138]

Like much of the legislation of the era, this cryptic little law wins no prizes for draftsmanship. Its incompleteness and ambiguity has generated an enormous amount of litigation,[139] but it does provide the basis for the most sensible solution that has yet been devised to square the constitutional requirement of just compensation with inevitable delays between valuation and payment. After its enactment the Brazilian courts began applying monetary correction, based upon coefficients derived from the general price index, cost-of-living index, and the construction cost index for the state of Guanabara, to all cases where there has been a delay of more than a year between valuation and payment, provided the judgment has not been executed. Yet even where compensation has already been deposited, the courts have been permitting a supplementary damage action to complement the award.[140] The Brazilian Supreme Federal Tribunal has interpreted the statutory phrase "final decision" to mean the permanent transfer of title following verification that the compensation has actually been paid.[141]

Brazil's highest court has also recognized that expropriation of corporate shares at nonmonetarily corrected book value is unjust to shareholders in an inflationary economy. In a recent decision involving the expropriation of all the stock of a French-owned bank in 1944, twenty years before Brazilian tax laws began to require sophisticated inflation adjustments of corporate balance sheets,[142] the Supreme Federal Tribunal held that compensation of shareholders at 1944 cruzeiro balance sheet values for assets acquired long before 1944 could not be squared with the constitutional precept of just compensation. The court therefore remanded the case to the state courts to permit revaluation in accordance with the real value of the expropriated bank's assets.[143] In other recent cases involving expropriation of corporate shares, Brazilian lower courts have been awarding compensation on the basis of monetarily corrected book value, going concern value, or both.[144]

In the 1963 case of *Farkas G., Desiderio,* the Chilean Supreme Court recognized that the constitutional provision requiring indemnification for expropriation would be violated if monetary depreciation between the date of valuation and date of payment were ignored. Instead of monetarily correcting the initial valuation, the Supreme Court awarded the condemnee only about 37 percent of the interim increase in the cost-of-living index since the initial valuation.[145] A 1972 decision of the court of Concepción employed the technique of reappraisal to correct for intervening monetary depreciation.[146] After 1973, when the inflation rate soared to an annual rate of 337 percent, the Chilean courts decided to adopt the Brazilian approach of monetary correction. Since then the Chilean Supreme Court has been readjusting condemnation awards in accordance with changes in the consumer price index between the month prior to the date of valuation and the month prior to the date of effective payment.[147] This case law orientation was confirmed in Constitutional Act No. 3 of Sept. 11, 1976, art. 1 (16) (IV), which requires that condemnation awards "maintain a constant purchasing value."

The Mandatory Ordinance of 1943, which still largely regulates eminent domain in Israel, provides for the assessment of compensation as of the date the government agency publishes a notice of its intent to condemn. Because this has been so unfair to the condemnee in the context of Israel's galloping inflation, in 1975 the Israeli government directed the Lands Administration to operate with monetary correction. The government's directive states that: "[C]ompensation shall be a sum equal to the value of the rights in the land, linked to the consumer price index. . . . The value of the rights shall be increased proportionately to the rise in the consumer price index last published before the payment of the compensation over the index published for the month in which the notice was published."[148] Although this directive does not apply to all Israeli condemnations, it has eliminated much of the unfairness resulting from inflation.

Construction Cost Indexation: The French Approach

For a brief period of time the French legislature also provided for indexation of condemnation awards. A 1962 statute required courts to appraise property for condemnation purposes at its value one year prior to the inquest determining that the taking is for a public purpose. This value had to be revised in accordance with variations in the construction cost index between that date and the date of the judgment fixing the amount of compensation. If the amount of compensation paid or deposited were revised on appeal, however, variations in the construction cost index subsequent to payment or deposit were to be ignored.[149] There was considerable unhappiness with this provision, because the construction cost index was published irregularly, and many judges found the task of performing the calculations burdensome. Consequently, many courts merely paid lip-service to the statute and proceeded to value the property as of the date of judgment, as was their practice under the prior law.[150] In 1965 this brief, unsatisfactory experience with indexed awards was ended by repeal, and France formally returned to valuing expropriated property as of the date of the decision of the court of first instance.[151]

The Brazilian system of monetary correction of condemnation awards is an attempt to correct for changes in the purchasing power of money between the date of valuation and the date of payment. The French indexation technique was a curious effort to push the valuation date back in time to prevent the imminence of the public improvement from influencing the value of the property, and then to bring that value forward in time by correcting for increases in the cost of construction. The implicit assumption, that land prices and building costs increase at the same rate, was a dubious one.

SUMMARY

No country appears to have worked out an entirely satisfactory approach to the elimination of inflation-related distortions of eminent domain proceedings. Brazil's monetary correction approach appears to be the most practicable technique, but it suffers from four drawbacks. First, if one postulates that an eminent domain award constitutes just compensation only if it is sufficient to enable the condemnee to purchase a similar asset, monetary correction will often provide inadequate compensation. Until recently, monetary correction of eminent domain awards was based upon coefficients drawn from the general price index. If real property values rise more slowly than the general price index, the condemnee can replace his property and have funds to spare; if, however, real property values rise more rapidly, his monetarily corrected award will be insufficient to purchase a comparable asset. During inflation, real property values generally rise more rapidly than a general price index because of capital flight from financial assets to real assets to insure greater protection against inflation. It would be fairer to the condemnee for a court to utilize an index of real property values in the locale of the condemnation rather than a general price index that excludes land values, but such an index is generally nonexistent.

Second, though nothing in the Brazilian monetary correction statute would appear to exclude the possibility of correcting an award where less than a year has elapsed, the Supreme Federal Tribunal has so construed it.[152] With Brazil's annual inflation rate running in excess of 100 percent annually in 1980–81, a few months delay in the payment of an award can reduce the value of the award considerably. Clearly, some time lapse must be allowed for between the date of final judgment and payment without triggering monetary correction, but thirty days would seem more than sufficient in the Brazilian context.[153]

Third, the Brazilian government, disturbed by the sizeable judgments resulting from monetary correction of long unpaid condemnation awards, enacted a statute preventing the courts from applying monetary correction retroactively prior to 1965 in all cases whose judgment had not become a final prior to July 2, 1971.[154] This statute is a regrettable regression toward sanctioning disguised confiscation. Nevertheless, the Brazilian Supreme Federal Tribunal has refused to declare it unconstitutional.[155] The Brazilian courts have been sidestepping this statutory barrier, however, by permitting an independent damage action for monetary depreciation where an eminent domain award has long remained unpaid.[156]

Fourth, concern about the inflationary feedback from its vast system of monetary correction resulted in a 1977 law that restricts monetary correction of eminent domain awards to changes in the value of indexed government bonds (ORTNs).[157] Readjustment of these bonds was originally based upon the wholesale price index; however, in recent years the adjustment mechanism has been deliberately manipulated to keep the increase in value of these bonds well below that registered by the wholesale or consumer price indexes.[158]

The revaluation approach adopted by the courts of Argentina and several other countries is fairer to the condemnee because it corrects for appreciation of condemned property rather than for monetary depreciation. Still, if taken literally, this approach requires new appraisals at every stage of the appellate process, which is expensive and time-consuming. To avoid this problem, the Argentine courts have been revaluing awards with an eye to the consumer price index.[159]

An alternative approach, utilized in California, is to invalidate the condemnation whenever a condemnation award remains unpaid for more than thirty days.[160] This solution would still be potentially unfair to condemnees unless their property were valued as of the date of the judgment. The difficulty with this solution is that in many countries the bureaucracy cannot work that fast. The number of condemnation suits would increase drastically, as condemnors refiled suits. Moreover, some countries, such as Brazil, have senseless automatic appeal requirements.

Despite its drawbacks, many of which are easily remedied, monetary correction would seem to be the most practical approach to assuring just compensation during inflation. Because it is designed to compensate the condemnee for depreciation in the purchasing power of money, rather than appreciation in the property, it may have the effect of preventing certain condemnees from replacing their property with something comparable. Yet the same thing can easily happen under normal procedures during a stable economy. Given the alternatives, monetary correction seems an efficient, manageable, and relatively equitable way for courts to deal with the problem of maintaining just compensation in an inflationary economy.

DAMAGE LIMITATION PROVISIONS

Statutory ceilings on the amount of damages that can be recovered in certain types of actions are not uncommon. The economic havoc that inflation can wreak on such statutes is vividly illustrated by the decision of the United States Court of Appeals for the District of Columbia in the case of *Tramontana v. S.A. Emprêsa de Viação Aérea Rio Grandense.*[161] Tramontana was killed in 1960 when the U.S. Navy plane in which he was traveling collided with a Varig plane in Rio de Janeiro. His widow sued Varig in a United States federal court for $250,000, alleging Varig's negligence. Plaintiff's cause of action was based on Brazilian law. Rather than defend the lawsuit, Varig invoked a damage limitation provision of Cr$100,000 in Article 102 of the Brazilian Air Code and requested that judgment be granted in its favor for all of the plaintiff's claim that exceeded $170 (the dollar equivalent at the 1963 exchange rate). The damage limitation provision, enacted in 1938 to protect Brazil's infant airline industry, was originally equivalent to about U.S. $5,675, or approximately $12,332 in 1963 dollars. Judge McGowan's reasons for sustaining the $170 verdict are strikingly unconvincing:

> We have seen nothing that would suggest that Brazil's concern for the financial integrity of her local airlines should be deemed to be less genuine now than when Article 102 was enacted, simply because of the depreciation of the cruzeiro. The failure to amend that provision may reflect a conscious desire to avoid enlarging the potential liability of local airlines during a period of general economic difficulty. It may represent an unwillingness to contribute to the inflationary spiral by adjusting "prices" fixed by statute, which the government can control. In any event, we are not satisfied that the fact of inflation itself—with the result that 100,000 cruzeiros are worth now considerably less than when the limitation was enacted—should be deemed to render obsolete Brazil's legitimate interest in limiting recoveries against her airlines.[162]

The court's opinion not only begs the question; even worse, it begs the wrong question. One can construct a respectable case for the proposition that Varig, a large, thriving international airline, required much less protection against liability suits in 1963 than in 1938. One can also construct a compelling case for the proposition that the suspension of the Cr $100,000 liability limitation on wrongful death actions against Brazilian airlines in 1963 would not have affected the Brazilian inflation rate one iota.[163] Nevertheless, the real issue is not whether Brazil has a legitimate interest in limiting liability against its airlines; of course, Brazil, like any sovereign nation, has a legitimate interest in protecting the fiscal integrity of its airlines. Rather the real issue is: Given the 98.7 percent fall in the cruzeiro's purchasing power between 1938 and 1963, what value should a U.S. court place in 1963 on a Cr$100,000 limitation enacted in 1938?

Judge McGowan cannot really be faulted for answering the wrong question, for he responded to the question plaintiff's counsel raised. The wiser opinion, however, was Judge Fahy's brief concurrence:

> I concur . . . that the forum law governing damages for wrongful death occurring in the District of Columbia does not govern this case, and that the Brazilian limitation of recoverable damages applies. However, were it not for the fact that the plaintiff seems to concede that should the District of Columbia limitation not apply the limitation found in the Brazil Air Code governs the amount of the recovery, I would leave the amount of recovery open for determination on the basis of more ample information as to what the Brazilian law, as applied by the courts of Brazil, would permit to be recovered in this case.[164]

Had counsel for the plaintiff bothered to research Brazilian law, he could have presented the following arguments and alternatives to the court: (1) that the damage limitation provision invoked by Varig did not apply to an airplane collision where the plaintiff was not a passenger in the defendant's airplane;[165](2) that on May 8, 1963 the Brazilian legislature had amended the Air Code to make it accompany inflation; the Cr$100,000 limitation was changed to 150 times the minimum wage, increasing the recovery limit from $170 to $5,080;[166] and (3) that the Brazilian courts and legislature had eschewed the nominalist principle with respect to tort indemnities, government bonds, and back tax debts.[167]

If the damage limitation provision applied, a dubious proposition foolishly conceded by plaintiff's counsel, the most equitable solution would have been to permit the plaintiff to recover the same value that Cr$100,000 had in 1938. This would be $11,253 via the straight cruzeiro monetary correction approach, or $12,332 by conversion first into 1938 dollars and then converting the purchasing power of 1938 dollars into 1963 dollars.

There are two alternative solutions that would have worked rough justice. One alternative would have been to apply the 1963 Air Code amendment retrospectively to permit recovery of the dollar equivalent of Cr$3,150,000 (about $5,080). The other would have been to link the recovery limitation to the monetary correction coefficients set out in that 1963 income tax statute for correcting the value of a fixed asset acquired in 1938.[168] The recovery limitation would then have been increased to Cr$2,963,000 or $4,779. It is well known, however, that the coefficients of monetary correction in the 1963 tax law were arbitrarily set and failed to correct sufficiently for inflation. Nonetheless, either solution would have been far preferable to the $170 judgment.

Many of the American states used to limit recovery in in wrongful death actions to $5,000;[169] however, today only Kansas retains any dollar limitation on recovery. Mexico and Ethiopia have extremely low limits on the amount that can be recovered for nonpecuniary injuries in tort cases.[171] Frequently, maximum limits upon compensation are used to mitigate the severity of strict liability. They are also said to be designed to facilitate the purchase of liability insurance,[172] though insurance can obviously be purchased without such limitations.

As the Brazilian experience suggests, unless legislatures index or revise pecuniary damage limitation provisions frequently, inflation will badly distort these measures. Indeed, in an inflationary economy failure to adjust the pecuniary sums contained in such limitations may effectively destroy the plaintiff's cause of action. The problem is not limited to damage limitation provisions. Legislatures should index jurisdictional limits for courts, fines, penalties, and other fees to prevent inflation from distorting values originally chosen.

Gold-linked limitations of liability in international transportation conventions and the conversion of damages expressed in foreign currency, two problems that relate to the general themes of this chapter and to the *Tramontana* case specifically, are discussed in chapter 8, *infra.*

CONCLUSIONS

Preservation of the principle of *restitutio in integrum* in an inflationary economy requires modification of a number of traditional legal rules. First, in countries where periodical rents or pensions are used to compensate tort plaintiffs for lost earnings or future medical expenses, pensions should be indexed to the cost-of-living index. An alternative, but less desirable measure, would be to permit the courts to revise pension awards to account for intervening inflation. In countries where lump sum awards are used, courts should take future inflation into account, either directly in calculating the amount of the award, or indirectly, by refusing to reduce the award to present value.

Second, all statutes that contain pecuniary damage limitations should be linked to a price index, or periodically revised by the legislature. Third, as in Israel, the legal interest rate should be indexed or allowed to float at a realistic level. Alternatively, the amount of damages plus interest should be monetarily corrected to prevent the onus of monetary depreciation from falling on the shoulders of an involuntary creditor.

Perhaps the simplest approach is to scrap the concept of a fixed rate of legal interest and substitute an interest rate that is consistently positive by 3 or 4 percent. This means the legal interest rate would be comprised of the variations in a general price index plus 3 or 4 percent. If the price index increases at an annual rate of 15 percent between the date of the breach, tort, or taking and effective payment, the plaintiff would be entitled to interest at an annual rate of 18 or 19 percent. This eliminates the present incentive of the defendant to delay litigation as much as possible to take advantage of a negative legal interest rate.

Another means of accomplishing nearly the same result is by monetarily correcting the damage award. Damages for breach of contract or tort would be calculated as of the date of the breach, or as of the day of the taking for condemnation. The principal plus interest would then be monetarily corrected in accordance with a coefficient derived from a general price index. This technique is slightly more favorable to the victim in that it adjusts interest as well as the principal for monetary depreciation. The monetary correction approach eliminates the distortions generated by inflation and affords the plaintiff in a tort or contract suit or the condemnee as full and complete a recovery as he would have received in a stable economy.

The monetary correction approach does not, however, adjust for changes in relative prices. If the price of land, the subject matter of the contract, a converted piece of property, or medical expenses, rises more rapidly than the general price index, the monetary correction approach will leave the plaintiff with an insufficient sum to repair the damage or replace the condemned or converted property. In this event, the approach of many of the civil law countries of assessing damages as of the date of the trial is more advantageous than the monetary correction approach. If there is a protracted appeal, however, the plaintiff is frequently left with an inadequate fixed legal interest rate as his only protection against monetary depreciation during the interval between the time of the trial and the date of effective payment. The debt of value theory, with its continual reassessment of damages until payment, clearly provides much better protection to the plaintiff in this situation.

There are decided drawbacks to an approach that requires continual judicial reassessments of damage. It is uneconomic and wasteful to require busy courts to revalue damages previously assessed. In certain circumstances, assessing contract damages as of the date of trial or appeal allows the plaintiff to speculate at the defendant's expense. If one has to opt for a single approach, indexation of the legal interest rate seems to offer the most practical and fair means to prevent inflation from distorting damage awards. Nevertheless, fairness suggests that the better solution would is to afford the plaintiff the right to opt for revaluation or indexation, depending upon his assessment of the circumstances.

NOTES

1. 2 F. Harper & F. James, The Law of Torts § 25.11, pp. 1323–24 (1956); Note, *Fluctuating Dollars and Tort Damage Verdicts,* 48 Colum. L. Rev. 264, 265–67 (1948) [hereafter cited as Colum. Note]; Annot., *Changes in Cost of Living or in Purchasing Power of Money as Affecting Damages for Personal Injuries or Death,* 12 A.L.R. 2d 611 (1950).

2. F. Mann, The Legal Aspect of Money 108–15 (3d ed. 1971) *But see* the text to note 4, *infra.*

3. [1956] 1 W.L.R. 471, 474.

4. These cases, decided during the 1920s, are cited in 2 F. Harper & F. James, *supra* note 1, at pp. 1324–25, fn. 7; Colum. Note, *supra* note 1, at 267–69.

5. Tent. Draft No. 19, March 30, 1973 § 911(j), p.100.

6. In the United States courts and juries generally have discretion to award prejudgment interest on damage claims, but practice varies from state to state. *See* C. McCormick on Damages §§ 54–56 (1935). Generally U.S. courts will not award prejudgment interest on nonpecuniary claims, such as pain or suffering, or on pecuniary claims which are unliquidated or not readily ascertainable. The theory is that the defendant should not be liable for interest on those claims which he cannot reasonably be expected to calculate the amount owed. D. Dobbs, Remedies § 3.5, p. 165 (1973); Comment, *Judgments: Interest on Judgments—Limitation on Recovery of Prejudgment Interest,* 56 Minn. L. Rev. 739, 740 (1972). Where the claim is liquidated or readily ascertainable, U.S. courts generally grant prejudgment interest at the legal rate. However, the rule is to award only simple interest rather than compound interest. D. Dobbs, *supra,* at 164. English courts have the power to award interest for all or part of the period between judgment and the date a claim arose, though it is generally not the practice to do so on unliquidated damage claims, except for personal injuries. F. Mann, *supra* note 2, at 70. Because English courts have shifted the time for assessing damages in fatal accident cases from the date of the accident to the date of trial, a recent decision of the Court of Appeal sensibly divided the award into two parts for the purpose of awarding prejudgment interest. Interest on actual pecuniary loss prior to trial was assessed at half the usual nine percent annual rate. Because future pecuniary losses had not yet occurred, the English court quite properly refused to assess interest on that part of the award. Cookson v. Knowles, [1977] 3 W.L.R. 279, 284.

7. For example, during the 19th century and early part of the twentieth century, French courts frequently assessed damages as the date of the tort. Derrida, *Dommages-Intérêts,* 3 Ency. Dalloz Droit Civil § 108 (2 ed. 1975); Gendrel, *Influence de la Dépréciation Monétaire sur le Droit de la Responsabilité Civile,* in Influence de la Dépréciation Monétaire sur la Vie Juridique Privée 143, 152–53 (P. Durand, ed. 1961). But the unfairness of this rule to the plaintiff during severe inflation eventually caused the French courts to modify it. The critical decision was that of

the *Chambre des Requêtes* of March 24, 1942, [1942] Gaz. Pal. I, 224; [1942] J.C.P. II, 1973. Since 1942 French courts have uniformly assessed tort damages as of the date of judgment.

8. The term *Wertschuld* was invented in 1925 by Arthur Nussbaum to differentiate between pecuniary and value obligations. Because he felt the term "value-debt" was obscure in English, Professor Nussbaum decided to translate *Wertschuld* as "adaptable debt." A. NUSSBAUM, MONEY IN THE LAW NATIONAL AND INTERNATIONAL 180 (rev. ed. 1950). Debt of value seems clearer than adaptable debt, and the text proceeds on that basis.

9.

> There is no conceptual uniformity; the notion varies according to the exigencies of the monetary picture and . . . in accordance with the criteria which the writers prefer. . . . [T]he preferable notion is that which characterizes [debts of value] as obligations whose object does not originally constitute a nominal sum, but depends upon the circumstances on future elements, variable and exogenous to the juridical relationship. However, they do not constitute a homogeneous category. Mugel has separated them into three groups: (1) credits of reparation; (2) credits of reimbursement; and (3) credits of unjust enrichment.

O. GOMES, TRANSFORMAÇÕES GERAIS DO DIREITO DAS OBRIGAÇÕES 112 (1967). For recent further criticism of the concept of the debt of value, *see* MAYDELL, GELDSCHULD UND GELDWERT 99 (1974); HORN, GELDWERTVERÄNDERUNGEN, PRIVATRECHT UND WITTSCHAFTSORDNUNG 12 (1975).

10. F. MANN, *supra* note 2, at 103–106; A. NUSSBAUM, *supra* note 8, at 180–81.

11. Derrida, *supra* note 7, at § 114 and cases cited therein; F. MANN, *supra* note 2, at 105.

12. Cass., Jy. 7, 1938, [1938] Pas. Bel. I, 261.

13. Cass., Aug. 10, 1946, [1946] Rev. Dir. Comm. II, 103; T. ASCARELLI, PROBLEMAS DAS SOCIEDADES ANÔNIMAS E DIREITO COMPARADO 202–3 (1945).

14. As to Belgian law, see F. MANN, *supra* note 2, at 107–108. For Italian law, which schizophrenically regards the expenses of renting a car after an automobile accident as a debt of value, but considers the expenses of repair, once paid, as a pecuniary obligation, *see* Montel, *Gastos por Reparación, Devaluación Monetaria y Resarcimiento del Daño,* in A. MONTEL, PROBLEMAS DE LA RESPONSIBILIDAD Y DEL DAÑO 125 (F. Sobrao Martínez, trans., 1955).

15. For the evolution of Argentine case law and doctrine, *see* E. BANCHIO, OBLIGACIONES DE VALOR 133–38 (1965); for a resume of current Brazilian case law, *see* Wald, *A Inflação e as Indenizações,* 233 Rev. For. 21 (1971).

16. The cases are collected in Malvar, *Deudas de Valor y de Dinero. La Desvalorización Monetaria y el Proceso. Oportunidad para Alegarla,* [1968–VI] J.A. 138–39.

17. J.A. v. Cámara del Bien Raíz, 67 Just. Urug. No. 7907 (Juzgado Letrado del Trabajo de 2d Turmo, Feb. 1, 1973); Galván Freijo de Reyes v. Dominguez, 66 Just. Urug. No. 7890 (1st Instance, Aug. 26, 1971); E.F.M. v. B.F.S., 67 Just. Urug. No. 8036 (1st Instance, Apr. 24, 1973); Carnelli, *La Desvalorización Monetaria en la Reparación del Daño Extracontractual,* 68 Rev. D.J.A. 276 (1969) and cases cited therein.

18. Onda S.A. v. CUTCSA, 69 Just. Urug. 8171 (Sup. Ct., Je. 5, 1974). How-

ever, to the extent that the tort claim is liquidated, Law No. 14.500 of Feb. 25, 1976 now provides for readjustment in accordance with the variations in the consumer price index between the date of the tort and the date of payment. The Uruguayan Supreme Court has refused to apply this statute retroactively, tenaciously adhering to nominalist theory. Ferrari, Britos et al v. Frigorífico Modelo S.A., 75 Just. Urug. No. 8623 (Sup. Ct., May 13, 1977).

19. J. Lopez-Santa Maria, Le Droit des Obligations et des Contrats et l'Inflation Monétaire 39–41 (1980). Cohen, Mario César, 66 R.D.J. 203 (4th sec. 1969); Lama, Abraham, 67 R.D.J. 424 (Pt. 2, 4th sec., Sup. Ct., Oct. 16, 1970), Escobar, Angelica, 71 R.D.J. 278 (Pt. 2, 4th sec., Sup. Ct., Oct. 8, 1974).

20. Yardenia Ltd. v. Ofer Bros. Ltd. et al, [1976] (I) P.D. 31; Horowitz v. Ports Authority of Israel, [1978] II 32 P.D. 256. These cases are discussed in Gilad, *On Linkage and Revaluation,* 15 Israel L. Rev. 79 (1980).

21. Adjudication of Interest Law (Amendment No. 3) 1978, changing the statute's name to the Adjudication of Interest and Linkage Law. The complete statute, as amended is translated in 14 Israel L. Rev. 520–23 (1979).

22. This assumption is explicitly stated in the note of Dr. Veléz Sársfield, drafter of the Argentine Civil Code, to Article 619, which provides legal interest as the sole remedy for damages resulting from delay in satisfying pecuniary obligations:

> We abstain from projecting laws to settle the much debated question regarding the obligation of the debtor, when there has been an alteration in the currency, because that alteration would have to be ordered by the national legislative body, an almost impossible occurrence. . . . If we had to legislate, supposing currency alterations, we would accept the article of the Austrian Code. [The article referred to states: If the intrinsic value of money is altered, the person who received it must reimburse the full value which it had at the time of the loan.]

23. Gendrel, *supra* note 7, at 170–72.

24. Until recently Italian cases and doctrine were split on the issue of whether entry of a damage award converted a debt of value into a pecuniary debt. E. Quadri, Questioni Giuridiche Sull'Inflazione 49–74 (1981). *See also* 4 R. Nicolo & M. Richter, Rassegna di Giurisprudenza sul Codice Civile §1223 (52–53). This division was settled by an *en banc (sezioni unite)* decision of Italy's highest court, the *Corte di Cassazione,* holding that a damage award does not loose its character as a debt of value until it has been paid. Cass., Jan. 9, 1978, n. 57, Giust. Civ. I, 7, (1978). For commentary on this decision, *see* E. Quadri, *supra,* at 77–83.

25. See E. Banchio, *supra* note 15, at 129–49.

26. The Brazilian doctrine and cases are collected in J. Chacel, M. Simonsen, & A. Wald, A Correção Monetária 176–213 (1970). Brazil has recently enacted a statute requiring monetary correction of all judgment debts, including costs and awards of attorneys' fees, until the date of effective payment. Money correction begins on the day of judgment unless the suit is to collect a liquid and certain debt, in which case money correction runs from the date of maturity. Law No. 6.899 of Apr. 8, 1981. For Chilean law, see B. Gesche Müller, Jurisprudencia Dinamica: La Desvalorizacion Monetaria y Otros Problemas en el Derecho 47–79

(1971); J. Lopez-Santa Maria, Obligaciones y Contratos frente a la Inflacion 106–52 (2d ed. 1980).

27. Law No. 14.500 of Feb. 25, 1976.

28. For surveys of the different systems, *see* H. McGregor, *Personal Injury and Death,* in 11 Int'l Ency. Comp. L. c. 9, §§48–52; Fleming, *Damages: Capital or Rent?,* 19 U. Toronto L. Rev. 295 (1969). Periodic payments are being increasingly used in common law countries through workers' compensation and no-fault automobile insurance statutes. *See* Comment, *Variable Periodic Payments of Damages: An Alternative to Lump Sums Awards,* 64 Iowa L. Rev. 138 (1978). There is also increasing, though still limited, use in the U.S. of structured settlements to spread payments out over extended periods of time. *See* J. Granelli, "Structuring the Settlement," The Nat'l L. J., Feb. 16, 1981, at p. 1, cols. 1–3.

29. 60 R.D.J. 407 (2d Part, 1st Sec. 1963).

30. 60 R.D.J. at 418–19. This case is an isolated and unfollowed decision. Chilean courts rarely award pensions except for support or in labor cases, and both types of pensions are automatically readjusted. J. Lopez-Santa Maria, *supra* note 26, at 102–06.

31. McGregor, *supra* note 28, at § 66; Fleming, *Inflation and Tort Compensation,* 26 Am. J. Comp. L. 51, 59 (1978).

32. *E.g.,* de Oliveira v. Rio Light S.A., R.E. No. 57.505, 45 R.T.J. 115 (2d Term 1967); Silva Ramos v. Rêde Ferroviária Federal S.A., 45 R.T.J. 421 (1st Term 1968). The case law evolution is traced in considerable detail in J. Chacel, M. Simonsen, & A. Wald, *supra* note 26, at 188–206.

33. *Súmula* No. 490 of Dec. 3, 1969, published in the Diário da Justiça da União Federal on Dec. 10, 1969, p. 5.931.

34. Code of Civil Procedure of 1939, arts. 911 & 912, as amended by Decree-Law No. 4.565 of Aug. 11, 1942; Code of Civil Procedure of 1973, art. 602.

35. *E.g.,* Viação Nove de Julho Ltda. v. Cromopel-Comércio e Indústria de Papel e Papelão S/A, A.C. No. 169.923, 395 Rev. Trib. 183, 186 (1st Civ. Cam. S.P. 1968). Law No. 6.205 of Apr. 29, 1975 prohibits the use of the minimum wage for monetary correction "for any legal purposes whatsoever," except for wage, social security, and fringe benefit adjustments. Adjustments for other purposes must now be made on the basis of changes in the value of Readjustable Treasury Bonds. Law No. 6.423 of Je. 17, 1977.

36. Corr. Gand, Feb. 21, 1959, [1959–60] R.W., col. 1368, and Gand, Je. 25, 1959 [1959–60] R.W., col. 1362 (indexing a pension to the cost-of-living in the same fashion as employees salaries are adjusted); Corr., Brussels, Nov. 30, 1959 and Oct. 26, 1960, [1961] J.T. 404 (pension indexed to an unspecified price index). *See generally,* Levie, *Quelle Est la Forme la Plus Adéquate du Payement des Indemnités Dues du Chef d'Accidents de Droit Commun?,* [1961] J.T. 399.

37. McGregor, *supra* note 28, at § 87.

38. *Compare* Civ. Brussels (9th ch.), Apr. 17, 1970, [1970] J.T. 395 (invalidating an indexed alimony award for violation of the nominalist principle) *with* Civ. Brussels (14th ch.), Apr. 3, 1970, [1970] J.T. 396 (upholding a similarly indexed alimony award). *See also* Dalcq, *La Responsabilité Délictuelle et Quasi Délictuelle, Examen de Jurisprudence* (1963 à 1967), [1968] R.C.J.B. 329 371–72, David-Constant, *Erosion Monétaire et Droit Privé,* 37 Annales de Droit 443, 452 (1977).

39. Cass. Crim., Mar. 20, 1952, [1952] D. Jur. 413; Cass. Civ., May 2, 1952, [1952] D. Jur. 413; 50 Rev. Trim. Dr. Civ. 468 (1952).

40. Cass., lre Civ., June 27, 1957 [1957] D. Jur. 649 (1957); [1957] J.C.P. II,10093, discussed in chap. 5, *supra,* in text to notes 77 and 78.

41. Ordonnance No. 58–1374 of Dec. 30, 1958, art. 79; as amended by Ordonnance No. 59–246 of Feb. 4, 1959, art. 14, discussed in chap. 5, *supra,* in text to notes 79–81.

42. Cass., Ch. Crim., Jy. 5, 1961, [1961] J.C.P. II, 12369; [1961] Gaz. Pal.II.3. nov., noted 60 Rev. Trim. Dr. Civ. 120 (1962).

43. Law of Jy. 10, 1963.

44. Law No. 72–73 of Jan. 3, 1972, amending art. 208 of the Civil Code.

45. Savatier, *Les Indemnités Allouées aux Victimes d'Accidents Corporels ne Peuvent-Elles, depuis la Loi du 13 Juillet 1963, Consister en une Rente Viagère Indexée?,* [1972] J.C.P. I, 2443 (Doct.); Note of Savatier, [1973] J.C.P. II, 17393.

46. *E.g.,* H. Mazeaud, *Les Rentes Flottantes et la Réparation des Accidents,* [1951] D. Jur., Chron. 17; Esmein, *Des Indemnités Variables selon les Indices Économiques,* [1949] J.C.P. I, 781; Savatier, *supra* note 45; Pierre-François, *L'Indexation Judiciaire des Rentes Viagères Allouées en Réparation d'un Préjudice de Responsabilité Délictuelle,* [1972] D.S. Jur. Chron. 229 (1972).

47. Trib. de grande Instance de Fontainebleau, Mar. 3, 1972, [1972] J.C.P. II, 17089 (pension indexed to the national consumer price index). Poiters, Ch. Correct., Jan. 12, 1973, [1973] J.C.P. II, 17393 (pension linked to the trimestral hourly wage index); Poiters, Ch. Civ. lre, Jan. 17, 1973, [1973] J.C.P. II, 17393 (pension linked to the trimestral hourly wage index); Agen, Trib. Correct., Jan 12, 1973, [1973] J.C.P. II, 17493 (pension indexed to the European Unit of Account).

Previously, other lower courts had tried to circumvent anti-indexing decisions of the *Cour de Cassation* by the *solution bâtarde* of awarding the plaintiff a lump sum but requiring investment of that amount in an indexed annuity. LE ROY, L'EVALUATION DU PREJUDICE CORPOREL § 90 (4th ed. 1966), cited in McGregor, *supra* note 28, at 687.

48. Sourdonnier v. Gallien, Cass., Ch. mixte, Nov. 6, 1974, [1975] J.C.P. II, 17978, with note by Savatier.

49. Law No. 74–1118 of Dec. 27, 1974.

50. J. CHACEL, M. SIMONSEN, & A. WALD, *supra* note 26, at 206–13.

51. McGregor, *supra* note 28, at 797.

52. *Id.*

53. Art. 567(2) provides: "When the circumstances upon which [an award] is based are appreciably altered, whether as to the establishment of the income, its amount, or duration, or whether as to the dispensal or imposition of guarantees, any party whatsoever is permitted to demand a corresponding modification in the judgment or accord." Art. 551 provides: "When the law permits the updating of pecuniary payments because of fluctuations in the value of money, one shall take into account, in the absence of some other legal criterion, the price indexes, in order to reestablish the relation between the payment and the quantity of merchandise to which it was equivalent on the date when the obligation was constituted."

54. Hellner, *Indexing of Tort Awards in Sweden,* 26 AM. J. COMP. L. 71, 72 (1977).

55. *Id.* at 73–77.

56. Fleming, *supra* note 31, at 54–55.

57. Palmer, *Accident Compensation in New Zealand: The First Two Years,* 25 AM. J. COMP. L. 1, 29 (1977).

58. For pro and con discussions of the Model Act, *compare* Henderson, *Periodic Payment of Bodily Injury Awards,* 66 A.B.A.J. 734 (1980) *with* Corboy, *Structured Injustice: Compulsory Periodic Payment of Judgments,* 66 A.B.A.J. 1524 (1980).

59. Model Act for the Periodic Payment of Judgments, sect. 5.

60. *Id.* at sect. 7.

61. *Id.* at sect. 10.

62. An analogous provision in California's 1975 Medical Injury Compensation Reform Act, which provided for periodic payment of awards in excess of $50,000 in medical malpractice cases, has recently been declared unconstitutional on equal protection grounds. American Bank and Trust Company v. Community Hospital of Los Gatos-Saratoga, Inc., 163 Cal. Rptr. 513 (1980).

63. Insurance companies strongly prefer lump sum awards for administrative convenience. Fleming, *supra* note 28, at 320–21. Plaintiffs with capitalistic values prefer the lump sum, as do their lawyers, who would rather be paid out of a cash fund. *Id.* at 296–97. In an inflationary economy these preferences for a lump sum settlement are greatly increased, particularly if the defendant has to fund a pension by purchasing fixed-income securities.

64. *E.g.,* Parente v. Bell, [1968] Argus L.R. 174, 177 (Australia); O'Brien v. McKean, 118 C.L.R. 540, 42 A.L.J.R. 223 (Australian High Ct. 1968); Gand, Nov. 24, 1970, [1971] Rev. Gen. Ass. et Resp. 8639 (Belgium); Trib. Pol. Liege, May 6, 1974, [1974] Pas. Bel. III, 49 (Belgium); Mallett v. McMonagle, [1969] 2 All E.R. 178, [1970] A.C. 166 (H.L.); Young v. Percival, [1974] 3 All E.R. 677; Fletcher v. Autocar and Transporters Ltd., [1968] Q.B. 322; Sleeman v. Chesapeake & Ohio Ry., 414 F.2d 305 (6th Cir. 1969); Johnson v. Penrod Drilling Co., 469 F.2d 897 (5th Cir. 1972), *cert. denied,* 423 U.S. 839; Williams v. United States, 435 F.2d 804 (1st Cir. 1970); Frankel v. Heym, 466 F.2d 1226 (3d Cir. 1972); Johnson v. Serra, 521 F.2d 1289 (8th Cir. 1975). The French cases are collected in 1 H. & L. MAZEAUD & A. TUNC, TRAITÉ THÉORIQUE ET PRATIQUE DE LA RESPONSIBILITÉ CIVILE 279–81 (6th ed. 1970).

65. Halloran v. New England Telephone & Telegraph Co., 95 Vt. 273, 115 A. 143, 144, 18 A.L.R. 554 (1921); Normand v. Thomas Theatre Corp., 349 Mich. 50, 84 N.W.2d 451, 457 (1957); Willard v. Hutson, 234 Ore. 148, 378 P.2d 966, 975–76, 1 A.L.R.3d 1092 (1963); Barnett v. Trinity Universal Ins. Co., 286 So.2d 770 (La. App. 1973); Scruggs v. Chesapeake & Ohio Railway Co., 320 F. Supp. 1248 (W.D. Va. 1970); Mitchell v. Mulholland (no. 2), [1972] 1 Q.B. 65 (C.A.); Gand, Nov. 9, 1967, [1969] B.A. 591 (Belgium); Gand, Feb. 24, 1970, [1970] J.T. 393 (Belgium).

One state in the United States, Rhode Island, has adopted a statute expressly authorizing the admission of evidence concerning future inflation. R.I. GEN. LAWS ANN. §10–7–1.1(3) (Supp. 1975) provides in pertinent part: "In determining said award, evidence shall be admissible concerning economic trends, including but not limited to projected purchasing power of money, inflation and projected increase or decrease in the costs of living."

66. [1971] A.C. 115, [1970] 1 All E.R. 365.

67. *Compare* the opinion of Edmund Davies, L.J. in Mitchell v. Mulholland, [1972] 1 Q.B. at 78 *with* Megaw, L.J. in Young v. Percival, [1974] 3 All E.R. at 683–86. Nevertheless, at the present time English courts are applying the Young v. Percival view of Taylor v. O'Connor and refusing to consider future inflation. *See* Cookson v. Knowles, [1977] 3 W.L.R. 279, 283 (C.A.).

68. 2 F. HARPER & F. JAMES, *supra* note 1, § 25.11, at 1325–26.

69. *See* Comment, *Damages for Loss of Future Income: Accounting for Inflation,* 6 S.F.L. REV. 311, 320–21 (1972); Note, *Future Inflation and the Undercompensated Plaintiff,* 4 LOY. CHI. L.J. 359, 370 (1973).

70. 282 F.2d 34 (2d Cir. 1960), *cert. denied,* 364 U.S. 870 (1960). In a subsequent opinion, Yodice v. Koninklijke Nedenlansche Stoonboot Maatschappij, 443 F.2d 76, 79 (2d Cir. 1971), Judge Friendly observed that if higher rates of inflation persist, the McWeeney approach may have to be modified.

71. I.R.S. Rev. Rul. 65–124, 26 CFR 1.104–1.

72. P. SAMUELSON, ECONOMICS 272 (9th ed. 1973); Sargent, *Anticipated Inflation and the Rate of Interest,* 86 Q. J. ECON. 212, 212–13 (1972).

73. 382 F. Supp. 1271 (D. Conn. 1974), *aff'd in part, rev'd in part,* 524 F.2d 384 (2d Cir. 1975); noted 37 OHIO ST. L. J. 138 (1976); 62 CORN. L. REV. 803 (1977).

74. In the recent case of Doca v. Marina Mercante, 634F.2d 30 (2d Cir. 1980), the Second Circuit reaffirmed the approach of Feldman v. Allegheny Airlines but suggested use of a discount rate of 2 percent. American courts frequently use a discount rate of 4 percent. *See* 1 S. SPEISER, RECOVERY FOR WRONGFUL DEATH §8.4, at 711 & fn. 33 (2d ed. 1975). English judges frequently use 4 or 5 percent. *See* Mallet v. McMonagle, [1969] 2 All E.R. at 190, [1970] A.C. at 176 (vote of Lord Diplock).

75. Andrews v. Grand & Toy Alberta Ltd., [1978] 2 S.C.R. 229, 83 D.L.R. (3d) 452; Thornton et al v. Board of School Trustees of School District No. 57 (Prince George), [1978] 2 S.C.R. 267, 83 D.L.R. (3d) 480; Arnold v. Teno [1978] 2 S.C.R. 287, 83 D.L.R. (3d) 609; Keizer v. Hanna [1978] 2 S.C.R. 342, 82 D.L.R. (3d) 449.

76. Rea, *Inflation, Taxation and Damage Assessment,* 58 CAN. BAR REV. 280, 284–85 (1980).

77. The U.S. cases are divided on whether discounting to present value is required for future pain and suffering and medical expenses. The majority of the cases hold that the jury should not be required to reduce an award for future pain and suffering to present value. J. STEIN, DAMAGES AND RECOVERY PERSONAL INJURY AND DEATH ACTIONS § 171 (1972). There are few cases which have considered whether future medical expenses need be discounted to present value, and they are nearly evenly divided. Yost v. West Penn. Ry., 336 Pa. 407, 9 A.2d 368 (1939) and Renner v. Sentle, 151 Pa. Super. Ct. 231, 30 A.2d 220 (1943) specifically hold that future medical expenses should not be discounted to present value. Hughes v. Brown, 109 Ga. App. 578, 136 S.E.2d 403 (1964) specifically holds the opposite. The most thorough discussion of the point is Frankel v. U.S., 321 F. Supp. 1331 (E.D. Pa. 1970), *aff'd sub nom.* Frankel v. Heym, 466 F.2d 1226 (3d Cir. 1972). The court stated that the rule of Yost v. West Penn Rys. Co., *supra,* is normally a salutary rule, but refused to apply it to an award for the expenses of institutional care for the remainder of the victim's life. The court reasoned that the payments for institutional care were more like payments for future earnings, and that the liquidity

concern articulated in the Yost case simply did not apply. The logical inconsistency between discounting future earnings but refusing to discount future medical expenses and pain and suffering has been cogently criticized in Leasure, *How to Prove Reduction to Present Worth,* 21 Ohio St. L. J. 204, 206–207 (1960).

78. 434 P.2d 665 (Alaska 1967). Most American courts insist on discounting to present value and regard failure to do so as reversible error. *See, e.g.,* United States v. English, 521 F.2d 63 (9th Cir. 1975). Swiss courts on the other hand, have been utilizing the failure to discount approach to inflation. McGregor, *supra* note 28, at §86.

79. 434 P.2d at 671–72.

80. Pierce v. New York Cent. R.R. Co., 304 F. Supp. 44 (W.D. Mich. 1969); Schnebly v. Baker, 217 N.W.2d 708, 728 (Iowa 1974); Hampton v. State Highway Comm., 209 Kan. 565, 498 P.2d 236 (1972).

81. *See* Comment, *Investment and Management of Trust Funds in an Inflationary Economy,* 126 U. Pa. L. Rev. 1171 (1978).

82. *See* Galbis, *Inflation and Interest Rate Policies in Latin America, 1967–76,* 26 IMF Staff Papers 334 (1979).

83. McGregor, *supra* note 28, at §§55, 86. Lord Parker has reported that in the northern part of England, all those awarded five figure sterling damage awards were drawing public assistance in a few years. *Compensation for Accidents on the Road,* 18 Curr. Leg. Prob. 1, 5 (1965).

84. Comment, *Future Inflation, Prospective Damages, and the Circuit Courts,* 63 Va. L. Rev. 105, 125–30 (1977).

85. The suggestion was made by the government in Frankel v. U.S., *supra* note 77. The District Court rejected the suggestion as requiring legislative authorization, but added: "An amendment to the Federal Tort Claims Act to provide for periodic payments when future, long range damages are significant seems desirable."

86. There are in most countries a series of rules that tend to prevent attainment of the ideal of complete indemnification. For example, damages may be limited to those that are reasonably foreseeable, or the innocent party may have a duty to mitigate damages.

87. F. Mann, *supra* note 2, at 100; A. Nussbaum, *supra* note 8, 174–175, 180.

88. Hauser, *Breach of Contracts during Inflation,* 33 Tul. L. Rev. 307, 308 (1959). Nevertheless, most commercial lenders do factor into the interest rate the likelihood of default.

89. Law No. 14.500 of Feb. 25, 1976 (Uruguay) and Law No. 6.899 of Apr. 8, 1981 (Brazil).

90. *E.g.,* López Cabana, *La "Indexación" de las Deudas Dinerarias,* [1976] J.A. III 788; Bustamante Alsina, *Deudas de Dinero y Deudas de Valor. Alcance de la Distinción y Posibildad de Suprimirla,* 149 La Ley 952 (1973); Darió, *Incumplimiento de una Obligación Dineraria y Depreciación Monetaria,* 29 J.A. 799 (1975); Borda, *Las Deudas de Dinero y la Desvalorización Monetaria,* [1975] La Ley C 793; Carranza, *Las Deudas Dinerarias Frente a la Desvalorización de la Moneda,* J.A. Doctrina 191 (1974).

91. Vieytes de Fernández v. Provincia de Buenos Aires, [1976] La Ley D 241, (Sup. Ct., Sept. 23, 1976); Valdez v. Gobierno Nacional, [1976] La Ley D 248 (Sup. Ct., Sept. 23, 1976); Maturana v. Elma, La Ley, Sept. 5, 1977, p. 6 (CN Fed., Apr.

22, 1977); La Amistad S.R.L. v. Iriarte, La Ley, Sept. 19, 1977, p. 1 (CNCiv., *en banc,* Sept. 9, 1977); CNCom, *en banc* Apr. 13, 1977, La Ley, Apr. 22, 1977, p. 1.

92. *See* chap. 3, *supra,* note 16.

93. There have been few reported Chilean cases dealing with this problem. In Enrique Pérez Moscoso v. Pablo Valdés Ossa, 62 R.D.J. 9 (pt. 2, 3d sec., Sup. Ct., Apr. 2, 1965), the Labor Court of Santiago monetarily corrected the damages owed an employee for breach of a labor contract because the unpaid salary had an alimentary character, a result confirmed by the Supreme Court in denying an appeal. The opposite result was reached in an unpublished decision of the Court of Appeals of Concepción of Apr. 15, 1974, which relied upon the nominalist theory of the Civil Code to reject a request for readjustment of a sum owed because of breach of a service contract. Cited in Alvarez Nuñez, *Las Obligaciones de Dinero en el Código Civil,* 41 Rev. Der. 43, 51 fn. 8 (Jan.–June 1974). In Blanco v. Carvacho, 72 R.D.J. 49 (pt. 2, 1st sec., Sup. Ct., May 20, 1975), the Supreme Court required monetarily corrected restitution of the portion of the purchase price already paid upon annulment of a sales contract. The court considered adherence to the nominalist principle tenable only when there is an express legal provision requiring payment or repayment in an equal number of currency units, such as Civil Code Article 2199, which is generally considered to be the source of the nominalist principle in the Chilean Civil Code. Article 2199 has however, been explicitly revoked by Decree-Law No. 455 of May 25, 1974, art. 25. *See* chap. 5, *supra,* at notes 99–102 and the accompanying text. Recent doctrinal writing has taken the position that damages stemming from monetary depreciation after breach of contract are compensable under Chilean law. Alvarez Nuñez, *supra;* Gesche Müller, *La Compensación de la Desvalorización Monetaria en el Cumplimiento de las Obligaciones,* 41 Rev. Der. 7 (1974); López-Santa María, *Indemnizaciones de Perjuicios y Desvalorización de la Moneda,* 67 R.D.J. 149 (pt. 1, No. 8, 1970).

94. Article 1224 of the Italian Civil Code provides:

> Damages in Pecuniary Obligations. In obligations having as their object a sum of money (1277 *ff.*), legal interest [set at 5% per annum by art. 1284] is due from the day of the default even if it was not due previously and even if the creditor does not prove that he has suffered any damage. . . . The creditor who proves to have suffered greater damages is entitled to additional compensation. This is not due if the rate of interest to be paid after default was agreed. THE ITALIAN CIVIL CODE (Beltramo, Longo, & Merryman, trans. 1969).

The cases are collected in 4 R. NICOLO & M. RICHTER, *supra* note 24, 442–43; 2 E. LAPORTA & G. TAMBURRINO, ÇODICE CIVILE COMMENTATO 2590–94 (1963).

95. *E.g.,* Trib. Milano, Je. 5, 1980, [1981] Giur. Ital. I, 2.

96. Tedeschi, *On the Date for Assessing Damage,* 13 ISRAEL L. REV. 10, 22 (1978).

97. Art. 106 of the Swiss Code of Obligations; F. MANN, *supra* note 2, at 100–01. During the hyperinflation that followed World War I, the German courts created a rebuttable presumption that the creditor had been damaged, but under present conditions of moderate inflation, the creditor must prove his damages. *Id.* at 101.

98. *Id.* at 158, fn. 8.

99. Law No. 75–619 of Jy. 11, 1975.

100. *See* E. QUADRI, *supra* note 24, at 11, 23.

101. Treitel, *Remedies for Breach of Contract (Courses of Action Open to a Party Aggrieved),* in 7 INT'L ENCY. COMP. L. c. 16 § 69 (1976). Of course, damages for breach may frequently include more than the value of the subject matter of the contract. Most countries will also permit recovery of reasonably foreseeable consequential damages resulting from the breach.

102. *Id.;* F. MANN, *supra* note 2, at 105–106.

103. 5 CORBIN ON CONTRACTS § 1005 (2d ed. 1964); Hauser, *supra* note 88, at 313.

104. Generally, interest will not be allowed on unliquidated prejudgment contract claims, though there are a substantial number of exceptions. 5 CORBIN ON CONTRACTS §1048 (2d ed. 1964); 2 WILLISTON ON CONTRACTS § 1413 (3d ed. by W. Jaeger 1968).

105. F. MANN, *supra* note 2, at 103–108; Treitel, *supra* note 101, at § 71. As a practical matter "day of judgment" generally means the date at which evidence with respect to damages is presented to the court rather than the date the court actually renders its decision. Yadin, *"The Date of Judgment" for the Assessment of Compensation for Damage to Movable Property,* 13 ISRAEL L. REV. 111, 114 (1978). Any appreciable delay between that date and the actual date of payment may result in further damage from monetary depreciation.

106. Argentina: A. MORELLO, INDEMNIZACION DEL DAÑO CONTRACTUAL 132–35 (1967); Belgium: F. MANN, *supra* note 2, at 107; Brazil: J. CHACEL, M. SIMONSEN, & A. WALD, *supra* note 26, at 176–88; Italy: 4 R. NICOLO & M. RICHTER, *supra* note 24, at § 1223(59), p. 423–24.

107. Law No. 21.488 of Dec. 30, 1976, arts. 1–2.

108. *Id.,* art. 2.

109. Adjudication of Interest and Linkage Law, art. 8, (Amendment No. 3) 1978, translated in 14 ISRAEL L. REV. 520–23 (1979).

110. Law No. 16.640 of 1967, translated in K. KARST & K. ROSENN, LAW AND DEVELOPMENT IN LATIN AMERICA 354–55 (1975). A 1963 constitutional amendment had permitted deferred compensation, conditioned upon judicial review and annual readjustment of the unpaid balance for inflation. This provision was amended in 1967 to permit the use of inflationary confiscation. *See* Thome, *Expropriation in Chile under the Frei Agrarian Reform,* 19 AM. J. COMP. L. 489, 496, fn. 36, 499 (1971).

111. United States v. Miller, 317 U.S. 369 (1943); United States v. Klamath and Moadoc Tribes, 304 U.S. 119 (1938); 6 A. NICHOLS ON EMINENT DOMAIN §27.25 (rev. 3d ed. by J. Sackman, 1976).

112. *E.g.,* United States v. 161.99 Acres of Land, 512 F. 2d 65 (5th Cir. 1975); United States v. 158.76 Acres of Land, 298 F.2d 559 (2d Cir. 1962). *But see* the Missouri Supreme Court's decision in City of St. Louis v. International Harvester Company, 350 S.W.2d 782 (1961), invalidating a taking that had occurred in 1946, but where compensation was not actually paid until 1956. Because the condemned land had substantially appreciated in the interim ten-year period, the Missouri court held that the compensation was not just and ordered revaluation as of the date compensation had been effectively paid.

113. Annot., *Changes in Purchasing Power of Money as Affecting Compensation in Eminent Domain Proceedings,* 92 A.L.R.2d 772 (1963). The author of this Annotation

attempts to rationalize this rule of the federal courts in terms which seem more naive today than when written in 1963:

> [I]t has been further held in these cases that interest "at a proper rate" is a good measure by which to ascertain the amount to be added to the fair market value of the property taken, . . . and that the two amounts added together are the measure of the total due. So, although the rule possibly could be read to permit consideration of significant changes in the purchasing power of the dollar in computing the amount of the proper supplementary allowance required to make the former owner whole, the holdings that the allowance of interest on the award is sufficient for this purpose makes it unlikely that a contention that a further allowance should be made to offset a decline in the dollar's purchasing power would be favorably received.
>
> Since the application of this federal rule compensates an owner of property taken in eminent domain for loss resulting from a withholding of money due him (including as a practical matter any loss attributable to a decline in the purchasing power of that sum), and leaves him in no worse position than the holder of any sound interest-bearing security payable in a fixed amount, barring catastrophic, runaway inflation, there would seem to be no compelling reason for a federal court in a condemnation proceeding to consider depreciation in the purchasing power of the dollar between the time of the taking and the time of the trial as a separate factor which should be reflected in an award. 92 A.L.R.2d at 775–76. [Footnotes omitted]

The legal interest rate paid on eminent domain awards varies from state to state, but it is commonly fixed at 6 percent. *See* 3 NICHOLS ON EMINENT DOMAIN §8.63 (rev. 3d ed. by J. Sackman, 1976). Recent decisions indicate a reluctance of appellate courts to sanction higher interest rates utilized by trial courts to reflect inflation. *E.g.,* United States v. 100 Acres of Land, 468 F.2d 1261 (9th Cir. 1972), *cert. denied,* 414 U.S. 822 and 864 (1973); Township of Wayne in County of Passaic v. Cassatly, 137 N.J. Super. 464, 349 A.2d 545 (1975), *cert. denied,* 70 N.J. 137, 358 A.2d 184 (1976); *In re* Washington Heights—Highbridge Park Community Development Area, 369 N.Y.S.2d 932, 82 Misc. 2d 557 (Sup. Ct., Spec. Term, N.Y. City. 1975). *But see* United States v. Blankinship, 543 F.2d 1272 (9th Cir. 1976), suggesting that the 6 percent interest figure employed by Congress in the Declaration of Taking Act is only a floor rather than a ceiling on the proper interest rate. "[A] rate no greater than 6 percent in some instances will contravene the Fifth Amendment." *Id.* at 1276. The Court went on to suggest that the proper interest rate should be that paid on treasury bills during the period between the date of the taking and the date of payment.

114. [1969] 3 All E.R. 172, [1970] A.C. 874.

115. Under English eminent domain law reinstatement is one of the ways by which an owner can elect to be compensated. The facts of this case were peculiar in that the condemnee did not actually acquire title to a new site until 1963, and the reinstatement did not actually take place until 1965. Apparently there was some unreasonable delay attributable to the condemnee, and the case was tried pursuant to a stipulation that reinstatement could have been reasonably accomplished by 1961.

116. Mann, *The Relevant Date for the Assessment of Compensation,* 85 L. Q. REV. 516, 521 (1969).

117. SI 1978/1741, cited in Lassman, *Interest on Debts-I,* 129 NEW L.J. 447 (1979).

118. DeLeeuw v. Ville de Lierre, Cass. 1st Ch., Oct. 21, 1966, [1967] J. T. 241 (upholding against constitutional challenge a taking valued as of 1949, even though in 1958, when the condemnation judgment was rendered, property values had increased by a factor of 1.7; the debt of value theory was not even discussed).

119. Cass. 1re Ch., Jan. 15, 1965, [1965] J.T. 296.

120. *See* 4 G. ZANOBINI, CORSO DI DIRITTO AMMINISTRATIVO 273 (1958); Ardizzone, *Espropriazione per Pubblica Utilità (procedimento),* 15 ENCI. DEL DIRITTO 835, 867–71 (1971); Trib. Sup. Acque, Nov. 14, 1949, [1950] Foro It. I, 1270 (1950); Trib. Genova, May 26, 1948, [1948] Foro It. I, 1080 (1948).

121. Ardizzone, *supra* note 120, at 867; Cass. Civ., Apr. 3, 1973, [1973] Rep. Gen. Giur. It. 1130; Cass. Oct. 12, 1960, n. 2679, in [1961] Foro Amm. II, 73; Cass. Apr. 8, 1952, n. 944, [1953] Foro It. I, 663. The Italian courts have, however, circumvented this obstacle to receipt of just compensation by permitting supplementary damage suits under Article 1224 of the civil code. *See* note 137 *infra* and the accompanying text.

For the historical evolution of the theory that expropriation is a forced sale, *see* Mann, *Outlines of a History of Expropriation,* 75 L.Q. REV. 188, 204–206 (1959).

122. Admn. Gral. de Obras Sanitarias de la Nación v. Torquinst y Bernal, 241 Fallos, [1959] III J.A. 509, 92 La Ley 77 (Sup. Ct. Arg. 1958); Gobierno Nacional v. Dumas, [1947] III J.A. 174, 47 La Ley 865 (Sup. Ct. Arg. 1947); Gobierno Nacional v. Iribarren de Olariaga, 49 La Ley 287 (Sup Ct. Arg. 1947); Picard v. União Federal, Embargos R.E. 51.670, 81 R.D.A. 220, 32 R.T.J. 484 (Braz. Sup. Fed. Trib. *en banc* 1964); *Súmula* No. 416 (Braz.) and cases cited therein.

123. The cases are collected in Rosenn, *Expropriation, Inflation, and Development,* 1972 WIS. L. REV. 845, 863, fn. 93.

124. Provincia de Santa Fé v. Nicchi, [1967] IV J.A. 115, 115–16, 127 La Ley 164 (1967).

125. *See, e.g.,* Azpillaga de Rodriguez Moreno v. Municipalidad de la Capital, CNCiv., Sala D, Feb. 22, 1977, La Ley, May 19, 1977, p. 5 (using the cost-of-living index). A recent statute, Law No. 21.499 of Jan. 21, 1977 codifies the case law by explicitly requiring indemnification for monetary depreciation between the date of dispossession and the date of effective payment, but the statute does not indicate how monetary depreciation is to be calculated.

126. As to Germany and Austria, *see* F. MANN, *supra* note 2, at 116–17. Prior to 1957, when French legislation moved the valuation date forward from the date of initiating the condemnation process to the date of judgment, the *Cour de Cassation* had been confirming appellate decisions ordering revaluation of awards to include loss stemming from monetary depreciation during the condemnation proceedings and appeals. P. JOSSE, LES TRAVAUX PUBLICS ET L'EXPROPRIATION 311–12 (1958).

127. F. MANN, *supra* note 2, at 117.

128. *See* chap. 4, *infra,* at notes 60–63 and accompanying text.

129. García de Enterría, *Expropiación Forzosa y Devaluación Monetaria,* 80 Rev. Admin. Pub. 9, 12–14 (May–Aug. 1976).

130. Ley de Expropiación Forzosa of Dec. 16, 1954, art. 58.

131. Cassinelli Muñoz, *Ajuste de la Compensación Expropiatoria a las Variantes Monetarias Luego de su Fijación Judicial,* 71 Rev. D.J.A. 112 (1972).

132. Municipio de Montevideo v. Pedro Rivero, 64 Just. Urug. 7615 (Trib. Apel. Civ. 2d Term, Sept. 24, 1971); Municipio de Montevideo v. Marín, 70 Just. Urug. 8255 (1st Instance, Oct. 15, 1974).

133. The cases are collected in Rosenn, *supra* note 123 at 862, fn. 88.

134. *Id.* at 863.

135. The *Súmula,* instituted in 1964, contains approximately 600 legal rules which have been laid down by constant decisions of the Brazilian Supreme Federal Tribunal. *Súmula* 416 stated: "For delay in the payment of the expropriation price, complementary compensation in addition to interest is improper."

136. J. CHACEL, M. SIMONSEN, & A. WALD, *supra* note 26, at 239–41.

137. Cass. Feb. 19, 1964, n. 374, in [1964] Giust. Civ. I, 1447; Cass. July 5, 1954, n. 2333, in [1954] Giur. Compl., Cass. Civ. 5, 244; Trib. of Rome, Jan. 18, 1980 [1980] Foro It. I, 1457; 4 R. NICOLO & M. RICHTER, *supra* note 24, at 447; 2 E. LAPORTA & G. TAMBURRINO, *supra* note 94, at 2614–15 (1963).

138. Law No. 4.686 of Je. 21, 1965.

139. J. CHACEL, M. SIMONSEN, & A. WALD, *supra* note 26, at 225–38; Moniz de Aragão, *A Correção Monetária na Desapropriação,* 23 Rev. Dir. Proc. Ger. 83 (1970); Ferraz, *Desapropriação: Indicações de Doutrina e Jurisprudência,* 22 Rev. Dir. Proc. Ger. 344, 416–25 (1970).

140. Rosenn, *supra* note 123 at 869. These supplementary tort damage suits have been routinely converted into successful requests for monetary correction. *Id.*

141. Ignez Corrêa Constantino v. Prefeitura Mun. de São Paulo, R.E. 63.395, 231 Rev. For. 75, 52 R.T.J. 711 (Sup. Fed. Trib. *en banc* 1969).

142. See chap. 9, *infra,* at notes 40, 95–109 and the accompanying text.

143. Estado de Minas Gerais v. Banco União Sucrière de L'Aisne S.A., R.E. 38.644, 67 R.T.J. 382 (Sup. Trib. Fed. *en banc* 1973).

144. The cases are collected in Tácito, *Desapropriação de Ações no Direito Brasileiro,* 126 Rev. Dir. Admin. 1, 9–17 (1976). *Compare* the measures employed in Austria and England to compensate shareholders for the nationalization of their stock, described in E. LANGER, LES NATIONALISATIONS EN AUTRICHE 137–63 (1964); Cairns, *Some Legal Aspects of Compensation for Nationalized Assets,* 16 L. & CONT. PROB. 594 (1951).

145. 60 R.D.J. 333 (pt. 2, 1st sec., Supreme Court, Nov. 7, 1963).

146. Macera Dellarossa, Carlos v. Fisco, 69 R.D.J. 4 (2d part, 1st sec., Court of Concepción, Jan. 10, 1972).

147. Margarita y Pedro Juan del Canto Puissegur, 71 R.D.J. 157 (pt. 2, 1st sect., Sup. Ct., Nov. 19, 1974); López Sabino v. Consejo de Defensa del Estado, 71 R.D.J. 137 (pt. 2, 1st sec., Sup. Ct., Oct. 7, 1974); Emilio Ciuffardi y otro v. Corporación de Mejoramiento Urbano, 71 R.D.J. 129 (pt. 2, 1st sec., Sup. Ct., Aug. 22, 1974).

148. Yalkut Hapirsumim 2158 of Oct. 20, 1975, quoted in Tedeschi, *supra* note 96, at 40.

149. Law No. 62–848 of Jy. 26, 1962, art. 22, [1962] S.L. 238.

150. Sirat, *Les Modifications Récentes du Régime de L'Expropriation,* [1965] J.C.P. I, 1958.

151. Law No. 65–559 of Jy. 10, 1965, art. 3, [1965] D.S.L. 225.

152. The cases are collected in Ferraz, *supra* note 139, at 416–17.

153. During the periods immediately following the overthrow of Isabel Perón in Argentina and Salvador Allende in Chile, when prices were rising at three percent per day, thirty days would seem far too much. In the context of the German inflation of 1923 or the Hungarian inflation of 1945–46, any delay would have been unfair.

154. Law No. 5.670 of Jy. 2, 1971.

155. da Rocha v. Central Eléctrica de Furnas, S.A., Emb. No. 69.304, 111 R.D.A. 225 (Sup. Trib. Fed. *en banc* 1971).

156. A.I. No. 26.768, Rev. Dir. Proc. Ger. Rio 137 (8th Cam. Civ. T.J.E.R. 1975) (Mar.–Jy. 1975); A.C. No. 88.785, D. Just., Mar. 31, 1975 (Sup. Trib. Fed.).

157. Law No. 6.423 of Je. 17, 1977. This statute applies to pecuniary obligations, and it is possible that the Brazilian courts will interpret it as inapplicable to eminent domain awards on the theory that these are debts of value.

158. See chap. 5 *supra,* at note 98.

159. *See* Rosenn, *supra* note 123, at 876.

160. CAL. CIV. PRO. CODE §§ 1251 and 1252 (West 1954).

161. 350 F.2d 468 (D.C. Cir. 1965), *cert. denied,* 383 U.S. 943.

162. 350 F.2d at 472.

163. Until recently, Brazil's highest tort verdict was only Cr$350,000 (then about U.S. $75,000), granted in September of 1970 by the Tribunal of Justice of the State of São Paulo to the widow of a judge murdered in 1961 at the order of a dissatisfied litigant. Jornal do Brasil, Sept. 22, 1970, p. 24, 1st Cad. The verdict is far greater than the typical wrongful death award in Brazil.

164. 350 F.2d at 478.

165. The statutory scheme is translated in K. KARST & K. ROSENN, *supra* note 110, at 508–9. Because of the poor draftsmanship, there has been much controversy about the application of the damage limitation provisions in collisions where the plaintiff was a passenger in plane other than the defendant's. There is a strong doctrinal current against limited liability. T. AZEREDO SANTOS, DIREITO DA NAVEGAÇÃO (Marítima e Aérea) 490–17 (1964); 2 AGUIAR DIAS, DA RESPONSABILIDADE CIVIL 826–827 (4th ed. 1960); Lemos Sobral, *A Responsabilidade Civil no Abalroamento Aéreo,* 132 Rev. For. 36 (1950); Vale, *O Nôvo Código do Ar,* 223 Rev. For. 12, 19–20 (1968). The controversy has finally been resolved by the new Brazilian Air Code, Decree-Law No. 32 of Nov. 18, 1966, as amended by Decree-Law No. 234 of Feb. 28, 1967. Art. 132 of this law establishes a limit of 400 times the highest prevailing minimum wage for wrongful death or injury from a negligent aircraft collision.

166. Law No. 4.221 of May 8, 1963.

167. *See* generally J. CHACEL, M. SIMONSEN, & A. WALD, *supra* note 26.

168. Resolução No. 3/63 of the National Economic Council of Jan. 24, 1963.

169. McGregor, *supra* note 28, at §32.

170. Except for pecuniary loss sustained by an heir at law, Kansas limits wrongful death recoveries to $25,000. 1 S. SPEISER, *supra* note 74, at § 7.2, p. 63 (Cumm. Supp. 1978). For similar provisions in other countries, *see* 2 S. SPEISER at § 16.1 *et seq.*

171. Ethiopia limits the recovery for non-pecuniary injuries *(dommage moral)* to E $1,000 (U.S. $400), while Mexico limits nonmaterial injuries to one-third of

the amount awarded for material loss, which is in turn limited to 27,375 pesos for total incapacitation, and 18,250 pesos for wrongful death. McGregor, *supra* note 28, at § 34.

172. H. Stoll, *Consequences of Liability: Remedies,* 11 INT'L ENCY. COMP. L. c. 8, § 159.

8

VALUE MAINTENANCE IN THE INTERNATIONAL SPHERE

Maintaining the economic value of legal arrangements during inflation takes on an additional layer of complexity in the international area. In addition to protecting the purchasing power of domestic currency against changes, one also has to consider the possibility of changes in the purchasing power and exchange rates of foreign currencies. These changes can fundamentally alter the economic assumptions upon which international transactions have been negotiated. They can also distort damage awards, bestowing a windfall on one party at the expense of the other.

This chapter will focus on two related international problems. The first problem involves the various consensual techniques utilized to maintain real economic value in international transactions. The second involves the conversion of damages measured in foreign currencies into the currency of the forum. Both problems have become more complicated and more important with the demise of the Bretton Woods system of fixed exchange rates pegged to gold. Legally, gold has become just another commodity. The two currencies that were at one time considered "as good as gold" for international payments, the U.S. dollar and the British pound, have been badly battered by continual balance of payments deficits. The stark reality is that there is no longer any simple standard of reference for defining value in international transactions.[1]

GOLD CLAUSES

Prior to World War II, the most popular technique for preserving the value of international transactions was the gold clause. The reasons for this popularity were simple. People conceived of the value of money in terms of the amount of gold into which it could be converted, and currency exchange rates were expressed in terms of gold. Although gold clauses were generally prohibited by statute during the monetary turmoil that followed World War I and the onset of the Great Depression, most of these statutes, particularly in Europe, permitted use of gold clauses in international transactions.[2] French case law went even further. The same judges who strained so hard to invalidate gold clauses in domestic contracts went to the opposite extreme in the international area. Through a reasoning process that may charitably be described as tortured, French courts reached the astonishing conclusion that gold clauses were valid even in contracts governed by the substantive law of a country like the United States or Canada, which had prohibited all gold clauses, irrespective of whether contained in domestic or international agreements.[3]

Prior to World War II, gold clauses had fallen into disuse, even in international transactions. The reasons are not entirely clear. Probably disaffection with gold clauses was in part due to the perception that they were too inflexible for creditors to count on enforcement in periods of monetary crisis,[4] and in part to recognition that better maintenance-of-value techniques, such as denominating a loan in U.S. dollars, were available. Yet even though they failed to reappear in private international transactions after World War II, gold clauses have occasionally surfaced in loans by governments and international agencies. Gold clauses have also been a conspicuous feature in loans made by the Soviet Union[5] and have been implicit in loans by the International Monetary Fund to member countries.[6]

Before gold was demonetized,[7] it made little sense to tie the value of an international transaction to gold. For several decades the price of monetary gold remained constant despite substantial world inflation. As the next section suggests, after demonetization it makes more sense to link international values to gold, but not much more. Gold has become essentially another commodity, and a highly speculative one at that. The unsuitability of gold clauses as a maintenance-of-value device is starkly revealed in the only area in which gold clauses are presently of any importance—limitation of liability in international conventions.

GOLD CLAUSE LIMITATIONS IN INTERNATIONAL CONVENTIONS

Gold clauses presently pose a perplexing problem because a substantial number of international conventions, particularly those dealing with air and maritime transportation, contain liability limitations expressed in terms of gold. Typical is the following provision contained in the 1929 Warsaw Convention on Air Transport:

> 1. In the carriage of persons the liability of the carrier for each passenger is limited to the sum of two hundred and fifty thousand francs. . . .
>
> 5. The sums mentioned in francs in this Article shall be deemed to refer to a currency unit consisting of sixty-five and a half milligrammes of gold of millesimal fineness nine hundred. These sums may be converted into national currencies in round figures. Conversion of the sums into national currencies other than gold shall, in the case of judicial proceedings, be made according to the gold value of such currencies at the date of judgment.[8]

The gold franc of the Warsaw convention, frequently referred to as the Poincaré franc, has been utilized to limit liability in all post 1924 international conventions involving air or maritime transportation and in two oil pollution treaties. The *franc de germinal,* a gold franc with 10/31 of a gram of gold millesimal fineness of nine hundred, has been used in several other kinds of transport conventions. Two transport conventions signed in 1924 use the gold pound sterling to limit liability.[9] The 1960 Paris Convention on Third Party Liability in the Field of Nuclear Energy limits liability in terms of the European Monetary Agreement unit, a fictitious unit containing .88867088 grams of gold, equivalent to the 1934 U.S. gold dollar.[10]

The purpose of tying these international liability limitation provisions to gold was twofold: (1) to insure uniformity, and (2) to protect the real value of the limitation from the vagaries of currency fluctuations;[11] but the delegates who negotiated these conventions never contemplated a two-tier gold price or the possibility that gold might someday be demonetized. Gold was the lodestone by which all currency compasses were set, and it seemed the one sure reference point for an international maintenance-of-value agreement. With the ending of the London Gold Pool in 1968 and the subsequent substantial spread between the official parity and the free market price for gold, a controversy quickly developed about which price reference should be used for converting these gold-linked liability limitations into national currencies. Should the conversion rate be the official monetary parity price or the free market price for gold?

The scant case law is divided on this question. The first judicial consideration of the issue was by the Supreme Court of the Netherlands in *Hornlinie v. Société Nationale des Pétroles Aquitaine.*[12] The dispute grew out of a collision that occurred in 1967 in Dutch territorial waters between German and French ships. The parties agreed that the collision was caused by the French ship, and that damages were limited to 2,313,360 Poincaré francs by Article 3 of the 1957 Brussels Convention Relating to the Limitation of Liability of Owners of Sea-Going Ships. They disagreed about whether these gold francs were to be converted into dollars (and then to guilders) at the official rate of $35 an ounce or the free market rate in 1969, when the action was initiated, of $44.46 an ounce. The Dutch Arrondissements Court decided to use the official gold parity as the conversion rate, and the Supreme Court sustained that determination.

The Netherlands Supreme Court acknowledged that there was nothing in the legislative history of the Convention to show that the delegates even thought about the possibility of a divergence between the free market and the official price for gold. It also acknowledged that neither price was likely to achieve to the delegates' purposes in utilizing the Poincaré franc: uniformity and the maintenance-of-value. Nevertheless, the court decided to use the official gold parity rate on the theory that it would better promote the goal of uniformity, and would avoid having the value of the limitation fluctuate in accordance with the fortuity of the gold price on the date of payment of the obligation. The court concluded:

> [A]s long as international arrangements exist between a substantial majority of the countries which are parties to the Convention, regarding the mutual relations between their currencies whereby a joint valuation of gold is the basis proceeded from, the general tenor of the Convention—viz. the promotion of uniformity . . . is better achieved by a rating of the franc which links-up with those international monetary arrangements than by a conversion on the basis of the daily prices of gold which are sometimes widely divergent and vary on the various free gold markets; That furthermore a choice for the conversion of the franc on the basis of the prices of gold on the free market would, in view of the fluctuating character of these prices, lead to the unsatisfactory result that the amount of the limited liability would vary according to the day on which the debtor makes this amount available or gives security thereof. . . .[13]

The Dutch court's determination to adopt the official gold parity rate has also been followed by the Paris Tribunal de Grande Instance in *Association Aéronautique du Centre Interclub de Saint-Cyr-Beynes v. Dame Veuve Thiérache,*[14] a 1973 decision involving application of the Warsaw Convention. Subsequent events, however, have seriously undermined the underlying premise of both these decisions. There is no longer an international monetary arrangement linked to gold, nor is there an official gold price that will produce uniformity with respect to the limitation of liability provisions. As can be seen from Table 3, which compares the number of a country's currency units in a SDR using official par values versus actual exchange rates on April 30, 1975, par value has become an artificial, meaningless concept. Moreover, under the Second Amendment to the IMF Articles of Agreement, which went into effect in 1978, no member nation is permitted to maintain the value of its currency in relation to gold.

Three cases that have considered the issue of converting gold value liability limitations in the post-1971 era of floating exchange rates have rejected the result reached in the *Hornlinie* and *Association Aéronautique*

TABLE 3 COMPARISON OF PAR VALUES AND EXCHANGE RATES IN TERMS OF SDRs OF NINE IMF MEMBERS ON APRIL 30, 1975

Country	*Par Value in Grams of gold per unit*	*Par Value in Units per SDR*	*Units per SDR on April 30, 1975 on Basis of Valuation of SDR*
Brazil	0.0480363	18.5000	9.68945
Burma	0.186621	4.76190	7.74941
Chile	0.00807883	110.000	4,717.47
Colombia	0.455733	1.94998	37.5412
Germany, Fed. Rep.	0.242806	3.66000	2.95214
India	0.118489	7.50000	9.91847
United Kingdom	2.13281	0.416667	0.527576
United States	0.736662	1.20635	1.24144
Uruguay	0.120091	7.40000	2,892.56

SOURCE: J. GOLD, FLOATING CURRENCIES, GOLD, AND SDRs: SOME RECENT LEGAL DEVELOPMENTS I6 (IMF Pamphlet No. 19, 1976)

cases. In the 1974 case of *Transarctic Shipping Corp., Inc. Monrovia, Liberia v. Krogerwerft,* [15] the German courts were faced with the same problem as the Dutch courts in *Hornlinie.* In calculating the bond required to limit a shipowner's liability under the 1957 Brussels Convention, the German Commercial Code mandated use of the "parity" of the Deutschmark (DM) in relation to gold. The District Court at Hamburg used the central rate for the DM, fixed in June of 1973 in terms of SDRs. Since at that time the SDR was defined in terms of a quantity of gold, the SDR rate could be recalculated in terms of gold. The Regional Court reversed the District Court and applied the par value. The Higher Regional Court ultimately reinstated the decision of the District Court, reasoning that the par value of the DM in relation to gold had become meaningless since the EEC countries had established their joint float ("the snake"), and that the purposes of the liability limitation would best be served by applying the central rate. While using the central rate did promote uniformity with respect to other members of the "snake", it did not promote uniformity with respect to other countries. Some important countries, such as the United States, have never declared a central rate. Even for countries declaring central rates, substantial differentials existed between countries whose currencies traded at a premium and those trading at a discount. Nor did the solution of the *Transarctic* case provide significant protection against inflation. Because of upward revaluation of German currency since the par value was established in 1969, utilization of central rate resulted in a liability limitation 13.7 percent lower than the par value would have produced.

In 1974 the Athens Court of Appeals held that the gold clause liability limitation in the Warsaw Convention was to be determined by reference to the free market price of gold.[16] The court reasoned that because Article 22 of the Convention required conversion into national currencies in accordance with "the gold value of such currencies at the date of judgment," the drafters must have contemplated a fluctuating gold price rather than a stable official price of gold. This reasoning is far from convincing. What the drafters of the convention contemplated was an international system in which official devaluations of fixed exchange rates were possible after consultation with the International Monetary Fund, a far cry from freely floating exchange rates.

In the 1973 case of *Saga v. Sagoland,*[17] the Swedish General Average Assessor decided that it was impossible to place a fixed value on the maritime liability limitation because both the free market price of gold and the exchange rates of currencies both fluctuate. He decided to use the free market gold price on the ground it produced more adequate compensation for the injured party.

It is impossible to solve this dilemma in terms of the intent of the drafters of these international conventions, for they never considered the possibility that exchange rates might be divorced from gold.[18] Nor is it possible to solve the dilemma in terms of promoting uniformity, unless one interprets the conventions to refer to the last official gold parity prior to the United States' closing of the "gold window" in 1971. This solution, however, dispenses with one of the primary reasons for expressing damage limitation provisions in gold: to insure that the real value of the limitation would be maintained. As the Dutch Court pointed out in *Hornlinie,* the free market gold price is a fortuitous maintenance-of-value arrangement, for it fluctuates in accordance with production, international monetary decisions, and demand by jewelers, dentists, and speculators rather than the internal purchasing power of currencies. On the other hand, the pre-1971 official gold price was an even less effective maintenance-of-value device, for it remained constant at $35 an ounce for thirty-seven years, a period during which the U. S. consumer price index increased by more than 200 percent.

The damage limitations in these international transport conventions, even if valued in terms of the free market price of gold, are quite low in comparison with damage awards in developed countries like the United States. They are often ridiculously low if gold is valued at $35 an ounce.[19] Because damage limitation provisions prevent innocent plaintiffs from receiving complete indemnification, it makes sense to construe these international conventions in a way that minimizes derogation from a complete recovery, particularly when the underlying purpose of uniformity can no longer be served. Therefore, the free market price of gold is the more appropriate reference.

If a court decides to use the free market price of gold, it must then decide when is the most appropriate time for determining the free market price of gold. The Athens Court of Appeals and the Swedish General Average Assessor determined the free market gold price at different times. The former used the price of gold on the Athens Stock Exchange on the date of the lower court judgment, while the latter applied the free market price at the date of collision.[20] The day of judgment, whose use is dictated by the language of the Warsaw Convention, has the disadvantage of inviting delay by the defendant if the price of gold is declining. On the other hand, the price of gold on the day of the collision or crash may be unfair to the plaintiff in a period of declining gold prices. Because the plaintiff is the innocent party and the damage limitation provisions come into play only to prevent the plaintiff from receiving full compensation, the fairest solution would be to choose the market price at the date of judgment or date of the tort, whichever is higher.

Some of the more recent international conventions have attempted to avoid the post-1971 difficulties with gold par values by stipulating that liability limitations stated in Poincaré francs shall be converted on the basis of the "official value" of the forum country's currency.[21] For some countries, however, the gold value of currency defined in domestic legislation is even more unrealistic and meaningless than IMF par values. For example, pursuant to a statute adopted in 1875, the official value of the Norwegian krone has remained at .4 gram of fine gold, but the par value for purposes of the IMF was set by the Norwegian government at slightly more than .1 gram of fine gold.[22] Other recent international conventions have attempted to resolve the gold value problem by stipulating liability limitations in SDRs, a development discussed separately, *infra.*[23]

MULTIPLE CURRENCY CLAUSES

A second technique for protecting the value of international transactions is the multiple currency clause, sometimes referred to as an optional currency clause. Such clauses effectively grant the creditor the option of being repaid in one of a number of designated currencies, thereby shifting the risk of currency devaluation or revaluation to the debtor. They also facilitate multinational securities offerings, making a single bond issue readily marketable in several countries simultaneously.

Multiple currency clauses have taken a variety of forms. Some grant the creditor the option of demanding repayment in a stipulated number of currency units in several countries, such as $1,000 in the United States, 2,100 DM in West Germany, or 4,500 francs in France. Others permit the creditor to demand repayment only in one country or currency, but grant the creditor the option of determining the number of units of that currency in accordance with the exchange rates fixed at the time of the issuance of the debt instrument. Thus, the creditor may be given the option of receiving $1,000 in the United States, or the equivalent in U.S. dollars of 2,100 German DM or 4,500 French francs.[24] If there is any change in exchange rates among the designated currencies, the creditor will almost always elect repayment in the strongest currency, *i.e.,* the one least devalued or most revalued.

Multiple currency clauses used to be common when the world's major currencies were on a gold or gold exchange standard. Although multiple currency clauses have been upheld in most countries,[25] the U. S. Supreme Court in 1939 construed the 1933 Gold Clause Resolution to deny holders of bonds in which one of the optional currencies of payment was the U.S. dollar the ability to elect repayment in any currency which would increase the dollar amount of the obligation.[26] Because most investors during the post-World War II era wanted dollar-linked obligations, multiple currency clauses declined in popularity. They enjoyed a limited revival during the late 1950s, when multiple currency bonds were issued in Luxembourg, Switzerland, the United Kingdom and West Germany, but the West German and Dutch revaluations of 1961 brought home vividly to borrowers how much more expensive multiple currency bonds can be than conventional offerings.[27] Since 1970 there have been a number of bond issues denominated in the European Monetary Unit (Ɇ), which is in effect a multiple currency clause payable in any of the six original EEC currencies.[28] On October 28, 1977 the U.S. Gold Clause Resolution was prospectively repealed,[29] thereby making it lawful to include the dollar as an optional currency in multiple currency obligations. It is doubtful, however, that this repeal will produce a substantial increase in the use of multiple currency clause obligations, for most prospective international borrowers deem unacceptable the potential exchange risk loss.

The multiple currency clause protects the creditor against the risk of exchange rate fluctuations, provided that the designated optional currencies are numerous and contain some of the world's strongest currencies. If the creditor's own currency is one of the designated payment options, the creditor is protected from exchange loss even if all the designated currencies are devalued in relation to a nondesignated currency. In addition, the creditor has a speculative advantage. If any of the denominated currencies appreciates relative to the creditor's own currency, the creditor can reap that speculative advantage by demanding repayment in the appreciated currency. A multiple currency clause, however, will not necessarily protect the creditor from the risk of inflation. If all the optional repayment currencies decline in purchasing power, a not unlikely scenario in this time of worldwide inflation, the real value of the obligation will diminish. It is possible that shifting exchange rates will result in the exchange rate differential between the strongest repayment currency and the creditor's own currency offsetting the decline in the purchasing power of the creditor's own currency, but this would be both fortuitous and unlikely.

THE EUROPEAN UNIT OF ACCOUNT

The European Unit of Account (EUA) is an artificial currency developed to protect international lenders from the risks of currency depreciation without affording the speculative advantage normally associated with multiple currency clauses. The value of the EUA was originally defined as equal to the unit of account of the now-dissolved European Payments Union. This was set in 1950 at 0.88867088 grams of fine gold, a sum conveniently equal to the gold value of the U.S. dollar when officially pegged to gold at $35 an ounce. Obligations denominated in EUAs are never payable in gold or in EUAs. As its name implies, the EUA is only a unit of account. Subscriptions, premiums, repayment of principal and interest of EUA obligations are payable in any of the nine EEC currencies.[30] The conversion rate between the EUA and the EEC currencies of payment varies with the par value of that currency in relation to gold or the SDR. A change in the par value of any currency of payment does not change the value of the EUA. For example, if the DM is revalued upward in relation to gold or the SDR, this simply means that a creditor of an obligation expressed in EUAs who demands payment in marks will receive fewer marks.

The value of the EUA varies only if two changes occur with respect to the values of reference currencies. These conditions are that: (1) the gold or SDR values of all reference currencies must have changed from their base values (par values in effect at the date the obligation denominated in EUAs was issued), and (2) a majority of the reference currencies must have changed in the same direction.[31] If both these conditions have been met, the value of the EUA in terms of gold or SDRs changes in the same direction as the majority of reference currencies. The new value of the EUA varies in direct proportion to the variation in the par value of the currency among the majority that has varied least.

The EUA was designed to strike an equitable balance between the interests of borrowers and lenders by providing a stable unit of account. Borrowers almost always subscribe to obligations denominated in EUAs by making payments in their national currencies. Because the reference currencies fluctuate against each other within a 2.25 percent band, the borrower receives the maximum amount of his national currency by converting subscriptions on the basis of the reference currency which trades at the highest premium in relation to the official parity.[32] At the time the borrower is repaying principal or interest, the lender has the option of choosing the reference currency in which he will be paid. Unlike the multiple currency clause lender, the EUA lender will not necessarily elect to be paid in the currency which has been most revalued upward, for the rate at which EUAs are converted into that currency will reflect that revaluation. Instead, the rational lender will elect to be repaid in the currency whose exchange rate has most appreciated in comparison with its official parity.[33]

Because the EUA is indexed to the reference currency that has varied least in the direction in which the majority of the reference currencies have moved, borrowers generally find EUA-denominated obligations less onerous than those containing multiple currency or gold clauses. The extreme variations of revaluation and devaluation are eliminated, and the exchange risks are apportioned between lenders and borrowers. The EUA, however, like the multiple currency clause, provides no protection against the risk of inflation. Moreover, the stability and the desirability of the EUA have been impaired by floating exchange rates and the economic difficulties of several EEC members. Since 1971 effective exchange rates have fluctuated with wider margins on either side of official parities, enabling bondholders to obtain substantial premiums by electing repayment in currencies trading at rates several percentage points above official parities. Though the EUA has been the most popular of the composite currency units, it accounts for only a small percentage of the Eurobonds issued.[34]

In 1975 the European Economic Community began using a unit of account for its internal affairs. Somewhat confusingly, this unit was also called the European Unit of Account, but is now referred to as the European Currency Unit (ECU). The ECU has been set up as a currency basket containing the following fixed quantities of these nine currencies:

0.828 German marks	0.217 Danish krone
1.15 French francs	109 Italian lira
0.0885 British pounds	3.66 Belgian francs
0.00759 Irish pounds	0.140 Luxembourg francs
0.286 Dutch florins	

These amounts do not fluctuate; however, the percentage weight of each currency will fluctuate with exchange rate changes. As one currency appreciates vis-à-vis other currencies in the basket, less of that appreciating currency is required to purchase the entire basket and its fixed amount represents a proportionately greater share of the total basket.[35] The ECU has been used in the denomination of receipts and contributions to the European Development Fund and the European Coal and Steel Community, and has become the basis for the new European Monetary System, which officially went into effect on March 13, 1979.

CURRENCY COCKTAILS

In the face of floating exchange rates and sinking dollars and pounds, international bankers and financiers have sought to devise stable units of account. This quest has produced a multinational analogue of the mutual fund, blending several different currencies into composite units of account called "currency cocktails" or "currency baskets".

The European Composite Unit

One of the most famous of the currency cocktails is the European Composite Unit (Eurco), which is based on the nine EEC currencies. The number of units of each currency in the Eurco are fixed at:

.90 German marks
1.20 French francs
.075 British pounds
80.00 Italian lire
.35 Netherlands guilders
4.50 Belgian francs
.20 Danish kroner
.005 Irish pounds
.50 Luxembourg francs

The value of the Eurco fluctuates daily in accordance with the weighted average of the exchange rates of the nine EEC currencies. The weight assigned to each currency was originally based upon the size of each country's economy; however, concern that investors might be put off by the large weights assigned to relatively weak currencies led, in 1973, to a downward revision of the weights of the British and Irish pounds and the Italian lire.[36] As with the EUA, the borrower selects the currency in which it will receive the proceeds of the subscriptions, while the lender elects the currency in which he will be repaid.

Like the EUA, the Eurco is designed to harmonize the interests of borrowers and lenders by creating a relatively stable unit of account. By spreading the exchange risk over nine component currencies, the value of a loan denominated in Eurcos is more stable than a loan in any one of these nine EEC currencies. Nevertheless, the Eurco, because its value changes in accordance with daily fluctuations in exchange rates, is somewhat more volatile than the EUA, whose value is linked to the official parity rate of the currency that moves least in the direction of general movement. The strong currencies have to offset the weak ones. When most of the reference currencies move in the same direction against a reference currency, the Eurco-denominated security becomes unduly advantageous for either borrowers or lenders. If the currency basket is dominated by the strong currencies, the Euroco will work to the lender's advantage. If dominated by the weak currencies, the Euroco will favor the borrower. This greater volatility is reflected in the slightly higher interest rates carried by Eurco loans in comparison with EUA loans. The Eurco, like the multiple currency clause and the EUA, provides no protection to the lender against the risk of inflation. The bloom has gone from the Euroco as far as the Eurobond market is concerned. In 1974 U.S. $68 million worth of Euroco-denominated bonds were issued, representing 1.5 percent of the total amount of Eurobonds issued. During the 1975–77 period World Bank data show no Euroco-denominated Eurobonds issued.[37]

The Special Drawing Right

In 1969 the International Monetary Fund (IMF) created the SDR, a new reserve asset.[38] The unit of value of this "paper gold" was originally pegged to the gold value of the dollar. Following the 1971 decision of the United States to allow the dollar to float and to end official convertibility of dollars into gold, the IMF changed the value of the SDR from a fixed quantity of gold to an elaborate currency cocktail. Between July 1974 and December 1980 the value of the SDR was determined by reference to a weighted average of the currencies of sixteen member nations with more than 1 percent of the world's exports of goods and services during a five-year period. The relative currency weights were broadly proportional to each country's share of the world's exports. These weights were revised by the IMF on July 1, 1978, and the Saudi Arabian riyal and the Iranian rial were substituted for the Danish krone and the South African rand. Since January 1, 1981, the SDR has been valued by reference to the weighted average of the currencies of the five member nations with the largest exports of goods and services during the 1975–79 period. The U.S. dollar has the greatest weight at 42 percent, followed by the Deutschmark at 19 percent, the French franc, Japanese yen, and British pound, with weights of 13 percent each.[39]

SDRs are valued in terms of the exchange rate market prices for the U.S. dollar; the rate of SDRs to other currencies then becomes a function of the dollar exchange rate as well as the representative exchange rates for other currencies. Thus, the value of the SDR in terms of any country's currency fluctuates with daily changes in exchange rates of the above five nations' currencies.

In recent years the SDR has been substituted for gold as a maintenance-of-value device for international conventions. The four protocols to the Warsaw Convention adopted at the International Conference on Air Law at Montreal in 1975 substituted the SDR for the Poincaré franc in liability limitation provisions for countries that are members of the IMF.[40] The value of the SDR in terms of a national currency is to be calculated in accordance with the valuation method applied by the IMF for its operations and transactions at the date of judgment. Countries that do not belong to the IMF have liability limits stated in terms of a unit of account defined as "sixty-five and a half milligrammes of gold of millesimal fineness nine hundred." Conversion of this gold unit of account into national currency is governed by the law of the country concerned.[41] The 1976 Convention on Limitation of Liability for Maritime Claims follows the same procedure for expressing liability limitations.[42] The Convention on Civil Liability for Oil Pollution resulting from Exploration of Seabed Mineral Resources, signed in London on May 1, 1977, allows each operator to limit his liability for each installation to 30 million SDRs for five years, and to 40 million SDRs thereafter.[43]

A number of countries and international organizations have used the SDR as an indexing device. As of mid-1981 fifteen countries have pegged their exchange rates to the SDR.[44] Since 1975 the Suez Canal Authority has been charging tolls in terms of SDRs.[45] Several Eurobond issues have utilized the SDR as their unit of account and the U.S. dollar as their currency of payment.[46] The authorized capital of the recently created Arab Monetary Fund is 250 million Arab dinars, a unit of account equal to 3 SDRs.[47] Both the Organization of Petroleum Exporting States (OPEC) and the International Air Transport Association agreed in 1975 to express their respective prices for oil and air fares in SDRs, but the decisions have yet to be implemented.[48] Since 1975 several banks have been offering loans, time deposits, and future contracts denominated in SDRs.[49] If the value of the dollar declines sharply in foreign exchange markets, it is quite possible that the SDR will eventually become the preferred unit of account in international transactions.

One difficulty with using the SDR to index contracts and loans is its complexity. Its value has to be recomputed daily to reflect changes in the exchange rates of the five currencies that make up its market basket. The second difficulty is that the IMF changes the market basket of the SDR from time to time. If the "frozen" SDR (the market basket in effect at the date of issuance of the obligation) is selected as the unit of account, the parties run the risk that the IMF will discontinue calculation of the daily value of the old SDR when the IMF switches to a new definition of the market basket. If the "variable" SDR is selected as the unit of account, uncertainty is increased; the parties must run the risk that subsequent changes might adversely affect their economic positions. Consequently, the SDR is little used for long-term international loan agreements or bonds.

Substitution of the SDR for gold as a maintenance-of-value device in international conventions would appear to be a step in the right direction. Preserving the value of a limitation of liability provision by linking it to gold has always been a dicey proposition. *A fortiori* this is the case today. Still, the SDR provides no protection against the realistic possibility that the purchasing power of some or all of the five reference currencies will undergo inflationary erosion. The SDR's value is pegged to exchange rates. Like any other currency cocktail, the SDR does nothing to safeguard the purchasing power of the currencies upon which it is based. If worldwide inflation continues, the real value of these international liability limitations may have been better protected if tied to the free market price of gold rather than to the SDR.

OTHER FORMS OF VALUE MAINTENANCE

There are a wide variety of techniques to maintain value in international transactions besides gold clauses, multiple currency clauses, composite units of account, and currency cocktails. One of the most common practices is the simplest: denomination of a loan or bond in a hard currency, such as the U.S. dollar, Swiss franc, or the DM. In the last few years a substantial market for variable interest rate medium-term loans in Eurocurrencies, especially Eurodollars, has developed.[50] The great bulk of international obligations are still simply denominated in dollars, despite the general unease over the infirmity of U.S. currency, with interest rates linked to a spread over the interbank offered rate. A dollar loan eliminates any risk to an American creditor from devaluation of the dollar; however, the risk of depreciation in the dollar's internal purchasing power remains with the creditor. A dollar loan spares an American debtor any risk of loss from devaluation of the dollar. On the other hand, the dollar loan imposes a risk from devaluation or revaluation on non-U.S. creditors and debtors, who must calculate the likelihood that the exchange rate of their own currency will appreciate or depreciate in relation to the dollar.

An interesting variation on dollar borrowing that has not yet caught hold is the Arab Currency-Related Unit (Arcru). All Arcru transactions are made in dollars, but the value of the Arcru depends on the U.S. dollar exchange rate for the currencies of twelve Arab countries. The base valuation for the Arcru was set to equal one U.S. dollar on June 28, 1974. Subsequent valuations disregard the two strongest and two weakest of the twelve Arab currencies, considering only the average movement of the remaining eight equally weighted currencies. The Arcru is designed to protect borrowers and lenders from having events in a single Arab country disproportionately influence the cost of their financing or investment. As of 1977, only one issue of bonds denominated in Arcrus had been issued.[51]

The great majority of intergovernmental loans are simply denominated in the currency of the lending government and contain no additional maintenance-of-value device.[52] Many lending institutions, particularly in hard currency countries, routinely make loans only in their own currencies. Others attempt to hedge any exchange risks by offsetting borrowing and lending risks in several different currencies.[53] Swap arrangements between central banks commonly contain guarantees immunizing the other party from any exchange losses resulting from devaluation of the net debtor's currency.[54]

The courts of many countries have been far slower than the international lending community to acknowledge the need for the development of maintenance-of-value techniques. In lawsuits that involve obligations measured in foreign currencies, the courts have generally ignored changes in value caused by inflation. The need for greater sensitivity to preservation of the value of transnational obligations becomes readily apparent in the next section, which focuses on one of the most confused areas of the law—the conversion of foreign currencies into the currency of the forum.

CONVERSION OF FOREIGN CURRENCIES

During the heyday of the gold or gold exchange standard, whether an obligation was discharged in the same currency by which it was measured was an insignificant question.[55] Exchange rates fluctuated only within the narrow margins between gold points. With the demise of the gold standard, however, the question suddenly became important, for currency exchange rates began to fluctuate sharply. Although there are exceptions,[56] the courts of most countries cannot render a judgment for an amount expressed in a foreign currency.[57] Consequently, courts have been forced to develop rules for the conversion of foreign currency obligations into domestic currency. The great majority of these decisions have opted for conversion either at the exchange rate in force at the date of the tort or of breach, or the exchange rate in effect at the day of judgment.[58]

Perhaps in no country is the law with respect to conversion of foreign currency obligations as confused as in the United States, where a 1792 statute has been interpreted as requiring that all judgments entered by

U.S. courts be expressed in dollars.[59] Considerable credit for the confusion belongs to Mr. Justice Holmes, whose reputation for legal brilliance has happily survived the two leading Supreme Court opinions he authored on conversion of foreign monetary obligations. The first was *Hicks v. Guinness,*[60] where a German defendant failed to pay a debt for 1,079.35 marks, due and payable in the United States to an American creditor in 1916. The Supreme Court unanimously held that the proper date for conversion was the day of breach. This result made eminent sense. Because the mark had become worthless by the day of judgment, judgment-day conversion would have effectively deprived the creditor of any remedy. Rather than analyze the relevant policy considerations, Holmes' opinion simply states: "The debt was due to an American creditor and was to be paid in the United States. When the contract was broken by a failure to pay, the American firm had a claim here, not for the debt, but, at its option, for damages in dollars. It no longer could be compelled to accept marks."[61] The opinion is silent as to why or how default converted a mark obligation into a dollar obligation. The second case was *Deutsche Bank Filiale Nurnberg v. Humphrey,*[62] decided the following year, where Holmes reached the opposite result. In this case a German bank had failed to repay a demand deposit held in Germany for an American depositor, who had demanded it in 1915, when the mark's exchange rate was U.S. $.205. The court held that the proper date for the conversion was the day of judgment, when the mark's exchange rate had plummeted to U.S. $.000000000000215.[63] Consequently, judgment for the plaintiff was entered for the munificent sum of one cent, while costs of $321 were awarded to the defendant.[64] Holmes' opinion distinguished *Hicks* on the highly formalistic ground that the defendant bank owed no duty to the plaintiff under American law.[65] The effect of *Deutsche Bank* and *Hicks* is to make the amount of recovery in foreign currency obligations sued on in the federal courts of the United States depend upon the fortuity of whether the cause of action arises under U.S. or foreign law. This absurd rule has been subjected to scathing criticism.[66]

American courts generally apply the judgment-date rule,[67] while English courts generally follow the breach-date rule.[68] New York state courts have also adopted the breach-date rule.[69] Yet it is not uncommon for American courts to manipulate these conversion date rules to achieve a reasonably just result.[70] English courts have recently reacted against the rigidity of the breach-date rule by permitting judgments to be rendered in foreign currency in circumstances when it has seemed just to do so.[71] As the next section shows, both the breach-date and the judgment-date conversion rules are far too mechanical and simplistic to compensate plaintiffs adequately, particularly in an era of continuous inflation and floating exchange rates.

Inadequacies of Breach-Date and Judgment-Date Conversion

Conversion at the exchange rate in effect on the day of breach or tort grants a windfall to the breaching party or tortfeasor if between day of breach (or tort) and day of judgment the foreign currency in which damages are calculated (currency of account) has been devalued in relation to the currency of the forum. Conversely, the breach-date rule grants the plaintiff a windfall if between breach and judgment the currency of the forum has been devalued in relation to the currency of account. Conversion at the exchange rate in effect on the day of judgment has just the opposite effect. If, between breach and judgment, the currency of the forum has been devalued in relation to the currency of account, the day of judgment rule presents the defendant with a windfall. If, between breach and judgment, the currency of account has been devalued in relation to the currency of the forum, the day of judgment rule presents the plaintiff with a windfall.

Inflation further complicates the problem of conversion of foreign currency obligations, for exchange rates frequently do not reflect relative changes in domestic purchasing power of different currencies, particularly in the short run. The facts of *Paris v. Central Chiclera, S. de R.L.*,[72] where a supplier sued a U.S. buyer in federal court for default on a contract to purchase bubble gum, are illustrative. The contract was made in Mexico and called for payment in pesos. The trial court assessed damages at 83,149.20 Mexican pesos. In December 1947, the time of the breach, the exchange rate stood at 4.7 pesos to the U.S. dollar. In 1951, when judgment was entered, the exchange rate stood at 8.62 pesos to the dollar. The U.S. Court of Appeals for the Fifth Circuit modified the District Court's judgment to require the use of the exchange rate in effect at the date of judgment. This reduced the Mexican plaintiff's recovery by 40 percent and accorded the American defendant a benefit of more than $8,000 for failing to meet his contractual obligations. The breach-date rule, which was urged by the dissent, would have overcompensated the plaintiff by 10 percent, because the decline in the peso's exchange rate exceeded the decline in domestic purchasing power of the peso between breach date and judgment date.[73]

Day-of-judgment conversion forces the foreign plaintiff to bear the entire risk of exchange rate devaluation and inflation in his own currency. If there is such inflation or devaluation, the damage award is likely to be only a fraction of his actual loss. In this circumstance, the defendant has a substantial incentive to delay the litigation as much as possible. On the other hand, if the foreign plaintiff's currency is appreciating relative to the currency of the forum, the defendant can mitigate damages by prompt settlement. Day-of-breach conversion immunizes the foreign plaintiff from the risk of inflation in his own currency only if the currency of the forum is stable and the exchange rate mirrors the purchasing power differential. If, however, the forum currency is depreciating, breach-date conversion is likely to undercompensate the plaintiff.[74]

There is an analogous problem if the foreign creditor obtains a judgment abroad and then sues for recognition and enforcement of that foreign judgment. Anglo-American courts will convert the foreign judgment into pounds or dollars at the exchange rate prevailing on the date of the foreign judgment.[75] This rule exposes the foreign creditor to the same hazards as judgment-day conversion, plus the added risks of exchange rate devaluation and inflation between the date of the original judgment and eventual payment.

Granting Judgment in a Foreign Currency

The British have recently tried to cope with the conversion problem by permitting the courts, in cases involving breach of a contract whose proper law and currency of account is foreign, to render judgment in the foreign currency of account.[76] This eliminates the need to convert the obligation into the currency of the forum. If the defendant fails to pay the judgment, conversion at the then existing exchange rate may be necessary at the time of execution of the judgment. This solution would place the plaintiff in the same position he would have been in had he been able to sue the defendant in the country in whose currency the obligation is denominated, assuming that legal interest rates are similar. If there is an interest rate differential, the plaintiff may be correspondingly better or worse off than if he had sued abroad.[77]

For more than 150 years, the requirement of conversion of foreign money obligations into sterling had generally worked to the advantage of foreign creditors because English courts compute damages as of the day of breach, and the pound had been extraordinarily stable during the nineteenth and first part of the twentieth century. The pound, however, softened dramatically in the post–World War II era,[78] making breach-date conversion a source of substantial unfairness to many foreign litigants seeking justice in British courts.

In 1975 the Court of Appeal in London became the first English court to repudiate the long-established rule that Anglo-American courts can render judgment only in domestic currency. In *Schorsch Meier G.m.b.H v. Hennin*[79] a German company sued an English customer for nonpayment of invoices for goods sold and delivered. The currency of account and the proper law of the contract were German. At the date payment was due, the exchange rate was £ 1 = DM 8.3. By the time suit was filed, devaluation of the pound resulted in an exchange rate of £1 = DM 5.85. Relying on Article 106 of the Treaty of Rome,[80] the German plaintiff sought judgment in DM to avoid loss of approximately one-third of its claim. Lord Denning's opinion for the Court of Appeal declared that the essential reason for rendering judgments only in sterling, its unequaled stability, had vanished. The opinion interpreted Article 106 to stand for the following proposition:

> It is the duty of the debtor to pay his debt to the creditor in the currency of the contract according to its terms. If he delays and sterling depreciates, the creditor ought not suffer loss as a result of the debtor's delay. The debtor ought to bear the burden of his own default. The English courts would be acting contrary to the spirit and intent of the Treaty if they made a German creditor accept payment in depreciated sterling. In order to comply with the Treaty, they should give judgment that the defendant do pay the stated sum in Deutschmarks or its sterling equivalent at the time of payment.[81]

This reading of Article 106, which was designed to "guarantee that the foreign exchange necessary for the performance of a contract in the currency specified will be made available,"[82] is dubious and has been cogently criticized.[83]

The House of Lords reached a similar result in the celebrated case of *Miliangos v. George Frank (Textiles) Ltd.,*[84] which involved a suit by a Swiss manufacturer against a British buyer for failure to pay for a purchase of yarn invoiced in Swiss francs. Between the date of the breach and the date of the trial, the pound had been devalued by approximately 40 percent vis-à-vis the Swiss franc. Utilization of the breach-date conversion rule would have reduced the plaintiff's recovery to £ 42,000, while rendering judgment in Swiss francs would have provided the plaintiff with the equivalent of £ 60,000. Britain's highest court decided to abandon the requirement of breach-date conversion, reaffirmed by the House of Lords as recently as 1961,[85] primarily because it often produced unjust results now that the world's major currencies, including the pound, were floating. The House of Lords was also influenced by two additional factors: (1) the development of procedures for enforcement of judgments in foreign currencies, and (2) judicial confirmation of London commercial arbitration awards in U.S. dollars. Although the Treaty of Rome did not apply to this case because Switzerland is not a member of the EEC, Lord Wilberforce's opinion contains dicta disapproving the Court of Appeal's reliance on Article 106 in the *Schorsch Meier* case.[86]

The House of Lords recently extended the *Miliangos* approach to claims for damages arising from tort and breach of contract. In the case of *The Despina R*,[87] a Greek ship managed by a New York firm was damaged by a collision near Shanghai. Plantiff paid for part of the repairs in four different currencies: Chinese renmimbi yuan, Japanese yen, pounds sterling, and U.S. dollars. Applying the principles of *restitutio in integrum* and reasonable foreseeability, the House of Lords awarded damages in dollars because plaintiff had purchased the other currencies involved with dollars, and a dollar award produced a fairer result than any of the other currencies involved. In the companion case of *The Folias,*[88] a French charterer sued the Swedish ship owners for reimbursement for cargo damage claims resulting from failure of the ship's refrigeration system. The French charterer had paid the claims of the cargo receivers in Brazilian cruzeiros, which had depreciated sharply against the French franc. The charter party was governed by English law and provided for arbitration in London. The charterer claimed that it was entitled to damages in the amount of the French francs used to purchase the Brazilian cruzeiros, or alternatively in U.S. dollars, the currency of the charter party. In affirming an award of damages in French francs, the House of Lords held that where a contract governed by English law failed to specify a currency of account and payment for all transactions arising thereunder, damages were to be awarded in the currency that most accurately expressed the plaintiff's loss. "In ascertaining which this currency is, the court must ask what is the currency, payment in which will as nearly as possible compensate the plaintiff in accordance with the principle of restitution, and whether the parties must be taken reasonably to have had this in contemplation."[89]

The technique of rendering judgment in a foreign currency will generally produce the same result as the judgment-day conversion rule and is subject to the same criticisms. It is, however, superior to the judgment-day rule whenever the foreign currency of account is appreciating relative to the currency of the forum. If the creditor is granted the option of seeking breach-date conversion or a judgment in foreign currency, much of the potential unfairness to foreign creditors disappears. There may be some unfairness to the debtor if the legal interest rate of the forum exceeds that of the foreign currency in which the judgment is rendered. This could prove substantial if the following three factors coalesce: (1) legal interest rates reflect inflation rates, (2) the currency of account is stable, and (3) the currency of the forum is highly inflationary. Under these circumstances courts should be careful to utilize an interest rate that reflects the cost of borrowing in the currency of account.[90]

Rendering judgment in a foreign currency does not avoid the potential unfairness to plaintiffs and defendants resulting from inflation between the date of breach and the date of actual payment. If there is substantial inflation in the currency of account, the plaintiff will be undercompensated. If the currency of the forum has been devalued by more than the domestic inflation rate in the country of the currency of account, the plaintiff will be overcompensated. If the currency of the forum has been devalued by less than the domestic inflation rate in the country of the currency of account, the plaintiff will be undercompensated. If the currency of the forum has been revalued upward by more than the inflation rate in the currency of account and the plaintiff maintains the option of being able to sue in the currency of the forum, breach-date conversion will overcompensate the plaintiff. Rendering judgment in the currency of account is essentially a nominalist solution that ignores changes in the purchasing power of the relevant currencies.

A Suggested Monetary Correction Approach

If a damage award is to serve its basic function of making the plaintiff whole, courts cannot ignore changes in the purchasing power of money. If courts are willing to discard the fiction of nominalism, a compensatory damage award could be achieved by two routes. Damages could be assessed in the currency of account at the date of the breach. One monetary correction technique would be to gross up this amount by a coefficient reflecting the change in a general price index of the currency of account between the date of the breach and the date of judgment (or payment, if there is a significant delay). This grossed up amount would then be converted into the currency of the forum at the exchange rate prevailing at the date of payment.

A second monetary correction technique would be to convert the damages assessed from the currency of account to the currency of the forum at the exchange rate prevailing at the day of breach. The award would then be grossed up by a coefficient reflecting the change in the forum's general price index between the date of the breach and the date of judgment (or payment, if there is a significant delay).

If the exchange rate mirrors the differential in inflation rates between the currency of account and the currency of the forum, the alternative techniques should produce identical results. Persuading a court accustomed to thinking in nominalist terms to adopt either solution is likely to be a difficult task, but a court is likely to be less resistant to monetary correction of the currency of account. Courts have, on occasion, been willing to treat foreign money as a commodity rather than as money,[91] and, by so doing, avoid triggering the nominalist principle. On the other hand, courts may be more reluctant to accept as reliable coefficients derived from price indexes with which they are wholly unfamiliar.

To avoid overcompensating plaintiffs, courts should attempt to net out any inflationary component from an award of interest. Because normal interest rates usually include a so-called real rate of interest plus a component for anticipated inflation, it would be unfair to the defendant to permit additional compensation for anticipated decline in the purchasing power of the currency during the course of a procedure which fully protects the award from monetary depreciation.

CONCLUSIONS

There is currently no generally accepted standard of value for international transactions. Gold and the U.S. dollar have ceased to perform that function, and no substitute standard is on the horizon. Thus far, maintenance-of-value techniques have been largely directed toward protecting creditors against the risk of loss from changes in exchange rates. Such techniques were largely developed in an era when exchange rates were linked to gold, whose value was assumed to be stable. In an age of demonetized gold, worldwide inflation, and floating exchange rates, it makes little sense to conceive of the value to be maintained in medium and long-term transnational transactions as the value of any given exchange rate. It makes much more sense to devise maintenance-of-value techniques that will preserve the purchasing power of the currency lent. None of the composite arrangements, such as the EUA, the European Monetary Unit, or the SDR seem likely to play the role of gold or the dollar, though it appears likely that the SDR will have an increasing role as a means of account for certain kinds of international transactions. If the trend toward chronic worldwide inflation continues, some effort may be made to build a more complex reference unit geared to international commodity prices.

There is increasing evidence that courts are not oblivious to the injustice perpetrated through mechanical application of antiquated rules in deciding cases that involve foreign currency obligations. The recent recognition by the British courts that floating exchange rates require discarding of traditional nominalist assumptions augurs increased sophistication about the real economic effects of judicial decisions. Although the solution of the House of Lords in the *Miliangos* case is far from ideal, it is an enormous improvement over the prior state of the law.

Eventually legislatures and courts may be persuaded to consider maintaining the real value of foreign monetary obligations by reference to price indexes. If a breakthrough in the stronghold of nominalism is achieved in the area of monetary obligations expressed in foreign currency, the monetary correction approach is likely to spread quickly into purely domestic transactions.

NOTES

1. Silard, *Maintenance-of-Value Arrangements in International Transactions,* 5 L. & Pol. Int'l Bus. 398, 413 (1973).

2. G. Delaume, Legal Aspects of International Lending and Economic Development Financing 267 (1967).

3. *Id.* at 114–15 and cases cited therein.

4. *Id.* at 267. *See also* Silard, *supra* note 1, at 424–25.

5. Delaume, *Gold and Currency Clauses in Contemporary International Loans,* 9 Am. J. Comp. L. 199, 200 (1960).

6. Evan, *New Socio-Economic Groupings and the Expanding Domestic International Dualism in the Light of Some of the Newer Monetary Law Developments,* Int'l L. Assoc., Am. Branch, Proc. & Comm. Reports 73, 78–79 (1969–70).

7. *See* chap. 3, *supra,* at pp. 55–57.

8. Convention for the Unification of Certain Rules Relating to International Transportation by Air, art. 22, signed at Warsaw Oct. 12, 1929, T.S. 876, 137 L.N.T.S. 11, as amended by the Protocol to Amend the Convention for the Unification of Certain Rules Relating to International Carriage by Air, done at the Hague, Sept. 28, 1955, art. 22, 478 U.N.T.S. 371. The Warsaw Convention limited liability for death or injury of a passenger to 125,000 Poincaré francs. This was doubled by the Hague Protocol. The Guatemala Protocol, opened for signature in 1971, 10 Int'l Legal Mat. 615 (1971) will raise this figure to 1,500,000 francs. *See* Heller, *The Warsaw Convention and the "Two-Tier" Gold Market,* 7 J. World Trade L. 126 (1973).

9. Asser, *Golden Limitations of Liability in International Transport Conventions and the Currency Crisis,* 5 J. Mar. L. & Com. 645, 646 (1974).

10. Arcari, *Gold Clauses in International Conventions* (Int'l Inst. Unification of Priv. Law, study LVII–Doc. 1/Rev. U.D.P.), at p. 3 (1973); Jeanprêtre, *La Conversion des Limitations de Responsabilité Exprimées en Or dans les Conventions Internationales,* 65 S.J.Z. 185 (1969).

11. Heller, *The Value of the Gold Franc—A Different Point of View,* 6 J. Mar. L. & Com. 73, 91–92 (1974); Asser, *supra* note 9, at 664.

12. 7 Europ. Transp. L. 933 (Netherlands Sup. C., Apr. 14, 1972). Much of the opinion is also reproduced in Asser, *supra* note 9, at 659–61 and 4 Netherlands Yearbook Int'l L. 408 (1973).

13. As translated in 7 Europ. Transp. L. at 960–61.

14. Decision of Feb. 10, 1973, 27 Rev. Fr. Dr. Aérien 212 (1973).

15. 9 Europ. Transp. L. 701 (1974), discussed in J. Gold, Floating Currencies, Gold, and SDRs: Some Recent Legal Developments 17–33 (IMF Pamphlet No. 19, 1976).

16. Judgment No. 256 of Jan. 10, 1974, cited in Comment, *Legal Problems in Compensation under the Gold Clauses of Private International Agreements,* 63 Geo. L. J. 817, 824 (1975) [hereafter cited as Georgetown Comment].

17. Lower Court, Goteborg, Sweden, Oct. 2, 1973, cited in *id.* at 825. Hagberg, *Gold Value Clauses in International Transport Conventions,* 5 INT'L BUS. LAW. 253, 257 (1977) suggests that the limitation of liability would not have arisen had the General Average Assessor correctly calculated the amount of liability. There was no appeal.

18. Hornlinie v. Société Nationale Pétrole Aquitaine, 7 EUROP. TRANSP. L. 933, 942–46, 951, 958 (1972).

19. GEORGETOWN COMMENT, *supra* note 16, at 818–19.

20. *Id.* at 825.

21. *E.g.,* Athens Convention Relating to the Carriage of Passengers and Their Luggage by Sea of December 13, 1974, art. 9; Brussels Convention on Civil Liability for Oil-Pollution Damage of Nov. 29, 1969, art. V(9); Geneva Convention on Limitation of Shipowner's Liability in Internal Navigation of May 1, 1973, art. 9.

22. Smith, *Legal Principles in Monetary and Credit Policy,* 18 SCAN. STUD. IN LAW 179, 184, 216 (1974).

23. *See* 278–80 *infra*.

24. *See* G. DELAUME, *supra* note 2, at 267–70; Silard, *supra* note 1, at 429–30. *See also* Nussbaum, *Multiple Currency and Index Clauses,* 84 U. PA. L. REV. 569 (1936).

25. *See* chap. 5, *supra,* at notes 41–54 and the accompanying text.

26. Guaranty Trust Co. v. Henwood, 307 U.S. 247 (1939); Bethlehem Steel Co. v. Zurich Ins. Co., 307 U.S. 265 (1939). Limits on the potential reach of these decisions is explored in Stevenson, *Legal Aspects of the Public Offering of Foreign Securities in the United States Market,* 28 GEO. WASH. L. REV. 194, 198–200 (1959).

27. Silard, *supra* note 1, at 429.

28. Van Ballegooijen, *The Units of Account in Eurobonds,* 22 NETHERLANDS INT'L L. REV. 51, 61–62 (1975). Because the Belgian and Luxembourg francs have the same value, subscribers to Ɇ bonds have the option of demanding repayment in five currencies: (1) Italian lire, (2) German mark, (3) Dutch guilder, (4) French franc, and (5) Belgian or Luxembourg francs. *Id.*

29. Pub. L. 95–147, §4(c), Oct. 28, 1977, 91 Stat. 1229.

30. Originally, there were seventeen reference currencies that also served as repayment media. These were the currencies of the countries which belonged to the former European Payments Union: Austria, Belgium, Denmark, France, Germany, Greece, Iceland, Ireland, Italy, Luxembourg, the Netherlands, Norway, Portugal, Sweden, Switzerland, Turkey, and the United Kingdom. Blondeel, *A New Form of International Financing: Loans in European Units of Account,* 64 COLUM. L. REV. 995, 997 (1964).

31. Originally, a change in the par value of two-thirds of the seventeen reference currencies was required to change the gold value of the EUA. *See id.* at 1000. Only those countries which have not adopted floating exchange rates independent of the rest of the EEC enjoy full reference status. The EUA agreements state if gold is replaced as the universal monetary common denominator, the EUA is to be defined on the basis of the new common denominator. Since the new common denominator of the international monetary system is the SDR and the EUA is the equivalent of the SDR when defined in terms of gold, it has been possible to

consider 1 SDR = 1 EUA. *Recent Development of Units of Account Designed to Serve Borrowers and Lenders,* 6 IMF Survey 346 (1977). *See* also Statement of J. Blondeel, in PROTECTION AGAINST INFLATION AND EXCHANGE RISK: THE ROLE OF INDEXATION 37 (Proc. of the Saltsjobaden Conf., Jy. 4–6, 1974).

32. Lusztig & Schwab, *Units of Account and the International Bond Market,* 10 COLUM. J. WORLD BUS. 74, 76 (Spring 1975).

In the first EUA bond issues, the borrower permitted subscribers to choose the currency in which subscriptions would be made. Because this option frequently worked to the borrower's disadvantage, subsequent practice has generally been for the borrower to choose a strong currency, such as the German mark, as the currency of subscription, forcing subscribers from outside that denominated currency to convert their own currencies into that currency in order to enter the EUA. van Ballegooijen, *supra* note 28, at 54–55.

33. Lusztig & Schwab, *supra* note 32, at 76.

34. In 1975 U.S. $388,000,000 worth of Eurobonds were denominated in EUAs, representing 3.7 percent of the total amount of Eurobonds issued that year. By 1977 EUA-denominated Eurobonds had dropped to U.S. $34,000,000, only 0.2 percent of the total amount of Eurobonds issued. 7 IMF Survey 236 (1978). In 1979 $253,000,000 worth of Eurobonds were denominated in ECUs, again only 0.2 percent of the total. *See* Morgan Guaranty Trust Co. of N.Y., World Financial Markets, Jy. 1980, at p. 13.

35. Dixon, *The European Unit of Account,* 14 COMMON MARKET L. REV. 191 (1977).

36. Lusztig & Schwab, *supra* note 32, at 76.

37. 7 IMF Survey 236 (1978); 6 IMF Survey 347 (1977).

38. *See* chap. 3, *supra* notes 88–89 and the accompanying text.

39. IMF, 34 INT'L FIN. STATISTICS 5 (May 1981). *See also* Effros, *Maintenance of Value in the General Account and Valuation of the SDR in the Special Drawing Account of the IMF,* 6 GA. J. INT'L & COMP. L. 493, 515–16 (1976).

40. Fitzgerald, *The Four Montreal Protocols To Amend the Warsaw Convention Regime Governing International Carriage by Air,* 42 J. AIR L. & COM. 273, 323–30 (1976); Treves, *The Monetary Clauses in the 1975 Montreal Protocols to the Warsaw Air Convention;* in INTERNATIONALES RECHT UND WIRTSCHAFTSORDNUNG 795 (W. Flume et al., eds. 1977).

41. *See, e.g.,* art. II of Additional Protocol n.2.

42. Arts. 6–8. The text of the Convention is printed at 8 J. MAR. L. & COM. 533 (1977).

43. Art. 6 § 1. *See also* Dubais, *The 1976 London Convention on Civil Liability for Oil Pollution Damage from Offshore Operations,* 9 J. MAR. L. & COM. 61, 66 (1977).

44. Countries which have been pegging their exchange rates to the SDR include Burma, Equitorial Guinea, Guinea, Guinea-Bissau, Iran, Jordan, Kenya, Malawi, Mauritius, São Tomé & Principe, Seychelles, Sierra Leone, Uganda, Viet Nam, Zaire, and Zambia. IMF, 34 INT'L FIN. STATISTICS 11 (Je. 1981).

45. J. GOLD, *supra* note 15, at 48.

46. The first of these SDR Eurobond issues were successfully marketed in 1975 by Alusuisse International N.V., Sveriges Investeringsbank, and Electricité de France. *Id.* at 59–60. In 1975 U.S. $173,000,000 worth of Eurobonds were denomi-

nated in SDRs. This represented 1.6 percent of the total amount of Eurobonds issued that year. According to data collected by the World Bank, no SDR-denominated Eurobonds were issued in 1976 or 1977. 7 IMF Survey 236 (1978).

47. The Arab Monetary Fund, established on February 2, 1977 by agreement of 20 Arab states, is designed to promote exchange stability, to develop Arab financial markets, to make loans to member states, and to pave the way for a unified Arab currency. *Arab Monetary Fund to Provide Loans, Technical Assistance to Member States,* 7 IMF Survey 69–70, (1978).

48. J. Gold, *supra* note 15, at 48–50.

49. *Id.* at 62–64.

50. *See* chap. 6 *supra,* at pp. 171–72.

51. 6 IMF Survey 347 (1977).

52. G. Delaume, *supra* note 2, at 258; Silard, *supra* note 1, at 414–15.

53. Silard, *supra* note 1, at 417–18.

54. *Id.* at 419–20.

55. The discussion in this section talks in terms of only two currencies: the currency of account *(moneta in obligatione)* and the currency of the forum *(moneta fori).* There are a number of cases where matters are much more complicated. A contract may be governed by the law of country A, use the currency of country B as its currency of account, provide for payment in country C, and be sued upon in country D. For some of the fascinating conflicts of laws problems engendered, *see* Krispis, *Money in Private International Law,* [1967–I] Recueil des Cours 191.

56. According to Mann, countries which permit judgments to be rendered in foreign currencies include Austria, Brazil, Denmark, Egypt, Germany, Italy, Norway, Poland, and Switzerland. F. Mann, The Legal Aspect of Money 351 (3d ed. 1971). Great Britain should be added to the list. Miliangos v. George Frank (Textiles) Ltd., [1976] A.C. 443, [1975] 3 W.L.R. 758, [1975] 3 All E.R. 801. Most of the countries which permit judgments to be rendered in foreign currencies do not permit execution in foreign currencies. Normally the defendant can pay the foreign money judgment in the currency of the forum at the exchange rate in effect on the day of payment. F. Mann, *supra,* at 351.

57. A. Lowenfeld, The International Monetary System 247 (1977).

58. The literature criticizing the existing state of the law is extensive. *See, e.g.,* F. Mann, *supra* note 56, at 350–76; A. Nussbaum, Money in the Law National and International 340–445 (rev. ed. 1950); Becker, *The Currency of Judgment,* 25 Am. J. Comp. L. 152 (1977); Dach, *Conversion of Foreign Money,* 3 Am. J. Comp. L. 155 (1954); Drake, *The Proper Rule in Fluctuating Exchanges,* 28 Mich. L. Rev. 229 (1930); Evan, *Rationale of Valuation of Foreign Money Obligations,* 54 Mich. L. Rev. 307 (1956); Comment, *Conversion Date of Foreign Money Obligations,* 65 Colum. L. Rev. 490 (1965).

59. Evan, *supra* note 58, at 310, fn. 8. That statute is the Coinage Act of 1792, 1 Stat. 246, 31 U.S.C. § 371 (1970), which provides: "The money of account of the United States shall be expressed in dollars . . . ; and all accounts in the public offices and all proceedings in the courts shall be kept and had in conformity to this regulation." It is, however, by no means clear that this statute should be interpreted as barring U.S. courts from rendering judgments in foreign currency. Becker, *supra* note 58, at 158.

60. 269 U.S. 71 (1925).

61. *Id.* at 80.

62. 272 U.S. 517 (1926).

63. The last sentence of Holmes' opinion confusingly suggests that the proper time for conversion is the date suit was filed. "It is generally held that the concluding three words of Mr. Justice Holmes are due to an obvious error and that he meant to and did apply the rate of exchange prevailing at the date of judgment." F. MANN, *supra* note 56, at 355. For a fascinating account of why a decree pursuant to judgment-date conversion was entered after an opinion apparently calling for day-of-filing conversion, see Jones, *The Spurious Judgment Day Rule for Converting Foreign Currency into Dollars When Suit Is Brought upon an Obligation Governed by Foreign Law: Deutsche Bank Filiale Nurnberg v. Humphrey Revisited,* 3 INT'L LAW. 277 (1968).

64. *Id.* at 283.

65. 272 U.S. at 518–19.

66. *See* the literature cited in note 58 *supra.*

67. *E.g.,* Tramontana v. S.A. Emprêsa de Viação Aérea Rio Grandense, 350 F.2d 468 (D.C. Cir. 1965), *cert. denied,* 383 U.S. 943; Gutor International AG v. Raymond Packer Co., Inc. 493 F.2d 938, 943 (1st Cir. 1974); RESTATEMENT (SECOND) OF CONFLICT OF LAWS § 144 (1971) and cases cited therein.

68. Re United Railways of the Havana and Regla Warehouses Ltd., [1961] A.C. 1007, [1960] 2 All E.R. 332 (H.L.); Evan, *supra* note 58, at 323; Becker, *supra* note 58, at 155.

69. F. MANN, *supra* note 56, at 358–60; Evan, *supra* note 58, at 323.

70. *E.g.,* Librairie Hachette, S.A. v. Paris Book Center, Inc., 62 Misc. 2d 873, 309 N.Y.S.2d 701 (Sup. Ct., N.Y. Cty. 1970); Evan, *supra* note 58, at 325–36; Becker, *supra* note 58, at 153–54.

71. *Infra,* notes 76–89 and the accompanying text.

72. 193 F.2d 960 (5th Cir. 1952).

73. Breach-date conversion would have given the plaintiff U.S. $17,691, which would have permitted the purchase of 152,500 pesos in 1951. Because of an intervening Mexican inflation of about 67 percent (the Mexican price index increased from 243 in December of 1947 to 405 in mid-1951), the plaintiff required 138,582 in 1951 pesos to enjoy the same purchasing power as 83,149 in 1947 pesos. Note, *Dollar Damage Awards to Foreign Plaintiffs: Conversion and Revaluation of Foreign Currencies,* 61 YALE L.J. 758, 761 (1952). This calculation, ignores any interest on the award. If Mexican interest rates were positive during this period, the 10 percent windfall might turn into a modest deficit.

74. *Id.* at 762. There is the possibility, however, that the plaintiff's own currency might be undervalued with respect to the currency of the forum, so that the exchange rate would remain the same despite the relative depreciation in the forum country's currency.

75. Foreign Judgments (Reciprocal Enforcement) Act of 1933, 23–24 Geo. 5, C. 13 (England); RESTATEMENT (SECOND) OF CONFLICT OF LAWS § 144, Comment (g) and cases cited therein.

76. Miliangos v. George Frank (Textiles) Ltd., *supra* note 56.

77. In the *Miliangos* case, *id.,* the Swiss plaintiff would have received approximately twice as much interest had the English courts applied the interest rates

prevailing in England rather than Switzerland. Bowles & Phillips, *Judgments in Foreign Currencies: An Economist's View,* 39 MODERN L. REV. 196, 198 (1976).

78. The story of the pound's decline is sketched in A. LOWENFELD, *supra* note 57, at 45–82.

79. Schorsch Meier v. Hennin, [1975] Q.B. 416.

80. Art. 106 of the Treaty of Rome provides: "Each member state undertakes to authorize, in the currency of member state in which the creditor or the beneficiary resides, any payments connected with the movement of goods, services or capital, and any transfers of capital and earnings, to the extent that the movement of goods, services, capital and persons between member states has been liberalized pursuant to this treaty."

81. [1975] Q.B. at 426.

82. *See* Point 2 of the Answer to Written Question No. 705/74 of the Commission of the European Communities, Jan. 30, 1975, Official J. of the Europ. Comm. No. C 170/9, Jy. 28, 1975, reproduced in A. LOWENFELD, *supra* note 57, at 280.

83. White, *Judgments in Foreign Currency and the EEC Treaty,* J. BUS. L. 7 (Jan. 1976).

84. *Supra* note 56.

85. In re United Railways of Havana and Regla Warehouses Ltd., *supra* note 69.

86. [1975] 3 All E.R. at 810–11.

87. [1979] 1 All E.R. 421; [1978] 3 W.L.R. 804.

88. *Ibid.*

89. [1979] 1 All E.R. at 429–30.

90. In the *Miliangos* case, *supra* note 56, the negative English interest rate (7.5 percent annually) over a three-year period would have increased the award about £ 30,000. The appropriate Swiss interest rate would have increased the award by only £ 15,000. Bowles & Phillips, *supra* note 77, at 198. The British court, therefore, awarded interest at prevailing rate in Switzerland for a loan of Swiss francs. J. GOLD, *supra* note 15, at 36, fn. 71.

91. A. NUSSBAUM, *supra* note 58, at 340–41.

9

INCOME TAXATION AND INFLATION

Inflation distorts the tax structure in myriad ways. Although the real value of *ad valorem* taxes, such as sales taxes, is little affected by inflation, the real value of other taxes, such as real property or nominally specific excise taxes, is substantially reduced.[1] Examination of the effect of inflation on all types of taxes would require an entire treatise and is beyond the scope of this book. Instead, this chapter will focus on the effects of inflation on progressive income taxation, where the distortions are the most important and complex.

The inequities accompanying the redistribution of income through inflation may be compounded by an income tax system that fails to make allowances for the effects of substantial changes in the purchasing power of a nation's currency. The distribution of tax burdens and benefits undergoes a multiplicity of distortions in an inflationary economy, for inflation affects virtually all types of income. The tax systems of most countries are based on the principle of nominalism, which assumes that one dollar or franc is always equal to any other dollar or franc, regardless of when earned or received.[2] They are also based upon conventional accounting concepts, such as historical cost depreciation, FIFO inventory valuation, and accrual basis reporting of gains and losses, all of which paint a distorted picture of real income during inflation.

The net effect of the failure to adjust an income tax for inflation is a substantial reallocation of the fiscal burdens and benefits that the legislature built into the tax structure. Even in stable economies, the allocation of the benefits and burdens in any tax system is unlikely to be ideal from the standpoint of economic efficiency or equity. Few would quarrel with the proposition that virtually any tax system could be improved, though even fewer would agree on the way in which this should be accomplished. Possibly some tax systems might be improved by the failure to adjust them to significant inflation; however, it will be shown that the failure to adjust for inflation makes progressive income taxes more regressive and makes income taxation generally more inequitable.

In addition to compounding inequities, failure to adjust an income tax system to inflation may have a number of undesirable social and economic consequences. For example, inadequate depreciation schedules may lead to declines in productivity and decapitalization of business enterprises. Sharp increments in effective tax rates may promote a significant rise in the rate of tax evasion. Unequal opportunities for evasion may exacerbate existing social tensions and lead to greater tax regressivity.

Adjusting income taxation to inflation is not without its costs. Elimination of "bracket creep," which automatically shifts individual taxpayers into higher tax brackets even though real income remains constant, destroys the countercyclical or automatic stabilizing effect of a progressive income tax. Elimination or deferral of taxation on the paper profits resulting from the increases in the nominal value of inventories may exacerbate the tendency of business firms to hedge against inflation by wasteful inventory stockpiling. Permitting only certain taxpayers to readjust their incomes for inflation may be even more inequitable than denying such adjustments to all; however, any reform program that attempts to eliminate all inflation-induced distortions may be impossible to administer. There are also conceptual difficulties in defining real income; during periods of economic stability, gains and losses resulting from speculation on price changes have traditionally been considered an important component of business income and loss. Whether the costs outweigh the benefits of inflation adjustments depends to a large degree on the magnitude and persistency of a country's inflationary experience.

This chapter begins by describing the ways in which inflation distorts modern income tax statutes. No particular country's income tax statute is used throughout the chapter. Instead a composite model of a modern income tax statute is drawn from the experience of a number of countries in which the income tax serves as an important source of government revenue. The chapter then examines the various statutory techniques that have been developed in these countries to adjust their tax systems to inflation, and concludes with an assessment of the comparative advantages and disadvantages of income tax inflation adjustments.

INFLATION-INDUCED DISTORTIONS OF BUSINESS INCOME

Depreciation

One of the principal sources of distortion in the taxation of business income results from the use of historical cost as the basis for calculation of depreciation deductions. The function of depreciation is to allocate the costs of a productive asset over its entire economically useful life. Modern income tax statutes commonly afford holders of productive wasting assets a deduction for depreciation reserves established in accordance with conventional accounting techniques. Establishment of a depreciation reserve requires estimation of the asset's useful life and its salvage value. The amount that can be charged each year varies in accordance with the accounting technique employed,[3] but tax statutes generally restrict the total depreciation deduction to the historical cost of the asset less its estimated salvage value.

In an inflationary economy such accounting conventions result in the taxation of illusory gains. The assumption that money—the basic measuring unit of the balance sheet—has a constant value is simply not true. As prices rise, the real value of sums charged to a depreciation reserve decreases. At the end of the asset's useful life, the purchasing power of the sums charged against income as depreciation is insufficient to recover fully the real costs of the asset. Another illusory gain results from estimating salvage value in constant currency units. When a fully depreciated asset is sold for more than its estimated salvage value, as is common during inflation, most tax systems regard the difference between the realized salvage value and the originally estimated salvage value as taxable gain.[4]

These illusory gains can be illustrated by supposing that a firm pays $100 for a machine with an estimated useful life of ten years and an estimated salvage value of $10. Further suppose that the total rate of inflation during this ten-year period is 100 percent. At the end of the ten-year period the machine is sold for $20. The firm will have deducted a total of $90 to depreciate a machine with a real cost of $200. If the machine generated $250 in income over its useful life, taxable income would have totalled $160. At a 50 percent tax rate, $80 would have been paid in income tax. If all net income were distributed as a dividend, $40 worth of capital would have been distributed as an illusory profit, and the $80 tax on net income would have taxed away an additional $40 worth of capital. The gain of $10 (the difference between the estimated salvage value and the actual sale price) represents another fictitious profit stemming from inflation's doubling of the nominal salvage value. Hence, restriction of depreciation recovery to historical cost less estimated salvage value imposes a tax on capital by failing to permit a firm to write off fully its real costs.

Illusory Gains and Losses from the Sale or Disposition of Property

When an asset is sold for more than its net basis, part or all of the gain on the sale will be illusory if there has been inflation between the date of the acquisition of the asset and its sale. This is because the currency units in which the asset's cost is stated will be worth less in real terms than the currency units in which the sale price is stated, and more nominal units than were originally spent will be necessary to recover the seller's original cash investment. For example, suppose that a farm in the United States were purchased for $30,000 in 1967 and sold for $60,000 in 1976. Because the inflation rate in the United States was approximately 75 percent between 1967 and 1976, $22,500 of the $30,000 nominal gain was illusory. In order to recover his original investment of $30,000 in 1967 dollars, the seller needed $52,500 in 1976 dollars. If the seller were taxed on the entire nominal gain at a rate higher than 25 percent, the income tax, in effect, would have become a tax on capital.

This same type of nominalist illusion leads to fictitious inventory profits. During inflation, the most commonly used accounting conventions for inventory valuation, FIFO or average cost, considerably overstate taxable profits. FIFO (first in, first out) generates the greatest amount of illusory profits during inflation, for it presumes that the first units sold were the first units acquired. The average cost accounting method generates less illusory inventory profit than FIFO during inflation, for it permits the seller, in effect, to write up to the average unit cost the carrying cost of inventory acquired earlier. Suppose a firm's entire inventory consists of three widgets purchased at different times and prices. The widget purchased on January 1 cost $20, that purchased on June 1 cost $25, and that purchased on November 1 cost $30. The firm sells a single widget on December 1 for $40. FIFO accounting would require reporting a "profit" of $20 ($40–$20). Average cost accounting would require reporting a "profit" of $15 ($40–25). If it is to continue in business, however, the firm must replace its inventory, and during inflation a firm generally must pay more to replace goods than it originally paid to acquire them. If a firm is to maintain the same dividend, reinvestment, and inventory levels, it will have to use some of its taxable inventory profit to replenish its stock. If our widget firm were operating in a stable economy with a tax rate of 50 percent, it could have used $10 of the $40 received to pay its income tax, $20 to replace the product sold, and $10 for dividends or reinvestment. If, however, widget prices rise by 50 percent between January and November, so that it costs $30 to replace the product sold, under FIFO the firm's taxable profit remains $20, or $15 under average cost. Even though the firm must now replace its inventory, there is no source of funds available for dividends or reinvestment under FIFO, while there is only $2.50 under average cost.

If inflation becomes acute, firms may be forced to reduce the size of their inventory in order to pay the taxes levied on illusory inventory gains. These inventory gains are illusory in the sense that they include unrecovered capital costs. As in the case of unrecovered depreciation, the illusion is a by-product of the unrealistic assumption that the currency units used to measure acquisition costs and sales receipts are of equivalent value. In an inflationary economy, the longer inventory is held, the greater the illusory profit on its sale.[5]

LIFO (last in, first out), an accounting method whose use is not permitted for tax purposes in most countries, generates the least illusory profit during inflation, for it presumes that the first units sold were the last units acquired. Under LIFO accounting, our widget firm would have reported a profit of only $10 ($40–$30). Because the time elapsed between acquisition and sale of inventory is much shorter, a firm will have to use much less of its inventory profit to replace goods sold. Only under very tight supply conditions, when firms are forced to dip deeply into stocks acquired some time ago, does LIFO result in significant illusory inventory profits.

Working Capital

A third important source of distortion in the taxation of business income stems from the failure of most tax systems to permit a deduction for the maintenance of the real value of working capital. Every firm must maintain a certain amount of its assets in cash, checking account balances, or similar liquid assets in order to carry on its day-to-day activities. Inflation steadily erodes the real value of this working capital, but very few countries will permit firms to deduct this real loss. If a firm is to continue in business, however, part of its paper profits must be used to replenish the real value of working capital. Replenishment of the real value of working capital is a real cost of earning income, and the failure to permit firms to charge that cost against gross income results in a substantial overstatement of taxable income for most firms.

Gains and Losses from Borrowing and Lending

In inflationary economies, lending institutions and other creditors frequently find themselves in the awkward position of having lent money at negative interest rates, *i.e.,* at rates less than the inflation rate.[6] Although in real economic terms such transactions result in losses to the lenders, most income tax laws not only deny firms a deduction for their losses, but compound the injury by taxing the interest as income. Conversely, firms fortunate enough to borrow at negative interest rates realize real economic gains from being able to repay in depreciated currency. Most income tax laws not only fail to tax borrowers on such real gains, but also compound the benefit by permitting deduction of negative interest payments.

Time Lags between Reporting and Receipt of Income

A fifth source of distortion stems from time lags between the receipt and the reporting of income. Many business firms use the accrual method for reporting income and losses. Currency depreciation between the time gains are accrued and the time payments are actually received causes part of firms' reported income to be illusory, though such illusory gains are normally offset by time lags between income accrual and payment of the tax. Firms receiving advance payments, such as a magazine publisher with prepaid subscriptions, may allocate equal portions, perhaps minus interest, to the entire period for which advance payments have been received, thereby underreporting the real value of that income during inflation.

Conversely, firms that are able to write off losses well in advance of their actual occurrence or to carry back losses to offset income earned in prior years realize gains via inflation. This is because they are able to charge losses suffered in depreciated currency against income earned in more valuable currency. Firms that carry losses forward or write off a loss experienced in the past against present income loose some of the real economic value of that writeoff because of inflation.

Disparate Impact of Inflation on Business Firms

Finally, the capriciousness with which inflation skews the taxation of business income constitutes a further source of distortion. The income of some firms is much more seriously affected by inflation than others, producing inequitable discrimination in effective tax rates. Thus, firms whose fixed assets consist primarily of machines that have to be replaced every few years are more detrimentally affected by inflation than firms whose fixed assets consist primarily of real estate. Similarly, firms that operate primarily with borrowed working capital are normally much less adversely affected by inflation than firms that generate working capital internally.[7] A recent study found that if the economic impact of inflation were properly accounted for on the balance sheets of fifty-four U.S. corporations (thirty industrials and twenty-four utilities), taxable income would have increased for nine and declined for twenty-one of the industrial corporations; all twenty-four of the utilities would have shown increases in taxable income with more than seventeen doubling their net incomes).[8]

Some countries tax the income of business entities in accordance with progressive tax brackets instead of a flat rate.[9] In these countries, inflation further distorts business income taxation by increasing the effective tax rates. This type of distortion is analyzed in the next section in the context of personal income taxation.

INFLATION-INDUCED DISTORTIONS OF PERSONAL INCOME

Personal income taxation shares some of the inflationary distortions which affect business income taxation, such as illusory gains or losses on the sale of property or from borrowing and lending. In addition, people who hold cash or similar financial assets suffer real losses analogous to the depreciation of working capital for business firms. There are, however, other distortions that are more properly treated as aspects of personal income taxation, namely the fixing of personal exemptions or family allowances, deductions, and progressive tax brackets in nominal terms.

Exemptions, Tax Brackets, and Fixed Deductions

Exemption levels, tax brackets, and certain fixed deductions must be continually adjusted to prevent inflation from modifying effective tax rates, thereby distorting the allocation of tax burdens and benefits implicit in the legislature's determination of such levels and brackets. Failure to adjust personal exemptions during inflation progressively lowers the real value of the exemptions. The larger the family, the greater the increase in effective tax rates from the declining real value of personal exemptions. Failure to adjust the width of progressive tax brackets during inflation increases effective tax rates because increases in nominal income automatically catapult taxpayers into higher tax brackets without any corresponding increase in real income. This shifting effect can be seen clearly in Table 4 and Figure 1. Table 4 shows the substantial increases in effective U.S. tax rates from inflation between 1972 and 1979 had the tax law remained constant. Figure I graphically depicts the dramatic decline in real disposable (after-tax) income of British taxpayers between 1961 and 1973 from inflation had tax rates and exemptions remained constant. Failure to adjust the value of nominally stated deductions during inflation progressively undermines the real value of such deductions.

Tax Receipts and Time Lags

In an inflationary economy, lags between the time income is earned and when taxes are paid substantially reduce the real value of taxes collected. Taxpayers who earn the bulk of their income toward the end of the fiscal year are taxed more heavily than those who earn the bulk of their income toward the beginning of the year. To the extent taxes are withheld, the impact of this time lag is reduced. On the other hand, withholding pro-

TABLE 4 IMPACT OF INFLATION ON U.S. INCOME TAX BURDENS IN 1979, ASSUMING NO CHANGES IN THE 1972 TAX LAW
(1979 Dollars)

Single returns

1979 Levels of wage income[1]	*1972 Income tax*		*Hypothetical 1979 Income tax*	
	Amount	*Effective tax rate*	*Amount*	*Effective tax rate*
2,500	0	0	n.a.	n.a.
5,000	216	4.3	509	10.2
7,500	640	8.5	1,006	13.4
10,000	1,000	11.0	1,448	14.5
12,500	1,496	12.0	1,807	14.5
15,000	1,900	12.7	2,341	15.6
20,000	2,829	14.1	3,461	17.3
25,000	3,809	15.2	4,738	19.0
30,000	4,875	16.3	6,179	20.6
40,000	7,285	18.2	9,460	23.7
50,000	10,092	20.2	13,214	26.4
100,000	28,100	28.1	32,463	32.5

Joint returns with two dependents

1979 Levels of wage income[1]	*Reduction from change in law*[2]	*Change due in inflation*	*Total change*	
			In amount of tax	*In effective tax rate*
2,500	0	0	0	0
5,000	0	0	0	0
7,500	−255	234	−21	−0.3
10,000	−608	613	5	0.1
12,500	−599	723	124	1.0
15,000	−385	630	245	1.6
20,000	−401	701	300	1.5
25,000	−483	926	443	1.8
30,000	−549	1,163	614	2.0
40,000	−770	1,930	1,160	2.9
50,000	−861	2,925	2,064	4.1
100,000	−1,236	6,681	5,445	5.4

NOTE: Deductible expenses assumed to equal 23 percent of gross income.

1. Equivalent real incomes are derived from the consumer price index: 1972 = 125.3; 1973 = 133.1; 1974 = 147.7; 1975 = 161.2; 1976 = 170.5; 1977 = 181.5; 1978 = 195.4; 1979 (estimated) = 214.15.

2. The refundable portion of the earned income credit is not included.

SOURCE: Offiice of the Secretary of the Treasury, Office of Tax Analysis; June 17, 1979

duces distortions of its own because it is impractical to require withholding on all forms of income. Taxpayers who are not required to pay withholding taxes on all or part of their incomes enjoy a lower effective tax rate than taxpayers whose taxes are withheld. In addition, the real value of tax refunds from overwithholding is substantially pared by the time lag between the earning of the income and receipt of the refund.[10]

When the inflation rate exceeds the penalty for late tax payments, it becomes profitable (assuming one sparks no criminal prosecution) for taxpayers to borrow from the government at negative interest rates by failing to pay taxes on time. For example, in Brazil prior to November 1962 the penalty for delay in payment of taxes was only 10 percent plus 12 percent annual interest, or a maximum of 22 percent in a year. There was also a ceiling of 50 percent, so that regardless of the number of years tax payments were delayed, the total penalty could not exceed 50 percent of the tax owed. With an inflation rate averaging more than 30 percent between 1959 and 1961, a nontaxable gain of 8 percent a year could be realized simply by not paying one's taxes on time.[11]

Miscellaneous Distortions

In addition to the principal types of business and personal tax distortions described above, most income tax codes contain an assortment of provisions that allow gains or losses to be shifted from one fiscal year to another. Familiar examples are loss carryover provisions, income averaging techniques, or taxation of retirement income. Inflation distorts loss carryback measures by increasing the real value of the benefits accorded. Losses incurred in current monetary units are used to offset income earned in more valuable monetary units. Inflation produces the opposite distortion for loss carryforward provisions. By lumping together current and past income with the same unit of account, inflation distorts income averaging. Smaller benefits are accorded to a greater number of taxpayers than originally intended. To the extent taxation is deferred until a taxpayer's retirement, the tax system is distorted by the government's receipt of its tax revenues in depreciated currency. To the extent retirement income is taxed when earned, the effective tax rate on retirement income is increased substantially by currency depreciation between the payment of the tax and the actual receipt of income.

Many tax codes also contain provisions that vary tax liability in accordance with nominally stated amounts. For example, in the United States the first $25,000 of corporate income is taxed at a preferential rate,[12] individual taxpayers residing abroad can exclude the first $15,000 of earned income,[13] and the first $100 of dividend income can be excluded from

Figure 1. Changes in Real Disposable Incomes with Constant Real Gross Incomes (1961–62 —1972–73) United Kingdom

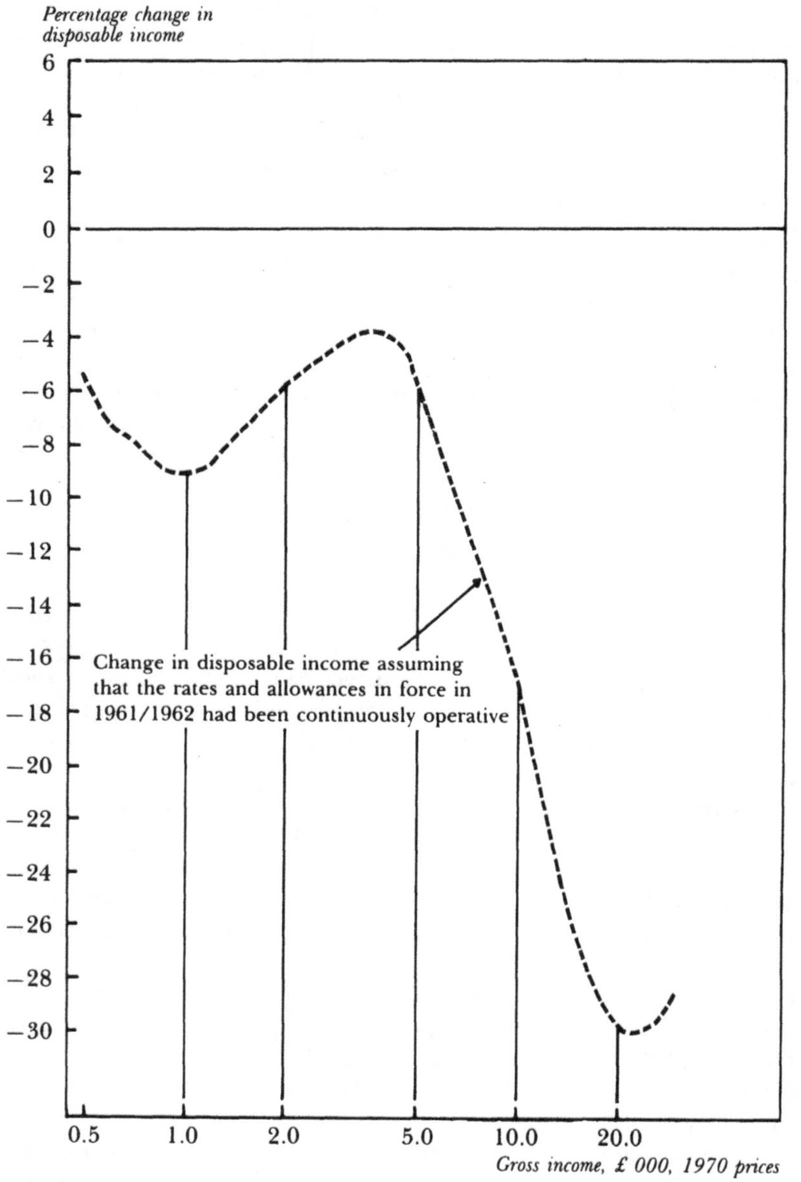

Source: Report of the Comm. on Fiscal Affairs of the OECD, The Adjustment of Personal Income Tax Systems for Inflation 36 (1976). The deflator used in constructing the graph was the consumer price index.

gross income.[14] In an inflationary economy the real economic value of such preferences is steadily eroded. Thus, by May of 1980 inflation had reduced the value of the $100 dividend exclusion, which was enacted in its present form in 1964, to approximately $26 in 1964 dollars.

THE EFFECTS OF INFLATIONARY DISTORTIONS

Increase in Effective Personal Income Tax Rates

The most obvious effect of the failure to adjust income taxation to compensate for inflationary distortions is a substantial increase in effective tax rates. The increase in effective tax rates resulting from the shifting to higher brackets of taxpayers with increased nominal incomes is commonly referred to as an "automatic stabilizer." Ordinarily, it tends to counteract inflationary pressure; the automatic increase in governmental tax receipts helps stabilize the economy by withdrawing funds from the consumer and reducing the need for the government to finance its operations in inflationary ways.[15]

Comparison of columns 2 and 4 of Table 4 further reveals that failure to adjust progressive income tax systems to inflation not only increases effective tax burdens, but also increases the degree of regressivity in the tax structure. At the lowest income level inflation would have increased effective tax rates by more than 100 percent, while at the highest income level the increase would have been less than 16 percent. This is partly because marginal tax rates generally increase more rapidly for lower income taxpayers than for taxpayers at higher income levels, where tax brackets become increasingly wider. This effect is most striking at opposite ends of the income scale. The family whose taxable income had previously fallen below the minimum taxable bracket incurs an infinite increase in real tax rates when inflation shifts it into a taxable bracket. On the other hand, the family already in the highest tax bracket suffers no shifting in marginal rates because of inflation. The decreasing rate of increase in marginal tax rates can be seen more clearly from Table 5.

The increase in regressivity is also caused by fixing exemptions and standard deductions in nominal terms. Both tend to be far more important to lower than to higher income taxpayers.[16] While itemized deductions rise with inflation, the standard deduction frequently contains minimum and maximum limitations expressed in nominal terms. These limitations either make the deduction worth less or cause it to be increasingly unavailable to lower income groups as they experience a rise in nominal income.[17] The importance of personal exemptions to low income families in large part explains why inflation would cause the tax of the married taxpayer with two

TABLE 5 CHANGES IN MARGINAL TAX RATES
UNITED STATES 1975

Taxable Income	*Rate of Increase of Marginal Tax Rates per $8,000 of Taxable Income*
$0 –$8,001	.57
$ 8,001–$16,001	.45
$16,001–$24,001	.21
$24,001–$32,001	.17
$32,001–$40,001	.14
$40,001–$48,001	.04
$48,001–$200,001	.025
Over $200,001	0

SOURCE: Calculated from Sec. 1(a) of the U.S. Internal Revenue Code for married taxpayers filing joint returns.

dependents at the $7,500 net income level in Table 4 to increase by 1,114.3 percent between 1972 and 1979, while the tax for the single taxpayer with the same net income would have increased by only 57.2 percent. The multiple between the rate of increase in the tax for a married taxpayer with two dependents and the single taxpayer falls quickly from 19.5 to 5.2 at a net income level of $12,500, and practically disappears at the higher income levels.

On the other hand, inflation has a tendency to make income taxation more progressive by increasing effective rates on capital gains and by taxing negative interest income. A greater percentage of the income of higher-bracket taxpayers is in the form of capital gains. Poorer taxpayers also hold fewer financial assets than higher income taxpayers, and are more likely to be debtors than creditors.[18] To the extent that an unadjusted income tax system affords debtors the benefit of a deduction for payment of negative interest and requires the creditor to pay tax on such income, its progressivity is likely to be enhanced.[19]

Inflation does not inevitably increase effective tax rates on personal income. The above discussion is predicated upon the assumption that legislatures take no action to counteract the increase in effective rates caused by inflation. From time to time most legislatures adopt widely heralded tax relief measures designed to offset the unvoted and unheralded tax increases produced by inflation. As can be seen from Figure 2, periodic changes by the British Parliament in the tax laws between 1961–62 and 1972–73 entirely compensated for inflation at the lowest and highest income levels, but only partially compensated for inflation in the middle brackets. The experience of the United States is similar. Table 6 reveals that despite several changes in the tax statute designed to offset the

Figure 2 Changes in Real Disposable Incomes with Constant Real Gross Incomes (1961–62—1972–73)[1] United Kingdom

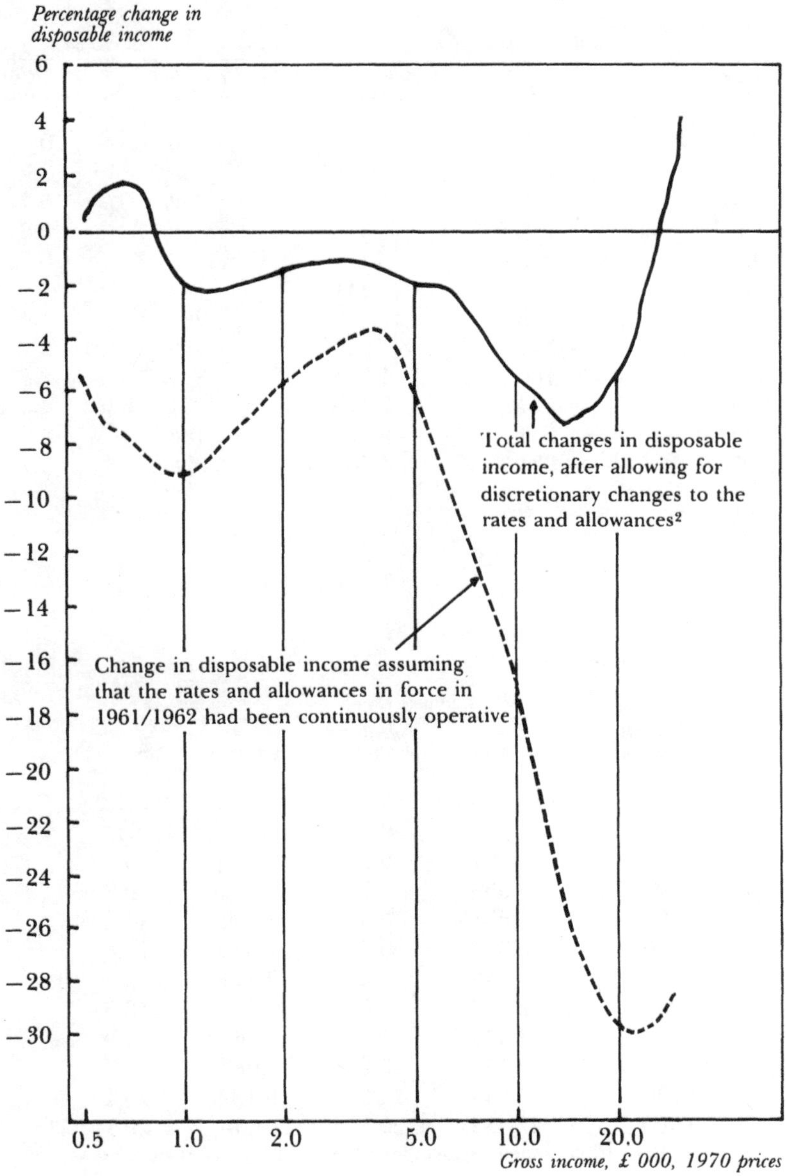

1. Married couple.
2. Vertical distance between curves represents discretionary changes due to changes in the tax allowances and rates.

NOTE: The broken line shows how the interaction between inflation and the personal income tax system would have changed the disposable income of the tax unit, assuming that no offsetting action was taken. The solid line modifies this position by allowing for the actual adjustment that was made to the tax allowances and rates during this period.

SOURCE: Report of the Comm. on Fiscal Affairs of the OECD, THE ADJUSTMENT OF PERSONAL INCOME TAX SYSTEMS FOR INFLATION 36 (1976). The deflator used in constructing the graph was the consumer price index.

TABLE 6 COMPARISON OF EFFECTIVE U.S. TAX RATES BETWEEN 1972 AND 1979 (1979 DOLLARS)

Single returns

1979 Levels of wage income[1]	*Reduction from change in law*[2]	*Change due to inflation*	*Total change: In amount of tax*	*Total change: In effective tax rate*
2,500	0	0	0	0
5,000	−259	293	34	0.7
7,500	−313	366	53	0.7
10,000	−272	348	76	0.8
12,500	−222	311	89	0.7
15,000	−293	441	148	1.0
20,000	−345	632	287	1.4
25,000	−374	929	555	2.2
30,000	−460	1,304	844	2.8
40,000	−574	2,175	1,601	4.0
50,000	−654	3,122	2,468	4.9
100,000	−671	4,363	3,692	3.7

Joint returns with two dependents

1979 Levels of wage income[1]	*1972 Income tax: Amount*	*1972 Income tax: Effective tax rate*	*Hypothetical 1979 Income tax: Amount*	*Hypothetical 1979 Income tax: Effective tax rate*
2,500	0	0	n.a.	n.a.
5,000	0	0	n.a.	n.a.
7,500	21	0.3	255	3.4
10,000	369	3.7	982	9.8
12,500	668	5.3	1,391	11.1
15,000	989	6.6	1,619	10.8
20,000	1,713	8.6	2,414	12.1
25,000	2,458	9.8	3,384	13.5
30,000	3,305	11.0	4,468	14.9
40,000	5,153	12.9	7,083	17.7
50,000	7,259	14.5	10,184	20.4
100,000	22,433	22.4	29,114	29.1

NOTE: Deductible expenses assumed to equal 23 percent of gross income.

1. Equivalent 1972 and 1979 real incomes are derived from the consumer price index: 1972 = 125.3; 1979 (estimated) = 214.15

SOURCE: Office of the Secretary of the Treasury, Office of Tax Analysis, June 17, 1979

effects of inflation, between 1972 and 1979 effective tax rates in the United States have risen from 1 to 5 percent for taxpayers with taxable earned income in excess of $12,500.[20]

Increase in Effective Tax Rates on Business Income

Inflation increases the effective tax rate on most businesses by bloating taxable profits. A great portion of these illusory profits stem from unrecovered depreciation and inventory gains. With an inflation rate of about 10 percent in 1974, the Secretary of the Treasury estimated that 68 percent of the reported net profits of U.S. nonfinancial corporations would disappear if profits were adjusted to reflect the costs of replacing inventory sold and the productive capacity consumed.[21] A more recent highly sophisticated study by Martin Feldstein and Lawrence Summers concluded that a 6.8 percent annual inflation had increased the 1977 tax burden on nonfinancial U.S. corporate income by more than $32 billion, a sum amounting to 69 percent of the real after tax capital income of the nonfinancial corporate sector. This means that inflation had raised the effective tax rate on this sector by 53.5 percent—from 43 percent to 66 percent—principally because of understated depreciation allowances.[22]

In a highly inflationary economy such as Brazil, the effect of inflation on effective tax rates prior to the adoption of a comprehensive adjustment scheme was even more striking. A study by Professors Werner Baer and Mario Simonsen found that in 1962 more than 43 percent of the reported profits of twenty large Brazilian industrial corporations in 1962 was attributable to unrecovered depreciation. They also calculated that more than half the reported profits of some 7,000 Brazilian firms between 1958 and 1962 resulted from illusory inventory gains. Since these firms held 77 percent of their net assets in working capital, in 1963, when the inflation rate was approximately 80 percent, they would have had to earn a net nominal after-tax profit of 61.6 percent on the value of their assets at the beginning of the fiscal year just to maintain the real value of their capital.[23] This posed a Catch 22 situation, for such earnings would have triggered steep excess profits taxes, rising as high as 50 percent. In addition, certain corporations were subjected to a further 30 percent tax on increases in their reserves in excess of paid-in capital. Thus, firms which attempted to replenish the real value of working capital found themselves subject to both excess profits taxes and the 30 percent additional tax on increases in their reserves.[24]

Decapitalization of Business Firms

Failure to permit inflation adjustments during severe inflation sharply increases risks of decapitalization of business firms. Corporate managers, to say nothing of investors and creditors, are sometimes deluded by fictitious, inflation-induced profits shown on their firms' balance sheets and use these profits as a source for dividends.[25] Because restrictions on dividend payments contained in corporation laws are framed in nominal terms, they offer scant protection against decapitalization in real terms. Prior to the institution of a comprehensive scheme for monetary correction of balance sheets in the mid-1960s, many Brazilian firms unwittingly decapitalized themselves through unrealistic dividend policies.[26] A 1980 study by Price Waterhouse of 215 large U.S. companies to which FAS 33 applies disclosed that if the earnings of firms in the retailing and utilities sectors were restated in constant dollars, dividend payouts amounted to 299 and 543 percent respectively of net earnings.[27] These figures indicate that firms in these sectors have been decapitalizing themselves by paying dividends on illusory profits.

A nominalist tax system in an inflationary economy also has a tendency to encourage business policies leading to bankruptcy. The tendency to decapitalize by unrealistic dividend policies is exacerbated by payment of taxes on illusory profits. Moreover, during inflationary periods, the tax structure encourages firms to finance as much of their operations as possible through increasing debt rather than equity. Even negative interest payments are deductible, and any gain on repayment of debts in depreciated currency is tax-free. Hence, it becomes more advantageous for business firms to increase debt rather than equity. The combination of unwitting decapitalization and increased leveraging has pushed many business firms over the brink of bankruptcy.[28]

Discouragement of Capital Investment and Savings

Another pernicious effect of inflation on a nominalist tax system is the discouragement of capital investment and savings. Adherence to conventional accounting principles, such as historical cost depreciation and inventory profits determined by FIFO or average cost, prevents firms from recovering their true capital costs. Inflation, therefore, discourages firms from making investments, particularly in capital intensive technologies with assets that have relatively long expected lives. Instead, it encourages firms to retain obsolete plant and equipment and to purchase inventory and capital assets with relatively short lives.[29] At the same time, firms have greater difficulty in attracting new equity capital because prospective investors eventually perceive that relatively low rates of tax on corporate profits and capital gains are in fact very high rates when inflation is factored in. Martin Feldstein and Joel Slemrod recently analyzed the $4.6 billion in nominal capital gains on corporate stock upon which U.S. individuals paid taxes in 1973. Their study revealed that the $4.6 billion gain, when adjusted for inflation, was actually a loss of nearly $1 billion.[30] The tax structure encourages spending and discourages savings by taxing savers on the nominal amount of interest income and permitting debtors to deduct the nominal amount of interest paid. This means that prospective investors insist upon higher rates of return, and that many investments that would have generated a sufficiently attractive rate of return in a stable economy will not be made in an inflationary economy.[31]

Increase in Tax Evasion

Substantial inflation has a decided tendency to increase the rate of tax evasion.[32] In Argentina high rates, coupled with the sentiment that paying an inflation tax and an income tax amounted to double taxation, spurred huge increases in the tax evasion rate.

> Tax ethics in Argentina, before inflation set in, were no better or worse than in the majority of the southern European countries, and perhaps they were better than in some of them. But . . . a feeling quickly spread that tax evasion was justified. The Argentine taxpayers became convinced that their only protection against a cheating government, which was debasing through inflation the value of their incomes and properties, was to use any method compatible with personal security to lower their contribution to the government.[33]

The large growth in the underground economies of the United States and England, two countries that have traditionally enjoyed a reputation for unusually high degrees of taxpayer compliance, is a phenomenon associated with continual inflation. No one knows with any degree of certainty the extent of evasion resulting from inflation's increase in effective tax rates, but estimates place the total at strikingly high levels.[34]

INFLATION ADJUSTMENT TECHNIQUES

Most countries make periodic changes in their tax structures to offset the effects of inflation. These have often been temporary, partial adjustments, such as permitting a one-shot fixed-asset revaluation or a cut in progressive tax rates. In recent years, however, a substantial number of nations have adopted a wide variety of techniques for automatically adjusting their income tax laws to inflation. The next two sections will describe and analyze the types of inflation adjustments that have been used to adapt business income and personal income taxation to inflation.

Business Income Tax Adjustment Techniques

Depreciation Adjustments

Many countries have enacted measures permitting or requiring firms to revalue their fixed assets, both to make balance sheets more realistic and to increase the amount of depreciation that can be written off for income tax purposes. There are basically two revaluation methods: (1) monetary correction of historical cost, and (2) valuation at current or replacement cost.[35]

The first technique involves writing up a depreciable asset's cost basis through multiplication by a coefficient derived from a general price index. Depreciation is then calculated as a percentage of the asset's monetarily corrected basis. Suppose an asset with a useful life of five years and no salvage value had been purchased in 1975 for $100. Further suppose straight line depreciation and a 20 percent inflation rate between 1975 and 1977. Under a monetary correction approach, the basis could be written up to $120, permitting the taxpayer to write off $24 in 1977. If the price index registered another 10 percent inflation in 1978, the taxpayer would be able to write off $26 (130 divided by 5). A variation of this technique is to correct monetarily only the annual depreciation deduction. Thus, straight-line depreciation for an asset costing $100 with a five-year useful life and no salvage value would be $20 a year in nominal terms. With a 20 percent inflation since the time of acquisition, the taxpayer would be allowed to write off $24, the same amount as in the prior example. If the price index registered another 10 percent inflation in 1978, the taxpayer would be allowed to write off 1.3 times $20 = $26. Whether one monetarily corrects the floating basis or the depreciation allowance, the resulting deduction is the same.[36]

Replacement-cost depreciation requires owners of depreciable assets to calculate depreciation on the current cost of replacing each depreciable asset. Technically, replacement-cost depreciation is not an inflation adjustment. Even if the value of money remains stable, the cost of replacing certain depreciable assets may increase or decrease. Nonetheless, replacement-cost depreciation acts as an inflation adjustment. In theory, replacement-cost depreciation involves an appraisal of the current value of each depreciable asset. Because machinery, plant, and equipment purchased years ago may be unavailable, in practice, replacement cost is often determined by applying coefficients derived from specific price indexes to groups of assets, or estimating the current economic value to the business of groups of assets by the income they generate.[37] Thus, if the cost of replacing the two-year old asset in our previous example were $100 in 1977, the taxpayer would be allowed to write off one-fourth of $100 in 1977. If the replacement cost remained the same in 1978 as it was in 1977 despite the extra year of use, the taxpayer could write off one-third of $100.

The more specific the index used to correct historical cost, the more the monetary correction method resembles the replacement cost method. Correspondingly, if an index is used to estimate replacement cost, the more generalized the index, the more the replacement cost method resembles the monetary correction method.[38]

Several variations on these two basic revaluation themes have been adopted by more than twenty countries since World War II.[39] Most have opted for some form of monetary correction of historical cost, but they have varied widely in the choice of an index. Brazil and Chile, which have built comprehensive inflation adjustments into their tax structures, mandate annual monetary correction of the historical cost of all depreciable assets. Brazil uses coefficients derived from the wholesale price index,[40] while Chile uses coefficients derived from the consumer price index.[41] Between 1945 and 1959 France permitted adjustment of fixed assets in accordance with coefficients derived from the construction materials, lumber, and steel products components of the wholesale price index.[42] During the 1950s, Japan provided for the revaluation of both depreciable and nondepreciable assets in accordance with coefficients derived from the wholesale price index, consumer price index, or a real estate price index.[43] Between 1948 and 1954 Austria gave taxpayers the option of monetarily correcting the cost of depreciable assets or correcting the depreciation allowance. These options should have theoretically produced the same result, but the wording of the latter alternative permitted taxpayers to take depreciation on assets that had already been fully depreciated.[44] After two supposedly once-and-for-all revaluation measures, in 1972 Argentina placed mandatory monetary correction of all depreciable assets on a permanent basis. This correction is now based upon coefficients derived from the wholesale price index for nonagricultural commodities.[45] After permitting a one-time readjustment of fixed assets to market value in 1974 and a 14 percent writeup for fiscal year 1977, Colombia recently adopted legislation permitting annual revaluation of fixed assets. In fiscal years 1978 and 1979, Colombian taxpayers were allowed to revalue their fixed assets annually by 60 percent of the increase in the consumer price index for wageearners. Starting in fiscal year 1980, taxpayers can revalue by 100 percent of the September to September increase in the consumer price index for wageearners.[46]

Taiwan permits business firms to revalue their fixed assets free from tax whenever the wholesale price index has risen by 25 percent above its January 1, 1967 level or 25 percent since the last revaluation.[47]

Only a few countries have adopted replacement cost revaluation for depreciation purposes. Immediately following World War II Belgium, Germany, and the Netherlands permitted one-shot revaluations based upon taxpayers' appraisals of replacement costs of assets acquired prior to the start of the war. Belgium limited the revaluation to two and one-half times 1939 values, less physical wear and tear, while the Netherlands limited revaluation to twice the 1949 depreciated book value.[48] The revaluation legislation adopted by West Germany in 1949 permitted fully depreciated assets to be written up to one-third their replacement cost.[49] In 1954 Mexico permitted all industrial and agricultural enterprises to revalue their fixed assets up to a limit of 40 percent over book value.[50]

A few countries have combined aspects of monetary correction and replacement-cost depreciation revaluation. In 1961–63 and again in 1973, Spain permitted monetary correction of the historical cost of fixed assets, tangible assets, and patents in accordance with coefficients published by decree.[51] Monetary correction could not exceed either fair market value or current replacement cost less accumulated depreciation. Alternatively, the taxpayer could establish a supplementary depreciation fund by allocating the difference between replacement cost and current book value over the remaining useful life of each depreciable asset.[52]

In 1976 Peru adopted a statute requiring firms to revalue their fixed assets periodically in accordance with coefficients derived from a price index for replacement of similar assets.[53] Such revaluations, which are presently being required annually, can be used for depreciation purposes, but the amount of revaluation gain is subject to a special tax. The rates for this special tax have varied from 2 to 4 percent in 1977, 3 to 10 percent in 1978, and 2 to 5 percent in 1979.[54]

Since 1973 Bolivia has authorized its Executive Branch to permit firms to revalue their assets for depreciation purposes whenever changes in exchange rates, the general price level, or prices of specific assets exceed 15 percent. An Executive Decree issued in 1977 required all firms to revalue their fixed assets of the end of 1976 by 5 to 300 percent, depending up date of acquisition. In no case, however, can the new value exceed current market value of the asset, and a 5 percent tax is levied on the revaluation gain.[55]

Uruguay has long required annual revaluation of fixed assets in accordance with replacement costs. Nevertheless, the tax authorities have used of a series of minimum and maximum coefficients; the minimum coefficients vary more or less with changes in the consumer price index, while the maximum coefficients are about 18 to 25 percent higher than the minimum coefficients.[56]

In 1975 Italy enacted a unique revaluation measure that allowed depreciable assets acquired prior to 1974 to be revalued in accordance with coefficients approximately derived from the consumer price index. Alternatively, a business firm could increase the book value of all of its assets by 50 percent of its net worth at the end of 1971. Sums resulting from either writeup method could be placed into a tax-free reserve, which could be used to issue bonus shares or increase existing par values. Under either method the book value of the revalued assets could not exceed their current market value.[57] While Italy appears to have joined two dissimilar inflation adjustments as alternatives, this conceptual marriage does have the advantage of aiding the firm with relatively few depreciable assets acquired prior to 1972.

Most of these asset revaluation measures have been transitory attempts to correct previous inflationary distortions. The majority have been optional and have required firms to capitalize the surplus generated by revaluation.[58] Most have accomplished little because they imposed a tax, ranging from 0.5 to 10 percent, on the revaluation gain.[59] Because revaluation represents neither a real profit to a firm nor a source of funds with which to pay the tax, many firms elected to forego the long-term benefits of revaluation. Even where revaluation was compulsory, many firms tried to evade it.[60] Imposing a tax on revaluation gains generally makes sense only in a purely formal, noneconomic context, because revaluation is nothing more than an accounting entry increasing the figure representing the value of the assets on the asset side of the balance sheet and a corresponding figure on the liability side.

One-shot revaluation measures have also been difficult to administer. Special returns or forms must be filled out requiring substantial data. Because of the nonrecurrent nature of these revaluation laws, inequitable discriminations against similarly situated taxpayers invariably result. If taxpayers have inside information about the timing of a revaluation measure, acquisition and sale dates can be manipulated to maximize tax advantages. Consequently, in South America, where inflation has been a perennial problem, nine countries have made revaluation of fixed assets a permanent part of their income tax legislation.[61]

Revaluation of fixed assets does have the additional advantage of eliminating most of the fictitious gains upon the sale of such assets. Ideally, the basis of every asset should be readjusted for monetary depreciation whenever it is sold. With one-shot fixed asset revaluations, there is ample opportunity for inflation to produce substantial fictitious gains between the date of sale and the last revaluation. The problem of capital gains will be treated more specifically under personal income taxation, *infra.*

Inventory Valuation Adjustments

Far fewer countries have permitted inflation adjustments for inventories than for depreciable assets. Correcting illusory inventory profits is conceptually more difficult than adjusting depreciation for inflation. Moreover, tax authorities have been justifiably concerned about the greater opportunities for manipulation of inventory figures.

One method of eliminating the great bulk of illusory inventory profits is the use of LIFO accounting. Most countries, however, will not permit

LIFO accounting to be used for tax purposes. Moreover, even in countries which permit the use of LIFO for tax purposes, many firms continue to use FIFO or average cost. One of the principal reasons for refusing to switch to LIFO in the United States has been the desire to display higher earnings to shareholders and prospective investors.[62]

Most of the methods that have been employed to correct inflationary distortions of inventory accounting have been *ad hoc* and fairly crude. Between 1947 and 1951 Austria evolved a rough technique that tied the amount of inventory adjustment to rates of inventory turnover. In 1947 firms were permitted to value inventories at twice their cost, on the theory that though the price index had increased by more than 100 percent, most inventories would have turned over at least once; however, for some unexplained reason, the total value of this reduction could not exceed two-thirds of taxable income.[63] In 1950 Austria again permitted inventories to be written up, this time by 15 percent, roughly half the rise in the wholesale price index in the prior year. This writeup had to be reduced whenever a firm turned over its inventory faster than twice a year. The theory was that the faster the turnover rate, the less a firm needed the tax-free inflation adjustment.[64] The Austrian statute sensibly recognized that inflation did not affect the inventory profits of all firms equally, but this crude adjustment scheme sought to differentiate inventory turnover on a value basis rather than on a quantity basis. Inventory turnover rates were obtained by adding the cost of opening inventory and inventory purchases, subtracting closing inventory, and dividing by opening inventory. This valuation technique tended to produce an artifically high rate of inventory turnover.[65] In 1951 Austria abandoned any attempt to correlate the inventory adjustment to changes in the price indexes for the relevant readjustment period. Firms were simply allowed to deduct 90 percent of the difference between the average cost of opening and closing inventory. Instead, the inventory deduction was reduced by 2.5 percent for each decimal by which a firm's annual rate of turnover exceeded three.[66] Had this method not suffered same deficiency in calculation of turnover rates as its predecessor, it would have been a fairly effective adjustment technique for most firms.

During the Fourth Republic, France adjusted inventories for inflation by setting up tax-free reserves for inventory replenishment. In 1949 firms were allowed to set up a nontaxable reserve consisting of the lesser of one-half the value of the 1948 closing inventory, or the difference between the 1948 opening and closing inventory. This crude adjustment was originally available only to manufacturing enterprises. The following year it was extended to commercial firms; however, the reserve was reduced for commercial firms that turned over their inventories faster than .5 times during a year.[67] In 1952 the French introduced the concept of essential inventory *(stock indispensable)* as a device for distinguishing between illusory inventory profits and real operating profits.[68] In theory each business firm was entitled to set up a tax-free reserve equal to the amount necessary to permit the firm to reconstitute or maintain the amount of inventory essential for the continuing functioning of the firm. This meant that if a firm had an essential inventory of 100 widgets carried on the books at a cost of 10 francs each, and the cost of replacing widgets increased to 15 francs each, a reserve of 500 francs could be deducted from taxable income. In practice, the system operated somewhat differently, for essential inventory was defined as average closing inventories for 1949 and 1950 (later extended to a five-year average) based upon quantity for raw materials and value for finished and semifinished products. If a firm expanded, reduced, or changed its activities, the tax definition of essential inventory simply did not correspond with reality. Moreover, the system gave rise to such an extraordinarily complex set of rules that only the larger French firms, as a practical matter, were able to take advantage of the special inventory reserve.[69] This system permitted French firms to eliminate virtually all illusory gains on those inventories defined as essential. According to the tax authorities, it also permitted elimination of real gains as well, particularly when firms financed their inventories on credit.[70] In 1959, when theoretically the franc was stabilized, this system of inventory adjustment was abolished. Since 1959 French tax law has permitted an adjustment for extraordinary increases in inventory costs. If the price of an item of inventory increases by more than 10 percent during a two-year period, the excess above 10 percent may be transferred to a temporary tax-free reserve *(provision pour hausse des prix).* At the end of the sixth year after any deduction has been taken, the amount added to the reserve must be restored to taxable income.[71]

The French adjustment for extraordinary increases in inventory prices was borrowed from West Germany, which permits establishment of an identical tax-free inventory valuation reserve in any year in which inventory prices increase by more than 10 percent.

The Scandinavian countries have given firms the option of creating tax-free inventory reserves up to a maximum percentage of closing inventory values. In Sweden these maximum percentages are 100 percent for compulsory storage inventories governed by special regulations, and 60 percent for other inventory items. In Denmark the maximum percentage is fixed at 30 percent. In Norway the maximum percentage is negotiated with the tax authorities, who usually limit the tax-free inventory reserve to 20 to 30 percent of closing inventories. In practice, the reserves set aside in one year are written back in the next, but a firm can immediately create a new reserve up to the maximum limit.[72]

Another type of inventory adjustment, an arbitrary flat rate method, was adopted by Uruguay in 1967. Businesses were entitled to deduct from gross income 40 percent of the value of opening inventories, provided the deduction did not exceed taxable income. This 40 percent deduction was reduced to 10 percent in 1968, raised to 15 percent in 1972, and upped to 25 percent in 1980.[73] The inventory deduction must be capitalized as a reserve for the maintenance of working capital. There are two basic problems with Uruguayan inventory deduction. First, the amount of the deduction is essentially arbitrary. There is no correlation between the percentage by which taxable profits can be reduced and the rate of inflation. Second, this type of inflation adjustment encourages firms to build up inventory well beyond the needs of the business and tends to stoke the fires of inflation by artificially stimulating demand for inventory goods.

An even more capricious method was adopted in England in Article 18 of the 1975 Finance Act, which allowed companies to value their closing inventories at the same figure as opening inventories plus 10 percent (increased to 15 percent in 1976) of their profits for fiscal year 1973.[74] From a theoretical standpoint, this inflation adjustment is a nightmare. It matters not whether the increase in inventories is attributable to inflation or simply a larger volume of inventory. The system encourages firms to stockpile inventories and penalizes those who cut back. It is advantageous to firms that operate on low profit margins and disadvantageous to those with high profit margins. Although intended as a transitory measure, the British promptly extended this form of inventory adjustment for three more years.

One of the crudest inventory adjustments was enacted in Argentina at the end of 1976.[75] Firms were permitted to revalue inventory at the cost of last purchase or the market price on December 31, 1976. Those firms taking advantage of the statute, however, were required to pay a tax of 8 percent of the amount of inventory writeup. This 8 percent toll charge amounted to a direct levy on illusory profits.

A more sophisticated inventory adjustment has recently been adopted by Australia and Israel.[76] Australia permits industrial and commercial firms to write up their initial inventory by one half the percentage increase in the goods component of the consumer price index during the fiscal year. Israel has virtually the identical measure; the only significant differences are that the write up is limited to manufacturing firms and is based upon the domestic industrial products component of the wholesale price index. From a conceptual standpoint the chief difficulties with these measures are: (1) they offer only partial relief from taxation of illusory inventory profits; (2) they fail to differentiate between inventory purchased with a firm's own funds and that purchased by borrowing; and (3) they invite firms to maximize the deduction by artificially building up inventory values at the start of the fiscal year. In addition, there is no good reason for limiting Israel's inventory adjustment to corporate manufacturing firms.

Conceptually, there are two methods which would entirely eliminate illusory inventory profits. These are the counterparts of replacement cost and monetary correction for asset revaluation, NIFO (next-in-first-out) and monetarily corrected FIFO. NIFO would tax a firm only on the difference between the price of goods sold and actual replacement cost. Monetarily corrected FIFO would adjust historical cost by the change in a general price index since the item entered inventory. If the replacement cost of inventory rises by exactly as much as the general price index, the two methods should produce identical results. If the price index rises by more than the replacement cost of the inventory, the monetarily corrected FIFO will shield the difference from taxation, giving the firm a tax-free real profit. If the price index rises by less than the replacement cost, monetarily corrected FIFO will tax the illusory gain represented by the difference.

A reasonable approximation can be obtained by revaluing opening inventories by average unit book prices at the close of inventory. For most firms this would be a simple and fairly effective way of eliminating inflationary inventory profits. Because of its greater administrative feasibility, the Australian Committee of Inquiry into Inflation and Taxation preferred this method over technically more accurate correction methods.[77]

Chile has adopted both NIFO and monetary correction for inventory revaluation. Prior to 1974, Chile from time to time permitted firms to write up their inventories to replacement costs. Since 1974 a tripartite system of inventory revaluation has become a permanent feature of Chile's comprehensive adjustment scheme, discussed below.[78] If a firm has actually ordered or purchased inventory items during the second half of the fiscal year, inventory sold is revalued according to the highest price actually paid for replacement. If inventory items have been replaced only during the first semester of the fiscal year, inventory sold is revalued according to the highest price actually paid for replacement, monetarily corrected by the change in the consumer price index during the second semester. If inventory items have not been replaced during the fiscal year, their book value is revalued by the increase in the consumer price index during the fiscal year. Imported inventory is revalued by correcting its original cost in accordance with changes in the exchange rate. Although there are difficulties in administering this complex adjustment provision, both from the standpoint of fraud prevention and the ascertainment of shifting values, it offers the most complete inventory adjustment yet instituted and virtually eliminates all inflationary distortion.

Gains and Losses from Borrowing and Lending

A complete inflation adjustment for gains and losses from borrowing and lending would allow lenders to reduce their taxable interest income by an amount corresponding to the diminution from inflation in the real value of their loan capital. If the interest rate were less than the inflation rate, lenders would be allowed to deduct the real losses incurred. Conversely, borrowers would be allowed to deduct from taxable income only real interest payments; monetary correction payments or their functional equivalents would be nondeductible. Moreover, if borrowers were fortunate enough to secure loans at negative interest rates, gains resulting from being able to repay in depreciated currency would be added to taxable income. No country has yet adopted such a complete inflation adjustment with respect to gains and losses by individuals, though Brazil and Chile have done so for business income as part of a comprehensive balance sheet adjustment.

Chile has come closest to a complete inflation adjustment for credit transactions by individual taxpayers. The Income Tax Law contains a general rule excluding from taxable income monetary correction gains on all credit instruments to the extent that such gains do not exceed the increase in the consumer price index.[79] Because interest is defined to exclude any readjustment of principal in accordance with the variation in the consumer price index,[80] debtors are denied an interest deduction for monetary correction payments. But they are not required to gross up their income by the gains resulting from borrowing at negative interest rates.

Brazil has no general rule making all monetary correction gains tax exempt. Instead, each statute authorizing monetary correction in particular types of transactions has contained a clause exempting that kind of monetary correction gain from tax.[81] In 1974 Brazil enacted a law exempting from income tax all monetary correction gains on investments by individuals, provided that the adjustment was based on indexed government bonds (ORTNs) and took place no more frequently than quarterly.[82] The same statute instituted a completely different regime for juridical entities. Starting with fiscal year 1975, all Brazilian legal entities have been required to include monetary correction gains as part of taxable income.[83] The statute also changed the manner of determining a firm's deduction for working capital, discussed in the next section, so that for some firms the effect of this reform is counterbalanced. As in Chile, Brazilian borrowers are normally denied a deduction for monetary correction payments.[84]

Prior to 1975 Israel specifically exempted monetary correction gains (called "linkage differences") from taxable income unless realized by a professional lender. Borrowers were correspondingly denied an interest deduction for monetary correction payments. This rule was changed by the Tax Reform Act of 1975, which generally taxes linkage gains, but exempts linkage gains on all bonds traded on the Tel Aviv stock exchange, government bonds, savings funds, and on foreign currency loans from nonresidents to Israeli borrowers.[85] Borrowers who are also holders of tax-exempt indexed bonds are permitted an interest deduction only to the extent the interest paid exceeds the tax-exempt interest and linkage gains received.

Austria, France, and the United Kingdom also exempt monetary correction gains from income tax under certain circumstances. Even though Austrian tax legislation is premised on nominalism, the tax authorities have determined that monetary correction gains are not taxable as interest to a private lender.[86] France characterizes gains from indexation of credit instruments as tax-exempt if received by individuals, provided the credit instrument is not held as a business asset. Gains resulting from indexation on redemption of an indexed bond held as a business asset are treated as taxable gain on the disposition of capital asset.[87] In 1975 the United Kingdom initiated two indexed savings programs, National Savings Certificates for people of retirement age and Save-As-You-Earn (SAYE) deposits for people over the age of sixteen. Both programs are designed to maintain the real economic value of savings by readjusting the face amount each month in accordance with variations in the Retail Price Index. Amounts attributable to indexation, as well as bonuses if held to maturity, are tax-exempt.[88]

For a time Finland employed precisely the opposite approach, exempting interest on ordinary savings deposits but fully taxing both the interest and monetary correction on indexed savings accounts. The theory behind this reversal was quite logical. Tax exemption was designed to compensate ordinary savers for inflation, and such compensation was unnecessary for holders of indexed accounts.[89] In 1957 the Finns introduced two classes of indexed savings accounts: fully indexed and fully taxable Class A accounts, and half-indexed and fully tax-exempt Class B accounts. The Class B accounts, which bore a slightly higher interest rate, were created to attract depositors with high marginal tax rates. When all indexed deposits became tax-free in 1964, Class B accounts ceased to be an economically viable proposition and were formally abandoned in 1966. The fully indexed deposits were eliminated in 1968 when Finland abandoned indexation.[90]

For a brief period Colombia also exempted monetary correction from taxation. Between 1972, when Colombia established a monetarily corrected housing finance system, and 1974, all gains to lenders and savers attributable solely to monetary correction were exempt from income tax. Since 1974 these gains have been taxed, but at reduced capital gains rates.[91]

In tax systems premised on the nominalist principle, courts and tax authorities have regarded monetary correction payments as interest taxable to the creditor and deductible by the debtor.[92] If, however, a monetary correction payment is contingent on the current level of a price index at the date of maturity of an obligation, the debtor may not be permitted to treat such expense as accrued interest.[93]

Although borrowers reap real economic gains if they are able to borrow at negative interest rates, only one country, Argentina, has sought to tax individual taxpayers on such gains. The notion that individual taxpayers ought to consider their borrowing as a source of taxable income has not been palatable even in countries like Brazil and Chile, which have military governments and widespread indexation. Nevertheless, Argentina's military government recently enacted a special tax of 8.5 percent per semester on the outstanding balance of most loans with the National Financial System. The tax is levied on the borrower "to increase the cost of credit so that it will approximate the inflation rate. . . ."[94] This measure does not directly tax borrowers on the amount of their gains from borrowing at negative interest rates because the tax rate is fixed regardless of the actual inflation rate, and the tax is levied on the amount of the debt rather the gain. Nonetheless, it recognizes the principle that borrowers do realize income from borrowing at negative interest rates, and is therefore an attempt to tax some of that gain.

Working Capital

Brazil has pioneered an explicit inflation adjustment for working capital. The practice started in 1964 with Law No. 4.357, which allowed a deduction for changes in a firm's own real "working capital" for the sole purpose of computing the excess profits tax for 1965. The Brazilian concept of a firm's own real working capital differed in several important respects from the traditional accounting notion of current assets less current liabilities. The minuend of current assets included all assets except fixed assets, shares or other firms of equity interest in other firms, and credits whose real value was protected against domestic inflation, such as accounts payable in foreign currency or adjusted by an index clause. The subtrahend included current liabilities except capital accounts and loans whose real value was protected against domestic inflation. The only taxable profit for purposes of the excess profits tax was an increase in a firm's own working capital by more than the annual inflation rate, as measured by the wholesale price index.[95]

In 1965 Brazil for the first time permitted firms to set up, for income tax purposes, a tax-free reserve for the maintenance of the real value of their own working capital, defined in precisely the same manner as in 1964 for the excess profits tax. The privilege of deducting a working capital maintenance reserve was restricted to firms that increased sales by at least 5 percent over 1964 levels and had not increased prices of their domestic products by more than 15 percent in 1965.[96] This attempt to utilize a tax incentive to constrain inflation worked poorly in practice, in large part due to the government's gross underestimation of the inflation rate for 1965.[97] By 1966 the reserve for the maintenance of working capital had been expanded into a comprehensive balance sheet readjustment.

Comprehensive Balance Sheet Adjustments

Brazil, Chile, Argentina, and Uruguay have enacted comprehensive legislation designed to tax business firms on their real income during inflation. These comprehensive adjustment mechanisms, which have evolved from prior partial adjustments, attempt to take into account the effect of inflation on both liabilities and assets. A basic assumption is that elimination of illusory profits from taxation should be offset by including real gains resulting from the ability to repay loans in depreciated currency.

The Brazilian Approach

Brazilian Decree Law No. 62 of 1966 was the logical outgrowth of prior legislation authorizing monetary correction of fixed assets and a reserve for working capital. The law permitted firms to create a partial balance sheet or *balancette* for fiscal year 1968 for the purpose of monetarily correcting balance sheets. Simplified somewhat, the asset side included only fixed assets, along with corresponding depreciation, amortization, or depletion schedules, and credits whose real value was unaffected by domestic inflation.[98] Fixed assets were to be corrected by applying to each asset's historical cost coefficients derived from the wholesale price index. Capital accounts were to be corrected by applying price index coefficients to the opening balance sheet values. Foreign currency obligations and credits were to be corrected by the present exchange rate, while indexed obligations and credits were to be revalued according to the terms of their index clauses. If the sum of the corrected capital and foreign currency and indexed obligations exceeded the corrected fixed assets and hard currency credits, the difference could be used to offset taxable income. On the other hand, if the corrected asset side of the *balancette* exceeded the corrected liabilities, the difference was to be used to offset deductible losses or to increase taxable income.

The mechanics of Decree Law No. 62 can be seen more clearly by considering the following simplified hypothetical balance sheet:

Assets	Liabilities
Cash (C)	Current liabilities (L)
Receivables (R)	Hard-currency loans (F)
Hard-currency credits (H)	Net worth (N)
Fixed assets (A)	

If the firm's fixed assets were all purchased on the date of the closing of the balance sheet for the prior year, the coefficient of monetary correction (c) will be the same for the fixed assets and for net worth, and if the exchange rate differential (e) is the same for all the foreign loans and credits, the calculation of the *balancette* can then be represented by

$$c(N - A) + e(F - H).$$

Since N – A = C + R + H – L – F, the amount that can be deducted or added to profits can, when one goes through the computations, be written as

$$c(C + R - L) + (e - c)(F - H).$$

If c is equal to e, as frequently happens over the long run, the deduction permitted by Decree-Law No. 62 is almost identical with that permitted for "working capital" by Law No. 4.357. If, however, these two factors differ over the short run, Decree-Law No. 62 presents a more accurate picture of the effect of inflation on the firm's real position. If the firm has no deferred credits or deferred liabilities, the deduction permitted by Decree-Law No. 62 corresponds to what is necessary to preserve working capital (in the traditional accounting sense of the difference between current assets and current liabilities) from inflationary erosion.[99]

The underlying theory of Decree-Law No. 62 was that a firm operating with its own capital suffers real losses from inflation, while a firm fortunate enough to operate with the unprotected capital of third parties derived real gains from inflation. Conceptually, these gains and losses should be offset against each other, and the balance should be added to or subtracted from taxable income. Normally, the higher a firm's equity ratio, the more valuable the deduction afforded by Decree-Law No. 62. Although this statute went a long way toward taxing business firms only on their real economic gains during inflation, it did not permit firms to revalue their inventory.

The balance sheet correction provided for in Decree-Law No. 62 was obligatory only for government-controlled, mixed capital (partly private and partly governmentally owned) firms; for all others it was optional. This meant that only firms with relatively low debt to equity ratios would have corrected their balance sheets. Nevertheless, the Brazilian Treasury was sufficiently frightened by the complexity and the projected revenue loss that it never issued the regulations necessary for the statute's implementation.[100] Decree-Law No. 62 graced Brazilian statute books for nearly two years without ever taking effect.

In December 1968, Decree-Law No. 62 was replaced by Decree-Law No. 401, a half-way measure that conditioned an optional deduction of a reserve for the maintenance of the real value of a firm's "own working capital" upon purchase of indexed government bonds (ORTNs) in an amount equal to 15 percent of the deduction taken during fiscal 1969 and 1970.[101] Firms were also permitted to revalue land and construction components of corporate fixed assets beyond the limit of monetary correction upon payment of a 15 percent tax on the additional revaluation.[102]

Decree-Law No. 401 was also never entirely implemented. The Treasury's fear of a substantial revenue loss and the undermining of its fiscal incentives program led Brazil to adopt for four years the Chilean approach of imposing a 20 percent limit on the deduction for a firm's own working capital. The deduction could be suspended entirely if the National Monetary Council deemed it necessary. Another curious amendment denied the privilege of setting up a "working capital" reserve to firms that operated at a loss.[103] This restriction made no sense, for a nonprofitable firm may suffer as much from inflation as a firm that earns a profit, and losses can be carried forward for three years in Brazil for tax purposes.

In 1974 Brazil returned to the approach of Decree-Law No. 62. Decree-Law No. 1.338 of July 23, 1974 required all legal entities to adjust their balance sheets for inflation for fiscal year 1975, but the method of calculating a firm's own working capital differed in a few significant respects from Decree-Law No. 62. All monetary correction gains or losses, as well as all exchange rate gains or losses, with the exception of monetary correction of fixed assets, were deemed taxable. A firm's own working capital was determined by subtracting from net worth its fixed assets net of depreciation. If the firm's own working capital were positive, that sum could be deducted from taxable income, after being monetarily corrected by coefficients derived from the wholesale price index. If the firm's own working capital were negative, that sum, after being monetarily corrected, had to be added to taxable income.[104]

Decree-Law No. 1.338 came close to providing a complete inflation adjustment for Brazilian balance sheets, though it too neglected the problem of inventory adjustment. But it made many Brazilian firms, particularly those with large foreign currency loans, unhappy. The wholesale price index had been rising far more rapidly than the rate of cruzeiro devaluation, producing substantial real economic gains that would now be subject to tax. Equally unhappy were firms that had been operating largely on borrowed capital. Moreover, a number of jurists argued that taxation of negative working capital was unconstitutional. The law generated so much controversy that the tax authorities modified the statute by the issuance of a *portaria* effectively nullifying the requirement that negative working capital be subjected to tax.[105]

Portaria No. 544 reinstated the system of Decree-Law No. 401 for firms operating with negative working capital. Increased liabilities resulting from monetary correction or exchange rate changes on loans used to acquire fixed assets had to be offset against the reserve set up to revalue fixed assets. Monetary correction of a firm's negative working capital was treated as taxable income only to the extent that it reduced the tax-free reserve resulting from monetary correction of loans or exchange rate losses on loans used to acquire fixed assets.[106]

On December 26, 1977, Brazil enacted Decree-Law No. 1.598, which reformulated the tax treatment of monetary correction for corporate balance sheets in order to conform with the 1976 Corporation Law.[107] As under the never implemented Decree-Law No. 62 of 1966, corporations are required to set up a *balancette* for monetary correction. Simplifying somewhat, the asset side of this *balancette* consists of monetarily corrected permanent assets, including fixed assets (with corresponding depreciation, amortization, or depletion schedules) and investments in other corporations. The liabilities side consists of net worth entries, including capital, reserves, and accumulated profits or losses. Each entry is to be monetarily corrected in accordance with variations in the index for indexed government bonds (ORTNs).[108] If the *balancette*'s corrected liabilities exceed corrected assets, the difference is deductible from taxable income. If corrected assets exceed corrected liabilities, the difference is added to taxable income. To the extent this difference represents unrealized gains, however, the taxpayer can place such sums in a special account captioned "Unrealized Inflationary Profit" and defer payment of tax until such time as the gain is realized.[109] Deferred tax payments are monetarily corrected by the same index as ORTNs.

The Brazilian comprehensive adjustment is less comprehensive than it should be, for it does not adjust for inventories, except for real property held by real estate companies. Nevertheless, this comprehensive adjustment has caused a substantial tax "loss" to the Brazilian Treasury and has been one of the factors cited for passage of Decree-Law No. 1.704 of October 23, 1979, which elevated the basic corporate income tax rate from 30 to 35 percent and imposed a 5 percent surtax for firms with net profits above Cr$30 million.

The Chilean Approach

Chile's approach to monetary correction of corporate balance sheets developed differently from Brazil's. Between 1959 and 1964 Chilean companies were permitted to "adjust their net worth annually into current money in accordance with the variations experienced by the consumer price index between the month prior to the date of the balance sheet and the same month of the previous year."[110] This optional adjustment became mandatory between 1964 and 1974. The increase in value from the net worth revaluation went into a tax-free reserve that had to be charged first against revaluation of the book value of depreciable fixed assets and then against revaluation of securities.[111] Only if a balance remained could that reserve be used to offset current income. Because of the government's fear of too great a revenue loss, this offset could not exceed 20 percent of net taxable income.

Chile's partial adjustment mechanism had several disadvantages. It left the book values of Chilean firms unchanged, making financial statements increasingly unrealistic as inflation continued apace. It failed to make any readjustment for inventory. The 20 percent limitation on the use of the revaluation reserve as a deduction from current taxable income was purely arbitrary and subjected many firms to tax on illusory profits. Firms with relatively few fixed assets but relatively large amounts of cash or inventory were especially discriminated against by this limitation.

The Chilean balance sheet adjustment was significantly revamped by Decree-Law No. 824 of December 27, 1974, which requires firms to deduct the total amount of their net worth revaluation from taxable income.[112] This statute eliminated the revaluation reserve concept, requiring firms to revalue directly their fixed assets, shares in other companies,[113] indexed and foreign currency credits and liabilities, and inventory. Fixed assets, regardless of whether acquired with foreign currency or indexed loans, must be revalued in accordance with coefficients taken from the consumer price index. Indexed or foreign currency loans and credits must be revalued in accordance with their respective indexes or exchange rates, and closing inventory must be written up to replacement cost.[114] The amounts by which a firm's assets are revalued must be added to taxable income, while the amounts by which its liabilities are revalued must be charged against taxable income.[115]

This comprehensive revaluation mechanism eliminates the chief defects in the previous partial mechanism and has the effect of taxing firms on their real incomes, assuming that the consumer price index and the foreign exchange rates are suitable proxies for the inflation rate. Firms that derive real economic gains from financing their investments by loans in domestic currency are taxed on those gains by having to include in profits the amount by which those assets have to be written up to reflect currency depreciation during the course of the fiscal year. Firms that suffer real economic losses from inflation's diminution of the value of their unprotected loans or financial assets are permitted to deduct such losses from profits. The net worth deduction permits firms to maintain the real value of the initial net worth by adding to their capital free from tax a sum representing the inflationary erosion of their net worth during the fiscal year. The chief difficulty with this approach is that it subjects heavily leveraged firms to immediate tax on unrealized inflationary gains, an unfair measure that could tip some firms into bankruptcy.

Implementation of the Chilean comprehensive adjustment has had a few problems, despite circulation of detailed rules and regulations by the tax authorities. The principal problem has been the initial revaluation necessary to put the new system into operation. This revaluation was authorized only upon payment of a 35 percent tax on revaluation gains, a rate deemed excessive by many Chilean firms. Consequently, few firms have adequately revalued their balance sheets. Revaluation has been a particular problem with respect to inventories, which probably have become a source of a fair amount of tax evasion. In other respects, the new system has worked smoothly. In its first year of operation comprehensive balance sheet revaluation produced losses of 2.28 billion pesos for 40,044 taxpayers, and gains of 938 million pesos for 23,412 taxpayers. These figures signified a diminution of the tax base of 1.34 billion pesos, which meant a revenue loss equal to 33 percent of the total amount collected in 1975 and 19 percent of the tax revenues budgeted for 1976.[116]

The Argentine and Uruguayan Approaches

In 1978 Argentina, influenced by the experiences of Brazil and Chile, added a quasi-comprehensive balance sheet adjustment to its income tax law.[117] Starting with fiscal year 1978 (or 1979 if the taxpayer so opts), all legal entities are required to adjust their balance sheets annually for inflation by creating a special *balancette* for "monetary net worth" *(capital proprio monetario)*. This *balancette* is created by excluding from normal corporate balance sheets certain assets and liabilities, some of which are corrected for inflation under previously enacted legislation. Excluded from the asset side of this *balancette* are: (a) real property and all depreciable personal property; (b) nonincome producing personal property; (c) intangibles; (d) shares in other companies and payments for future capital contributions; (e) inventories of standing or cut timber; (f) capital contributions not yet paid in; (g) debts owed by related parties or whose terms differ from normal arm's length transactions; (h) research and development expenses to the extent allowed as deductions; and (i) foreign investments producing foreign source income. Excluded from the liability side of this *balancette* are: (a) disallowable or excess reserves; (b) advances for future capital contributions; (c) debts owed to related parties where the terms differ from arm's length transactions; and (d) certain sums owed foreign parents by Argentine subsidiaries.[118]

Liabilities are then subtracted from assets and multiplied by the percentage change in the wholesale price index between the last month in the current fiscal year and the last month of the prior fiscal year. If the result is positive, that sum must be subtracted from taxable income; if negative, the difference must be added to taxable income. In addition, taxpayers required to adjust their balance sheets for inflation must include within taxable income certain gains that are normally tax-exempt, such as interest on government bonds, monetary correction on debt instruments and savings deposits, and increases in the value of securities and foreign currency. Any increase in taxable income resulting from this comprehensive inflation adjustment can be spread over a three-year period, provided dividend distributions are postponed.

In 1979 Uruguay adopted a quasi-comprehensive balance sheet adjustment along the lines of that adopted the previous year in Argentina.[119] This measure requires Uruguayan firms to create a similar *balancette* for monetary correction. Simplifying somewhat, this *balancette* is created by excluding from the asset side of ordinary balance sheets assets devoted to the production of nontaxable income, fixed assets, and investments in other firms not represented by shares. Liabilities are then subtracted from assets and the difference is adjusted by the percentage increase in the wholesale price index between the prior and current fiscal years. The Uruguayan balance sheet adjustment is being phased in over a three-year period. In 1981 the adjustment is limited to 30 percent of the index change, a figure that rises to 100 percent by 1983. If the assets on the *balancette* exceed liabilities, the difference, after monetary correction, is subtracted from taxable income; if liabilities exceed assets, the corrected difference must be added to taxable income.

Both the Argentine and Uruguayan balance sheet adjustments are less precise and comprehensive than the global adjustments presently being used in Brazil and Chile. Indeed, the term "monetary net worth" is a misnomer. Because the *balancette* includes inventory as well as monetary assets, the Argentine and Uruguayan approach is really closer to working capital adjustments than to net worth adjustments. The principal advantages of the Argentine and Uruguayan approach is that it is somewhat simpler to calculate than the more comprehensive Brazilian and Chilean balance sheet adjustments. Its principal defect is that it subjects heavily leveraged firms to tax on unrealized gains stemming solely from inflation, although the three-year deferral feature makes it less unfair than the Chilean law in this regard.

Personal Income Tax Adjustment Techniques

Essentially two types of automatic inflation adjustment schemes have been utilized in the taxation of personal income. The most popular technique has been to link tax brackets, exemption levels, and nominally-expressed deductions to a general price index or its functional equivalent. The second technique, adopted by only one Swiss canton, is to deflate current income to currency units of a base year, calculate the income tax in those units, and then reflate the tax to current currency units.

Indexing Brackets, Deductions, and Exemptions

Sixteen countries have adopted some form of indexation of their personal income tax in order to maintain the real economic value of tax brackets, exemption levels, and nominally-expressed deductions, or some combination thereof. The degree to which these measures have corrected inflationary distortions varies considerably.

Automatic Indexation of Brackets, Deductions, and Exemptions

As of 1980, Chile, Australia, Argentina, and Colombia were the only countries that automatically and fully index tax brackets, deductions, and exemption levels. In addition, five states in the United States have recently automatically indexed their state income tax laws.

The pioneer was Chile, which in 1954 began expressing tax brackets, exemption levels, and deductions previously fixed in nominal terms as multiples of the minimum wage *(sueldo vital).*[120] Until 1972 the minimum wage generally had been adjusted each year to reflect the increase cost of living for the previous twelve months, though there were periods of austerity and prosperity in which the adjustment had been lower or greater than the inflation rate. Beginning in 1975 the basic tax unit *(unidad tributaria basica)* replaced the minimum wage as the measuring stick for tax rates, exemptions, and deductions. The basic tax unit, originally fixed at one-half the 1972 minimum wage, is now automatically adjusted each month to reflect the variation in the consumer price index.[121]

In June 1976 Australia adopted legislation automatically indexing its personal income tax to changes in the consumer price index, net of indirect taxes, during the twelve month period ending March 31. The adjustment includes tax brackets, exemptions, and most, though not all, of the deductions expressed in nominal amounts. Like the Canadian indexation legislation, Australian brackets, exemption levels, and deductions do not decline in the event of a decrease in the consumer price index. Australia's indexation scheme went into effect for the first time in fiscal year 1977–78.[122]

Argentina began indexing exemptions and deductions to the consumer price index in 1973, but not until 1977 did it take the additional step of automatically indexing the tax brackets.[123] For a time Argentine legislation adjusted exemptions and deductions in accordance with the rise in the consumer price index for the previous year; however, with prices rising by 183 percent in 1975, the year lag in indexation would have produced a sharp increase in effective tax rates for lower income taxpayers had not special legislation been adopted adding an additional 100 percent to exemption and deduction levels. The statutory scheme was altered in 1976 to adjust exemptions and deductions, as well as brackets, in accordance with the average change in the consumer price index during the year of payment of the tax.[124] Thus, indexation in Argentina occurs with considerably less lag than in Australia, and slightly greater lag than in Chile, which has reduced the lag to only two months. Paradoxically, adoption of indexation in Argentina did not have the effect of preventing inflation from increasing effective tax rates. Between 1960 and 1976 deductions and exemptions had been increasing far more rapidly than the consumer price index because of discretionary adjustments.[125]

In 1977 Colombia adopted legislation, effective in fiscal year 1978, automatically indexing all values expressed in nominal terms in the income tax law, including personal income tax brackets and exemption levels, by 60 percent of the September to September increase in the consumer price index for wageearners. In 1979 this readjustment coefficient was increased to 100 percent of the annual change in the consumer price index.[126]

Five states in the United States have recently enacted legislation automatically indexing their state income taxes for inflation. Starting in 1980, Arizona annually adjusts dollar amounts for deductions, exemptions, and tax rates in its personal income tax by the percentage change in the state consumer price index.[127] Starting in 1979, Colorado adjusts tax brackets, the standard deduction, and personal exemptions annually in accordance with coefficients derived from the "best statistics available," taking into consideration the percentage change in the consumer price index for Denver and the commodity indexes published in the *Wall Street Journal.*[128] Since the end of 1978, Minnesota has fully indexed its personal income tax brackets to the consumer price index for the Minneapolis-St. Paul area; credits and exemptions have been indexed only for tax years beginning after December 31, 1980.[129] An initiative petition to index personal income tax brackets and exemption levels to the consumer price index was approved in Montana, effective for tax years beginning after 1980.[130] In 1980 South Carolina enacted a law, effective for tax years beginning after 1981, indexing tax brackets, deductions, and exemption levels to changes in the consumer price index.[131]

Partial Automatic Indexation Measures

Six countries and four states in the United States have adopted measures indexing some, but not all, of the nominally expressed values in their personal income tax laws. Denmark and Canada automatically index tax brackets and exemption levels each year. Uruguay had a similar scheme in force until 1974, when the personal income tax was all but abolished. Sweden and Belgium take a different tack, annually indexing their tax brackets but not their deductions and exemption levels. The United Kingdom and Peru take still a different tack, indexing deductions and exemption levels each year but not their tax brackets.

In 1969 Denmark began automatically adjusting tax brackets and personal exemptions, but not fixed deductions in accordance with changes in the consumer price index (net of indirect taxes and government subsidies). For each 4 point increase in the consumer price index, brackets and exemptions were increased by 3 percent.[132] This stange adjustment mechanism would have produced steady increases in the real value of brackets and exemptions, for as the price index rose, 4 index points represented an increasingly smaller percentage increase in the consumer price level. In 1972, the tax law was amended to increase brackets and exemptions by 3.5 percent for every 3 point increase in the index with reference to the index number of 90. Simultaneously, the base of the consumer price index was shifted to make the price level on January 1971 equal to 100. The Danish adjustment system also requires the Danish Parliament to vote each year as to whether the basic rates established in 1969 should be modified, though they cannot be increased by more than 5 percent above 1969 levels. The system was again modified in 1974 to index tax brackets and personal exemption levels to the index for hourly wages of industrial workers. Because this index reflects price changes, union power, and productivity increases, Denmark's indexation scheme goes well beyond adjusting for inflation. It is designed to prevent the tax burden from increasing even if real income increases.[133]

In 1974 Canada began automatically indexing its tax brackets and exemptions in accordance with the twelve-month average change in the consumer price index for the period ending September 30. In the event of a decline in the consumer price index, brackets and exemption levels remain at the levels of the previous year. Canada has not yet indexed deductions fixed in nominal terms, such as the standard $100 medical and charitable deductions.[134]

Between 1968 and 1973 Uruguay employed the same kind of adjustment measure as Canada. Technically, only personal exemption and dependent allowances were adjusted for annual changes in the consumer price index; however, the result was the same as in the Canadian system because personal tax brackets in Uruguay were expressed as multiples of the personal exemption. The measure is now moot, because Uruguay virtually abolished its personal income tax as of January 1, 1974.[135]

In 1979 Sweden began expressing tax brackets, but not exemptions and deductions, in terms of a basic unit that is automatically adjusted each year for changes in the consumer price index between August of the prior year and August of the taxable year. For purposes of calculating the basic tax unit, the effect of the value-added tax is excluded from the index.[136]

In 1976 Belgium enacted legislation providing for indexation of its personal income tax. Lower income brackets are fully indexed in accordance with changes in the consumer price index. Middle income brackets are only partially indexed, and high income brackets are not indexed at all.[137]

In 1978 the United Kingdom began to index deductions and exemptions (excluding child allowances) by the same percentage as the increase in the retail price index for the prior calendar year. Tax brackets, however, remain unindexed.[138]

In 1972 Peru adopted a statute fixing personal exemptions and deductions as multiples of the minimum wage prevailing in Lima and Callao at the beginning of each calendar year. Because the minimum wage is largely determined on basis of changes in the cost of living index, Peru has *de facto* indexation for deductions and personal exemptions. There is, however, no indexation of tax brackets.[139]

Four states in the United States have recently instituted partial indexation of their personal income tax laws. For taxable years ending on or before November 30, 1980, the brackets in California's state income tax are indexed for any changes in the California consumer price index in excess of 3 percent. Tax brackets are fully indexed for taxable years beginning 1980, but the 3 percent floor is to be reimposed for taxable years starting on or after January 1, 1982. California has also fully indexed its standard deduction to changes in the California consumer price index.[140] Iowa has enacted legislation phasing in complete indexation of tax brackets in accordance with changes in the implicit GNP deflator. Brackets are to be adjusted by one-fourth the percentage change in the GNP deflator in 1979, one-half the percentage change in 1980 and 1981, and are to be fully indexed after January 1, 1982.[141] Starting on January 1, 1981, Oregon began indexing its $1,000 personal exemption but not its tax brackets to changes in the consumer price index for Portland.[142] Starting with calendar year 1980, Wisconsin has indexed the tax brackets in its state income tax to the U.S. all urban consumer price index. There is, however, a ceiling of 10 percent on any increases resulting from such indexation, and the standard deduction is not indexed.[143]

Discretionary Indexing Measures

Six countries have adopted indexation statutes that grant discretion to the tax authorities to index certain combinations of brackets, deductions, and/or exemption levels. Some grant broad discretion to the tax authorities, while others spell out precisely under what circumstances and to what extent this discretion may be exercised.

Brazil has long had a discretionary indexing mechanism that is largely automatic in practice. Between 1961 and 1964 exemptions and tax brackets were expressed in terms of multiples of the minimum wage, but the minimum wage was neither changed enough nor at the proper times for income tax purposes. In 1964 Brazil began indexing tax brackets, exemptions, and deductions in accordance with coefficients derived from the wholesale price index. Between 1964 and 1968 cruzeiro values expressed in the tax law had to be monetarily corrected every time the price index rose by more than 10 percent in a single year, or 15 percent in a three-year period. Legislation adopted in 1968 grants the Minister of Finance discretion to correct monetarily all values in the tax laws expressed in cruzeiros, a power used each year to update all values expressed in cruzeiros in the income tax laws.[144] On occasion, however, this power is used to redistribute tax burdens. For example, in 1973 and 1974 brackets for highest levels were adjusted in accordance with the wholesale price index, while the lower level brackets and the exemptions were increased by significantly more. For 1980, despite an inflation rate in excess of 100 percent, Brazilian tax authorities adjusted all brackets, exemptions, and deductions by only 45 percent, producing a substantial increase in effective tax rates.

The Netherlands has a partial, quasi-automatic adjustment scheme. Law No. 259 of April 23, 1971, provides for the annual readjustment of tax brackets, family allowances, and age and disablement deductions by multiplying these figures by a coefficient derived from the consumer price index. The manner in which this coefficient is derived is unique. First, the price index must be adjusted to eliminate the effects of tax changes and subsidies assumed to be directly related to the price of goods. Second, the average price index number from the eighteenth to the seventh month prior to the start of the year in question is divided by the average price index number from the thirtieth to the nineteenth preceding month. Third, the resulting coefficient is sent to the Finance Minister, who has the discretion to reduce the coefficient by up to 20 percent, a discretion normally utilized to the hilt. Moreover, from time to time this adjustment has been suspended by statutory regulation.[145]

In 1966 Iceland provided for annual indexing exemptions, certain deductions, and tax brackets to a special tax index. The tax index was to have been constructed by averaging the increase in prices and real income, but in practice the system has proven highly discretionary. In 1968 and 1969, when nominal incomes fell and the consumer price index rose by 13 percent and 22 percent respectively, no adjustment was made. Nevertheless, as a general rule, annual adjustments have exceeded or equaled the rise in the consumer price index.[146]

In 1967 Luxembourg adopted a measure that requires the government to revise the nominal tax structure whenever the consumer price index during the first six months of the year exceeds by 5 percent its average during the first six months of the previous year. In practice the authorities have adjusted brackets and deductions more frequently. Since 1972 the tax brackets and deductions have been adjusted by the change in the consumer price index.[147]

The French system resembles that of Luxembourg. Since 1968 French law has required restructuring of the personal income tax whenever the consumer price index rises by more than 5 percent in a year. The authorities have considerable discretion in adjusting the system, and have exercised it from time to time to lower tax rates and increase the width of the tax brackets. Except for the lowest income brackets, these changes have almost always lagged well behind the actual inflation rate.[148]

In 1975 Israel joined the burgeoning group of countries indexing their income taxes to the consumer price index. Prior to 1975 Israeli income tax legislation exempted, at the discretion of the Finance Minister, cost-of-living allowances in wages and salaries. Tax credits, exemptions, and deductions are now fully indexed to the consumer price index, but the

Finance Minister has discretion to reduce the amount of adjustment to the tax brackets. During much of the post-1975 period, that authority has been exercised to reduce the rate of indexation by approximately one-third.[149]

Adjustment to the Base Year

The Swiss canton of Basel-Land requires current taxable income to be restated in terms of 1953 francs. This deflation is accomplished by use of coefficients derived from the consumer price index. The tax liability is then calculated in 1953 francs, which are then inflated to current francs by the use of coefficients derived from the consumer price index. This system maintains an existing tax structure in real economic terms, but it is sufficiently cumbersome that it has not been adopted in other countries.[150]

CAPITAL GAINS

Only a few countries have enacted measures specifically designed to eliminate taxation of illusory capital gains. Many countries do not tax capital gains; those that do often tax such gains at lower rates than ordinary income. Taxation of capital gains at preferential rates is sometimes justified as a crude form of compensation for inflation.[151] To the extent that tax systems permit businesses to revalue their fixed assets and to use that stepped-up basis for calculation of capital gains, the great bulk of fictitious profits stemming from inflation are eliminated.[152] The privilege of asset revaluation, however, has generally been denied to individuals.

Four types of inflation adjustment have been utilized in capital gains taxation. The first method, monetary correction of the capital asset's historical cost basis, is technically much superior as a device for eliminating illusory inflation gains from taxation. This technique has been used in Chile and is currently being used in seven countries: Israel, Argentina, Brazil, France, Sweden, Colombia, and Ireland. The second method, a percentage reduction in the tax rate for the length of time the asset has been held, is currently employed only in Belgium, though it was utilized in Israel prior to 1975. The third method, stepping up the original cost basis by a certain percentage for the length of time the asset has been held, is currently used in Belgium, Denmark, Norway, and France, and was utilized in Argentina prior to 1972 and in Colombia prior to 1978. The fourth method, reducing the amount of gain subject to tax by a percentage for the length of time the asset has been held, is currently used in Spain, Finland and Mexico, and is also used in combination with the first method in Brazil and Sweden for real property.

Monetary Correction of Historical Cost

Israel

Israel has treated capital gains derived from real property transactions somewhat differently from other capital gains. The former are subject to a Land Appreciation Tax *(Mas Shevach),* whose rates vary between 20 and 40 percent, depending upon the percentage of profit on the sale. Prior to 1975, the tax was reduced by 0.5 percent for each month the asset had been held beyond the twenty-fourth month up to a maximum of thirteen years. For each additional year the asset had been held the tax was reduced by one percent. The latter are subject to the Capital Gains Tax *(Mas Rivchei Hon),* whose maximum rate was also 40 percent. Prior to 1975, the tax rate on the sale of nondepreciable personalty was reduced by 3.5 percent for each year the asset had been held.[153]

In 1975 Israel enacted a reform that eliminated 90 percent of the gain attributable solely to inflation from taxation. All long-term capital gains are divided into real and inflationary components in accordance with changes in the consumer price index (or the foreign exchange rate for assets purchased with foreign currency) between the date of acquisition and the date of sale.[154] Individuals are taxed at ordinary income rates on the real component of their capital gains and at a flat 10 percent on the inflationary component. Legal entities are taxed at a flat rate of 61 percent on the real component of their capital gains, and a flat 10 percent of the inflationary component. In no event can the entire tax, whether levied on individuals or legal entities, exceed 50 percent of the total gains.[155]

Argentina

During the 1960s Argentina's capital gains tax contained a crude, flat percentage inflation adjustment. The cost basis of automobiles and real property could be increased by 25 percent for each year from the year of purchase to the year of sale.[156] Since 1972 Argentina has provided for monetary correction of a capital asset's adjusted basis between the date of acquisition and the date of sale in accordance with coefficients derived from the wholesale price index for nonagricultural commodities.[157]

Brazil

Brazil treats the capital gains of legal entities as ordinary income, which means that corporate capital gains are adjusted for inflation through the comprehensive balance sheet adjustment. With respect to individuals, capital gains taxation is more complex. Between 1946 and 1966 Brazil imposed a capital gains tax on gains realized by individuals, a tax that was widely evaded by transferring property by using agreements to sell in lieu of deeds. In 1964, as part of the introduction of a more generalized program of monetary correction, Brazilians were permitted to opt for monetary correction of their original cost basis in accordance with coefficients derived from the wholesale price index. The amount of monetary correction was taxed at 5 percent, and the regular income tax was imposed upon the difference between the monetarily-corrected cost and the selling price.[158] This capital gains tax was eliminated at the end of 1966, but reinstated in part in 1974 for persons who entered into more than three real estate transactions in a year, or six in three years (in 1977 these figures were reduced to three transactions in one year, or five in three years). Such persons are taxed on the resulting gain, which is computed by monetarily correcting the historical cost basis by coefficients derived from the wholesale price index.[159] In 1978 the capital gains tax was extended to all gains in excess of Cr$4,000,000 (then about U.S. $191,000) realized by individuals from real estate transfers. To avoid taxation of inflationary profits, the taxpayer was not only permitted to adjust his historical cost basis by monetary correction coefficients, but was also permitted to reduce his taxable gain by 10 percent for each year he owned the property. In 1980 this reduction privilege was reduced from 10 to 5 percent.[160]

France

Since 1964 France has imposed a capital gains tax on sales of real property held by individuals for speculation. In order to take account of normal price increases, taxpayers may increase their cost basis by 3 percent for each year the property has been held up to five years. For each year the property has been held beyond the fifth year the basis may be increased by 5 percent.[161] In addition, individual sellers of unimproved land for building purposes are given the option of increasing their cost basis by 25 percent or by their actual outlays for capital improvements and expenses of acquisition.[162]

In 1976 France adopted a more generalized capital gains tax that utilizes both monetary correction and flat percentage rate inflation adjustment techniques. All short-term capital gains (realty held less than two years or personalty held less than one year) are taxed at ordinary income rates. Medium-term capital gains are divided into two categories. Gains resulting from the sale of real estate held by individuals for two to ten years for speculation continue to be calculated by the preexisting system of readjusting the cost basis by 3 or 5 percent *per annum,* depending upon the length of the holding period. Taxable capital gains resulting from the sale of personalty held between one and ten years, or from the sale of real property held between two and ten years without a speculative purpose, are calculated by adjusting the historical cost basis in accordance with coefficients reflecting the change in the consumer price index between the date of the sale and the date of acquisition. All long-term capital gains, which require that the asset be held for more than ten years, are first calculated as medium-term capital gains. The net taxable gain is then reduced by 3.33 percent for unimproved land for building purposes and by 5 percent for other property, for each year held beyond the tenth.[163]

Sweden

Sweden imposes a capital gains tax on sales of personal and real property. For personalty, the portion of the gain includible in taxable income declines in accordance with the holding period. Three-fourths of the gain is subject to tax for property held between two and three years, but only one-fourth is subject to tax if the holding period is between four and five years. If the asset has been held more than five years, the includible portion falls to 10 percent, unless one can show that the gain does not exceed 5 percent of the sales price. Since 1967 all real property gains have been taxable if the property has been held less than two yers, while only three-fourths are taxable if held longer than two years. The basis of real property is readjusted by the percentage change in the consumer price index since the time of acquisition.[164]

Colombia

In recent years Colombia has employed a variety of techniques for adjusting its capital gains tax for inflation. A 1974 tax reform measure permitted taxpayers to choose between two revaluation methods for movable fixed assets: (1) writing up present basis to current market value, or (2) writing up last year's basis by 8 percent. For 1975 and 1976 taxpayers were permitted to write up the bases of these assets by 8 percent each year. During 1977 that revaluation percentage was upped to 14 percent. During 1978 taxpayers could revalue their fixed assets by 60 percent of the increase in the consumer price index for wageearners. In 1979 this revaluation coefficient was increased to 100 percent of the increment in the consumer price index.[165]

Ireland

In 1978 Ireland began indexing the historical cost basis of capital assets for the calculation of its capital gains tax. Assets sold on or after April 8,

1978 have their cost basis adjusted by the percentage change in the consumer price index between mid-February of the year of acquisition and mid-February of the year of sale.[166]

Chile

Prior to abolition of the capital gains tax in 1975, Chile adjusted capital gains for inflation in the same manner as Argentina. Between 1964 and 1974, sales of capital assets that had been revalued for the purposes of the net worth adjustment used these stepped-up bases for the determination of taxable gains; unrevalued capital capital assets were monetarily corrected by the percentage change in the consumer price index between the date of acquisition and the date of sale.[167]

Percentage Reduction of the Tax

Belgium is the only country presently varying its capital gains tax as an inflation adjustment. Belgium reduces its capital gains tax on individuals from 30 to 15 percent if the asset has been held for more than five years.[168] Prior to 1975 Israel used to reduce its capital gains tax rate by 0.5 to 1 percent a month for each month real assets had been held, and 3.5 percent a year for nondepreciable personalty.[169]

Percentage Increase in Historical Cost Basis

Four countries currently permit taxpayers to adjust their original cost of a capital asset by a flat percentage for each year the asset has been held beyond a certain minimum period. This method was also used in Argentina and Colombia until more sophisticated inflation adjustments were adopted.[170]

Belgium

In addition to reducing its tax rate for assets held more than five years,[171] Belgium also permits individuals to step up the cost basis of real property by 5 percent for each year the property has been held. Even though taxed on their gains from property sales at ordinary income rates, real estate dealers have been accorded the privilege since 1973 of stepping up their cost basis by 5 percent a year for each year they have held real property, up to a maximum of 50 percent.[172]

Denmark

Denmark permits taxpayers to revise upward the historical cost basis of real property by use of specific coefficients which increase proportionately with the length of the holding period. These coefficients are modified from time to time. Presently, land and buildings acquired prior to 1966 can be written-up by 120 percent for the purpose of computing one's capital gains tax.[173]

Norway

In 1971 Norway adopted an inflation adjustment similar to Sweden's adjustment for personalty. Initially, the adjustment was limited to real property, the basis of which could be readjusted upward by 5 percent for each year beyond five that the property was held. In 1975 this adjustment provision was extended to all capital assets. The adjustment rises to 6 percent a year from the twenty-first to thirtieth year of the holding period, and to 7 percent for each year thereafter. In no case, however, can the total basis adjustment exceed three times an asset's historical cost.[174]

France also permits individuals who have capital gains from the sale of speculative real property to readjust their cost basis by 3 to 5 percent a year, depending upon the holding period.[175] Prior to 1972 in Argentina and 1978 in Colombia the cost basis of capital assets could be written up by varying percentages for the purpose of calculating capital gains tax.[176]

Percentage Reduction in the Amount of Taxable Gain

Spain, Finland, and Mexico reduce the amount of gain subject to capital gains tax by a certain percentage for the length of time the asset has been held. Brazil and Sweden also utilize this method of adjustment for real property in conjunction with monetary correction of historical cost.

Spain

Spain reduces the capital gain subject to tax by 5 percent for each year the asset has been held beyond the threshold period. This threshold is set at one year for property acquired by inheritance and three years for property acquired by purchase.[177]

Finland

Finland allows individuals to reduce the amount of gain subject to tax by 20 percent for each year the property has been held beyond five years.

Gains derived from the transfer of personal property are free from tax if the asset has been held for at least five years.[178]

Mexico

Mexico reduces the amount of gain subject to capital gains tax by 10 percent for each year real property has been held beyond six years. The maximum amount that can be excluded, however, is 50 percent of the gain.[179]

SUMMARY

As the preceding text indicates, a substantial number of countries have perceived of the need to adjust their capital gains tax for inflation. The methods chosen have varied considerably, and some countries employ several simultaneously. The flat percentage rates used to exclude gain from tax, to reduce the tax itself, or to adjust the cost basis are obviously only appropriate for those years in which the inflation happens to correspond to the percentage fixed in the statute. Monetary correction of the historical cost is only slightly more complicated, but is a much superior technique for insuring that only real gains will be taxed.

The present Israeli scheme is a curious compromise. It recognizes that part of all capital gains are illusory, and therefore reduces tax rate to 10 percent on that component of the gain. Although more justifiable than a 5 to 10 percent tax on the surplus generated by revaluation of fixed assets or inventory, because the taxpayer at least has a ready source of funds available to pay the tax, the Israelis are nevertheless levying a tax on a fictitious profit. The result is that Israel taxes capital gains more heavily than ordinary income, a short-sighted disincentive to capital formation.

From a technical standpoint all of these statutes might be improved by differentiating between the portion of the capital gain resulting from the taxpayer's use of his own funds and that portion resulting from the use of borrowed funds. A full adjustment for inflation is justifiable for the former, but is not for the latter. This is particularly true if the tax system permits a deduction for all interest paid, even if the real rate is negative.

The Chileans discovered that the great bulk of capital gains disappeared with full indexation. They, therefore, decided that it made little sense to incur the expense of administering a tax that produced so little revenue and may have deterred capital investment. They, therefore, abolished the capital gains tax, a decision that has much to commend it.

TECHNICAL PROBLEMS OF INFLATION ADJUSTMENTS

Some of the serious technical problems involved in adjusting income taxation to inflation have already been mentioned, but they are sufficiently important to warrant a closer look. They are problems concerning the determination of the appropriate standard of value, expurgation, timing, and delinquent tax payments.

The Appropriate Standard of Value

The ongoing debate between advocates of current-value (replacement-cost) accounting and monetary-correction (price level) accounting has had accounting standards committees in many countries turning somersaults.[180] In May 1974 the United Kingdom's Accounting Standards Steering Committee advocated supplementation of conventional historical-cost financial statements with monetarily-corrected versions. After many years of wrangling, the Accounting Standards Committee on March 31, 1980 finally adopted SSAP 16, which requires most large companies to supplement their annual financial statements for years beginning after December 31, 1979 with income statements and balance sheets prepared on a current value basis. The Australian Institute of Chartered Accountants proposed adoption of monetary-correction accounting in December 1974; six months later it reversed itself and proposed current-value accounting. Australia presently requires disclosure of current-value accounting as supplementary information to financial statements. In July of 1975 the Canadian Institute of Chartered Accountants proposed supplementation of historical cost balance sheets with monetary-correction accounting; in December of 1979 the Institute reversed itself and issued an exposure draft endorsing current-value accounting. In December of 1974 the U.S. Financial Accounting Standards Board (FASB) also proposed monetary-correction accounting. In March of 1976 the FASB proposal was torpedoed by the Securities and Exchange Commission's Accounting Release 190, requiring corporations with total assets in excess of $100 million to supplement their conventional financial statements with footnotes disclosing current replacement costs of depreciable assets and inventory. The FASB finally resolved its dilemma by riding both horses. In 1979 it issued FAS 33, requiring public companies with total assets in excess of $1 billion or with inventories, plant and equipment in excess of $125 million, to file supplementary financial statements on both monetary-correction and current-value bases.[181]

Whether current-value accounting is more appropriate than monetary-correction depends to a large extent upon the purposes for which the information is being used. If one is primarily concerned with affording investors a more realistic notion of the value of a company's assets, there are definite advantages to current-value accounting. On the other hand, if one is primarily concerned with eliminating inflationary distortions from income taxation, the problem is more complex.

If one conceptualizes the problem as finding a method to permit business firms to recover their real capital costs for wasting assets, the simplest solution would be to amend the tax code to permit an immediate writeoff of the cost of all depreciable assets.[182] Since the expenditure and the deduction would be in currency units of the same year, inflationary distortions would be minimized. In some cases, however, the depreciation write-off would exceed current taxable income, and a method would have to be devised to adjust unused depreciation in a carryforward provision. This approach runs counter to the essential nature of a depreciation deduction, which involves allocation of part of the cost of wasting assets to each year of their income producing life. This necessarily involves estimation of an asset's useful life and salvage value in setting up a depreciation schedule. If one intends a depreciation schedule to permit firms to set aside a tax-free reserve sufficient to permit replacement of the depreciable asset,[183] it would seem more appropriate to use replacement cost than a general price index as a standard of value. The price of replacing one firm's assets may double during a given period, while the cost of replacing those of another firm's may quadruple. Use of the same price index for revaluation gives one firm an unfair tax advantage over the other. Of course, it would then also seem more appropriate to use replacement-cost accounting than historical-cost accounting in a stable economy, for relative prices may be changing even though the general price level remains constant.

From a tax standpoint, it is preferable to conceptualize the problem as finding a method to permit business firms to charge against taxable income the real costs of earning such income. In such a case it would seem more appropriate to correct the historical cost of depreciable assets by coefficients derived from a general price index. Any changes in relative prices of depreciable assets are ignored except for the purpose of calculating gains or losses at the time of the sale or disposal of the asset.

The monetary-correction approach to depreciation has the virtue of being much easier than replacement cost to compute and administer, because the latter method presents difficult questions of judgment as to the actual worth of used productive capacity. Moreover, the replacement-cost approach tends to eliminate from taxation any real gain or loss upon the sale of a depreciable asset.

Replacement-cost inventory accounting not only eliminates the taxation of all illusory inventory profits, but also makes tax-exempt real capital gains when the replacement cost of inventory items rises more or less than the general price level. Whether these real gains should be taxed depends to a large extent on whether the business firm is regarded as being committed to the purchase of these particular inventory items. Thus, a shoe store whose shoes have risen in price more rapidly than the general price level is no better off economically from this increase in the value of its inventory because it has to purchase more shoes in order to remain in business. But an entity whose business consists of liquidating the stock of bankrupt merchants with no commitment to any particular type of inventory realistically realizes a gain that should be taxed whenever it sells inventory whose price has risen since purchase by the store.

The Appropriate Index

There is little agreement about which index or indexes most appropriately adjust income taxation to inflation. The practices of the group of countries that have permitted some form of indexing vary considerably. Some of the countries that have permitted replacement-cost adjustments of fixed assets have allowed the taxpayer to reappraise those assets in any reasonable manner, while others have approximated replacement costs from price indexes. [184] The countries that have institutionalized some form of income tax indexation have adopted a variety of different indexes. Some link personal income taxes to the consumer price index,[185] while others use the wholesale price index, the minimum wage, or the consumer price index net of indirect taxes and/or subsidies.[186] Business income taxation is indexed to the consumer price index in Chile and Uruguay and to the wholesale price index in Argentina and, until recently, in Brazil. To a large extent this great variety reflects the strengths and weaknesses of particular price indexes in various countries.[187] It also reflects the different solutions reached in the ongoing debate about whether a tax system should attempt to correct for changes in the general price level or for changes in relative prices in revaluing inventory and fixed assets.[188]

Which index is most appropriate for indexing a progressive personal income tax depends upon both theoretical and practical considerations. The purpose of indexing the tax legislation should be to prevent inflation from changing the real tax burden imposed on any given real income. There are two conceptually different approaches to achieving this goal. One is to define income in terms of consumption opportunities. In other words, a taxpayer's income would remain constant in real terms if its nominal amount permitted purchase of the same quantity and quality of goods. The other is to define income in terms of total national output, which would include savings as well as consumption. The former approach implies adoption of a consumption deflator like the consumer or wholesale price index, while the latter approach presupposes adoption of an output deflator like the implicit GNP deflator.[189]

There are several technical reasons for preferring adoption of an output index like the implicit GNP deflator. First, as a measure of total output, the GNP deflator more closely corresponds to the definition of income in income tax legislation than does a measure of consumption opportunities.[190] Second, inflation affects the consumption opportunities of taxpayers differently. Attempting to maintain the real tax burden on any particular taxpayer, or group of taxpayers, requires the use of multiple price indexes. Using different indexes for different groups in order to adjust tax brackets and exemption levels "would create a mare's nest of endless haggling over which groups were being treated preferentially. Given the insolubility of the index number problem, no number of economists, lawyers, and accountants could really prove to any group that its claims were invalid."[191] Moreover, if it costs 20 percent more to purchase the same market basket of goods in New York City than it does in Austin, the taxpayer who resides in New York should pay less income tax on the same nominal income as the taxpayer who resides in Texas. Use of multiple price indexes poses nightmarish administrative problems, particularly in large countries like the United States, where population mobility is extremely high. Third, the GNP deflator is far more comprehensive than the other price indexes and is thus a far better proxy for money. The wholesale price index has too narrow a universe, covering only price changes in selected commodities at their first important level of commercial transaction. Important areas of price change, such as construction costs, real estate, government expenditures, military production, and securities, fall outside its coverage. Moreover, by focusing on list prices rather than actual prices, the wholesale price index has a tendency to overstate the inflation rate during an economic downturn and understate the inflation rate during an upswing. The consumer price index is limited to retail purchases of a selected group of items by a selected group of consumers (generally urban families with two to four children and working class income). Prices and expenditure patterns may differ significantly for other groups of consumers. Important prices, such as those of land and securities, are not covered by the consumer price index.[192]

Technically, the national income deflator, which measures net national product at factor costs, would be an even better index for a progressive tax system than the implicit GNP deflator. Because it measures national output net of depreciation, the national income deflator more closely corresponds to the concept of taxable income. For income tax purposes the GNP deflator overweights the fixed investment components of national output by using gross rather than net investment.[193] Nonetheless, the variation between the national income deflator and the implicit GNP deflator is generally so small that it is probably preferable to trade off the slight improvement in technical accuracy for the greater recognition of the GNP deflator.[194]

Despite the technical superiority of the implicit GNP deflator, no country has yet indexed income tax adjustments to it. There are several explanations for the failure to do so. The implicit GNP deflator is a relatively new concept; even in a system of highly developed economic reporting like the United States, deflators calculated quarterly have been available only since 1947. The consumer and wholesale price indexes are better known and understood. Generally, these indexes are available monthly, while in many countries the GNP deflator is available only annually. In countries with advanced economic reporting systems, the GNP deflator is available only quarterly and lags behind the wholesale and consumer price indexes by three months to a year. Perhaps the biggest deficiency of the GNP deflator for indexing purposes is that it is a Paasche index, which means that the relative weight given to each component changes every year in accordance with changes of the relative magnitude of that component as a percentage of total gross national product. As a result, sequential year comparisons with the implicit GNP deflator are difficult.[195] Moreover, in many countries national accounts data are so shaky that it is difficult to have much confidence in any index based on them.

The choice of an index has usually been dictated by practical rather than theoretical considerations. In countries undergoing rapid inflation, a revaluation coefficient based on any price index is generally obsolete by the time it is promulgated by the tax authorities. Allowing taxpayers to derive their own coefficients from the indexes, however is likely to be chaotic. Even in countries long accustomed to living with inflation, few persons understand the nature of price indexes. If the consumer price index or the wholesale price has been publicly identified as synonymous with the inflation rate, it may be preferable to adopt that index for income tax purposes rather than to try to familiarize taxpayers with another, even if it is technically preferable. In many instances the differences in inflation rates registered by the various indexes are simply not that significant.[196]

Expurgation for Terms of Trade and Indirect Taxes

Changes in the terms of trade affect a consumer or wholesale price index in a qualitatively different way from domestic price changes. If domestic inflationary pressures cause these price indexes to rise, the country's aggregate real income remains unaffected. If a substantial rise in important prices relative to export prices causes these indexes to rise, however, the country's aggregate real income will decline. This point was brought home to the Brazilians when the quadrupling of oil prices sent Brazil's bill for imported oil soaring from $710 million in 1973 to $2.8 billion in 1974, producing a huge balance-of-payments deficit and a sharp surge in the inflation rate. In such circumstances indexation would have seriously reduced government tax revenues. The rise in oil prices boosted the wholesale price index substantially, but the extra income went to foreigners. Since tax brackets were linked to the wholesale price index, taxpayers were effectively insulated (at least for tax purposes) from the national decline in real income resulting from the oil hike. In 1975, faced with the prospect of income tax revenues bearing a disproportionately large share of the burden caused by the oil price increase, the Brazilian government decided to purge the wholesale price index for indexation purposes from the effects of "inflationary accidents."[197] It is, however, extraordinarily difficult to isolate the effect of changes in important prices on the domestic price level, and there is some reason to believe that Brazilian expurgation of the price index may have been excessive. Furthermore, it is not clear why at least part of the decline in real income should not be borne by the government sector.[198]

When the price of exports rises relative to imports, the opposite problem occurs. The government's income tax yields will increase, but the domestic price level may stay the same. Because of the progressivity of the tax rates, the government may arguably receive a disproportionately large share of the extra income generated by exports. Neither of these problems presents itself if indexation is based upon the implicit GNP or national income deflators, which net out the terms of trade.[199]

Australia and The Netherlands have decided to purge the consumer price indexes used to index personal income taxes of the effects of all indirect taxes. There are two related arguments for doing so: fairness and resource allocation. The fairness argument is that if indirect taxes increase, thereby pushing up the price index, the taxpayer receives a corresponding benefit through the quality or quantity of public goods and services. No such *quid pro quo* attaches to a price increase stemming from inflationary pressures, such as excess demand. The resource allocation argument is that it is inefficient for the government to give with one hand and take with the other. To the extent an increase in indirect taxes is offset by a decline in personal income taxes, the taxpayer effectively avoids the impact of the indirect tax increase.[200]

Australia recently introduced a new aspect to expurgation. Starting in 1979, the effects of increases in the price of domestically produced oil to maintain parity with imported oil were eliminated from the price index used to adjust its income tax.[201] The justification for this kind of expurgation is also resource allocation. The government wishes to discourage the oil consumption by allowing the price of domestically produced crude to rise to the international level. To the extent that this price rise is offset by a decline in personal income taxes because of indexation, the effectiveness of the measure is lessened.

Timing

One of the thorniest problems is that of timing. During the course of an inflation, price levels are constantly changing. The value of $100 received today is less than that of $100 received last month. The taxpayer who received the bulk of his income in the beginning of the year receives more real income than the taxpayer who received the same nominal income towards the end of the year, though they pay equivalent amounts of tax. This kind of discrimination is most unfair with respect to a taxpayer whose entire income is subject to withholding tax, for his effective tax rate is considerably higher than that of a taxpayer with similar nominal incomes who can liquidate his tax liability the following year in depreciated currency. Moreover, some taxpayers can time certain transactions, for example, the sale of a building or receipt of fees and commissions, so that income will be received in the beginning rather than at the end of a fiscal year. Since withholding generally falls most heavily on wage earners and salaried middle-income groups, failure to adjust for this inflationary distortion in the timing of tax payments has a regressive effect.

Time lag distortions of business income might be eliminated by requiring each firm to adjust its daily receipts, disbursements, depreciation, inventory, and net reinvestment to end-of-the-year currency units, but the administrative burden would be intolerable. As a practical matter, the comprehensive balance sheet adjustments used in Argentina, Brazil, and Chile closely approximate a complete daily adjustment into end-of-the-year cruzeiros or pesos. Assuming there are no capital additions or withdrawals, the adjustments to daily receipts will tend to be canceled out by the adjustments to daily disbursements.

The theoretical problems of adjusting personal income to end-of-the-year currency units are more difficult than for business income. If taxpayers are required to adjust receipt of income into end-of-the-year currency units, fairness would seem to require that disbursements be similarly adjusted. Personal disbursements for food, clothing, shelter, and transportation traditionally have not been deductible for income tax purposes, and the record keeping requirements for individuals would be unreasonably complicated.

Chile has adopted a comprehensive set of measures designed to restate all gains and losses into end-of-the-year currency units. In general, taxpayers must make monthly provisional income tax payments. The difference between the amount paid and the total tax actually due at the close of the fiscal year has to be readjusted by the increase in the consumer price index between the second month prior to the date the provisional payment was made and the second month prior to the end of the fiscal year. If there is a balance owing to the fisc, that sum, readjusted for price index changes, must be paid in its entirety at the time of the filing of the annual return. If there is a refund owing the taxpayer, that sum can be applied to future tax payments, or returned to the taxpayer with monetary correction.[202] All professional income and losses must be readjusted by coefficients derived from the consumer price index to reflect price changes between the month in which the gain or loss is realized and the end of the fiscal year.[203] Losses can be carried forward two years and the value of the loss can be adjusted by the change in the consumer price index between the date of the loss and the date it is actually charged against income.[204]

Argentina has recently adopted legislation to adjust for timing distortions. Amounts carried over from prior years because of limitations on deductions, deductions made in prior years which have subsequently become disqualified, and nonrecognized gains in corporate reorganizations which fail to meet statutory nonrecognition requirements must all be revalued in accordance with the percentage change in the wholesale price index. All carry-over losses are subject to similar monetary correction.[205]

Perhaps because, until recently, Brazil's inflation rate had been under greater control than Chile's and Argentina's, Brazil has not moved as far with respect to correcting for timing distortions. In 1974, however, Brazil did begin monetary correction of withholding payments in order to convert all tax payments to end-of-the-year cruzeiros.[206]

Monetary Correction of Delinquent Tax Payments

A serious and chronic problem of tax administration in an inflationary environment is tax delinquency. With high rates of inflation, many taxpayers find it cheaper to borrow back taxes from the government than to pay the prevailing interest rates.

Many countries have attempted to resolve this problem by increasing the number of taxpayers and types of income subject to withholding, requiring monthly or quarterly estimated tax payments, shortening the lag time for tax payments, and increasing late penalties and interest charges for back taxes.[207] Brazil, Chile, Israel, and Argentina have gone further and have instituted monetary correction of back tax debts.

Brazil instituted monetary correction of back tax debts in 1964 in a successful attempt to reduce the massive amount of tax evasion and to curb the tradition of dilatory payment of taxes. All tax debts, including those whose payment has been suspended by administrative or judicial proceedings, are subject to monetary correction in accordance with coefficients derived from the wholesale price index.[208] Since 1967 late penalties have also been subjected to monetary correction.[209] Interest, however, has remained exempt.[210] If the taxpayer deposits with the Treasury the amount he is disputing and subsequently prevails, he is entitled to receive his deposit back with monetary correction. Similarly, excess withholding tax payments are returned to the taxpayer with monetary correction.

Chile introduced monetary correction of tax payments in 1965. Prior Chilean tax law permitted a taxpayer to discharge his tax liability in three equal installments during the year subsequent to the year in which his income was earned. A 1965 reform gave the taxpayer the option of paying all of his tax when filing his declaration (between January and March) or grossing up his tax liability by half of the percentage increase in the consumer price index during the year in which the income was earned.[211] In 1966 the system was modified to gross up installment liabilities by 80 percent of the past year's price index increment, and to gross up taxes fully paid at the time of filing of the declaration by 40 percent. In 1967 these percentage readjustments were increased to 100 and 50 percent respectively. This system was replaced by one which charged the late taxpayer interest of 3.6 percent a month (now reduced to 1.5 percent per month), a flat 5 percent penalty, plus monetary correction on the unpaid balance from the date due to the date of actual payment.[212]

Israel began indexing back tax debts in 1975. In addition to payment of interest and penalties, Israel now requires the delinquent taxpayer to index his back taxes to the cost-of-living index starting six months after the end of the fiscal year in which the taxes were due. Tax refund payments are correspondingly indexed.[213]

Argentina instituted monetary correction of tax debts in 1976.[214] All unpaid tax obligations must be updated in accordance with variations in the wholesale price index between the date the obligation is actually paid and the month prior to the due date. All credits that the government owes to the taxpayer, as well as all amounts prescribed as fines and penalties, are subject to similar monetary correction.

CONCLUSIONS

On first impression the case for adjusting income taxation for inflation appears overwhelming. Regardless of how much the tax structure diverges from some ideal, it is difficult to construct any principled argument justifying reallocation of tax benefits and burdens in the haphazard manner resulting from inflation. Instead of governmental revenues increasing automatically with inflation, indexation forces legislatures to go on record and vote up tax increases. Because it eliminates the automatic growth in governmental revenue, it has even been argued that indexation may serve as a brake on inflation, forcing the government to justify additional expenditures.[215] Automatic adjustments avoid the need for larger, more disruptive adjustments at future dates. Moreover, indexation prevents legislatures from palming off those discretionary adjustments as "tax cuts." Because the rate of increase in marginal tax rates diminishes as taxable income increases, inflation tends to make a progressive income tax structure more regressive. By eliminating the shifting of taxpayers into higher brackets without any increase in real income, indexation counters this regressive effect.

The arguments most commonly raised against indexation are less than convincing. First, it is argued that indexation destroys the automatic stabilizing mechanism of a progressive income tax. Because tax revenues rise more rapidly than aggregate income during inflationary periods, and fall more rapidly during recessionary periods, a progressive income tax has a built-in countercyclical feature, cushioning the effects of swings in the business cycle.[216] To a limited extent this criticism of indexation may be valid. Tax yields will not rise as much in a boom period, nor fall as much during a recession, if there is indexation. This assumes there is only a short time lag between the change in the general price level and the change in tax revenues. It is by no means clear, however, that a reduction in tax revenues due to indexing would occur at the same time as an expansion of economic activity from inflation. In post-war Canada, economists have observed that general price-level increases have lagged behind economic expansion by about 9 to 18 months. On several occasions the inflation rate did not reach its maximum until well after a cyclical downturn had begun.[217] Recent studies have concluded that indexing the personal income tax would have had very little destablizing effect on the United States and Canadian economies. Indeed, under certain circumstances, an indexed system may actually be more stabilizing than an unindexed system.[218]

Second, it is argued that the administrative burdens of indexation are too great. There is some truth to this contention, particularly if depreciable assets must be restated each year in terms of replacement costs. Nevertheless, the experiences of Argentina, Brazil, Chile, and Israel indicate that monetary correction is manageable. If the tax authorities publish monetary correction coefficients, taxpayers need only multiply nominal values on their returns by the proper coefficients.

Third, it is argued that indexation implies continued toleration of serious inflation. Yet this implication is far from clear. It seems just as plausible to interpret a decision to index the tax system as evidence of awareness of the distortions caused by inflation and an unwillingness to see governmental revenues swell automatically.

Fourth, it is argued that government tax revenues will be substantially diminished by indexation, while a large percentage of governmental expenditures are either actually or practically indexed. Consequently, most governments will likely resort to inflationary techniques to finance their deficit. This argument is also questionable. It is true that indexing will prevent governmental revenues from increasing automatically in real terms during an inflationary period without a corresponding increase in real income. Indexing does not, however, mean that the government cannot maintain the same level of real revenue. All it means is that the legislature will have to raise rates or levy new taxes to increase real tax revenues beyond the level of any increase in national income.

None of these arguments really go to the heart of the matter. Whether the tax system should be indexed depends upon the answers to two questions: (1) Is inflation improving or worsening the present tax structure? (2) Can correction of undesirable inflationary tax distortions be corrected more easily and wisely by *ad hoc* legislation rather than by indexing? Neither of these questions has easy answers.

In some respects indexation makes the tax system more progressive, but in other respects it makes it more regressive. Preventing the shifting of lower income taxpayers into higher brackets has a progressive effect. Adjusting all withholding payments to end-of-the-year currency units also has a progressive effect. Wage-earners generally must liquidate their tax liability immediately through withholding, while the wealthiest taxpayers are able to pay their taxes later in depreciated currency. Because upper-income taxpayers are likely to have more capital gains than lower-income taxpayers, use of a floating basis readjustment for capital gains is regressive. Because creditors, as a class, are likely to be more wealthy than debtors, as a class, taxing only real interest income and permitting a deduction for real capital lost through lending at a negative rate makes the tax structure more regressive. Large corporations are likely to be the chief beneficiaries of inventory and depreciation adjustments. If a comprehensive net worth or "working capital" adjustment similar to that used in Argentina, Brazil, or Chile were adopted, highly leveraged corporations would pay higher tax bills. In short, from the viewpoint of tax equity, indexing is very much a mixed bag.

The most convincing argument for indexing the income tax is that it helps insure that firms and individuals are taxed only on real economic gains. This prevents the income tax from being converted into tax on capital. It also promotes equality by treating firms and individuals with similar real incomes alike. Under a system of nominal income taxation, all too often persons or firms with quite disparate real incomes are treated alike. A certain amount of disparate treatment is inevitable, but inflation exacerbates unequal treatment of similarly situated taxpayers.

Most countries which have adopted indexing have done so only partially, which makes indexing itself a new source of inequality. It is difficult to justify only indexing either business income or personal income and ignoring the other. Relative to other socio-economic groups as pensioners, landlords, or wage-earners, business firms are likely to be hurt least by inflation because increases in their incomes usually accompany the rise in the general price level. But some business firms are seriously hurt by inflation, while others profit from it. Affording only partial rather than comprehensive inflation adjustments may simply intensify the distortions generated by inflation.

Whether the legislature can do a more effective job by actually readjusting for inflation every few years instead of creating an automatic adjustment mechanism is a difficult question to answer in the abstract. Inflation is hardly the only distortion to an income tax, and to the extent the legislature is deprived of an important pressure for tax reform, it may fail to adjust existing inequities unrelated to inflation as often as it should. Nevertheless, nearly every time a legislature decides to reform the tax system, it adds several layers of complexity. Those who believe the tax structure in countries like the United States is already too complex may support indexing on the theory that the legislature generally does more harm than good when it revises the system. On the other hand, one concern expressed by several economists at a recent conference on indexation of the U.S. income tax was that Congress might so botch the process of enacting an indexation provision that the income tax would be even worse than it is now.[219]

Finally, whether indexing the income tax is worth the candle is in good part a function of the inflation rate. With an annual inflation rate of less than 5 percent, a good case can be made for the proposition that indexing is too troublesome to bother with. With an inflation rate hovering between 5 and 10 percent a year, however, the distortions become sufficiently pronounced to outweigh the administrative burden. For countries like Argentina, Brazil, and Chile, inflation was distorting the operation of the income tax so much and so fast that *ad hoc* legislative modification was hardly a meaningful alternative.

Postscript: Since type was set on this book, the United States adopted the Economic Recovery Tax Act of 1981, which provides that income tax brackets, the zero bracket amount, and the personal exemption shall be indexed to increases in the consumer price index, commencing in 1985. In addition, Mexico's new income tax law, which went into effect on January 1, 1981, contains a special balance sheet adjustment for inflation.

NOTES

1. *See generally* INT'L FISCAL ASSOC., L'INFLATION ET LA FISCALITÉ, 62a CAHIERS DE DROIT FISCAL INTERNATIONAL (1977) [hereafter cited as L'INFLATION ET LA FISCALITÉ]; V. TANZI, INFLATION AND THE PERSONAL INCOME TAX: AN INTERNATIONAL PERSPECTIVE 8–11 (1980). If real property values are continuously reassessed, the real property tax will stay abreast of inflation, albeit with some lag. Value added and excise taxes are by no means unaffected by inflation, particularly as it distorts the values of credits against these taxes.

2. *See* Dach, *Tax Aspects of Inflation: A Study in Monetary Nominalism,* 9 AM. J. COMP. L. 657 (1960).

3. Three of the most commonly used techniques are straight-line, sum-of-the-years-digits, and double-declining balance. Straight-line depreciation involves charging off the difference between cost and salvage value in equal annual installments over the asset's estimated useful life.

The double-declining balance method applies twice the straight-line rate annually to the unrecovered cost of the asset, whose value is reduced each year by the amount of the depreciation deduction of the previous year. Approximately 10 to 15 percent of the cost remains unrecovered in the last year with this method. This unrecovered depreciation may then be charged off as salvage value, or the owner of the asset may convert to straight-line depreciation when that method becomes more advantageous.

The sum-of-the-years-digits method involves charging off a fraction of the difference between cost and salvage value each year. The numerator of the fraction in the first year is the number of years of useful life, and it decreases by one each successive year. The denominator of the fraction always equals the sum of all the numbers in the numerator.

Because the latter two methods permit earlier recovery of the bulk of an asset's cost, their use reduces the degree to which inflation produces fictitious profits.

There is considerable variation in the rapidity with which the tax systems of the industrial nations permit recovery of the cost of depreciable assets. The United Kingdom and Canada permit the fastest writeoffs; the United States lags far behind most countries. *See* Sanden & Crawford, *The Treatment of Capital Recovery Allowances in the U.S. and Other Countries,* 1 INT'L TAX J. 265, 269 (1975). *See also* G. Kopits, INTERNATIONAL COMPARISON OF TAX DEPRECIATION PRACTICES (OECD Report 1975).

4. Many countries would consider this capital gain. Under Section 1245, added to the United States Internal Revenue Code in 1962, this excess depreciation would be taxed as ordinary income rather than as capital gain. *See generally* Schapiro, *Recapture of Depreciation and Section 1245 of the Internal Revenue Code,* 72 YALE L. J. 1483 (1963).

5. This assumes that the cost of replacing items in inventory is rising, though not necessarily at the same rate as the general price level.

6. A study of interest rates charged by Brazilian banks between 1952 and 1966 found that the real rate of interest (the nominal interest rate deflated by the wholesale price index) was negative in twelve out of the fifteen years in this period. Indeed, in 1963, a year in which the rate of inflation accelerated from 53.2 to 73.5 percent, the real rate of interest being charged by Brazilian banks on commercial loans was −30.4 percent. Christoffersen, *Taxas de Juro e a Estrutura de um Sistema de Bancos Comerciais em Condições Inflacionárias,* 23 Rev. Bras. Econ. 5, 28 (Abr./Jun. 1969). The average real interest rate paid on savings deposits in the ten-year period between 1967 and 1976 was −23.7 percent in Argentina and −31.9 percent in Uruguay. *See* Galbis, *Inflation and Interest Rate Policies in Latin America, 1967–76,* 26 IMF STAFF PAPERS 334, 356 (1979).

7. This assumes that the borrowing firm's effective rate of interest less the value of the tax deduction for its interest expense is less than the rate of inflation.

8. Davidson & Weil, *Inflation Accounting: Implications of the FASB Proposal,* in INFLATION AND THE INCOME TAX 81, 89–94 (H. Aaron, ed. 1976) [hereafter cited as BROOKINGS CONFERENCE]. A recent estimate of the effect of price level adjustment of the income of a sample of ten banks showed the median percentage change in income was −43.04 percent. *See* Falkenstein, *Price Level Accounting: Bad News for Bank Earnings,* Rep. R–17A–5 (Legg Mason Washington Service, Sept. 1975), cited in *id.* at 94, fn. 16.

9. *E.g.*, MEXICAN INCOME AND COMMERCIAL RECEIPTS TAX LAWS, art. 346 of the Income Tax Law, 115 (CCH Span.-Eng. ed. 1978); Colombia, Income Tax Law, arts. 55–57 (1968) (modified to a flat rate on corporations by Decree No. 2053, Sept. 30, 1974); Liberian Income Tax Statute, Liberian Code of Laws, Tit. 35, §120 (Supp. 1958–61).

10. This paring can become guillotine-like for the taxpayer forced to sue for a refund.

11. Rosenn, *Adaptations of the Brazilian Income Tax to Inflation,* 21 STAN. L. REV. 58, 70–71 (1968).

The Japanese experience suggests that if interest and penalties for delay are very high, taxpayers will also be reluctant to pay delinquent taxes. In July 1948 Japan increased the interest rate on overdue taxes to 36.5 percent a year, and the delay penalty to 73 percent a year, only to discover that these high rates themselves contributed to increased delinquencies. Hirao and Aguirre, *Maintaining the Level of Income Tax Collections Under Inflationary Conditions,* 17 IMF STAFF PAPERS 277, 292–93 (1970).

12. U.S. Internal Revenue Code §11.

13. *Id.* §911. Until 1976 U.S. taxpayers continuously present in a foreign country for seventeen out of eighteen months were entitled to exclude $20,000 annually from gross income, while taxpayers who were bona fide residents of foreign countries for three consecutive years were entitled to exclude $25,000 a year from gross income. The exclusion is now limited to $15,000, except for employees of charitable organizations, who may exclude up to $20,000 per year.

14. *Id.* §116(a). These three examples by no means exhaust the number of nominal sum limitations contained in the United States Internal Revenue Code. There are numerous other such limitations. Lubell & Lavin, *Indexation of the Tax Law: A "Fresh-Start" Adjustment,* 58 TAXES 355 (1980), shows what has happened to the real value of 19 nominally stated provisions of the U.S. Internal Revenue Code

since enactment. For a comprehensive study of the provisions in the United Kingdom's tax law expressed in nominal terms and hence distorted by inflation, *see* Hudson, *The Indexation of the Tax System,* in INDEXING FOR INFLATION 111 (T. Liesner and M. King eds. 1975).

15. *See* P. SAMUELSON, ECONOMICS 356–58 (9th ed. 1973).

16. Von Furstenberg, *Individual Income Taxation and Inflation,* 28 NAT'L TAX J. 117 (1975).

17. For example, in the United States the standard deduction was set at 10 percent but limited to $1,000 between 1944 and 1969. Between 1964 and 1969 the minimum standard deduction was set at $200 plus $100 for each exemption. In 1969 Congress enacted legislation increasing the standard deduction to 15 percent, with a maximum limitation that reached $2,000 by 1972. The minimum deduction was replaced with a low-income allowance, which reached $1,300 in 1972. *Id.* at 122. It is now called the zero bracket and set at $3,200 for a married taxpayer with two dependents.

18. Comment, *Inflation and the Federal Income Tax,* 82 YALE L. J. 716, 739 (1973) [hereafter cited as YALE COMMENT].

19. As long as a tax system permits a deduction for all interest expense, the wealthier taxpayer will derive greater benefit from that deduction than will the poorer taxpayer. Once lenders have come to anticipate the actual inflation rate, a new borrower who agrees to pay an inflation-adjusted interest rate receives no benefit from inflation if his marginal tax rate is zero. Moreover, if the borrower is a low-income taxpayer who takes a standard deduction, he receives no particular tax benefit from borrowing. But the higher the borrower's marginal tax rate, the greater the tax benefits he receives from borrowing. These benefits increase along with the anticipated inflation rate. *See* Tanzi, *Inflation, Indexation and Interest Income Taxation,* BANCA NAZIONALE DEL LAVORO Q. REV. 64, 70–71 (Mar. 1976).

20. Between 1960 and 1975 periodic tax reforms resulted in a slight decrease in the aggregate effective U.S. tax rate on personal income—from 12.2 percent to 11.3 percent. Sunley and Pechman, *Inflation Adjustment for the Individual Income Tax,* in BROOKINGS CONFERENCE, *supra* note 8, at 153, 156–57. If Congress had not modified the tax laws between 1960 and 1975, the effective tax rate on personal income during this period would have increased from 10.7 percent to 16.2 percent. *Id.* at 159. Some of this increase (from 10.7 percent to 12.2 percent), however, is attributable to the combination of progressive tax rates and an increase in real personal income. Aaron, *Inflation and the Income Tax: An Introduction,* in BROOKINGS CONFERENCE, *supra* note 8, at 1, 21.

21. Palmer, *Accounting the Way to Real Profits,* N.Y. Times, Apr. 25, 1976, III, at p. 20, cols. 2–5.

22. Feldstein and Summers, *Inflation and the Taxation of Capital Income in the Corporate Sector,* 32 NAT'L TAX J. 445 (1979). Because of inflation, depreciation was found to be understated by $39.7 billion, raising corporate income taxes by $19 billion. Illusory inventory profits added another $7 billion in corporate income taxes. The balance stemmed from a complex calculation of the net effect of inflation on corporate shareholders and creditors.

23. Baer & Simonsen, *Profit Illusion and Policy-Making in an Inflationary Economy,* 17 OXFORD ECON. PAPERS 279 (New Ser. 1965). *See also* Simonsen, *O Impôsto de*

Renda e a Inflação, in FUNDAÇÃO GETÚLIO VARGAS E COMISSÃO DE REFORMA DO MINISTÉRIO DA FAZENDA, ANTEPROJETO DE CÓDIGO DO IMPÔSTO DE RENDA 217, 220 (1965).

24. Rosenn, *supra* note 11, at 72.

25. It has been suggested that this is precisely what happened to the Consolidated Edison Company of New York, Inc., which had to suspend its dividend payments in 1974. Hunt, *Funds Position: Keystone in Financial Planning,* 53 HARV. BUS. REV. 106 (My.–Je. 1975).

26. L. GORDON & E. GROMMERS, UNITED STATES MANUFACTURING INVESTMENT IN BRAZIL 85 (1962); M. SIMONSEN, A EXPERIÊNCIA INFLACIONÁRIA NO BRASIL 52 (1964). The annual increase in real investment in working capital in Brazilian firms declined impressively during galloping inflation, falling from 14 percent in 1959 to −13 percent in 1963. 2 MINISTÉRIO DO PLANEJAMENTO E COORDENÇÃO ECONÔMICA, POLÍTICA MONETÁRIA E MERCADO DE CAPITAIS 17 (prel. vers. 1967).

27. *See* Hart, *Accounting for Inflation in the United States,* 33 NAT'L TAX J. 247, 255 (1980).

28. Tideman & Tucker, *The Tax Treatment of Business Profits Under Inflationary Conditions,* in BROOKINGS CONFERENCE, *supra* note 8, at 33, 36–38.

29. Gramlich, *The Economic and Budgetary Effects of Indexing the Tax System,* in BROOKINGS CONFERENCE, *supra* note 8, at 271, 282–85; Parker & Zieha, *Inflation, Income Taxes and the Incentive for Capital Investment,* 29 NAT'L TAX J. 179 (1976).

30. Feldstein & Slemrod, *Inflation and the Excess Taxation of Capital Gains on Corporate Stock,* 31 NAT'L TAX J. 107 (1978).

31. The adequacy of the present rate of capital formation is a matter of debate in the United States, as is the enormously complex question of the relationship between the decline in productivity experienced in the United States since 1966 and the tax structure. *Compare* Feldstein, *Taxes, Inflation and Capital Formation,* 32 NAT'L TAX J. 347 (1979) *with* Musgrave, *Tax Policy and Capital Formation,* 32 NAT'L TAX J. 351 (1979).

32. Hirao & Aguirre, *supra* note 11, at 283; Mishan & Dicks-Mireaux, *Progressive Taxation in an Inflationary Economy,* 48 AM. ECON. REV. 591 (1958).

33. Alemann, *Economic Development of Argentina,* in ECONOMIC DEVELOPMENT ISSUES 1, 22 (Comm. for Econ. Develop. Supp. Paper No. 21, 1967).

34. In 1967 Delfim Neto, then Finance Minister, conservatively estimated the rate of tax evasion in Brazil at about equal to 50 percent of total tax collections. O Globo, Dec. 4, 1967, at 14. Some 250,000 Argentine taxpayers took advantage of a 1970 amnesty provision to declare the previously unreported sum of 8,820 million pesos (then a little more than U.S. $2.5 billion), about equal to the nation's total annual budget. *Argentina: Dagnino's Lucky Break,* Latin America, May 8, 1970, at 151. In 1979 the U.S. Internal Revenue Service estimated U.S. unreported income for 1976 at $130 billion, about 7 percent of Gross National Product (GNP), but most outside estimates are considerably higher, ranging from 10 to 20 percent of GNP. Lohr, "How Tax Evasion Has Grown," N.Y. Times, Mar. 15, 1981, sect. 3, p. 1, cols. 2–4. In 1979 the head of Great Britain's Inland Revenue estimated tax evasion at £10 billion, 7.5 percent of GNP. Ilersic, *Tax Evasion in the United Kingdom,* 27 CAN. TAX J. 693 (1979).

35. *See* Lent, *Adjusting Taxable Profits for Inflation: The Foreign Experience,* in

BROOKINGS CONFERENCE, *supra* note 8, at 195. Accelerated depreciation can also be used as an inflation adjustment. The faster one can depreciate an asset under conventional historical cost techniques, the less distortion caused by inflation to depreciation schedules.

36. YALE COMMENT, *supra* note 18, at 722–23.

37. *See* U.S. Securities and Exchange Commission, Proposed Amendments to Regulation S-X Regarding Replacement Cost Disclosure (Aug. 1975). An Australian Committee of Inquiry recommended adoption of "replacement cost" depreciation, calculated in accordance with coefficients derived from the implicit GNP deflator. INFLATION AND TAXATION 581–85 (Report of Comm. of Inquiry into Inflation and Taxation, May 1975) [hereafter cited as INFLATION AND TAXATION]. FAS 33, the accounting standard recently adopted for U.S. large corporations by the Financial Accounting Standards Board, offers four methods for estimating current costs: (1) index historical cost of existing plant to price indexes specific for its industry; (2) price its assets at current vendor's prices; (3) estimate current buying prices of smaller used assets; or (4) estimate the cost of a new plant of equivalent productive capacity and adjust that figure for the age of the old plant. Each of these methods poses administrative difficulties for firms. *See* Connor, "Displaying Real Figures," Wall St. J., Jan. 7, 1980, at p. 12, col. 3.

38. Lent, *supra* note 35, at 204.

39. Austria, Belgium, France, Germany, and Italy also adopted similar measures after World War I. Lent, *supra* note 35, at 195, fn. 1.

40. Rosenn, *supra* note 11, at 98. Until the end of 1973, the Brazilian system of monetary correction of fixed assets was peculiar in that sums resulting from monetary correction were considered to be new investments with the same useful life as the underlying depreciable assets. Therefore, monetary gains were written off over a period extending beyond the life of the underlying assets, which helped reduce tax revenue loss. Casanegra de Jantscher, *Taxing Business Profits during Inflation: the Latin American Experience,* 2 INT'L TAX J. 128, 140 (1976). This peculiar feature was eliminated from Brazilian law by Decree-Law No. 1.302 of Dec. 31, 1973. Monetary correction gains on depreciable assets are now written off over the remaining useful life of the underlying asset.

41. Chile, Ley sobre Impuesto a la Renta, Decree-Law No. 824 of Dec. 27, 1974, as modified by Decree-Law No. 910 of Feb. 24, 1975, art. 17(1).

42. Holzer & Schonfeld, *The French Approach to the Post-War Price Level Problem,* 38 ACCOUNTING REV. 382, 383 (1963); Tabatoni, *France,* in FOREIGN TAX POLICIES AND ECONOMIC GROWTH 275, 310–15 (Conf. Rep. of Nat'l. Bur. of Econ. Research & Brookings Inst. 1966).

43. *See* Davidson and Yasuba, *Asset Revaluation in Income Taxation in Japan,* 13 NAT'L TAX J. 45 (1960). The 1950 Japanese statute made revaluation of practically all durable assets optional. Maximum reappraisal value was calculated by multiplying book value by a coefficient derived from a price index which varied with the nature of the asset. Depreciable assets were revalued by coefficients from the wholesale price index, land by an urban land price index, and other assets by the consumer price index. *Id.* at 48–49.

Because a 6 percent tax, payable over three years for corporations and five for individuals, was levied on the write-up of depreciable assets, very few taxpayers revalued their assets. A similar statute passed in 1951 was also taken advantage of by few firms; response to a similar 1953 statute was equally disappointing. In 1954 Japan passed a statute making revaluation compulsory for the depreciable assets of large corporations. The tax on revaluation gains was cut drastically. A similar statute was enacted for smaller businesses in 1957. *Id.* at 56.

44. The coefficients used to correct depreciable assets in Austria during this period corresponded roughly rather than precisely to changes in the wholesale price index. Kollaritsch, *Austria's Answer to Inflationary Profits and Taxation,* 36 ACCOUNTING REV. 439, 440–41 (1961).

45. The two once-and-for-all optional measures, Laws 15.272 of 1959 and 17.335 of 1967, as well as accompanying decrees and regulations, are discussed in considerable detail in H. LOPEZ SANTISO, FLUCTUACIONES MONETARIAS Y ESTADOS CONTABLES 72–87 (1969) and Atchabahian, *Business Operations in Argentina,* B.N.A. TAX MANAGEMENT PORTFOLIO NO. 253 (2d) A30–31 (1976). The source of the revaluation coefficients in these two laws is unclear. Revaluation was placed on a permanent basis by Law No. 19.742 of Jy. 25, 1972, as regulated by Decree 8.626 of Dec. 7, 1972. Revaluation is tax free; one-half of the resulting sums must be capitalized and the other half maintained in a reserve for future losses.

46. The 1974 one-time revaluation was authorized by Decree No. 2.247 of 1974, art. 51; the 14 percent revaluation for 1977 by Law No. 54 of 1977, art. 3; annual indexation of 60 percent of change in the consumer price index by Law No. 54 of Dec. 23, 1977, arts. 1 and 2; and 100 percent annual indexation by Law 20 of Apr. 16, 1979.

47. *Business Operations in Taiwan,* B.N.A. TAX MANAGEMENT PORTFOLIO NO., p. A–10 (1975).

48. Lent, *supra* note 35, at 196.

49. Holzer & Schonfeld, *The German Solution of the Post-War Price Level Problem,* 38 ACCOUNTING REV. 377, 379 (1963). Partly depreciated assets were to be written up to one-third the replacement cost, plus two-thirds replacement cost, times the following fraction:

$$\frac{\text{undepreciated useful life}}{\text{the ordinary useful life.}}$$

Land and buildings had to be carried at 1935 assessed values. *Id.* at 378.

50. Lent, *supra* note 35, at 200.

51. Law No. 76 of Dec. 23, 1961. Decree No. 445–63 of Feb. 28, 1963 contained the revaluation coefficients, and the Ministerial Decision of Apr. 30, 1963 contained the regulations for implementation. Subsequent legislation extended this measure into 1964; it was renewed by Decree-Law No. 12 of Dec. 1, 1973. *See Spain-Revaluation of Assets,* 3 EUROP. TAXATION 127 (1963) and *Tax Modifications in Spain,* 14 EUROP. TAXATION 101, 102–03 (1973).

52. FOREIGN TAX LAW ASSOC., SPANISH INCOME TAX SERVICE 9, 18 (rev. 1969).

53. Decree-Law No. 21.694 of Nov. 16, 1976. Peru's prior revaluation law, Decree-Law No. 18.815 of 1971, required all fixed assets (except for buildings) acquired prior to the end of 1967 to be revalued by 55 percent, those acquired by 1968 by 10 percent, and those acquired by 1969 by 5 percent. Buildings owned by the end of 1969 were to be revalued by 15 percent, and those acquired in 1969

were to be written up by 9 percent. These percentages bore no resemblence to the Peruvian inflation rate.

54. Massone, *Adjustments of Profits for Inflation—Developments in Latin America,* 35 BULL. INT'L FISCAL DOCUM. 3, 13–14 (pt. 1, 1981). Decree-Law No. 22.493 of Apr. 11, 1979 prohibits the Executive Branch from setting the tax on revaluation gains at more than 10 percent of the increase in the cost of living.

55. Decree-Law No. 11.154 of Oct. 26, 1973, as amended by Decree-Law No. 12.853 of Sept. 12, 1975; Supreme Decree No. 14.460 of Mar. 25, 1977 contains a variety of revaluation coefficients, set out in Martí, *Latin American Tax Up Date,* 10 LAW. AM. 448, 457 (1978).

In 1972 Bolivia required all firms to revalue their imported capital assets by 60 percent, the percentage by which the Bolivian peso had been devalued that year. Domestically produced fixed assets had to be revalued by 20 percent (subsequently raised to 50 percent), the amount the tax authorities estimated the general price level would rise because of the peso's devaluation. Casanegra de Jantscher, *supra* note 40, at 135–36.

56. Law No. 13.420 of Dec. 2, 1965; Massone, *supra* note 54, at 14.

57. *See* 15 EUROP. TAXATION 282 and 308 (1975).

58. Even countries like Brazil tax any revaluation surplus that is distributed to shareholders instead of being capitalized. Recurso No. 77.060, 4th Cam., 1st Conselho de Contribuintes (1976).

59. These rates are collected in tabular form in Lent, *supra* note 35, at 209.

60. In France only 10 to 12 percent of all businesses, and only one-third of all corporations, elected to revalue. In Japan only 22 percent of juridical entities opted for revaluation prior to the year it became compulsory. In Indonesia, which imposed a 10 percent revaluation tax, no company appears to have revalued. *Id.* at 208. Even though revaluation was made compulsory in Korea in 1958 and the tax on revaluation gains was only 1 percent, the majority of all business corporations and practically all sole proprietorships failed to revalue. *See Korean Accounting Revaluation Laws,* 40 ACCOUNTING REV. 622, 624 (1965). Very few Brazilian firms took advantage of the opportunities to revalue afforded by five statutes enacted between 1946 and 1958; not until monetary correction of fixed assets became compulsory in 1964 and the tax on revaluation gains reduced from 10 to 5 percent (with the option of avoiding the tax entirely by subscribing to government bonds, paying 6 percent annual interest plus monetary correction) was there a rush to revalue. Rosenn, *supra* note 11, at 74–82.

61. Casanegra de Jantscher, *supra* note 40, at 137, lists eight countries: Argentina, Bolivia, Brazil, Chile, Colombia, Ecuador, Paraguay, and Uruguay. To these should be added Peru. Decree-Law No. 21.694 of Nov. 16, 1976 has required all commercial and industrial firms to revalue their fixed assets periodically according to coefficients set by the Executive. Revaluation sums are subject to a 4 percent tax and must be capitalized.

62. A 1973 survey found that more than twice as many U.S. firms were using FIFO than LIFO, even though LIFO would have lowered taxes for nearly all surveyed firms. Aaron, *supra* note 20, at 1, 12–13. A Commerce Department survey showed that in 1974 there were 250 major U.S. companies in the process of converting from FIFO to LIFO. Wolman, "Profits: True and False," N.Y. Times,

Oct. 27, 1974, sec. III, at p. 1, at p. 2, col. 2. In 1975 the U.S. Internal Revenue Service ceased to bar a firm using LIFO from issuing financial statements disclosing what earnings would have been under FIFO accounting. *See IRS Gives in on Proper Disclosure of Former FIFO Figures when LIFO Is Elected,* 42 J. TAXATION 175 (1975).

63. Kollaritsch, *supra* note 44, at 442.

64. The writeup was to be reduced by 2.5 percent for each decimal by which a firm's annual turnover rate exceeded two. Thus, if the turnover rate were 2.1, the writeup would be reduced to 13.5 percent. *Id.* at 442–43. At a turnover rate of six times a year, illusory inventory profits were considered negligible.

65. *Id.* at 443.

66. *Id.* at 443–44.

67. Holzer and Schonfeld, *supra* note 42, at 384–85.

68. The essential inventory concept has also been employed from time to time in Italy and the Netherlands. Lent, *supra* note 35, at 202, 205.

69. WORLD TAX SERIES, TAXATION IN FRANCE 313 (1966) [hereafter cited as WORLD TAX—FRANCE].

70. Decocq, *L'Influence de la Dépréciation Monétaire sur le Droit Commercial et le Droit Fiscal des Affaires,* in INFLUENCE DE LA DÉPRÉCIATION MONÉTAIRE SUR LA VIE JURIDIQUE PRIVÉE 257, 282 (P. Durand, ed. 1961).

71. WORLD TAX—FRANCE, *supra* note 69, at 315–16.

72. INFLATION AND TAXATION, *supra* note 37, at 541–43.

73. Casanegra de Jantscher, *supra* note 40, at 138–39. For fiscal years 1977 and 1978 the 15 percent gross income deduction could not exceed either 10 percent of the value of the inventory at the close of the fiscal year, or net taxable income. Decree No. 175 of Apr. 5, 1978. For fiscal year 1979 the 25 percent deduction cannot exceed either 15 percent of closing inventory or net taxable income. Decree No. 73 of Feb. 6, 1980.

74. Strain, *Inflation and Taxation: World Developments,* 25 CAN. TAX J. 40, 43–44 (1977); Arnold, *United Kingdom Stock Relief: LIFO Revisited,* 24 CAN. TAX J. 363 (1976).

75. Law No. 21.489 of Dec. 30, 1976.

76. Australian Income Tax Assessment Law, section 82 B-D; Israeli Law for the Encouragement of Industry of Jy. 30, 1978, discussed in Pick, *New Measures Reflecting Inflation in the Israeli Tax Legislation,* 32 BULL. INT'L FISCAL DOCUM. 547 (1979).

77. INFLATION AND TAXATION, *supra* note 37, at 566–76. This method is similar to that introduced recently to revalue inventories in Great Britain, which allows firms to reduce closing to opening inventory values, after adjustment for changes in volume. Remarks of Arnold Lovell of the British Treasury, in BROOKINGS CONFERENCE, *supra* note 8, at 229.

78. Decree-Law No. 824 of Dec. 31, 1974, art. 41(3), as modified by Decree-Law No. 1.604 of Nov. 24, 1976, art. 11(e) and (f). For a more detailed description of inventory valuation in Chile prior to the Decree-Law 1.604 modifications, *see* A. RENCORET B., EL IMPUESTO SOBRE LA RENTA 131–32 (1975).

79. Ley sobre Impuesto a la Renta, Decree-Law No. 824 of Dec. 27, 1974, as modified by Decree-Law No. 910 of Feb. 24, 1975, art. 17 (25). Article 20(2)

incorporates the following definition of interest, contained in Decree-Law No. 455 of 1974, art. 4:

> For all legal and fiscal purposes, in pecuniary credit transactions interest is the quantity which the creditor has the right to collect from the debtor, by virtue of law or contract, above and beyond the value of the capital originally lent in money with the same purchasing power. . . .
>
> In order to determine the value of the capital originally lent in money of the same purchasing power, the numerical sum originally lent shall be readjusted in accordance with the variation registered by the consumer price index as determined by the National Institute of Statistics or the organ which replaces it. . . .

80. Decree-Law No. 455 of 1974, art. 4, *id.*

81. For example, Law No. 4.357 of Jy. 16, 1964, art. 1. §6 made gains from updating the nominal value of Readjustable Treasury Bonds tax-free. Laws No. 4.357, art. 7, §3 and 4.506 of Nov. 30, 1964, art. 20, §4 exempted monetary gains on deposits made to contest tax assessments successfully. Law 4.380 of Aug. 21, 1964, art. 57 exempted monetary correction on the outstanding balance of real estate contracts, mortgages, and deposits made under the auspices of the national housing finance system. Law No. 4.728 of Jy. 14, 1965, the so-called Capital Markets Law, arts. 26, §3; 27, §1; and 28, §3 exempted from tax all gains resulting from monetary correction of the principal of debentures or other corporate obligations, bills of exchange *(letras de câmbio),* and bank deposits and loans, provided their format complies with the conditions and restrictions imposed in the Capital Markets Law.

The statutes permitting monetary correction of credit instruments contemplated periodic readjustments of the outstanding balance of the debt after publicationof the price indexes for the relevant readjustment period. This proved impractical, and the practice of prefixing the monetary correction rate became widespread. The amount that corresponded to the official inflation adjustment remained tax-exempt until Decree-Law No. 403 of Dec. 30, 1968 imposed a sliding-scale withholding tax on the entire amount of prefixed monetary correction. See chap. 6, *supra,* at notes 67–71 and accompanying text.

82. Decree-Law No. 1.338 of Jy. 23, 1974, art. 13. Prefixed monetary correction and monetary correction received by individuals from ordinary private contracts is not exempt from taxation. d'Almeida Jr. & Neviani, *Brazil,* in L'INFLATION ET LA FISCALITÉ, *supra* note 1, at 271, 278.

In 1980 a compulsory loan was levied upon tax-exempt income, including monetary correction, of individuals in excess of Cr$ 4,000,000 (then about U.S. $77,500). Decree-Law 1.782 of Apr. 16, 1980, as amended by Decree-Law No. 1.790 of Je. 9, 1980. Even though this so-called loan bears 3 percent annual interest and monetary correction, it has substantial tax aspects since the official monetary correction rate has been running at approximately half the actual inflation rate.

83. Decree-Law No. 1.338 of Jy. 23, 1974, art. 14.

84. Special legislation has recently been adopted permitting certain borrowers to deduct monetary correction payments. Thus, Decree-Law No. 1.410 of Jy. 31, 1975 permitted to borrowers from financial institutions under control of the

federal government for projects relating to certain industries that the government wished to stimulate, such as steel and petrochemicals, to deduct monetary correction payments in excess of 20 percent during financial year 1975.

85. Yoran & Zuckerman, *Israel,* in *Les Encouragements Fiscaux Utilisés comme Instruments de Politique des Pouvoirs Publics,* 61A CAHIERS DE DROIT FISCAL INT'L 375, 377 (1976); J. Bachrach, *Business Operations in Israel,* B.N.A. TAX PORTFOLIO NO. 250(2d) A36 (1974) and Changes and Additions, p. 9 (1976); Pick, *Israel,* in L'INFLATION ET LA FISCALITÉ, *supra* note 1, at 377, 385. Amendment No. 32 to the Income Tax Ordinance, enacted in 1978, made it clear that all court awarded linkage differentials were fully taxable. The Minister of Finance recently exempted all court awarded linkage differentials in personal injury cases retroactive to April 1, 1979. Yoran, *"Linkage or Revaluation" or "A General or a Specific Index?,"* 15 ISRAEL L. REV. 106, 108 (1980).

86. Mayer, *Österreich,* in L'INFLATION ET LA FISCALITÉ, *supra* note 1, at 231, 232–33.

87. WORLD TAX-FRANCE, *supra* note 69, at 498–99.

88. OECD, INDEXATION OF FINANCIAL ASSETS 15–17 (1975).

89. S. MUKHERJEE AND C. ORLANS, INDEXATION IN AN INFLATIONARY ECONOMY: A CASE STUDY OF FINLAND 50–54 (1975).

90. *Id.* at 52–56; OECD, *supra* note 88, at 17–20.

91. *See* Colombian Decree-Law 19.308 of Mar. 7, 1972; Decree 677 of May 2, 1972; Decree 120 of 1974, discussed in Martí, *Taxation,* 7 LAW. OF THE AM. 415, 430 (1975); and Decree 2053 of 1974, art. 102, discussed in Perenzin, *Business Operations in Colombia,* B.N.A. TAX MANAGEMENT PORTFOLIO NO. 260(2d) A 19 (1975).

92. Galper & Mendenhall, *United States,* in L'INFLATION ET LA FISCALITÉ, *supra* note 1, at 321, 330; Meeles, *Netherlands,* in L'INFLATION ET LA FISCALITÉ, *supra* note 1, at 461, 464–65.

93. *See* Utility Trailer Manufacturing Company v. United States, 212 F. Supp. 773 (S.D. Calif. 1962), where a company had issued indexed notes, called "Registered Inflation Provision Notes," paying 6 percent interest annually. The principal was readjusted on maturity in accordance with the increase in the consumer price index since issuance, but could not fall below 100 percent of the obligation's face value. The company sought to deduct each year as "discount expense" an amount representing the increments in principal for variations in the consumer price index that year. The court refused to permit accrual of this readjustment expense because its amount was uncertain and contingent. Although it might be good accounting practice to set aside a reserve to meet the contingency of increased debt on maturity, this was not controlling for tax purposes. The court was unclear as to whether the readjustment should be considered principal or interest; however, its opinion does suggest the increase in principal should be deductible when actually paid.

94. Law No. 21.308 of May 7, 1976.

95. Law No. 4.357 of Jy. 16, 1964, art. 27.

96. Law No. 4.663 of Je. 3, 1965, art. 5.

97. *See* Rosenn, *supra* note 11, at 88–89.

98. Also included were shares or other equities in other corporations. Decree-Law No. 62, art. 4.

99. This analysis draws upon that of Mario Simonsen and Augusto Jefferson Lemos, in "A Inflação e a Legislação Tributária Brasileira" 35–36 (mimeo prepared for Curso de Advogados de Emprêsa of CEPED 1967).

100. J. Chacel et al, Correção Monetária 105 (1970).

101. Decree-Law No. 401 of Dec. 29, 1968.

102. Firms could also purchase nontransferable Readjustable Treasury Bonds in double the amount of the revaluation tax in lieu of paying the tax.

103. Decree-Law No. 433 of Jan. 23, 1969, arts. 1 & 2. The 20 percent limitation was removed by Decree-Law No. 1.302 of Dec. 31, 1973.

104. Decree-Law No. 1.338 of Jy. 23, 1974, art. 15(4) and (5).

105. Technically, a *portaria,* which is an intraministerial decree, cannot modify a law, but Brazilians often resort to paralegal techniques to resolve legal quandaries. *See* Rosenn, *The Jeito: Brazil's Institutional Bypass of the Formal Legal System and Its Developmental Implications,* 19 Am. J. Comp. L. 514 (1971).

106. Portaria 544 is explained in detail in C. Botelho de Morães, Comentários às Novas Alterações do Impôsto de Renda 186–93 (1975).

107. Law No. 6.404 of Dec. 15, 1976. The Corporation Law instituted a new system of monetary correction of corporate balance sheets. It requires firms to correct annually, in accordance with officially recognized indexes for monetary depreciation, their net worth and their fixed assets, including investments, depreciation or depletion reserves, and deferred assets. Sums resulting from monetary correction of net worth are allocated to a special reserve for capitalization through issuance of stock dividends after the next general stockholder's meeting. Counterentries of monetary correction of both net worth and fixed assets are made to a monetary correction account, the balance of which is deducted from profits if positive, or added to profits if negative.

108. Decree-Law No. 1.598 of Dec. 26, 1977, arts. 39–40. The calculation of monetary correction adjustment for ORTNs is discussed in chap. 6, *supra,* at notes 31–33 and the accompanying text.

109. Decree-Law No. 1.598 of Dec. 26, 1977 arts. 51–53.

110. Net worth was defined as the difference between assets and current liabilities, without taking into account the fiscal year's profit or loss. Law No. 15.564 of Feb. 14, 1964, art. 35. This section began with Law 13.305 of 1959 inserting art. 26 *bis* into Law No. 8.419 of Apr. 10, 1946. *See* A. Rencoret B., *supra* note 78, at 125.

111. Law No. 15.564 of 1964, art. 35. Depreciable assets were to be revalued in accordance with coefficients from the consumer price index, unless acquired with foreign currency loans. To the extent these loans remained unpaid, assets purchased with these loans were to be readjusted by the change in the exchange rate between acquisition and that in force on the day of the balance sheet's close. Securities were to be readjusted by the most recent stock exchange quotations.

112. Arts. 32(1) and 41(1). This language was eliminated from art. 41(1) by Decree-Law No. 1.604 of Nov. 24, 1976, art. 11(c), but art. 32(1) of Decree-Law No. 824 was left unchanged.

113. Decree-Law No. 1.604 of Nov. 24, 1976, art. 11(a) and (i), now requires firms which do not habitually buy and sell securities to exclude the value of shares, bonds, and debentures for the purpose of calculating their net worth adjustment.

114. Chilean Decree-Law No. 824, art. 41(3). The various techniques for determining replacement cost of inventory in Chile are described at p. 319, *supra.*

115. Decree-Law No. 824, art. 32.

116. ORGANIZACION DE LOS ESTADOS AMERICANOS, INFLACION Y TRIBUTACION 69–74 (1978) [hereafter cited as OAS STUDY].

117. Law No. 21.894 of Oct. 27, 1978.

118. *Id.* at art. 2.

119. Law No. 14.948 of Nov. 7, 1979.

120. Chilean Law No. 11.575 of Aug. 14, 1954. *See* Carvallo Hederra, *Incidencia de la Inflación en el Sistema Tributario,* 5 Rev. Der. Econ. 145, 147 (Nos. 19 and 20, 1967).

121. OAS STUDY, *supra* note 116, at 25.

122. Income Tax (Rates) Act 1976, No. 57, Je. 4, 1976; Bratby & Orrock, *Australia,* in L'INFLATION ET LA FISCALITÉ, *supra* note 1, at 201, 214.

123. Laws No. 20.046 of Dec. 28, 1972 and No. 21.481 of Dec. 30, 1976.

124. OAS STUDY, *supra* note 116, at 28–29.

125. *Id.* at 26–28.

126. Law No. 54 of 1977, art. 1, as amended by Law No. 20 of 1979, art. 1.

127. ARIZ. LEGIS. SERV., LAWS 1980, ch. 44.

128. 16 COL. REV. STAT. 1973, § 39–22–103.5 (1979 Supp.).

129. WEST MINN. STAT. ANN., §§ 290.06 (2d) and (3g) (1980 Supp.).

130. LAWS OF MONT., §§ 15–591, 15–595, and 15–596 (1980).

131. 5 CODE OF LAWS OF S. CAR. ANN. 1976, §§ 12–7–150, 12–7–160, and 12–7–170 (1980 Supp.).

132. INFLATION AND TAXATION, *supra* note 37, at 194–96; V. TANZI, *supra* note 1, at 38–39; Petrei, *Inflation Adjustment Schemes under the Personal Income Tax,* 22 IMF STAFF PAPERS 539, 546 (1975).

133. Tanzi, *Adjusting Personal Income Taxes for Inflation: The Foreign Experience,* in BROOKINGS CONFERENCE, *supra* note 8, at 215, 226. The correction factor is now 2.1 percent for each full three point rise in the hourly earnings index above its March 1974 level of 141.9. OECD, Report by Comm. on Fiscal Affairs, THE ADJUSTMENT OF PERSONAL INCOME TAX SYSTEMS FOR INFLATION 50–51 (1976) [hereafter cited as OECD REPORT].

134. 21–22 Eliz. II c. 30, Sect. 15, Jy. 27, 1973; Allan, Dodge, and Poddar, *Indexing the Personal Income Tax: A Federal Perspective,* 22 CAN. TAX J. 355, 358 (1974).

135. V. TANZI, *supra* note 1, at 27, 29. Uruguayan Decree-Law No. 14.252 of Aug. 22, 1974 eliminated the taxation of all personal income except that derived from the conduct of a business or industry. 25 FOREIGN TAX BI-WEEKLY BULL. 15 (Nos. 33–34, Dec. 25, 1974 and Jan. 1, 1975).

136. V. TANZI, *supra* note 1, at 29.

137. Belgian Law of Jan. 5, 1976 (The Program Law), described in Spruyt, *Belgique: Modifications Apportées par la Loi du Janvier 1976 au Regime d'Imposition des Revenues Professionels,* 31 BULL. INT'L FISCAL DOCUM. 17, 23–24 (1977) and Dupont, *Belgique,* in L'INFLATION ET LA FISCALITÉ, *supra* note 1, at 251, 253–54. Between Apr. 1 and Dec. 31, 1976, indexation was temporarily suspended as to incomes in excess of BF 42,700 per month. J. Malherbe, *Business Operations in Belgium,* B.N.A. TAX

MANAGEMENT PORTFOLIO No. 93 (4th)(1972), Changes and Additions 2 F(C) (1/3/77).

138. Finance Act of 1977, sect. 22(2).

139. Decree-Law No. 19.653 of 1972. *See also* OAS STUDY, *supra* note 116, at 25–26.

140. West. CALIF. ANN. REV. & T. CODE, §§ 17041 and 17171 (1979 Supp.).

141. IOWA CODE ANN., §§ 422.4 and 422.5 (West. 1980 Supp.). The inflation adjustment is to be set at 100 percent of the change in the implicit GNP for any year in which the unobligated state fund has a balance in excess of $60 million, any of the phase-in-provisions to the contrary notwithstanding.

142. ORE. REV. LAWS, ch. 240, sec. 3 (1979).

143. WIS. STAT. ANN., § 71.09 (1980 Supp.). The statute is not clear whether this 10 percent cap is an annual or cumulative limitation.

144. Decree-Law No. 401 of Dec. 30, 1968, art. 29. This provision is interpreted in art. 573 of the Brazilian Income Tax Regulations (Decree No. 76.186 of Sept. 2, 1975) to support the following proposition: "The values expressed in cruzeiros in these Regulations will be updated annually by the Minister of Finance, ignoring fractions less than Cr$1 (one cruzeiro)."

145. With inflation in excess of 10 percent in 1974, the Dutch decided to suspend operation of the automatic adjustment for the year and to instead raise basic exemptions levels by 8.3 percent. This was done to preserve revenue and give the lower income groups more of the benefits of any adjustment. In 1976 the adjustment was suspended only for upper income levels. OECD REPORT, *supra* note 133, at 50–51; Meeles, *supra* note 92, at 466–67.

146. Petrei, *supra* note 132, at 542–43; INFLATION AND TAXATION, *supra* note 37, at 212–13; V. TANZI, *supra* note 1, at 39–40.

147. INFLATION AND TAXATION, *supra* note 37, at 199–200; V. TANZI, *supra* note 1, at 31.

148. Petrei, *supra* note 132, at 546; Meary, *France,* in L'INFLATION ET LA FISCALITÉ, *supra* note 1, at 351, 355–56.

149. Pick, *supra* note 76, at 549; Tanzi, *supra* note 133, at 224; Klimowsky, *Israeli Tax Reform on Indexed Income and Capital Gains,* 1976 BRIT. TAX REV. 71, 72–73. Prior to 1975 Israel exempted a cost-of-living component of wages and salaries.

150. Petrei, *supra* note 132, at 541.

151. For example, when Senator McGovern proposed that the United States tax capital gains like ordinary income, Nixon Administration officials defended preferential treatment partly on the ground that the bulk of capital gains stem solely from inflation and are hence illusory. YALE COMMENT, *supra* note 18, at 716. Canada's Finance Minister gave the following explanation for the decision to subject only half of all capital gains to taxation: "[A]t the time of tax reform, it was decided that only one half of capital gains would be taxable, partially in recognition . . . of inflation." Cited in V. TANZI, *supra* note 1, at 42.

152. *See* notes 39 to 61 *supra* and the text thereto.

153. J. Bachrach, *supra* note 85, at A–11, A–22.

154. If a capital asset, such as good will, has no cost basis, the inflationary component of the gain is calculated in accordance with the following formula:

$$IG = SP \times \frac{I_s - I_m}{I_s}, \text{ where}$$

IG is the inflationary gain;

SP is the sale price;

I_s is the index number at the date of the sale; and

I_m is the index number at the middle of the holding period. Klimowsky, *supra* note 149, at 73.

155. The holding period is two years for real estate and one year for other long-term capital gains. However, if an asset is sold between twenty-four and thirty-six months (twelve and twenty-four months for personalty) after acquisition, for the purpose of calculating the inflationary component of the gain, the date of acquisition is deemed to have moved forward by the number of full months remaining between the sale and the end of the 36th month. J. Bachrach, *supra* note 153, at Changes and Additions 6(1) (March 28, 1977); Rafael, *Tax Reform in Israel,* 30 BULL. INT'L FISCAL DOCUM. 505, 508 (1976).

156. Argentine Capital Gains Tax Law *(Impuesto a los Beneficios Eventuales),* art. 5. This inflation adjustment was originally limited to the period between the date of purchase and Dec. 31, 1960 and was subsequently extended to Dec. 31, 1966.

157. Argentine Law No. 19.414 of Dec. 31, 1971, art. 5. If an asset has been revalued for depreciation purposes, that valuation is used as the cost basis for capital gains purposes. If the asset has not been revalued, the updated cost basis is determined by first deducting 2 percent per year from historical cost of the value allocated to buildings or construction, then multiplying by a coefficient determined by the Tax Board from the wholesale price index. Argentina's new capital gains tax law, Law 21.284 of Ap. 2, 1976, has retained this system. Atchabahian, *supra* note 45, at A36–37.

158. Brazilian Law No. 4.357 of Jy. 16, 1964, art. 4. The law granted a reduction of the tax due of 2 percent for each year the taxpayer had owned the property prior to the sale. *Id.* §1. In addition, the taxpayer had the option of paying the 5 percent tax on monetary correction gains in cash or subscribing in twice the amount due to Readjustable Treasury Bonds paying annual interest of 6 percent plus monetary correction. *Id.* at §§2 and 6.

159. Brazilian Decree-Law No. 94 of Dec. 30, 1966, art. 2 abolished the tax for individuals, but legal entities continued to be required to include capital gains as ordinary income. Decree-Law No. 1.381 of Dec. 23, 1974, as amended by Decree-Law 1.510 of Dec. 27, 1976, reimposed the tax by treating individuals making the prescribed number of real estate transactions as if they were legal entities. *See generally,* Juocys, *Income Tax on Real Estate Transactions in Brazil,* 31 BULL. INT'L FISCAL DOCUM. 491 (1977).

160. Decree-Law No. 1.641 of Dec. 7, 1978, as amended by Decree-Law No. 1.790 of Je. 9, 1980.

161. DALLOZ, CODE GÉNÉRAL DES IMPOTS 35A (1975); 25 FOREIGN TAX LAW BI-WEEKLY BULL. 8 (Nos. 1 and 2, May 15 and 24, 1974).

162. WORLD TAX-FRANCE, *supra* note 69, at 550. If the land were acquired prior to 1959, the seller could increase his basis by revaluing in accordance with coefficients determined for revaluation of business firms' depreciable assets. *Id.* at 551. And if the land had been acquired prior to 1950, the seller had the option of taking 30 percent of the sales price as his basis. *Ibid.*

163. Law No. 76–660 of Jy. 19, 1976, arts. 3–5.

164. Price Waterhouse, *Doing Business in Sweden* 27–28 (Dec. 1974).

165. Colombian Decree No. 2.247 of 1974; Law No. 54 of 1977; Law No. 20 of 1979.

166. INT'L BUREAU OF FISCAL DOCUM., 2 GUIDES TO EUROPEAN TAXATION: THE TAXATION OF COMPANIES IN EUROPE—UNITED KINGDOM 66–67 (No. 2, 1981) [hereafter cited as GUIDES TO EUR. TAX.]; V. TANZI, *supra* note 1, at 49.

167. Law No. 15.564 of Feb. 14, 1964, art. 54.

168. J. Malherbe, *supra* note 137, at A–53. There is no tax if the property has been held for more than eight years. *Ibid.*

169. *Supra* at note 153 and the accompanying text.

170. *Supra* at notes 156 and 165 and the accompanying text.

171. *Supra* at note 168 and the accompanying text.

172. J. Malherbe, *supra* note 137, at Changes and Additions 8 F(C) (Mar. 28, 1977).

173. FOREIGN TAX LAW ASSOC., DANISH INCOME TAX SERVICE, chap. 13, at 17 (Oct. 1973); Kjaer, *Denmark,* in L'INFLATION ET LA FISCALÍTE, *supra* note 1, at 295, 298; A. Spang-Hanssen & E. Trolle, *Business Operations in Denmark,* B.N.A. TAX MANAGEMENT PORTFOLIO No. 181–2d, p. A–16 (1980).

174. Odegard, *Norway,* in L'INFLATION ET LA FISCALITÉ, *supra* note 1, at 451, 455.

175. *Supra* at notes 161–63 and the accompanying text.

176. *Supra* at notes 156 and 165 and the accompanying text.

177. Lampreave Perez, *Espagne,* in L'INFLATION ET LA FISCALITÉ, *supra* note 1, at 305, 315.

178. Räihä, *Finland,* in L'INFLATION ET LA FISCALITÉ, *supra* note 1, at 341, 343.

179. MEXICAN INCOME AND COMMERCIAL RECEIPTS TAX LAWS, *supra* note 9, art. 70.

180. Currently, primary financial statements must be presented on a monetarily corrected basis in Argentina, Brazil, and Chile. Supplemental financial statements on a current value basis are required or recommended, at least for major corporations, in Australia, Canada, West Germany, the Netherlands, New Zealand, South Africa, the United Kingdom, and the United States. Hauworth, *A Comparison of Various International Proposals on Inflation Accounting: A Practitioner's View,* 16 INT'L J. OF ACCOUNTING 63 (Fall 1980). For a helpful presentation of the issues, *see* T. FIFLIS & H. KRIPKE, ACCOUNTING FOR LAWYERS 395–456 (2d ed. 1977).

181. Hart, *supra* note 27, 249–50.

182. For example, sect. 174 of the U.S. Internal Revenue Code permits immediate deduction of research and development expenditures, which theoretically should be allocated over the invention's useful life. Great Britain permits firms to write off 100 percent of the cost of certain plant and equipment in the first year. 2 GUIDES TO EUR. TAX. *supra* note 166, at 60–61.

183. Firms generally do not actually deposit these funds in an account specifically earmarked for replacement of inventory or depreciable assets. If they did actually deposit such funds in accounts that bore interest at the rate of inflation, normal depreciation methods would partially adjust for the effect of inflation. *See* YALE COMMENT, *supra* note 18, at 720–21, suggesting that straight line depreciation

accounts for almost half the total intervening inflation, and accelerated depreciation more than half, if depreciation allowances were set aside at interest rates equal to the inflation rate. But these calculations fail to take into account the income tax on the interest earned.

184. *See* notes 48–57, *supra,* and the accompanying text.

185. Argentina, Australia, Belgium, Canada, Chile, Colombia, Israel, Luxembourg, the Netherlands, Sweden, and seven U.S. states index their personal income tax laws to the consumer price index.

186. Prior to the start of 1981, Brazil had been indexing on an expurgated version of the wholesale price index. Since then it has been linking the value of Readjustable Treasury Bonds to a recently created national consumer price index. Peru indexes to its minimum wage, a measure once employed by Brazil and Chile. The Netherlands indexes to the consumer price index after netting out indirect taxes and subsidies, a method also used by Denmark until 1974.

187. *See, e.g.,* Rosenn, *supra* note 11, at 97–101.

188. *See* notes 35–38 and 63–78 *supra* and the accompanying text.

189. For arguments on both sides of this question, *compare* Denison, *Price Series for Indexing the Income Tax System,* in BROOKINGS CONFERENCE, *supra* note 8, at 233, 246–49, *with* Gordon, *Comments, id.* at 264–66.

190. Denison, *supra* note 189, at 248.

191. Blinder, *Comments,* in BROOKINGS CONFERENCE, *supra* note 8, at 261, 262.

192. *See* chap. 2, *supra,* at p. 30.

193. Denison, *supra* note 189, at 249.

194. *Id.* at 256, Table 9–2, col. 8.

195. In 1969 the U.S. Office of Business Statistics began publishing a fixed-weight implicit GNP deflator, thereby making it more useful as an inflation adjustment. Comment, *The Feasibility of Adjusting for Inflation in Computing Taxable Income,* 49 WASH. L. REV. 873, 893–94 (1974).

196. *See* Denison, *supra* note 189, at 256–57.

197. "Inflação, Correção Monetária e Índices de Preços," 29 Conj. Econ. 91, 93 (Sept. 1975). The expurgation extended to all "inflationary accidents", characterized as seasonal fluctuations, droughts, frosts, and oil imports. Brazilian wages are indexed, and expurgation was undoubtedly motivated more by concern about producing a wage-price spiral than concern about a diminution in tax yields.

198. For arguments on both sides of this issue *compare* Denison, *supra* note 189, at 258–59, *with* INFLATION AND TAXATION, *supra* note 37, at 176–83 and Gordon, *supra* note 189, at 265.

199. Denison, *supra* note 189, at 259.

200. INFLATION AND TAXATION, *supra* note 37, at 167–76; Ruppe, *General Report,* in L'INFLATION ET LA FISCALITÉ, *supra* note 1, at 89, 115.

201. Income Tax (Rates and Assessment) Amendment Act 1979, No. 43, Je. 14, 1979.

202. Chilean Decree-Law No. 824 of Dec. 27, 1974, arts. 95–97.

203. *Id.* at art. 51.

204. *Id.* at art. 31(3).

205. Law No. 21.911 of Dec. 19, 1978.

206. Brazilian Decree-Law No. 1.351 of Oct. 24, 1974, art. 1.

207. *See generally* Hirao and Aguirre, *supra* note 11, at 289–320.

208. Brazilian Law No. 4.357 of Jy. 16, 1964, art. 7.

209. Decree-Law No. 326 of May 8, 1967, art. 12; Regulamento do Impôsto sôbre a Renda e Proventos de Qualquer Natureza, Decree No. 76.186 of Sept. 2, 1975, art. 511.

210. *Id.* at art. 511(9).

211. Hirao and Aguirre, *supra* note 11, at 303.

212. Price Waterhouse, *Doing Business in Chile* 26 (Jan. 1975); *Id.* (May 1975 Supp.) at p. 4.

213. Pick, *supra* note 85, at 381–84.

214. Law No. 21.281 of Apr. 2, 1976.

215. OECD REPORT, *supra* note 133, at 16–17.

216. P. SAMUELSON, *supra* note 15, at 356.

217. Allan, Dodge, and Poddar, *supra* note 134, at 368.

218. Bossons & Wilson, *Adjusting Tax Rates for Inflation,* 21 CAN. TAX J. 189, 190–93 (1973); Pierce & Enzler, *The Implication for Economic Stability of Indexing the Individual Income Tax,* in BROOKINGS CONFERENCE, *supra* note 8, at 173.

219. BROOKINGS CONFERENCE, *supra* note 8, at 329.

10

INDEXATION: INFLATIONARY ANESTHESIA OR ADRENALINE?

Indexation is not a cure for inflation, nor is it meant to be. The aims of indexation are much more modest. Its primary purpose is the alleviation of many of the economic ills and distortions caused by inflation, thereby making it easier to live with inflation. Secondarily, it is intended to facilitate implementation of stabilization measures. Whether this form of inflationary anesthesia aggravates the disease is a much debated question. Detractors claim that indexation will exacerbate existing inflationary pressures, decrease the willingness of the body politic to accept austerity measures necessary to eradicate inflation, and institutionalize the existing rate of inflation. Proponents claim that indexation helps eliminate inflation by depriving the government and special interest groups of financial incentives from its continuance and by reducing the unfairness and misallocation of resources normally attributable to inflation. They also contend that indexation makes stabilization measures politically more palatable by permitting avoidance of the recession and unemployment normally accompanying such measures.

This chapter will assess the desirability of adopting comprehensive indexation in highly developed economies. Because no modern developed country has ever adopted comprehensive indexation, the chapter begins by considering the theoretical implications of a perfectly indexed economy. It then compares the experiences of Brazil, Finland, and Israel, three countries with widespread indexation schemes, and proceeds to examine the implications of these experiences for developed economies. The chapter concludes with a proposal for adoption of partial indexation in developed countries suffering from substantial inflation, and with an analysis of the costs and benefits of this proposal.

THEORETICAL IMPLICATIONS OF A PERFECTLY INDEXED ECONOMY

Although no country has ever completely indexed its economy, one can imagine a free market economy in which the redistributive effects of inflation were entirely neutralized by complete indexation. If the price level were to rise by 10 percent during a given period, all contracts, leases, wages, fees, taxes, pensions, insurance and welfare payments, bank deposits, and other charges would automatically rise by 10 percent. Even cash might be stamped with a date of issuance and indexed accordingly. The object of a perfectly indexed legal structure would be to insure that all kinds of income and expenditures change at precisely the same rate, thereby completely neutralizing all of inflation's wealth-redistributive effects.[1] With no change in relative prices, no one would be either hurt or helped by inflation. All income and expenditures would be automatically readjusted to compensate for changes in the purchasing power of money.

If it were possible to construct an ideal inflation index and devise a legal structure that would automatically link every monetary transfer to that index, at least three different scenarios might result. The first is that inflation might spiral upward at rapidly increasing rates because complete indexation would immediately telegraph to the rest of the economy inflationary pressures felt in one sector. With no unindexed contracts or automatic stabilizing mechanisms in the tax structure to act as inflationary shock absorbers, the economic system might be precariously unstable. Indeed, if inflationary pressures are experienced in such an economy, there may not be sufficient friction to attain a new equilibrium. Like a Rube Goldberg device, an increase in one set of prices because of a bad harvest or increases in the price of oil imports might trigger wage increases, which, in turn, would activate further price rises. These would trigger devaluation and result in a continuous price-wage spiral.

The second scenario is that inflation might cease because it is pointless. If neither the government nor any other societal group is able to profit from it, inflation loses its *raison d'être.* In this scenario, inflation might spiral upward for a time. Eventually, both government and private groups would realize that a perfectly indexed system had made it impossible to gain any economic advantage from inflation and would cease behaving in ways that produce inflationary pressures. At this point inflation would disappear from the economic scene.

A third scenario might also revolve around a gradual reduction in the inflation rate as societal groups eventually recognize the futility of trying to gain an economic advantage from inflation. Unlike the second scenario, however, in this version indexation itself would continue to produce a basic inflationary feedback, making it impossible to eliminate inflation entirely. In order to wring the last few percentage points of inflation from an economy, indexation itself would have to be eliminated.

Which of these scenarios is most probable depends in good part on the theory that one uses to explain the causes of inflation.[2] To the monetarist, who views inflation's cause as expansion of the money supply in excess of productivity gains, complete indexation will eventually result in the second scenario—elimination of inflation—provided that the rate of monetary expansion is limited to the rate of growth in real output. This proviso contains the monetarist's basic premise: reduction in the rate of growth of the money supply curtails inflation. From this point of view, indexation is essentially a catalytic agent that makes this reduction in the money supply feasible by depriving the government and other societal groups of the opportunity to profit from inflation. If the government is deprived of the additional revenues from the "inflation tax" resulting from the creation of fiat money, the automatic increase in effective tax rates, and the satisfaction of debts in depreciated currency, it will have no incentive to promulgate inflationary policies.[3] Similarly, if labor unions are assured that their real wage rates will not be eroded by inflation, they will not build into collective bargaining agreements expectations of price changes based upon prior rates of inflation. Consequently, it should be possible to reduce the inflation rate by appropriate stabilization measures without significantly increasing the unemployment rate.[4] In short, indexation makes it easier to fight inflation.

Even monetarists disagree, however, about the effect of indexation of money. Morag, a distinguished Israeli economist, argues that indexation of cash and the excess of bank deposits over loans will result in an infinite expansion of the money supply and a concomitant infinite rise in the general level of prices.[5] On the other hand, Lemgruber, a Brazilian economist, advocates indexation of the money stock (M_1) to the extent practicable on the theory that failure to index money still leaves the government with a substantial incentive to try to collect an inflation tax.[6]

Support for Morag's view can be derived from the post-World War II experience of Hungary, which experienced the highest rates of inflation yet recorded. Between August of 1945 and July of 1946 inflation averaged 19,800 percent per month, with the highest monthly rate reaching the mind-boggling figure of 4.2×10^{16}. On January 1, 1946 the Hungarian government issued a decree indexing tax liabilities to the official price index, by this time published on a daily basis. This decree created a new unit of account called the tax *pengö.* To safeguard the value of its tax revenues, on January 10, 1946 issued another decree requiring commercial and savings banks to open accounts denominated in tax *pengö.* Private citizens and corporations were also permitted to make demand deposits in tax *pengö,* thereby providing complete indexation of demand deposits. This measure was tantamount to indexing cash, for the huge bulk of cash balances was thrown into these tax *pengö* accounts. With steadily shrinking base upon which to levy the inflation tax, the Hungarian government issued huge quantities of paper money in a desperate attempt to attract real resources. The result was the complete collapse of the currency.[7]

To the Keynesians, who read the quantity theory of money equation from right to left, as though written in Hebrew, indexation is likely to result in the first scenario—an accelerating inflationary process. If inflation is the result of consumers bidding up the price level by attempting to buy more goods and services than can be physically produced, prices should continue to rise until taxes absorb the excess spending capacity or the finiteness of the money supply itself effectively limits the excess demand. But under a perfectly indexed system, the money supply will increase with inflation and the automatic stabilizing mechanism will have disappeared from the income tax. Removal through indexation of the friction and inertia incident to imperfectly anticipated inflation will, under Keynesian reasoning, push inflation into high gear.[8]

To the "cost-push" school, who generally view inflation as caused by certain societal groups seeking to expand their share of national income at the expense of other groups, complete indexation is likely to produce the skyrocketing inflation of the first scenario. They argue that the illusion of a stable currency moderates these demands for a larger share of the pie by permitting the government to inflate the pie's nominal size. If there were complete indexation, the struggle for a larger share of the pie would be intensified.[9] Cost-push adherents attributing the cause of inflation to rising commodity or fuel prices contend that indexation would rapidly transmit those price pressures throughout the economy and send wages and prices spiralling upward.

> An automatic across the board indexing system would have promptly translated skyrocketing commodity prices not only into higher interest rates but into higher wages. Thus it would have put relentless cost-push pressure on the general price level. Under the present system, one has at least a fighting chance to avoid converting the 1973–74 "soft-core" inflation . . . into a "hard-core" price-wage spiral reaching well into the future.
>
> Because of its uneven impacts, then, our existing system throws sand into the gears of inflation. Indexing would oil the gears and speed the process of inflation.[10]

To the structuralists who view inflation as caused by either an inelastic supply of food for domestic consumption or import inelasticity, total indexation is also likely to result in the first scenario's steadily accelerating inflationary spiral. Because indexation will not affect the structual imbalances seen as the causes of inflation, each new round of price increases triggers further increases in wages and prices. On the other hand, "supply siders" view the second or third scenarios as most likely, for indexation would give savers and investors greater incentives and would prevent automatic tax increases. If the resulting increase in savings is properly channeled, productivity should increase, and inflation should *pro tanto* decrease.

Some economists of various schools view indexation as a source of inflationary feedback that will prevent an economy from ever entirely eliminating inflation as long as indexation continues. They view the third scenario as most likely on the theory that indexation itself becomes an autonomous source of inflation.[11]

This wide divergence in economic theory and predicted outcome explains why there is little agreement among economists about the desirability of adopting comprehensive indexation. Of course, no economist seriously urges that any country try to convert its economy into a perfectly indexed system. Such a proposal would be impractical for two reasons. First, the transaction costs of implementing such a proposal would be astronomical. Just the cost of constructing and maintaining an index sufficiently accurate to measure the inflation rate would be enormous. At very high rates of inflation index numbers would have to be reported on a weekly, or even daily basis, to prevent price lags. The cost of readjusting all money transactions occurring in a complex economy on a weekly or daily basis would be prohibitive.

Second, total indexation would deprive the economy of the myriad benefits of the price system. Any change in relative prices in a perfectly indexed system would automatically set off a chain reaction that would ultimately result in the restoration of the previous set of relative prices. As a consequence, producers would be deprived of important signals about relative demand changes normally communicated through the price system. Elimination of this feedback mechanism would substantially increase the extent to which producers misjudge the demand for particular products, thus leading to an increasingly inefficient allocation of resources.

These practical and theoretical limitations make it difficult to take seriously any proposal urging that an economy be completely indexed.

COMPREHENSIVE INDEXATION—THE EXPERIENCES OF BRAZIL, FINLAND, AND ISRAEL

Three countries with substantial experience with broad-spectrum indexation are Brazil, Finland, and Israel. The country with the most comprehensive system of indexation is Brazil, which has indexed its tax system, government and corporate bonds, savings and time deposits, mortgage and bank loans, construction contracts, insurance, leases, pensions, public utility rates, social security, wages, and even all judgments, court costs, and awards of attorneys' fees.[12] Prior to 1968, Finland indexed government and corporate bonds, pensions, insurance, savings and time deposits, construction contracts, mortgages and bank loans, leases, and collective bargaining agreements.[13] Israel currently indexes its tax system, government and corporate bonds, pensions, insurance, savings deposits, mortgage and bank loans, and collective bargaining agreements.[14] In addition, all three countries have adopted minidevaluation policies that result, in practice, in rough indexation of their foreign exchange rates.[15]

The Brazilian Experience

For a time Brazilian economic performance subsequent to the introduction of indexation in 1964 was most impressive. During the first quarter of 1964, inflation had been galloping at an annual rate of 144 percent. The annual economic growth rate had fallen to 3 percent, a rate so low that when population growth was subtracted, per capital income was actually declining. At this point the military ousted the inept Goulart regime and entrusted economic planning to a group of imaginative technocrats, who rejected traditional economic austerity measures advocated by the IMF on the ground that these would have caused a recession. Instead they instituted a gradual stabilization program. This program was principally intended to remedy the host of economic distortions generated by several decades of continuous inflation. Indexation was designed to play the crucial but temporary role of facilitating living with inflation during the gradual stabilization period.[16] From 1967 to 1973 Brazil's economic success was so spectacular that economists refer to the period as "The Brazilian Miracle." The annual real rate of growth in GNP averaged a phenomenal 10 percent, and the annual inflation rate, as measured by the cost-of-living index for Rio, gradually declined to 13.7 percent in 1973.[17]

The goals of Brazilian indexation measures were decidedly diverse. At least five different goals can be identified: (1) restoration of relative prices as a guide to efficient allocation of resources, a goal underlying indexation of most financial instruments, long-term contracts, rentals, loans, insurance, and savings deposits; (2) allowing the government to engage in noninflationary debt financing, a goal underlying the issuance of indexed government bonds (ORTNs); (3) rationalization of the tax structure to increase government revenues, a goal underlying indexation of the income tax; (4) containing inflation by preventing wages from pushing up prices, a goal underlying wage indexation; and (5) neutralization of the effects of inflation on the balance-of-payments current account without the dislocations and speculation accompanying massive devaluations, a goal underlying indexation of the exchange rate. For a time indexation appeared to have been remarkably successful in achieving these diverse goals in Brazil. Indeed, Brazilian experience with indexation was regarded as so successful that a number of economists recommended adoption of similar programs in other countries suffering significant inflationary pressures. Nonetheless, it is difficult to know how much of the success is properly attributable to indexation.

Monetary correction is widely credited with reviving Brazil's moribund insurance and construction industries and permitting the establishment of an impressive housing finance program. The credit is, to a large extent, deserved, but most of the funds flowing through the National Housing System are the result of forced savings, such as a retirement fund financed by involuntary contributions by employers of 8 percent of each employee's salary.[18] Part of the credit for revitalization of the construction industry belongs to changes in the laws governing mortgage foreclosure and rent control.[19]

The government bond market, which had virtually disappeared prior to 1964, has flourished since 1965. Some, but by no means all, of the credit for this success belongs to indexation. Part is attributable to the unduly generous rates of return initially offered via the dollar exchange rate option.[20] Part is attributable to the simple fact that since 1964 the government has been scrupulously repaying its bonds—a radical departure from past practice. Part is also attributable to the placement of a substantial percentage of government bonds with quasi-involuntary lenders, who purchased such bonds in lieu of paying income tax obligations or used them to meet Central Bank reserve requirements. There have also been large purchases by government-controlled entities. Moreover, in recent years a large part of the government debt has been financed although issuance of nonindexed short-term treasury bills because monetary correction, calculated on quarterly averages, has been too cumbersome for open-market operations.[21]

Indexation has not worked particularly well in Brazil with respect to interest rates in credit transactions. Many businessmen have been unhappy about the uncertainty regarding the ultimate cost of credit. A large number of loan transactions remained unindexed because of a mutual desire of borrowers and lenders to fix interest costs in advance. These loans were simply wrapped in the verbal cellophane of "prefixed monetary correction" to circumvent usury restrictions. In addition, a substantial number of mortgagors have had difficulty in keeping up with the monetarily corrected mortgage payments. The Brazilians have resolved this problem as well as can be expected, but the problem persists.

Brazil's economic planners anticipated that monetary correction would eventually bring down interest rates by increasing the savings rate.

They also expected that reforms in the Capital Market Law and more realistic corporate accounting techniques would stimulate active markets for stocks and long-term bonds, thereby permitting corporations to obtain financing more cheaply. The planners were correct in their assumptions about the increase in the savings rate, which jumped from a paltry 3.6 percent of Gross Domestic Product in 1962–66 to an impressive 10.6 percent in 1968–72.[22] How much of this large increase in the savings rate is fairly attributable to monetary correction, however, is unclear. Some of the increase is attributable to forced savings, the increase in political stability, and the decline in the inflation rate. The increase in the savings rate has not resulted in a corresponding decline in interest rates. Despite a sharp decrease in the inflation rate and the sharp increase in the savings rate during the late 1960s and early 1970s, Brazilian interest rates have enigmatically remained extraordinarily high.[23] In recent years the government has been forced to introduce a series of measures designed to reduce these high rates of interest. After a brief speculative flurry, the stock market has languished in the doldrums of investor disinterest and distrust. It has been suggested that the attractiveness of indexed government bonds, indexed deposits and prefixed monetarily corrected bills of exchange has discouraged equity investment.[24] Despite the legalization of bonds and convertible debentures utilizing monetary correction, very few corporations have been either willing or able to market indexed long-term debt instruments. Because of the high cost of capital in the domestic market, many Brazilian firms have found it cheaper to borrow Eurodollars abroad. As a result, Brazil's foreign debt has skyrocketed from $3.8 billion into $54 billion in mid-1980, creating a new set of economic problems for the country.

Income tax collections have soared in real terms since the institution of monetary correction.[25] Yet it is far from clear how much of this increase is fairly attributable to indexation. Monetary correction lowered the rate of tax evasion by making the system more equitable and the costs of noncompliance more expensive;[26] however, some of this resulting gain to the government was offset by elimination of the inflation tax collected by the government prior to the institution of monetary correction.

Perhaps the most vigorously criticized aspect of monetary correction in Brazil has been wage indexation. Although it appeared well-suited to protecting real wages and productivity gains from inflationary erosion, Brazilian wage indexation has proved to be more a manipulative device than an automatic inflation adjustment. It was utilized from 1964 to 1967 to force many Brazilian workers to accept substantial declines in real income, and to part with some of their productivity gains thereafter.[27] In practice, Brazilian wage indexation has been a highly discretionary incomes policy, much more akin to wage and price controls than to what is normally thought of as wage indexation.[28] In this sense, indexation was undoubtedly useful in the fight against inflation.

The Brazilian government had been able to get away with underestimating the inflation and productivity rates for wage purposes for so many years only because of a combination of three unusual factors: (1) for all practical purposes, strikes were outlawed;[29] (2) labor unions were legally permitted to function only under the aegis of government-controlled labor courts and were dependent upon the government for financial support; and (3) the franchise in presidential elections was restricted to generals.[30] The easing of political repression in 1979 has been accompanied by a rash of strikes. The government has attempted to placate this labor unrest by adoption of an automatic wage indexation statute that redistributes income from higher paid to lower paid workers.[31]

The clearest indexation success story in Brazil is the introduction of the "trotting peg" exchange rate; the system of a fixed exchange rate was supplanted by monthly or bimonthly minidevaluations based upon inflation rate differentials between Brazil and its major trading partners. Under the prior system the existing exchange rate was maintained until exporters could no longer compete in world markets; devaluations were then massive and produced very substantial economic dislocations. These included large-scale currency speculation, capital flight, and sharp increases in the prices of imports. The "trotting peg" device helped stimulate a dramatic increase in exports, which have risen impressively since implementation of the "trotting peg."[32]

In recent years, however, Brazilian exchange rate policy has been more a creeping and leaping peg than a trotting peg. Systematic underestimation of the differential in inflation rates between Brazil and its major trading partners eventually produced a substantially overvalued cruzeiro; much of the stimulation of exports has stemmed from generous tax incentives and credit subsidies accorded to Brazilian exporters. Under pressure from its trading partners to cut back on these export incentives to avoid dumping charges, Brazil devalued the cruzeiro on December 7, 1979 by 30 percent, eliminated some of the tax incentives, and lowered the amount of subsidized credit. Although this "maxi-devaluation" was presented as a one-time remedial measure, during 1980 the cruzeiro was devalued by less than half the domestic rate of inflation rate. Despite a record increase in exports in 1980, Brazil encountered severe balance-of-payments difficulties because of its large oil import bill and the cost of servicing its $54 billion foreign debt. By imposing a 25 percent tax on the purchase of foreign exchange and reinstituting tax incentives for exports, Brazil effectively reverted to a policy of multiple exchange rates. During the initial half of 1981, however, the pace of devaluation has accelerated, which may indicate that Brazil has resumed its "trotting peg" exchange policy.

Monetary correction has been clearly successful in revitalizing a substantial number of legal institutions that had either malfunctioned or ceased to function entirely because of chronic inflation. Readjustment of tort and contract damage awards has restored the traditional balance of rights inherent in tort and contract law.[33] The constitutional guaranty against confiscation of private property has been resuscitated by indexing the value of condemnation awards.[34] Rent control legislation, which had also undermined the constitutional guaranty of property, was made more equitable to landlords by monetary correction of original rental values. Consequently, rent control legislation has become much less of a disincentive to the construction of badly needed rental units, and the courts are no longer crowded with sham lawsuits seeking to evade the unrealistic norms of the rent control laws.[35] Similarly, Brazilian public utility rate legislation had been undermining the constitutional guaranty of private property by determining rates as a percentage of historical cost, a concept that inflation had rendered meaningless. Because public utilities could not earn a fair return, they were unable to attract new funds for expansion and maintenance of existing facilities. During the early 1960s, public utility service in Brazil was charitably described as "deplorable." Moreover, the government was gradually forced to acquire failing public utilities, whose steadily increasing operating deficits helped to fuel inflation. Monetary correction has largely resolved this problem as well. Since 1964 public utilities have been using monetarily corrected asset values for rate-making purposes,[36] and the improvement in public utility service has been dramatic.

In 1974, however, the Brazilian "miracle" sank in a sea of Arab oil. Brazilian industrialization has revolved around the automobile industry. Because the nation has to import 80 percent of its petroleum, the quadrupling of oil import prices has dealt Brazil a hard economic blow. The injury to the economy has been exacerbated by severe droughts and frosts, diminishing agricultural production, particularly that of coffee. The annual economic growth rate slowed, averaging only 6.4 percent in 1975 and 1976, while the annual inflation rate simultaneously accelerated to more than 40 percent. With natural disasters and increased import prices generating strong inflationary pressures, Brazilians discovered that indexation was itself acting as an inflationary lever. The increased income from oil prices was going to foreigners, while natural disasters reduced aggregate national income. By counteracting the resulting price increases, indexation artificially inflated the size of the shrinking economic pie. The government, therefore, decided to purge the index of the effect of these "inflationary accidents."[37] Expurgation was dropped for a time and reinstituted in September of 1979 solely for oil imports.

The post-1973 upsurge in the inflation rate has resulted in considerable pressure on the government to reduce the rate of monetary correction on loans from governmental agencies. As did its Israeli counterpart during the 1960s, the Brazilian government succumbed to the pressure. During 1975 and 1976 monetary correction on mortgage loans from the National Housing Bank (BNH) was reduced to 75 percent of the increase in the wholesale price index. At the same time the National Development Bank (BNDE) limited monetary correction on its loans to basic industries to 20 percent annually, roughly half the then prevailing inflation rate.[38] Agricultural loans have frequently been made without monetary correction, or at a small fraction of the ORTN adjustment rate. As part of the austerity measures instituted in 1980, certain loan subsidies have been eliminated, and the rate of monetary correction in others has been raised, but agricultural loans continue to be made at a fraction of the ORTN adjustment rate. These measures have not only entailed substantial subsidies to favored borrowers, but they have also disrupted the automatic nature of monetary correction of credit instruments. Because these loans come largely from social security trust funds and savings deposits, which by law are supposed to earn real rates of return, the government either has to make up the amount of these subsidies through tax revenues or else change the rules of the game.

In January of 1980 the surge in inflation caused the Brazilian government to revise the rules of monetary correction once again. *Ex post* monetary correction was prohibited, and monetary correction was prefixed two months in advance in accordance with a presumed rate of inflation, set at approximately half the actual inflation rate. As a result, the interest rate on all indexed lending turned sharply negative.

Brazil thus turned monetary correction into an inflation control device. By limiting all indexation, except for wages, to a predetermined rate, the government attempted to brake Brazil's galloping inflation. The policy was a clear failure. Not only was it unsuccessful as a strategy for reducing the inflation, but it also resulted in a substantial lowering of the savings rate and a drying up of credit and investment. In November 1980 the Brazilian government dramatically jettisoned this ill-fated prefixed monetary correction policy and returned to *ex post* monetary correction. Significantly, instead of returning to the *status quo ante,* when the ORTN was linked to an expurgated version of the wholesale price index, Brazilian monetary correction is now tied to an unexpurgated national consumer price index.[39] Whether the government will resist the urge to manipulate the national consumer price index, which was created in 1979 for wage indexation purposes, remains to be seen.

The Finnish Experience

Finland would seem to be the ideal laboratory in which to study the effects of comprehensive indexation. It is the sole country to adopt a comprehensive system of indexation only to later abandon it almost completely. Even more intriguing is evidence that Finland is gradually returning to broad scale indexation. Yet here, too, the lessons of the Finnish experience for other countries are difficult to discern.

Indexation in Finland resulted from the galloping inflation that followed World War II. The nation suffered heavy damage from German troops, and the terms of its armistice with Russia required that Finland cede 12 percent of its territory and pay a huge indemnity. In 1945, to compensate those who migrated to other parts of Finland when their land was conveyed to Russia, the government issued ten-year bonds. Because the annual inflation rate averaged more than 40 percent from 1945 to 1947, the government decided simple justice required that the evacuees' bonds be protected from inflation by linking them to the wholesale price index.[40]

In 1946 the Finnish Public Pension Institute began making loans with principal and interest adjusted by 50 percent of the variation in the wholesale price index. The following year, private life insurance companies adopted a similar policy with respect to their loans. Before long, indexation had spread to bank and government loans, and by 1955, time deposits were being indexed. By 1967 the great majority of the bonds issued by the government and financial institutions were indexed; however, only a little over 30 percent of all nonfinancial corporate bonds were indexed. Thus, as in Brazil and Israel, most of the private corporations were reluctant to assume the risks of indexation.

Indexation of credit transactions did not create the repayment difficulties that so often plagued borrowers in Brazil and Israel. This was largely because creditors did not shift the full burden of monetary depreciation to the debtor through indexation. The usual practice was to split the inflation risk by indexing only one-half the obligation; in some cases only one-fourth the obligation was indexed. Indexation did increase the real rate of interest, and by so doing probably increased the savings and investment rates; however, there is little data on the subject. Some Finns believe that indexation made little difference; others, particularly those associated with savings banks, believe that indexed savings accounts attracted substantial amounts of savings that would have otherwise been spent on durable goods.[41]

The most controversial aspect of indexation in Finland was its application to wages. Finnish labor unions, unlike their Brazilian counterparts, were not docile creatures of the state. They exercised their right to strike when collective bargaining broke down. Since 1955, when postwar emergency powers legislation lapsed, the Finnish government has had no power to set wages directly.

Wage indexation was introduced in collective bargaining agreements in 1948 in an attempt to contain inflation by holding soaring wage increases to more moderate levels. The first two-year agreement, which covered virtually all workers, provided for a 5.5 percent increase in wages for each full 5 percent rise in the index. At the insistence of the labor unions, a special cost-of-living index that included black market prices was constructed for indexing purposes. No wage increase resulted from this initial indexation agreement, principally because Finland abolished price controls in 1949, causing a sharp drop in black market prices. After expiration of the collective agreement in 1950 and a 7.5 percent general wage increase, followed shortly by another 15 percent negotiated increase, wage indexation was reinstated.

During 1950 and 1951 the Finnish government escalated its battle against inflation into a war against the index. Calculating that a 5 percent rise in the index would trigger wage increases that would cost the entire nation some 10 million marks, the government concluded that it made economic sense to spend anything less than that to keep the index from rising. Therefore, it spent approximately 5 million marks in the second half of 1950 subsidizing staples such as bread, butter, and sugar, and reducing import duties and taxes. The results of these measures were a few months stay of execution of a 5 percent general wage increase, a shortage of coffee, and union distrust of the government. After extensive work stoppages produced a wage increase, the government, knowing that publication of the November 1950 index would trigger a new wage increase, announced a wage freeze. The government was promptly deposed.[42]

Indexation was restored in October 1951 after institution of comprehensive price controls. For the next four years, inflationary pressures were much less, and the new government was able to avoid triggering a wage increase by astutely managing the index with a shrewd mixture of production increases, lowered tariffs, and price controls. Skill in index management became a widely valued indicia of governmental competence. In October 1954, when it appeared that the index was about to trigger an automatic wage increase, the crisis toppled the government. The new regime expanded price controls and convinced the unions and employers to replace indexation with wage renegotiation whenever the index rose an agreed upon amount.

Wage indexation was reinstated in 1957, during a period of high unemployment and substantial inflation. Because of their weak bargaining position, unions were persuaded to accept a government proposal for automatic increases of only two-thirds of the increase in the cost-of-living index; however, the base period was moved backwards almost two years to sweeten the deal. This agreement produced a few small wage increases in 1958, but expired in 1959 with the index well below the next threshold level. There was no wage indexation for the next four years, but collective agreements negotiated in 1963 included provision for flat-rate increases in hourly earnings triggered by the index reaching prescribed numbers. Unlike past index clauses, this had a noticeable inflationary effect because it automatically translated an increase in sales tax into an automatic wage increase.[43]

Finland's last indexed central agreement was to have covered the 1966 to 1968 period. It was aborted in 1968 by the Stabilization Agreement in which the unions exchanged a pledge of wage restraint for price controls. The agreement, like the Economic Special Powers Act of 1968, was motivated by a desire to avoid a strong inflationary surge after a 24 percent devaluation of the Finnish mark. There was also real concern that the country would not be able to obtain the economic benefits of the devaluation if indexation set off a chain reaction of price increases, a problem that would have been obviated had the Finns indexed to the implicit GNP deflator or purged the cost-of-living index of import prices.

The Finns seem to agree that indexation is highly desirable for long-term contracts, and post-1968 legislation is steadily permitting readoption of indexation in such contracts. Indexation was never banned for insurance and pensions, but there have been serious problems in maintaining indexed insurance and pension benefits without correspondingly indexed investments.

The Finnish experience is difficult to evaluate because the government devoted so many resources to holding down the index and to maintaining a system of price controls. Yet a few conclusions are clear. Wage indexation was not a source of significant inflationary pressure in Finland. To the contrary, during most of the period when indexation was in force, average real earnings did not increase as rapidly as the cost-of-living index.[44] Nor did the partial indexation of loans, bonds, or bank deposits generate significant inflationary pressures. On the whole, the system worked smoothly. The greatest difficulty with the Finnish experiment was the government's policy of squandering resources to "buy points" on the index. This inefficient allocation of resources was accentuated by maintenance of a broad range of price controls during much of the period.

The Israeli Experience

Indexation was part of the colonial legacy bequeathed to the state of Israel by the British. In order to promote labor peace during World War II, the Palestinian colonial government encouraged the inclusion in collective bargaining agreements of an automatic cost-of-living adjustment, a feature which remains central to Israeli indexation to the present day.

Wage indexation in Israel, as was the case in Finland, is based upon a periodically renewable collective bargaining agreement between a central trade union organization and an employers' federation. These agreements contain a cost-of-living allowance that rises whenever the cost-of-living index exceeds a stipulated amount. Except in periods of very rapid inflation, the adjustment is biannual. The cost-of-living allowance is not paid on 100 percent of every employee's earnings; earnings that exceed a continuously readjusted limit are excluded. Thus, one study showed that between 1957 and 1969 the average wage was only 40 to 60 percent of what it would have been had there been complete indexation without a ceiling.[45]

During the late 1940s and 1950s, when the cost-of-living wage adjustment was made quarterly, the Israeli government reacted to indexation by combating the index in precisely the same fashion as the Finnish government. A special department within the Ministry of Finance bought index points by skillfully rigging short-term subsidies, permitting certain items to bear unduly high weights, and making sophisticated changes in the way seasonal variations were taken into account.[46] This practice of manipulating the index was abandoned in 1959, largely because more frequent market basket surveys and a shift to a biannual cost-of-living adjustment made it less worthwhile.

The Israeli experience with wage indexation between 1954 and 1970 provides little support for the proposition that such a device is inflationary.[47] Average real wages increased fairly steadily at about 5 percent per year under the Israeli system, while the annual inflation rate between 1954 and 1970 was less than 10 percent.

The problem of devaluations has been a real one, however, for Israel imports about one-third to one-half of its Gross Domestic Product, and until 1975 had a system of infrequent, massive devaluations. The basic benefits from devaluation flow from its tendency to encourage exports and discourage imports, benefits which will be vitiated if labor costs are raised to compensate for the increase in import prices. In order to preserve the economic advantages of devaluation, a partial exclusion of devaluation effects has usually been negotiated between employers and unions. Thus, in 1970, organized labor agreed to forego the cost-of-living adjustment that would have resulted from a heavy increase in import prices. Since adoption of the Brazilian "trotting peg" exchange rate approach, Israeli unions have agreed to limit their cost-of-living allowance to only 70 percent of the increase in the cost-of-living index.[48]

During the early 1950s, a number of Israeli companies issued bonds linked to the price of their products. In 1955, the government, which had been issuing dollar-linked bonds, decided to offer purchasers the option of a bond fully linked to the cost-of-living index. With the exception of short-term (up to eighteen month) obligations, subsequent government bonds have been indexed to the cost-of-living index.

Since the sharp upsurge in the inflation rate following the 1973 war, the Israeli government has become increasingly disenchanted with indexed bonds. It reduced the percentage of indexation in its obligations from 100 to 80 percent in 1977, and the Minister of Finance announced plans to cease indexation of government bonds entirely.

As in Brazil, political pressures have compelled the Israeli government to relax indexation of loans from government agencies to Israeli borrowers. Softening the rigors of indexation because of hardship to borrowers began in 1962, when the Israeli pound was devalued by 67 percent. Beginning in 1955 the government had extended its borrowers the option of linking their obligations either to the exchange rate or to the cost-of-living index. Most opted for the exchange rate linkage, unrealistically anticipating that Israel could maintain its overvalued exchange rate indefinitely. When the long-postponed devaluation came, the outcry from debtors whose obligations were increased by 67 percent from one day to the next was so deafening that the government modified the linkage provisions, granting borrowers the option of retroactive conversion to cost-of-living indexation or an extension of time for repayment.[49] The relative price stability of the 1960s lulled the Israeli government into such a state of false security about inflation that it decided to suspend indexation of government loans in 1967 upon payment of an insurance premium of 3 to 4 percent of the loan's face amount. With the consumer price index increasing more than tenfold between 1973 and 1979, the government has been heavily subsidizing its borrowers in recent years.

Indexation has been a conspicuous feature of Israeli nongovernmental financial markets ever since 1955. In contrast to Brazil, where only 10 to 20 percent of the total portfolio of assets held by the public are indexed, 50 to 60 percent of the assets held by the public are indexed to the cost-of-living index in Israel.[50] Bank loans, savings deposits, insurance policies and premiums, mortgages, and corporate bonds are routinely indexed.[51]

Indexation of debt obligations is generally more equitable in Israel than in Brazil or Finland. Not only does the creditor receive the entire amount of the increase in the index, but the monetary correction adjustment is calculated on the rise in the index from the month preceding the date of issue to the month prior to redemption or interest payment. Moreover, index figures are available with a time lag of only two weeks.[52] In contrast, Brazilian monetary correction has been calculated on three-month averages with a time lag of two months before such averages are available. Thus, if the inflation rate rises, Brazilian monetary correction gives the borrower an unfair advantage because the initial linkage is established at an index number much lower than the actual price level. During a period of declining inflation the converse is true. In Finland monetary correction on most government bonds was triggered only when the index climbed above threshold levels of 5 percent, and the amount of monetary correction was generally limited to one-half the percentage increases in the index.

Until 1975, inflation adjustments in the Israeli income tax were essentially confined to tax exemption for the cost-of-living allowance in collective bargaining agreements and the amount of loan payments corresponding to monetary correction, plus a gradual reduction in capital gains tax on real estate transactions in accordance with the length of the holding period. In 1975, Israel began taxing cost-of-living allowances and monetary correction gains with the exception of those stemming from government bonds, bonds traded on the Tel Aviv Stock Exchange, savings deposits, or foreign currency loans from nonresidents.[53] The exemption for monetary correction gains was replaced with automatically indexed personal exemptions, deductions, and credits, all of which were tied to the cost-of-living index. Tax brackets were also indexed, but the minister of finance was given discretion to reduce the amount by which these are adjusted to avoid too great a revenue loss. During 1975 this discretion was exercised to reduce the bracket adjustment to only 70 percent of the increase in the cost-of-living index.[54] Capital gains were divided into real and inflationary parts by monetarily correcting the assets' basis in accordance with changes in the cost-of-living index and reducing the tax rate on the inflationary component to 10 percent.[55] Unlike Brazil, Israel has not permitted firms to revalue physical assets or to adjust corporate balance sheets to eliminate inflationary distortions. Such legislation has, however, recently been proposed in Israel and may soon be adopted.

SUMMARY

It is important to recognize that in all three of these countries a substantial part of the economy has remained unindexed. None has attempted to index cash or sight deposits, and Israel has never indexed time deposits. Finland never indexed its income tax system, and Israel has only partly indexed its income tax laws. A wide range of financial markets, most prices, business profits, and the earnings of independent workers and professionals have not been determined by indexation. Even within the indexed sectors of the economies of these three countries, the adjustment mechanisms have marched to the beat of different indexes. Some Israeli bonds have been linked to the cost-of-living index, others to the dollar exchange rate, and still others to the prices for products produced or sold by the issuer.[56] Finnish bonds were linked to a broader assortment of indexes, such as the wholesale price index (or its domestic subindex), the cost-of-living index, the export price index, or the exchange rate.[57] Until June

1977, when legislation was enacted to consolidate the proliferation of monetary correction devices, Brazil had a dozen different indexation coefficients operating simultaneously.[58] Thus, construction costs were linked to a construction cost index; bonds, certain mortgages, bank loans, insurance, and taxes were linked to an expurgated version of the wholesale price index; wages were indexed with a complex formula based upon the average real wage prevailing in the past twelve months and one-half the estimated inflation rate for the coming year; rents, certain mortgage payments, and fines were indexed to the minimum wage until 1975; and condemnation awards were indexed to a composite index derived from a weighted average of the wholesale price index, the cost-of-living index for Rio de Janeiro, and the construction cost index.

In none of these countries has indexation been fully automatic. Instead, governments from time to time have taken measures to influence the index numbers for political and economic reasons. Only Brazil has blatantly tampered with the indexes themselves,[59] but both Finland and Israel have resorted to "buying points" on the cost-of-living index by subsidizing the prices of overrepresented goods.[60] In addition, some of the index adjustments have been only partial.[61] Thus, even the countries with the most widely indexed economies have deviated rather substantially from the paradigm of the fully and automatically indexed economy.

Brazil, Finland, and Israel are developing nations with historical rates of inflation considerably higher than those prevailing in highly developed nations. The capital markets of all three countries are fairly thin; the government is the chief financial intermediary. Price controls are a more or less permanent part of the economic landscape. Brazil's entire experience with indexation has been under military dictatorship, while Israel's economy has been on a wartime footing since independence was declared in 1948. What lessons can the experiences of these countries have for developed nations with free market economies like the United States?

IMPLICATIONS OF THE BRAZILIAN, FINNISH, AND ISRAELI EXPERIENCES FOR THE DEVELOPED NATIONS

Despite the substantial differences in economic, political, and social conditions, at least seven lessons that can be drawn from the Brazilian, Finnish, and Israeli experiences have relevance to the highly developed nations. These seven lessons relate to: (1) the administrative feasibility of broad-scale indexation, (2) the need to safeguard the integrity of the index, (3) expurgation of the index, (4) the difficulty of limiting indexation to one sector, (5) the utility of indexing the exchange rate, (6) the reluctance of the private sector to issue indexed obligations, and (7) the need for special constraints on governmental spending.

Administrative Feasibility

The first important lesson to be drawn from the experiences of these countries is that broad-scale indexation is administratively feasible. People can and do compute their obligations on the basis of coefficients derived from price indexes. Accountants and lawyers have been busier because of monetary correction, but business and financial life in Brazil and Israel is hardly chaotic because of it. Even in the extraordinarily complicated area of corporate income taxation, the Brazilians (as well as the Chileans) have shown that monetary correction can work.

The Integrity of the Index

A crucial problem in an extensively indexed economy is maintainance of the integrity of the index-making process. If billions of dollars turn on one index point, enormous political pressures are brought to bear on the index-makers. It is not accidental that Brazil, Finland, and Israel have all witnessed governmental attempts to manipulate the index. For technical reasons price indexes require continual adjustment and updating. Since these mechanisms are so little understood, it is extremely important to devise safeguards for the integrity of the index. One desirable measure to insure the independence of the index-makers would be to insulate them from the political processes by designating the index preparing group an autonomous agency along the lines of the U.S. Federal Reserve Board, or by constituting them as a quasi-judicial body. Another measure might be to grant the judiciary jurisdiction to protect the integrity of the index-making process.

The Expurgation of the Index

There is no single price index that is clearly preferable to all other indexes for the purpose of indexation. At very high rates of inflation the choice of an index may not make much difference.[62] Most countries have elected to use the consumer or wholesale price index for pragmatic and historical considerations rather than technical concerns. If the consumer or wholesale price index is used for indexation purposes, it should be purged of price increases resulting from deterioration in a nation's terms of trade, devaluation, and natural disasters. If this expurgation does not occur, indexation may itself become a significant source of inflationary pressure, as the experience of all three countries confirms.[63] It also makes eminent sense to eliminate indirect taxes from the index; otherwise a large part of any increase in indirect taxes will be neutralized by indexation, as the Finns discovered in 1963 when they increased the sales tax. If the implicit GNP deflator is used for indexation purposes, no expurgation is necessary.

The Difficulty of Limiting Indexation to a Particular Sector

Indexation is not a device that is easily cabined. Once part of an economy is indexed, there is a strong tendency for indexation to spread to other parts. All three countries began by indexing government bonds. Since financial markets are interrelated, once the government begins to index bonds, private corporations are forced to offer comparable returns. There is then pressure to index savings and time deposits to avoid financial disintermediation. Such indexation in turn requires that bank and mortgage loans be indexed. If mortgage loans are indexed, it is logical for insurance companies to issue indexed policies and for landlords to insist on indexed rentals. It is also logical for wages to be indexed so that wage earners can be assured of the ability to meet their mortgage or rental payments. Thus, devising an economic Maginot line to contain indexation is no easy task.

On the other hand, not all financial instruments will be indexed. Many companies and individuals much prefer to lend or borrow at fixed rates rather than undergo the uncertainty of indexation. Massive shifts of preferences between the indexed and unindexed sectors of the economy are likely to occur from time to time, creating liquidity crises for one sector or the other. To the extent the government solves the crisis by extending credit to the sector in a financial bind, inflationary pressures will be augmented.

The Need to Index the Exchange Rate

Brazil and Israel have discovered that their position as indexed economies in a nonindexed world seriously complicates economic management problems. If exchange rate devaluation lags behind the domestic inflation rate, as it so frequently does in countries with fixed exchange rates, substantial short-term capital is likely to flow into the country, attracted by the high yields available on indexed obligations. In addition, indexation tends to retard the flight abroad of domestic capital in search of protection from inflation. Both factors tend to improve the country's balance of payments, but servicing large quantities of foreign debt may place severe strain on the country's foreign exchange reserves in future years. Much of this foreign capital is particularly sensitive to fluctuations in inflation and exchange rates. Both Brazil and Israel found it desirable to link their exchange rates to a "trotting peg" and to try to maintain tight controls on capital inflows and outflows.

The "trotting peg" can be viewed as "a necessary complement of the indexation system" for the financial sector.[64] Even with the "trotting peg," Brazil has had large surpluses in its capital account of its balance of payments because of large nominal interest rate differentials. Consequently, it has had to adopt a series of regulations pertaining to the terms and interest rates on foreign loans to avoid major economic imbalances resulting from massive shifts of these funds.[65] Furthermore, because they increase the money supply, massive inflows of foreign capital can aggravate existing inflationary pressures. Thus, the presence of an indexed financial market makes maintenance of successful monetary policy in an inflationary economy even more difficult.[66]

Reluctance of Private Corporations to Issue Indexed Obligations

Few Brazilian, Finnish, and Israeli corporations have issued indexed bonds or debentures, although they have shown no reluctance to borrow from the government at indexed rates. This attitude in part stems from fear that a potential issuer's earnings might not rise as fast as the index because of changes in relative prices due to market forces or price controls. It also stems from confidence that if the government is the creditor, debtors can expect relaxation of indexation exigencies if they run into serious economic difficulties. Past behavior of Brazilian and Israeli governments toward its borrowers indicates that this confidence in governmental leniency is fully justified.

The Need for Special Constraints on Governmental Spending and Lending

Brazil and Israel both managed to reduce their inflation rates sharply with broad-scale indexation in effect. Both have also managed, however, to increase their inflation rates to all-time highs with broad-scale indexation in effect. Since 1973 inflation rates in Brazil and Israel have gradually surged, hitting historic highs in excess of 100 percent annually in 1980–81. This suggests that despite indexation, governments can still be expected to attempt to collect an inflation tax, but that much higher levels of inflation are required in order to produce the desired revenue. It also suggests a need for special constraints on governmental spending and lending to prevent attempts to resort to inflationary financing.

A variety of proposals to limit governmental spending are currently being debated in the United States.[67] They fall essentially into three categories. One is a constitutional amendment to mandate a balanced budget or to prohibit budgetary deficits unless sanctioned by an extraordinary majority of Congressmen. Two is to limit federal expenditures to a percentage of GNP. Three is to limit the rate of increase in the money supply. Chile has recently chiseled one of them into constitutional granite in Article 64 of its 1980 Constitution:

> Congress may not approve any new expenditure from public funds without simultaneously indicating the source of funds to pay for such expenditure.
>
> If Congress approves a project with a source of funds insufficient to pay for its costs, the President of the Republic, in promulgating the law, and with a prior favorable report from the agency or institution that is to collect the new revenue and the Comptroller-General of the Republic, shall proportionately reduce all expenditures, regardless of their nature.

All these proposals reflect a lack of confidence in legislative ability to restrain governmental spending without some kind of extraordinary limitation. All have serious difficulties in passing between the Scylla of placing the country in an economic straightjacket and the Charybdis of allowing easy circumvention of spending limitations.

In order for a balanced budget scheme to be effective, there must be detailed accounting mechanisms for the budget process and an enforcement mechanism with real teeth. Despite triple-digit inflation, Brazil has a substantial budgetary surplus. This feat has been accomplished by having substantial governmental expenditures off record and forcing the banking system to accord large amounts of subsidized credit to favored borrowers. Similar problems are inherent in limiting governmental expenditures to a given percentage of GNP or to limiting increases in the money supply. There is little agreement about how GNP and the money supply are to be measured. Moreover, Congress can easily shift large amounts of current expenditures to the private sector by regulation, thereby subverting the entire scheme. Any serious attempt at policing these schemes is likely to drag the judiciary into the kind of conflict with Congress that will leave the former badly bruised. Nevertheless some form of limitation on Congressional spending and lending is desirable, particularly if comprehensive and indexation is adopted.

SHOULD DEVELOPED COUNTRIES INDEX?

In July 1974 Milton Friedman published a provocative proposal in *Fortune Magazine* advocating comprehensive indexation of the economy of the United States.[68] More specifically, Friedman's proposal called for indexing the federal income tax and all government securities (with the exception of short-term bills and notes) to the consumer price index. It also called for removal of all legal restraints on voluntary indexation for the private sector and encouragement of the use of index clauses in long-term contracts. Friedman's proposal attracted widespread attention and controversy, but has yet to result in implementing legislation. Such legislation should be enacted, for Friedman's proposal is a sound one. It would, however, be an even better proposal if slightly enlarged.

AN ENLARGEMENT OF FRIEDMAN'S INDEXATION PROPOSAL

The basic components of Friedman's proposal for revising the income tax statute are indexation of personal exemptions, the standard deduction, low-income allowance, and tax brackets. Moreover, the historical cost basis used in the calculation of capital gains and depreciation would be similarly indexed, and the cost of inventories would be adjusted to eliminate fictitious gains. Finally, the $25,000 line between normal tax and surtax on corporate income would be monetarily corrected. The principal difficulty with this proposal is that it does not go far enough in eliminating inflationary distortions from the tax system. A major source of income tax distortion caused by inflation is not eliminated, for the proposal fails to recognize that those who can borrow at negative interest rates realize real gains, while lenders suffer corresponding real losses. Finally, Friedman does not indicate what the legal obstacles to index clauses are or how they should be removed.

Friedman's proposal can be improved by recommending adoption of the comprehensive balance sheet adjustments used by Brazil and Chile, for they are the best techniques yet devised to eliminate from the taxation of business income the distortive effects of inflation.[69] All nominally expressed sums in the tax law should be indexed instead of only the $25,000 corporate surtax trigger. Certain timing adjustments should be made, such as indexation of back tax debts, refunds, loss carry forward or carry back provisions, and deferred income. It would also be a significant improvement if monetary correction gains on interest income were eliminated from personal income tax. While theoretical consistency would require denial of an interest deduction to individual borrowers for monetary correction payments on loans, this is probably not politically viable.

While indexing demand deposits is likely to be highly inflationary, it makes sense to allow banks and savings and loan associations to offer monetary correction of savings left on deposit for at least six months. This will require that mortgages and loans from these institutions be correspondingly indexed. In order to compete, state-chartered lending institutions will have to offer similarly indexed deposits and loans.

The index adopted for the purpose of monetarily correcting the income tax and government bonds should be the implicit GNP deflator, which has certain slight mechanical advantages over the consumer price index. Private parties, however, should remain free to link their contracts to any index or subindex if they wish; indeed, if they prefer not to link their contracts to any index, that option should remain open. It seems senseless to interfere with freedom of contract to secure an illusory uniformity. Indexation plainly does not make sense in all economic contexts, and there is no justification for imposing it if the parties prefer some other arrangement.

The use of index clauses in long- and medium-term contracts should be encouraged in order to facilitate longer-term agreements and to discourage litigation if the pace of inflation quickens. Therefore, legislation should be adopted requiring the use of index clauses in all contracts that are to be performed over more than a one-year period, unless the parties specifically agree not to include such a clause. This requirement would red flag the inflation risk for the contracting parties and specifically force them to reallocate it. Congress should define monetary correction as a return of capital, thereby excluding the possibility that any federal or state court consider such an inflation adjustment as interest for the purpose of state usury laws. It should also repudiate the nominalist presumption for the purpose of calculating damages in contract, tort, and eminent domain cases; all damage awards should be monetarily corrected. Congress's powers under the interstate commerce clause and the regulation of the value of money clause (Article I, Section 8, Clause 5) are sufficiently broad enough to support such legislation even though its effect would be to change a series of substantive state law rules. In order to avoid giving indexation an unfair competitive advantage, the Brazilian concept of prefixed monetary correction should be read into nonindexed credit arrangements for the purposes of tax and usury laws. This means that if the annual inflation rate were 7 percent, an unindexed loan bearing an annual interest rate of 14 percent should be treated for tax and usury purposes as if it were a loan bearing interest at 7 percent *per annum.* The other 7 percent should be regarded as nontaxable monetary correction.

There is no need to propose indexation of social security benefits, which are already indexed in the United States, as in many countries. Indexation of pension benefits is also desirable as a matter of equity, and in many instances pensions are already indexed. Frequently, however, indexed pension and social security systems are actuarially unsound. In part this is the result of having received insufficient contributions; in part it is the result of the unavailability of indexed securities in which to invest reserves.

Nor is there any need to propose legislation indexing the exchange rate or permitting indexation of private contracts. The exchange rates of many highly developed countries, including the United States, are now floating and are thereby indexed by the market. Contractual index clauses are lawful in most countries. Only a few, such as Finland, France, Greece, and West Germany, have a general rule restricting the freedom of contracting parties to insert index clauses into their agreements.[70]

THE DESIRABILITY OF THIS PARTIAL INDEXATION PROPOSAL

One reason for adopting this kind of partial indexation proposal is to improve the fairness of the nation's legal system during an inflationary period. Indexation reduces the redistribution of wealth and income resulting from inflation; helps preserve the institution of private property, particularly financial assets, from insidious confiscation; deprives people of economic incentives to delay payment of obligations; prevents inflation from eroding the value of long-term obligations; and offers savers the opportunity to protect the value of their capital.

A second reason for adopting this kind of proposal is that it reduces economic distortions that typically occur during inflation. It helps prevent the misallocation of resources that occurs when investment dollars flee from money or financial assets into gold, land, diamonds, luxury apartments, or foreign currency in an effort to preserve economic value. Capital and financial markets can continue to operate despite relatively high levels of inflation. Thus, indexation helps permit the price system remain an efficient allocator of resources despite inflation.

A third reason is that this proposal makes the government more democratic. Indexation tends to force legislators to vote real tax increases if they believe that such increases are called for instead of surreptitiously collecting the inflation tax. Public accountability of government representatives is decidedly enhanced during a period of inflation if there is indexation.

A fourth reason for indexation is that it substantially improves the quality of economic information available to the public. Monetarily corrected corporate balance sheets more accurately depict the real economic position of the firm. Indexation destroys the "nominalist illusion," forcing people to think in terms of real costs and gains. Consequently, economic decision-making in an inflationary economy becomes more rational.

IS INDEXATION INFLATIONARY?

The principal objection to indexation is that it causes acceleration of inflation. In the words of the 1967 Annual Report of the U.S. Council of Economic Advisors: "[I]f all unions—and other groups in society—were to succeed in tying compensation to consumer prices, the arrangement would become a vast engine of inflation, which, once it began to roll, would continue to gain speed."[71]

Whether indexation is likely to accentuate, diminish, or have no effect on inflationary pressures is a much debated question. Casual empiricism is an uncertain guide; the experiences of Brazil, Finland, and Israel are equivocal. All three heavily indexed economies were able to reduce galloping inflation rates to quite moderate levels; on the other hand, all three experienced sharply increased inflation rates while broad-scale indexation was in effect. How one ultimately resolves the issue is largely a function of what is seen as the causes of inflation, whether a stabilization program has been instituted, and what sets of assumptions are made about people's behavior during inflation. It is also a function of the time frame selected. Many who maintain that indexation is not, in the long run, a source of inflation will admit that indexation may cause an economy's inflation rate to climb faster in the short run.

The indexation debate really revolves around three areas: (1) credit transactions, (2) taxes, and (3) wages.

Credit Transactions

A common argument for the proposition that the indexation of debt instruments is noninflationary is that such indexation will increase the savings rate by increasing the real rate of interest. This will take money away from consumption goods, thereby reducing the inflation rate by dampening demand. But this argument is too simplistic. Whether demand will be lessened depends upon what is done with the increased savings. If the increased savings are channeled into increased capital goods spending or housing construction, there will be no decrease in demand. In order for the argument to succeed, one must show that with indexation the savings rate will rise and the investment rate will fall. That this can be demonstrated is extremely unlikely.[72]

Another argument that the use of indexed debt instruments tends to lower the inflation rate is that some lenders will accept a lower rate of return in exchange for contractual insurance against the risk that the inflation rate may turn out to be higher than anticipated over the life of the loan. Those lenders averse to running the risk of underestimating the inflation rate should be willing to pay a premium in the form of accepting a lower interest rate on an indexed bond or loan.[73] The problem with this argument is that it ignores the possibility that this group of risk-averse lenders will be counterbalanced by a like group of risk-averse borrowers; theoretically, the latter group should be willing to pay a similar premium in the form of higher interest rates for protection from the risk that they have overestimated the inflation rate.

Robson has argued convincingly that indexation will make a difference in the inflation rate only if borrowers and lenders have different expectations about what the inflation rate will be.[74] If expectations are the same and all other factors are equal, the real interest rate on indexed bonds and loans should be identical with the real rates on nonindexed debt instruments. If expectations are different, borrowers who anticipate that the inflation rate will be less than that implicitly factored into the nominal market interest rate on nonindexed bonds and notes will issue indexed bonds and notes. To these borrowers, indexing means a drop in the perceived real interest rate, which implies an increase in investment demand. Correspondingly, lenders who anticipate that the inflation rate prediction in the going nominal interest rate is too low will buy indexed bonds and notes. To these lenders, indexing means an increase in the perceived real interest rate, which implies an increase in the savings rate. Under Robson's analysis, it is impossible to tell whether indexation of credit transactions is inflationary or not because investment and savings will both rise. In the long run, debt indexation should increase capital formation, which, in turn will have an anti-inflationary effect.[75]

Robson's analysis ignores the tax implications, which can decidedly change the picture. Some countries specifically exempt indexation gains from taxation, while taxing nonindexed gains in their entirety.[76] If they need not pay income tax on monetary correction gains, lenders should be content with far lower rates of return on indexed obligations.[77] With a marginal tax rate of 40 percent on interest income and an annual inflation rate of 10 percent, a lender would have to charge an annual interest rate of 20.7 percent to receive a real return equivalent to that realized by charging 4 percent a year interest in a noninflationary period. If the loan were indexed and the inflation adjustment were tax-exempt, a total nominal yield of 14 percent a year would be sufficient. If the borrower is denied a corresponding deduction for the inflation adjustment, as happens in certain countries,[78] the attractiveness of indexed financing relative to nonindexed financing also becomes a function of the borrower's marginal tax rate. One would anticipate that most of the high marginal rate lenders would purchase indexed securities or make indexed loans, while most of the high marginal rate borrowers would issue nonindexed bonds or notes. If the credit market becomes almost entirely indexed, denial of a tax deduction for monetary correction payments makes debt financing less attractive to many companies. A similar disincentive to debt financing results from the comprehensive balance sheet adjustments required by Brazilian and Chilean tax legislation. On the other hand, granting a tax exemption on indexation gains to lenders may effectively foreclose firms from raising capital by selling equity. This should be anti-inflationary by lessening demand for credit and reducing interest rates. Under certain circumstances, then, the way the tax system treats monetary correction gains can be decisive in determining the relative attractiveness of indexed and nonindexed debt instruments and the effective cost of credit.

If usury laws in force exempt indexation gains, indexation should also have an anti-inflationary effect in lowering the cost of capital to firms. This is because indexation avoids the need to resort to costly simulations to circumvent the usury laws. This reduction in transaction costs should be translated into lower costs of operating capital.

In the short run, whether indexing credit instruments reduces or raises effective interest rates depends to a large extent on whether the anticipated inflation rate is exceeded by the actual inflation rate. Ignoring the tax aspects, if lenders anticipate that the inflation rate for the next year will be 10 percent and require a 4 percent real return, they will try to set interest rates at 14 percent. If the inflation rate for next year were 20 percent, adoption of indexing would have increased effective interest rates by 10 percent (counting the index adjustment as interest). On the other hand, if the inflation rate for the next year were 5 percent, adoption of indexing would have decreased effective interest rates by 5 percent. In the long run, however, efforts will be made to compensate for miscalculations. Realistically, one cannot expect lenders to lose part of their capital without making an effort at recoupment. In the following year, shrewd lenders are likely to overestimate the rate of anticipated inflation to make up for last year's losses and to provide a margin of safety. They may decide to shorten the term of their loans, or to leave the lending business. Any of these reactions is likely to drive up interest rates.

These considerations become crucial if indexation is introduced as an integral feature in a stabilization program, as was the case in Brazil. During stabilization, introduction of restrictive fiscal and monetary policies to reduce the existing rate of inflation adversely affects borrowers, who are locked into fixed rate contracts based on the assumption that the present level of inflation will continue. Indexation makes it politically easier to institute stabilization policies by minimizing the concern that borrowers will be unable to meet their obligations.[79]

Professors Baer and Beckerman argue that indexation of financial instruments is inflationary on two empirical grounds. First, there will be liquidity crises as investors shift preferences between the indexed and unindexed sector, and governments will tend to bail out the sector in difficulty through inflationary creation of credit. Second, a government will be lax in insisting upon complete indexation of financial instruments when it is a creditor, and such governmental subsidies to borrowers are inflationary.[80] These arguments are not wholly convincing. Although the governments of Brazil and Israel (as well as Chile) have from time to time engaged in an inflationary credit expansion to bail out particular groups or institutions, it is difficult to see why indexation should bear the onus for the government's behavior. Governments typically subsidize certain borrowers without indexation, just as they typically subsidize societal groups during periods of hardship. If liquidity crises are going to appear because there are both indexed and unindexed sectors, it seems as logical to blame the lack of total indexation for the inflationary pressures resulting from a governmental bailout as it is to blame indexation. Moreover, not every government bailout or subsidy is inflationary. Whether governmental bailouts or subsidies are inflationary depends upon how they are financed.

Income Taxation

It is commonly argued that indexation of the tax structure is inflationary because it destroys the automatic stabilizing mechanism of a progressive income tax. Because state revenues rise more rapidly than aggregate income during inflationary periods and fall more rapidly during recessionary periods, a progressive income tax has a built-in countercyclical feature, cushioning the effects of swings in the business cycle.[81] To a limited extent this criticism of indexation may be valid. Tax yields will not rise as much in a boom period, nor fall as much during a recession, if there is indexation. This assumes there is only a short time lag between the change in the general price level and the change in tax revenues. It is by no means clear that a reduction in tax revenues due to indexing would occur at the same time as an expansion of economic activity from inflation. In postwar Canada, economists observed that general price-level increases lagged behind economic expansion by about nine to eighteen months. On several occasions the inflation rate did not reach its maximum until well after a cyclical downturn had begun.[82] Recent studies have concluded that indexing the personal income tax would have had very little destabilizing effect on the United States and Canadian economies. Indeed under certain circumstances, an indexed system may actually be more stabilizing than an unindexed system.[83] At galloping rates of inflation, the automatic stabilizing mechanism of a progressive income tax loses any real significance, and unless the tax system is indexed or often modified to prevent sharp rises in effective rates, tax evasion increases so much that the entire system breaks down.

Another common contention is that government tax revenues will be substantially diminished by indexation, while a large percentage of governmental expenditures are either actually or practically indexed. This will result in budget deficits, and governments are likely to resort to inflationary techniques to finance their deficit. This is questionable. It is true that indexing will prevent governmental revenues from increasing automatically in real terms during an inflationary period without a corresponding increase in real income, but indexing does not mean that the government cannot maintain the same level of real revenue. All it means is that the legislature will have to raise rates or levy new taxes to increase real tax revenues beyond the level of any increase in national income. Whether the legislature will be willing to go on record and vote new tax increases depends upon popular perceptions of the appropriate level of taxation, or perhaps more accurately, on legislators' perceptions of their constituencies' perceptions about the appropriate level of taxation.

Given the present mood of the taxpaying public in countries like the United States, depriving the government of the ability to collect the inflation tax is likely to force a reduction in governmental expenditures. If a legislature has to vote additional taxes for additional expenditures, indexation is likely to have a significant anti-inflationary effect. On the other hand, a legislature can always continue its spending patterns without voting new taxes by deficit spending. If revenues fail to rise automatically, continuation of such spending patterns may mean even more inflation.

Wages

Neither Friedman's proposal nor this amplification of it would require wage indexation, which is probably the most hotly debated aspect of comprehensive indexation. On the other hand, neither would prohibit any type of wage indexation. Nonetheless, any partial indexation proposal is likely to result in an increase in the number of collective bargaining agreements containing escalator clauses. Indexation of savings and time deposits quickly leads to indexed mortgages, loans, and rental agreements, resulting in more workers demanding that wages and salaries be indexed to insure that the percentage of their income required to cover mortgage, rent, or loan payments will not become progressively greater.

Wage indexation is often said to be inflationary because it pushes up wages at a faster rate than would prevail with nonindexed collective bargaining agreements. The contention is that time lags in the renegotiation of collective bargaining agreements brake existing inflationary pressures whereas indexation would eliminate the lags and accelerate the inflationary process. If small percentage changes in the price index trigger the readjustment mechanism, indexation may trigger several wage increases during the course of a year. Because collective bargaining agreements normally last at least a year, indexation will cause wages paid under indexed contracts to rise faster than nonindexed contracts, thereby provoking a wage-price spiral.[84] But this argument assumes that the nonindexed contracts do not contain clauses providing for reopening of negotiations if inflation rises by a given percentage. It further assumes that the unions will not seek to regain ground lost to inflation plus some additional territory as a kind of buffer zone when the contract is ultimately renegotiated. Neither assumption may be tenable.

A second reason wage indexation is said to be inflationary is that it enables union leaders to "whipsaw" management into higher wage increases. The argument is that if some unions have indexed contracts and others do not, the unions with the contracts that produce the lower overall wage increase will in the next bargaining session pressure management into eliminating the disparity.[85] But this argument assumes that management will not be able to use the same argument to whipsaw union leaders into accepting a lower wage increase.

As many countries discovered in 1974, indexation of wages to the consumer or wholesale price index can be quite inflationary if the price index is being pushed up by a quadrupling of the price of oil imports, a rise in import prices resulting from currency devaluation, or bad harvests. Transferring income to workers from other sectors will not offset the adverse change in the terms of trade; all it will do is lead to a further round of price and wage increases. Similarly, if workers are protected against a loss in real income stemming from devaluation, much of the benefit to a country's balance of payments from devaluation will disappear. This kind of indexation will eventually result in more devaluation and corresponding wage and price increases. Similarly, if the price index rises because of a bad harvest, granting wage increases to compensate for this rise in the price of food will only lead to higher food prices and a further round of price increases.[86] These special cases of inflationary pressures generated by wage indexation can be prevented by substituting the GNP deflator for the consumer or wholesale price index or purging these indexes for import prices and bad harvests.[87]

The monetarists argue that wage indexation will have an anti-inflationary effect which will make it politically easier for governments to institute stabilization measures. The argument assumes that there is only a temporary trade-off between the increase in unemployment and reduction in the rate of inflation resulting from reducing the rate of monetary expansion. During stabilization programs unions demand wages that are too high because workers anticipate more inflation than actually occurs. Employers are forced to lay off workers because the reduction in aggregate demand produced by monetary contraction makes it impossible to set prices sufficiently high to meet these inflated wage demands. If wages were indexed, the unions would not demand wage increases to cover future inflation because this would be automatically corrected. With indexation, real wage levels and employment levels should remain constant during a period of stabilization.[88]

Monetarists assume that if a certain rate of monetary expansion has been consistently maintained, the average rate of inflation will become correctly anticipated with employment stable at its "natural" level and with prices and wages rising at approximately the same rate. Yet if one views the economy as subject to repeated "autonomous shocks" that cause particular prices and wages to accelerate or decelerate, it is improbable that labor or management would ever have confidence in the accuracy of their expectations about the anticipated rate of inflation. If this is so, wage indexation might make the general price level more sensitive to price and cost pressures developing in particular parts of the economy, setting off an increase in the rate of inflation and a rise in the level of unemployment.[89]

In practice, wage indexation has generally been less than a complete inflation adjustment. Most escalator clauses in collective bargaining agreements cover only basic rates of pay rather than the entire pay package; overtime, expense allowances, bonuses, and productivity hikes are almost always excluded. Typically, the price index must move above a certain threshold in order to trigger an automatic pay hike, or the agreement calls for an annual cost-of-living adjustment. Frequently, cost-of-living adjustments contain a cap or ceiling.[90]

Wage indexation has also been less than a complete inflation adjustment, because it lags behind the increase in the cost of living. As soon as a wage earner is restored to a real income peak by indexation, inflation causes his wage to slide down the slope once more. Moreover, unless the tax system is indexed, a wage increase may increase an employee's marginal tax rate. If this happens, a wage increase exceeding a simple cost-of-living adjustment will be necessary to enable him to maintain the same real disposable income.

During the 1960s Brazil devised a method to maintain real income stability but has since abandoned it.[91] The theory behind the Brazilian wage formula was that nominal wages should be automatically adjusted each year to compensate for three factors: (1) the actual inflation rate in the past year, (2) productivity increases, and (3) one-half the predicted inflation rate during the next year. During the first six months following adjustment, workers enjoy an increase in real income. This gradually disappears as inflation progresses, so that by the middle of the wage period, real wages are approximately equal to the average real wage during the previous period. Real wages then gradually decline during the final half of the next year. If inflation and productivity rates are projected fairly accurately, and if inflation is more or less spread out evenly over the year, the Brazilian wage formula will prevent inflation from eroding real income.[92] In practice, the Brazilian government deliberately underestimated the projected inflation rate to hold down wage increases.[93] With political liberalization, the formula has been replaced with a new automatic indexation measure that redistributes income to the lowest paid workers.[94]

CONCLUSIONS

There is substantial support for the proposition that indexation is a highly useful form of inflationary anesthesia. It does reduce the unfairness and misallocation of resources that would otherwise be generated by inflation, thereby making it easier to coexist with inflation. By depriving the government of the ability to collect the inflation tax and making gradual stabilization more feasible, indexation is also a useful form of inflationary anesthesia. Inflation is essentially a political problem, and indexation makes it politically more feasible for countries to swallow some of the painful austerity measures necessary to reduce inflation to minimal levels.

There is also substantial evidence that indexation can become an inflationary adrenaline, particularly if wages are indexed to the consumer or wholesale price index. A decline in the terms of trade, a substantial increase in the prices of imports, poor harvests, or other natural disasters may require cuts in real income that will be postponed through indexation. In such circumstances, the index must be purged to prevent indexation from fueling additional inflation. Similarly, if wages are indexed in such a fashion that they increase more rapidly than cost-of-living and productivity gains, as has been the case in Italy, indexation itself becomes a source of inflationary pressure.

If there is a sharp surge in the inflation rate, indexation may result in a short-run increase in the rate of future price increase that would have been repressed for a time in a nonindexed economy. But this differential is only temporary. The nominalist illusion does not last forever, and people soon strive to recoup any losses in real income. In the long run, the recoupment process may add a layer of padding against future price increases that would not have been included in an indexed economy.

If the legal system bars index clauses or if people lack confidence in the accuracy of their country's price indexes, alternative devices will be employed to maintain the real economic value of contractual arrangements. For example, wage agreements and leases will be renegotiated frequently. Long-term credit transactions will become short-term. More people will resort to commodity and foreign currency clauses.

If the legal system insists on strict adherence to the nominalist principle in the face of serious inflation, society will move closer to barter and away from money: "It must be recognized that no legislator can eliminate barter. If he makes it too difficult for the parties to secure for a monetary obligation such protection as may be required, he will merely drive them into barter transactions of a somewhat old-fashioned type."[95] The costs in terms of economic inefficiency from the shift from index clauses toward barter are enormously high.

Indexation is far from a panacea for the ills of inflation. Unquestionably, far better than indexation would be price stability, but elimination of inflation seems a highly unlikely scenario, unless perhaps legislatures could be persuaded to enact legislation indexing the salaries of legislators in reverse so that their salaries would decline by the percentage increase in the price index. Indexation inevitably produces its own distortions, undesirable side effects, and increased transaction costs. No matter which index is employed for indexation purposes, there will be imperfections and distortions. No matter how often prices are adjusted, indexation will lag behind actual price changes. Considerable study needs to be done to determine at what rate of inflation the costs of a substantial indexation program exceed its benefits. Present estimates suggest that if the inflation rate is running below 5 percent a year, requiring a substantial amount of indexation is probably not worth the administrative costs, but that if inflation is persistently running above 8 or 9 percent a year, the advantages of indexation begin to exceed its costs. Unhappily, in all too many countries indexation is an idea whose time has come.

NOTES

1. Fane, *The Case for Indexation,* in INDEXING FOR INFLATION 1 (T. Liesner & M. King, eds. 1975).

2. For a discussion of various theories of the cause of inflation, *see* chap. 1, *supra,* at pp. 7–10.

3. Friedman, *Monetary Correction,* in ESSAYS ON INFLATION AND INDEXATION 25, 29 (H. Giersch, et al., 1974) [hereafter cited as INDEXATION ESSAYS].

4. *See* note 88 *infra* and the accompanying text.

5. A. MORAG, ON TAXES AND INFLATION 159 (1965).

6. Lemgruber, *An Analysis of Friedman's Hypotheses on Monetary Correction,* in INDEXATION, THE BRAZILIAN EXPERIENCE 56, 70–73 (M. Nadiri & A. Pastore eds., Occasional Papers of the Nat'l Bur. of Econ. Research, Vol. 4, No. 1 Winter 1977) [hereafter cited as BRAZILIAN INDEXATION].

7. Bomberger & Makinem, *Indexation, Inflationary Finance, and Hyperinflation: the 1945–1946 Hungarian Experience,* 88 J. POL. ECON. 550 (1980).

8. Giersch, *Index Clauses and the Fight against Inflation,* in INDEXATION ESSAYS, *supra* note 3, at 1, 5.

9. *See* Jackman & Klappholz, *The Case for Indexing Wages and Salaries,* in INDEXING FOR INFLATION 19, 22–23 (T. Liesner & M. King, eds. (1975).

10. "Has the Time Come for Indexing?", Wall St. J., Je. 20, 1974, cited in Morley, *Indexing and the Fight against Inflation,* in BRAZILIAN INDEXATION, *supra* note 6, at 76, 82–83.

11. M. SIMONSEN, INFLAÇÃO: GRADUALISMO X TRATAMENTO DE CHOQUE 191 (1970); Baer and Beckerman, *The Trouble with Index-Linking: Reflections on the Recent Brazilian Experience,* 8 WORLD DEVELOPMENT 677 (1980). *Cf.* Fishlow, *Indexing Brazilian Style: Inflation without Tears?,* 1 BROOKINGS PAPERS ON ECON. ACTIVITY 261, 270 (1974); "Correção Monetária e Realimentação Inflacionária," 30 Conj. Econ. 88 (Je. 1976).

12. *See generally* J. CHACEL, M. SIMONSEN, & A. WALD, CORREÇÃO MONETÁRIA (1970); Kafka, *Indexing for Inflation in Brazil,* in INDEXATION ESSAYS, *supra* note 3, at 87–93; Fishlow, *supra* note 11.

13. *See generally* S. MUKHERJEE & C. ORLANS, INDEXATION IN AN INFLATIONARY ECONOMY: A CASE STUDY OF FINLAND (1975).

14. Kleiman, *Monetary Correction and Indexation: The Brazilian and Israeli Experience,* in BRAZILIAN INDEXATION, *supra* note 6, at 141, 144–53.

15. Since 1968, Brazil has utilized the "trotting peg" to devalue every ten days to two months to reflect the differential in inflation rates between Brazil and her principal trading partners. For a detailed study, *see* Da Silva, *The Basis of the Minidevaluation Policy,* in BRAZILIAN INDEXATION, *supra* note 6, at 101. Israel adopted a similar policy in 1975.

Finland indexed its foreign exchange rate directly to the exchange rates of its major trading partners. On November 1, 1977, Finland amended its Currency Act to replace the linkage of the par value of its currency to gold with a new concept called the external value of the mark. This is expressed as a currency index number reflecting the average change in the exchange rates for currencies which in the past 3 years have accounted for not less than 1 percent of the total value of Finnish foreign trade. The index is weighted by the percentage of each country's participation in Finnish foreign trade. Puro, *The Amendment of the Currency Act,* 52 BANK OF FINLAND MONTHLY BULL. 20 (No. 2., Feb. 1978).

16. Kafka, *The Brazilian Stabilization Program, 1964–1966,* 75 J. POL. ECON. 596, 605–12 (No. 4, pt. 2, Supp. Aug. 1967).

17. It has been subsequently revealed that this 13.7 percent inflation rate reported for 1973 was the product of recording the prices of certain commodities at official prices, even though none was obtainable at such prices. A World Bank study has placed the inflation rate for 1973 at 26.6 percent, a figure the government has reportedly conceded is more accurate. Several of the labor unions have instituted suits in the labor courts for a 34.1 percent wage restoration because of the government's index dishonesty. Vidal, "Brazilian Labor Federation Brings Court Action against Government," N.Y. Times, Dec. 11, 1977, sec. I, p. 64, cols. 3–6.

18. The Fund for the Guarantee of the Time of Service (FGTS) was instituted in 1966 by Law No. 5.107. It requires employers of all employees who opt for the FGTS to deposit 8 percent of the employee's salary in a bank account in the employee's name. These accounts bear interest and monetary correction, and funds corresponding to these accounts are administered and employed by the National Housing Bank (BNH). J. CHACEL et al., *supra* note 12, at 128.

19. Lefcoe, *Monetary Correction and Mortgage Lending in Brazil: Observations for the United States,* 21 STAN. L. REV. 106, 112 (1968).

20. *See* chap. 6, *supra,* at note 8.

21. *Id.* at note 29.

22. Ness, *Financial Markets Innovation as a Development Strategy: Initial Results from the Brazilian Experience,* 22 ECON. DEVELOPMENT & CULT. CHANGE 453, 465 (Apr. 1974).

23. *Id.* at 456–57. Most spectacular has been the real growth in indexed passbook savings accounts, which have grown in real terms by an average of 39.3 percent annually between 1970 and 1978. *See* Baer & Beckerman, *supra* note 11, at Table 4.

24. Overholt, *The Future of Brazil: An Overview,* in THE FUTURE OF BRAZIL 1 (W. Overholt, ed. 1978).

25. Between 1965 and 1971 the number of returns filed increased by a factor of 22, while the amount collected, converted into dollars, nearly doubled. In 1965, 354,000 returns were filed showing a total tax liability of U.S. $719.5 million. In 1970 the number of returns filed totalled 7,100,000 with a total tax liability of $1.1 billion. Novitski, "April 15 in Brazil Is Tax Time, Too," N.Y. Times, Mar. 28, 1971, p. 22, col. 1.

26. Other factors contributing to the increase in income tax collections including the distributing of forms gratis instead of requiring taxpayers to buy their returns, the increase in the number of trained revenue agents, and the unprecedented and widely publicized imprisonment of notoriously delinquent taxpayers.

27. Fishlow, *supra* note 11, at 267–68; Macedo, *A Critical Review of the Relation between the Post-1964 Wage Policy and the Worsening of Brazil's Size Income Distribution in the Sixties,* in BRAZILIAN INDEXATION, *supra* note 6, at 117, 122–25. Since 1975, when the wage formula was altered to correct for inflation in the past twelve rather than twenty-four months, wage policy has become fairer to workers.

28. Morley, *supra* note 10, at 91.

29. Law No. 4.330 of Je. 1, 1964 regulated the right to strike in such restricted terms that most strikes are illegal. D. MARANHÃO, DIREITO DO TRABALHO 377 (2d ed. 1972).

30. *See* Steiner and Trubek, *Brazil—All Power to the Generals,* 49 FOREIGN AFFAIRS 464 (1971).

31. *See* chap. 5, *supra* note 67 and the accompanying text.

32. Fishlow, *supra* note 11, at 276.

33. *See* chap. 7, *supra,* at pp. 225, 226–27, 235.

34. *Id.* at pp. 243–44.

35. *See* Rosenn, *Controlled Rents and Uncontrolled Inflation: the Brazilian Dilemma,* 17 AM. J. COMP. L. 239 (1969).

36. J. CHACEL et al., *supra* note 12, at 42–45, 249–51.

37. "Inflação, Correção Monetária e Índices de Preços," 29 Conj. Econ. 91, 93 (Sept. 1975). "Inflationary accidents" were characterized as seasonal fluctuations, droughts, frosts, and oil imports.

38. *See* chap. 6, *supra,* at notes 72–73 and accompanying text.

39. *Id.* at note 74 and accompanying text.

40. This account of the Finnish indexation experience is largely drawn from S. MUKHERJEE & C. ORLANS, *supra* note 13.

41. *Id.* at 79–80.

42. *Id.* at 34–35.

43. *Id.* at 48.

44. *Id.* at 46, Fig. 3.

45. Kleiman, *supra* note 14, at 171, fn. 10.

46. Rubner, *The Abdication of the Israeli Pound as a Standard of Measurement for Medium and Long-Term Contracts,* 28 REV. ECON. STUDIES 69, 74 (Oct. 1960); Kleiman, *supra* note 14, at 149.

47. Kleiman, *supra* note 14, at 154.

48. *Id.* at 156.

49. *See* chap. 6, *supra,* at note 44 and accompanying text.

50. Kleiman, *supra* note 14, at 159.

51. Sarnat, *Monetary Risk, Stagflation, and the Uneasy Case for Indexation,* in INFLATION AND CAPITAL MARKETS 179, 201 (M. Sarnat ed. 1978).

52. Kleiman, *supra* note 14, at 150.

53. *See* chap. 9, *supra,* at note 85.

54. *Id.* at note 149.

55. *Id.* at notes 154–55.

56. *See* chap. 6, *supra,* at notes 8, 12, 34 and the accompanying text.

57. *Id.* at notes 20–21 and the accompanying text.

58. "Correção Monetária e Realimentação Inflacionária," 30 Conj. Econ. 88, 89 (Je. 1976).

59. *See* chap. 6, *supra,* at notes 32–33 and the accompanying text.

60. *See* chap. 2, *supra,* at note 17.

61. Many bonds, loans, savings deposits, and, occasionally, wage adjustments were only partly indexed in Finland. *See* chap. 6, *supra,* at notes 20–21. Brazilian wage policy has deliberately underindexed wages. *See* notes 27–29 *supra* and the accompanying text. And the Finnish and Israeli cost-of-living adjustments for wages have often been only partial. *See* pp. 383, 385.

62. Fishlow, *supra* note 11, at 263.

63. This experience is also confirmed by the sharp rises in inflation rates in 1974 in several Western European countries that index wages to the consumer price index. Ross-Skinner, *The Failure of Indexation,* DUN'S REVIEW 76–79 (Sept. 1977). Indexation tied to the consumer price index under these circumstances means that the nation is trying to maintain the same level of income for everyone despite an actual drop in national income. This can be done only through inflation. Bernstein, *Indexing Money Payments in a Large and Prolonged Inflation,* in INDEXATION ESSAYS, *supra* note 3, at 71, 73–75. *See also* chap. 9, *supra,* at pp. 346–47.

64. Lemgruber, *Inflation in Brazil,* in WORLDWIDE INFLATION: THEORY AND RECENT EXPERIENCE 395, 421–22 (L. Krause & W. Salant eds. 1977).

65. Foreign loans must be registered with the central bank and must now have a minimum term of eight years with a grace period of thirty months. The central bank carefully scrutinizes the interest rates and repayment schedules of foreign currency loans and refuses to register those whose terms fail to meet its guidelines. *See* Skola, *Foreign Loans in Brazil: Theory and Practice*, 15 INT'L LAW 73 (1981).

66. OECD, REPORT BY COMM. ON FINANCIAL MARKETS, INDEXATION OF FIXED-INTEREST SECURITIES 29 (1973); Cline, *Brazil's Aggressive Response to External Shocks,* in WORLD INFLATION AND THE DEVELOPING COUNTRIES 102, 112 (W. Cline ed. 1981).

67. The advantages and disadvantages of these proposals are explored in THE CONSTITUTION AND THE BUDGET: ARE CONSTITUTIONAL LIMITS ON TAX, SPENDING, AND BUDGET POWERS DESIRABLE AT THE FEDERAL LEVEL? (W. Moore and R. Penner eds. 1980).

68. In expanded form this article has been published as *Monetary Correction,* Occasional Paper No. 41 of the Institute of Econ. Affairs, London (1974) and reprinted in INDEXATION ESSAYS, *supra* note 3, at 25–61.

69. *See* chap. 9, *supra,* at pp. 322–28.

70. *See* chap. 5, *supra,* at pp. 142–48.

71. COUNCIL OF ECONOMIC ADVISORS, ANNUAL REPORT 129 (1967).

72. Morley, *supra* note 10, at 81.

73. Arvidsson, *Should We Have Index Loans?,* in INFLATION 112, 113 (D.C. Hague, ed. 1962).

74. Robson, *Index-Linked Bonds,* REV. ECON. STUDIES 57 (Oct. 1960).

75. Morley, *supra* note 10, at 81.

76. *See* chap. 9, *supra,* at pp. 320–21. Finland for a time did just the opposite with respect to savings account interest. Fully indexed accounts were fully taxable, while nonindexed accounts were tax-free. *Id.* at 321.

77. *See* chap. 6, *supra,* at note 3 and the accompanying text.

78. *See* chap. 9, *supra,* at pp. 320–22.

79. Morley, *supra* note 10, at 82.

80. Baer & Beckerman, *supra* note 11.

81. OECD, REPORT BY COMM. ON FISCAL AFFAIRS, THE ADJUSTMENT OF PERSONAL INCOME TAX SYSTEMS FOR INFLATION 16–17 (1976).

82. P. SAMUELSON, ECONOMICS 356 (9th ed. 1973).

83. Allan, Dodge, and Poddar, *Indexing the Personal Income Tax: A Federal Perspective,* 22 CAN. TAX. J. 355, 368 (1974).

84. H. DOUTY, COST OF LIVING ESCALATOR CLAUSES AND INFLATION 52 (1975).

85. Garbarino, *The Economic Significance of Automatic Wage Adjustments,* in NEW DIMENSIONS IN COLLECTIVE BARGAINING 154, 169 (H. Davey, H. Kaltenborn, and S. Ruttenberg eds. 1959).

86. Bernstein, *supra* note 63, at 71, 74–75.

87. *See* chap. 9, *supra,* at pp. 346–48.

88. For a more elaborate analysis, see Morley, *supra* note 10, at 77–79; Peel, *On the Case for Indexation of Wages and Salaries,* 30 KYKLOS 259, 260 (Fasc. 2, 1977).

89. Braun, *Indexation of Wages and Salaries in Developed Economics,* 23 IMF STAFF PAPERS 226, 228–30 (1976).

90. *Id.* at 239.

91. In algebraic terms the pre-1968 wage indexation formula used in Brazil was:

$$W_{n+1} = 0.5(\bar{W}_n + \bar{W}_{n-1})(1 + r_{n+1})(1 + 0.5i^e_{n+1})p_n,$$

where

W_{n+1} = the nominal wage to apply in the next twelve months
$\bar{W}_n$ = the real wage prevailing in the past year
r = the rate of anticipated productivity increase
i^e_{n+1} = the rate of expected inflation
p_n = the price index at the end of period n.

Law No. 5.451 of Je. 14, 1968 substituted a formula which corrected any subestimation of the projected inflation rate during the past pay period by using the actual inflation rate. The post-1968 version of the formula was:

$$W_{n+1} = 0.5\left[\bar{W}_n\left(\frac{1 + 0.5i_n}{1 + 0.5i^e_n}\right) + \bar{W}_{n-1}\right](1 + r_{n+1})(1 + 0.5i^e_{n+1})p_n,$$

where i_n is the actual rate of inflation experienced during the most recent wage period. Fishlow, *supra* note 11, at 267; Macedo, *supra* note 27, at 117.

92. Even this kind of approach will not assure that real disposable income remains constant unless progressive income tax brackets are also indexed. Otherwise, increases in nominal income will push taxpayers into higher brackets, thereby decreasing real disposable income. If one wishes to avoid this effect with an unindexed tax system, wage increases must do more than merely retain the same real income. This problem is explored in greater detail in chap. 9, *supra,* at pp. 304–06 and the accompanying text.

93. This was not the way this wage policy worked out in practice because the inflation rate for 1965 was estimated at only 10 percent, about 55 percent lower than was actually experienced. By using the average real wage of the prior

twenty-four months (shortened to twelve months in January of 1975) and deliberately underestimating the projected inflation rate, the Brazilian government used this formula-approach to reduce real wages substantially.

94. *See* chap. 5, *supra,* at pp. 141–42.

95. F. Mann, The Legal Aspect of Money 162 (3d ed. 1971).

APPENDICES

APPENDIX A

Cost-of-Living Escalation Clause in the Collective Bargaining Agreement between the Dayton Public Service Union Local No. 101 and the City of Dayton, Ohio, March 16, 1973

For the term of this Agreement each employee covered by the Agreement shall receive a cost-of-living allowance to be determined in accordance with the Official Consumer Price Index for Urban Wage Earners and Clerical Workers published by the Bureau of Labor Statistics, U.S. Department of Labor (1967 = 100). Such allowance will be granted subject to the following conditions.

A. The base for computation shall be the Index of 126.2. The amount shall be computed and paid quarterly. The first adjustment to be paid in April, 1973 shall be based upon the change occurring in said Index from September through December, 1972 and applied to the quarter January through March, 1973. The second payment shall be based upon the change occurring in the Index from the base through March, 1973 and shall be paid in July, 1973 for the quarter ending June, 1973. Subsequent adjustments shall be made quarterly.

B. Adjustments will be up or down, but in no event shall a reduction be made below the 126.2 base.

C. Adjustments will be one cent (1¢) per hour adjustment for each 0.4 change in the Index.

D. Such adjustment shall not be applied to overtime or premium pay.

E. Quarterly payments will be made to those employees on the payroll at the end of the quarter for which payment is made. Employees separated from employment during the quarter for which payment is made, are eligible for proportional payment provided the employee makes application within thirty (30) days after his last day worked.

F. No adjustments, retroactive or otherwise, shall be made due to any revision which may later be made in the published figures for the Bureau of Labor Statistics Consumer Price Index for any base month.

G. The parties to this Agreement agree that the continuance of the cost-of-living allowance is dependent upon the availability of the monthly Consumer Price Index in its present form and calculated on the same basis as the Index for January, 1971 unless otherwise agreed upon by the parties.

H. The maximum adjustment is limited to eight (8¢) cents per hour increase during any one calendar year, provided, however a minimum increase of five (5¢) cents per hour is guaranteed for each calendar year.

APPENDIX B

No. R.............

CHRISTIANSEN CORPORATION
Christiansen Plan—Inflation Provision Debenture
Due July 1, 1972

Chicago, Illinois
July 1, 1952

§ 1.1. CHRISTIANSEN CORPORATION, a Delaware corporation (hereinafter called "the Company"), for value received hereby promises to pay to the registered holder, on July 1, 1972, in such coin or currency of the United States of America as at the time of payment shall be legal tender for the payment of public and private debts, at its principal office in the City of Chicago and State of Illinois a sum of money (hereinafter called the "Maturity Value") the amount of which is to be determined in accordance with the provisions of section 1.2 of this Debenture, together with interest from the date hereof payable to the registered holder of this Debenture at the said principal office of the Company on January 1 and July 1 of each year, such interest payments to be calculated at a rate of 4 1/2% per annum on a sum of money (hereinafter called the "Prepayment Value") the amount of which is to be determined in accordance with the provisions of section 1.2 of this Debenture.

This Debenture is being issued in the sum of $............. (hereinafter called the "Face Amount").

§ 1.2. Since it is the purpose of the Company to pay to the holder of this Debenture at maturity, or any prior date of payment, and to pay interest on, an amount in dollars equivalent to the purchasing power of the Face Amount on June 15, 1952, such payments of principal and interest shall be made in amounts which will provide within the limits expressed below for changes in the purchasing power of the Face Amount due to price changes as measured by changes in the "Consumer's Price Index for Moderate Income Families in Large Cities-Combined Adjusted Series" (all Items), which index is now being published monthly in the "Monthly Labor Review" of the Bureau of Labor Statistics of the United States Department of Labor and is hereinafter referred to as the "BLS Consumers' Price Index". As used in this Debenture "Base Index" shall mean the index number for all items of the BLS Consumers' Price Index published by the aforesaid Bureau of Labor Statistics as the final official index number for June 15, 1952. "Index Number" shall mean the final official index number for all items of the BLS Consumers' Price Index as published at any specified date by the Bureau of Labor Statistics.

(*a*) The Maturity Value of this Debenture shall be at least 100% of the Face Amount and not more than 150% of the Face Amount. Within these limits the Maturity Value shall be determined by multiplying the Face Amount by a factor obtained by dividing the Index Number for January 15, 1972, by the Base Index, such factor to be determined to the nearest one-hundredth.

(*b*) The Prepayment Value of this Debenture shall be at least 100% of the Face Amount and not more than 150% of the Face Amount. Within these limits the

Prepayment Value shall be determined semiannually as of January 15 and July 15 of each year by multiplying the Face Amount by a factor obtained by dividing the Index Number for January 15 and July 15 respectively by the Base Index, such factor to be determined to the nearest one-hundredth. The Prepayment Value as determined from the Index Number for January 15 of each year shall, for all purposes including, without limitation, the payment of interest, be considered the Prepayment Value of this Debenture from March 15 to and including September 14 of such year. The Prepayment Value as determined from the Index Number for July 15 of each year shall for all purposes, including, without limitation, the payment of interest, be considered the Prepayment Value of this Debenture from September 15 of such year to and including March 14 of the year succeeding such July 15.

(*c*) It is recognized that the base period of the BLS Consumers' Price Index may be changed from time to time and that such changes may result in the publication of Index Numbers not directly comparable with the Base Index as defined above. In the event of any such change in the BLS Consumers' Price Index, Maturity Value and Prepayment Value shall be determined in accordance with the following provisions in order to utilize the Index Numbers which will be published:

(1) As used in this Debenture

(*i*) "New Index" means any index published regularly by the Bureau of Labor Statistics, its successor agency or other United States governmental organization which is designed to reflect changes in the cost of living to consumers due to price changes. In the event that more than one index is published by the Bureau of Labor Statistics, its successor agency or other United States governmental organization, which indices are designed to reflect changes in the cost of living to consumers due to price changes, the Bureau of Labor Statistics, its successor agency, or other United States governmental organization, shall be requested to certify to the Company which published index is most comprehensive in coverage and most nearly comparable with the BLS Consumers' Price Index. The index so certified shall be considered the "New Index" for purposes of this Debenture and such certification shall be final and binding on the Company and the registered holder of this Debenture. In the event that the Bureau of Labor Statistics, its successor agency, or other United States governmental organization refuses to certify to the Company which published index is most comprehensive in coverage and most nearly comparable with the BLS Consumers' Price Index, the Company and the registered holder of this Debenture agree that a third party shall be appointed by American National Bank and Trust Company of Chicago, a national banking association, now located at 33 North La Salle Street, Chicago, Illinois, who shall certify as to what published index is most comprehensive in coverage and most nearly comparable with the BLS Consumers' Price Index. The index so certified shall then be considered the "New Index" for purposes of this Debenture and such certification shall be final and binding on the Company and the registered holder of this Debenture.

(*ii*) "New Index Number" means any index number published by the Bureau of Labor Statistics or its successor agency or other United States governmental organization in the "New Index".

(*iii*) "Revised Base Index" means the number found in accordance with the provisions of this section 1.2(c) which will be comparable with the New Index Number.

(2) At the time the New Index becomes effective the Bureau of Labor Statistics, its successor agency, or other United States governmental organization publishing the New Index shall be requested to supply a conversion factor by means of which the Base Index may be redetermined on a basis comparable with the New Index Numbers. The finding of the Bureau of Labor Statistics, its successor agency, or other United States governmental organization with respect to this conversion factor shall be final and binding upon the Company and the registered holder of this Debenture. The number obtained by applying the conversion factor to the Base Index (obtained to the nearest one-hundredth) shall be the Revised Base Index.

(3) In the event that the Bureau of Labor Statistics, its successor agency, or other United States governmental organization publishing the New Index is unable or refuses to supply a conversion factor, the Revised Base Index shall be determined by multiplying the Base Index by a factor obtained by dividing the New Index Number published for the last month that the old index number is official by the old index number for the last month in which the old index number is official. In the event that a New Index Number is not published for the last month in which the old index number is official, the Revised Base Index shall be determined by multiplying the Base Index by a factor obtained by dividing the New Index Number first published by the Bureau of Labor Statistics, its successor agency, or other United States governmental organization publishing the New Index by the last index number published by any of the aforesaid organizations prior to the change.

(4) Maturity Value and Prepayment Value will be determined as of the dates and as described in sections 1.2(a) and 1.2(b) substituting the Revised Base Index for the Base Index and the New Index Number for the Index Number.

(*d*) Changes in the name, methods of compilation, publication, or United States governmental agency directing the publication of the BLS Consumers' Price Index or any New Index as determined by section 1.2(*c*)(1)(i) other than changes in the base period or other changes herein provided for shall in no way affect the obligations of this Debenture or the methods of determining Prepayment Value and Maturity Value as described in this section 1.2.

(*e*) In the event that during the term of this Debenture the Bureau of Labor Statistics, its successor agency, or other United States governmental organization ceases to publish an index designed to reflect changes in the cost of living to consumers due to price changes, the Maturity Value and Prepayment Value of this Debenture shall be determined in accordance with the provisions of this section 1.2 for the last date of publication of BLS Consumers' Price Index or New Index. Such Maturity Value and Prepayment Value as determined of that date shall remain unchanged for the duration of the term of this Debenture.

APPENDIX C

Convertible Debentures with Monetary Correction Issued in 1970 by UNIPAR, a Brazilian Petrochemical Corporation

1.0—Type of Debentures—This shall be a bearer debenture, regulated by Decree No. 177-A of Sept. 15, 1893, with the following clauses:

(a) monetary correction, in accordance with the terms of Article 26 of Law No. 4.728 of July 14, 1965, as amended by Article 5 of Decree-Law No. 614 of June 6, 1969; and

(b) convertibility into shares, in accordance with the terms of Article 44 of Law 4.728 of July 14, 1965.

2.0—Nominal Value and Monetary Correction of the Principal:

2.1—Nominal unit value—Each debenture shall have the initial nominal value in the first trimester of 1970 of NCr $254,10.

2.2—Monetary correction—The nominal value of the debenture shall be subject to trimestral monetary correction on an identical basis with that applicable to the Readjustable Treasury Bonds (ORTN), regulated by Article 1 of Law No. 4.357 of July 14, 1964.

2.2.1—The trimestral correction shall take place on the first day of each trimester and shall remain in force, until the next correction, for all purposes of calculating interest, redemption, and conversion into shares.

2.2.2—The correction shall end on the day of conversion, the date marked for redemption, or at maturity of the debenture, whichever occurs first.

3.0—Series and Quantity of Obligations—The issue shall consist of one series of 165,250 debentures.

4.0—Issue and Distribution

4.1—The total value of the issue: NCr $41.990.025,00

4.2—Placement, type and distribution—The debentures shall be placed at par, by their nominal value, and offered for public subscription through institutions or intermediaries which constitute part of the distribution system of the capital market.

4.3—Provisional receipts and guarantees—The corporation shall provisionally deliver to subscribers receipts or guarantees, which shall later be substituted for the definitive certificates.

4.4—Term of payment—The debentures shall be placed for payment during the period of twelve months, adjusting the value of the installment payments in accordance with monetary correction of the principal and with prorating of the interest.

5.0—Interest—The debenture shall bear interest at the rate of 9% per annum, calculated on the readjusted nominal value.

5.1—Time and method of payment: The interest shall be paid in trimestral installments on the last day of the month of March, June, September, and December of each year, upon delivery of the detachable coupon which accompanies the debenture.

5.2—Termination of Interest Liability—The obligation to pay interest shall terminate on the day of conversion, the date marked for redemption, or on maturity, whichever shall occur first.

6.0—Maturation of the Debentures and Redemption of the Issue—All the obligations shall become due by December 31st, 1976, but the corporation shall redeem the issue on the following dates and percentages:

(a) by December 31st, 1974: 20%

(b) by the 31st of December, 1975: an additional 40%;

(c) by the 31st of December, 1976: the remaining 40%

6.1—Method of redemption—The corporation may redeem its debentures through purchase on the Stock Exchange or by lot, if necessary, in order to complete the percentages indicated above.

6.2—Redemption price—The debentures which are redeemed through lot shall be paid according to their adjusted nominal value on the day marked for redemption upon presentation of the certificate accompanied by all of the interest coupons which have matured since the trimester of redemption. The principal to be paid on redemption of the debenture with coupons which have matured and have been already detached shall be reduced by the same percentage of interest represented by the detached coupons. . . .

7.0—Anticipatory Redemption—As of January 1st, 1973, the corporation may anticipatorily redeem the issue, either in whole or in part, on the date interest falls due, so long as it gives 90 days prior notice and assures the opportunity to exercise the option of converting the debentures into shares.

7.1—Lottery—In the case of the anticipatory redemption of part of the issue, the selection of the debentures to be redeemed shall be made by lot. . . .

7.2—Premium for anticipatory redemption—The debentures which have been anticipatorily redeemed within the terms of item 7.0 shall be paid in accordance with their updated nominal value, increased by 3%.

8.0—Guaranty—The debentures shall be guarantied by all of the company's assets which are free and clear of any lien, and shall have preference over any other certificate of debt of the corporation.

8.1—Special obligations—In addition, the corporation obligates itself, until the final redemption of all of the debentures issued:

(a) not to create real rights of guaranty in favor of third parties which take priority over real rights which guarantee the debentures in circulation;

(b) not to assume new obligations vis-à-vis third parties which elevate the total of its liabilities beyond the following limits:

(i)—the principal of the debentures in circulation, including any new issue of debentures, shall not exceed the total net worth of the corporation;

(ii)—the total of the current liabilities of the corporation—including the debentures in circulation and other debts of the company, shall not exceed 150% of its net worth;

(iii)—the total of the debentures with a monetary correction clause or a foreign currency clause shall not exceed 120% of the corporation's net worth.

(c) not to assume new obligations whose amortization and interest charges reduce to less then 1.5 the relation between the company's surplus (foreseen in its financial projections, and after attending to all of its other obligations) and the annual total of charges for interest and amortization of the debentures with monetary correction clauses. . . .

10.0—Convertibility into Shares—While attached to the coupon which represents the right to subscribe to shares, the debenture may, at the option of its bearer, be converted into stock of the corporation in accordance with the following rules:

10.1—Time of conversion—The right of conversion may be exercised starting from 90 days from the date of the issuance of the security and until the date of its maturity. In case of redemption, whether or not anticipatory, the right of conversion may be exercised until 30 days after publication in the press of the debentures which have been selected for redemption.

10.2—Date of Conversion—For all purposes the date of conversion shall be considered as the date on which the debenture was presented for conversion at corporate headquarters on any working day. Starting from the close of business on that date, the bearer of the debenture shall enjoy all of the rights of a shareholder, and the corporation shall deliver the share certificates within a maximum period of 60 days.

10.3—The minimum number of shares into which each debenture shall be converted—As long as it is united with a detachable coupon which represents the right to subscription in shares, each debenture shall be converted, independently of any other payment by the bearer, in the following minimum quantities of shares, in accordance with the date of conversion:

(i) until December 31st, 1973: 125 shares; *(ii)* in 1974: 114 shares; *(iii)* in 1975: 109 shares; *(iv)* in 1976: 104 shares.

10.4—Updating the number of shares—The minimum number of shares referred to in the previous section shall be updated, on the date of conversion, through the application of the following formula:

$$\text{No. of shares} = \frac{\text{Value of the debenture} \div \text{Capital of the shareholders} \times \text{factor}}{\text{No. of shares of social capital}}$$

The definition of the terms in this formula is the following:

(a) "No. of shares" is the updated number of shares on the date of conversion into which the debenture is to be converted.

(b) "Value of the debenture" is the nominal updated value of the debenture in the trimester in which the date of conversion occurs.

(c) "Capital of the shareholders" is the value of the capital paid in by the shareholders to the corporation for acquisition of shares (nominal value plus any premium), monetarily corrected from the date of payment until the date of the conversion, through the application of coefficients of monetary correction of the Readjustable Treasury Bonds (ORTNs) adopted in the correction of the debentures of this issue;

(d) "Factor" shall be one of the following, in accordance with the date of

conversion: *(i)* until December 31st, 1973: 2.0; *(ii)* in 1974: 2.2; *(iii)* in 1975: 2.3; *(iv)* in 1976: 2.4.

(e) "Number of shares of social capital" is the total of the shares with a nominal value of NCr $1.00 into which the social capital of UNIPAR is divided on the date of conversion.

In any case, the number of shares into which the debenture shall be converted shall not be inferior to that set out in the prior article, except for the conversion of debentures which are presented with the coupon of matured interest detached, in which case the number of shares shall be reduced by the same percentage as the matured interest.

10.5—Class of shares: Each debenture or group of debentures simultaneously delivered by the same bearer for conversion shall be converted into one third common stock and two thirds non-voting preferred stock. . . . If the number of shares into which the debenture is converted, (or group of debentures) is not divisable by 3, the remainder shall be converted into preferred stock.

10.6—Interest—The debentures presented for conversion shall bear interest until the date of conversion, which shall be paid in money at the same time as the delivery of the share certificates.

11.0—Coupon for the Right to Subscribe to Shares—The right to subscribe to shares, corresponding to the convertibility of the debenture into shares, shall be the object of a coupon attached to the debenture which may be detached and negotiated separately from the debenture.

11.1—The date of the exercise of the right—The subscription right represented by the detached coupon of the debenture may be exercised from July 1st, 1971 (except in the case of anticipation authorized by UNIPAR) until December 31st, 1974. Detached coupons which are not presented for subscription by December 31st, 1974 shall lose all value.

11.2—Date of subscription—For all purposes the date of subscription shall be considered as the date on which the coupon was presented on any business day at the corporate headquarters for the exercise of the subscription right, jointly with the payment of the price of the shares to be subscribed, in cash or with a certified check in the name of the corporation. As of the close of business on that date, the bearer of the coupon shall enjoy all the rights of a shareholder, and the corporation shall deliver the share certificates within a maximum period of 60 days.

11.3—The price of the subscription of shares—Each detached coupon shall give the right to subscription of the number of shares provided for in the following sections, at the price equivalent to the nominal updated value of each bearer debenture of this issue in force on the date of subscription.

11.4—The minimum number of shares—The bearer of the detached coupon shall have the right to subscribe, at the price referred to in the previous section, to the following minimum quantities of shares, in accordance with the date of subscription:

(i) in 1971: 147 shares; *(ii)* in 1972: 135 shares; *(iii)* in 1973: 125 shares; *(iv)* in 1974: 115 shares.

11.5—Updating the number of shares—The minimum number of shares referred to in the previous item shall be updated, on the date of subscription, in accordance with the formula set out in item 10.4, applying, however, the following factors:

(i) in 1971: 1.7; *(ii)* in 1972: 1.85; *(iii)* in 1973: 2.0; *(iv)* in 1974: 2.2.

11.6—Class of shares—The subscribed shares shall be common and preferred, in the proportion of 1/3 and 2/3, respectively, as provided in item 10.5.

12.0—Place of Payment—The debentures of the issuing corporation shall be paid at its corporate headquarters, or at financial institutions authorized by it, which shall be announced in the press.

13.0—Conversion or Subscription through an Act of the Directors—The conversion of debentures into shares under the conditions provided for in item 10.0, or the subscription of shares in the terms of item 11.0, shall be independent of the approval of the general shareholders meeting of UNIPAR, and shall be effectuated by company management at the request of the holder of the debenture or the detached coupon which represents the right of subscription.

Appendix D

Index Clause Used in Term Life Insurance Policy Issued by TIAA in the U.S. in 1980

AGREEMENT FOR COST OF LIVING BENEFIT

Attached to and made part of policy at date of issue. Agreement Date is the date of issue of the policy. Agreement Years and Anniversaries are computed from the Agreement Date. Initial Consumer Price Index: 216.6

TIAA will pay an Insurance Benefit defined herein upon receipt of due proof that the death of the Insured occurred prior to the termination of this Agreement. Payment will be made to the beneficiary of the policy. Any amount payable under this Agreement is in addition to the proceeds payable under the policy.

Definitions

The Initial Consumer Price Index as used in this Agreement will be the Consumer Price Index-All Items, published by the U.S. Department of Labor's Bureau of Labor Statistics for June of the calendar year preceding the calendar year of the Agreement Date. The Initial Consumer Price Index applicable to this Agreement is set forth above.

The Current Consumer Price Index as used in this Agreement will be the Consumer Price Index-All Items, published by the U.S. Department of Labor's Bureau of Labor Statistics for June of the calendar year preceding the calendar year of the Agreement Anniversary at the beginning of the Agreement Year for which the CPI Factor is to be computed.

The CPI Factor will be determined by subtracting the Initial Consumer Price Index from the Current Consumer Price Index, and dividing the result by the Initial Consumer Price Index.

If the Consumer Price Index preparation and publication is transferred to some bureau or agency of the United States Government other than the U.S. Department of Labor's Bureau of Labor Statistics, the definition of Consumer Price Index is hereby automatically changed to refer to such succeeding bureau or agency.

If the base year of the Consumer Price Index is changed by the Bureau of Labor Statistics after the date of this Agreement, then the Initial Consumer Price Index will be adjusted to the new base for purposes of determining all subsequent CPI Factors.

If the Consumer Price Index becomes unavailable, is no longer published, or is altered so that it is, in the opinion of TIAA, no longer appropriate or usable in connection with this Agreement, then substitute factors for the CPI Factors will be determined in a manner that is mutually acceptable to TIAA and to the insurance supervisory official of the State in which the Agreement is delivered and will be used during the subsequent Agreement Years.

Insurance Benefit

The Insurance Benefit to be paid under this Agreement in the event of the death of the Insured while this Agreement is in force will be the amount determined by multiplying the CPI Factor for the current Agreement Year times the amount of insurance which would be payable under the policy to which this Agreement is attached if death occurred during the current Agreement Year. The amount of insurance under the policy for the purpose of this definition is:

a. for Lifetime, Endowment and Term Insurance policies the Face Amount; and
b. for Decreasing Term policies the amount determined by the Schedule of Insurance.

If the CPI Factor for any Agreement Year is a positive number, the amount of Insurance Benefit under this Agreement will be not less than $1,000 nor more than two times the amount of insurance provided by the policy as of the date of death of the Insured.

If the CPI Factor for any Agreement Year is zero or a negative number, there will be no Insurance Benefit under this Agreement for that Agreement Year, and no premium will be payable for that Agreement Year.

Premiums

The premiums under this Agreement are payable annually beginning with the premium due on the first Agreement Anniversary and on each subsequent Agreement Anniversary while this Agreement remains in force. The premium payable on the Agreement Anniversary for any Agreement Year while this Agreement is in force will be equal to the product of the premium rate per $1,000 shown in the Table of Premium Rates below for the Insured's age nearest birthday on the Agreement Anniversary at the beginning of the Agreement Year multiplied by the Insurance Benefit provided by this Agreement for the Agreement Year and divided by one thousand.

Payment of the premiums required hereunder will not affect any cash, loan, paid-up or extended insurance values under the policy. The Automatic Premium Loan Provision, if any, included in the policy to which this Agreement is attached will not be applicable to premiums due under this Agreement.

APPENDIX E

Index Clause Used in Homeowner's Policy Issued by Continental Insurance Companies in the United States in 1980

5. Automatic Adjustment of Limit(s) of Liability for Residence Locations Owned by *Named Insured:* The limit of liability applicable to a residence location owned by the *named insured* listed in the Declarations as covered under Section I is subject to adjustment to reflect changes in the construction cost index for residences published by the organization whose indices are approved specifically for this purpose by the state official exercising jurisdiction over this insurance. Adjustment will be made in accordance with the following provisions:

5a. The percent of change in the index from the published index in effect as of the inception date of the policy (or in effect under 5d below) and listed in the Declarations shall be ascertained.

5b. When there is cumulative change in the published index equal to four percent (4%) or more of the index listed in the Declarations, the company at next premium due date (but not more often than once each 12 months) will increase (or reduce) the appropriate limit of liability by the net percentage change, rounded to the nearest $1,000. No change in limit will be made if the calculated change is less than $500.

5c. The adjusted limit of liability rounded to the nearest $1,000 and the adjusted premium will be applicable to the next policy period. The index which is used in the adjustment in limit(s) shall be furnished to the *named insured.*

5d. Whenever a location limit is added or changed by endorsement, adjustment shall be made according to the most recently published index, which shall appear on the endorsement and shall become the index governing subsequent adjustments under these provisions.

5e. In case of loss in excess of the limit of liability applicable to the location, such amount of insurance shall be adjusted by increasing the limit stated in the Declarations to reflect the percentage increase, if any, that the construction cost index for the month next preceding the date of loss exceeds the index most recently applied in the Declarations. Such adjusted amount, after rounding in accordance with provision 5b, shall be the revised limit of the company's liability at such location, subject to all other provisions of provision F.

SELECTED BIBLIOGRAPHY

BOOKS

AARON, H., ed., INFLATION AND THE INCOME TAX (Washington, D. C.: Brookings, 1976).

ADVISORY COMMISSION ON INTERGOVERNMENTAL RELATIONS, INFLATION AND FEDERAL AND STATE INCOME TAXES (Washington, D.C.: U. S. Gov't Printing Office, 1976).

ASCARELLI, T., LA MONETA (Padova, Dott. A. Milani, 1928).

——— PROBLEMAS DAS SOCIEDADES ANÔNIMAS E DIREITO COMPARADO (São Paulo: Saraiva, 1945).

——— STUDI GIURIDICI SULLA MONETA (Milan: Giuffre, 1952).

BACH, G., THE NEW INFLATION: CAUSES, EFFECTS, CURES (Providence: Brown Univ. Press, 1973).

BANCHIO, E., OBLIGACIONES DE VALOR (Buenos Aires, 1965).

BRECKINRIDGE, S., LEGAL TENDER (Chicago: Univ. of Chicago Press, 1903).

BRESCIANI-TURRONI, C., THE ECONOMICS OF INFLATION (London, Allen & Unwin, 1937).

CANDILIS, W., VARIABLE RATE MORTGAGE PLANS (Am. Bankers Assoc., Res. Paper No. 7, 1971).

CHACEL, J., SIMONSEN, M., & WALD, A., CORREÇÃO MONETÁRIA (Rio de Janeiro: APEC, 1970).

COLANDER D., ed., SOLUTIONS TO INFLATION (New York: Harcourt, Brace, Jovanovich, 1979).

COLLIER, R., PURCHASING POWER BONDS AND OTHER ESCALATED CONTRACTS (Taipei, Taiwan: Buffalo, 1969).

DELAUME, G., LEGAL ASPECTS OF INTERNATIONAL LENDING AND ECONOMIC DEVELOPMENT FINANCING (Dobbs Ferry, N.Y.: Oceana, 1967).

DOUCET, J., L'INDEXATION (Paris: Libraire Générale de Droit et de Jurisprudence, 1965).

DURAND, P., ed., INFLUENCE DE LA DÉPRÉCIATION MONÉTARIE SUR LA VIE JURIDIQUE PRIVÉE (Paris: R. Pichon et R. Durand-Auzias, 1961).

EDEL, M., FOOD SUPPLY AND INFLATION IN LATIN AMERICA (New York, Praeger, 1969).

FELLNER, W., CLARKSON, K., & MOORE, J., CORRECTING TAXES FOR INFLATION (Washington, D. C.: Amer. Enterprise Inst., 1975).

FERRERE-LAMAISON, D., EL DINERO EN LA TEORIA JURIDICA (Montevideo, 1974).

FISHER, I., STABLE MONEY: A HISTORY OF THE MOVEMENT (New York: Adelphi, 1934).

FLUME, W., HAHN, H., KEGEL, G., & SIMMONDS, K., eds., INTERNATIONALES RECHT UND WIRTSCHAFTSORDNUNG: FESTSCHRIFT FÜR F. A. MANN (Munich: Beck, 1977).

Galbraith, J., Money: Whence It Came, Where It Went (Boston: Houghton Mifflin, 1975).

Gesche Müller, S., Jurisprudencia Dinamica: La Desvalorizacion Monetaria y Otros Problemas en el Derecho (Santiago: Editorial Jurídica, 1971).

Giersch, H. et al., Essays on Inflation and Indexation (Washington, D. C.: Amer. Enterprise Inst., 1974).

Gomes, O., Transformações Gerais do Direito das Obrigações (São Paulo: Editôra Revista dos Tribunais, 1967).

Gonnard, R., Histoire des Doctrines Monétaires dans Ses Rapports avec L'Historie des Monnaies (2 vols. Paris: Libraire du Recueil Sirey, 1935).

Griffiths, B., Inflation: The Price of Prosperity (New York: Holmes & Meier, 1976).

Gurfinkel de Wendy, L., Depreciacion Monetaria. Revaluacion de Deudas Dinerarias (Buenos Aires: Ed. Depalma, 1976).

Hargreaves, E., Restoring Currency Standards (London: P.S. King & Son, 1926).

Harris, S., The Assignats (Cambridge, Mass.: Harvard Univ. Press, 1930).

Hawtrey, R., The Gold Standard in Theory and Practice (London: Longmans, Green, 5th ed., 1947).

Helfferich, K., Money, Trans. L. Infield, (New York: Adelphi, 1927).

Hepburn, A., A History of Currency of the United States (New York: MacMillan, 1903).

Hirsch, F., & Goldthorpe, J., The Political Economy of Inflation (Cambridge, Mass.: Harvard Univ. Press, 1978).

Hirschberg, E., The Nominalistic Principle (Ramat-Gan, Israel: Bar-Ilan Univ., 1971).

——— The Impact of Inflation and Devaluation on Private Legal Obligations (Ramat-Gan, Israel: Bar-Ilan Univ., 1976).

Hubrecht, G., La Dépréciation Monétaire et L'Exécution des Contrats: Stabilisation du Franc et Valorisation des Créances (Paris: Dalloz, 1928).

Hurst, J. W., A Legal History of Money in the United States, 1774–1970 (Lincoln: Univ. of Nebraska Press, 1973).

Int'l Fiscal Assoc., L'Inflation et la Fiscalité, 62A Cahiers de Droit Fiscal International (Amsterdam: Int'l. Bur. Fiscal Doc., 1977).

Jud, G., Inflation and the Use of Indexing in Developing Countries (New York: Praeger, 1978).

Karst, K., & Rosenn, K., Law and Development in Latin America (Berkeley, Calif.: Univ. of California Press, 1975).

Kemp, A., The Legal Qualities of Money (New York: Pageant Press, 1956).

Krause, L., & Salant, W., eds., Worldwide Inflation: Theory and Recent Experience (Washington, D.C.: Brookings, 1977).

Liesner, T. & King, M., eds., Indexing for Inflation (London: Heinemann, 1975).

Lopez-Santa Maria, J., Le Droit des Obligations et des Contrats et L'inflation Monétaire (Paris: Centre National de la Recherche Scientifique, 1980).

Lowenfeld, A., The International Monetary System (New York: Matthew Bender, 1977).

MANN, F., THE LEGAL ASPECT OF MONEY, (London, Oxford Univ. Press, 3d ed. 1971).

MANNE, H., & MILLER, R., eds., GOLD, MONEY AND THE LAW (Chicago: Aldine, 1975).

MEDEIROS DA FONSECA, A., CASO FORTUITO E TEORIA DA IMPREVISÃO (Rio de Janeiro: Forense, 3d ed. 1958).

MORAG, A., ON TAXES AND INFLATION (New York: Random House, 1965).

MORGAN, D., OVERTAXATION BY INFLATION: A STUDY OF THE EFFECTS OF INFLATION ON TAXATION AND GOVERNMENT EXPENDITURE, AND OF ITS CORRECTION BY INDEXING (London: Inst. of Econ. Affairs, 1977).

MUKHERJEE, S., & ORLANS, C., INDEXATION IN AN INFLATIONARY ECONOMY: A CASE STUDY OF FINLAND (London: PEP, 1975).

NESS, W., A INFLUENCIA DA CORREÇÃO MONETÁRIA NO SISTEMA FINANCEIRO (Rio De Janeiro: IBMEC, 1977).

NUSSBAUM, A., MONEY IN THE LAW: NATIONAL AND INTERNATIONAL (Brooklyn, N. Y.: Foundation Press, rev. ed. 1950).

OECD, INDEXATION OF FINANCIAL ASSETS (Paris: OECD, 1975).

——— REPORT BY COMM. ON FINANCIAL MARKETS, INDEXATION OF FIXED-INTEREST SECURITIES (Paris: OECD, 1973).

——— REPORT BY COMM. ON FISCAL AFFAIRS, THE ADJUSTMENT OF PERSONAL INCOME TAXES FOR INFLATION (Paris, OECD, 1976).

OLIVECRONA, K., THE PROBLEM OF THE MONETARY UNIT (New York: Macmillan, 1957).

ORGANIZACION DE LOS ESTADOS AMERICANOS, INFLACION Y TRIBUTACION (Washington, D.C.: OAS, 1978).

PRIMER CONGRESO NACIONAL DE ABOGADOS CHILENOS, EL DERECHO ANTE LA INFLACION (Santiago: Editorial Jurídica, 1955).

QUADRI, E., QUESTIONI GIURIDISCHE SULL'INFLAZIONE (Bari: Cacucci Editore 1981).

REPORT OF COMMITTEE OF INQUIRY INTO INFLATION AND TAXATION (Mathews Comm.), INFLATION AND TAXATION (Canberra, Australia, 1975).

ROLFE, S., GOLD AND WORLD POWER (New York: Harper & Row, 1966).

SHAW, W., THE HISTORY OF CURRENCY (New York: B. Franklin, 2d ed. 1896).

TANZI, V., INFLATION AND THE PERSONAL INCOME TAX: AN INTERNATIONAL PERSPECTIVE (Cambridge: Cambridge Univ. Press 1980).

TRIGO REPRESAS, F., OBLIGACIONES DE DINERO Y DEPRECIACION MONETARIA (La Plata: Editora Platense, 1965).

VON MEHREN, A., & GORDLEY, J., THE CIVIL LAW SYSTEM (Boston: Little, Brown, 2d ed. 1977).

WACHTER, S., LATIN AMERICAN INFLATION: THE STRUCTURALIST-MONETARIST DEBATE (Lexington, Mass.: Lexington Press, 1976).

WALD, A., A CLÁUSULA DE ESCALA MÓVEL (Rio de Janeiro: Editôra Nacional de Direito, 2d ed. 1959).

WALLACE, W., & W. CULLISON, MEASURING PRICE CHANGES: A STUDY OF THE PRICE INDEXES (Richmond: Fed. Reserve Bank of Richmond, 4th ed. 1979).

YEAGER, L., INTERNATIONAL MONETARY RELATIONS: THEORY, HISTORY AND POLICY (New York: Harper & Row, 2d ed. 1976).

ARTICLES

Allan, Dodge, and Poddar, *Indexing the Personal Income Tax: A Federal Perspective,* 22 CAN. TAX J. 355 (1974).

Alvarez Nuñez, *Las Obligaciones de Dinero en el Código Civil,* 41 REV. DER. 43 (Chile, Jan.–Je. 1974).

Andersen, *Les Instruments Juridiques de la Politique des Prix,* 37 ANNALES DE DROIT 351 (Belgium, 1977).

Andersen, *Compensation for Inflation under Alternative Regulatory Formulas—A Rejoinder,* PUB. UTIL. FORT. 32 (Dec. 6, 1979).

Annotation, *Changes in Purchasing Power of Money as Affecting Compensation in Eminent Domain Proceedings,* 92 A.L.R. 2d 772 (1963).

——— *Changes in Cost of Living or in Purchasing Power of Money as Affecting Damages for Personal Injuries or Death,* 12 A.L. R.2d 611 (1950).

Arvidsson, *Should We Have Index Loans?,* in INFLATION 112 (D. C. Hague, ed. 1962).

Asser, *Golden Limitations of Liability in International Transport Conventions and the Currency Crisis,* 5 J. MAR. L. & COM. 645 (1974).

Backman, *Cost-of-Living Escalator Clauses—Here and Abroad,* 10 LAB. L. J. 615 (1959).

Baer, *The Inflation Controversy in Latin America: A Survey,* 2 LAT. AM. RES. REV. 3 (1967).

Baer & Beckerman, *Indexing in Brazil,* 2 WORLD DEVELOPMENT 35 (Oct.–Dec. 1974).

——— *The Trouble with Index-Linking: Reflections on the Recent Brazilian Experience,* 8 WORLD DEVELOPMENT 677 (1980).

Baer and Simonsen, *Profit Illusion and Policy-Making in an Inflationary Economy,* 17 OXFORD ECON. PAPERS 279 (New Ser. 1965).

Becker, *The Currency of Judgment,* 25 AM. J. COMP. L. 152 (1977).

Bergsten, *Resource Scarcity: Cartelization and Contrived Shortages,* 24 AM. U. L. REV. 1128 (1975).

Bernstein, *Indexing Money Payments in a Large and Prolonged Inflation,* in ESSAYS ON INFLATION AND INDEXATION 71 (H. Giersch et al., 1974).

Bianchi, *Sobre Inflación e Imprevisión,* [1977] III J. A. 619 (Argentina).

Blinder, *Indexing the Economy through Financial Intermediation,* in STABILIZATION OF THE DOMESTIC AND INTERNATIONAL ECONOMY 69 (K. Brunner & A. Meltzer, eds. 1977).

Blondeel, *A New Form of International Financing: Loans in European Units of Account,* 64 COLUM. L. REV. 995 (1964).

Bomberger & Makinen, *Indexation, Inflationary Finance, and Hyperinflation: The 1945–1946 Hungarian Experience,* 88 J. POL. ECON. 550 (1980).

Borda, *Las Deudas de Dinero y la Desvalorización Monetaria,* [1975] LA LEY C 793 (Argentina).

Bossons, *Indexing Financial Instruments for Inflation,* 22 CAN. TAX J. 107 (1974).

Bowles & Phillips, *Judgments in Foreign Currencies: An Economist's View,* 39 MODERN L. REV. 196 (1976).

Braithwait, *The Substitution Bias of the Laspeyres Price Index,* 70 AM. ECON. REV. 64 (1980).

Braun, *Indexation of Wages and Salaries in Developed Economies,* 23 IMF STAFF PAPERS 226 (1976).

Buchanan and Tideman, *Gold, Money and the Law: The Limits of Governmental Monetary Authority,* in GOLD, MONEY AND THE LAW 9 (H. Manne and R. Miller, eds. 1975).

Call, *Money and the Sliding Scale Clause in Contracts,* 24 MO. L. REV. 44 (1959)

Carranza, *Las Deudas Dinerarias Frente a la Desvalorización de la Moneda,* [1974] J. A. DOCTRINA 191 (Argentina).

Carvallo Hederra, *Incidencia de la Inflación en el Sistema Tributario,* 5 REV. DER. ECON. 145 (Chile, Nos. 19–20, 1967).

Casanegra de Jantscher, *Taxing Business Profits During Inflation: The Latin American Experience,* 2 INT'L TAX J. 128 (1976).

Chaplin, *Redistributing the Cost of Inflation,* 34 U. MIAMI L. REV. 301 (1980).

Comment, *Adjustable Interest Rates in Home Mortgages: A Reconsideration,* 1975 WIS. L. REV. 742.

——— *Contractual Flexibility in a Volatile Economy: Saving U.C.C. § 2–615 from the Common Law,* 72 N.W. U. L. REV. 1032 (1978).

——— *Conversion Date of Foreign Money Obligations,* 65 COLUM L. REV. 490 (1965).

——— *Damages for Loss of Future Income: Accounting for Inflation,* 6 U. S. F. L. REV. 311 (1972).

——— *Fluctuating Dollars and Tort Damage Verdicts,* 48 COLUM. L. REV. 264 (1948).

——— *Future Inflation and the Undercompensated Plaintiff,* 4 LOY. CHI. L. J. 359 (1973).

——— *Future Inflation, Prospective Damages, and the Circuit Courts,* 63 VA. L. REV. 105 (1977).

——— *Inflation and the Federal Income Tax,* 82 YALE L. J. 716 (1973).

——— *Investment and Management of Trust Funds in an Inflationary Economy,* 126 U. PA. L. REV. 1171 (1978).

——— *Legal Problems in Compensation under the Gold Clauses of Private International Law Agreements,* 63 GEO. L. J. 817 (1975).

——— *Pre-Assessment Inflation as a Factor in Damages,* 48 CIN. L. REV. 999 (1979).

——— *Termination of Two-Tier Gold,* 7 L. & POL. INT'L BUS. 273 (1975).

——— *The Energy Crisis and Economic Impossibility in Louisiana Fuel Requirements Contracts: A Gameplan for Reform,* 49 TUL. L. REV. 605 (1975).

——— *The Feasibility of Adjusting for Inflation in Computing Taxable Income,* 49 WASH. L. REV. 873 (1974).

——— *The Unit of Account: Enforceability Under American Law of Maintenance-of-Value Provisions in International Bonds,* 71 YALE L. J. 1294 (1962).

——— *Variable Periodic Payments of Damages: An Alternative to Lump Sum Awards,* 64 IOWA L. REV. 138 (1978).

Cooper, *Effects of Inflation on Private Contracts: France, 1916–1926,* 6 DET. L. REV. 63 (1936).

Crosby, *Impact of Inflation and Income Taxes on Future Damages in Personal Injury and Death Cases,* 21 TRIAL LAW. GUIDE 196 (1977).

Dach, *Conversion of Foreign Money,* 3 AM. J. COMP. L. 155 (1954).

———*Tax Aspects of Inflation: A Study in Monetary Nominalism,* 9 AM. J. COMP. L. 657 (1960).

———*Floating-Rate Loans in the Euro-Market,* 19 AM. J. COMP. L. 700 (1971).

———*Validity of Price-Index Clauses under the Gold Coin Joint Resolution,* 13 GEO. WASH. L. REV. 328 (1945).

David-Constant, *Erosion Monétaire et Droit Privé,* 37 ANNALES DE DROIT 443 (Belgium, 1977).

Dawson, *Effects of Inflation on Private Contracts: Germany, 1914–1924,* 33 MICH. L. REV. 171 (1934).

———*The Gold Clause Decisions,* 33 MICH. L. REV. 647 (1935).

Dawson and Cooper, *The Effect of Inflation on Private Contracts: United States, 1861–1879,* 33 MICH. L. REV. 706 (1935).

——— *The Inflation in the North, 1862–1879,* 33 MICH. L. REV. 852 (1935).

Dawson & Coultrap, *Contracting by Reference to Price Indices,* 33 MICH. L. REV. 685 (1935).

Day, *A Reform of the European Currency Snake,* 23 IMF STAFF PAPERS 580 (1976).

Dean, *Provision for Capital Exhaustion and Changing Price Levels,* 65 HARV. L. REV. 1339 (1952).

Delaume, *Gold and Currency Clauses in Contemporary International Loans,* 9 AM. J. COMP. L. 199 (1960).

Denison, *Price Series for Indexing the Income Tax System,* in INFLATION AND THE INCOME TAX 233 (H. Aaron, ed. 1976).

Denz, *Lease Provisions Designed to Meet Changing Economic Conditions,* 1952 U. ILL. L. F. 344.

Deschenaux, *La Révision des Contrats en Droit Suisse,* 30 J. COMP. LEGIS. 55 (3d Ser., Pts. 3 & 4 1946).

Dixon, *The European Unit of Account,* 14 COMMON MARKET L. REV. 191 (1977).

Drake, *The Proper Rule in Fluctuating Exchanges,* 28 MICH. L. REV. 229 (1930).

Eder, *Legal Theories of Money,* 20 CORN ELL L. Q. 52 (1934).

Evan, *Rationale of Valuation of Foreign Money Obligations,* 54 MICH. L. REV. 307 (1956).

Fane, *The Case for Indexation,* in INDEXING FOR INFLATION 1 (T. Liesner & M. King, eds. 1975).

Faustini, *Wage Indexing and Inflation in Italy,* BANCA NAZIONALE DEL LAVORO Q. REV. 364 (Dec. 1976).

Fellner, *The Controversial Issue of Comprehensive Indexation,* in ESSAYS ON INFLATION AND INDEXATION 63 (H. Giersch et al., 1974).

Fishlow, *Indexing Brazilian Style: Inflation Without Tears?,* 1 BROOKINGS PAPERS ON ECON. ACTIVITY 261 (1974).

Fleming, *The Impact of Inflation on Tort Compensation,* 26 AM. J. COMP. L. 51 (1978).

Friedman, *Monetary Correction,* in ESSAYS ON INFLATION AND INDEXATION 25 (H. Giersch et al., 1974).

Formuziz & O'Donnell, *Inflation and the Valuation of Future Economic Losses,* 38 MONT. L. REV. 297 (1977).

Galbis, *Inflation and Interest Rate Policies in Latin America, 1967–76,* 26 IMF STAFF PAPERS 334 (1979).

Garbarino, *The Economic Significance of Automatic Wage Adjustments,* in NEW DIMENSIONS IN COLLECTIVE BARGAINING 154 (H. Davey et al., eds. 1959).

García de Enterría, *Expropiación Forzosa y Devaluación Monetaria,* 80 REV. ADMIN. PUB. 9 (Spain, May–Aug. 1976).

Genberg and Swoboda, *Inflation and Indexation: A Survey of the Issues,* in PROTECTION AGAINST INFLATION AND EXCHANGE RISK: THE ROLE OF INDEXATION 7 (Proc. of the Saltsjobaden Conf., July 4–6, 1974, Int'l Center for Monetary and Banking Studies, Geneva).

Gendrel, *Influence de la Dépréciation Monétaire sur le Droit de la Responsabilité Civile,* in INFLUENCE DE LA DÉPRÉCIATION MONÉTAIRE SUR LA VIE JURIDIQUE PRIVÉE 143 (P. Durand, ed. 1961).

Gesche Müller, *La Compensación de la Desvalorización Monetaria en el Complimiento de las Obligaciones,* 41 REV. DER. 7 (Chile, Jan.–Je. 1974).

Giersch, *Index Clauses and the Fight against Inflation,* in ESSAYS ON INFLATION AND INDEXATION 1 (H. Giersch et al., 1974).

Gilad, *On Linkage and Revaluation,* 15 ISRAEL L. REV. 79 (1980).

Gold, *Floating Currencies, Gold and SDRs* (IMF Pamphlet No. 19, 1976).

——— *Floating Currencies, SDRs, and Gold: Further Legal Developments* (IMF Pamphlet No. 22, 1977).

——— *Law and Reform of the International Monetary System,* 10 J. INT'L. & ECON. 371 (1975).

Gordon, *The Demand for and Supply of Inflation,* 18 J. L. & ECON. 807 (1975).

Gramlich, *The Economic and Budgetary Effects of Indexing the Tax System,* in INFLATION AND THE INCOME TAX 271 (H. Aaron, ed. 1976).

Guastavino, *El Derecho Civil ante la Inflación,* 116 LA LEY 1080 (Argentina, 1964).

Hagberg, *Gold Value Clauses in International Transport Conventions,* 5 INT'L BUS. LAW. 253 (1977).

Hamel, *Clauses d'Échelle Mobile et le Droit Monétaire Français,* REV. ÉCONOMIQUE 167 (France, 1955).

Harberger, *The Dynamics of Inflation in Chile,* in MEASUREMENT IN ECONOMICS: STUDIES IN MATHEMATICAL ECONOMICS IN MEMORY OF YEHUDA GRUNFELD 219 (C. Christ, ed. 1963).

Hauser, *Breach of Contracts Damages during Inflation,* 33 TUL. L. REV. 307 (1959).

——— *The Use of Index Clauses in Private Loans,* 7 AM. J. COMP. L. 350 (1958).

——— *Index Clauses in Private Loans since the Advent of the Fifth French Republic in 1958,* 13 AM. J. COMP. L. 606 (1964).

Hein, *A Note on the Use of Index Clauses Abroad,* 15 J. FINANCE 546 (1960).

Heller, *The Value of the Gold Franc—A Different Point of View,* 6 J. MAR. L. & COM. 73 (1974).

Hellner, *Indexing of Tort Awards in Sweden,* 26 AM. J. COMP. L. 71 (1978).

Hirao & Aguirre, *Maintaining the Level of Income Tax Collections under Inflationary Conditions,* 17 IMF STAFF PAPERS 277 (1970).

Hudson, *The Indexation of the Tax System,* in INDEXING FOR INFLATION 111 (T. Liesner & M. King, eds. 1975).

Jackman and Klappholz, *The Case for Indexing Wages and Salaries,* in INDEXING FOR INFLATION 19 (T. Liesner & M. King, eds. 1975).

James, *International Cooperation in the Field of Money: A Strand of Economic History,* in MONEY AND THE LAW: PROCEEDINGS THE INSTITUTE OF MONEY AND LAW (NYU School of Law, 1945).

Jeanprêtre, *La Conversión des Limitations de Responsabilité Exprimées en Or dan les Conventions Internationales,* 65 S.J.Z. 185 (Switzerland, 1969).

Kafka, *Indexing for Inflation in Brazil,* in ESSAYS ON INFLATION AND INDEXATION 87 (H. Giersch et al., 1974).

——— *The International Monetary System in Transition-Part I,* 13 VA. J. INT'L. 135 (1972).

Kleiman, *Monetary Correction and Indexation: The Brazilian and Israeli Experience,* in INDEXATION, THE BRAZILIAN EXPERIENCE 141 (N. Nadiri and A. Pastore, eds., Occasional Papers, Nat'l Bur. Econ. Res., Vol. 4 No. 1, Winter 1977).

Klimowsky, *Israeli Tax Reform on Indexed Income and Capital Gains,* 1976 BRIT. TAX REV. 71.

Krispis, *Money in Private International Law,* [1967] 1 RECUEIL DES COURS 191.

Lefcoe, *Monetary Correction and Mortgage Lending in Brazil: Observations for the United States,* 21 STAN. L. REV. 106 (1968).

Lemgruber, *Inflation in Brazil,* in WORLDWIDE INFLATION: THEORY AND RECENT EXPERIENCE 395 (L. Krause & W. Salant eds., 1977).

Lent, *Adjusting Taxable Profits for Inflation: The Foreign Experience,* in INFLATION AND THE INCOME TAX 195 (H. Aaron, ed., 1976).

Levy, *"Sliding Scale" or "Indexation" Clauses in French Law,* 16 AM. U. L. REV. 35 (1966).

López Cabaña, *La "Indexación" de Deudas Dinerarias,* [1976] III J. A. 788 (Argentina).

Lubell & Lavin, *Indexation of the Tax Law: A "Fresh Start" Adjustment,* 58 TAXES 355 (1980).

Lusztig & Schwab, *Units of Account and the International Bond Market,* 10 COLUM. J. WORLD BUS. 74 (Spring 1975).

Maier, *The Politics of Inflation in the Twentieth Century,* in THE POLITICAL ECONOMY OF INFLATION 37 (F. Hirsch and J. Goldthorpe, eds. 1978).

Mann, *The Relevant Date for the Assessment of Compensation,* 85 L. Q. REV. 516 (1969).

Marnierre, *Observations sur L'Indexation comme Mesure de Valeur,* 76 REV. TRIM. DROIT CIV. 54 (France, 1977).

Marx, *Compensation for Inflation under Alternative Regulatory Formulas,* PUB. UTIL. FORT. 23 (Je. 7, 1979).

Massone, *Adjustments of Profits for Inflation—Developments in Latin America,* 35 BULL. INT'L FISCAL DOCUM. 3 & 51 (pts. I & II, 1981).

Mazeaud, *Les Rentes Flottantes et la Réparation des Accidents,* [1951] D. JUR. CHRON. 17 (France).

McClintock, *The Probable Legal Consequences of Inserting Price-Index Clauses in Long-Term Obligations,* 18 HASTINGS L. J. 959 (1967).

McKay, *The Legal Problems of Inflation,* 1975 N.Z.L.J. 395.

Meichsner, *The Gold Standard and Monetary Law,* in INTERNATIONALES RECHT UND WIRTSCHAFTSORDNUNG: FESTSCHRIFT FÜR F. A. MANN 757 (W. Flume et al., eds. 1977).

Meiselman, *World-Wide Inflation: A Monetarist View,* in THE PHENOMENON OF WORLD-WIDE INFLATION 69 (D. Meiselman & A. Laffer, eds. 1975).

Mishan & Dicks-Mireaux, *Progressive Taxation in an Inflationary Economy,* 48 AM. ECON. REV. 591 (1958).

Moore, *Inflation and Statistics,* in CONTEMPORARY ECONOMIC PROBLEMS 1980, 167 (W. Fellner, ed. 1980).

Morag, *Value-Linking of Loans in Israel,* in FISCAL AND MONETARY PROBLEMS IN DEVELOPING STATES 148 (D. Krivane, ed. 1967).

——— *For an Inflation-Proof Economy,* 52 AM. ECON. REV. 177 (1962).

Moreno, *Sistemas Legales de Reajustes en los Valores Monetarios,* 2 REV. DER. ECON. 57 (Chile, No. 6, 1964).

Morley, *Indexing and the Fight against Inflation,* in INDEXATION, THE BRAZILIAN EXPERIENCE 76 (M. Nadiri & A. Pastore, eds., Occasional Papers, Nat'l. Bur. Econ. Res., Vol. 4, No. 1, Winter 1977).

Morris, *English Judgments in Foreign Currency: A "Procedural" Revolution,* 41 L. & CONTEMP. PROB. 44 (1977).

Ness, *Financial Markets Innovation as a Development Strategy: Initial Results from the Brazilian Experience,* 22 ECON. DEVELOP. & CULT. CHANGE 453 (1974).

Noirel, *L'Influence de la Dépréciation Monétaire dan les Contracts de Droit Privé,* in INFLUENCE DE LA DÉPRÉCIATION MONÉTAIRE SUR LA VIE JURIDIQUE PRIVÉE 100 (P. Durand, ed. 1961).

Note, *Dollar Damage Awards to Foreign Plaintiffs: Conversion and Revaluation of Foreign Currencies,* 61 YALE L. J. 758 (1952).

——— *U.C.C. § 2–615; Sharp Inflationary Increases in Cost as Excuse from Performance,* 50 N.D. L. REV. 297 (1974).

Nowotny, *Inflation and Taxation: Reviewing the Macroeconomic Issues,* 18 J. ECON. LITERATURE 1025 (1980).

Nussbaum, *Comparative and International Aspects of American Gold Clause Abrogation,* 44 YALE L. J. 53 (1934).

——— *Multiple Currency and Index Clauses,* 84 U. PA. L. REV. 569 (1936).

——— *The Meaning of Inflation,* 58 POL. SCI. Q. 86 (1943).

Oliphant, *The Theory of Money in the Law of Commercial Instruments,* 29 YALE L. J. 606 (1920).

Page, *International Experience of Indexing,* in INDEXING FOR INFLATION 97 (T. Liesner & M. King, eds. 1975).

Page & Trollope, *An International Survey of Indexing and its Effects,* NAT'L INST. ECON. REV. 46 (Nov. 1974).

Parker & Zieha, *Inflation, Income Taxes and the Incentive for Capital Investment,* 29 NAT'L. TAX J. 179 (1976).

Pasquesi, *Protecting Clients from Inflation,* 19 PRAC. LAW. 83 (1973).

Pastore, Almonacid, Barros, *Reflections on the Brazilian Experience with Indexation,* in INDEXATION, THE BRAZILIAN EXPERIENCE 8 (M. Nadiri and A. Pastore, eds., Occasional Papers, Nat'l Bur. Econ. Res., Vol. 4, No. 1, Winter 1977).

Patinkin, *What Advanced Countries can Learn from the Experience with Indexation,* in INDEXATION, THE BRAZILIAN EXPERIENCE 177 (M. Nadiri and A. Pastore, eds., Occasional Papers, Nat'l Bur. Econ. Res., Vol. 4, No. 1, Winter 1977).

Peel, *On the Case for Indexation of Wages and Salaries,* 30 KYKLOS 259 (Fasc. 2, 1977).

Petri, *Inflation Adjustments Schemes under the Personal Income Tax,* 22 IMF STAFF PAPERS 539 (1975).

Pierce & Enzler, *The Implication for Economic Stability of Indexing the Individual Income Tax,* in INFLATION AND THE INCOME TAX 197 (H. Aaron, ed. 1976).

Pierre-François, *L'Indexation Judiciare des Rentes Viagères Allouées en Réparation d'un Prejudice de Responsabilité Delictuelle,* [1972] D. S. JUR. CHRON. 229 (France).

Portes, *Inflation under Central Planning,* in the POLITICAL ECONOMY OF INFLATION 73 (F. Hirsch & J. Goldthorpe, eds. 1978).

Rashba, *Debts in Collapsed Foreign Currencies,* 54 YALE L. J. 1 (1944).

Rea, *Inflation, Taxation and Damage Assessment,* 58 CAN. BAR REV. 280 (1980).

Robinson, *Readjustable Mortgages in an Inflationary Economy—A Study of the Israeli Experience,* 5 J. INT'L. L. & ECON. 169 (1971).

Rodhe, *Adjustment of Contracts on Account of Changed Conditions,* 3 SCAN. STUD. IN LAW 151 (1959).

Roe, *Finance, Rules and the Indexation of Brazilian Government Bonds,* 12 VAND. J. TRANSNAT'L L. 1 (1979).

Rosenn, *Adaptations of the Brazilian Income Tax to Inflation,* 21 STAN. L. REV. 58 (1968).

——— *Adjusting Taxation of Business Income for Inflation: Lessons from Brazil and Chile,* 13 TEXAS INT'L L. J. 165 (1978).

——— *Controlled Rents and Uncontrolled Inflation: The Brazilian Dilemma,* 17 AM. J. COMP. L. 239 (1969).

——— *Expropriation, Inflation, and Development,* 1972 WIS. L. REV. 845.

——— *Protecting Contracts from Inflation,* 33 BUS. LAW 729 (1978).

——— *The Effects of Inflation on the Law of Obligations in Latin America,* 2 B. C. INT'L & COMP. L. REV. 269 (1979).

——— *The Constitutional Guaranty Against Diminution of Judicial Compensation,* 24 U.C.-L.A. L. REV. 308 (1976).

Rozental, *Variable-Return Bonds—The French Experience,* 14 J. FINANCE 520 (1959).

Rubner, *The Abdication of the Israeli Pound as a Standard of Measurement for Medium and Long-Term Contracts,* 28 REV. ECON. STUDIES 69 (Oct. 1960).

Salant, *International Transmission of Inflation,* in WORLD-WIDE INFLATION 167 (L. Krause & W. Salent, eds. 1977).

Sarnat, *Monetary Risk, Stagflation and the Uneasy Case for Indexation,* in INFLATION AND CAPITAL MARKETS 179 (M. Sarnat, ed. 1978).

Schwartz, *Sales Law and Inflations,* 50 S. CAL. L. REV. 1 (1976).

Schwartz, *Secular Price Change in Historical Perspective,* 5 J. MONEY, CREDIT & BANKING 243 (1973).

Sergio de Castro Spikula, *Inflation and Financial Discipline in Chile,* in CHILE AND ECONOMIC POLICY 275 (J. C. Mendez, ed. 1979).

Silard, *Maintenance-of-Value Arrangements in International Transactions,* 5 L. & POL. INT'L BUS. 398 (1973).

Simonsen, *Correção Monetária—a Experiência Brasileira,* 29 CONJUNTURA ECONÔMICA 65 (Jy. 1975).

——— *Inflation and the Money and Capital Markets of Brazil,* in THE ECONOMY OF BRAZIL 133 (H. Ellis, ed. 1969).

Smit, *Frustration of Contract: A Comparative Attempt at Consolidation,* 58 COLUM. L. REV. 287 (1958).

Smith, *Legal Principles in Monetary and Credit Policy,* 18 SCAN. STUD. IN LAW 179 (1974).

Stahl, *The Rise and Fall of Index Loans in Sweden,* SKANDINAVISKA ENSKILDA BANKEN Q. REV. 14 (No. 1, 1975).

Strain, *Inflation and Taxation: World Developments,* 25 CAN. TAX J. 40 (1977).

Sunley and Pechman, *Inflation Adjustment for the Individual Income Tax,* in INFLATION AND THE INCOME TAX 153 (H. Aaron, ed. 1976).

Tanzi, *Adjusting Personal Income Taxes for Inflation: The Foreign Experience,* in INFLATION AND THE INCOME TAX 215 (H. Aaron, ed. 1976).

——— *Inflation and the Incidence of Income Taxes on Interest Income: Some Results for the United States, 1972–1974,* 24 IMF STAFF PAPERS 500 (1977).

——— *Inflation, Indexation and Interest Income Taxation,* BANCA NAZIONALE DEL LAVORO Q. REV. 64 (Mar. 1976).

Tedeschi, *On the Date for Assessing Damage,* 13 ISRAEL L. REV. 10 (1978).

Tendler, *Indexation et Ordre Public,* [1977] D. S. CRON. 245 (France).

Terrar, *A Consumer Oriented Approach to Regulation of Public Utility Prices by the Cost of Living Council,* 23 CATH. U. L. REV. 61 (1973).

Tideman & Tucker, *The Tax Treatment of Business Profits under Inflationary Conditions,* in INFLATION AND THE INCOME TAX 33 (H. Aaron, ed. 1976).

Toulemon, *Évolution de la Jurisprudence en Matière de Clauses d'Échelle Mobile et des Clauses de Variation suivant Indices,* 4 REV. TRIM. DROIT COMM. 663 (France, 1951).

Tracy, *Maintaining Value of Social Security Benefits during Inflation: Foreign Experience,* 39 SOC. SECURITY BULL. 33 (Nov. 1976).

Triffin, *Basic Considerations in International Monetary Reform,* INFLATION, TRADE, AND TAXES 119 (D. Belsley et al., eds. 1976).

U.N. Fiscal and Fin. Branch, Bur. of Econ. Affairs, *Index Clauses in Deferred Payments,* 2 ECON. BULL. LAT. AM. 73 (No. 2, Oct. 1957).

Van Ballegooijen, *The Units of Account in Eurobonds,* 22 NETHERLANDS INT'L L. REV. 51 (1975).

Van Hecke, *Currency,* in 3 INT'L ENCY. COMP. L. 36 (1972).

Vasseur, *French Monetary Depreciation and Methods Used to Remedy It,* 30 TUL. L. REV. 73 (1955).

——— *L'Indexatión a L'Étranger,* REV. ÉCONOMIQUE 275 (France, No. 2, 1955).

Viaux, *L'Indexation des Valeurs Mobilières dan la Pratique,* REV. ÉCONOMIQUE 249 (France, No. 2, 1955).

Von Furstenberg, *Individual Income Taxation and Inflation,* 28 NAT'L TAX J. 117 (1975).

Wald, *Inflação e as Indenizações,* 233 REV. FOR. 21 (Brazil, 1971).

Watkins, *The Economic Aspects of Inflation,* 33 MICH. L. REV. 153 (1934).

White, *Judgments in Foreign Currency and the EEC Treaty,* J. BUS. L. 7 (Jan. 1976).

Whitley, *Mortgages: The Case for Index-Linking,* NAT'L INST. ECON. REV. 75 (Nov. 1974).

Yadin, *"The Date of Judgment" for the Assessment of Compensation for Damage to Movable Property,* 13 ISRAEL L. REV. 111 (1978).

——— *Problems of Devaluation before Israeli Courts,* in INTERNATIONALES RECHT UND WIRTSCHAFTSORDNUNG: FESTSCHRIFT FÜR F. A. MANN 847 (W. Flume et al., eds. 1977).

INDEX

www.ingramcontent.com/pod-product-compliance
Lightning Source LLC
LaVergne TN
LVHW101454200926
848483LV00001B/124